THE ROUGH GUIDE TO

The Dordogne & the Lot

written and researched by

Jan Dodd

with additional contributions by

Amanda Lawrence and Darren Longley

ROUGH GUIDES

roughguides.com

Contents

OPPOSITE A DOVECOTE SURROUNDED BY POPPIES, LOT VALLEY **PREVIOUS PAGE** SNUFFLING FOR TRUFFLES

Introduction to

The Dordogne & the Lot

It was in the green, secluded valleys of the Dordogne and the Lot that prehistoric people penetrated deep into limestone caves to paint the world's earliest masterpieces of pot-bellied ponies, mammoths and muscular bison. Later occupants of the area expressed their faith in the Romanesque churches found on many a hilltop, and in the array of abbeys and towering cathedrals, while the legacy of a more bellicose era lies in the medieval fortresses perched on pinnacles of rock.

In addition to this richly layered history, the Dordogne and the Lot are endowed with a tremendous variety of scenery, from the dry limestone plateaux of the *causses*, sliced through with narrow gorges, to densely wooded valleys and serried ranks of gnarled grape vines. Through these landscapes slide the great rivers that unify and define this region: the **Vézère**, running swiftly through its deeply cloven valley, hurtles into the **Dordogne** which in turn flows placidly out to the Atlantic coast. Further south the serpentine **Lot** writhes its way across the country to join the mighty **Garonne**, which along with its tributaries, the **Tarn** and **Aveyron**, marks this region's southern border.

It's an area best savoured at its own unhurried pace; there is always something to catch the eye, some forgotten corner to stumble upon, a market or a village *fête*. That isn't to say the region is undiscovered – indeed, some sights are numbered among the most visited in France – but its heartland is still steeped in what the French call the *douceur de vivre*, the gentle way of life.

Where to go

The principal northern gateway to the Dordogne and the Lot is the charming city of **Brive-la-Gaillarde** (usually shortened to Brive), whose cosy café culture emanates the spirit of the south, a hint of pleasures to come. West lies **Périgueux**, where an

FOOD AND DRINK IN THE DORDOGNE AND THE LOT

The Dordogne and the Lot are blessed with some of the most sought-after delicacies in the culinary world, including the celebrated **black truffle** and rich **foie gras** (fattened duck or goose liver pâte). Deep in the oak forests, *cèpes* cluster in generous numbers and hordes of wild *sangliers* (boars) roam. On the high limestone *causses* lie secluded dairy farms, where **goats' cheese** reaches its apogee in the creamy *cabecou*, while swathes of delicate violet flowers – the **saffron crocus** – thrive in the harsh conditions. Between the neatly combed vineyards **walnut** plantations provide barrels of precious walnut oil and the region's famous dessert, *tarte aux noix*. Accompanying this copious feast are the rich, dark **wines** of Cahors and the fragrant, golden Montbazillac of Bergerac. South of the Lot valley the landscape changes to the baking fields of the Quercy Blanc and temperatures shift up a gear to ripen acres of yellow sunflowers, heaps of melons and orchards dripping with peaches, plums and apricots.

extraordinary Byzantine-style cathedral stands above a tangle of medieval lanes. The city is the capital of a broad sweep of rolling pasture and woodland known as **Périgord Vert** (Green Périgord). This region's loveliest river is the Dronne and its most appealing town water-bound **Brantôme**, known for its rock-cut sanctuaries and plethora of restaurants. East of here is castle-country: **Château de Puyguilhem** stands out for its elegant Renaissance architecture, while the **Château de Hautefort** is one of the grandest castles in the Dordogne and Lot.

South of Périgueux, in an area known as **Périgord Pourpre** (Purple Périgord) thanks to its wine production, vines cloak the slopes of the lower Dordogne valley around the pleasant riverside town of **Bergerac**. The star of this area is the river itself, which loops through two immense meanders near **Trémolat** to create a classic Dordogne scene.

FACT FILE

- The area covered by this Guide amounts to some 22,000 square kilometres, about the size of Wales, but has a population of under a million, one of the lowest population densities in metropolitan France.

- The French Air Force has special permission to perform occasional low-level flying practice in the Lot valley, on the premise that there is less chance of tragedy should an accident occur.

- The economy is based on tourism and agriculture, primarily **wine** production. Bergerac has 120 square kilometres of vines while the Cahors' vineyards amount to about 43 square kilometres. Originally planted by the Romans in 50BC they are said to be the oldest in France.

- The region boasts three **World Heritage Sites** – the Vézère valley, with its prehistoric cave art, the entire Causses du Quercy and a dozen or so sites listed under the pilgrims' route to Santiago de Compostela.

- The iconic French **jam**, Bonne Maman, with its distinctive red-checked lid, is made in Biars, in the northern Lot.

- During a *fête*, when the soup course comes to a close, it is *de rigueur* for gentlemen to tip a glass of Cahors wine into the empty bowl, swill it round and drink it down in one, to the boisterous cheers of their companions.

- The Causses du Quercy is known to **astronomers** the world over as the black triangle because it has the lowest light pollution in France.

- **Pigeonniers** – vernacular structures originally built as pigeon lofts and often highly ornamental – encapsulate the Quercy landscape. The oldest were constructed on stilts in order to facilitate the collection of manure. They are still built as architectural features today and nearly every sizeable house has one.

East of Trémolat the colour scheme changes again as you enter the **Périgord Noir** (Black Périgord), named for the preponderance of evergreen oaks with their dark, dense foliage. Here you'll find the greatest concentration of Périgord cottages with their steep, stone-covered roofs, and dramatic fortresses perched high above the river. Here, too, are the walnut orchards and flocks of ducks and geese, the source of so much of the produce featured in the region's markets. Of these the most vivid is **Sarlat**'s, held among the fine medieval and Renaissance houses built in honey-coloured stone. Close by, the beetling cliffs of the **Vézère valley** are riddled with limestone caves where prehistoric artists left their stunning legacy.

Upstream from Sarlat, the abbey-church of **Souillac** offers remarkable Romanesque carvings, while the nearby pilgrimage town of **Rocamadour**, set halfway up a cliff face, is equally compelling. Further east is the **Château de Castelnau**, a supreme example of medieval military architecture, and the Renaissance **Château de Montal**, with its exquisite ornamental detailing.

Shadowing the Dordogne to the south, the Lot flows through comparatively wild country where, even in high summer, it's possible to find quiet corners. The departmental capital, **Cahors**, is home to France's best surviving fortified medieval bridge, **Pont Valentré**, while upstream the perched village of **St-Cirq-Lapopie** provides the valley's most dramatic sight. From near here the pretty Célé valley cuts northeast to **Figeac**, which boasts a highly rewarding museum, dedicated to Champollion, the man who unravelled the mystery of hieroglyphics. West of Cahors, the atmospheric villages of **Monflanquin** and **Monpazier** represent outstanding examples of *bastides* (see box, p.244), poignant echoes of a

violent past. South of the river both landscape and colour change yet again, while temperatures (see box below) ramp up a gear to ripen the sunflowers, vineyards and orchards of the **Quercy Blanc**. You have only to glance at an empty field, bleached by the sun, lavishly dusted with white stone and perhaps decorated with a vernacular *borie* (dry-stone hut), to perceive the reason for its sobriquet.

The highlights of the Garonne valley to the south are the Romanesque carvings of the abbey-church at **Moissac** and the river's dramatic gorges around the attractive old town of **St-Antonin-Noble-Val** and the evocative ruined fortress of **Najac**.

When to go

Winters are variable in this diverse region. In the north they are generally wet, while in the southern regions they can be short and very dry indeed – on sunny days it's possible to sit outside even in December. January and February, however, can see temperatures plummeting to well below zero. **Spring** is usually the wettest period although some years see glorious weather. Temperatures begin to pick up around April and can reach the mid-30s in high **summer**, though usually hover in the high 20s. **Autumn** is longer and drier than spring, bringing sunny weather until the end of October.

The most important factor in deciding when to visit is the **holiday seasons**. By far the busiest period is July and August, peaking in the first two weeks of August, when hotels and campsites are bursting at the seams and top-rank sights are absolutely heaving. Conversely, from November to Easter many places close down completely. Overall, the **best time to visit** is September and early October, with May and June coming a close second.

AVERAGE DAILY TEMPERATURE AND RAINFALL

	Jan	Feb	Mar	Apr	May	Jun	Jul	Aug	Sep	Oct	Nov	Dec
CAHORS												
Max/min (°C)	9/1	12/2	15/5	18/7	22/12	24/13	28/14	29/15	25/12	20/9	13/4	10/2
Rainfall (mm)	66	71	73	69	66	71	47	44	59	68	71	76
SARLAT												
Max/min (°C)	8/1	11/2	14/4	16/6	20/10	23/11	26/14	27/13	2312	18/9	12/4	9/3
Rainfall (mm)	73	78	79	80	85	78	59	64	65	79	78	77

Author picks

Our authors have admired prehistoric caves and charming villages, consumed far more cheese and wine than is strictly necessary and developed excellent canoeing skills – it's a hard job, but someone's got to do it. Here are their favourite things to do, see and eat:

❶ **Truffle markets** Between December and March, the area's countless wonderful town and village markets are given an exotic foodie twist with the arrival of the delicious, and expensive, fungi (see p.71).

❷ **River trip** The Dordogne and Lot's many rivers offer superb water-bound activities, though it's hard to beat a trip in a canoe along the Vézère river, and in particular the stretch between Montignac and Les Eyzies (see p.142).

❸ **Must-see medieval** With its solid, soaring towers and graceful arches, the all-powerful Pont Valentré (see p.207) in Cahors is a masterpiece of medieval architecture.

❹ **Underground church** The Dordogne's most unique ecclesiastical treasure, the church of St-Jean (see p.64) in Aubeterre-sur-Dronne is a stupendous twenty-metre high chamber carved into the rock face.

❺ **Black tipple** So-named because of its dark colour and strong taste, the black wine of Cahors (see p.204) is harvested from what are reputedly some of the oldest vineyards in the country, and is worth sampling any time of the year.

❻ **Cool cave** Glittering stalactites, prehistoric cave paintings and hundreds of bats are three very good reasons to make a beeline for the Grotte de Villars (see p.67) hidden away amid the lush Périgord Vert.

❼ **Giddy up** The racetrack at Arnac-Pompadour (see p.80) is one of France's most spectacular, and a great place to watch magnificent thoroughbreds in action.

❽ **Cracking castle** One of the grandest of the region's myriad enchanting châteaux, Hautefort (see p.72) is a superb example of French Renaissance architecture at its best.

Our author recommendations don't end here. We've flagged up our favourite places – a perfectly sited hotel, an atmospheric café, a special restaurant – throughout the guide, highlighted with the ★ symbol.

17

things not to miss

It's not possible to see everything that the Dordogne and Lot has to offer in one trip – and we don't suggest you try. What follows is a selective and subjective taste of the region's highlights: spectacular castles, quaint villages and eye-catching architecture. Each highlight has a page reference to take you straight into the Guide, where you can find out more.

1 ST-CIRQ LAPOPIE
Page 212
Tumbling down a sheer cliff and reflected in the serpentine waters of the Lot, this higgledy-piggledy village is officially France's favourite.

2 TRUFFLE MARKET, LALBENQUE
Page 270
Lalbenque holds the largest truffle market in southwest France every Tuesday afternoon in winter – the streets are suffused with the unique scent of the fungi.

3 CADOUIN ABBEY
Page 114
The astonishing Cadouin Abbey was once a major pilgrimage site.

4 SARLAT
Page 121
Lose yourself in Sarlat's old centre – an intriguing maze of narrow medieval lanes.

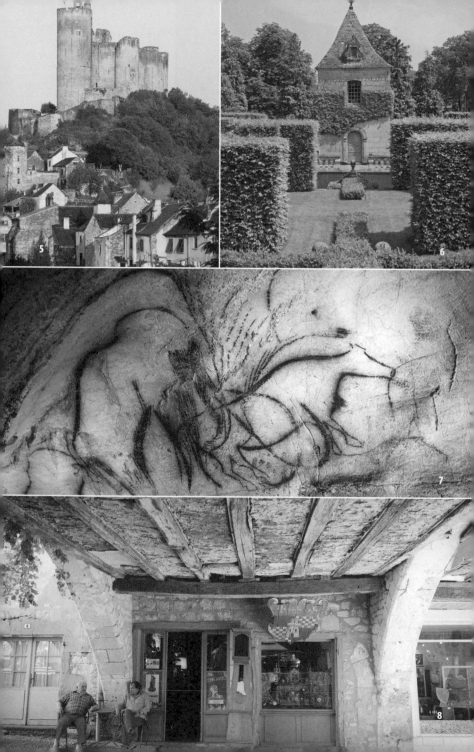

5 CHÂTEAU AT NAJAC
Page 282
The fairy-tale château of Najac set on top of a hill with an impressive view dominates the Aveyron.

6 THE GARDENS OF MANOIR D'EYRIGNAC
Page 128
Explore these ornate gardens dating back to the eighteenth century

7 PREHISTORIC CAVES
Page 130
The caves and rock shelters around Les Eyzies contain stunning examples of prehistoric art.

8 MONPAZIER
Page 246
One of the region's best-preserved *bastide* towns, in the typical grid-style, with many buildings dating from the thirteenth century.

9 ROCAMADOUR
Page 174
Cliff-side pilgrimage town which will take your breath away – if you avoid the peak-season crowds.

10 PARC NATUREL RÉGIONAL DES CAUSSES DU QUERCY
Page 198
Explore swathes of wild limestone plateau, carved by imposing rivers and dotted with grazing sheep.

11 CANOEING
Page 33
Drifting along in a canoe is a perfect way to get some gentle sightseeing done.

12 LOCAL PRODUCE
Page 29

Famous gastronomic treats from the region include foie gras, walnut oil, goats' cheese and truffles.

13 PONT VALENTRÉ
Page 207

The Pont Valentré in Cahors is an outstanding example of a fortified medieval bridge.

14 VINEYARD VISITS
Page 204

From grand chateaux like Lagrezette to tiny, family-run concerns, a visit and tasting at a wine château provides a memorable experience.

15 CORDES-SUR-CIEL
Page 280

The picturesque medieval hill-town of Cordes-sur-Ciel, the pearl of the *bastides*, perches on a rocky pinnacle.

16 ST-ANTONIN-NOBLE-VAL
Page 277

Take in St-Antonin-Noble-Val and the medieval houses from its glorious heyday sheltering under towering limestone cliffs.

17 CAHORS
Page 200

Trapped in a tight meander of the Lot river, glorious Cahors is rich in history. Wander through the labyrinth of medieval streets surrounding the double-domed cathedral.

12

13

14

15

16

17

Itineraries

The following itineraries are designed to lead you up, down and round about the enduringly beautiful Dordogne and Lot – picking out the area's prettiest towns and villages, most impressive medieval architecture and tastiest food and drink.

LE GRAND TOUR

❶ Aubeterre-sur-Dronne Two marvellous churches – one a remarkable subterranean cavern – are the highlights of this gorgeous little hillside town on the Charente border. **See p.64**

❷ Périgueux A rich confection of Roman remains, old-town Renaissance buildings and grand ecclesiastical architecture makes a visit to Périgueux imperative. **See p.47**

❸ Bergerac Hop aboard a traditional *gabare* for a scenic river cruise before heading to one of the town's many excellent bars to indulge in a glass or two of Bergerac wine. **See p.89**

❹ Trémolat and Limeuil Defined by the two dramatic bends at Trémolat and Limeuil, this is the prettiest stretch of the Dordogne River. **See p.109 & p.110**

❺ Les Eyzies Be prepared to be dazzled by some of the world's finest prehistoric cave art, most impressively at the Font-de-Gaume and Abri du Cap Blanc caves. **See p.131**

❻ Sarlat Run through with handsome medieval houses and honey-coloured Renaissance stone buildings, Sarlat is perhaps the Dordogne's most alluring town. **See p.121**

❼ Rocamadour Not only is Rocamadour possessed of a breathtaking cliff-top location, but it's one of the country's most important pilgrimage sites. **See p.174**

❽ Figeac Straddling the River Célé, this town boasts a raft of splendid medieval architecture and a quite superb museum of writing. **See p.220**

❾ Moissac The Romanesque carvings of the abbey-church of St Pierre rate among the most impressive in the country, not least those on its magnificent tympanum. **See p.261**

GASTRONOMIC ODYSSEY

❶ Foie gras, Thiviers Undoubtedly the region's culinary star, the fattened liver of duck or goose is best eaten on its own in succulent slabs, though is also delicious pan-fried with a fruit compôte; learn more at the Maison du Foie Gras museum. **See p.68**

❷ Truffles, Sorges Evocatively known as the "black diamonds of the Périgord", these expensive black fungi crop up in all sorts of dishes, from rich Périgourdin sauces to the humble omelette – head to the museum in Sorges to see some whoppers. **See p.71**

❸ Montbazillac Sample a drop of this sumptuously sweet white wine at the eponymous château, just outside Bergerac, or in any number of the surrounding wineries. **See p.96**

❹ Cèpes, Monpazier These plump, brown mushrooms can be sampled just about anywhere in the Dordogne, but you'll find an abundance of them around Monpazier and Villefranche-du-Périgord. **See p.246**

ABOVE SAFFRON AND APRICOT JAM; TAKING A BREAK NEAR LIMEUIL (P.110)

❺ Le Bugue market Pitch up at any town or village in the Dordogne and Lot and you'll find a terrific food market taking place, but this one in pretty Le Bugue is one of the best. **See p.139**

❻ Walnuts, Beynac Though traditionally used as an oil, the humble but wonderfully versatile walnut can be found in breads, cakes and desserts. For more nutty kicks, follow the Route de la Noix between Argentat and Beynac. **See p.129**

❼ Cabécou cheese, Rocamadour The region boasts few speciality cheeses, but this is a beauty; a little flat medallion of goats' cheese, typically served on toast or a bed of lettuce with walnut oil. **See p.180**

❽ Saffron, Cajarc Numerous farms in the region produce this age-old spice, but your best bet is to make a beeline for the marvellous saffron fair in Cajarc at the end of October. **See p.216**

MEDIEVAL DORDOGNE

❶ Château Jumilhac Nestled amid thick woodland in the lush Périgord Vert region, Jumilhac is a classic fairy-tale castle, complete with requisite towers, turrets and ramparts. **See p.70**

❷ Châteaux Beynac and Castelnaud Situated on opposing sides of the Dordogne river, these two magnificent, semi-ruined castles are pre-eminent among the region's many châteaux. **See p.156 & p.160**

❸ Cadouin Attractive village known for its twelfth-century Cistercian abbey, though it's the adjoining cloister, with stunningly carved capitals, that is the real show-stealer. **See p.114**

❹ Monpazier The most complete of the *bastide* towns, with intact medieval gates, a fine church and a perfect looking central square. **See p.246**

❺ Eymet Laid out on a classic *bastide* chequerboard plan, Eymet is centred on a handsome, arcaded main square lined with half-timbered houses. **See p.99**

❻ Pont Valentré A formidable construction straddling the Lot river in Cahors, this is perhaps the finest example of a fortified medieval bridge in the entire country. **See p.207**

❼ St-Antonin-Noble-Val Set against a stunning backdrop of white limestone cliffs, St-Antonin's medieval heritage is writ large throughout the village. **See p.277**

❽ Cordes-sur-Ciel Heavily fortified in its heyday, this charming, mist-clad hilltop village is now home to artisans and craftspeople of many persuasions. **See p.280**

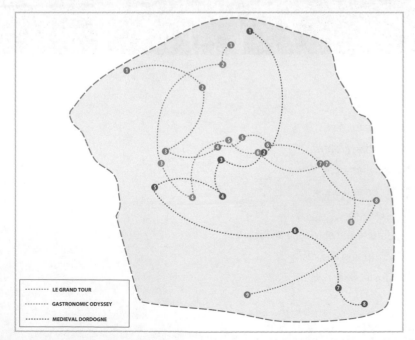

LE GRAND TOUR

GASTRONOMIC ODYSSEY

MEDIEVAL DORDOGNE

GEESE IN THE DORDOGNE

Basics

Getting there

The Dordogne and Lot is easy to reach by air, with several airlines flying there from numerous UK airports. Travelling overland is another, possibly more attractive option, with the Eurostar making the journey from London to Paris, from where you can connect to the fast and efficient TGV services. Alternatively, both the Channel Tunnel and cross-Channel ferries allow you to make the journey by car. From the US, Canada, Australia, New Zealand and South Africa, you'll have to fly to Paris, and take an onward connection from there, be it by plane or train.

Fares increasingly depend on how far in advance you can book: the earlier the cheaper. But they will also depend on the **season**, with the highest prices generally from June to August, Christmas and the New Year; fares drop during the "shoulder" seasons – roughly September to October and April to May – and you'll get the best prices during the low season, November to March.

Most airlines prefer you to book online these days, and you can find some great deals, but always check the small print as most budget airline bookings are non-changeable and non-refundable. Another option is to contact a general flight or travel agent – these have similar deals on flights and services, and some are particularly geared towards youth, student and independent travel. Other specialist tour operators can book you onto a variety of breaks or themed tours.

Flights from the UK and Ireland

Flying time to the Dordogne and the Lot from the UK or Ireland is between one and a half and two hours, depending on your departure airport. There are currently four airlines flying from the UK directly to the Dordogne and the Lot, almost all of which fly to Bergerac: Ryanair (Wryanair.com) flies from London Stansted, Bristol, East Midlands and Liverpool (it also flies to Rodez, which is just 60km southeast of Figeac); Jet2 (Wjet2.com) flies from Leeds Bradford; and Flybe (Wflybe.com), which flies from more than half a dozen regional airports across the UK. The only other airport currently used in the Dordogne is Brive; CityJet (Wcityjet.com) has flights from London City and Dublin. Tickets with all these airlines can be obtained from as little as £50–60 return, including tax.

Flying to Bordeaux is another option, being just a short train ride away from the Dordogne: easyJet (Weasyjet.com) links London Gatwick, Luton, Liverpool and Bristol with the city, while Ryanair offers flights from Edinburgh to Bordeaux. In addition, British Airways (Wba.com) offers daily direct flights to Bordeaux. Aer Lingus (Waerlingus .com) also has direct flights from Dublin to Bordeaux.

Flights from the US and Canada

The only direct flights from the US or Canada to the region is the weekly **Montréal–Bordeaux** service offered by Air Transat (Wairtransat.com). However, most major airlines operate scheduled flights to **Paris**, from where you can take a domestic flight (check there's no inconvenient transfer between Charles de Gaulle and Orly airports) or transfer to the rail network. Air France (Wairfrance.com) has the most frequent and convenient service, with daily flights from more than half a dozen US cities, but their fares tend to be pricey. Other airlines offering services to Paris from a variety of US cities include: American Airlines (Waa.com) from New York, Chicago, Dallas and Miami; Delta (Wdelta.com) from Atlanta, Chicago, Cincinnati, Houston and New York; and United (Wunited.com) from Chicago and New York. **Air Canada** (Waircanada.ca) offers direct services to Paris from Montréal and Toronto.

Thanks to such intense competition, transatlantic **fares** to France are fairly reasonable. A typical return fare to Paris, flying midweek outside peak season, costs around US$700 from Houston or Los Angeles and US$550 from New York. From Canada, prices to Paris start from Can$850 from Montréal and Toronto or Can$950 from Vancouver. Air Transat's return fares on the non-stop Montréal–Bordeaux route start at around Can$900.

Flights from Australia, New Zealand and South Africa

There are scheduled flights to Paris from Sydney, Melbourne, Brisbane, Perth and Auckland, all of which involve at least one stop en route. Alternatively, you can fly via another European hub and get a connecting flight to Bordeaux from there. Flights

---

TRAVELLING WITH PETS FROM THE UK

For information about travelling with pets from the UK to France, consult Wdefra.gov .uk/wildlife-pets/pets/travel/pets/index .htm or contact the Pet Travel Scheme (PETS) helpline (T0870 241 1710).

via Asia or the Gulf States with a transfer or overnight stop in the airline's home port are generally the cheapest option. The cheapest return **fares** start at around Aus$1700 from Sydney, Perth and Darwin and NZ$2300 from Auckland.

From South Africa, Air France operates direct flights to Paris from Johannesburg, and Cape Town. With other airlines you'll be routed through another European hub such as London, Amsterdam, Madrid or Frankfurt, from where you can pick up a connecting flight to Bordeaux. From South Africa, you're looking at anything upwards of R7500 from Johannesburg and R9000 from Cape Town.

By train

Eurostar operates high-speed passenger trains daily from St Pancras International to the Continent via the **Channel Tunnel**; most but not all services stop at either Ebbsfleet or Ashford in Kent (30min from London). Services depart roughly every hour (from around 5.30am to 8pm) for Paris Gare du Nord (2hr 20min), most of which stop at Lille (1hr 30min). You can connect with TGV trains to the southwest at either station.

Standard **fares** from London to Paris start at £69 for a non-refundable, non-exchangeable return. "Semi-flexible" tickets (which are exchangeable and refundable, subject to various conditions and upon payment of a fee) start at £125. Otherwise, you're looking at around £245 for a fully refundable ticket with no restrictions. Ticket prices are often significantly lower for those under 26, and all tickets go on sale four months in advance – you need to be quick to snap up the cheapest fares.

Note that Inter-Rail, Eurail and Eurodomino **rail passes** entitle you to discounts on Eurostar trains. It's possible to take your **bike** on Eurostar (see p.27).

A BETTER KIND OF TRAVEL

At Rough Guides we are passionately committed to travel. We believe it helps us understand the world we live in and the people we share it with – and of course tourism is vital to many developing economies. But the scale of modern tourism has also damaged some places irreparably, and climate change is accelerated by most forms of transport, especially flying. All Rough Guides' flights are carbon-offset, and every year we donate money to a variety of environmental charities.

Rail passes

Rail Europe (Ⓦ raileurope.co.uk) issues a number of **rail passes** for travel within France and for trips combining France with other European countries. Note that these passes must be purchased in your home country.

If you plan to visit several countries and are a European resident, the best bet is an **Inter-Rail Pass** (Ⓦ interrailnet.com), which entitles you to unlimited travel within the specified period and geographical area. The passes (Global and One Country Passes) come in over-26 and (cheaper) under-26 versions, and cover 30 European countries. The France Rail Pass allows between three and eight days of unlimited travel within a month (€170 for three days, €264 for eight days); first-class passes and cheaper passes for children, those under 26 and seniors are also available. For non-European residents there are various **Eurail passes** (Ⓦ eurail.com), covering either several countries or just France.

By car from the UK

If you have the time and inclination, then travelling to the Dordogne by car – a distance of some 850km from London – is certainly an attractive proposition.

Ferries from the UK and Ireland

The ferries plying the waters between Dover and Calais offer the cheapest means of getting to the other side, and are particularly convenient if you live in southeast England, from where the quickest crossings take 1hr 30min. Operators on this route include P&O Ferries (Ⓦ poferries.com) and My Ferry Link (Ⓦ myferrylink.com), formerly Sea France. If your starting point is west of London, it may be worth heading to one of the south-coast ports and catching a ferry to Brittany or Normandy. Brittany Ferries (Ⓦ brittany-ferries.co.uk) operates plentiful services from Portsmouth to Caen, Cherbourg and St Malo; the quickest crossing from Portsmouth is around three hours. If you're coming from the north of England or Scotland, you could consider the overnight crossing from Hull to Zeebrugge (Belgium) operated by P&O Ferries, though it'd be quicker just to drive down to the south coast and take a ferry there.

Another option is to take a ferry from Portsmouth to Santander or Bilbao (Brittany Ferries) in northern Spain. Crossing times are long (24–32hr), but the route north into the Dordogne is a relatively short one, roughly 250km.

From Ireland, putting the car on the ferry from Cork to Roscoff (P&O Ferries) or Rosslare (near Wexford) to Roscoff or Cherbourg (ⓦ irishferries .com) in Brittany cuts out the drive across Britain to the Channel. The crossing takes around fourteen hours from Cork and eighteen hours from Rosslare.

Return fares on the Dover–Calais route start at around £70 for a car and four passengers, while the voyage from the south coast to northern Spain costs around £700 return for a car and four people. From Ireland return fares for a car and two adults start at around €300 on the Cork to Roscoff route. Most ferry companies also offer fares for foot passengers, typically around £20 return on cross-Channel routes; accompanying bicycles can usually be carried free in the low season, though there may be a small charge during peak periods.

An easy way to compare prices and get an overview of possible routes is via Ferry Savers (ⓦ ferrysavers.com) and EuroDrive (ⓦ eurodrive .co.uk), both of which offer cut-price fares; the latter caters only for people taking their cars across the Channel.

The Channel Tunnel

Alternatively, there are the drive-on drive-off shuttle trains operated by **Eurotunnel** (ⓣ 0870 535 3535, ⓦ eurotunnel.com). The service runs continuously between Folkestone and Coquelles, near Calais, with up to four departures per hour at peak times (one every two hours from midnight to 6am) and takes 35min (slightly longer at night), though you must arrive at least 30min before departure. It is possible to turn up and buy your ticket at the check-in booths, but you'll pay the highest rate on the day. Standard **fares** start at £47 one way if you book far enough ahead and/or travel off peak, rising to £149 on the day. Fully refundable and changeable FlexiPlus fares cost £199 return.

AutoTrain

If you don't want to drive too far when you've reached France, you can take advantage of SNCF's **AutoTrain**, booked through Rail Europe (ⓣ 0844 848 4050, ⓦ raileurope.co.uk). This entails putting your car on a train at Paris Bercy station, which then travels overnight for the journey south to Brive; meanwhile, you make your own way down – preferably by train too – whereupon you meet your car at the destination; you do, though, have two days to collect it, useful if you want to hang around in Paris for a day, or wish to make a detour. The

service operates most days between early June and early September, and is reduced to two or three services per week during the rest of the year. The cheapest non-flexible tickets start at around £90 one way, just for the car.

Agents and tour operators

There are a vast number of travel agents and tour operators offering holidays in Dordogne and the Lot, the majority of which are geared to providing trips centred around outdoor activities such as cycling and canoeing, or food and wine. You'll also find operators listed on the Holiday France website (ⓦ holidayfrance.org.uk), run by the Association of British Tour Operators to France.

AGENTS AND OPERATORS

Adventure Center US ⓣ 1 800 228 8747, ⓦ adventurecenter.com. American hiking and "soft adventure" specialists. Their eight-day "Dordogne Discovery" includes a bit of canoeing, walking and cycling, while "Flavors of the Dordogne" (also eight days) is a deluxe gastronomic experience.
Affair Travel UK ⓣ 020 3504 0248, ⓦ affairtravel.com. Offers a range of luxury, villa-style self-catering accommodation in the Dordogne and Lot.
Arblaster & Clarke UK ⓣ 01730 263 111, ⓦ winetours.co.uk. Britain's biggest wine-tour specialist offers any number of superb tours of the magnificent Bordeaux vineyards, located right on the Dordogne's doorstep.
Backroads ⓣ 1 800 462 2848 or ⓣ 510 527 1555, ⓦ backroads .com. Luxury cycling and walking tours of the Bordeaux vineyards and the Dordogne and Vézère valleys. Family trips too.
Cycling for Softies UK ⓣ 0161 248 8282, ⓦ cycling-for-softies .co.uk. An easy-going cycle holiday operator offering a seven-day Dordogne and Garonne trip. Accommodation and restaurants tend to be top-end, including the occasional Michelin-starred restaurant.
Cyclomundo ⓣ 33 450 872109, ⓦ cyclomundo.com. French-based outfit which defines itself as the "bike rider's travel agency", specializing in custom-made "biking à la carte" trips for serious cyclists. Guided and self-guided trips.
Equestrian Escapes UK ⓣ 01829 781123, ⓦ equestrian-escapes .com. Offers five-day horseback holidays in the northern part of the Dordogne, catering to all levels, from beginners to advanced.
Eurocamp UK ⓣ 0844 406 0402, ⓦ eurocamp.co.uk. Self-drive, go-as-you-please holidays with tent or mobile home.
Exodus UK ⓣ 0845 287 2396, ⓦ exodus.co.uk. Eight-day Dordogne Family Adventure trips, involving canoeing on the Dordogne and Vézère rivers, and cycling, plus there's a bit of culture thrown in too. Accommodation in campsites. There's also a nine-day Dordogne Gastronomic Cycling trip, which, unsurprisingly, entails lots of exercise and lots of food.
France Afloat US ⓣ 0870 011 0538, ⓦ franceafloat.com. UK-based French canal and river cruising specialist leading trips on the Garonne Canal around Moissac and Agen, and the Canal du Midi.
French Travel Connection Australia ⓣ 02 9966 1177, ⓦ frenchtravel.com.au. Australia-based online agent offering everything

to do with travel to and around France, including accommodation, canal boats, walking tours, train travel, cookery classes, car rental and more.

The International Kitchen US ☎ 1 800 945 8606 or ☎ 312 467 0560, ⓦ theinternationalkitchen.com. "Cooking school vacations" in a Bordeaux wine château or in the Dordogne or the Quercy.

Lot Cycling Holidays UK ☎ 0844 888 2340, ⓦ lotcyclingholidays .com. Seven-day cycling tours of the Lot are available with this private, French-based agency, with accommodation based in Mas de Flory for the whole week.

North South Travel UK ☎ 01245 608 291, ⓦ northsouthtravel .co.uk. Friendly, competitive travel agency, offering discounted fares worldwide – profits are used to support projects in the developing world, especially the promotion of sustainable tourism.

Peregrine Adventures Australia ☎ 03 8601 444, ⓦ peregrine .net.au. Small-group adventure specialist offering guided and independent walking and cycling holidays in the Dordogne.

STA Travel US ☎ 1 800 781 4040, UK ☎ 0871 230 0040, Australia ☎ 134 782, New Zealand ☎ 0800 474 400, South Africa ☎ 0861 781 781; ⓦ statravel.com. Worldwide specialists in low-cost flights and tours for students and under-26s, though other customers are welcome.

Getting around

France has the most extensive train network in Western Europe. The nationally owned French train company, the SNCF (Société Nationale des Chemins de Fer), runs fast, modern trains between all the main towns in the Dordogne and Lot, and even between some of the minor ones. In rural areas where branch lines have been closed, certain routes (such as Agen to Villeneuve-sur-Lot) are covered by buses operated by the SNCF or in partnership with independent lines. It's an integrated service, with buses timed to meet trains and the same ticket covering both. To really do the region justice, however, you'll need your own transport.

By rail

SNCF has pioneered one of the most efficient, comfortable and user-friendly railway systems in the world. Pride and joy of the French rail system is the high-speed **TGV** (*train à grande vitesse*; ⓦ tgv .com). The quickest way to reach the Dordogne by train is to take a TGV from Paris Montparnasse to Bordeaux (3hr), some of which continue on along the main line to Agen and Montauban. From Bordeaux, you take an Intercité train across to Périgueux. Alternatively, take a TGV from Paris to Libourne, with an onward connection to Périgueux.

Brive, meanwhile, is served by a handful of direct Intercité trains each day from Paris Austerlitz. Elsewhere, the majority of trains you will use here are designated TER (*Train Express Régional*) which cover shorter distances and stop at more and smaller stations. A scenic branch traces much of the Dordogne valley linking Bordeaux with Bergerac and Sarlat, while three north–south axes cross the Dordogne and Lot valleys (Périgueux–Agen, Brive–Cahors–Montauban and Brive–Figeac–Toulouse). In all these cases, schedules are thin, with often big gaps between trains, so it's imperative to check timetables in advance. Paper copies of **timetables** are available free at most stations, or check ⓦ voyages-sncf.com. *Autocar* (often abbreviated to *car*) at the top of a column means it's an SNCF bus service, on which rail tickets and passes are valid.

Tickets

Tickets for all SNCF trains can be bought online with a credit card through ⓦ sncf.com, which has an English-language option, or by phone and at any train station (*gare SNCF*). Here you can buy tickets at the ticket office, or one of the yellow touch-screen machines (in English). If boarding at a smaller station (such as Le Bugue), which has neither machines nor a ticket office, you can buy your ticket from the guard on the train. All tickets – but not passes or internet tickets printed out at home – must be **validated** in the orange machines located at the entrance to the platforms; it is an offence not to follow the instruction *Compostez votre billet* (Validate your ticket).

Fares

Fares are cheaper if you travel off peak (*période bleue* or blue period) rather than during peak hours (*période normale* or *période blanche*, normal or white period) – in general, peak period means Monday mornings and Friday and Sunday evenings. A leaflet (*le calendrier voyageurs*) showing the blue and white periods is available at train stations. For longer journeys it's worth checking the advance special discount offers, known as *tarifs Prem's* (one-way fares from €22 on TGVs), on the SNCF website. A limited number of these are available on some main lines and can be bought online between two months and two weeks in advance. Even cheaper internet-only TGV fares can be purchased through ⓦ idtgv.com on services from Paris to Bordeaux and Toulouse; tickets go on sale four months before departure and you'll have to be able to print out your ticket. Try to book in advance for all TGV trains, as **seat reservations** are obligatory, and are included in the ticket price, though note that you will have to pay extra for them if you are travelling on an Inter-Rail pass. Anybody under 26 is entitled to a discount of 25 percent off all blue-period trains in France.

By bus

Travelling around the Dordogne and Lot region by bus is not particularly recommended. A very limited timetable serves a few routes, and whatever bus services there are, are usually governed by the needs of schoolchildren rather than tourists.

The most convenient **bus services** are those operated as an extension of rail links by SNCF, which run between train stations and serve areas not accessible by rail. In addition to SNCF buses, private, municipal and departmental buses can be useful for local and some cross-country journeys, though be prepared for early starts and careful planning if you want to see much outside the main towns.

Timetables for SNCF services are available at Ⓦsncf-voyages.fr, but times for services run by private companies can be frustrating to track down. Ⓦfrance-week-end.com has links to bus timetables by department, and Ⓦmopy.fr is a good source for the south of the region, but it's frankly easiest just to ask at the local tourist office.

Larger towns usually have a *gare routière* (bus station), often next to the *gare SNCF*, though this is often little more than just a couple of bus stands. However, the private bus companies don't always work together and you'll frequently find them leaving from an array of different points (here, too, the local tourist office should be able to help).

One final thing to note is that many rural bus services only operate *sur réservation* or "on demand". This means that you need to phone the operating company by 6pm the day before you wish to travel (or by 6pm on Friday for travel on Monday). Such services are usually indicated by a telephone icon in the bus timetable.

By car

Driving in the Dordogne and Lot can be a real pleasure – and is often the only practical means of reaching the more remote sights. There are three **autoroutes** in the area: the A20 cuts south from Limoges to Toulouse via Cahors; the A62 runs along the Garonne from Bordeaux to Toulouse; and the A89 links Bordeaux with Périgueux and Brive. Motorway **tolls** are payable in cash or by credit card (get in the lane marked CB) at the frequent tollgates (*péages*). The Michelin website (Ⓦviamichelin.fr)

details the cost of tolls on any particular journey. Slower and more congested are the toll-free national roads (marked, for example, N21 or RN21 on signs and maps). The smaller *routes départementales* (marked with a D) are generally uncongested and make for a more scenic drive, though may occasionally be in relatively poor condition.

For up-to-the-minute **information** regarding traffic jams and roadworks on *autoroutes*, ring the 24hr, multilingual service Autoroutel (☎08 92 70 70 01; €0.34 per min) or consult Ⓦasf.fr. Traffic information for other roads can be obtained from the Bison Futé recorded information service (☎08 00 10 02 00; free, Ⓦbison-fute.equipement.gouv.fr) in French only.

At the time of writing, petrol prices were hovering around €1.40 a litre for unleaded (*sans plomb*), slightly more for four-star (*super*) and €1.20 a litre for diesel (*gazole* or *gasoil*); you'll find prices lowest at out-of-town hypermarkets. Note that in rural areas most petrol stations close at night, on Sundays and on bank holidays, and some may also close on Mondays. Some stations are equipped with 24hr pumps, but these only work with French bank cards.

If you run into **mechanical difficulties** you'll find garages and service stations in the Yellow Pages of the phone book under *"Garages d'automobiles"*; for **breakdowns**, look under *"Dépannages"*. If you have an accident or theft, you should contact the local police – and keep a copy of their report in order to file an insurance claim. Within Europe, most vehicle **insurance** policies cover taking your car to France; check with your insurer. However, you're advised to take out extra cover for motoring assistance in case your vehicle breaks down; contact your insurer or one of the motoring organizations listed below for a quote.

Rules of the road

US, Canadian, Australian, New Zealand and all EU **driving licences** are valid in France, though an International Driver's Licence makes life easier. The minimum driving age is 18 and you must hold a full (not a provisional) licence. Drivers are required to carry their licence, insurance papers and vehicle registration document (*carte grise*) with them in the car.

Since the French drive on the right, drivers of right-hand drive cars must adjust their **headlights** to dip to the right. This is most easily done by sticking on black glare deflectors, which can be bought at motor accessory shops and at the Channel ferry ports or the Eurostar terminal. Motorcyclists must drive with their headlights on, and must also wear a **helmet**.

All non-French vehicles must display their **national identification letters** (GB, etc), either on the number plate or by means of a sticker, and all vehicles must carry a red warning triangle, fluorescent jacket and a single- use breathalyser. **Seat belts** are compulsory front and back, and children under 10 years are not allowed to sit in the front of the car. It is illegal to use a hand-held **mobile phone** while driving.

The law of *priorité à droite* – **giving way** to traffic coming from your right, even when it is coming from a minor road – has largely been phased out. However, it still applies on a few roads in built-up areas and the occasional roundabout, so it pays to be vigilant at junctions, especially in rural areas where old habits die hard. A sign showing a yellow diamond on a white background gives you right of way, while the same sign with a diagonal black slash across it warns you that vehicles emerging from the right have priority. *Stop* signs mean you must stop completely; *Cédez le passage* means "Give way".

Unless otherwise indicated, **speed limits** are: 130kph (80mph) on *autoroutes*; 110kph (68mph) on dual carriageways; 90kph (55mph) on other roads; and 50kph (31mph) in towns. In wet weather, and for drivers with less than two years' experience, these limits are 110kph (68mph), 100kph (62mph) and 80kph (50mph) respectively, while the town limit remains constant. The legal blood **alcohol limit** is 0.05 percent alcohol (0.5 grams per litre), and police frequently make random breath tests, as well as saliva tests for drugs. There are stiff **penalties** for driving violations, ranging from on-the-spot fines for minor infringements, to the immediate confiscation of your licence and/or car for more serious offences.

Car rental

To rent a car in France you must be over 21 and have driven for at least one year. **Car rental** in France costs upwards of €50 for a day and €200 for a week for the smallest car, but is usually cheaper if arranged before you leave home or online. You'll find the big firms represented in most of the bigger towns, while a few of these also have desks at Bergerac and Brive airports. Local firms can be cheaper but most don't offer one-way rentals. Unless you specify otherwise, you'll get a car with manual transmission.

The **cost** of car rental includes the minimum car insurance required by law. Under the standard contract you are liable for an excess (*franchise*) for any damage to the vehicle. This starts at around €500 for the smallest car and can be covered by credit card.

CAR RENTAL AGENCIES

Alamo ⓦ alamo.com.
Argus Car Hire ⓦ arguscarhire.com.
Auto Europe ⓦ autoeurope.com.
Avis ⓦ avis.com.
Budget ⓦ budget.com.
Dollar ⓦ dollar.com.
Enterprise ⓦ enterprise.com.
Europcar ⓦ europcar.com.
Europe by Car ⓦ europebycar.com.
Hertz ⓦ hertz.com.
Holiday Autos ⓦ holidayautos.com.
National ⓦ nationalcar.com.
SIXT ⓦ e-sixt.com.
Thrifty ⓦ thrifty.com.

By scooter and motorbike

Though they're not built for long-distance travel, scooters are ideal for pottering around the local area. You also don't need a licence to drive them, just a passport or some form of ID. A few places that rent out bicycles often also rent out scooters; you can expect to pay at least €40 a day for a 50cc machine, less for longer periods. For anything more powerful you'll need a full **motorbike** licence. Rental prices are around €70 a day for a 125cc bike. Expect to leave a hefty deposit by cash or credit card – over €1000 is not unusual – which you may lose in the event of damage or theft. Crash helmets are compulsory on all bikes, and the headlight must be switched on at all times.

Cycling

Bicycles (*vélos*) have high status in France, where cyclists are given respect both on the roads and as customers at restaurants and hotels. In addition, local authorities are actively promoting cycling, not only with urban cycle lanes but also with comprehensive networks in rural areas (frequently using disused railways). Tourist offices can usually provide maps of local routes.

Most towns have well-stocked retail and **repair shops**, where parts are normally cheaper than in Britain or the US. However, if you're using a foreign-made bike with nonstandard metric wheels, it's a good idea to carry spare tyres.

The **train** network runs various schemes for cyclists, all of them covered on the website ⓦ velo .sncf.com. It's possible to take your bike for free on all TER trains in the region – make sure you arrive in good time to get a slot in the bike rack. Folding bikes travel free on TGV and Intercite services if they're packed into a bag measuring no more than 120cm by 90cm; for non-folding bikes you'll have to pay a €10 fee, which you can do either beforehand by calling ☎ 36.35, or when you buy your ticket at the station. If you board the train without a bike reservation, you are liable to incur a €45 fine and you will also be asked to leave the train at the next station.

Eurostar allows you to take your bicycle as part of your baggage allowance, provided it's dismantled and packed in a bike bag, again measuring no more than 120cm by 90cm. However, the company encourages people to register their bikes and send them unaccompanied with their registered baggage service for £25 one way, with a guaranteed arrival time of 24 hours; you can register your bike, which does not need to be dismantled, from ten days before departure. **Ferries** usually carry bikes free (though you may need to register it), as do some **airlines** such as British Airways, while others charge – check when making your booking.

Bikes – either mountain bikes (*vélos tout-terrain* or VTT) or hybrid bikes (*vélos tout-chemin* or VTC) – are widely available to **rent** from campsites and hostels, as well as from specialist cycle shops and some tourist offices for around €15–20 per day. As for **maps**, a minimum requirement is the IGN 1:100,000 series (see p.38) – the smallest scale that carries contours. The UK's national cyclists' organization, the CTC (☎0844 736 8451, ⓦctc.org.uk), can suggest routes and supply advice for members (£41 a year, or £66 for a family of four and £16 for under-18s and students under 26 years). They run a particularly good insurance scheme. Companies offering specialist bike touring **holidays** are listed on p.23. All cyclists are required by law to wear a reflective safety jacket at night outside urban areas and in the daytime during periods of poor visibility, or risk being fined up to €35.

By boat

Boating is a leisurely way to explore the Lot and Garonne valleys. From April to September the **River Lot** is navigable for motorboats from St-Cirq-Lapopie downstream to Luzech (65km), and from Fumel down to its confluence with the Garonne (78km). From October through to March the current is too swift and the river too high to be safe. But the Lot is a capricious river at any time, so it pays to follow the guidelines provided by rental companies carefully.

The other option is to potter along the **Garonne Canal**, which tracks the Garonne eastwards from Castets-en-Dorthe, near Langon, to Toulouse (190km), where it joins the Canal du Midi. You can also combine the Garonne Canal with the River Lot and the **River Baïse** south to Nérac.

Boats are usually rented by the week, though shorter periods are also available outside the July and August peak. **Rates** range from €800 to €2500 per week for a four- to ten-person boat, depending on the season and level of comfort. No licence is required, but you'll receive instruction before taking the controls. You should also be given a **carte de plaisance**, guaranteeing that the boat is insured and in good working order.

BOAT RENTAL COMPANIES IN THE LOT

Babou Marine ☎ 05 65 30 08 99, ⓦ baboulene-jean.fr.
Le Boat ☎ 0844 463 3594, ⓦ leboat.co.uk.
Locaboat Plaisance ☎ 03 86 91 72 72, ⓦ locaboat.com.
Lot Navigation ☎ 05 65 24 32 20, ⓦ lot-navigation.com.
Nautic ☎ 04 67 94 78 93, ⓦ nautic.fr.
Nicols ☎ 02 41 56 46 56, ⓦ nicols.com.

Accommodation

Throughout the Dordogne and Lot, there's an excellent spread of hotels and, increasingly, chambres d'hotes, which are complemented by some smart campsites and a smattering of hostels. In general you'll be able to get a simple double for around €40, though sometimes with shared facilities, while €50 should secure a reasonable level of comfort. At most times of the year you can turn up in any town and find a room or a place in a campsite, but it's best to book in advance.

Problems may arise between mid-July and the end of August, when the French take their own vacations en masse. During this period, hotel and hostel accommodation can be hard to come by – particularly in the most popular towns, such as Sarlat – and you may find yourself falling back on local tourist offices for help. Some offer a **booking service**, though they can't guarantee rooms at a particular price, and all provide lists of hotels, hostels, campsites and bed-and-breakfast possibilities. With **campsites**, you can be more relaxed about finding an empty pitch somewhere for a tent, though it may be more difficult with a caravan or camper van.

Hotels

Most French hotels are **graded** from zero to five stars. The price more or less corresponds to the number of stars, though the system is rather simplistic, having more to do with ratios of bathrooms-per-guest and so forth than genuine quality.

What you get for your money varies enormously between establishments. Paying under €40, you take your chances somewhat: there won't be soundproofing and the showers (*douches*) and toilets (WC or *toilettes*) may well be communal (*dans le palier*). However, you should have your own bidet and washbasin (*lavabo*), often partitioned off from the rest of the room in an area referred to as a *cabinet de toilette*. Over €40 should get you a room with its own bath or shower though not necessarily toilet, and, though the decor may not be anything to write home about, comfortable furniture. For around €60 you can expect a decent en-suite room with smart furnishings, while anything over €80 should give you something approaching luxury. **Single rooms** – if the hotel has any – are only marginally cheaper than doubles, so sharing always slashes costs, especially since most hotels willingly provide rooms with **extra beds** for three or more people at good discounts.

Breakfast, which is not normally included, will add between €6 and €15 per person to a bill, sometimes more – though there is no obligation to take it. Unless otherwise stated, all hotels listed in this guide offer free **wi-fi**.

Note that many family-run hotels close down for two or three weeks a year. In smaller towns and villages they may also close for one or two nights a week, usually Sunday or Monday. Details are given where possible in the Guide, but dates change from year to year and some places will close for a few days in low season if they have no bookings. The best precaution is to phone ahead to be sure.

A useful option, especially if you're driving and looking for somewhere late at night, are the modern **chain hotels** located at motorway exits and on the outskirts of major towns. Among the cheapest (from around €35 for a three-person room with communal toilets and showers) are the one-star Formule 1 chain (Ⓦ hotelformule1.com) and the slightly more comfortable Ibis Budget (formerly Etap; Ⓦ ibisbudgethotel.ibis.com).

There are also a number of well-regarded **hotel federations** in France, the biggest and most useful of which is **Logis** (Ⓦ logishotels.fr), an association of over three thousand hotels nationwide; standards are generally good, though occasionally can be a bit erratic. Two other, more upmarket federations worth mentioning are the Châteaux & Hôtels Collection (Ⓦ chateauxhotels.com) and Relais du Silence (Ⓦ relaisdusilence.com), both of which offer high-class accommodation in beautiful older properties, often in rural locations.

Bed-and-breakfast and self-catering

Predominantly in country areas, but increasingly found in towns, are *chambres d'hôtes*, **bed-and-breakfast accommodation** in someone's house, château or farm. Though the quality can vary, on the whole the standards are very high, and in many cases, the properties are blessed with an abundance of charm and character. Moreover, the owners may also provide traditional home cooking and a great insight into French life. In general, prices range between €50 and €100 for two people including breakfast; payment is almost always expected in cash. Some offer meals on request (*tables d'hôtes*), usually evenings only, while others are attached to *fermes auberges*, farm-restaurants serving local produce.

If you're planning to stay a week or more in any one place it might be worth considering renting **self-catering accommodation**. This will generally consist of self-contained country cottages known as *gîtes* or *gîtes ruraux*. Many *gîtes* are in converted barns or farm outbuildings, though some can be quite grand.

You can get lists of both *gîtes* and *chambres d'hôtes* from **Gîtes de France** (Ⓦ gites-de-france .com). They also publish annual guides such as *Nouveaux Gîtes Ruraux, Chambres et Tables d'Hôtes* and *Chambres d'Hôtes de Charme*, and more comprehensive regional or departmental guides that include photos. All these guides are available online or from departmental offices of Gîtes de France, as well as from local bookshops and tourist offices. Tourist offices will also have lists of places in their area that are not affiliated to Gîtes de France.

You'll also find self-catering accommodation, much of it foreign-owned, on Ⓦ frenchconnections .co.uk, Ⓦ cheznous.co.uk and Ⓦ bvdirect.co.uk; or try one of the agents listed in the Travel Shop section of the official French tourist office website, Ⓦ franceguide.com.

DEPARTMENTAL OFFICES OF GÎTES DE FRANCE

Aveyron/Lot/Tarn et Garonne Château de Bernussou, 12200 Villefranche de Rouergue ☎ 05 65 75 55 66, ✉ info @gitesdefrance-reservation-altg.com.

Corrèze Immeuble Consulaire, BP 30, 19001 Tulle ☎ 05 55 21 55 61, ✉ gites-de-france@correze.chambagri.fr.

Dordogne 25 rue Wilson, BP 2063, 24002 Périgueux ☎ 05 53 35 50 24, ✉ dordogne.perigord.tourisme@wanadoo.fr.

Lot-et-Garonne 11 rue des Droits-de-l'Homme, 47000 Agen
☎ 05 53 47 80 87, ✉ gites-de-france.47@wanadoo.fr.

Hostels, foyers and gîtes d'étape

At around €14–20 per night for a dormitory bed, usually with breakfast thrown in and the opportunity to prepare your own meals in a shared kitchen, **youth hostels** – *auberges de jeunesse* – are invaluable for single travellers on a budget; per-person prices of dorm beds are given throughout the Guide.

Most hostels are run either by the municipality or by the French **hostelling association**, the Fédération Unie des Auberges de Jeunesse (FUAJ). Many can be reserved online through the FUAJ website. To stay at FUAJ hostels you normally have to show a current HI (Hostelling International) **membership card**. It's usually cheaper and easier to join before you leave home, provided your national Youth Hostel association is a full member of HI. Alternatively, you can purchase an HI card in certain French hostels for €7.

Unfortunately, there aren't that many youth hostels in the Dordogne and Lot region. Sometimes, as is the case in Villefranche-de-Rouergue and Périgueux, hostel accommodation is provided in workers' hostels (**Foyers de Jeunes Travailleurs**). These tend to be functional and centrally located, with good canteens. Other hostels, most notably that at Cadouin, are more beautifully sited, though you might have to factor in the cost of a taxi in order to get there.

In the countryside, hostel-style **gîtes d'étape** are aimed primarily at hikers and long-distance bikers. Often run by the local village or municipality, they are less formal than hostels and provide bunk beds, primitive kitchen and washing facilities from around €15. They are marked on the large-scale IGN walkers' maps and listed in the individual Topo guides (see p.304). For more information check out the Gîtes de France booklet *Gîtes d'Étapes et de Séjours* (€10), and in *Gîtes d'Étape et de Refuges*, published by Rando Éditions, downloadable at ⓦ gites-refuges.com; €5 for the southwest region.

Camping

Practically every village and town in France has at least one **campsite** to cater for the thousands of people who spend their holiday under canvas. Most sites open from around Easter to September or October. The vast majority are graded into four **categories**, from one to four stars, by the local authority. One- and two-star sites are very basic, with toilets and showers (not necessarily with hot water), but little else, and standards of cleanliness are not always brilliant. At the other extreme, four-star sites are far more spacious, have hot-water showers and electrical hook-ups. Most will also have a swimming pool – sometimes heated – washing machines, a shop and sports facilities, and will provide refreshments or meals in high season. At three-star sites you can expect a selection of these facilities and less spacious plots. A further designation, **Camping Qualité** (ⓦ campingqualite .com), indicates those campsites with particularly high standards of hygiene, service and privacy, while the Clef Verte (ⓦ laclefverte.org) label is awarded to sites (and hotels and hostels) run along environmentally friendly lines. For those who really like to get away from it all, **camping à la ferme** – on somebody's farm – is a good, simple option. Lists of sites are available at local tourist offices.

Though **charging systems** vary, most places charge per pitch and per person, usually including a car, while others apply a global figure. As a rough guide, two people with a tent and car might pay as little as €10 at a simple municipal site to as much as €35 at a four-star in a prime location. In peak season and if you plan to spend a week or more at one site, it's wise to book ahead, and note that many of the big sites have caravans and chalet bungalows for rent.

The Fédération Française de Camping et de Caravaning (ⓦ ffcc.fr) has some 1200 affiliated sites and publishes an annual guide covering ten thousand campsites, details of which can also be found on the excellent Camping France website ⓦ campingfrance.com. If you'd rather have everything organized for you, a number of companies specialize in **camping holidays**, including Eurocamp (see p.23).

Lastly, a word of **caution**: never camp rough (*camping sauvage*, as the French call it) on anyone's land without first asking permission. If the dogs don't get you, the guns might – farmers have been known to shoot first and ask later. On the other hand, a politely phrased request for permission will as often as not get positive results. Camping on public land is not officially permitted, but is widely practised by the French, and if you are discreet you're not likely to have problems.

Food and drink

The cuisine of the Dordogne and Lot region is predominantly simple, country cooking (cuisine de terroir), revolving

around duck and goose, garlic, a host of mushrooms, walnuts and whatever else the land has to offer. It's the sort of cuisine best sampled in little family-run places, where it's still possible to eat well for €15 or less. That said, every restaurant worth its salt offers a **menu du terroir**, featuring local specialities. Expensive **gastronomique** restaurants throughout the region, and most mid-priced establishments, also offer a smattering of fish dishes. The food glossary is on p.309.

Breakfast and light meals

The standard hotel breakfast comprises cereals, yoghurt, bread and/or pastries, jam, orange juice and a jug of coffee or tea, and usually costs anywhere between €6–10. More expensive hotels typically offer fresh fruit, cheeses and hot and cold meats in addition to the above. If you're not staying in a hotel (or don't want to fork out that much), head to a café-bar and grab a croissant or *pain au chocolat* (a chocolate-filled, light pastry) with coffee or hot chocolate, which will cost around €4.

At **lunchtime**, and sometimes in the evening, you'll find places offering a *plat du jour* (daily special) at between €9 and €13, or *formules*, a limited menu, typically offering a main dish and either a starter or dessert for a set price. *Croques-monsieur* and *croques-madame* (variations on the toasted-cheese sandwich), along with *frites*, *gaufres* (waffles) and fresh-filled baguettes are good lunchtime snacks. You could also try a **crêpe** (pancake with a filling) – the savoury buckwheat variety (*galettes*) are the main course; sweet, white-flour crêpes are dessert. **Pizzerias**, usually *au feu de bois* (wood-fired), are also very common.

For **picnics**, the local outdoor market or supermarket will provide you with almost everything you need. Cooked meat, prepared snacks, ready-made dishes and assorted salads are also available at charcuteries (delicatessens), which you'll find in some villages, and in most supermarkets. You'll find boulangeries (bakeries) just about everywhere – often several in one village – and it's here you can pick up some delicious breads and, usually, a mouthwatering array of cakes and pastries too.

Restaurant meals

There's no difference between restaurants (or *auberges* or *relais* as they sometimes call themselves) and brasseries in terms of quality or price range. The distinction is that **brasseries**, which resemble cafés, serve quicker meals at most hours of the day, while **restaurants** tend to stick to the traditional meal times of noon to 2pm, and 7pm to 9pm or 9.30pm. In touristy areas in high season, and for all the more upmarket places, it's wise to make reservations – easily done on the same day in most cases.

When hunting for places to eat, don't forget that **hotel restaurants** are open to non-residents, and can be very good value. In country areas keep an eye out for **fermes auberges**, farm restaurants where the majority of ingredients are produced on the farm itself. These are often the best places to sample really traditional local cuisine at very reasonable prices; a four-course meal for between €15 and €35 is the norm, including an apéritif and wine, but reservations are a must.

Prices, and what you get for them, must be posted outside. Normally there's a choice between one or more **menus fixes** – with a set number of courses and a limited choice – and choosing individually from the *carte* (menu). *Menus fixes*, often referred to simply as *menus*, are normally the cheapest option, typically around €14–18 at lunchtime (*le déjeuner*) for a two- or three-course menu, rising to €20–30 or more at dinner (*le dîner*). Going **à la carte** offers greater choice and, in the better restaurants, unlimited access to the chef's inventiveness – though you'll pay for the privilege.

In the vast majority of restaurants a **service charge** of fifteen percent is included in prices listed on the menu – in which case it should say *service compris* (*s.c.*) or *prix nets*. Very occasionally you'll see *service non compris* (*s.n.c.*) or *servis en sus*, which means that it's up to you whether you leave a tip or not. Wine (*vin*) or a drink (*boisson*) is sometimes included in the cost of a *menu fixe*. Otherwise, the cheapest option will be the house wine, usually served in a jug (*pichet*) or carafe; you'll be asked if you want *un quart* (0.25 litre), *un demi* (0.5 litre) or *un litre* (1 litre).

One final note is that you should always call the waiter or waitress *Monsieur* or *Madame* (*Mademoiselle* if a young woman), never *Garçon*.

Vegetarian food

On the whole, **vegetarians** can expect a fairly lean time in the Dordogne and Lot region. That said, in the very best restaurants you'll often find one or two fantastically creative vegetarian dishes on the menu, typically featuring *cèpes* (mushrooms) as the star ingredient. Otherwise your best bet is to head for a crêperie or pizzeria, while Chinese or North African restaurants can be good standbys. Occasionally they'll be willing to replace a meat dish on the fixed-price menu (menu fixe); at other times you'll have to pick your way through the carte. Remember to ask "Je suis végétarien(ne); est-ce qu'il y a quelques plats sans viande?" (I'm a vegetarian; are there any non-meat dishes?) **Vegans**, however, should probably forget about eating in restaurants and stick to self-catering.

Drink

In France **drinking** is done at a leisurely pace whether it's a prelude to food (apéritif), or a sequel (digestif), and cafés are the standard places to do it. Every bar or café has to display its full price list, including service charges. You normally pay when you leave, and it's usually perfectly acceptable to sit for hours over just one cup of coffee. Note that the minimum age for buying alcohol is 18, though younger teenagers may drink wine in a restaurant if with their parents.

Wine

French wine (vin), drunk at just about every meal or social occasion, is unrivalled in the world for its range, sophistication, diversity and status. The house wine served in restaurants can be very good value in this wine-producing region, or opt for a bottle of AOP (appellation d'origine protégée) wine if you want a more sophisticated taste. You can buy a very decent bottle of wine for €6 in a shop or from the producer, while €10 and over will get you something worth savouring. A glass of wine in a bar will typically cost around €3 to €5.

The best way of **buying wine** is directly from the producers (vignerons) at their vineyards or at Maisons or Syndicats du Vin (representing a group of wine-producers), or Coopératifs Vinicoles (producers' co-ops). At all of these you can usually sample the wines first. The most interesting option is to visit the vineyard itself, where the owner will often include a tour of the chais in which the wine is produced and aged. The most economical method is to buy en vrac, which you can do at some wine shops (caves), filling a plastic five- or ten-litre container (generally sold on the premises) straight from the barrel. Supermarkets often have good bargains, too.

There are strict limitations on the extent to which wine-growers can interfere in the natural process – it's illegal even to water vines. The result is that, far more than in other countries, French wines are the product of a very specific bit of land or terroir, and there will often be significant differences in taste between the wines of two neighbouring producers. This makes tasting wines a real joy, and even if you're not an expert, it's well worth trying to establish which grape types you particularly like or dislike, and whether you like your wine fruity or dry, light or heavy. Waiters and wine producers are usually delighted to give you advice in making a choice.

For basic wine vocabulary, see p.313.

Beer

Light Belgian and German **beers**, plus various French brands from Alsace, account for most of the beer you'll find. Draught beer (à la pression) – very often Kronenbourg – is the cheapest drink you can have next to coffee and wine; une pression (usually 0.33 litre) will cost around €3. For a wider choice of draught and bottled beer you need to go to special beer-drinking establishments such as the English- and Irish-style pubs found in larger towns and cities. A small bottle at one of these places can cost up to twice as much as a demi in an ordinary café-bar. Buying bottled or canned beer in supermarkets is much cheaper.

Spirits and liqueurs

Strong alcohol, including **spirits** (eaux-de-vie), such as cognac and armagnac, and **liqueurs** such as locally made walnut liqueurs (vins de noix), are always available. Refreshing pastis – the generic name for aniseed drinks such as Pernod or Ricard – is served diluted with water and ice (glace or glaçons). Among less familiar names, try Poire William (pear brandy), or Marc (a spirit distilled from grape pulp). Measures are generous, but they don't come cheap: the same applies for imported spirits such as whisky (Scotch). Two drinks designed to stimulate the appetite – un apéritif – are Pineau (cognac and grape juice) and Kir (white wine with a dash of cassis – blackcurrant liqueur – or with champagne instead of wine for a Kir Royal). For a post-meal digestif, don't miss out on armagnac, oak-aged brandy from the south of the Garonne but available in bars and restaurants throughout the region. **Cocktails** are served at most late-night bars, discos and clubs, as well as at upmarket hotel bars; they usually cost at least €5.

Soft drinks

On the **soft drink** front, you can buy cartons of unsweetened fruit juice in supermarkets, although in cafés, the bottled (sweetened) nectars such as apricot (jus d'abricot) and blackcurrant (cassis) still hold sway. Fresh orange or lemon juice (*orange/citron pressé*) is a much more refreshing choice on a hot day. Other soft drinks to try are syrups (*sirops*) of mint, grenadine and other flavours mixed with water. The standard fizzy drinks of lemonade (*limonade*), Coke (*coca*) and so forth are all available. Bottles of **mineral water** (*eau minérale*) and spring water (*eau de source*) – either sparkling (*gazeuse*) or still (*plate*) – abound. But there's not much wrong with the tap water (*l'eau de robinet*) which will always be brought free to your table if you ask for it.

Coffee, tea and hot chocolate

Coffee is invariably espresso – small, black and very strong. *Un café* or *un express* is the regular; *un crème* is with milk; *un grand café* or *un grand crème* are large versions. In the morning you could also ask for *un café au lait* – espresso in a large cup or bowl filled up with hot milk. *Un déca* is decaffeinated. Ordinary **tea** (*thé*) – Lipton's nine times out of ten – is normally served black (*nature*) or with a slice of lemon (*au citron*); to have milk with it, ask for *un peu de lait frais* (some fresh milk). *Chocolat chaud* – **hot chocolate** – unlike tea, lives up to the high standards of French food and drink and is available at any café. After meals, **herb teas** (*infusions* or *tisanes*), are offered by most restaurants – most commonly *verveine* (verbena), *tilleul* (lime blossom), *menthe* (mint) and *camomille* (camomile).

Festivals

It's hard to beat the experience of arriving in a small French village, expecting no more than a bed for the night, to discover the streets decked out with flags and streamers, a band playing in the square and the entire population out celebrating the feast of their patron saint. As well as the country-wide Fête de la Musique (June 21) and Bastille Day (July 14), there are any number of festivals – both traditional and of more recent origin – throughout the Dordogne and Lot.

The region's cathedrals, churches and châteaux make superb venues for festivals of **music** and **theatre**. All the major towns, and many of the smaller ones, put on at least one such festival a year, usually in summer, when you can often catch free performances in the streets. Anyone interested in

contemporary theatre should make a beeline for Périgueux in early August, when international mime artists gather for Mimos, one of France's most exciting and innovative festivals.

Popular local culture is celebrated in the Félibrée, a festival established in 1903 to promote and safeguard the local *Occitan* (or *Oc*) language and culture. The **Félibrée** takes place on the first Sunday in July, when there is a procession, an *Occitan* Mass and – of course – a blow-out Périgordin meal. Nowadays the celebrations also continue for around ten days either side of the Félibrée itself in the form of folk concerts, crafts demonstrations, theatre and so forth. It takes place in a different town in the Dordogne *département* each year; contact the tourist office in Périgueux for the latest information.

More recent introductions are the **historical spectaculars** held at places such as Castillon-la-Bataille, where the final battle of the Hundred Years War is re-enacted by hundreds of local thespians. Such events may be touristy, but the atmosphere – most are held at night – and general enthusiasm more than compensate.

In such dedicated **wine** country, there are inevitably festivals coinciding with the grape harvest, when each village stages its own celebrations.

For details of the region's most important and interesting festivals, see the boxes at the beginning of each chapter of the Guide.

Sports and outdoor activities

The Dordogne and Lot region offers a terrific range of sports and outdoor activities, including hiking, cycling, trekking and waterborne diversions such as canoeing and kayaking. By far the most popular spectator sport in the region is rugby, particularly in Brive, but you'll find a team of some description in just about every town.

Walking

Walking is undoubtedly the best way to enjoy this region of France. Well-maintained long-distance paths known as *sentiers de grande randonnée*, or simply **GRs**, cut across country, signed with red and white waymarkers and punctuated with campsites and *gîtes d'étapes* at convenient distances. Some of the main routes in the region are the GR6, linking Ste-Foy-la-Grande in the west to Figeac; the GR36, which wanders southeast from Périgueux via Les Eyzies and Cahors to the Gorges de l'Aveyron; and the GR65, the great pilgrimage route passing through Figeac, Cahors and Moissac on the way to Santiago de Compostela in Spain.

The entire GR65 and parts of the GR36 and GR6 are described in a **Topo-guide** (available outside France in good travel bookshops), which gives a detailed account of the route, including maps, campsites, refuges, sources of provisions, etc. In France, the guides are available from bookshops and some tourist offices, or direct from the principal French walkers' organization, the Fédération Française de la Randonnée Pédestre (W ffrandonnee.fr).

In addition, many tourist offices produce guides to their local footpaths; where there is no tourist office, try asking at the *mairie*. For recommendations on walking **maps**, see p.38.

Cycling

The region's minor roads and demarcated **cycling** routes provide plenty of opportunities for cyclists; it's best to avoid main roads if you want to enjoy yourself, particularly in the high season. Among the long-distance routes, there's the "Grand Traversée du Périgord" running 180km from Mareuil in the far northwest via Brantôme, Périgueux and Les Eyzies to Monpazier. In the Lot-et-Garonne, the "Véloroute" follows the River Lot 80km from Aiguillon northeast to Fumel and Bonaguil. Many tourist offices can provide details of cycle paths in their area, while the French Federation of Cycling has lots of useful information on their website (W ffct.org). For recommendations on cycling **maps**, see p.38.

Canoeing and kayaking

Canoeing is hugely popular in the Dordogne and Lot region, and in the summer months every navigable river has outfits renting canoes and organizing excursions. Those along Dordogne itself are the busiest, particularly the stretch between La Roque-Gageac and Beynac, where you pass beneath some of the region's most dramatic castles, and the Vézère, where you can stop off at various points to visit the valley's prehistoric sights. Other, quieter options include the River Lot, through the Aveyron gorges and the smaller Dronne, Dropt and Célé rivers.

You can **rent** two- to three-person canoes and single-seater kayaks on all these rivers; every tourist office also stocks lists of local operators. Although it's possible to rent by the hour, it's best to take at least a half-day and simply cruise downstream. The company you book through will provide transport as required. Prices vary according to what's on offer, but you can expect to pay anywhere between €15–25 per person for a day's canoe rental, and around €4 more for a kayak.

On the Dordogne and Lot rivers you can make **longer excursions** of up to two weeks, either accompanied or on your own, sometimes in combination with cycling or walking. Various tour operators offer canoeing packages or you can book direct with the local company. Two of the biggest along the Dordogne valley are Canoës Loisirs (T 05 53 28 23 43, W canoes-loisirs .com) and Copeyre Canoë (T 05 65 37 33 51, W copeyre.com).

The length of the canoeing **season** depends on the weather and the water levels. Successive droughts have caused some rivers almost to dry up in recent summers. Better to come in spring or early summer to be on the safe side. Most operators function daily in July and August, on demand in May, June and September, and close between October and April when the rivers are too high for inexperienced canoeists. One or two, however, stay open throughout the year. All companies are obliged to equip you with lifejackets (*gilets*) and teach you basic safety procedures. You must be able to swim.

Horseriding

Horseriding is an excellent way of enjoying the countryside. Practically every town in the Dordogne and Lot, and many farms, have equestrian centres (*centres équestres*) where you can ride with a guide or unaccompanied – depending on your level of experience – on the marked riding trails that span the region. Local and departmental tourist offices can provide details, or you can contact the Comité National du Tourisme Équestre (W ffe.com).

Rock climbing and caving

In the limestone regions of the Dordogne and Lot **rock climbing** (*escalade*) and **caving** (*spéléologie*) are popular activities. Several local canoe rental outfits, such as Couleurs Périgord and Kalapaca offer beginners' courses and half-day or full-day outings. Further information is available from tourist offices or the national federations; for rock climbing (W ffme.fr), and for caving (W ffspeleo.fr).

Swimming

There are several pebbly beaches which give access to the water along the Dordogne and Lot rivers, but it's often too shallow or fast-flowing to be ideal for **swimming**. An alternative is to head for one of the real or artificial lakes, which pepper the region. Many have leisure centres (*bases de plein airs*) at which you can rent pedaloes, windsurfers and dinghies, as well as larger boats and jet-skis (on the bigger reservoirs). It's worth noting, however, that in high summer, when the water is at its lowest, pollution warnings have been issued on rivers and lakes in the region. Check with local tourist authorities for the current situation. Many hotels and campsites also have their own swimming pools for guests to make use of. One thing to be aware of is that some impose strict rules on what sort of swimming costumes can and can't be worn: for men, long or baggy swimming shorts are often outlawed.

Rugby and football

Despite the influence of France's footballing prowess, **rugby** remains the most important and closely followed field game throughout this region. In season (mid-September to mid-May) virtually every town worth its salt boasts a team and if you go along to a match you'll soon get swept up in the camaraderie; unless it's a final, tickets are easy to buy at the gate and are reasonably priced (around €10–15). The top two teams to look out for are Sporting Union Agen, who play in the First Division (Top 14), and Brive, one-time European Cup champions, though they have struggled recently and currently play in the Second Division (Pro D2).

In the absence of a professional football team hereabouts, you'll have to make the short trip to Bordeaux to watch any football of substance. First Division team **FC Girondins** (Ⓦgirondins.com) play at Stade Chaban-Delmas, in the city's southwestern suburbs, with tickets starting at just €10, going up to €50 for the best seats in the ground. Illustrious players such as Zidane, Deschamps, Wiltord and Lizarazu – all members of France's winning 1998 World Cup squad – have all played for Bordeaux at one time or another.

Boules

Once the preserve of elderly men in berets, **boules**, and its variant *pétanque* (in which contestants must keep both feet on the ground when throwing), has been growing in popularity in recent years and broadening its appeal to include more young people and women. There is even a world championship and talk – not all of it in jest – of getting *boules* recognized as an Olympic sport.

Shopping and markets

The quickest and most convenient places to shop are the hypermarkets and supermarkets you'll find in and around every major town. Even some villages have a "superette". But more interesting by far are the specialist food shops and, of course, the markets which are still held at least once a week in towns throughout the region.

Many of these **markets** have been held on the same day for centuries. One of the region's biggest and best is that at Sarlat, but the competition is fierce and it's worth including several market days in your itinerary. Other terrific markets are held in Brantôme, Brive, Cahors, Le Bugue, Périgueux and Ribérac, among many other towns and villages. In recent years the hordes of visitors in summer have meant an inevitable increase in the volume of generic tack sold at the biggest markets, but they still boast more than enough enticing local produce and genuine craftsmanship to be unmissable.

In winter time, you'll also find most towns in the Dordogne and Lot hold *marchés aux gras* when whole fattened livers of duck and goose are put up for sale alongside the other edible bits of the fowl. Often these events double up as truffle markets and are one of the few places in France where **bargaining** is acceptable. For a list of the region's most important and interesting markets, see the boxes at the beginning of each chapter of the Guide.

Travel essentials

Costs

Although prices have been rising steadily in recent years, the Dordogne and Lot is not an outrageously expensive place to visit, especially compared to many other parts of France, such as the regions further south towards the coast, and east towards the Alps. When and where you go, however, will make a difference: in prime tourist spots, hotel prices can go up by a third during July and August.

For a reasonably comfortable existence, including a double room in a mid-range hotel, lunch and dinner in a restaurant, plus moving around, café stops and museum visits, you need to allow around €100/£80/US$125 a day per person. But by counting the pennies, staying at youth hostels or camping, and being strong-willed about extra cups of coffee and doses of culture, you could manage on around €60/£40/US$75 a day each, to include a cheap restaurant meal.

Youth and student discounts

Once obtained, various official and quasi-official youth/student ID cards soon pay for themselves in savings. Full-time students are eligible for the **International Student ID Card** (ISIC; Ⓦ isic.org or Ⓦ statravel.co.uk in the UK), which entitles you to special air, rail and bus fares, and discounts at museums, theatres and other attractions. It also gives you access to a free 24-hour helpline to call in the event of a medical or legal emergency. You have to be 25 or under to qualify for the **International Youth Travel Card**, while teachers are eligible for the **International Teacher Card**, offering similar discounts. They are available through universities and student travel specialists such as STA Travel, USIT and Travel CUTS.

Taxes

The majority of goods and services in France are subject to **value-added tax** (*taxe sur la valeur ajoutée* or *TVA* in French), usually at a rate of 19.6 percent, which is included in the price. Most local authorities also levy a **tourism tax** on hotel and *chambre d'hôte* accommodation – called a *taxe de séjour* – generally not more than €1 per person per night depending on the category; in some areas this tax only applies in peak season. While the tax is not included in room rates, it must be clearly indicated as a separate item.

Crime and personal safety

In the more rural parts of the Dordogne and Lot region crime is extremely rare. However, it obviously makes sense to take the normal **precautions**: don't flash wads of notes around; carry your bag or wallet securely; never leave cameras, mobile phones or other valuables lying around; and park your car overnight in a monitored parking, garage or, at the very least, on a busy and well-lit street. It's wise to keep a separate record of cheque and credit card numbers, and the phone numbers for cancelling

them. Finally, make sure you have a good insurance policy.

There are two main types of **police** in France – the Police Nationale and the Gendarmerie Nationale. The former deals with all crime, parking and traffic affairs within large and mid-sized towns, where you will find them in the Commissariat de Police. The Gendarmerie Nationale covers the rural areas.

If you need to **report a theft**, go to the local Gendarmerie or Commissariat de Police (addresses of commissariats are given in the Guide for the major towns), where they will fill out a *constat de vol*. The first thing they'll ask for is your passport, and vehicle documents if relevant. Although the police are not always as cooperative as they might be, it is their duty to assist you if you've lost your passport or all your money.

If you have an **accident** while driving, you must fill in and sign a *constat d'accident* (declaration form) or, if another car is also involved, a *constat aimable* (jointly agreed declaration); these forms should be provided with the car's insurance documents. The police can impose on-the-spot fines for minor **driving offences** and take away your licence for anything more serious.

Drugs

Drug use is just as prevalent in France as anywhere else in Europe – and just as risky. People caught smuggling or possessing drugs, even just a few grams of marijuana, are liable to find themselves in jail. Should you be **arrested** on any charge, you have the right to contact your consulate, though don't expect much sympathy.

Racism

Unfortunately, **racist attitudes** are not uncommon in France, particularly towards the country's Arab and black communities. Visitors to the Dordogne and Lot are extremely unlikely to experience any aggression or open hostility, but may encounter an unwelcome degree of curiosity or suspicion from shopkeepers, hoteliers, bar and club owners and the like. Carrying your passport at all times is a good idea.

If you suffer a **racial assault**, contact the police, your consulate or one of the local anti-racism organizations (though they may not have English-speakers): SOS Racism (29 rue Bergeret, 33000 Bordeaux; ☎05 56 31 94 62, Ⓦ sos-racisme.org); and Mouvement contre le Racisme et pour l'Amitié entre les Peuples (MRAP; Paris ☎01 53 38 99 99, Ⓦ mrap.asso.fr).

Electricity

The **electricity** supply in France is almost always 220V, using plugs with two round pins. If you need a transformer, it's a good idea to buy one before leaving home, though you can find them in big department stores.

Entry requirements

Citizens of European Union (EU) countries can travel freely in France, while those from Australia, Canada, New Zealand and the United States, among other countries, do not need a visa for a stay of up to ninety days. However, the situation can change and it's advisable to check with your nearest French embassy or consulate before departure.

All non-EU citizens who plan to remain longer than ninety days should apply for a **long-stay visa**, for which you will have to show proof of – among other things – a regular income or sufficient funds to support yourself and medical insurance. For further information about visa regulations consult the Ministry of Foreign Affairs website: ⓦ diplomatie .gouv.fr.

The website ⓦ embassyworld.com has a list of embassies and consulates in France.

Gay and lesbian travellers

In general, France is more liberal on homosexuality than many other European countries. The legal age of consent is 15 and civil unions between same-sex couples were made legal in 1999. That said, gay couples are not allowed to adopt children and same-sex marriages remain illegal.

On a day-to-day level, the French mostly consider sexuality to be a private matter, and homophobic assaults are extremely rare. Neverthe-less, **gays** tend to be discreet outside specific gay venues, **lesbians** even more so. You can expect to be received with tolerance, but not necessarily a warm welcome.

USEFUL CONTACTS

Dykeplanet ⓦ dykeplanet.com. Sells *Le dykeGuide*, a French-language guidebook published annually and aimed at lesbians primarily. Available at FNAC stores and major booksellers or from the publishers.

> ### EMERGENCY NUMBERS
> Police ❶17; Ambulance ❶15; Fire ❶18 or call ❶112 for all emergencies.

Spartacus International Gay Guide ⓦ spartacusworld.com. Has an extensive section on France and contains some info for lesbians.
Têtu ⓦ tetu.com. France's best-selling gay/lesbian magazine, with events listings and contact addresses; you can buy it in bookshops, newsagents or through their website, which is also an excellent source of information.

Health

Visitors to the Dordogne and Lot region have little to worry about as far as health is concerned. No vaccinations are required, there are no nasty diseases to be wary of and tap water is safe to drink. The worst that's likely to happen is a case of sunburn or an upset stomach from eating too much rich food – or a hangover from all that wonderful wine. If you do need treatment, however, you should be in good hands: the French health-care system is rated one of the best in the world.

Under the French health system, all services, including doctor's consultations, prescribed medicines, hospital stays and ambulance call-outs, incur a charge which you have to pay upfront. **EU citizens** are entitled to a refund (usually between 70 and 100 percent), providing the doctor is govern-ment registered (*un médecin conventionné*) and provided you have a European Health Insurance Card (EHIC; *Carte Européenne d'Assurance Maladie*). Note that everyone in the family, including children, must have their own cards, which are free. In the UK you can apply for them online through the Depart-ment of Health website (ⓦ dh.gov.uk), by phone (❶0845 606 2030) or by post – forms are available from post offices. Even with the EHIC card, however, you might want to take out some additional insurance to cover the shortfall. A stay in hospital, for example, can still leave you with a hefty bill. All **non-EU visitors** should ensure they have adequate medical insurance cover.

For minor complaints go to a **pharmacie**, signalled by an illuminated green cross. You'll find at least one in every small town and even some villages. They keep normal shop hours (roughly Mon–Sat 9am–noon & 3–6/7pm), though some stay open late and, in larger towns, at least one (known as the *pharmacie de garde*) is open 24 hours according to a rota; details are displayed in all pharmacy windows.

For anything more serious you can get the name of a **doctor** from a pharmacy, local police station, tourist office or your hotel. Alternatively, look under "Médecins" in the Yellow Pages (*Pages Jaunes*) phone directory. The consultation fee is in the region of €23–25. You'll be given a statement of treatment (*Feuille de Soins*) for later insurance claims. Any prescriptions will be fulfilled by a pharmacy and must be paid for; little price stickers (*vignettes*) from each medicine will be stuck on the *Feuille de Soins*.

In serious **emergencies** you will always be admitted to the nearest general hospital (*centre hospitalier*). Phone numbers and addresses are given in the Guide for all the main cities. The national number for calling an ambulance is ☎15.

Insurance

Even though EU citizens are entitled to health-care privileges in France, it's advisable to take out an insurance policy before travelling to cover against theft, loss and illness or injury. Before paying for a new policy, however, it's worth checking whether you are already covered: some all-risks home insurance policies may cover your possessions when overseas, and many private medical schemes include cover when abroad. In Canada, provincial health plans usually provide partial cover for medical mishaps overseas. Students will often find that their student health coverage extends during the vacations and for one term beyond the date of last enrolment.

A typical **travel insurance policy** usually provides cover for the cost of medical treatment and damage caused by accidents, as well as cancellation or curtailment of your journey. Cover for lost or stolen cash, cheques and possessions usually costs a little extra. Most policies exclude so-called dangerous sports unless an extra premium is paid: in the Dordogne and Lot this would include rock climbing and pot-holing and sometimes such apparently benign activities as canoeing, so it's best to check the small print carefully. Many policies can be chopped and changed to exclude coverage you don't need.

If you need to **make a claim**, you should keep receipts for medicines and medical treatment, and in the event you have anything stolen, you must obtain an official statement from the police (called *un constat de vol*).

Internet

Wireless internet (wi-fi) is increasingly the norm in even the cheapest French hotels, and more often than not, it's free. Internet cafés are not so common these days, though most cafés will have wi-fi available – you'll just be obliged to buy a drink. Unless specified otherwise, all accommodation establishments listed in this guide have wi-fi.

Laundry

Laundries are still reasonably common in French towns – just ask in your hotel, or the tourist office, or look in the phone book under "*Laveries automatiques*" or "*Laveries en libre-service*". They are usually unattended, and while some have machines for changing notes, it's prudent to come armed with small change. Washing powder (*la lessive*) is always available on site. Machines are graded in different wash sizes, costing in the region of €4 to €5 for 7kg. Most hotels forbid doing any laundry in your room, though you should get away with just one or two small items.

Mail

French **post offices**, known as La Poste and identified by bright yellow-and-blue signs, are generally open from around 9am to 5pm or 6pm Monday to Friday, and 9am to noon on Saturday. Those in smaller towns and villages usually also close from noon to 2pm.

You can receive mail using the **poste restante** system available at the central post office in every town. It should be addressed (preferably with the surname first and in capitals) "Poste Restante, Poste Centrale", followed by the name of the town and its postcode. You'll need your passport to collect your mail and will have to pay €0.60 per item; mail is kept for two weeks.

Stamps (*timbres*) are sold at *tabacs* and newsagents as well as post offices. For information

---

PUBLIC HOLIDAYS

January 1 New Year's Day
March/April Easter Monday
Ascension Day (forty days after Easter)
Pentecost or Whitsun (seventh Sunday after Easter)
May 1 Labour Day
May 8 Victory in Europe (VE) Day 1945
July 14 Bastille Day
August 15 Assumption of the Virgin Mary
November 1 All Saints' Day
November 11 Armistice Day 1918
December 25 Christmas Day

---

on postal rates, among other things, log on to the post office website ⓦ laposte.fr.

You can also change money at post offices, send faxes and do photocopying. To post your letter on the street, look for the bright yellow **postboxes** – make sure, where necessary, to put your letter in the box marked "étranger" (abroad).

Maps

In addition to the **maps** in this guide and the various free town plans you'll be offered along the way, the one extra map you might want is a good, up-to-date road map of the region. The best are the regional maps produced by Michelin (ⓦ michelinonline.co.uk) and IGN (ⓦ ign.fr). To cover the area encompassed by this guide, IGN's Dordogne map (1:200,000), and Michelin's Aquitaine and Midi-Pyrénées maps (1:200,000) are all worth seeking out. Alternatively, both companies issue large spiral-bound road atlases covering the whole of France at around the same scale.

If you're planning to walk or cycle, it's well worth investing in the more detailed IGN maps. The Carte de Randonnée (1:25,000) series is specifically designed for walkers, while the Carte de Promenade (1:100,000) is ideal for cyclists.

Money

France's currency is the **euro** (€), which is divided into 100 cents (also called *centimes*). There are seven notes – in denominations of 5, 10, 20, 50, 100, 200 and 500 euros – and eight different coins: 1, 2, 5, 10, 20 and 50 cents, and 1 and 2 euros.

For the most up-to-date **exchange rates** for these and other currencies, consult ⓦ xe.com.

The best way to access money in France is to use your **credit** or **debit card** to withdraw cash from an

ATM (known as *un distributeur de billets* or *un point argent*); most machines give instructions in several European languages. Note that there is often a transaction fee, so it's more efficient to take out a sizeable sum each time rather than making lots of small withdrawals.

Credit and debit cards are widely accepted in shops, hotels and restaurants, though some smaller establishments don't accept cards, or only for sums above a certain threshold. Visa – called Carte Bleue in France – is almost universally recognized, followed by MasterCard (also known as EuroCard). American Express ranks a bit lower.

You can **change cash** at most banks and main post offices, though only the latter will change travellers' cheques. There are money-exchange counters (*bureaux de change*) at French airports, major train stations and usually one or two in city centres as well, though they don't always offer the best exchange rates.

Newspapers and radio

The large number of Brits living in France has also led to an active English-language press in the country. Two monthly newspapers in English are *The Connexion* (ⓦ connexionfrance.com) and the broadsheet *The French Paper* (ⓦ thefrenchpaper .com). *The Connexion* publishes a Dordogne-specific newspaper, *The Advertiser*, monthly. They are available from newsagents (*maisons de la presse*) and, in larger towns, from street-side kiosks.

As for **RADIO**, Radio Liberté (ⓦ radioliberte.fr) broadcasts an English-language show with news during the week.

Opening hours and public holidays

Basic **hours of business** are 9am to noon and 2 to 6pm. Small food shops often don't reopen till halfway through the afternoon, closing around 7.30 or 8pm, just before the evening meal. Supermarkets also tend to stay open to at least 7pm.

The standard **closing day** is Sunday, though some food shops, particularly bakeries (boulangeries), and newsagents are open in the morning. Some shops and businesses, particularly in the rural areas, also close on a Monday.

Core **banking hours** are Monday to Friday 9am to noon and 2 to 4.30pm. Some branches close on Monday, while others stay open at midday and may also open on Saturday morning. All are closed on Sunday and public holidays.

Most tourist offices are open all day every day throughout July and August, but hours outside these months vary considerably. **Museums** tend to open around 9.30 or 10am, close for lunch from noon until 1 or 2pm, and then run through to 5 or 6pm. In summer some stay open all day and close later, while in winter, many open only in the afternoon. Museum closing days are usually Monday or Tuesday, sometimes both. Many state owned museums have one day of the week or month when they're free or half price.

Churches are generally open from around 8am to dusk, but may close at lunchtime and are reserved for worshippers during services (times of which will usually be posted on the door). Country churches are increasingly kept locked; there may be a note on the door saying where to get the key, usually from the priest's house (*le presbytère*) or someone else living nearby, or from the *mairie*.

France celebrates eleven **public holidays** (*jours fériés*), when banks and most shops and businesses (though not necessarily restaurants), and some museums, are closed.

Phones

Payphones (*cabines*) are increasingly rare, but where you do find one, you can make and receive domestic and international **calls** – look for the number in the top right-hand corner of the information panel. The vast majority of public phones require a **phone card** (*télécarte*), available from *tabacs* and newsagents; they come in 50 and 120 units (€7.50 and €15 respectively). You can also use **credit cards** in many call boxes.

Alternatively, you can pick up one of the many prepaid phone cards (*cartes téléphoniques*) that operate with a unique **code** (on sale at post offices, *tabacs*, newsagents and many supermarkets), and which can be used from both public and private phones. Symacom (ⓦ symacom.fr) generally gives the best rates and service, with its "Continental" cards priced at €7.50 and €15. Note, though, that

you pay a substantial charge on each connection, so these are only good value for a couple of long calls, not for many short ones.

French **telephone numbers** have ten digits. Numbers beginning ☎0800 or 0805 are free-dial numbers; those beginning ☎081 and ☎086 are charged as a local call; anything else beginning ☎08 is premium-rated. Numbers starting ☎06 and 07 are mobile numbers and therefore also expensive to call.

Mobile phones

If you want to use your **mobile/cell phone** in France, contact your phone provider before leaving home to check whether it will work locally, and what the call charges are.

French mobile phones operate on the European GSM standard, so many **US cellphones** won't work in France unless they are "tri band". The quickest and cheapest option is probably to change your phone and/or service provider.

If you're going to be in France for an extended time and plan to make a lot of local calls, consider buying a pay-as-you-go French **SIM card**. For this you'd have to make sure your phone is "unlocked", in other words it will work with other providers. Again, you'll get a local number. You can buy the kits (upwards of €15 for a starter kit including a SIM card and around €5 worth of calls credited to your account) at one of the high street shops run by the three main French operators, the largest of which are Orange and SFR, followed by Bouygues Télécom. One other option is to access a wi-fi facility and use your Skype account.

Smoking

Smoking is banned in all enclosed public spaces, including museums, restaurants, bars and nightclubs.

Time

France lies in the **Central European Time Zone** (GMT+1). This means it is one hour ahead of the UK, six hours ahead of Eastern Standard Time, and nine

---

CALLING HOME FROM ABROAD

Note that the initial zero is omitted from the area code when dialling the UK, Ireland, Australia and New Zealand from abroad.

Australia international access code + 61
New Zealand international access code + 64
UK international access code + 44
US and Canada international access code + 1
Republic of Ireland international access code + 353
South Africa international access code + 27

hours ahead of Pacific Standard Time. Between April and October France is eight hours behind eastern Australia and ten hours behind New Zealand; from November to March it is ten hours behind south-eastern Australia and twelve hours behind New Zealand. Daylight Saving Time (GMT+2) in France lasts from the last Sunday of March to the last Sunday of October.

Tipping

Hotels and almost all restaurants include a **service charge** of fifteen percent in their prices (*service compris*). It's therefore not necessary to leave an additional cash **tip** at restaurants unless you feel you have received service out of the ordinary; if so, an extra two or three percent is plenty. It's customary to tip porters, tour guides and taxi drivers one or two euros, and to leave the small change at cafés.

Tourist information

The French Government Tourist Office (Maison de la France, ⓦ franceguide.com) increasingly refers you to their website for information, though they still produce a number of useful brochures. For information specific to the Dordogne and Lot region, contact the regional or departmental tourist offices before you leave home.

Tourist offices

In the Dordogne and Lot region you'll find a tourist office – usually an **Office du Tourisme** (OT) but sometimes a **Syndicat d'Initiative** (SI) – in practically every town and many villages (addresses, contact details and opening hours are detailed in the Guide). For the practical purposes of visitors, there is little difference between them; sometimes they share premises and call themselves an OTSI. In small villages where there is no OT or SI, the *mairie* (town hall) will offer a similar service.

All these offices are well stocked with information, both locally and regionally, including hotels and restaurants, leisure activities, bike rental, markets and festivals, while those in the wine regions will provide information on local vineyards, and in peak season may also conduct vineyard tours; many can also book accommodation for you.

Most offices can provide a town/village plan and/or walking leaflets, while an increasing number now provide audio-guides (with English language) for self-guided town or village walks, though there will be a charge for this. Most, too, have maps and local walking guides on sale.

REGIONAL AND DEPARTMENTAL TOURIST OFFICES

Aquitaine ⓦ tourisme-aquitaine.info.
Aveyron ⓦ tourisme-aveyron.com.
Corrèze ⓦ correze.net.
Dordogne ⓦ dordogne-perigord-tourisme.fr.
Lot ⓦ tourisme-lot.com.
Lot-et-Garonne ⓦ tourisme-lotetgaronne.com.
Midi-Pyrénées ⓦ tourisme-midi-pyrenees.com.
Tarn-et-Garonne ⓦ tourisme-tarnetgaronne.com.

Travellers with disabilities

The French authorities have been making a concerted effort to improve facilities for disabled travellers. Though haphazard parking habits and stepped village streets remain serious obstacles for anyone with mobility problems, ramps and other forms of access are gradually being added to hotels, museums and other public buildings. All but the oldest hotels are required to adapt at least one room to be wheelchair accessible, and a growing number of *chambres d'hôtes* are doing likewise. Accessible hotels, sights and other facilities are gradually being inspected and, if they fulfil certain criteria, issued with a "Tourisme & Handicap" certificate. Listings produced by Logis (see p.28) and Gîtes de France (see p.28) indicate places with specially adapted rooms. It's essential to double-check when booking that the facilities meet your needs.

Most **train stations** now make provision for travellers with reduced mobility. Spaces for wheelchairs are available in first-class carriages of all **TGVs** for the price of the regular, second-class fare; note that these must be booked in advance. For other trains, a wheelchair symbol in the timetable indicates services offering special on-board facilities, though it's best to double-check when booking. SNCF also runs a scheme called Accès Plus, through which they assist travellers with disabilities, including ticket reservations, baggage assistance and a full reception service. You must, though, get in contact with them 48 hours in advance. Full details are on the website ⓦ accessibilite.sncf.com, which also includes a downloadable guide.

Drivers of **taxis** are legally obliged to help passengers in and out of the vehicle and to carry guide dogs. Ask at the local tourist office or *mairie* for further information on specially adapted taxis. All the big **car rental** agencies can provide automatic cars if you reserve sufficiently far in advance, while most agencies should also be able to able to offer cars with hand controls on request – again, make sure you give them plenty of notice.

If you can read French, there are some other excellent guides to make use of. The association Vacances Accessibles, ☎06 13 72 86 20, Ⓦhandiplage.fr) can provide the outstanding **guidebook**, *Le Guide de Globe Roller; Voyages Accessible dans le Lot* (2006), by local resident and wheelchair-user Jonathan Dupire. It details accessible accommodation, transport, attractions and other tourist facilities graded according to the level of mobility. The same organization also produces a booklet called *Handi-plus Aquitaine* (Ⓦhandiplusaquitaine.fr), which outlines suitable itineraries across the whole region. *Handitourisme*, published annually by Petit Futé (Ⓦpetitfute.com) covers the whole of France.

For general **information** about accessibility, special programmes and discounts contact one of the organizations listed below before you leave home.

CONTACTS FOR TRAVELLERS WITH DISABILITIES

Access Tourisme Service Ⓦaccess-tourisme.com. Organized and customized holidays for people with special needs, including adapted vehicle rental, accessible hotels and even travel companions if required.
Access Travel Ⓦaccess-travel.co.uk. Tour operator that can arrange flights, transfer and accommodation, including gîtes in Aquitaine. This is a small business, personally checking out places before recommendation.
Accessible Journeys Ⓦdisabilitytravel.com. Well-established travel agent offering both group tours and advice on independent travel for disabled travellers.
APF (Association des Paralysés de France) Ⓦapf.asso.fr. National association that can answer general enquiries and put you in touch with their departmental offices.

Work and study in Dordogne and the Lot

EU citizens are free to work in France on the same basis as a French citizen. This means you don't have to apply for a residence or work permit except in very rare cases – contact your nearest French consulate for further information. You will, however, have to apply for a Carte de Séjour from a police station within three months of your arrival – consular websites have details. **Non-EU citizens**, however, will need a work permit (*autorisation de travail*) and a residence permit; again contact your nearest French consulate or, if already in France, your local *mairie* or *préfecture* to check what rules apply in your particular situation. Whatever your nationality, once you have a work permit, you are entitled to exactly the same conditions as French workers, including the national **minimum wage** (SMIC), currently set at €9.40 per hour.

When **looking for a job**, a good starting point is to read one of the books on working abroad published by Vacation Work (Ⓦvacationwork.co.uk). You could also try the websites Ⓦmonster.fr and Ⓦjobs-ete.com, which focuses on summer jobs for students. Once in France, you'll find "Offres d'Emploi" (Job Offers) in the national and regional papers, or there's the national employment agency, pôle emploi (Ⓦpole-emploi.fr), with offices all over France and which advertises temporary jobs in all fields. Non-EU citizens will have to show a work permit to apply for any of their jobs.

A degree and a TEFL (Teaching English as a Foreign Language) or similar qualifications are normally required for **English-language teaching** posts. The online *EL Gazette* newsletter (Ⓦelgazette .com) is a useful source of information, as is the annual *Teaching English Abroad* published by Vacation Work. The TEFL website (Ⓦtefl.com) has a good database of English-teaching vacancies.

Foreign students pay the same as French nationals to enrol for a course and you'll be eligible for subsidized accommodation, meals and all the student reductions. French **universities** are fairly informal, but there are strict entry requirements, including an exam in French, for undergraduate degrees, but not for postgraduate courses. For full details and prospectuses, contact the Cultural Service of any French embassy or consulate.

Embassies and consulates can also provide details of **language courses** at French universities and colleges, which are often combined with lectures on French "civilization" and usually very costly. Numerous private language schools also offer French language courses, which are often cheaper than those run by the universities.

FURTHER CONTACTS

AFS Intercultural Programs Ⓦafs.org. Opportunities for high-school students to study in France for a term or full academic year, living with host families.
Campus France Ⓦcampusfrance.org. Government-run agency set up to promote French higher education abroad.
Erasmus Ⓦbritish-council.org/erasmus or contact their university's international office. EU-run student exchange programme enabling students at participating universities in Britain and Ireland to study in one of 31 European countries. Grants available for three months to a full academic year.
Language Courses Abroad Ⓦlanguagesabroad.co.uk.
World Wide Opportunities on Organic Farms (WWOOF) Ⓦwwoof.fr. Volunteer to work on an organic farm in return for board and lodging.

Périgueux and the north

PÉRIGUEUX AT NIGHT

1

Périgueux and the north

The north of the Dordogne *département* is its least known and most rural corner, a land with few people and large tracts of pasture and woodland, its intimate green valleys lending it the name of the Périgord Vert. The region is bounded to the south by the Périgord Blanc, defined by its limestone plateaux and wide, gentle valleys that cut a broad swathe across the heart of the Dordogne, following the course of the River Isle. On its way the river flows through Périgueux, capital of both Périgord Blanc and the whole département. It is easy to spend a day or two exploring the old city centre with its pineapple-capped cathedral and superb Roman remains, but it's in the countryside around that the region's best attractions lie.

One of the loveliest stretches is the **Dronne valley**, which shadows the Isle to the north. At **Brantôme** the Dronne's still, water-lilied surface mirrors the limes and weeping willows along its banks, before flowing on past the twin fortresses of **Bourdeilles** to **Ribérac**, a market town beloved by the British, and **Aubeterre** on the Charente border. As at Brantôme, the river-carved cliffs at Aubeterre were hollowed out into primitive churches by twelfth-century monks. Others built dozens of little Romanesque churches on the sunny hills around, while south of the Dronne their successors helped tame the marshy, insalubrious plateau of the **Double**. In doing so they created the pine and chestnut forests that blanket the area today.

Upstream from Brantôme, two tributaries of the Dronne lead northeast to the tiny village of **St-Jean-de-Côle** and the decorative, Renaissance pile of **Château de Puyguilhem**. Further northeast, there's no mistaking the warlike nature of **Jumilhac** castle's granite hulk. As a break from the châteaux trail, connoisseurs of foie gras should head south to the little museum in **Thiviers**, while truffle-lovers might like to press on to **Sorges**, where there's a marked path through truffle country and another small museum to explain it all. These two towns are close to the southeast border of the Périgord Vert, where the scenery becomes softer towards the lovely Auvézère valley. Here, in a spectacular spot high over the river, the **Château de Hautefort** marks a return to the Périgord Blanc.

East of Hautefort, across the border in the Corrèze *département*, **Brive-la-Gaillarde** lies on an important crossroads and provides an alternative to Périgueux as a gateway to the region. For such a large city, Brive has a surprisingly compact and enjoyable old centre with more than enough to detain you for a day or two. The countryside around also holds a few surprises, from the National Stud at **Arnac-Pompadour** to the appropriately named **Collonges-la-Rouge**, a village built with rich red sandstone, and neighbouring **Turenne**, another absurdly pretty village capped by the substantial remains of its eponymous fortress.

Festivals, events and markets p.49
Daumesnil: the Peg-leg General p.53
Follow the river p.56
Foie gras p.68

Voie Verte p.70
The Black Diamonds of Perigord p.71
Brive's markets and fairs p.79
Visiting the National Stud p.81

BRANTÔME

Highlights

① Périgueux From prehistoric and Gallo-Roman remains via Renaissance-era mansions to the cathedral's Byzantine extravagance, Périgueux has something for everyone. **See p.47**

② Brantôme Stroll the tree-shaded waterways, bridges and parks of this handsome town, then settle down to some serious eating. **See p.57**

③ Bourdeilles Perched precariously over the River Dronne, the château of Bourdeilles harbours a splendid collection of Renaissance furniture and religious statuary. **See p.60**

④ Aubeterre-sur-Dronne Though not the largest in the region, Aubeterre's subterranean church is both mysterious and awe-inspiring. **See p.64**

⑤ Grotte de Villars A rare opportunity to see displays of stalagmites and stalactites alongside prehistoric wall paintings in these wonderful caves. **See p.67**

⑥ Château de Hautefort Built to rival the châteaux of the Loire, Hautefort stands out for its elegance and architectural harmony. **See p.72**

⑦ Brive-la-Gaillarde Vibrant, energetic and with a beautifully restored city centre, rugby-loving Brive is worth a day's exploration. **See p.74**

HIGHLIGHTS ARE MARKED ON THE MAP ON P.46

PÉRIGUEUX & THE NORTH

HIGHLIGHTS

1. Périgueux
2. Brantôme
3. Bourdeilles
4. Aubeterre-sur-Dronne
5. Grotte de Villars
6. Château de Hautefort
7. Brive-la-Gaillarde

N

kilometres
0   10

Clermont-Ferrand
Argentat & Aurillac
River Corrèze
D940
A89
Tulle
Collonges-la-Rouge
Meyssac
Beaulieu-sur-Dordogne
River Dordogne
Figeac
Uzerche
A20
Brive-la-Gaillarde ⑦
Turenne
Sarrazac
Rocamadour
Cahors
Limoges & Paris
N20
Lubersac
National Stud
Beyssac
Varetz
Soullac
A20
D704
Arnac
Arnac-Pompadour
N89
Terrasson-la-Villedieu
Sarlat-la-Canéda
Domme
Limoges
Neyrac
Turnilhac-le-Grand
Périgord Vert
Hautefort ⑥
Thenon
Montignac
River Vézère
Les-Eyzies-de-Tayac-Sireuil
Agen
Chális
D21
Lanouaille
Excideuil
Tourtoirac
River Auvézère
Limoges
Châlis
River Isle
St-Jean-de-Côle
Thiviers
Corgnac-sur-l'Isle
Sorges
D705
Le Bugue
D710
Château de Puyguilhem
Grotte de Villars ⑤ Villars
Champagnac-de-Belair
Brantôme ②
Bourdeilles
Nontron
Mareuil
Périgueux ①
Vergt
Lalinde
Cahors
Bourdeilles
③ Lisle
A89
Neuvic
St-Astier
Mussidan
Bergerac
Agen
Vertella
Grand-Brassac
Bertric-Burée
Ribérac
Segonzac-de-Ribérac
Étang de la Jémoye
Ferme du Parcot
River Isle
La Double
River Dordogne
Ste-Foy-la-Grande
Marmande
St-Martial-Viveyrol
Bourg-du-Bost
Faye
Aubeterre-sur-Dronne ④
Échourgnac
Montpon-Ménestérol
D936
Angoulême
Poitiers & Paris
D674
Barbezieux-St-Hilaire
Chalais
La Roche-Chalais
River Dronne
Castillon-la-Bataille
St-Émilion
La Réole
Limoges
N10
Libourne
Bordeaux

Both Périgueux and Brive are major transport hubs, the latter especially so now that there are flights to the UK. In addition both cities have frequent flights to Paris. The two cities also have reasonable train connections, both to other towns in the region and to destinations beyond the Dordogne. Local bus services throughout the region, however, are very sporadic. For this reason, a car is pretty much essential if you wish to explore the more remote areas.

Périgueux

PERIGUEUX, capital of the Dordogne, is a small, busy market town for a province made rich by tourism and specialized farming. Its name derives from the Petrocorii, the local Gaulish tribe, but it was the Romans who transformed it into an important settlement. While a few **Roman remains** survive, it is the city's **medieval and Renaissance core** that gives Périgueux its particular appeal. Pretty, stone-flagged squares and a maze of narrow alleys harbour richly ornamented merchants' houses, while above it all rises the startlingly white spire of **St-Front Cathedral**, flanked by its cluster of pinnacled, Byzantine domes. It looks best at night – particularly from across the river – when floodlights soften the sharper edges and accentuate its exotic silhouette.

Périgueux's compact **historic centre** – much of it pedestrianized – sits on the west bank of the River Isle, occupying a rough square formed by the river, the tree-shaded cours Tourny to the north, boulevard Michel Montaigne to the west and cours Fénelon to the south. Though the hilltop **Cathédrale St-Front** provides a natural magnet, the surrounding streets hide some particularly fine Renaissance architecture as well as the **Musée d'Art et d'Archéologie du Périgord**, with its collection of Paleolithic tools, and a remnant of **medieval wall**. The main commercial hub is concentrated around rue Taillefer, running from the cathedral west to place Bugeaud, and along pedestrianized rue Limogeanne to the north. At the southwest corner of the old town lies the wide, place Francheville, from where rue de la Cité leads westwards towards Périgueux's other principal area of interest, **La Cité**, centred around a rather mutilated church. This is where you'll find the smart Gallo-Roman Museum, **Vesunna**, featuring the foundations of a Roman villa. Everything is within easy walking distance, making it possible to explore the city comfortably in a day.

Brief history

Périgueux began life some time after the fourth century BC as a fortified settlement inhabited by the **Petrocorii** ("Four Tribes"), whose craftsmen were noted for their ironwork. After 51 BC, however, the area came under Roman rule and a thriving town known as **Vesunna** (Vésone in French) began to develop, complete with amphitheatre, temples and luxurious villas. By the first century AD its population had reached an estimated twenty thousand, but the glory was shortlived. Vesunna, like many other towns, had neglected its defences under the *pax romana* and was caught unprepared by a succession of **barbarian invasions** in the third century. When Germanic tribes swept through the area in 275 AD, the population used stone from the surrounding civic monuments to construct defensive walls that helped the town survive, but in a much reduced state. As it faded it became known as La Cité des Pétrocores, then simply **La Cité**.

La Cité and Le Puy-St-Front

St Front arrived on the Périgueux scene some time in the fourth century to convert the local population to Christianity. After giving La Cité a new breath of life by founding what eventually became St-Étienne Cathedral, the saint was later buried on a neighbouring hilltop, or *puy*, where his tomb became a pilgrimage centre. By the thirteenth century it had spawned a small but prosperous town of merchants and artisans known as **Le Puy-St-Front**, which began to rival La Cité, now the seat of the counts of Périgord. Though the two communities were joined by an act of union

1

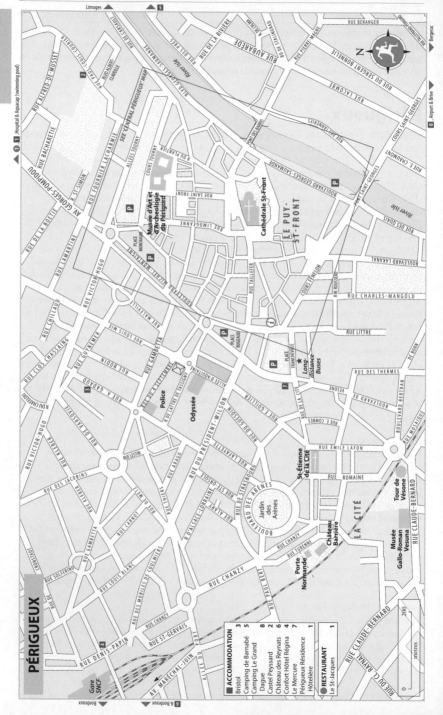

PÉRIGUEUX

■ **ACCOMMODATION**

Bristol	3
Camping de Barnabé	5
Camping Le Grand	
Dague	8
Castel Peyssard	2
Château des Reynats	6
Confort Hôtel Régina	4
Le Mercure	7
Périgueux Résidence	
Hôtelière	1

● **RESTAURANT**

Le St-Jacques	1

in 1240, they continued to glare at each other over their encircling walls – indeed, at the start of the **Hundred Years War** La Cité sided with the English and Le Puy with France. For a while following the Treaty of Brétigny in 1360, Périgueux, as it was now known, fell under English rule, but the loyal burghers of Le Puy soon rallied to Charles V, and by 1369 Périgueux had been liberated by Bertrand du Guesclin, who then chased the English back towards the coast. Even so, by the early fifteenth century the city was in ruins, its population decimated by war, plague and famine and its buildings crumbling through neglect.

With peace, however, came renewed prosperity and a building boom that left Périgueux its wonderful legacy of **Renaissance** architecture, though much was lost or damaged during the **Wars of Religion**: despite being predominantly Catholic, Périgueux was held by

FESTIVALS, EVENTS AND MARKETS

Where we haven't given a specific information number, contact the relevant tourist office.

First weekend in May Bertric Burée, near Ribérac: Snail Festival. Locals celebrate the snails by preparing and cooking them in their thousands; they are then consumed throughout the village by locals and tourists alike.

Second weekend in May St-Jean-de-Côle: Les Floralies (🖰floralies-saintjean.fr). Long-standing and highly rated festival, where the streets and squares of this pretty village are packed with flower stalls.

Mid-July and August Brive and around: Festival de la Vézère (🖰festival.vezere.com). Operas and classical concerts in the open air (with picnics) or in various châteaux and churches, including Arnac-Pompadour and Turenne.

July and August Périgueux: La Truffe d'Argent. A festival of French song open to amateurs, which takes place in the streets on Thursday evenings. Entrants are judged and take part in a final on the last night.

Mid-July to early August Hautefort and around: Festival du Pays d'Ans (☎05 53 51 13 63). A mix of classical concerts, jazz, opera and theatre held in the Château de Hautefort and other châteaux and churches hereabouts.

Late July Ribérac: Le Grand Souk. Aimed at fostering young talent from around the world, this five-day international music festival is a vibrant affair.

First week in August Périgueux: Mimos, the International Festival of Mime (🖰mimos.fr). One of France's most exciting and innovative contemporary art festivals, with more than 150 artists performing in over fifty shows; mostly street artists but also some ticketed events.

Second week in August Périgueux: New Orleans Music Festival (🖰mnop-festival.com). Jazz, gospel and blues concerts in a different area of the city each night.

Mid-August Brive-la-Gaillarde: Les Orchestrades (🖰orchestrades.com). Over ten days, some seven hundred young instrumentalists give free classical concerts in the streets of Brive culminating in a grand open-air concert when they all play a specially commissioned piece.

Last week of August Périgueux and around: Sinfonia en Périgord (🖰sinfonia-en-perigord .com). A ten-day celebration of Baroque and Renaissance music, with concerts in various venues in Périgueux, as well as in the nearby abbeys of Chancelade and Brantôme and the Château de Bourdeilles.

First weekend in November Brive: La Foire du Livre. One of the country's most prestigious literary gatherings. Held in Brive's market hall, it attracts some three hundred authors and artists presenting their new works, and around ten thousand book-lovers keen to snap up signed editions.

Mid-November Périgueux: Salon International du Livre Gourmand (🖰livre-gourmand.com). Biennial (2014, 2016 etc) book fair dedicated to wine and gastronomy. Events take place over four days in the theatre (1 allée d'Aquitaine), and include book exhibitions, cooking demonstrations and opportunities to sample the results.

MARKETS

The main weekly markets in this region are: Brântome (Fri); Brive (Tues & Sat); Excideuil (Thurs); Périgueux (Wed & Sat); Ribérac (Fri); and Thiviers (Sat). In winter many local towns hold foie gras, truffle and walnut markets, generally on the same day as their weekly market.

1

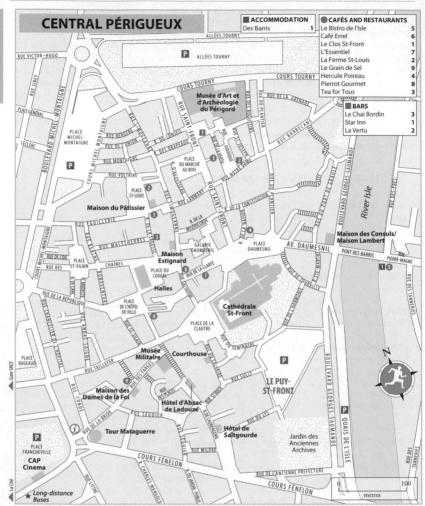

CENTRAL PÉRIGUEUX

■ ACCOMMODATION	
Des Barris	1

● CAFÉS AND RESTAURANTS	
Le Bistro de l'Isle	5
Café Errel	6
Le Clos St-Front	1
L'Essentiel	7
La Ferme St-Louis	2
Le Grain de Sel	9
Hercule Poireau	4
Pierrot Gourmet	8
Tea for Tous	3

■ BARS	
Le Chai Bordin	3
Star Inn	1
La Vertu	2

the Protestants for six years after 1575, during which time they vandalized many religious buildings, among them St-Étienne. This proved to be the final blow for La Cité, which fell into slow decline, culminating in the transfer of cathedral status to St-Front in 1669.

Modern Périgueux

La Cité and Le Puy-St-Front remained firmly inside their respective walls, separated by open space, up until the beginning of the eighteenth century, after which Périgueux began to expand into today's **modern city**. In the process the medieval walls gave way to wide boulevards, while in the nineteenth century the canal and railway brought further development to what was by then the capital of Périgord. The old city centre was left largely untouched, so that in 1979 some twenty hectares were designated a preservation district. Nevertheless, Périgueux is still the *département*'s most industrialized town: its biggest current claim to fame – a result of 1970s decentralization policies – is the printing works where all French postage stamps are produced.

Le Puy-St-Front

There's still a slight medieval air to **Le Puy-St-Front**, the district tumbling downhill from the cathedral west to place Francheville and to cours Fénelon in the south. Its confined and cobbled alleys harbour Périgueux's oldest buildings – the former homes of wealthy merchants – as well as the last remaining fragment of the medieval fortifications. Le Puy was originally surrounded by 28 defensive towers, of which only stout, circular **Tour Mataguerre** (July & Aug daily 9am–6pm; €2), protecting the southwest corner, remains. According to legend, it was named after an English captain imprisoned here during the Hundred Years War, but the present structure dates from the late fifteenth century, when it was rebuilt using leper labourers. Although there's little to see inside – just the prison and a simple guardroom above – the views from the roof are worth the climb.

Maison des Dames de la Foi

6 rue des Farges

From beside Tour Mataguerre, rue de la Bride runs into rue des Farges, where you'll find Périgueux's most venerable building, **Maison des Dames de la Foi**, dating from the late twelfth century. The name, "House of the Ladies of Faith", refers to a convent established in the seventeenth century for young Protestant women wishing to convert to Catholicism. Two hundred years earlier, during the Hundred Years War, it's said that du Guesclin stayed here while preparing to liberate nearby Chancelade Abbey from the English. Nowadays, you'd be forgiven for walking straight past, as the only evidence of its more illustrious history is the blocked-in window arches on the ground floor.

Musée Militaire

32 rue des Farges • Jan–March Wed & Sat 2–6pm; April–Dec Mon–Sat 2–6pm • €4 • ☏ 05 53 53 47 36

At the top of rue des Farges, the **Musée Militaire** contains a vast and rather chaotic array of military memorabilia, one of the foremost such collections in France. Covering everything from the Franco-Prussian War to the Gulf War and today's UN peacekeeping missions, the exhibits are of rather specialized interest, but there are some noteworthy pieces including some poignant sketches of trench life in World War I and memorabilia dating back to the French colonial wars in Indochina (today's Vietnam, Laos and Cambodia), among them a couple of tattered Viet Minh flags.

Hôtel d'Abzac de Ladouze

16 rue de l'Aubergerie

Rue de l'Aubergerie is known for its fortified fifteenth-century houses, of which **Hôtel d'Abzac de Ladouze** at no. 16, a typically dour building with an octagonal defensive tower, is the most interesting. The massive blind arch on the wall is evidence of much older foundations, while the incongruous ornamental balustrade above is a Renaissance addition. Note also the cockleshell carving on the side of the tower, indicating that the house once received pilgrims en route to Santiago de Compostela. Further down the street, at no.6, **Hôtel de Saltgourde** sports an impressive tower complete with a machicolated parapet.

Rue St-Roch to place de la Clautre

Rue St-Roch leads east from below Hôtel d'Abzac past several interesting houses, one retaining its wood-timbered upper storey, others their overhanging latrines or decorative arcaded windows, to **rue du Calvaire**. This was the road that criminals in the Middle Ages climbed on their way to the courthouse, identifiable by its studded Renaissance door. The condemned would then continue to the gallows on **place de la Clautre**, which also served as an execution ground during the Revolution. Nowadays it provides a more peaceful setting for a twice-weekly fresh-produce **market** (Wed & Sat mornings) against the backdrop of the cathedral.

1 **Cathédrale St-Front**
Daily 8.30am–7pm • Free

The domed and coned **Cathédrale St-Front** began life in the sixth century as a simple chapel over the tomb of St Front. Seven hundred years later – by then an important abbey – it was rebuilt after a fire and in the process the architects created one of the most distinctive Byzantine churches in France, modelled on St Mark's in Venice and on Constantinople's Church of the Holy Apostles.

Unfortunately, the cathedral of today is no beauty, thanks to the zealous attentions of the nineteenth-century restorer **Paul Abadie**, who went on to build Paris's Sacré-Coeur. The result is too regular, and the roof is spiked all over with ill-proportioned nipple-like projections; "a supreme example of how not to restore", Freda White tartly observed in her travelogue, *Three Rivers of France*. Nevertheless, the Byzantine influence is still evident in the interior's Greek-cross plan – unusual in France – and in the massive, clean curves of the domes. The bell tower also survived largely intact and is one of the few vestiges of the twelfth-century reconstruction. The adjoining cloister is not open to the public, but peek through the gates and you can see that, unusually, two sides are constructed in the Gothic style, and the other two in Romanesque.

North of the cathedral

North of the cathedral crowd the renovated buildings of the **Renaissance** city. The longest and finest street in this part of town is narrow **rue Limogeanne**, leading north from place de la Clautre via rue Salinière. Among the proliferating souvenir shops stand elegant mansions, now turned into swish boutiques, confectioners and delicatessens; its most notable facade belongs to **Maison Estignard** at no. 5, whose elaborate architecture – mullions, dormer windows and ornamental columns – is typical of the Renaissance. It's also worth popping into the more sober courtyard of no. 3 to see a salamander carved above the inner door; this was the insignia of Francis I (reigned 1515–47), who brought Italian Renaissance style to France. Opposite, impasse Limogeanne leads into a series of courtyards and passageways known as **galerie Daumesnil** after the famous general born at 7 rue de la Clarté in 1776.

Though nearby place du Coderc and place de l'Hôtel-de-Ville are both strong contenders, **Place St-Louis**, to the west of rue Limogeanne, is probably the prettiest of Périgueux's squares. In its southeast corner stands the handsome, turreted **Maison du Pâtissier** – built by a man who made his fortune from *pâté en croûte* (pâté in a pastry crust) – with a lovely Renaissance door bearing a fearsome warning on its lintel. There are more fine houses over to the east of rue Limogeanne on rue de la Constitution; from here the lanes begin to drop steeply to the river, where you'll find the semi-fortified fifteenth-century **Maison des Consuls** with the sixteenth-century **Maison Lambert** next door.

Musée d'Art et d'Archéologie du Périgord

22 cours Tourny • April–Sept Mon & Wed–Fri 10.30am–5.30pm, Sat & Sun 1–6pm; Oct–March Mon & Wed–Fri 10am–5pm, Sat & Sun 1–6pm • €4.50 • ☎ 05 53 06 40 70, ⓦ musee-perigord.museum.com

Set in a grand, nineteenth-century building at the top of rue St-Front, overlooking the broad, tree-lined allées de Tourny is the **Musée d'Art et d'Archéologie du Périgord**. First and foremost, the museum houses an extensive prehistoric collection, among its most prized exhibits a partially complete 90,000-year-old human skeleton, the oldest yet found in France, and a delicate engraving of a bison's head. However, many of the more fragile items on display are copies, and the museum's old-fashioned layout makes it hard to appreciate what's on offer. The fine and decorative arts section is largely forgettable, though the display of sculpture by the Transylvanian-born French sculptor Étienne Hajdu (1907–96) is worth musing over; his striking, bright white aluminium structures are loosely based on the work of renowned Romanian sculptor, Constantin Brancusi. Elsewhere, the cloister is packed with carved stones and decorative sculptures, some taken from the Cathédrale St-Front, as well as some beautiful Gallo-Roman mosaics.

La Cité

Remnants of the Roman town of Vesunna, now known as La Cité, lie southwest along rue de la Cité from place Francheville. Named after a local divinity, Vesunna was an important and prosperous town: by the first century AD it extended over some seventy hectares, complete with a forum, basilica, thermal baths and a seven-kilometre-long aqueduct. Today the most visible vestiges – a ruined amphitheatre, the remains of a temple complex and an excavated villa – lie scattered around the hulk of Périgueux's first cathedral, St-Étienne-de-la-Cité.

Church of St-Étienne

Approaching from the east, **St-Étienne**'s domes dominate La Cité. It was founded by St Front in the fourth century, then rebuilt in its present form, with a Romanesque nave comprising big square bays, some six hundred years later. The original building comprised four bays but two were destroyed, along with the bell tower, by Huguenots in 1577, leaving the church's west facade roughly truncated. The first bay you enter is the older of the two, dating from the eleventh century: the dome is more massive, the windows smaller and fewer and the stone less regular. The second bay was added a century later, then restored as an exact copy in the 1600s. Apart from being lighter and higher, its main feature is the line of decorative columns along the walls which stand out in the otherwise unornamented church.

Jardin des Arènes

Bd des Arènes • Daily: April–Sept 7.30am–9pm; Oct–March 7.30am–6.30pm • Free

The pretty **Jardin des Arènes**, a circular garden a few paces northwest of St-Étienne, conceals a few remnants – comprising an entrance arch and traces of the foundations – of an enormous **amphitheatre** capable of holding twenty thousand people or more. Built in the first century AD, it was dismantled two hundred years later to construct defensive walls, of which you can see a fragment, the **Porte Normande**, along nearby rue Turenne. In the panic, the walls were cobbled together with whatever came to hand: a column, some capitals, a carved lintel, all pilfered from neighbouring monuments.

DAUMESNIL: THE PEG-LEG GENERAL

A devoted follower of Napoleon Bonaparte, **Baron Pierre Daumesnil** (1776–1832) was fiery, impetuous, loyal, patriotic and, above all, brave. He first distinguished himself during the Italian campaign (1796–97) when he rescued the drowning Napoleon from a river during the Battle of Arcole. Then at Acre in 1799 Daumesnil threw himself in front of his hero when a bomb landed at Napoleon's feet. It failed to explode, but Daumesnil, by now a major, was less lucky at the **Battle of Wagram** in Poland in 1809, when his left leg was so badly mutilated that it had to be amputated. Three years later he was promoted to general and made **governor of the Château de Vincennes** – the country's largest arsenal – which he twice refused to hand over to the allied European armies fighting Napoleon. The second time, in 1815, he declared: "I will give up Vincennes when you give me back my leg." Nevertheless, Daumesnil was forced to retire a few months later following Napoleon's defeat at Waterloo, and he eventually died of cholera in 1832, though his wooden leg was preserved and is now on display in Paris's Musée de l'Armée. In Périgueux you'll find a statue of him towards the south end of boulevard Michel Montaigne, proudly pointing at his peg-leg.

1

Tour de Vésone

Daily: April–Sept 7.30am–9pm; Oct–March 7.30am–6.30pm • Free

Southeast of the gardens, past the empty carcass of the twelfth-century **Château Barrière** and across the train lines, you reach the neatly manicured **Jardin de Vésone** and Périgueux's most imposing Roman monument, the **Tour de Vésone**. This high, hulking circular tower was once the sanctuary of a temple dedicated to Vesunna's eponymous guardian goddess. The gaping breach on the north side is said to have been created when St Front exorcized the pagan gods; more prosaically, the bricks and stones probably went into local building works.

Vesunna

Jardin de Vésone • April–June & Sept Tues–Fri 9.30am–5.30pm, Sat & Sun 10am–12.30pm & 2.30–6pm; July & Aug daily 10am–7pm; Oct–March Tues–Fri 9.30am–12.30pm & 1.30–5pm, Sat & Sun 10am–12.30pm & 2.30–6pm • €6, audioguides available in English • ☎ 05 53 53 00 92, ⓦ vesunna.fr

Concealed within a magnificent modern glass building a few paces from the Tour de Vésone is **Vesunna**, an outstanding Gallo-Roman museum built around the well-preserved remains of a grand Roman villa, which were discovered by chance in 1959. Superbly conceived wooden walkways (note how the layout is cleverly mirrored in the ceiling painting) take you over the walls and into the heart of the site, which is dominated by the garden, ornamented with peristyles of varying height. Indeed, this villa was no humble abode. It was complete with at least sixty rooms, an underfloor central-heating hypocaust, thermal baths and colonnaded walkways. Around the walls you can see the remains of first-century murals of river and marine life, the colours still amazingly vibrant, and here and there, graffiti of hunting scenes, gladiatorial combat and even an ostrich – no doubt the work of some bored Roman teenager. The best views of the site are from the two balconies, which are otherwise laid out with exquisitely crafted pilasters and funerary monuments.

ARRIVAL AND DEPARTURE

PÉRIGUEUX

By plane Périgueux has a small domestic airport at Bassilac, 7km east of the city, with just two daily flights (Mon–Fri) to and from Paris Orly with Twin Jet (☎ 08 92 70 73 37, ⓦ twinjet.fr). There are no facilities – though rented cars can be picked up here if booked in advance – and no bus links, but a taxi into town will take less than twenty minutes (around €15).

By train The *gare SNCF* is on rue Denis Papin, roughly ten minutes' walk from the centre, or you can take bus #1 (direction "Boulazac") to place Bugeaud or St-Front (€1.50). Destinations Bordeaux (7–11 daily; 1hr–1hr 30min); Brive (4–6 daily; 1hr); Neuvic (3–5 daily; 20–30min); St-Astier (6–12 daily; 10–15min); Thiviers (7–11 daily; 20–50min).

By bus Long-distance buses leave from the bus stop on rue de la Cité, behind place Francheville. Most routes are operated by CFTA, which has an information office on site (☎ 05 53 08 43 13, ⓦ cftaco.fr). Tickets are available on board, €2 all routes.

Destinations Angoulême (Mon–Sat 2 daily, Sun 1 daily; 1hr 45min); Bergerac (school term Mon–Fri 4 daily; school hols Mon–Fri 3 daily; 1hr); Brantôme (Mon–Sat 2 daily, Sun 1 daily; 40min); Excideuil (school term Mon–Fri 4–5 daily; school hols Mon–Fri 3 daily; 1hr); Hautefort (Mon–Fri 1 daily; 40min); Neuvic (school term Mon–Fri 1–3 daily; 40min); Ribérac (school term Mon–Fri 4 daily; school hols Mon–Fri 3 daily; 1hr).

By car You can park for free along the river below St-Front Cathedral, or there's plenty of pay-parking along allées de Tourny, to the north of the centre, in place Montaigne to the east and underneath place Francheville.

GETTING AROUND AND INFORMATION

Bike rental Cycles Cums, across the river at 37 rte de Bergerac (☎ 05 53 53 31 56) or MBK at 15 cours Fénelon (☎ 05 53 53 44 62).

Car rental Near the train station, try: Ada-Autoloc 24, 4 bis avenue Henri Barbusse (☎ 05 53 05 40 28); Hertz, 1 Angle rue Puebla et Barbusse (☎ 05 53 54 61 80); Europcar, 7 rue Denis Papin (☎ 05 53 08 15 72); in the centre there's Avis, 18 rue Président Wilson (☎ 05 53 53 39 02). You can

also arrange to pick up cars at the airport.

Taxis Call Allo Taxi Périgueux (☎ 05 53 09 09 09). There are also taxi stands outside the train station and another on place Bugeaud.

Tourist office 26 place Francheville (June–Sept Mon–Sat 9am–7pm, Sun 10am–6pm; Oct–May Mon–Sat 9am–12.30pm & 2–6pm; ☎ 05 53 53 10 63, ⓦ tourisme -perigueux.fr). They offer excellent themed city tours (mid-June to mid-Sept; €6) covering medieval and Renaissance Périgueux, the Gallo-Roman city or with a focus on music or food and drink. Though the tours are predominantly in French, some guides also speak English; ask in advance.

ACCOMMODATION

The choice of hotels in central Périgueux is surprisingly stark. Most of those by the train station are a fairly grubby lot, and there's very little in the old city itself. There are, though, three or four decent options within walking distance of the centre. The following are marked on the map on p.48, unless otherwise stated.

HOTELS

Des Barris 2 rue Pierre Magne ☎05 53 53 04 05, ⓦhoteldesbarris.com; map p.50. Just across the river, this two-star *Logis* hotel has fourteen simple and fairly small rooms, two with views of the cathedral. The bathrooms are cramped and the furnishings could do with a bit of an overhaul, but otherwise it's reasonable value. There's also a worthwhile restaurant here if you don't fancy the short walk into the centre. Breakfast €7. **€55**

Bristol 37 rue Antoine Gadaud ☎05 53 08 75 90, ⓦbristolfrance.com. This welcoming, privately run place looks pretty bland from the outside, but inside it's perfectly agreeable, with airy, part-painted, part-wallpapered rooms. Separate toilet and bathroom facilities, featuring lots of big mirrors. Breakfast €9. **€76**

★ **Castel Peyssard** 15 rue Paul Louis Courier ☎05 53 35 91 91, ⓦhotel-castelpeyssard.com. Sitting pretty in the midst of a gorgeous landscaped park, this gleaming white stone château offers up the most luxurious stay anywhere in the city, albeit at a fair whack. Based on the owner's love of cinema (check out the staircase lined with photos of screen divas), each of the four beautifully upholstered rooms is themed – and decorated accordingly – on a famous film, namely; *The Tiger of Bengal*, *Indochina*, *Out of Africa* and *Cleopatra*, while two of these also incorporate the château's four corner turrets. To add to the glamour, there's a luxury spa on site too. **€185**

Château des Reynats 15 av des Reynats ☎05 53 03 53 59, ⓦchateau-hotel-perigord.com. In the village of Chancelade, roughly 5km northwest of central Périgueux, this nineteenth-century château has firmly established itself as one of the region's top hotels. Plush, immaculately turned-out rooms both in the château itself and the Orangerie annexe, with those in the latter fashioned in more contemporary style. There's a top-class restaurant here too. Closed Jan. **€165**

Confort Hôtel Régina 14 rue Denis-Papin ☎05 53 08 40 44, ⓦchoicehotels.fr. The only hotel in the vicinity of the train station worth considering, a pleasant two-star offering cheerful en-suite rooms with high ceilings with spotlights, and windows to match (double-glazed on the front). Triples and quads available too. Breakfast €8.50. **€67**

Le Mercure 7 place Francheville ☎05 53 06 65 00, ⓦmercure.com. Located on the corner of the city's most prominent square, *Le Mercure* is by some distance the smartest hotel in the centre, though you'll pay a small premium to stay here. The old facade conceals a shiny three-star with impeccably kept rooms decorated in cream and beige tones and with a few extras like tea- and coffee-making facilities. Breakfast €15. **€115**

Périgueux Résidence Hôtelière 38 av Georges Pompidou ☎05 53 35 70 70, ⓦprh-perigueux.com. This conveniently situated hostel/conference centre offers simple accommodation and good meals for those on a limited budget. All the rooms have twin beds and either a washbasin, or washbasin and toilet. There is an attractive garden, which is a haven of peace five minutes' walk from the city centre. Breakfast is €5.60, and half-board and full board are also available for stays of four days or more. Rooms with washbasin **€25pp**, **€28** for two sharing; rooms with washbasin and toilet **€28pp**, **€32** for two sharing

CAMPSITES

Camping de Barnabé 80 rue des Bains ☎05 53 53 41 45, ⓦbarnabe-perigord.com. Charming two-star campsite fifteen minutes' walk northeast of the city along the Isle in Boulazac. It has a lovely riverside location, with an overspill site on the other bank, linked by boat. Games room, plus bar with snack meals available in summer. Closed Oct to mid-March. **€16**

Camping Le Grand Dague Atur ☎05 53 04 21 01, ⓦlegranddague.fr. Lost in the hills 7km southeast of Périgueux, this spacious and immaculate four-star site is worth seeking out if you've got your own transport. A welter of facilities including TV lounge, shop, launderette, swimming pools and slides, playground and bike hire. Closed Sept–May. **€19**

EATING, DRINKING AND ENTERTAINMENT

Périgueux can call upon at least half a dozen genuinely first-rate restaurants, the majority of which are sprinkled around the old city. Similarly, the best of the bars and cafés are to be found in the lanes and squares of the old centre. There's further entertainment on place Francheville at the multiscreen CAP Cinema (☎08 92 68 01 21, ⓦcap-cine.fr/perigueux), while the Théâtre Odyssée (NTP) at 1 allée d'Aquitaine (☎05 53 53 18 71, ⓦodyssee-perigueux.fr) puts on a varied programme of theatre, dance, concerts and variety shows. The following are marked on the map on p.50, unless otherwise stated.

1

FOLLOW THE RIVER

Fed up with tramping the streets, you might like to explore Perigueux's greener side. If you're on a bicycle, or on foot, take to **La Voie Verte**, a 15km path winding from Marsac in the west of the city to Trélissac in the east. With car parks, picnic areas and information points along the way, it's popular with both locals and tourists. **La Voie Bleue** is the water-based alternative – a 21km paddle down the River Isle by canoe. For more details ask at the tourist office, or for canoe hire contact the clubs at Trélissac (☎ 05 53 08 63 95), Périgueux (☎ 05 53 04 24 08) or Marsac (☎ 05 53 04 11 57).

CAFÉS AND RESTAURANTS

Le Bistro de l'Isle 2 rue Pierre Magne ☎ 05 53 09 51 50, ⓦ lebistrotdelisle.fr. The dimly lit, all-black and blood-red interior may be a bit heavy-going, but there are unrivalled views of the cathedral through its big bay windows (and there is a terrace in the summer). The food here is sound; omelette with *cèpes*, Isle burger (duck breast, foie gras and balsamic syrup), and scallop risotto are some of the staple dishes, plus there's a reasonable choice of *menus*, starting at €15 for two courses at lunchtime, and €21 for three courses in the evening. Access via the *Des Barris* (see p.55). Daily noon–2pm & 7.30–10.30pm.

★ **Café Errel** 10 place du Coderc ☎ 05 53 09 52 51. Give the other places on this bright square a miss and make a beeline for this perky little café tucked away in the far corner. Then settle back at one of the four colourful outdoor tables with a strong espresso (varieties from as far afield as Rwanda and Guatemala) and watch all the comings and goings. Mon noon–6pm, Tues–Fri 8.30am–7pm, Sat 8am–7pm.

Le Clos St-Front 5 rue de la Vertu ☎ 05 53 46 78 58, ⓦ leclossaintfront.com. This elegant, bare-bricked-wall restaurant has a well-earned reputation for its inventive and well-priced *menus*, starting at €27. The dishes are beautifully presented, the *menu* changes approximately every six weeks and could include delights such as carpaccio of fresh figs and duck, or rabbit confit with sweet garlic and stewed beans. Daily noon–2pm & 7.30–10.30pm; closed Tues–Sun lunchtimes Oct–May.

L'Essentiel 8 rue de la Clarté ☎ 05 53 35 15 15, ⓦ restaurant-perigueux.com. As the city's sole Michelin-starred restaurant, *L'Essentiel* is, as you'd expect, a high-class, and pretty expensive, affair. The service and cooking here are outstanding, and you'll have a tough time choosing between the likes of caramelized sturgeon fillet with pumpkin coulis, or veal cooked with potato fondant and truffle butter, each dish meticulously prepared by chef Eric Vidal. The decor, meanwhile, is extremely attractive. *Menus* from €40. Tues–Sat noon–2pm & 7.30–10pm.

★ **La Ferme St-Louis** 2 place St-Louis ☎ 05 53 53 82 77. By far the most rewarding, and welcoming, of the many restaurants on this square, possessing a homely, stone-walled interior and sunny little terrace. The food is as seasonal as you could wish for and generously portioned, but if it all looks too tempting, try one or two of the house

specialities such as sweetbreads with vinegar, and scallops with red pepper and chorizo. The three-course Menu Terroir €25 (lunchtimes and evenings) is terrific value. Tues–Sat noon–2.30pm & 7–10pm; July & Aug also open Mon.

Le Grain de Sel 7 rue des Farges ☎ 05 53 53 45 22. Tucked away in a narrow street just along from the tourist office, this impeccable little restaurant uses fresh produce from the market to create original dishes. *Menus* from €21 for two courses at lunchtime to €40 for four courses, or let the chef choose for you with his surprise *menu* of five courses, for €48. Tues–Sat noon–2pm & 7.30–10pm.

Hercule Poireau 2 rue de la Nation ☎ 05 53 08 90 76. One of Périgueux's best-known restaurants, located down in a gorgeous, sixteenth-century stone-vaulted room with soft lighting and cheerful red-check fabrics. This is rich fare: house speciality is the luxurious *rossini de canard* (duck with a slice of foie gras in a truffle sauce). *Menus* from €29. Daily except Wed noon–2pm & 7.30–10pm.

★ **Pierrot Gourmet** 6 rue L'Hôtel de Ville ☎ 05 53 53 35 32. Although principally a gourmet deli and rotisserie, it also has a few attractive-looking tables for daytime diners. The food is crisp and fresh, and includes a range of wonderful yet simple dishes such as mushroom pâté and pears poached in red wine. Wash it down with a glass of Bergerac and you've got yourself a cracking little lunch. Tues–Sat 8.30am–7.30pm.

Le St-Jacques 38 av Georges Pompidou ☎ 05 53 35 70 70; map p.48. Situated in the *Résidence Hôtelière* (see p.55) but open to non-residents. Don't be put off by the slightly institutional atmosphere – this is one of Périgueux's best-kept secrets. As well as the spacious restaurant there is a terrace overlooking the peaceful garden. Tasty food is of outstanding value (lunchtime *menu* of three courses including coffee for €14) and the service efficient and friendly. If you fancy straying from the French wines, there are some first-rate New World wines. Daily except Wed noon–2pm, plus Thurs–Sat 7.30–10pm; closed Sun Oct–March.

Tea For Tous 28 rue Eguillerie ☎ 05 53 53 92 86. Sweet little tea shop featuring over seventy types of teas from all over the world, from English breakfast to Moroccan mint. Also serves delicious home-made savoury snacks and cakes and desserts such as apple and cinnamon crumble with red fruits, and crème brulée flavoured with Earl Grey. Tea with scones or cake costs €5.90. Tues 10am–3pm, Wed–Sat 10am–6pm.

BARS

Le Chai Bordin 8 rue de la Sagesse ☎ 09 81 89 40 65, ⓦ lechaibordin.com. Ostensibly a shop, *Le Chai Bordin* is actually a delightful little wine bar that makes for a terrific place to linger for an hour or two. Some six hundred varieties of both French and other foreign wines are available, many of these by the glass, with each one costing €2–4.50. Tues–Sun 10am–12.30pm & 3–8pm, Sat & Sun till 10pm.

Star Inn 17 rue des Drapeaux ☎ 05 53 08 56 83, ⓦ starinnfrance.com. Hidden away inside a marvellous early eighteenth-century building, this snug Anglo-Irish pub is patronized by a mixed crowd of local expats and Anglophiles, here to enjoy quiz nights (Friday), fish and chips (Thursday), darts, board games and a very popular English book exchange. Tues–Sat 7pm–1am.

La Vertu 11 rue Notre-Dame ☎ 05 53 53 20 75. Appealingly eccentric bar where, in summer, you can lounge in wooden deck chairs outside in the quiet square. As well as a good choice of wines and beer, *La Vertu* serves cocktails, tapas and ice creams. Opening times are erratic.

DIRECTORY

Books and newspapers Maison de la Presse, 11 place Bugeaud (Mon–Sat 6.30am–7.30pm, Sun 7.30am–noon), stocks the widest selection of English-language newspapers and magazines and has a decent selection of local guidebooks. Otherwise, try Librairie Marbot at 17 bd Montaigne, which also stocks a few English-language novels.

Hospital Central Hospitalier, 80 av Georges Pompidou (☎ 05 53 45 25 25, ⓦ hopitalperigueux.com), to the north of centre off bd Michel Montaigne.

Markets Périgueux's largest markets take place on Wednesday and Saturday mornings principally in place de la Clautre, place du Coderc and place de l'Hôtel de Ville (all fresh foods) and place Bugeaud (Wed only; clothes and household goods). There's also a small, daily fresh-food market in place du Coderc's covered hall (8am–1pm). In winter (mid-Nov to mid-March), stalls selling foie gras and truffles set up in place St-Louis for the annual *marchés au gras* (Wed & Sat morn).

Police Commissariat de Police, rue du 4 Septembre (☎ 05 53 06 44 44); Police Municipale, 2A rue Charles Mangold (☎ 05 53 08 49 33).

Post office The central post office is at rue du 4 Septembre, 24000 Périgueux (Mon–Fri 8.30am–6.30pm, Sat 9am–noon; ☎ 05 53 03 61 10).

Shopping The best place to look for regional produce is along rue Taillefer, where Pierre Champion (no. 21) sells local wines and truffles as well as duck and goose in all its guises; rue Limogeanne is packed cheek-by-jowl with tempting specialist shops, in particular chocolatiers and all manner of other artisan food shops. You can buy picnic food in the Monoprix supermarket on place Francheville.

Swimming pool Aquacap (☎ 05 53 02 90 29) at Champcevinel, northeast of the city centre, just after the main hospital, is Périgueux's watersports centre, with space for serious swimmers as well as slides, aquagym, swimming for babies, jacuzzi, sauna and hammam.

Brantôme

Thirty kilometres north of Périgueux, the beautiful town of **BRANTÔME** is often described as the "Venice of Périgord". Of course, it's nothing of the sort, though the river walks and waterside, along with a Benedictine **abbey** and some **troglodyte caves**, certainly draw the crowds. Moreover, it has some top-notch accommodation and restaurants.

Sitting prettily on an island, which was created around one thousand years ago when local monks dug a mill-stream across a tight meander of the Dronne, the town is surrounded by leafy gardens and parks. Brantôme's **old centre** is packed onto an almost circular island, seemingly tethered to the surrounding bank by its bridges. A modern bypass takes the worst of the traffic, but in summer it's still a bottleneck along the main road, rue Gambetta, which cuts north across the island to place de Gaulle on the far bank of the Dronne. The modern bridge directly in front of the abbey leads into rue Puy-Joli, Brantôme's main shopping street, where you'll find a variety of attractive **shops**, while the **café-bars** on place du Marché are a popular spot for a drink. A good day to be here is Friday, when the waterfront and surrounding streets are given over to the weekly market, which has been doing roaring trade for some 450 years. Between December and March the stalls are augmented with truffles, foie gras and walnuts.

1

The Benedictine abbey

The town owes its existence to some rock-shelters – where the first hermits set up home around the fifth century – and a spring now hidden behind the church and convent buildings of the former **Benedictine abbey** standing on the river's far north bank. The first church was built under the cliffs here sometime before 817 – according to local tradition, it was Charlemagne (742–814) who founded the abbey with the endowment of St Sicaire's relic, one of the infants massacred by Herod. It had a rocky start, but by its twelfth-century heyday the abbey supported 24 parishes and had spawned a thriving town. Nevertheless, things started going downhill again with the Hundred Years War and, after being rebuilt on several occasions, the abbey was finally abandoned after the Revolution. The present buildings, which date from the seventeenth century but were heavily restored two hundred years later, house the **Hôtel de Ville**, whose staring, serried windows still hint at ascetic institutional life.

The abbey **church** recalls some of this history. The death of St Sicaire is the subject of a stained-glass window behind the altar, while bas-reliefs to either side depict the Massacre of the Innocents and Charlemagne offering Sicaire's relic to the church.

The caves

After a quick look in the neighbouring chapterhouse, with its palm-frond vaulting, next stop is the **caves** (April–June & Sept daily 10am–6pm; July & Aug daily 10am–7pm; Feb, March & Oct–Dec Mon & Wed–Sun 10am–noon & 2–5pm; €5, tickets from tourist office), accessed through the northeast corner of the Hôtel de Ville. Despite being used as a quarry over the years, there's still considerable evidence of the monks' earlier troglodytic existence. The most interesting of the caves contains a large, rather crude **sculpture** of the Last Judgement, believed to date from the fifteenth century, in the aftermath of the Hundred Years War. Look out, too, for the pigeonniers, identifiable by several rows of niches carved into the rock face; not only were pigeons a valuable source of meat, but their droppings were traded as fertilizer.

Musée Desmoulin

Feb, March & Oct–Dec Mon & Wed–Sun 10am–noon & 2–5pm; April–June & Sept daily 10am–6pm; July & Aug daily 10am–7pm • €5, tickets from tourist office

Just by the entrance to the caves, you'll find the **Musée Desmoulin**, dedicated to the eponymous illustrator and painter. Much of Desmoulin's work was heavily influenced by spritualism, hence his well-known, if slightly spooky, medium drawings, many of which are on display here – typically pencil or charcoal portraits of women, or more specifically, women's faces. The artist later went on to paint more orthodox impressionist works, in particular, landscapes.

Jardin public

A later, more worldly generation of monks built themselves an Italianate walled garden, now a public **park**, to the south of the abbey and across the old stone bridge from the water mill. It's a pleasant picnic spot, and a walk along the balustraded **riverbanks** is a must. In summer you can also take a **boat trip** (April to mid-Oct; hourly trips 11am–6pm; 45min; €7) around the island from beside the old bridge. At 9pm on Friday evenings in July and August, the locals take part in a lively jousting competition – in boats.

ARRIVAL AND DEPARTURE   **BRANTÔME**

By bus Buses on the Périgueux–Angoulême route, timed to connect with TGV trains in Angoulême, stop on the Champs de Foire, at the south end of rue Gambetta.

Destinations Angoulême (Mon–Sat 3 daily; 1hr); Périgueux (Mon–Sat 3–4 daily, Sun 1 daily; 35min).

INFORMATION AND ACTIVITIES

Tourist office Currently located in the Hôtel de Ville though slated to move next to the parish church across the bridge (Feb, March & Oct–Dec Mon & Wed–Sun 10am–noon & 2–5pm; April–June & Sept daily 10am–6pm; July & Aug daily 10am–7pm; ☎ 05 53 05 80 52, ⍟ ville-brantome.fr).

Canoe rental Between April and September, you can rent canoes (reservations are recommended in high season) from

Allo Canoës, on the road to Bourdeilles (☎ 05 53 06 31 85, ⍟ allocanoes.com) or Brantôme Canoë, just out of the centre on the road east to Thiviers (☎ 05 53 05 77 24, ⍟ brantome -canoe.com). The latter also run rock-climbing classes for individuals or small groups, taught by a registered monitor.

Bike rental Bikes can be rented from L'Hermitage in Saint Julien de Bourdeilles (☎ 05 53 08 28 93, ⍟ lhermitage.eu), 4km west of Brantôme, though they can deliver bikes.

ACCOMMODATION

Camping Peyrelevade Av André Maurois ☎ 05 53 05 75 24, ⍟ camping-dordogne.net. Shady and sunny site just 1km east of town beside the river Dronne, with private beach, fishing and heated swimming pool. Children's playground, shop snack bar and camper van emptying facilities. Closed Sept–May. **€19**

Camping Puynadal ☎ 05 53 06 19 66, ⍟ camping -puynadal.com. Small, family-run site offering around 30 pitches, but it's well equipped with bar, restaurant, children's playground, sports facilities and swimming pool. Closed Sept–April. **€15**

Chabrol 57 rue Gambetta ☎ 05 53 05 70 15, ⍟ lesfrerescharbonnel.com. One of Brantôme's most popular hotels, in a superb location by the Pont des Barris, offers high-quality rooms decked out in lots of pretty florals combined with fine wood-carved furnishings; excellent service too. Closed mid-Nov to mid-Dec. Breakfast €12. **€75**

Coligny 8 place Charles-de-Gaulle ☎ 05 53 05 71 42, ⍟ hotel-coligny.fr. Across the river from *Chabrol*, this friendly hotel is the cheapest option in Brantôme, with eight good-sized, a/c rooms painted in strong violet and mauve colours, including one with access for the disabled. Closed Jan & Feb. Breakfast €7.50. **€60**

★ **Les Jardins de Brantôme** 33 rue Pierre de Mareuil ☎ 05 53 05 88 16, ⍟ lesjardinsdebrantome.com. Just outside the old centre, on the road to Angoulême, *Les Jardins* has seven sparkling rooms, one of which has level access and facilities for disabled persons. The remaining six rooms are set back from the main building at the top of the lush gardens, each with a patio-style door leading onto its own bit of terrace. Not cheap but worth every penny. Breakfast €12. **€130**

Maison Fleurie 54 rue Gambetta ☎ 05 53 35 17 04, ⍟ maison-fleurie.net. Homely, English-owned *chambre d'hôte* with five rooms (one a single), all named after a different flower and decorated accordingly; gentle pastel colours, floral print curtains and old-fashioned dressers are the order of the day here. You can also enjoy a small pool and quiet courtyard garden. Closed two weeks in Feb. **€70**

Moulin de l'Abbaye 1 rue de Bourdeilles ☎ 05 53 05 80 22, ⍟ www.moulinabbaye.com. If you're feeling self-indulgent, treat yourself to a night of unbridled luxury in this beautiful old mill to the west of the abbey. Nineteen rooms are spread between three buildings, though there's little to distinguish between them in terms of comfort offered. Closed Nov–April. Breakfast €22. **€190**

EATING AND DRINKING

Au Fil de l'Eau 21 quai Bertin ☎ 05 53 05 73 65, ⍟ www.fildeleau.com. Specialist fish restaurant, hence dishes such as pan-fried cuttlefish, fillet of sea-bream and roast pike-perch, in addition to *menus* with names like Menu du Capitaine and Menu Marin. The chocolate-brown interior is a handsome affair, but the place is at its best in fine weather, when tables are set out under the canopied terrace by the riverbank. *Menus* from €26. Daily noon– 2pm & 7–10.30pm; closed mid-Oct to March.

★ **Les Frères Charbonnel** in the *Chabrol* (see above). This hotel restaurant is in the gourmet class, but is still good value with *menus* from €32; for this expect sumptuous dishes like lemon sole with truffles and turbot with *cèpes* and walnut wine. The restaurant itself looks fantastic, as does the adjacent stone terrace, and even better are the views across the water. Daily noon–2pm & 7.30–10pm; Oct–June closed Sun eve & Mon, also closed mid-Nov to mid-Dec.

★ **Les Jardins de Brantôme** 33 rue Pierre de Mareuil ☎ 05 53 05 88 16, ⍟ lesjardinsdebrantome.com. The food at this cool, intimate restaurant is consistently superb; rabbit salad, pastry-encrusted lamb with garlic and thyme sauce, and scallops with beetroot and nut oil are the sort of mouthwatering dishes you can expect, with many of the ingredients culled from the chef's vegetable garden. *Menus* from €26. Daily noon–2pm & 7.30–10pm; closed Wed & Thurs lunchtime.

Les Saveurs 6 rue Georges Saumande ☎ 05 53 05 54 23, ⍟ restaurant-les-saveurs.com. Tucked away down a little side passage off place St Pierre, *Les Saveurs* is one of Brantôme's better-kept secrets. It's a gorgeous little place with hardwood flooring and wicker seating spread over two floors, plus a lovely garden terrace to the rear, and dishes like rabbit and foie gras with mango chutney, and *escargots* with forest mushrooms. *Menus* from €28. Daily noon–2pm & 7.30– 10pm; closed Mon, plus Wed and Sun eves Sept–April.

1

The lower Dronne valley

The country west of Brantôme and along the **River Dronne** remains largely undisturbed. It is tranquil, very beautiful and restoring, best savoured at a gentle pace, perhaps by bike or even by canoe along the river. **Bourdeilles**, the first sizeable town downstream from Brantôme, was the seat of one of Périgord's four baronies (see p.290), as its great tower testifies, while the Renaissance château next door contains a marvellous collection of furniture. From the foot of the castle, the Dronne meanders through water meadows to one of the Dordogne's most famous market towns, **Ribérac**. Though Ribérac itself holds little else of interest, it makes an agreeable base from which to visit a crop of Romanesque churches scattered in the countryside around. **Aubeterre-sur-Dronne**, with another, better-preserved troglodyte church and a splendid position, represents the final stop along the river.

Bourdeilles

BOURDEILLES, 16km down the Dronne from Brantôme by the beautiful D106 back road, is relatively hard to reach – perhaps the most appealing way is by canoe (see below). It's a sleepy backwater, an ancient village clustering round its **château** on a rocky spur above the river.

The château

Feb & March, Nov & Dec Sun–Thurs 10am–12.30pm & 2–5pm; April–June & Sept to Oct daily except Sat 10am–1pm & 2–6pm; July & Aug daily 10am–7pm • €7 • ☎ 05 53 03 73 36, ⓦ semitour.com

The château essentially comprises two buildings, the first of which is a thirteenth-century fortress. Entered via a heavily cobbled yard, it consists of a now empty banqueting hall – though the two enormous, unadorned fireplaces are worth a peek – and a sturdy octagonal **keep**, the top of which offers lovely views over the town and river below.

The other building, and the main reason for visiting, is the sombre-looking Renaissance residence begun by the lady of the house, Jacquette de Montbrun, wife of André de Bourdeilles, as a piece of unsuccessful favour-currying with Catherine de Médicis – unsuccessful because, though she passed through the area, Catherine never came to stay and so the château remained unfinished. The Renaissance château is now home to an exceptional collection of **furniture** and **religious statuary**. Among the more notable pieces are some splendid Spanish dowry chests; the gilded bedroom suite of a former Yugoslav king; and a sixteenth-century Rhenish *Entombment* whose life-sized statues embody the very image of the serious, self-satisfied medieval burgher. The showpiece room, however, is the overly elaborate *salon doré* (the room Catherine de Médicis was supposed to sleep in), which has retained its original decor, notably a fine oak-panelled wainscot comprising over sixty painted panels depicting the various properties owned by the Bourdeilles family, and the coffered ceiling bearing a riot of paintings, from flowers and insects to sphinxes.

INFORMATION AND ACTIVITIES   BOURDEILLES

Tourist office Place de la Tilleuls, just downhill from the château (April–Nov daily 2.30–5.30pm; ☎ 05 53 03 42 96, ⓦ bourdeilles.com).

Canoe rental Available by the bridge from Canoës Bourdeilles Loisirs (☎ 05 53 04 56 94; open all year).

ACCOMMODATION AND EATING

Hostellerie le Donjon Place de la Halle ☎ 05 53 04 82 81, ⓦ hostellerie-ledonjon.fr. A sweet little family-run residence directly opposite the tourist office offering seven modestly sized rooms fitted out in nicely carved wooden furnishings. Note, though, that all rooms are on the second floor and there's no lift. Whether you're staying here or not, the courtyard to the rear of the hotel is a top place to eat, with a menu that's heavily skewed towards North African influences, for example Moroccan chicken with herbs, and duck with tagine; *menus* from €21. The courtyard really comes alive on Thursday evenings throughout the summer, when there's free live music, either blues, jazz or folk. Restaurant open daily noon–2pm & 7–9.30pm, closed Mon in July & Aug, plus Tues rest of year. Hotel closed Oct–April. Breakfast €8. €65

Hostellerie les Griffons ☎ 05 53 45 45 35, ⓦgriffons .fr. Two hundred metres down from Lisle, the more upmarket *Griffons* occupies a fabulously picturesque spot in a sixteenth-century house beside the humpback bridge. The ten rooms are plushly carpeted in anthracite grey,

which looks great set against the partially exposed brickwork and occasional stone fireplace; all have a view of the river, though some are better than others. A small, kidney-shaped pool enclosed within a flowery walled garden rounds things off beautifully. Closed mid-Oct to Easter. Breakfast €12. €112

Moulin du Pont 8km downstream near the village of Lisle ☎ 05 53 04 51 75. If you don't fancy eating in Bourdeilles, head to the *Moulin du Pont* and grab a seat on the terrace with the weir on one side and the restaurant's trout ponds on the other. *Menus* from €14. Closed mid-Nov to Feb, plus Sun eve & Mon except in summer.

Ribérac and around

Surrounded by an intimate, hilly countryside of woods, hay meadows and drowsy hilltop villages, **RIBÉRAC**, 30km downstream from Bourdeilles, is a pleasant if unremarkable town whose greatest claim to fame is its Friday **market**, bringing in producers and wholesalers from all around. There's nothing really in the way of sights, but the country here is dotted with numerous **Romanesque churches** that provide a focus for leisurely wandering – the tourist office has a leaflet detailing these. Nowadays many are kept locked, but the route described here takes in a representative sample of those that are more likely to be open – hours tend to be 9am to 6/7pm daily.

Ribérac lies on the south bank of the Dronne. Its main street starts in the south as rue Jean Moulin, runs through the central **place Nationale** and then continues northwards as rue du 26 Mars 1944. From place Nationale, rue Gambetta heads east to **place Général de Gaulle** and the vast market square beyond.

The Romanesque churches

A couple of hundred metres from the centre on the hill to the east of town, Ribérac's own **Collégiale Notre-Dame** (July & Aug Fri–Sun 9am–6pm, ask at tourist office at other times; free), now an exhibition and concert hall, makes a good place to start exploring. It's a pleasing building, with its squat tower and semicircular apse designed on a grander scale than its country cousins, but the west end and interior have been extensively altered; if it's open, it's worth popping in to see the recently restored seventeenth- and eighteenth-century frescoes. The **church of St-Pierre** in the village of **FAYE**, 1km west of Ribérac on the D20, on the other hand, has great charm even though it's no architectural beauty. Its diminutive single nave seems barely able to carry the fortress of a tower above. There's more reason to stop at **BOURG-DU-BOST**, 6km further downstream, where the significantly chunkier **Notre-Dame** possesses a similarly haphazard mix of architectural styles and an almost identical tower. It also harbours some very faded twelfth-century murals: the four Evangelists inside the dome, and the twelve Apostles around the choir.

From here the route cuts north and climbs to an undulating plateau with good views back over the Dronne's river meadows, then meanders through a string of villages. The first one to aim for is **ST-MARTIAL-VIVEYROL**, roughly 15km due north of Ribérac. Its church more resembles a castle keep; the windows are reduced to narrow slits, there's just a single, simple door at ground level and the belfry doubles as a watchtower with, behind it, a guardroom along the length of the nave big enough to hold the whole village. Looping southeast around Ribérac, the **church of St-Pierre-et-St-Paul** in **GRAND-BRASSAC** is unusual in that sculptures were added over its north door. They show Christ in majesty flanked by St Peter and St Paul above a frieze of the Adoration with traces of earlier paintwork.

The last of the Romanesque churches, **St-Pierre-ès-Liens**, is also one of the most prettily sited. It lies in wooded country 6km south of Ribérac and is best approached

1

from the west with the roofs of **SIORAC-DE-RIBÉRAC** clustered behind. From the hastily erected rubble walls it's easy to see where, in the fourteenth century, the nave was raised a couple of metres and a guard tower added at the west end. Again, there are almost no windows and the walls are up to three metres thick – which explains why the nave is so surprisingly narrow.

ARRIVAL AND DEPARTURE — RIBÉRAC

By bus Buses for Périgueux and Angoulême stop on place Debonnière, a few paces north of the tourist office.

Destinations Angoulême (Mon & Fri 1 daily; 1hr); Périgueux (Mon–Fri 5 daily; school hols Mon–Fri 4 daily; 1hr).

INFORMATION AND ACTIVITIES

Tourist office Inside the Palais de Justice on place Général de Gaulle (July & Aug Mon–Fri 9am–12.30pm & 2–7pm, Sat 10am–12.30pm & 2–7pm, Sun 9.30am–12.30pm; Sept–June Mon–Fri 9am–12.30pm & 2–6pm, Sat 9am–12.30pm & 2–5pm; ☏ 05 53 90 03 10, ⍉ riberac.fr). The office doubles as a ticket office for SNCF, and in July and August they organize guided walks and farm visits.

Bike and canoe rental You can rent bikes at the *Terrasse de la Rivière* by the bridge on the Angoulême road, and at the campsite, beside the entrance to which Canoës Ribérac (mid-June to mid-Sept; ☏ 05 53 90 54 42, ⍉ canoriberac .free.fr) rents out canoes and pedal boats, and also organizes guided day-trips along the Dronne.

ACCOMMODATION

Camping de la Dronne Rte d'Angoulême ☏ 05 53 90 50 08, ✉ ot.riberac@wanadoo.fr. Cheap, mid-sized two-star site just across the Dronne on the Angoulême road, with reasonable facilities, including shower blocks, laundry and play area. Closed Sept–June. **€11**

Chambres Florence 5 place Général de Gaulle ☏ 05 53 90 93 38, ⍉ chambres-florence.com. In a spacious and elegant townhouse just across the square from the tourist office, this enthusiastically run *chambre d'hôte* has two rooms and a suite, variously accommodating exposed stone

walls, lovingly polished old parquet floors and roll-top baths, plus there's a gorgeous conservatory for breakfast and a small pool. Elsewhere, the boldly painted walls clearly take their cue from the in-house art gallery, Galerie le 5. **€58**

Rev'Hôtel Rte de Périgueux ☏ 05 53 91 62 62, ⍉ www .rev-hotel.fr. A kilometre east of town, this single-storey, two-star hotel won't win any awards for class, but it does offer cheap, convenient and comfortable rooms (two for disabled) and helpful service. Triples and quads available too. Breakfast €6. **€47**

EATING AND DRINKING

Café des Colonnes 17 place Général de Gaulle ☏ 05 53 90 01 39. You can't beat sitting under the trees with a coffee on the terrace of this venerable café, which has been keeping locals fuelled since 1832 – alternatively, head inside and park yourself down on one of the leather seats, and admire the old posters and photos dotted around the walls. Daily 8am–11pm.

Le Chabrot 8 rue Gambetta ☏ 05 53 91 28 59. Though sparingly furnished and decorated, this is a terrific local restaurant that offers mainly traditional fare as well as more unusual dishes, such as duck skewer with mash, salmon with polenta, and gazpacho with goat's cheese. The gourmet menu marries the various dishes with some first-rate local wines, for example, Montbazillac with the dessert. Express lunch *menu* for €12 and evening *menus* from €21. Daily noon–2pm & 7–9.30pm; closed Tues eve & Wed.

Le Citronnier 3 place Nationale ☏ 05 53 90 22 72. This refined, Anglo/Swiss-owned restaurant, tucked away in what is probably the oldest house in Ribérac, not only

specializes in fish (sea bass baked Provençal-style, bream, John Dory, turbot) but also prepares dishes that you're unlikely to find elsewhere, like *clafoutis* of local *cèpes*, and Quercy lamb in white wine and apple sorbet. Everything is seasonal and home-made and there is an extensive wine list of over 50 wines, including an impressive two pages of Bergeracs. As pretty as the restaurant is, the rear garden is the place to dine in summer. Lunch *menus* from €15, evening *menus* from €25. Daily noon–2.30pm & 7–10pm; closed Sun lunch in July & Aug & Sun eve rest of year.

Le Commensal 54 rue du 26 mars ☏ 05 53 90 46 28. Not the best of locations, on the busy main road to Angoulême, but here you'll find a warm welcome, tasteful decor and creative *menus* that change regularly. Périgord rabbit features heavily, typically with rosemary rillettes or saffron and wild rice, but otherwise you'll find the odd quirky dish like nutty chicken fritters in walnut oil. Three-course lunch *menus* from €12 and evening *menus* from €21. Tues–Sun noon–2pm & 7–10pm; Sept–June also closed Sat lunchtime & Sun eve.

CLOCKWISE FROM TOP LEFT CHURCH OF ST-JEAN (P.64), AUBETERRE-SUR-DRONNE; CHÂTEAU DE PUYGUILHEM (P.67); CA BRIVE IN ACTION (P.74)>

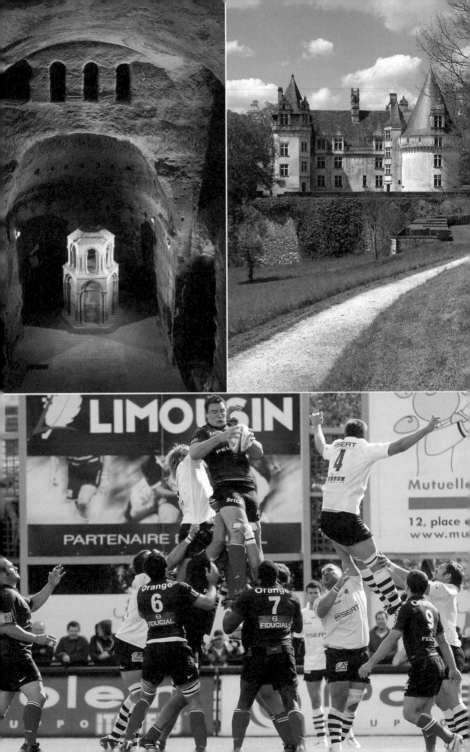

1

Aubeterre-sur-Dronne

Hanging on a steep hillside above the river, some 30km west of Ribérac, **AUBETERRE-SUR-DRONNE** is undoubtedly touristy, but it's extremely beautiful and well worth a few hours' exploration for its two wonderful churches, and ancient galleried and turreted houses.

Church of St-Jean

Rue St Jean • Daily: June to Sept 9.30am–12.30pm & 2–7pm; Oct to May 9.30am–noon & 2–6pm • €5, audioguide €1 • ☎ 05 45 98 65 06

The village's principal curiosity is the cavernous subterranean **church of St-Jean**, in the lower town northeast of Aubeterre's lime-shaded central square, **place Trarieux**. Carved out of the soft rock by twelfth-century Benedictine monks, it took at least a century to excavate the astonishing twenty-metre-high chamber and gallery above. Accessed via some eighty steps, it's from up here that you get the best views over the capacious baptismal font, designed for total immersion, and the two-tiered, hexagonal structure, possibly a reliquary, cut from a single piece of rock – its precise arches seem strangely out of place against the rough walls. The side-chapels are riddled with eerie, rock-hewn tombs, while a now blocked-off tunnel connects the gallery with the château on the bluff overhead. The chilly crypt, meanwhile, was discovered by chance after a lorry accidentally demolished this part of the square in 1961.

Church of St-Jacques

On the southwestern hillside, the upper town consists of a single street of houses culminating in the **church of St-Jacques**, where only the beautiful, sculpted west facade remains of the original twelfth-century church. The great tiered and decorated arch around the main door is lovely, but don't overlook the frieze of zodiacal signs on the smaller arch to the left: Taurus, Aries and Pisces are easy enough to recognize, then come Capricorn, Aquarius and Sagittarius. The other half of the frieze is missing. The remainder of the exterior is rather humble by comparison. Inside, the cold, but light-coloured brickwork is devoid of ornamentation, though the smooth circular arches separating the nave and aisles, and timber-beamed ceiling, are worth a look.

ARRIVAL AND INFORMATION
AUBETERRE

By train Chalais, which is on the Angoulême–Bordeaux train line, is 12km away; call ☎ 06 86 80 25 46 if you need a taxi.

By bus On weekdays there is a daily bus (7am in school term, 7.38am in school hols) to Angoulême, which departs from near the Chapelle des Minimes on rue du Minage, a five-minute walk uphill from the tourist office.

Tourist office Facing the town's main car park on place du Champ de Foire (April–June & Sept Mon–Sat 10am–noon & 2–6pm; July & Aug daily 10am–12.30pm & 2–7pm; Oct–March Mon–Sat 2–6pm; ☎ 05 45 98 57 18, ⓦ aubeterresurdronne.com).

Canoe hire In July and August, there's canoe rental down by the bridge (☎ 05 45 98 51 72).

ACCOMMODATION AND EATING

Cupcakes Place du monument aux morts ☎ 05 45 78 32 68, ⓦ cupcakes16.fr. Occupying a fabulous location next to the church of St-Jacques, the sunny, pebble-covered terrace of this family-run *salon du thé* is just the place to sample one of the owner's home-made sweet treats, be it a cupcake or a chunk of lemon drizzle, alongside a steaming hot cup of coffee. Three-course lunch *menus* (€14) are also served, as is wine. Tues–Sun 10am–6pm.

De France 24 place Ludovic Trarieux ☎ 05 45 98 50 43, ⓦ hoteldefrance-aubeterre.com. On the corner of the main square, this lovely nineteenth-century building has rooms of varying sizes and styles, though all feature thick wood-panelled flooring and heavily timbered ceilings; a couple of rooms share bathroom facilities. It's certainly not

an unattractive option, though it does sit above the village's most popular bar. Breakfast €6. **€55**

Municipal campsite ☎ 05 45 98 60 17. Just across the bridge, and adjacent to the river, this three-star municipal campsite has some good amenities; snack bar and grill, kids' play area, and a small sandy beach for volleyball and sunbathing. Closed Sept–May. **€19**

Du Périgord ☎ 05 45 98 50 46, ⓦ hostellerie-perigord .com. An appealing low-rise building down by the bridge on the Ribérac road, the *Périgord* offers bright, though not totally inspiring, rooms, with the occasional floral wallpaper and wicker furniture, and there's a pool, jacuzzi and sauna for good measure. Breakfast €8. **€65**

The Double region

1

South of the Dronne valley the landscape and atmosphere change dramatically as you enter the region known as the **Double**. This high, undulating plateau is strewn with lakes and brooding **forests** of oak, chestnut and pine, interspersed with pockets of vines, scattered farmhouses and an abbey at **Échourgnac**. The larger lakes, such as the **étang de la Jemaye**, have been developed for tourism, and in summer the Double is a popular destination for walkers, cyclists and nature-lovers; the best place to pick up information is Ribérac tourist office (see p.62).

GETTING AROUND   THE DOUBLE REGION

While there is no public transport in the Double, Neuvic is on the Périgueux to Bordeaux train line from where there are several services a day; they are also on the bus route (school term-time only) to Mussidan, though services are few and far between.

Échourgnac

Until the late nineteenth century the Double was largely uninhabited thanks to its poor soils and malarial marshes. Then Napoléon III decreed that it should be drained and planted with maritime pines in similar fashion to the great Landes forest further south. This work was partly carried out by Trappist monks who arrived from Port-Salut in 1868. They settled near the only village of any size, **ÉCHOURGNAC**, plumb in the middle of the plateau nearly 20km southwest of Ribérac, where they founded the **Abbaye de Notre-Dame de Bonne-Espérance**. Since 1923 the walled abbey has sheltered a small community of Cistercian sisters – these days numbering about thirty, some under a vow of silence – who not only continued in the monks' spiritual footsteps but also in their role as local cheese-makers. But the enterprising and energetic sisters didn't stop there. In their well-stocked **shop** opposite the church entrance (daily 2.30–5.30pm; ☎05 53 80 82 50, ⓦabbaye-echourgnac.org) you'll find the original Le Trappe Échourgnac, a firm, orange-crusted cheese with a smoky flavour, and a newer version laced with walnut liqueur, as well as jams, pâté, jellied sweets and handicrafts from missions around the world. You can also watch a video about the convent; the church is open during the same opening hours, except for when there are services.

Ferme du Parcot

May, June & Sept Sun visits at 2.30, 4 & 5.30pm; July & Aug daily 2.30, 4 & 5.30pm • Free • ☎05 53 81 99 28, ⓦparcot.pagesperso -orange.fr/

Five kilometres east of Abbaye de Notre-Dame de Bonne-Espérance, on the D41 from Échourgnac, the **Ferme du Parcot** has been preserved as a more typical example of local architecture. With walls of mud and straw on latticed timber frames, protected by a limestone plaster, these farm buildings are quite unlike the sturdy stone houses found elsewhere in the Dordogne. They date from 1841 and, from the grandeur of the barn, it seems the farmer was relatively affluent. In true rural style, however, the house itself, which was inhabited up to 1990, consists of just two very spartan rooms containing a few bits and pieces of furniture and old implements. The farm also marks the start of a gentle **nature trail** (2.5km; accessible all year) through the fields and forest to a fishing lake.

EATING AND DRINKING   ÉCHOURGNAC

Auberge de la Double ☎05 53 80 06 65. To fortify yourself before setting off on the trail, you can eat at the *Auberge de la Double* in Échourgnac, a little village inn which serves weekday lunches at €12 and a *menu* at €21 (Fri & Sat eves & Sun lunchtime). Closed Sun–Thurs eves & Dec.

1

Neuvic

It's worth dropping down to the **Isle valley**, which marks the edge of the Double to the south and east, to visit an imposing Renaissance château with a botanical garden on the outskirts of **NEUVIC**, roughly 15km east of Échourgnac. As you head east across the valley floor, a great bank of red-tiled roofs pinpoints the largely sixteenth-century **Château de Neuvic** (July & Aug daily tours except Mon at 3.30pm & 5pm; €5.50 including garden; ☎05 53 80 86 60, ⓦchateau-parc-neuvic.com), which now makes an unusually grand school for deprived children. Since the interiors have been extensively modified, there's not a lot to see beyond some badly damaged frescoes and an elegant eighteenth-century salon furbished with pastoral scenes. But it's the scale of the building, and particularly its handsome western facade, that grabs the attention. The best vantage point is from the **botanical garden** to the west of the château, which is also classed as a bird reserve (April–June, Sept & Oct 10am–noon & 1.30–6.30pm; July & Aug 10am–7pm, closed Thurs; €4.50), though you'll find your attention diverted by a wonderful collection of sculptures created by the pupils.

St-Jean-de-Côle

Twenty kilometres northeast of Brantôme, **ST-JEAN-DE-CÔLE** ranks as one of the loveliest villages in the Périgord Vert. An ancient church and château constitute its major sights and, with a couple of restaurants, it makes a good lunchtime stop. Tiny and very picturesque without being twee, St-Jean's unusually open, sandy square is dominated by the charmingly ill-proportioned late-eleventh-century **church of St-Jean-Baptiste**. The view as you approach is harmonious enough – layers of tiled roofs from the low, square market-hall to the steeply pitched belfry – but on entering the single, lofty bay it becomes apparent that the nave was never completed, due to a lack of funds. Beside the church stands the rugged-looking **Château de la Marthonie** (not open to the public), which dates from the twelfth century, but has since acquired various additions in a pleasingly organic fashion. Apart from a huddle of houses round the square, the rest of the village consists of a line of pastel-plastered cottages stretching west to a humpbacked bridge over the River Côle and the inevitable water mill. The whole ensemble makes a perfect backdrop for the Floralies **flower festival**, held on the second weekend in May.

INFORMATION   ST-JEAN-DE-CÔLE

Tourist office 19 rue du Château (mid-June to mid-Sept daily 10am–1pm & 2–6.30pm; mid-Sept to Oct & March to mid-June Wed–Sun 10am–1pm & 2–6pm; Nov–Feb Mon–Fri same times; ☎05 53 62 14 15, ⓦville-saint-jean-de-cole.fr).

EATING AND DRINKING

La Perla Café Place de l'Église ☎05 53 52 38 11. Take a seat at this warming outdoor café overlooking the church and fill up with one of their light lunches – for example duck salad (€14) – or just kick back with a coffee. May, June & Sept Wed–Sun 10am–6pm; July–Aug daily 10am–9pm.

Le Saint-Jean 7 rue de la Mairie ☎05 53 62 31 95, ⓦle-stjean.com. You'll eat well at the wisteria-covered St-Jean on the main road near the entrance to the square. It's an old-fashioned country place, nothing fancy but welcoming, and with appealing dishes such as calf sweetbreads in Périgueux sauce, and ravioli of foie gras with cream. Menus from €17. Daily noon–2pm & 7–10pm; closed Sun & Mon eve.

Château de Puyguilhem

May–Aug daily 10am–12.30pm & 2–6.30pm; Sept–April Wed–Sun 10am–12.30pm & 2–5.30pm • €5.50 • ☎ 05 53 54 82 18, ⓦ monuments-nationaux.fr

About 10km west of St-Jean, just outside the village of **VILLARS**, the **Château de Puyguilhem** is a perfect example of early French Renaissance architecture. It was erected at the beginning of the sixteenth century by the La Marthonie family of St-Jean-de-Côle on the site of an earlier and more military fortress. The lake that once filled the foreground has long gone, but the château still makes an enchanting prospect, with its steep roofs, stone balustrades, mullion windows, carved chimney stacks and an assortment of round and octagonal towers reminiscent of contemporaneous Loire châteaux.

Though the **interior** suffered more from neglect and pillaging, it too has been beautifully restored and contains some noteworthy pieces of furniture and Aubusson tapestries; the most impressive of the latter are located in the Great Hall, one tapestry depicting a rhinoceros, and another, a lion fighting a leopard. Its most remarkable features, however, are two magnificent fireplaces: the first, in the guardroom, depicts three Greek soldiers, while upstairs in the banqueting hall the theme is continued with six of the twelve Labours of Hercules. Both are heavily restored, but no less remarkable for that. The sculptors also went to work on the entrance hall and main staircase, leaving a wealth of oak, vine and acanthus leaves, thistles, fleur-de-lis and a few salamanders for good measure. Right at the top, it was the turn of the master carpenters, whose superb hull-shaped roof timbers have lasted five hundred years. Once done in the château, take a look at the pigeonnier, situated amongst the trees to the rear of the castle; it's a fine example of a French medieval pigeon house, this one consisting of hundreds of boulins (pigeon holes), each of which typically lodged a pair of birds.

Abbaye de Boschaud

The ruined Cistercian **Abbaye de Boschaud**, 3km away in the next valley south of the Château de Puyguilhem, merits a quick visit while you're in the area. Standing in the middle of a field, it's reached by a lane not much bigger than a farm track. Though the pure, stark lines of the twelfth-century architecture hold a certain appeal, the abbey's real charm rests in the fact that it is – for once – unfenced, unpampered and free.

Grotte de Villars

Daily: April–June & Sept 10am–noon & 2–7pm; July & Aug 10am–7.30pm; Oct & Nov 2–6pm • €7.50, visits by guided tour only • ☎ 05 53 54 82 36, ⓦ grotte-villars.com

In 1953 speleologists discovered an extensive cave system in the hills 3km north of Villars, now known as the **Grotte de Villars**. To date, around 13km have been explored, some 600m of which are open to the public on a forty-minute guided tour, but what is most unusual about the Villars cave is the combination of concretions and paintings. As impressive as these few paintings are – notably of horses and a still unexplained scene of a man and bison – the main reason for coming here is the variety of **stalagmites** and, in particular, **stalactites**. Some are almost pure white and as fine as needles, others ochre yellow or tainted red from the soil, and there are also cascades, semicircular basins and hanging curtains of semi-translucent calcium carbonate. The final cave contains the **paintings**, dating from 17,000 years ago, though they're only just discernible under the thick layer of calcite. Look out, too, for the claw marks further back from the entrance, where generations of tiny bear cubs have left their imprints – there are a handful of cave bear bones, including part of a jaw, on display near the reception area. There's a good chance, too, that you'll encounter one of the many resident pipistrelle bats as they swoop around the caves.

1

Thiviers

Not far east of St-Jean-de-Côle, and linked by a pleasant cycle ride along a disused train line, the small market town of **THIVIERS** sits on the main road and rail links between Périgueux, 40km to the south, and Limoges. The N21 bypasses the town these days, leaving its old centre – comprising a clutch of pretty, old houses round the church and along pedestrianized rue de la Tour – relatively peaceful. The one exception is during the Saturday **market**, when the streets present a lesson in local agriculture: walnuts, apples, Limousin beef, pork, duck and goose and all manner of associated foodstuffs. From mid-November to mid-March the *foies* come out in force

---

FOIE GRAS

It is generally agreed that it was the Egyptians who first discovered the delights of eating the **enlarged livers** of migratory geese and ducks gorging themselves in the Nile delta, and that it was the Romans who popularized the practice of force-feeding domesticated birds, generally with figs. For many the name (literally, "fat liver") is off-putting enough, let alone the idea of force-feeding the birds, while for others a slice of the succulent, pale rose-coloured liver is a pleasure not to be missed.

DUCK OR GOOSE?

Foie gras is produced throughout southwest France and also in Alsace, Brittany and the Vendée. However, the yellowish-hued livers from the Périgord, where the birds are traditionally fed on local yellow – as opposed to white – maize, and where producers jealously guard their methods of preparation, are particularly sought after. Périgord farmers now favour hybrid Mulard or Barbary **ducks** over the more traditional **geese** for a variety of reasons: they fatten more quickly, are easier to raise and force-feed, and the liver is easier to cook with. The softer goose livers, on the other hand, have a more delicate flavour and smoother texture. They are also larger – 600g to 700g for an average goose liver (*foie gras d'oie*) as opposed to 500g for duck (*de canard*).

PRODUCTION

The young birds are raised outside to the age of four months, after which they are kept in the dark and fed over one kilo per day of partly cooked maize for between two and three weeks. During this time the livers can quadruple in size. This **gavage**, or force-feeding, was traditionally carried out using a funnel to introduce the grain into the bird's throat and then stroking it down the neck by hand. Modern techniques follow the same principle but use a mechanized feeder. When done carefully, it's not nearly as terrible as it sounds and most small producers go to a lot of trouble not to harm their birds, if for no other reason than that a stressed bird will produce a rancid liver.

WHERE AND WHAT TO BUY?

All round, it's best to **buy** foie gras from small family concerns, either direct from the farm – local tourist offices can advise – or at the region's many *marchés aux gras* that take place from November to March. If you're buying fresh liver, choose one which is not too big, is uniform in colour and firm but gives slightly to the touch; the market price averages around €30–40 per kilo for foie gras of duck and €50–60 for goose. The alternative is the ready-prepared preserved version, of which there is a bewildering variety. The majority is de-veined, seasoned (wherein the secret recipes) and then sterilized by cooking briefly (*mi-cuit*) before being vacuum-packed or sealed in jars, either of which is preferable to the canned varieties; the tin taints the flavour. When choosing, check that it is locally produced and then look for the label *foie gras entier*, in other words consisting of one or more whole lobes, or simply *foie gras*, which is composed of smaller pieces but is still top-quality liver. Next step down is a *bloc de foie gras* made up of reconstituted liver (sometimes *avec morceaux*, visible pieces of lobe) pressed together. Below that come all sorts of *mousses*, *parfaits*, pâtés and so forth, each of which has to contain a specified minimum percentage of foie gras and to indicate this on the label.

at the *marché au gras*, some of them destined to go into the local speciality, *L'autre fois de Thiviers*, consisting of duck or goose liver robed in pâté. Thiviers' accommodation options make it a good base should you wish to make a detour to visit the **Château de Jumilhac** to the north.

Up until the 1920s Thiviers was an important centre for faience, a hundred or so pieces of which are displayed in the town hall (Sat 10am–noon & 3–5.30pm; free). But the pretty blue-and-white faience plays second fiddle to the town's prime concern – the history and production of **foie gras**, the subject of a small **museum** (€5) accessed via the tourist office, though it's expensive and not particularly stimulating, especially as there's nothing by way of English explanation.

ARRIVAL AND INFORMATION   THIVIERS

By train The *gare SNCF*, with services to Bordeaux, Périgueux and Limoges, is located on rue Pierre Sémard, just a few minutes' walk north of Thiviers' centre.
Tourist office 8 place du Maréchal Foch (Mon–Fri

10am–1pm & 2–6pm; Sat 9am–1pm & 3–6pm; July & Aug also open Sun 10am–1pm; ☎ 05 53 55 12 50, ⓦ officede tourismethiviers.com), also known as La Maison du Foie Gras on account of it housing the foie gras museum and shop.

ACCOMMODATION AND EATING

La Cuisine 25 rue Jean Jaurès ☎ 05 53 62 82 88, ⓦ la-cuisine-thiviers.blogspot.co.uk. The simple formula at this refreshingly colourful restaurant, just a short walk down from the main square, requires that you choose from one of three *menus* (€18–25), represented by dishes like truffle omelette, Lamb burger, and pork cheek in Bordeaux wine. Throw in some terrific wine and a convivial atmosphere, and you've got yourself a cracking night out. Tues–Sun lunch noon–2pm & 7.30am–10pm, closed Sun eve & Mon.

De France et de Russie 51 rue du Général Lamy ☎ 05 53 55 17 80, ⓦ thiviers-hotel.com. A warm welcome is assured at this ever-so-relaxing English-run hotel, which is particularly popular with pilgrims travelling the route to Santiago. A former eighteenth-century coaching inn, its rooms retain a pleasingly timeworn ambience, though the whole place is run through with the owner's personal, and occasionally quirky, touch – you can even play chess in the reception area or tinkle on the ivories in the lounge. In the building to the rear, two rooms have been specially adapted for wheelchair users. Breakfast €8. **€66**

Le Repaire ☎ 05 53 52 69 75, ⓦ campinglerepaire .com. A well-run three-star campsite beside an artificial lake on the D707 road towards Lanouaille, with lounge bar, pool and playground. Closed Sept–May. **€14**

St Roch Auberge 54 rue du Général Lamy ☎ 05 53 62 90 96. Awkwardly located on the roundabout at the bottom of the street, this pizzeria/pub doesn't look like much from the outside, or the inside for that matter, but the pizzas are loaded with great toppings and you can also sup on one or two of the more unusual Belgian beers. Moreover, you couldn't wish to meet a friendlier bunch of staff. Mon & Thurs–Sat 10am–3pm & 6–11pm, Tues & Wed 10am–3pm.

La Sablière 25 Promenade de la Sablière ☎ 06 61 63 73 19, ⓦ la-sabliere-perigord.com. Classy *chambre d'hôte* located around 1km north of town with four rooms, though they're basically mini-suites, three of which sleep four; fantastically comfortable beds, fine white linen and brilliant power showers are just some of the little luxuries that await. It's a little tricky to find as there are no signs; head north along the road towards Jumilhac and take a left at the turning for the abbatoir. **€80**

Jumilhac

In its upper reaches the Isle valley narrows down between steep, wooded banks to become a mini-ravine. One of its rocky bluffs, some 20km northeast of Thiviers, is home to the vast **Château de Jumilhac**. For more than two centuries Jumilhac has been closely associated with **gold**, and though the nearby mines closed in 2001, you can learn more about the history of gold here and further afield in the **Galerie de l'Or** (same hours as tourist office; free), a succinct but well-presented museum next to the tourist office overlooking the grassy square in front of the château. Visit in summer and you can even try your luck **panning for gold** in the River Isle (July & Aug; call the tourist office to reserve a half-day course; €18); it's not uncommon to find tiny specks, but don't expect to make your fortune.

1

VOIE VERTE

One of the lesser known walking and cycling routes in the region is the **Voie Verte (The Green Way)**, an 18km-long footpath and cycleway that follows a disused train line from Thiviers into the heart of the Périgord Vert. On a warm summer's day it's a delightful outing, taking in pretty villages like St-Jean-de-Côle and Milhac-de-Nontron, as well as rivers and viaducts, before winding up at Saint-Pardoux-la-Rivière. The tourist office can provide a leaflet/ handout illustrating the route, and bikes can be hired from Dordogne Cycle Hire in Thiviers (€15 per day; ⓦdordognecyclehire.com), who will also deliver to your accommodation. Trailer buggies and child seats are available too.

Château de Jumilhac

March–May & Oct daily 2–6pm; June–Sept daily 10am–7pm & Tues 9.30am–11.30pm; Nov–Feb Sun 2–5pm • €7, €9 including gardens • Reservations ☎ 05 53 52 42 97

While elements of the original thirteenth-century château remain – such as the stone-paved ground-floor rooms and the family chapel – the present structure largely owes its existence to an ironmaster, Antoine Chapelle, later count of Jumilhac, who made his fortune manufacturing arms for the future Henry IV during the Wars of Religion.

The body of the château is suitably uncompromising: the hard, grey stone allowed for little decorative detail, and what windows there are mostly consist of narrow slits. But the roof is another matter, adorned with no fewer than eight different **towers**, from great grey-slate wedges to pinnacled turrets and a jaunty pepper pot, topped off with delicate lead statues depicting the angels of justice or more mundane pigeon-shaped weather-vanes.

Inside, however, austerity reigns once again. This is particularly so in the cramped, ground-floor rooms, which date back to the thirteenth century, but also extends to the medieval rooms above, of which the much-vaunted **spinner's room** provides the focus of the tour. Not so much for its architecture – it's a small vaulted chamber decorated with naive frescoes of animals and flowers – but for the story attached. The spinner in question was Louise de Hautefort, wife of the then count of Jumilhac, who was imprisoned here for thirty years (1618–48) for her alleged infidelity. Not one to mope, Louise took to painting the walls and spinning to occupy her time. Or so it seemed. The shepherd who regularly called under her window, and from whom she bought her wool, was of course her lover in disguise, and the spindles were used to carry secret messages between them. According to one legend, the story ended in the lover being killed in a duel, while another has him retiring to a monastery. To give you some idea what all the fuss was about, there's a portrait of Louise, supposedly painted at the time of her release but still beautiful, defiantly holding her spindle aloft.

The two wings enclosing the courtyard were added later in the seventeenth century and are gradually being restored by the château's present owners, descendants of Antoine Chapelle, who bought it back from the state in 1927. The interior is demonstrably lighter in tone, thanks to the prevailing use of limestone – witness the handsome staircase – while the flooring is a pebble and stone mosaic encrusted in sand. The outstanding features here are two wooden fireplaces at opposing ends of the Grand Hall, which is otherwise dominated by paintings of various hunting scenes. Crossing the balustraded stone balcony to the opposite wing gives you superb views of the steeply sloping tree-lined square straight ahead.

INFORMATION

JUMILHAC

Tourist office Place du Château (April, May & Oct Mon–Fri except Wed 10am–12.30pm & 2–6pm; June & Sept Thurs–Mon 10am–12.30pm & 2–6pm; July & Aug daily 10am–1pm & 2.30–6.30pm; Nov–March Mon–Fri except Wed 2–5pm; ☎ 05 53 52 55 43, ⓦ pays-jumilhac.fr).

1

ACCOMMODATION AND EATING

La Chatonnière ☎ 05 53 52 57 36, ⓦ chatonniere.com. Beside the river just over a kilometre from Jumilhac, the three-star *La Chatonnière* campsite is a small, family-oriented affair, with extensive play spaces and a sandy beach to keep the little ones amused. Closed mid-Sept to mid-May. €22

Lou Boueïradour ☎ 05 53 52 50 47. If you're in Jumilhac around lunchtime, try the *Lou Boueïradour* restaurant, named after an implement used for blanching chestnuts, a few paces down from the château entrance. Although it doesn't look especially enticing, they've a few good-value regional *menus* from around €12 – alternatively just stop by for light refreshment after visiting the castle. Sept–June closed Wed eve.

Les Vignes de Chalusset 5km east of Jumilhac, signed off the St-Yrieix road ☎ 05 53 52 38 25. One of the most attractive places to stay, *Les Vignes de Chalusset* is a pretty and very welcoming *chambre d'hôte*, with a pool and extensive grounds. Meals available on request. €55

Excideuil

The old route between Périgueux and Limoges used to run up the Isle and Loue rivers to **EXCIDEUIL**, 17km southeast of Thiviers, where two huge medieval keeps still dominate the little market town. The **castle** was one of the region's most heavily fortified and for a while the viscounts of Limoges held court here. Following the Hundred Years War, however, the fortress lay in ruins until relatively recently, when restoration was carried

THE BLACK DIAMONDS OF PÉRIGORD

The **black truffle** of Périgord, *tuber melanosporum*, is one of those expensive delicacies that many people find overrated. This is mainly because it's usually served in such minute quantities or is combined with such strong flavours that its own subtle, earthy taste and aroma are completely overwhelmed. Really to appreciate the truffle, it should be eaten in a salad, omelette or simple pastry crust.

The truffle is a **fungus** that grows entirely underground, and a fussy one at that. It prefers shallow, free-draining limestone soils rich in organic matter, a sunny position and marked seasonal differences, and requires the presence of certain species of oak, or occasionally lime or hazelnut, around the roots of which it grows. It's greedy, too, absorbing so much of the nutrients and water available that the vegetation overhead often dies. This tell-tale ring of denuded earth is just one of the clues truffle-hunters are on the lookout for. Others include small, yellow truffle-flies hovering just above the soil, and the distinct smell – which is where the pig, or generally these days the more amenable dog – comes in.

Even now the **life cycle** of the Périgord truffle – the most prized out of more than forty different varieties – is not completely understood, and attempts to cultivate them artificially have so far proved unsuccessful. What is clear is that the spores are released in the spring and mature truffles are ready for harvest between December and early March. When ripe, the skin of a Périgord truffle is a deep purple-brown or black, while the lighter-coloured flesh is flecked with fine white veins. It should be firm to the touch and give off a pleasantly earthy aroma; an overripe truffle stinks.

The principal truffle markets take place at Périgueux, Sorges, Sarlat and Brantôme, and at Labenque near Cahors in the Quercy. Prices these days average around €800–1000 per kilo. In the past, however, truffles were so common that they were considered a pest by vine growers. Ironically, the fungus proved a life-saver for many local farmers when phylloxera hit in the late nineteenth century, ushering in the truffle's "golden age". Since the 1950s, the harvest has declined dramatically for a number of reasons – deforestation and rural depopulation among others – although a revival is well under way with up to 90 hectares of truffle trees being planted each year in the Dordogne since 2000.

If you want to learn more about truffles, then head to Sorges, 17km west of Excideuil, where the **Musée de la Truffe** (Feb to mid-June & Oct–Jan Tues–Sun 10am–noon & 2–5pm; mid-June to Sept daily 9.30am–12.30pm & 2.30–6.30pm; ☎ 05 53 05 90 11; €5) offers detailed explanations (in French only) of the truffle-growing process; from how the fungus forms to how to create your own truffle-oak orchard. There are also many preserved specimens for sale in the downstairs shop, which doubles as the tourist office (same hours).

1

out. It is now privately owned, so you can enter only the precinct, but it's an impressive sight, particularly if you approach from the west. From the castle, rue des Cendres leads north into the tight knot of streets concentrated around lovely place Bugeaud, with its stone duck fountain and the much-restored church, with its Gothic portal. This square and the nearby *halle* are the venue for a lively farmers' **market** on Thursday mornings, augmented in winter (Nov to early March) by an important *foire aux gras*. The tourist office can provide you with a leaflet outlining a walking tour of the village, which, even at an easy pace, should take no more than an hour.

ARRIVAL AND INFORMATION

EXCIDEUIL

By bus Buses stop beneath the castle on place du Château. Destinations Périgueux (school term Mon–Fri 4–5 daily, school holidays Mon–Fri 3 daily; 50min).

Tourist office 1 place du Château, which lies on the main road through town (May–Sept Mon–Sat 10am–1pm & 2–6pm, plus July & Aug Sun 10am–1pm; Oct–April Thurs–Sat 10am–1pm; ☎ 09 52 68 95 56, ✆ naturalementperigord .fr).

ACCOMMODATION AND EATING

Aux Delices d'Excideuil 2 place Burgeaud ☎ 05 53 62 46 65, ✆ auxdelicesdexcideuil.fr. The cool stone walls, grey shuttered windows and a delightful wrought-iron balcony mark this out as one of the loveliest buildings on the square. It also conceals a classy *chambre d'hôte*, with four smartly furnished rooms, though each with its own idiosyncracies. In warmer weather, breakfast is served on the flower-strewn garden patio. **€70**

Hostellerie du Fin Chapon Place du Château ☎ 05 53 62 42 38, ✆ lefinchapon.com. Next to the tourist office, and not long renovated, the *Hostellerie du Fin Chapon* offers good comfortable modern rooms in stock *Logis* chain-style fashion. Breakfast €8. **€50**

★ **Kitsch Kafe** 29 rue Jean Jaurès ☎ 05 53 52 21 62. The Anglo-Aussie proprietors of *Kitsch* certainly know a thing or two about coffee, which is lovingly prepared before being served in brightly coloured mugs – to be savoured, perhaps, with one of their sweet or savoury crumpets or home-made cupcakes. Wonderfully mismatched furnishings in the shape of 1960s formica-covered plastic tables and wooden chairs, as well as wall paintings and other cute collectables add to this gorgeous little café's undoubted charm. Mon–Fri 8.30am–5pm.

Municipal campsite ☎ 05 53 62 43 72, ✆ excideuil.fr. Prettily located municipal campsite by the river on the east side of town that's as basic as it gets, but suffices for a night or two. Closed Sept–June. **€10.50**

Le Rustic 1 place du Champ de Foire ☎ 05 24 17 50 24, ✆ lerustic.fr. There are few concessions to style in this easy-going brasserie/pizzeria just off boulevard Gambetta, but it's a friendly gaff and you can pick up very reasonably priced plates such as Perigourdine hamburger and salad or good old-fashioned fish and chips. Daily except Mon evening noon–2pm & 7.30–10pm.

Hautefort and around

Southeast of Excideuil you cross the pretty Auvézère valley, the route of the GR646 footpath, and enter the limestone plateaux of the Périgord Blanc. The views are magnificent, and nowhere more so than around **HAUTEFORT** and its eponymous **château**, standing on a south-facing promontory some 20km from Excideuil and 40km northeast of Périgueux.

Château de Hautefort

Daily: March & Oct to mid-Nov 2–6pm; April–May 10am–12.30pm & 2–6.30pm; June–Aug 9.30am–7pm, night visits on Wednesdays at 10pm; closed mid-Nov to Feb • €9 • ☎ 05 53 50 51 23, ✆ chateau-hautefort.com

The **Château de Hautefort** is a stunning sight from whichever direction you approach, a magnificent example of good living on a grand scale, endowed with an elegance that's out of step with the usual rough stone fortresses of Périgord. Indeed, when the then marquis de Hautefort rebuilt it in the mid-seventeenth century, his ambition was to create a château worthy of the Loire.

The original fortress, which was built some time around 1000, in the twelfth century belonged jointly to the famous troubadour **Bertran de Born** (see box, p.293) and his brother Constantin, until Bertran persuaded his overlord, Henry II of England, to grant him sole ownership in 1185. The following year Constantin took his revenge and left the place in ruins – at which point Bertran went off to become a monk. The château's recent history has been no less troubled. After decades of neglect, in 1929 Hautefort was bought and meticulously restored by the rather unfortunately named Baron Henri de Bastard and his wife. Then in August 1968, just three years after the work was completed, a **fire** gutted everything except the chapel in the southeast tower. A year later the indomitable baroness – her husband having died before the fire – set about the whole task again, and master craftsmen were called in to recreate everything from the staircases to the ornate chimneypieces. There's no disguising the fact that it's all brand-new, but the quality of work is superb.

The approach lies across a wide esplanade, flanked by immaculate topiary gardens, and over a drawbridge to enter a stylish Renaissance **courtyard** opening to the south. The two wings end in a pair of round towers, whose great bulk is offset by grey-slate domes topped with matching pepper-pot lanterns; the southwestern tower, nearest the entrance, is the only part of the medieval château still standing. While the main building is equally symmetrical, the overall impression is one of rhythm and harmony rather than severity.

About the only furnishings saved from the fire were four sixteenth-century tapestries, now on display inside, but the real highlight is the **great hall**. This monumental room provides the perfect setting for two huge chimneypieces. Exact copies of the originals and carved from local walnut, each took five thousand hours' work. The **chapel,** meanwhile, is worth a look for its pebble mosaic flooring, representing the family coat-of-arms, and the trompe l'oeil ceiling.

Musée de la Médecine

Place de Marquis J-F de Hautefort • March–May, Oct & Nov daily 10am–noon & 2–6pm; June–Sept daily 10am–7pm • €5.50 • Ⓦ musee-medecine-hautefort.fr

After you've finished in the château and its thirty-hectare park, it's also worth wandering through the village to visit the **Musée de la Médecine** in the midst of an open square and accessed via the tourist office. It occupies part of a hospice for the poor founded in 1669 by the same marquis who rebuilt the castle, as its architecture – particularly the domed central chapel – suggests. One of the ground-floor rooms presents an early-nineteenth-century ward (complete with silly-looking mannequins under the ministration of the Sisters of Charity). Here you'll find a reconstruction of a so-called tour, essentially a revolving cupboard in which abandoned children would be placed by mothers who could not, or did not wish to, care for their child – they would then ring the bell to inform the hospice of the new arrival; these could be found in hospices all over the region, including here at Hautefort, until their removal in 1847. As if this wasn't sobering enough, things get worse upstairs among the displays of brutal-looking medical implements through the ages (the gynaecological stuff doesn't bear thinking about), culminating in examples of dental surgeries up to 1970. There's also a section devoted to Louis Pasteur, inventor of the rabies and anthrax vaccines, among many other notable achievements. However, the absence of any English captioning ultimately renders this a rather frustrating visit.

Tourtoirac

March & Nov Sat & Sun 2–6pm; April & Oct daily 2–6pm; May, June & Sept daily 10am–1pm & 2–6pm; July & Aug daily 9.30am–7.30pm • €7.50 • ☎ 05 53 50 24 77, Ⓦ grotte-de-tourtoirac.fr

Only discovered in 1995, and opened as recently as 2010, the caves at **Tourtoirac**, 8km west of Hautefort, were never inhabited, but contain a rich array of stalactites and stalagmites, and have the advantage of being probably the only caves in France that offer access to the wheelchair-bound and elderly, via a lift. You can also visit the **abbey**

1

at Tourtoirac, parts of which date from the tenth century, and which houses an archeological museum (July–Aug daily 10am–12.30pm & 2.30–6pm) containing weapons and tools found during the course of excavations at the site.

ARRIVAL AND INFORMATION HAUTEFORT

By bus Public transport to Hautefort is almost non-existent, the only possibility being to catch a late afternoon bus from Périgueux (Mon–Fri at 5.20pm), with the return service departing from Hautefort at 6.30am the following morning.

Tourist office In the north wing of the old hospice on Place du Marquis J-F de Hautefort (June–Sept daily 10am–7pm; Oct to mid-Dec & mid-Jan to May Mon–Fri 10am–noon & 2–6pm; ☎ 05 53 50 40 27, ⓦ ot-hautefort.com).

ACCOMMODATION AND EATING

Auberge du Parc ☎ 05 53 50 88 98, ⓦ aubergeduparc -hautefort.fr. Although it's unlikely that you'll need, or want, to stay overnight in Hautefort, the *Auberge du Parc*, right under the castle walls, has five rooms, which are basic at best and rather on the dowdy side – though they're dead cheap. Closed mid-Dec to Feb. Breakfast €5.50. €40
Le Camping du Coucou ☎ 05 53 50 86 97, ⓦ campingducoucou.com. A lakeside campsite, less than 2km to the south of Hautefort in Nailhac, with superb

facilities including a grocery shop, TV lounge, playground, boulodrome and swimming pool. Closed Sept to Easter. €16 chalets €440 per week
Les Petits Plaisirs Place Eugène Le Roy ☎ 05 53 51 91 86. After visiting the castle, stop by at this sweet little café-cum-shop on the pretty little main square just below, where they serve crêpes, salads and charcuterie platters; or just indulge in a glass of wine. Daily except Tues 10am–7pm.

Brive-la-Gaillarde

A major road and rail junction, **Brive-la-Gaillarde** is the nearest thing to an industrial centre for miles around. That said, its largely pedestrianized old centre, enclosed within a circular boulevard shaded by plane trees, comes as a pleasant surprise after its sprawling suburbs. The town's cultural highlights include the much-restored **church of St-Martin**, the wide-ranging **Musée Labenche** and the local Resistance museum, the **Musée Edmond Michelet**, along with a handful of very smart restaurants.

It's thought that Brive earned its nickname *la Gaillarde* during the Hundred Years War when, for much of the time, it was a lone French stronghold surrounded by English. Opinions are divided, but the name "la Galliarde" (meaning strong, sprightly or bawdy) refers either to its fortifications or – the generally preferred option – the spirited, valiant nature of its people. The ramparts disappeared after the Revolution to make way for today's gardens and ring road, but the "Brivistes" themselves haven't changed, as they will happily tell you, citing past glories on the rugby field as the prime example. Brive also makes a convenient base for exploring the beautiful towns and villages around, and it's not that far to Lascaux and the upper reaches of the River Dordogne.

RUGBY IN BRIVE

Southwest France is without question the heartland of French rugby, and Brive one of its major centres. Founded in 1910, Club Athlétique Brive Corrèze Limousin (or CA Brive) enjoyed only moderate success until the 1990s, when, somewhat surprisingly, it emerged as a major European force. The club's greatest moment came in 1997, when it won the European Cup, beating Leicester Tigers in Cardiff. The following year they reached the final again, this time narrowly losing to Bath, and in 2000 contested the final of the French Cup, though this proved to be their last taste of success, as that same year they were relegated, following financial mismanagement. Since then they've yo-yoed between the top two divisions and, as of the 2012–13 season, played in Division 2. Brive play at the Stade Amédée Domenech, twenty minutes' walk east of the centre, with games usually taking place on either Saturday or Sunday and tickets costing as little as €10 (ⓦ cabriverugby.com).

OPPOSITE CHÂTEAU DE BOURDEILLES (P.60)>

1

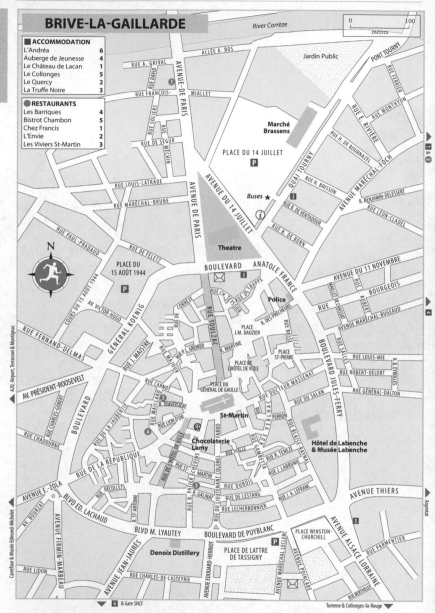

Church of St-Martin and place du Général-de-Gaulle

As a focus for wandering Brive's compact old streets, head first to the **church of St-Martin**, plumb in the middle of town. It was originally Romanesque in style; now only the transept, apse and a few comically carved capitals survive from that era. The most striking aspect of the church interior, however, is its outwardly slanting columns, which have supposedly given way in this manner due to the sheer weight of the central vault. It's said that St Martin, a Spanish aristocrat, arrived in pagan Brive in 407 AD on the feast of Saturnus, smashed various idols and was promptly stoned to death by the outraged onlookers. Supposedly, St Martin's unmarked tomb is among those in the tiny crypt, which is otherwise crammed with archeological remnants, reliquaries and other religious artefacts. **Place du Général-de-Gaulle** itself is dotted with a number of handsome turreted and towered houses, some dating back to the thirteenth century.

Musée Labenche

26 bd Jules-Ferry • Mon & Wed–Sun: April–Oct 10am–6.30pm; Nov–March 1.30–6pm • €5 • ☎ 05 55 18 17 70, ⓦ musee-labenche.com

The most impressive of the buildings on or just off place du Général-du-Gaulle is the sixteenth-century **Hôtel de Labenche**, now housing the enlightening **Musée Labenche**, whose prime focus is local art and history. As you enter, note the busts of the Labenche family leaning forward over each window. The museum's exhaustive collection encompasses wide-ranging geological and archeological finds, including stalagmites and cave-bear bones, some delightful Gallo-Roman bronzes complete with moulds, and a superb ethnographic section featuring a beautiful display of many-coloured accordions made in Brive by the Dedenis factory prior to 1939. The highlight, though, is a rare collection of **Mortlake tapestries**. The Mortlake workshop, under the supervision of Dutch weavers, was founded by James I of England in 1620, and though they were only in business until the end of that century, they produced a number of important, highly prized works. The most interesting of the ten tapestries presented here are *Fête de Nuit*, and *La Chasse au Loup*, the latter depicting a fox-hunting scene – both are still in exceptional condition and have retained their vibrant colours.

Musée Edmond Michelet

4 rue Champanatier • Mon–Sat 10am–noon & 2–6pm • Ask to borrow the audioguide in English • Free • ☎ 05 55 74 06 08, ⓦ museemichelet.brive.fr

Brive's second key museum, the **Musée Edmond Michelet**, occupies the former home of Edmond Michelet, one of Brive's leading *résistants*, who was arrested here in 1943 and deported to Dachau, where he remained until the camp was liberated in April 1945. Not long after, Michelet became a minister in de Gaulle's postwar government, rising to the post of Minister of Justice in 1959. Spread over three floors, the rooms portray the Resistance and deportations during World War II through personal effects, posters and objects of the time, though most affecting are the chilling photographs taken in the concentration camps. To get here take the main rue de la République west from St-Martin church as far as the ring road, from where the museum is signed straight ahead along avenue Émile Zola.

Denoix distillery and Chocolaterie Lamy

Founded in 1839, the **Denoix distillery** (Tues–Sat 9am–noon & 2.30–7pm; free; ☎ 05 55 74 34 27, ⓦ denoix.com) at 9 bd Maréchal Lyautey, is renowned throughout the region for its walnut-flavoured liqueurs, notably a very mellow tipple called Suprême Denoix, of which you can have a free taste here. They have also been busy resurrecting a local mustard, Moutarde Violette de Brive, which is made with grape must and spices and was first devised in the fourteenth century for Pope Clément VI, a native of Corrèze. Not surprisingly for this area, it goes very well with duck. For something a little sweeter, pay a visit to **Chocolaterie Lamy** (Mon 2–7pm, Tues–Sat 9am–noon & 2–7pm; ☎ 05 55 18 91 26), at 5 rue de l'Hôtel de Ville, which is really just a shop, but one where you can watch the delectable chocolates being made (demonstrations Thurs mid-June to Aug, 3pm; €3) and even learn how to make them yourself on half-day courses.

1

Jardins de Colette

April & Oct Wed–Sun 10am–12.30pm & 2–5.30pm; May, June & Sept Tues–Sun 10am–12.30pm & 2–6.30pm; July & Aug daily 10am–7pm • €6, audioguide €1 • ☎ 05 55 86 75 35, ⓦ lesjardinsdecolette.com

Ten minutes' drive west of Brive, at **Varetz**, are the lovely **Jardins de Colette**, so named after the eponymous, and controversial, French writer, who lived next door in Château de Castel Novel (now a hotel) between 1912 and 1923 with her second husband, Henry de Jouvenel. By means of plants and landscaping, the gardens aim to represent the places she lived, from her native Burgundy through to the Palais Royal in Paris. There are six in all, the most impressive of which is the Brittany garden, distinguished by its various rock formations, and the Provence garden, bursting with the typically distinctive colours of the region. The highlight – for kids at least – is an immense butterfly-shaped maze (a nod to Collette's beloved butterfly collection), made from double-plaited willow and dotted with educational signs outlining aspects of the writer's life. Once you're done wandering, take a cool drink on the terrace of the *salon du thé* overlooking the gardens. The gardens generally look their finest in June and early July.

ARRIVAL AND DEPARTURE

BRIVE-LA-GAILLARDE

By plane Brive airport (Brive-Vallée de la Dordogne; ☎ 05 55 22 40 00, ⓦ aeroport-brive-vallee-dordogne.com) is around 10km to the south of town in Nespouls. There is no public transport into Brive, so short of catching a lift, your only option is a taxi (☎ 05 55 24 24 24), which should cost around €15; if there aren't any waiting outside, go to the information desk. There are few other facilities to speak of here, save for a small café.

By train The *gare SNCF*, on the Paris–Toulouse and Bordeaux–Lyon main lines, is located on the south side of Brive, some ten minutes' walk along avenue Jean Jaurès from the centre. Alternatively, bus #3 makes the trip into the centre of town.

Destinations Arnac-Pompadour (3–4 daily; 40min); Bordeaux (3–4 daily; 2hr 30min); Cahors (5–8 daily; 1hr

10min); Paris Austerlitz (4–6 daily; 3–4hr 15min); Périgueux (3–5 daily; 1hr); Souillac (5–8 daily; 25min); Toulouse (6–9 daily; 2hr–2hr 30min).

By bus Buses depart from various spots round town, including the *gare SNCF*, though many buses around the *département* leave from place du 14 Juillet, just across from the tourist office; for information on timetables contact CFTA buses (☎ 05 55 17 91 19, ⓦ cftaco.fr).

Destinations Arnac-Pompadour (Mon–Fri 2 daily; 2hr); Beaulieu-sur-Dordogne (school term Mon–Sat 1–3 daily, school hols Mon–Sat 1–2 daily; 1hr–1hr 30min); Collonges-la-Rouge (Mon–Sat 1–4 daily; 25min–1hr); Meyssac (Mon–Sat 1–4 daily; 30min–1hr 5min); Turenne (Mon–Sat 1–3 daily; 20–40min).

GETTING AROUND AND INFORMATION

Car rental Avis, 56 av Jean Jaurès ☎ 05 55 24 51 00; Europcar, 52 av Jean Jaurès ☎ 05 55 74 14 41; National, 59 av Jean Jaurès ☎ 05 55 17 22 23; Hertz, 169 av Jean Jacques Rousseau ☎ 05 55 87 10 53. All of these companies also have desks at the airport.

Taxis Allo Brive ☎ 05 55 24 24 24.

Tourist office Place du 14 Juillet (April–June & Sept Mon–Sat 9am–12.30pm & 1.30–6.30pm; July & Aug

Mon–Sat 9am–7pm, Sun 11am–4pm; Oct–March Mon–Sat 9am–noon & 2–6pm; ☎ 05 55 24 08 80, ⓦ brive -tourisme.com). It occupies an old pumping station and water tower built in the form of a lighthouse, so you can't miss it; for €0.50 you can pop up to the top of the tower and enjoy the views of the market place below.

Internet access Net & Games, 5 rue Henri Marjory (Mon 2–11pm, Tues–Fri 11am–11pm, Sat 2pm–2am).

ACCOMMODATION

Central Brive is surprisingly short of decent hotels. Inevitably, there's a clutch of cheap places around the station, but otherwise the better hotels are randomly scattered on or close to the ring road; there are none in the old centre itself.

L'Andréa 39 av Jean Jaurès ☎ 05 55 74 11 84, ⓔ hotelandrea@wanadoo.fr. While it may not look terribly appealing from the outside, this privately run hotel, located some 200m down from the station, is perfectly fine in a rather off-beat sort of way. Reasonably modern, occasionally quirky, decor informs its decently sized en-suite rooms, and there's also a small terrace garden at

the back. Breakfast €6. **€45**

Auberge de Jeunesse 56 av Maréchal Bugeaud ☎ 05 55 24 34 00, ⓔ brive@fuaj.org. Pleasant, low-key HI hostel 25 minutes' walk across town from the train station, situated in its own little park-like area. Rooms comprise two, three or four beds, most with bathrooms and all with wi-fi, while other facilities include a lounge and kitchen area

1

which guests are free to use. Meals are available in season (April–Sept), as are snacks all year. Closed Dec and Jan. Breakfast €4.20. Rate per person includes sheets. **€14.60**

★ **Le Château de Lacan** Rue Jean Mace ☎05 55 74 79 79, ⓦchateaulacan.com. Hidden away, somewhat incongruously, in a residential area north of the centre, this superbly renovated twelfth-century mansion is the place for a splurge, offering thirteen rooms and two suites of the highest order, each and every one beautifully and thoughtfully integrated into this ancient building. And as well as going that extra mile – bottled water, fresh fruit and pastries in the rooms – the place is impeccably staffed too. **€240**

Le Collonges 3 place Winston Churchill ☎05 55 74 09 58, ⓦhotel-collonges.com. The rooms here are impressive, with smart, dark furniture, light brown, wicker-style carpeting and impeccable bathrooms, which all add up to a decent level of comfort. Despite its position on a busy road

junction, it's just a few paces from the old centre, and there are a couple of cafés and bars close by. Breakfast €9. **€73**

Le Quercy 8 bis Quai Tourny ☎05 55 74 09 26, ⓦhotelduquercy.com. Super slick hotel in a central location overlooking the market place. Each floor is colour themed, so if you really have a preference, there's black and white, lime green and beige, or silver and rose. There are some neat little touches like the reading lights on the headboards. Breakfast €10. **€95**

La Truffe Noire 22 bd Anatole-France ☎05 55 92 45 00, ⓦla-truffe-noire.com. The exterior could do with freshening up a bit, but apart from that, the nineteenth-century "Black Truffle" is a charming hotel, full of warm wood panelling and cosy inglenooks. True to its name, the rooms are fitted out mainly in black, though it's far from oppressive, with gold and beige thrown into the mix and glass-topped tables and wood-framed mirrors to further lighten the tone. Breakfast €12. **€117**

EATING AND DRINKING

Brive rates a small concentration of top-end restaurants, though a wander along the streets of the old town will yield somewhere to eat or drink every fifty yards or so, and in summer at least, this is the area to stake out. Otherwise, the bottom half of avenue de Paris and the area around the theatre offer further possibilities for drinking and general bonhomie.

Les Barriques 5 rue Maillard ☎05 55 17 18 40. There are few frills about this modern bar-brasserie, which sees lunchtime packed with office workers, and punters popping in for a quick bite at other times. It offers a limited range of dishes like quiche and croque monsieur (€6–10), or you can make your own salad from the self-service hors-d'oeuvre buffet. Not the sort of place where you linger over your meal. Mon–Sat 11.30am–10.30pm.

Bistrot Chambon 8 rue des Echevins ☎05 55 22 36 83. Bristling with colour and energy, this easy-going bistro tempts customers with a bewildering array of *formules*, *menus* and daily specials. Typical dishes include risotto with Perigourdin steak, stuffed pigs' trotters, and Limousine, apple cinnamon with caramel ice cream. Good fun, and popular with families. *Menus* €16–28. Tues–Sat noon–2pm & 7.15–10pm, Fri & Sat till 10.30pm.

★ **Chez Francis** 61 av de Paris ☎05 55 74 41 72. A favourite haunt of writers, actors and artists during

Brive's book festival. The walls, ceilings and lampshades are covered with messages of appreciation, which all adds to the mildly bohemian, occasionally eccentric, flavour of the place. The imaginative seasonal *menus* feature the best of local ingredients; at lunch you can have two courses with a glass of wine for €16.50, while the fixed *menus* are priced at €17 and €26. Tues–Sat noon–2pm & 7–10pm.

★ **L'Envie at Le Château de Lacan** Rue Jean Mace ☎05 55 74 79 79, ⓦchateaulacan.com. Château Lacan's utterly fantastic restaurant is the place to head for if you've only the time (and money) for one gastronomic treat in Brive. It's headed up by chef (and hotel owner) Cédric Nieuviarts, who consistently manages to conjure up a raft of magical dishes like roasted fillet of brill with sautéed cèpes and tarragon butter, beef fillet with truffle oil and rocket, and fig crumble with iced grand cru, often utilizing great local

BRIVE'S MARKETS AND FAIRS

The modern Marché Brassens, behind the tourist office on Place du 14 Juillet, is the venue for a huge **market** on Tuesday, Thursday and Saturday mornings, though the Saturday one is by far the biggest; the hall itself is usually reserved for foodstuffs, while the square itself is taken over with stalls selling clothes, textiles and other knick-knacks. On the first Saturday of each month between December and March, the fabulous *foires grasses* – for foie gras and truffles – are held in the same place. During the first weekend in November, the fruit and veg gives way to one of the country's most important book fairs, **La Foire du Livre**, which attracts a number of well-known authors and artists.

farm produce as well as pickings from the château's garden. Lunch *menus* from €20 and evening *menus* from €38. Alternatively, head up here for the gut-busting Sunday brunch (€43). Daily Mon–Sat noon–2pm & 7.30–10.30pm, Sun 11am–3pm.

Les Viviers St-Martin 4 rue Traversière ☎ 05 55 92 14 15. It's worth seeking out this restful little restaurant in a backstreet just west of St-Martin church for its wide-ranging *carte*, though the real draw is its fish, for example turbot in hollandaise sauce and roasted pike-perch. The two interior rooms are pretty formal compared with the jolly pavement terrace, lined with black and white checked tables and chairs. *Menus* from €26. Daily noon–2pm & 7.30–10pm; closed last two weeks in March.

Arnac-Pompadour

Some 30km northeast of Brive, among the green fields and apple orchards of southern Limousin, **ARNAC-POMPADOUR** is a must for anyone remotely interested in horses. The town is dominated by its massive, turreted château – from where Madame de Pompadour got her name – a fitting and stately backdrop to a national stud farm and one of the most picturesque racecourses in France.

The château

Guided tours: daily April–June & Oct at 10am, 3pm and 5pm; July & Aug also at 2pm and 4pm; rest of year Mon–Sat at 10am, 3pm and 5pm • €5.50, unaccompanied visit €4

Although there was a fortress of sorts here as far back as the eleventh century, the present château largely dates from the fifteenth century. When the Pompadour line died out in 1745, it was ceded to Louis XV who promptly bestowed the title on his mistress, the **Marquise de Pompadour**. Though she never bothered to visit, the marquise started breeding horses on her estate before being forced to sell for financial reasons in 1760; she nevertheless kept the title. On regaining possession of the castle the following year, Louis founded the Royal Stud, which became a **National Stud** in 1872. In between, the horses were sold off during the Revolution, but Napoleon I soon re-established the stud to keep his cavalry supplied. He sent four Arab stallions, booty from his Egyptian campaign, which were crossed with English thoroughbred mares to produce the first **Anglo-Arabs**. Although historically bred for military purposes, today these magnificent horses are ideally suited to eventing, owing to their powerful combination of speed, stamina and jumping ability.

The **château** was gutted by fire in 1834 and now houses the stud's headquarters. If you want to visit the château itself (albeit just three rooms), you must do so on a **guided tour** organized by Trois Tours de Pompadour. Otherwise, it's only possible to visit the gardens on an unaccompanied visit.

Chapelle St Blaise

Ask at the tourist office (see opposite) for information about opening hours

For those less enamoured of horses, pop along to Pompadour's own parish church, the **Chapelle St Blaise**, in the town centre just behind the château. Since its restoration in 2008, the chapel is home to over three hundred square metres of paintings depicting Old and New Testament scenes by the contemporary artist, André Brasilier, worth seeing for the scale of the work alone.

Abbey church of Arnac

Two kilometres northwest of Arnac-Pompadour, in the village of Arnac itself, the Romanesque **abbey church** (part of the Pompadour *domaines*) is chiefly of interest for its carved capitals, which sit atop the inwardly leaning columns, just about perceptible if you stand at the back of the church. Though the columns are exceptionally high, enlarged photos beside each one help identify the striking images, including Daniel in the lions' den.

VISITING THE NATIONAL STUD

Pompadour's stallions are housed in the **Écurie du Puy Marmont**, across the chestnut-shaded esplanade from the château (April–Sept daily; rest of year daily except Sunday; €5.50). During the spring breeding season (March–June) there are fewer stallions in the *écurie*, but this is the best time to visit the mares (*juments*) at the **Jumenterie de la Rivière** (afternoons only: April–June & Sept Tues–Sun, July & Aug Tues & Thurs; €5.50), 4km southeast near the village of Beyssac. In late spring (May–June) the fields around are full of mares and foals, the best being kept for breeding, the rest sold worldwide as two-year-olds. In each case you have to join a guided tour organized by Trois Tours de Pompadour, located inside the gatehouse of the château (☎ 05 55 98 51 10, ⓦ les3tours-pompadour.com). Times of the visits vary, so check first. They also sell tickets to the château and a "passport", with which you can visit two of the three sites for €10.

At any time of year, you will see horses being exercised round the magnificent oval track in front of the château. On numerous Sundays between May and September, there are **race meetings** (around €6), as well as dressage and driving events, shows and open days. A calendar of events is available from Trois Tours de Pompadour. A good time to be here is August 15, when the Pompadour *fête le cheval* takes place, with various races, dressage and jumping events.

ARRIVAL AND INFORMATION

ARNAC-POMPADOUR

By train Arnac-Pompadour lies on a minor train line between Brive and Limoges; the *gare SNCF* is 500m southeast of town on the D7 to Vigeois.
Destinations Brive (Mon–Fri 4 daily; 45mins); Limoges (Mon–Fri 3 daily; 1hr 15min).

By bus Buses from Brive (Mon–Fri 2 daily) stop by the château.
Tourist office In the gatehouse of the château (June–Sept daily 10am–12.30pm & 2–6pm; Oct–May Mon–Fri 10am–noon & 1.30–4.30pm; ☎ 05 55 98 55 47, ⓦ pompadour.net).

ACCOMMODATION

Camping Les Étoiles Allée du Stade, Saint-Sornin-Lavolps ☎ 05 55 73 01 27, ⓦ camping-pompadour.com. Spruce, well-shaded campsite by a small lake 2km south of town, with places for both tents and camper vans; there are also a handful of chalets sleeping between two and five. Closed Oct–April. **€18.50**, chalet **€300** per week

De l'Hippodrome 26 av du Midi ☎ 05 55 73 35 03. Opposite the turning to the road that leads down to the racecourse, this is pretty basic accommodation, but if you don't mind a cheap, no-frills option, then it does the job – it's perfectly clean and the hosts are very welcoming. Breakfast €6. **€43**

Turenne

TURENNE, 16km south of Brive, is the first of two very picturesque villages in the vicinity. In this case, slate-roofed, mellow stone houses crowd under the protective towers of a once-mighty fortress. At their peak during the fifteenth century, the viscounts of Turenne ruled over a vast feudal domain containing some 1200 villages. Virtually autonomous, it was one of the most powerful estates in France. The viscounts retained the right to raise taxes and mint their own coins, amongst other privileges, up until 1738 when Louis XV bought the viscountcy in the aftermath of the Fronde rebellion (see p.297).

Château de Turenne

April–June, Sept & Oct daily 10am–noon & 2–6pm; July–Aug daily 10am–7pm; Nov–March Sun 2–5pm • €4.50 • ☎ 05 55 80 90 66

Although Louis also ordered that the castle be demolished, two towers still sprout from the summit, one of which is occupied by the present owners of the château. From this first tower (known as the Tour d'Horloge, or Clock Tower), you walk along a gravel pathway through the neatly manicured gardens – which is where the main body of the castle once stood – to the round **Tour de César**, where a further 64 steps await. It's well worth climbing for the vertiginous views away over the ridges and valleys to the

1

mountains of Cantal. Although it's a stiff fifteen-minute climb up to the castle entrance, you do pass a number of elegant Renaissance houses and the all-important salt store, as well as a **church** hurriedly thrown up in 1662 during the Counter-Reformation to bring the local populace back to Catholicism; take a peek inside at the gilded altar and unusual mosaic ceiling.

ARRIVAL AND INFORMATION   TURENNE

By bus Buses from Brive stop on the main road near the tourist office booth.

Destinations Brive (school term Mon–Fri 1–2 daily; 20min); Collonges-la-Rouge (school term Mon–Sat 1 daily; 15min); Meyssac (school term Mon–Sat 1 daily; 20min).

Tourist office Place Belvedere (May, June & Sept Tues–Sun

10am–12.30pm & 3–6pm; July & Aug daily 9.30am–12.30pm & 2.30–6.30pm; ☎ 05 55 85 59 97, ⊚ brive-tourisme.com); here you can pick up walking maps of the village (€1), which are also available at the souvenir shop next to the lane that leads up to the castle. Guided walks of the village take place in July and August on weekdays at 9.30am and 11am (€5).

ACCOMMODATION AND EATING

Le Clos Marnis Place de la Halle ☎ 05 55 22 05 28, ⊚ closmarnis.online.fr. Quiet and homely bed and breakfast just a stride or two from the main square, housed within a barn-like building erected by the Guild of White Penitents in 1771. While the five rooms won't set the pulse racing, they're of a decent size and tidily furnished with low-slung beds, and there's a large open garden to chill in. **€60**

La Maison des Chanoines Rue Joseph Rouveyrol ☎ 05 55 85 93 43, ⊚ maison-des-chanoines.com. Along the path leading up to the church, this handsome sixteenth-century house has retained many of its fine Gothic flourishes, some of which have been incorporated into the four rooms and three suites (the latter in the building opposite). There are plenty of thoughtful touches too, like

tea- and coffee-making facilities and bedside wirelesses, while all the rooms have been designed so as they offer either a castle or countryside view. Breakfast €10. **€80**

La Vicomté Place de la Halle ☎ 05 55 85 91 32, ⊚ lavicomte.com. You can't miss the jolly facade (albeit with two rather disturbing-looking mannequins hanging out of the window) of *La Vicomté*, where the Dutch owner/chef crafts dishes like Waldorf salad with smoked salmon, ravioli with duck foie gras and grilled pork with violet mustard. The interior has a faintly medieval whiff about it, but if you're going to eat here, grab a seat on the bright stone terrace and take in the views up to the château. Main dishes around €14 or a traditional regional *menu* for €19. Tues–Sat noon–2pm & 7.30–10pm, Sun noon–2pm.

Collonges-la-Rouge

There's a great view back to Turenne as you head southeast on the D20 before cutting eastwards on pretty back lanes through meadows and walnut orchards to reach **COLLONGES-LA-ROUGE** some 10km later; alternatively, you can walk between the two on the GR446 footpath. The village is the epitome of bucolic charm, with its rust-red – even verging on mauve – sandstone houses, pepper-pot towers and pink-candled chestnut trees, although it's arguably more touristy than Turenne and crammed with artisan shops and souvenir stalls; it's best to arrive earlier or later in the day if possible. Though small-scale, there is grandeur about Collonges, for this is where the nobles who governed Turenne on behalf of the viscounts built their mini-châteaux, each boasting at least one tower – there's a wonderful view of the bristling roofs as you approach from the west.

On the main square the twelfth-century **church** is unusual in having two naves, of which the shorter, north nave – the one used today – was a later addition. They came in handy during the sixteenth century when Turenne supported the Huguenot cause; here at least, Protestants and Catholics conducted their services peacefully side by side. Outside, the timber-framed covered **market hall** still retains its old-fashioned baker's oven, which is fired up just once a year for the annual **Bread Festival** on the first Sunday of August.

Maison de la Sirène

Museum July–Aug daily 10.30am–12.30pm & 3–6pm • €2 • ☎ 05 55 84 08 03

On your way back up the main street, look out for the sixteenth-century **Maison de la Sirène**, diagonally opposite the tourist office, which is named after the little mermaid sculpted above the entrance. Though battered, she's still charming as she preens herself, comb in one hand and mirror in the other. The only house in the village that you can visit, it contains a small **museum** with archeological remains including a Merovingian sarcophagus, tools relating to local trades, and rooms arranged with typical rural furniture from the eighteenth and nineteenth centuries. The curator is a mine of information on the village and also gives guided tours; book through the tourist office.

ARRIVAL AND INFORMATION

By bus Buses from Turenne and Drive pass Collonges on their way to the terminus at Meyssac. They stop on the main road at the northern entrance to the village.

By car There are several car parks lining the main road above the village.

COLLONGES-LA-ROUGE

Tourist office Rue de la Barrière (April–June & Sept daily 10am–12.30pm & 2.30–6pm; July & Aug daily 10am–1pm & 2–7pm; Oct & March Mon–Sat 10am–noon & 2–5pm; Nov–Feb Mon–Sat 2–5pm; ☎05 55 25 47 57, ⓦot -collonges.fr).

ACCOMMODATION AND EATING

Camping Moulin de la Valane ☎05 55 25 41 59, ⓦmeyssac.fr. Just off the main road, halfway between Collonges and Meyssac, this is a large, sunny site with comprehensive facilities, among them a snack bar, lounge, laundry, tennis courts and heated pool with slides. Closed Sept–May. €15, chalets €370 per week

Le Cantou Rue de la Barrière ☎05 55 84 25 15, ⓦlecantou.fr. Take your pick from any number of restaurants lining the narrow streets of Collognes, but as the tightly packed ranks of busy tables on the vine-covered terrace attest, Le Cantou is one of the most popular. Light fills such as salads and *tartines* or a full three-course meal costing a very reasonable €20. July & Aug noon–2pm & 7.30–10pm; Sept–June closed eves & all day Mon.

La Maison Jeanne ☎05 55 25 42 31, ⓦjeannemaisondhotes.com. Just a short stroll down from the church on the quieter eastern side of the village, this gorgeous red sandstone building dating from the fifteenth-century is now a classy *chambre d'hôte*; five

individually styled and impeccably furnished rooms crammed with lots of homely touches such as potted plants, books and wall paintings. Breakfast (included) is a jolly affair, taken around the communal dining table. €95

Relais du Quercy ☎05 55 25 40 31, ⓦrelaisduquercy .com. If you want somewhere quieter to bed down for the night, then head 2km east to the village of Meyssac (a smaller town built in the same red sandstone) and this pleasant *Logis* hotel, which has two categories of room and a brightly coloured garden with pool. Closed three weeks in Nov. Breakfast €7.50. €68

Relais de St-Jacques de Compostelle ☎05 55 25 41 02, ⓦrestaurant-relaisstjacques.com. The village's most prominent hotel, just around the corner from the Mermaid's House, though it's not quite as grand as it sounds; ten, rather sparsely furnished rooms, though the views of the narrow streets are lovely and it's fairly priced. Closed Nov–Feb. Breakfast €8. €5

Bergerac
and around

BERGERAC

Bergerac and around

In its lower reaches the Dordogne slides wide and slow through a landscape of vine-planted hills. This is the heart of the Périgord Pourpre, a major wine-growing area that blends seamlessly into the Bordelais vineyards to the west. For centuries the region's most important market town, port and commercial centre has been Bergerac, the second largest city in the Dordogne *département*, but still a pleasantly provincial place with a clutch of worthwhile sights among its twisting lanes. The outlying areas, meanwhile, harvest a rich complement of stately châteaux, attractive *bastide* towns and some outstanding natural heritage.

The foremost sight in the wine region is the Renaissance **Château de Monbazillac**, clearly visible on the ridge to the south and surrounded by its prestigious vineyards, originally planted by monks in the Middle Ages, which produce a very palatable sweet white wine. The high country further south of Bergerac, where the gentle River Dropt marks the border of the Dordogne and Lot-et-Garonne *départements*, wasn't always such a bucolic scene, as a glance at the remaining fortifications of **Issigeac** and particularly **Eymet** – the ramparts built in the run-up to the Hundred Years War – goes to show. The prevailing sense of unease following more than a century of war, plague and famine is caught in the fifteenth-century frescoes of the Last Judgement in the little church of **Allemans-du-Dropt**. Further downstream, at **Duras** another semi-ruined château dominates the valley.

To the west of Bergerac the Dordogne valley becomes wider, busier and less attractive. Nevertheless, there are one or two appealing sights, notably the Gallo-Roman remains at **Montcaret** and the nearby **Château de Montaigne**, where the eponymous philosopher wrote his original, wide-ranging *Essais*. North of here, the **Forêt du Landais** stretches north across the top of the Périgord Pourpre. It's a pretty region of wooded hills, meandering streams and sparse habitation, good for wandering, though without any particularly compelling sights.

Upstream of Bergerac, the pure waters of the River Couze, a tributary of the Dordogne, have spawned a paper-making industry at **Couze-et-St-Front**, where traditional, handmade paper is still produced to this day. Further east, the Dordogne has carved two gigantic meanders at **Trémolat** and **Limeuil**. Here also the Périgord Pourpre gradually gives way to wooded hills on the western edge of the Périgord Noir. The change is perhaps most obvious in the landscapes south of the river, where the *bastide* town of **Beaumont** and the nearby abbey of **St-Avit-Sénieur** stand isolated on the edge of a high, open plateau. Just a few kilometres to the east, however, **Cadouin**'s abbey church sits in a hidden valley deep among the chestnut forests.

GETTING AROUND   **BERGERAC AND AROUND**

Overall, exploring this region by public transport is not easy. While the main towns along the Dordogne valley are well served by trains on the Sarlat–Bordeaux line, anywhere inland requires your own steam. What limited bus services do exist are planned around the needs of school children, not travellers.

Highlights

❶ **Bergerac** Surrounded by vineyards, this sleepy provincial town of cobbled squares and half-timbered facades makes for an atmospheric day's wander. **See p.89**

❷ **Bastides** The fortified towns of Eymet, Lalinde and Beaumont, with their arcaded central squares, retain a medieval atmosphere relatively untouched by tourism. **See p.99 & p.109**

❸ **Church of St-Eutrope**, **Allemans-du-Dropt** Fifteenth-century frescoes depict the Last Judgement in spine-tingling detail. **See p.100**

❹ **Montcaret** The elaborate mosaics in a fourth-century villa unearthed here provide ample evidence of luxury living Roman-style. **See p.105**

❺ **Cingle de Trémolat** A classic Dordogne meander, best viewed from the limestone cliffs to the north. **See p.109**

❻ **Canoeing the Dordogne** Don a life-jacket and take to the waters at Limeuil for a leisurely trip down either the Vézère or Dordogne rivers. **See p.110**

❼ **Cadouin** An exceptionally pretty village with unusual accommodation options and the main draw of an austere twelfth-century Cistercian abbey. **See p.113**

HIGHLIGHTS ARE MARKED ON THE MAP ON P.88

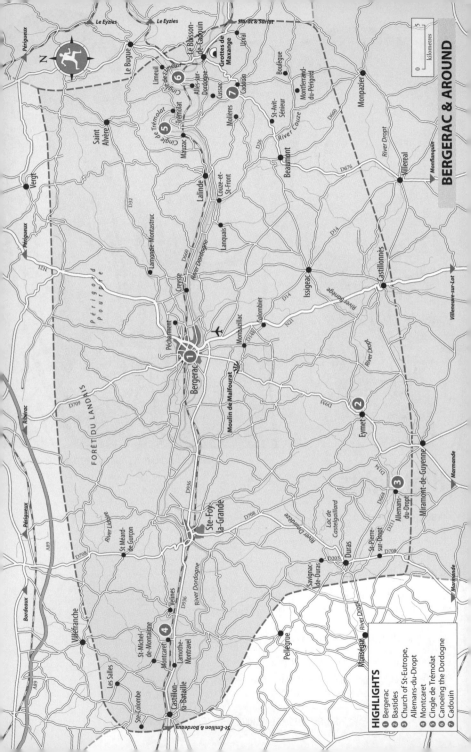

BERGERAC & AROUND

HIGHLIGHTS
1. Bergerac
2. Bastides
3. Church of St-Eutrope, Allemans-du-Dropt
4. Montcaret
5. Cingle de Trémolat
6. Canoeing the Dordogne
7. Cadouin

0   5 kilometres

Bergerac

Lying mostly on the Dordogne's north bank overlooking its wide flood plain, **BERGERAC** is a rather sleepy place for much of the year, but bursts into life for the summer tourist season, when cafés and restaurants spill out into the cobbled squares and alleyways. It suffered particularly badly during the Wars of Religion, but in recent years the old streets fanning out from the former port have been carefully restored to bring out the best in the rows of half-timbered cottages and more bourgeois, stone-built residences. Among several interesting and attractive reminders of the past, the main sights are a surprisingly rewarding **museum** devoted to tobacco and a former **monastery** which now houses an information centre on the local wines.

Although Bergerac sits astride the Dordogne, nearly everything of interest is located on the north bank. The best place to start is beside the old port where, in season, replica *gabares* (barges) pick up passengers for leisurely **river trips**. A short hop east of the port lies the entertaining **Musée du Tabac**, in the narrow lanes of the **vieille ville** which spreads gently uphill. A calm and pleasant area to wander, with numerous late-medieval houses and perfect pavement cafés, its main artery is the Grand Rue, which runs north from the central church of St-Jacques to join rue de la Résistance, the old town's northern perimeter; these two form Bergerac's principal shopping streets. Just beyond their junction, across the wide place de Lattre-de-Tassigny, stands another useful landmark, the **Notre-Dame church**.

Brief history

The largest town in the Dordogne valley, Bergerac owes its existence and prosperity to the **river**. By the twelfth century it was already an important bridging point and port, controlling the trade between its Périgord hinterland and Bordeaux, particularly the burgeoning **wine trade**. Things began to take off after Henry III of England sought to keep the townspeople sweet by giving them certain privileges in 1254: they were exempted from local taxes, given the right of assembly and allowed to export their wines to Bordeaux unhindered. Local burghers took advantage of the new dispensations to ship their own wines first, while the less privileged were forced to sell later, at disadvantageous prices, and were also charged a tax of five *sous* per barrel. Bergerac's wine aristocracy were thus able to corner the lucrative foreign market until the seventeenth century, when the technique of ageing wines was discovered.

The town's heyday came in the decades preceding the Wars of Religion (1561–98) when Bergerac was among the foremost centres of **Protestantism** in southwest France. One of many truces between the warring factions was even signed here in 1577, but in 1620 the Catholic Louis XIII seized the town and ordered that the ramparts and fortress be demolished. Worse was to come when Catholic priests arrived to bring Bergerac back into the fold. They met with mixed success – the majority of the Protestant population fled, principally to Holland, where they soon established a long and mutually profitable business importing Bergerac wines.

Since then wine has continued to be the staple of the local economy. Up until the railway arrived in the 1870s, the bulk of it was transported by river, leading to a thriving **boat-building** industry all along the Dordogne. Though most have long disappeared, a few sturdy *gabares* are still being built to cater to the tourist trade.

Musée du Tabac

Place du Feu • mid-March to mid-Nov Tues–Fri 10am–noon & 2–6pm, Sat 10am–noon & 2–5pm, Sun 2.30–6.30pm; mid-Nov to mid-March Tues–Fri 10am–noon & 2–6pm, Sat 10am–noon • €4 • ☏ 05 53 63 04 13

Rue de l'Ancien Pont leads northwards from portside rue Hippolyte Taine to the splendid seventeenth-century Maison Peyrarède, which houses the absorbing **Musée du Tabac**. Tobacco used to be a major crop in the Bergerac region, and indeed, Europe's major tobacco research centre is based here. While inevitably glossing over its more dire

2

medical effects, this is nevertheless a stunning collection of pipes, snuffboxes, cigar holders, tobacco jars, graters and various tools of the trade, garnered from all over the world. There are wooden graters etched with religious scenes, snuffboxes engraved with the busts of Napoleon and Marie Antoinette, blushing young beauties adorning porcelain pipe-bowls and hunting scenes fashioned out of meerschaum. Among many rare and beautiful pieces, the museum's prize possessions are an incredibly ornate Viennese meerschaum-and-amber cigar holder depicting a Sicilian wedding, and an intriguing machine, invented in the 1860s, for carving fourteen brier pipes at once. Look out, too, for the clay pipe in the ominous form of a skull with glittering glass eyes. The cool 1960s and 70s-era Gitanes posters, meanwhile, hark back to a time when smoking was regarded as a somewhat more glamorous activity.

Cloître des Récollets

A few paces along from the Musée du Tabac stands the **Cloître des Récollets**. This simple, galleried cloister dates from the early seventeenth century when, in the aftermath of the Wars of Religion, Louis XIII dispatched five monks of the Franciscan Récollets order to bring Protestant Bergerac back to the faith. They were not warmly welcomed – it took a visit by Louis himself, in 1621, to assure their authority – but by the end of the decade the Récollets had succeeded in founding a new chapel and

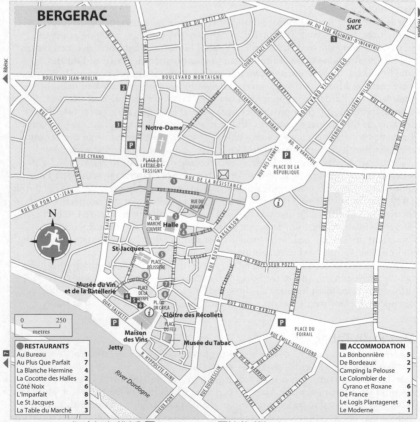

BERGERAC

● RESTAURANTS	
Au Bureau	1
Au Plus Que Parfait	7
La Blanche Hermine	4
La Cocotte des Halles	2
Côté Noix	6
L'Imparfait	8
Le St Jacques	5
La Table du Marché	3

■ ACCOMMODATION	
La Bonbonnière	5
De Bordeaux	2
Camping la Pelouse	7
Le Colombier de Cyrano et Roxane	6
De France	3
Le Logis Plantagenet	1
Le Moderne	4

2

FESTIVALS, EVENTS AND MARKETS

Where we haven't given a specific information number, contact the relevant tourist office.

July and August Bergerac: Les Mercredis du Jazz (ⓦ www.bergerac.fr). Free concerts by French jazz artists on Wednesday evenings on place de la Myrpe and the Cloître des Récollets.

Third weekend in July Duras: Fête de la Madeleine (ⓦ paysdeduras.com). This traditionally Basque festival is marked in Duras by cheap or free concerts in the castle courtyard, a firework display on the Monday night and plenty of wine-tasting.

Third Sunday in July Issigeac: Foire aux Paniers. Unique basket weavers' fair held on the place du Château. Some sixty artisans from all regions of France demonstrate their different techniques and styles.

Late July to mid-August Bergerac and around: Été Musical en Bergerac (ⓦ pays-de-bergerac .com). Performances of classical music, jazz and ballet in Bergerac, the Château de Biron, Monpazier, St-Avit and Cadouin.

Mid-July to mid-August Castillon-la-Bataille: La Bataille de Castillon (ⓦ www .batailledecastillon.com). Local citizenry stage a spectacular floodlit re-enactment of the battle that ended the Hundred Years War. Some five hundred actors and fifty cavaliers take part, performing every Sat and Sun evening for around six weeks; €22 per performance.

August Dropt valley: Itinérance Médiévale en Vallée du Dropt (ⓦ medieval.dropt.org). This four-week festival sees all kinds of events – gastronomic markets, parades in medieval costumes, joustings and concerts by torchlight – laid on in towns and villages along the Dropt valley (including Duras, Eymet, Issigeac and Cadouin).

Second or third weekend in August Duras: Fête du Vin (ⓦ cotesdeduras.com). Two-day wine-fest held beside the château with free tastings (you have to buy a glass at the entrance for €5). The festival features some good music too, with live jazz/blues on the Sunday afternoon.

Mid-Aug Bergerac: L'Assiette de Cyrano (ⓦ pays-de-bergerac.com). The old town is transformed into a gigantic outdoor restaurant for this magnificent food festival, also with free concerts every night.

Late September to early October Bergerac: Fêtes des Vendanges (ⓦ vins-bergerac.fr). Various festivities take place – starting with a procession of *gabares* – over one week to celebrate the end of the grape harvest.

MARKETS

The main markets in this region are at Bergerac (Wed & Sat); Le Buisson (Fri); Cadouin (Wed); Eymet (Thurs); Issigeac (Sun); Lalinde (Thurs); Ste-Foy-la-Grande (Sat); Trémolat (Tues).

---

monastery. Not that they had the last word. After the Revolution, Bergerac's remaining Protestant congregation bought the chapel and re-established a temple on the site, which is still used for regular Sunday-morning worship. The monks' vaulted grain and wine cellars now form an unusual setting for Bergerac's **Maison des Vins** (see p.93), which can be entered through the cloister.

Place de la Myrpe

On its north side the Cloître des Récollets opens onto Bergerac's most picturesque square, the cobbled, tree-shaded **Place de la Myrpe** (also spelt Mirpe), lined with stone and half-timbered labourers' cottages looking onto a badly weathered statue, erected in 1977, honouring Edmond Rostand's fictional hero **Cyrano de Bergerac** (see box, p.92) in typically haughty pose.

Musée du Vin et de la Batellerie

5 rue des Conférences • Tues–Fri 10am–noon & 2–5.30pm, Sat 10am–noon; mid-March to mid-Nov also open Sun 2.30–6.30pm • €3 • ☎ 05 53 57 80 92

The small **Musée du Vin et de la Batellerie** (Wine and Inland Waterways), just off place de la Myrpe, contains a rather motley collection of items related to viticulture, farming and the town's once bustling river trade. This latter section is the most interesting, with models of the *gabares* alongside some text (French only) on the practicalities of navigating the Dordogne. If you'd been wondering how non-motorized vessels used to make any progress at all going upriver against the flow, the answer is that they did so with difficulty. The river was only navigable upstream on about 150 days per year, and for a long time this relied on men hauling the boats from the riverbank – a practice banned in 1837 for humanitarian reasons.

Church of St-Jacques

Rue St-Jacques • Mon–Sat 2–7pm

Further uphill, along rue St-Jacques, stands the patchwork **church of St-Jacques**. The church, a stop on the route to Santiago de Compostela (see p.290), has had a chequered past, founded in the twelfth century but plundered and destroyed in the Hundred Years War and the Wars of Religion – only the campanile and balcony remain from the original church. Today's church is fairly modest, but has a certain grandeur in its narrow, high nave, topped by a precise rib-vaulted ceiling and lit by stained-glass windows.

Rue St-James to the market square

Rue St-James runs east from the church across the top end of pedestrianized **place Pélissière**, the old tanners' quarter but now dotted with cafés and ice cream parlours. This square, too, boasts its own statue of Cyrano, a more recent incarnation from 2005 and bearing an uncanny, and somewhat cartoonish, resemblance to Gérard Depardieu. From here pretty **rue des Fontaines** continues uphill past prosperous fourteenth- and sixteenth-century houses – no. 29 on the corner with rue Gaudra is particularly noteworthy with its large, arched windows and carved capitals – to the **market square**. The covered *halle* is the focus of a vast market on Wednesday and Saturday mornings, with more stalls on the square outside the church of Notre-Dame.

Church of Notre-Dame

Place de Lattre de Tassigny • Mon–Sat 8.30am–6pm

The **church of Notre-Dame** was built in 1865 as the town's congregation grew too large for the church of St-Jacques. Designed by Paul Abadie of Sacré-Coeur fame, it does impress for the resolutely Neo-Gothic style of its architecture, though the twee

---

CYRANO DE BERGERAC

In 1897, the poet and playwright Edmond Rostand penned his most successful play, **Cyrano de Bergerac**. It tells the story of a guardsman and poet, renowned for his bravery and intellect, who falls in love with his cousin Roxane, but feels unable to declare his feelings because of his unattractive looks – in particular his large, protruding nose. Instead, he writes letters to her on behalf of one of his cadets, the handsome but dim-witted Christian, who has also fallen for her charms. First attracted by Christian's looks, Roxane falls in love with the soul revealed in the letters – not discovering until it is too late that it is in fact Cyrano's soul. Rostand's play has since been the subject of numerous adaptations, perhaps most famously the 1990 French film version staring Gérard Depardieu.

The lead character was inspired by a seventeenth-century soldier, playwright and free-thinking philosopher called Savinien de Cyrano, who was born in Paris and only decided to embellish his name while serving in a Gascon company. It seems Cyrano was well able to match the Gascon reputation for swaggering boastfulness and impetuosity. Not only was he a famous duellist, but many of his works were so outspoken that they had to be withheld from publication until after his death.

miniature columns and Nativity-scene sculptures on its main facade border on greeting-card kitsch. The long, high and grey interior does little to inspire, though it's worth a look to view two large oil paintings in the east chapel: *The Adoration of the Shepherds*, attributed to a pupil of Leonardo de Vinci, and *The Adoration of the Magi* from the Venetian School.

ARRIVAL AND DEPARTURE BERGERAC

By plane Bergerac's airport is in Roumanière (☎05 53 22 25 25, ⓦbergerac.aeroport.fr), 5km southeast of the city on the Agen road. There's a restaurant and an ATM here but nothing else. Moreover, there's no public transport to the centre and taxis (around €15) are often in short supply. If there aren't any outside, you can order one from Abeilles Bergerac Taxis; call ☎05 53 23 32 32. Another option is to wait by the car park exit and try and grab a lift from someone heading into town.
Airlines Flybe (ⓦflybe.com); Ryanair (ⓦryanair.com); Transavia (ⓦtransavia.com); Twinjet (ⓦtwinjet.fr).
By train The *gare SNCF* is located at the north end of cours Alsace Lorraine, ten minutes' walk from the old town.
Destinations Bordeaux (6–12 daily; 1hr 15min–1hr 30min); Le Buisson (4–8 daily; 40min); Castillon-la-Bataille (6–12 daily; 40–50min); Couze (1–2 daily; 15min);

Lalinde (4–8 daily; 15–20min); Lamothe-Montravel (1–3 daily; 35–40min); Libourne (6–12 daily; 45min 1hr); St-Émilion (3–7 daily; 40min); Ste-Foy-La-Grande (6–12 daily; 20min); Sarlat (4–8 daily; 1hr 20min–1hr 30min); Trémolat (3–7 daily; 30min).
By bus Most buses around the region depart from outside the *gare SNCF*.
Destinations Eymet (Mon–Fri 1–2 daily; 50min–1hr 20min); Issigeac (Mon–Fri 1–2 daily; 45min); Lalinde (school term Mon–Sat 1–3 daily; 40min); Périgueux (school term Mon–Fri 4 daily; school hols Mon–Fri 3 daily; 1hr); Port de Couze (as for Lalinde; 30min).
By car You'll find free parking in the cobbled area beside the old port and on place du Foirail, a short walk east of the town centre.

GETTING AROUND

Bike rental First choice should be the friendly and helpful Apolo Cycles, 31 bd Victor-Hugo (☎06 20 64 59 25, ⓦapolo-cycles.com); they can also do drop-offs at your hotel (€15 per day). Otherwise, there's Périgord Cycles, 11 place Gambetta (☎05 53 57 07 19; Tues–Sat 9am–noon & 2–7pm), which also does repairs.
Car rental Near the train station, try Avis, 26 cours

Alsace Lorraine (☎05 53 57 69 83), or Europcar, 3 av du 108e Régiment-d'Infanterie (☎05 53 58 97 97) and at airport (☎05 53 61 61 61); Hertz at airport (☎05 53 27 10 51); Ucar, 31 bd Victor Hugo (☎05 53 61 08 16, ⓦapolo-cars.com).
Taxis There's a taxi stand outside the station. Otherwise, call ☎05 53 23 32 32.

INFORMATION AND TOURS

Tourist office 97 rue Neuve d'Argenson (July & Aug daily 9.30am–7.30pm; Sept–June Mon–Sat 9.30am–1pm & 2–7pm; ☎05 53 57 03 11, ⓦbergerac-tourisme.com). There's one internet terminal (15min free), plus free wi-fi. In summer they also open an annexe in the Cloître des Récollets (July & Aug daily 10.30am–1pm & 2.30–7pm; same number as above). Both offices organize guided tours of the old town several times a week (July & Aug; 1hr 30min; €4.50).
Maison des Vins 2 place du Docteur Cayla (Feb–June & Sept–Dec Tues–Sat 10.30am–12.30pm & 2–6pm; July & Aug daily 10am–7pm; free; wine-tasting lessons July & Aug Wed in French and Fri in English; €5; reservations required; ☎05 53 58 63 13, ⓦvins-bergerac.fr) – enter

either through the cloister or at street level on the riverfront. As well as tasting and selling wines, they provide wine-tasting lessons and produce the *Route des Vins de Bergerac*, a handy guide to visiting the vineyards around the town. In addition there are interesting displays about the history of the Bergerac appellation.
River trips Périgord Gabarres, Le Quai Salvette (April–Oct; €8; ☎05 53 24 58 80, ⓦgabarres.fr). In season, replica *gabares* pick up passengers for leisurely 1hr river trips beside the old port along the Dordogne to a nature reserve that is home to herons, cormorants and kingfishers, among other wildlife; commentary is bilingual. Departures are at least four times daily and up to once an hour in July and August (10am–8pm).

ACCOMMODATION

For a modestly sized town, Bergerac has a fairly broad range of accommodation, offering an appealing mix of hotels and *chambres d'hôtes*, many of the latter clustered in or around lovely Place de la Myrpe. There's no hostel in Bergerac, though there is a well-located campsite very close to the centre.

2

THE WINES OF BERGERAC

The **Bergerac wine region** extends along the north bank of the Dordogne from Lamothe-Montravel in the west to Lalinde in the east, and south as far as Eymet and Issigeac. It comprises no fewer than thirteen different *appellations*, of which over half the total output is red wine, although the region's most famous wine is the sweet white Monbazillac.

There is evidence of wine production around Bergerac since Roman times, but the vineyards really began to develop in the thirteenth century to supply the English market. Demand from Holland, for sweet white wines in particular, led to a second spurt in the sixteenth century and then again after the Wars of Religion, when Protestant émigré merchants virtually monopolized the market in Monbazillac wines. By the nineteenth century vines covered 100,000 hectares around Bergerac, only to be decimated by phylloxera in the 1870s; the area under AOP wines today covers a mere 12,000 hectares.

Pre-eminent among the Bergerac wines is **Monbazillac**. This pale golden, sweet white wine is blended from Semillon, Sauvignon and Muscadelle vines grown on the chalky clay soils of the valley's north-facing slopes. As with Sauternes, a key element is the cold, autumn-morning mists which lead to the development of *Botrytis cinerea*, or "noble rot", on the grapes. The result is an intensely perfumed, concentrated wine best consumed chilled with foie gras, desserts or as an apéritif. Though they can't compare to the finesse of Sauternes, even a top-quality Monbazillac is eminently affordable at around €15 a bottle.

Pécharmant, the best of the local reds, is often compared unfavourably to Bordeaux wines, though some now rival a number of less prestigious St-Émilions. Pécharmant wines are produced from Cabernet Sauvignon, Cabernet Franc and small quantities of Malbec or Merlot grapes, grown on the most favourable pockets of sand and gravel soils found to the north and east of Bergerac. They are thus far more complex and full-bodied than other Bergerac reds, and some will age well up to seven years.

You can sample the range of local AOP wines at Bergerac's Maison des Vins. Alternatively, many producers offer **tastings and visits** to their *chais* – for a full list see the brochure *Route des Vins de Bergerac* available at the Maison des Vins (see p.93) or Bergerac tourist office (see p.93).

★ **La Bonbonnière** 15 place de la Myrpe ☎ 05 53 61 82 04, ⊛ labonbonniere.net. Bergerac's loveliest square is full of fine medieval buildings, though few possess as much character as this cosy, cottage-like *chambre d'hôte* run by engaging host, Simone. There are four rooms, one of which is an attic room, each replete with beautiful detail, from the wooden beams running through the partially exposed stone walls, to colourful handwoven textiles and all sorts of oddball knick-knacks. Breakfast is taken around the communal kitchen table, which only adds to its charm. €68
De Bordeaux 38 place Gambetta ☎ 05 53 57 12 83, ⊛ hotel-bordeaux-bergerac.com. In terms of facilities, if not character, this is probably Bergerac's top hotel, boasting a sizeable pool and plush bar. The rooms are bright and handsomely furnished and the bathrooms are spankingly clean – ask for a room at the back, which are quieter and have views of the pool and small garden. Breakfast €9. €55
Camping la Pelouse 8bis rue J-J Rousseau ☎ 05 53 57 06 67, ⊛ entreprisefrery.com/camping-la-pelouse. In a beautiful position on the peaceful south bank of the river, a short walk west from the Vieux Pont, this is a cheap and friendly municipal site but with fairly basic facilities. Closed Oct–April. €12, mobile homes €550 per week
Le Colombier de Cyrano et Roxane 17 place de la Myrpe ☎ 05 53 57 96 70, ⊛ lecolombierdecyrano.fr. This lovely little *chambre d'hôte* in a flagstone sixteenth-century cottage is adorned with blue shutters, flower boxes and a tiny blue wooden door. Bursting with colour, the two en-suite rooms offer touches of Baroque extravagance, while one – only a touch more expensive – has its own private terrace with wicker chairs and a hammock. €69
De France 18 place Gambetta ☎ 05 53 57 11 61, ⊛ hoteldefrance-bergerac.com. This three-star has an unpromising modern exterior but don't let that put you off; the twenty rooms are pleasing on the eye and there's a high level of comfort on offer. In addition, there's an open-air pool at the back to enjoy. Breakfast €9. €69
★ **Le Logis Plantagenet** 5 rue du Grand Moulin ☎ 05 53 57 15 99, ⊛ lelogisplantagenet.com. Restored fourteenth-century house with three very elegant, light-filled double rooms – all beams, wood floors, rugs and country-style furnishings imported from Italy – as well as two beautiful sitting rooms, a kitchen (where guests are free to avail themselves of tea and coffee) and a courtyard garden for breakfast. €85
Le Moderne 19 av du 108e Régiment-d'Infanterie ☎ 05 53 57 19 62, ⊛ hotel-restaurant-le-moderne.fr. For those arriving late or leaving early by train, this hotel bang

opposite the station is just the job. Twelve slightly boxy en-suite rooms, though they're well maintained and have a/c; note that those rooms at the front look directly onto the busy main road, and there's a lively bar below. Breakfast €8. **€50**

EATING AND DRINKING

When it comes to places to eat, the streets of old Bergerac present a promising hunting ground – you'll find a bunch of terrific restaurants clustered around place du Marché Couvert, and several more located further down towards the river. Bergerac is hardly your typical party town, hence the paucity of drinking establishments, though there are one or two bars and cafés where you can linger over a mid-morning cappuccino or a beer at sundown.

CAFÉS AND RESTAURANTS

★ **La Blanche Hermine** Place du Marché-Couvert ☎ 05 53 57 63 42. An excellent rendition of a Breton crêperie offering a dozen or so savoury buckwheat *galettes* (€6–9), like the *Périgordine* (duck breast and peaches), and a similar number of sweet crêpe desserts (€3–6); don't miss the house special Gourmandise, a scrummy caramel and salty butter pancake. Tues–Sat noon–2am & 7–10pm.

La Cocotte des Halles 14 place du Marché-Couvert ☎ 05 53 24 10 00. Just inside one corner of the market hall, you'll find this easy-going place – all plastic chairs and tables – packed to the gills every lunchtime with locals filling up on surprisingly sophisticated dishes like pear and roquefort cheese salad, or dried fillet of duck with prunes, nuts and raisins; there's a fresh fish dish each day too. The no-frills two-course *menu* costs €12. Mon–Sat noon–2am & 7–10pm.

Côté Noix Place Pélissiere ☎ 05 53 57 71 38, ⓦ cotenoix.fr. One of the few places in Bergerac where you can sit down for a quick bite to eat, this place makes for a good lunchtime pit-stop; sandwiches, salads, crumbles and ice cream, plus hot and cold drinks including tea, coffee and smoothies. Tues–Sat 10am–6pm.

L'Imparfait 8 rue des Fontaines ☎ 05 53 57 47 92, ⓦ imparfait.com. Bergerac's longest-standing and most refined traditional restaurant is an attractive high-ceilinged, stone dining room complete with fireplace, though in summer diners migrate to the well-shaded terrace. The menu changes daily, but revolves around fresh fish and meat, subtly flavoured by a talented chef; the veal sweetbreads are a bit of a house speciality. *Menus* from €26. Daily noon–2pm & 7–10pm. Closed mid-Dec to mid-Jan.

Le St Jacques 30 rue St-James ☎ 05 53 23 38 08, ⓦ lesaintjacques.info. This place has a charming shaded garden at the back complete with outdoor fireplace and stone walls strewn with lanterns and candles. The sophisticated menu is small but varied, from the local duck breast in a sweet Bordeaux sauce or lightly fried foie gras with stewed apples and nuts, to Scottish salmon with guacamole. Reckon on €30 à la carte. Wed–Sun noon–2pm & 7–10pm, plus Tues 7–10pm.

★ **La Table du Marché** 21 place de la Bardonnie ☎ 05 53 22 49 46, ⓦ www.table-du-marche.fr. If you've only time for one meal in Bergerac, then make it *Table du Marché*, whose young chef, Stéphane Cuzin, oversees dazzlingly adventurous dishes like cucumber gazpacho, nougat foie gras with walnuts and pistachios, and hake with spring onion and grilled pepper sorbet. The black and white decor gives the venue a sharp, contemporary feel, as does the open kitchen where you can watch your food being prepared. *Menus* from €19. Mon–Sat noon–2pm & 7.30–10pm.

BARS

Au Bureau 9 rue de la Résistance ☎ 05 53 74 81 72. Indeed, this well attended pub/brasserie is just the sort of place people visit to escape the office, typically for a burger and fries washed down with a pint of strong Belgian ale. It's not fancy, but then it doesn't have to be. Daily 10.30am–midnight.

Au Plus Que Parfait 12 rue des Fontaines ☎ 05 53 61 95 11. Great-looking pub across the street from *L'Imparfait*, where you'll receive a warm welcome and a choice of seven or eight Belgian beers on tap and dozens more by the bottle. There's plenty of entertainment too, from games nights and salsa to occasional live music on Saturday evenings. Daily 9am–1am, Fri & Sat till 2am.

DIRECTORY

Books and newspapers Bergerac's fantastic independent bookshop, La Colline Aux Livres on place du Marché-Couvert (Tues–Sat 9.30am–1pm & 2–7pm; ☎ 05 53 57 90 97), has a small selection of books in English. With so many Brits residing here, many of the *tabacs* stock English newspapers.

Hospital Central Hospitalier Samuel Pozzi, 9 bd du Professeur Albert Calmette, the eastern extension of rue du Professeur Pozzi (☎ 05 53 63 88 88).

Markets There's a fresh-food market from Monday to Saturday in the central *halle*, while Bergerac's main market takes place on Wednesday and Saturday mornings in the *halle* and the roads and squares around it. There's also a small organic market on Tuesday mornings in front of the town hall. Place de la Myrpe is the venue for a flea market on the first Sunday of the month.

Police Commissariat de Police, 37 bd Chanzy (☎ 05 53 74 74 17).

Post office The main post office is at 36 rue de la Résistance (Mon–Fri 8.30am–8pm, Sat 8.30am–12.30pm).

Monbazillac and around

Six kilometres south of Bergerac, **MONBAZILLAC** is the name not only of a village but also, more famously, of a château and a sweet white wine similar to those of the Sauternes in the Bordeaux region. After whetting your appetite at Monbazillac, investigate some of the area's private **vineyards**. There are two good options to the east of Monbazillac near the village of **Colombier**.

Château de Monbazillac

Daily: April–May & Oct 10am–12.30pm & 2–6pm; June–Sept 10am–7pm; Nov–Dec & Feb–March Tues–Sun 10am–noon & 2–5pm; guided tours in July & Aug daily at 11.30am & 3pm • €6.70 • ☎ 05 53 61 52 52, ⓦ chateau-monbazillac.com

Visible from across the valley floor, the handsome sixteenth-century **Château de Monbazillac** sits invitingly atop a low hill, surveying the gentle slopes of its long-favoured vineyards below. An eye-catching blend of Renaissance residence and mock-medieval fortress, its corners reinforced by four sturdy towers, the château was a Protestant stronghold during the Wars of Religion. Surprisingly, it has survived virtually intact and now contains many richly furnished rooms; although few original furnishings remain, it is nevertheless an impressive collection. The pick of the rooms are located on the ground floor, notably the grand salon with its beautifully decorated ceiling, herringbone parquet flooring of oak, pine and cherry wood and a Renaissance fireplace with heraldic sculptures. There's another fine fireplace in the adjoining *petit salon*, this one clad in walnut and featuring an unusual tryptych. The so-called Library Tower, meanwhile, is just that, well-stocked with books as well as a family tree of the D'Aydies', the founders of the castle. Better still is the superbly vaulted cellar with its many wine-related displays including a cabinet full of antique bottles specially labelled for the Dutch market, the oldest of which dates from 1920.

Cave de Monbazillac showroom and Maison de Tourisme

The Château de Monbazillac and its vineyards have been under the ownership of the local wine producers' co-operative, the **Cave de Monbazillac** (Mon–Sat: Jan & Feb 10am–12.30pm & 2–6pm; March–June 10am–12.30pm & 1.30–7pm; July & Aug 9am–7pm; Sept–Dec 10am–12.30pm & 1.30–7pm; ☎05 53 63 65 00), since 1960. You can taste, and buy, its famous velvety sweet white wine both at the château or at the main **showroom** located 2km west on the D933 Bergerac–Marmande road. Alternatively, you can sample a similar variety of wines, as well as view a small exhibition on the local vineyards, at the **Maison de Tourisme** (Tues–Sat 2–5pm; free; ☎05 53 58 63 13), just 500m up the road from the château.

Château de la Jaubertie

Mon–Sat 10am–5pm • Free • ☎ 05 53 58 32 11, ⓦ chateau-jaubertie.com

The first of the châteaux you come to on the D14E, after about 4km, is the sixteenth-century **Château de la Jaubertie**, which was supposedly built by Henry IV for his mistress, Gabrielle d'Estrée, and later belonged to a doctor of Marie Antoinette. Now owned by an English family – the Rymans – the estate produces a variety of very reasonable wines under the Bergerac *appellation*, the most prominent of which is the *Bergerac Blanc Sec*.

Domaine de l'Ancienne Cure

Shop Mon–Sat 9am–7pm, plus Sun in July & Aug • ☎ 05 53 58 27 90, ⓦ domaine-anciennecure.fr

The **Domaine de l'Ancienne Cure** in the village of Colombier, overseen by Christian Roche, has won any number of awards for its high-quality, and mostly organic, Monbazillac, Bergerac and Pécharmant wines – their three cuvées, namely the Jour du Fruit, L'Abbaye and the highly concentrated L'Extase are all fantastic; a bottle of the latter, which is harvested only in vintage years, will set you back around €20. You can visit the *chais* by appointment, but tastings are available at any time at their shop just below the village on the main N21 Bergerac–Agen road, right by the Issigeac turning.

Château de Bridoire

April–June & Sept–Oct Sat & Sun 10am–12.30pm & 1.30–6pm; July & Aug daily 10am–7pm • €8 • ☎ 05 53 58 11 74,
ⓦ chateaudebridoire.com

Four kilometres west of Monbazillac, in Ribagnac, the **Château de Bridoire** recently opened to the public for the first time following some twenty years of painstaking restoration work. A private estate since 1979, the work remains far from complete though, and there's little to see beyond a re-created kitchen, billiards room and a few other, mostly empty, rooms on the ground floor. Still, it's a lovely site, and there's lots of fun to be had in the surrounding grounds, where a series of medieval and traditional French games and activities have been laid out, such as Jeu d'Oies (snakes and ladders with geese), Jeu de la Boulie, archery, croquet, and an enormous chess board. Incorporated within the outer wall are the stables, complete with horses.

EATING AND DRINKING   MONBAZILLAC AND AROUND

Tour des Vents ☎ 05 53 58 30 10, ⓦ tourdesvents.com. Three kilometres west from the Cave de Monbazillac showroom, the well-rated *Tour des Vents* sits beside the Moulin de Malfourat, a ruined windmill perched on the highest point for miles around. Though it's not an attractive building, the views from the restaurant's picture windows and terrace are superb – and the food is first rate; *menus* start at €32, or fans of foie gras can try a selection of four kinds for €25. Tues–Sat noon–2pm & 7.30–10pm, Sun noon–2pm; Sept–June also closed Tues lunchtime.

Pécharmant

East of Bergerac, if you leave the river valley at Creysse and head north, you're soon back among vine-covered hills. Some of this region's best red wines are produced around the village of **PÉCHARMANT**, 6km northeast of Bergerac; indeed, the wines here are certainly a cut above the surrounding Côtes de Bergerac and Bergerac *appellations*.

Domaine du Haut-Pécharmant

Mon–Sat 9am–noon & 3–7pm • ☎ 05 53 57 29 50, ⓦ haut-pecharmant.com

The family-run **Domaine du Haut-Pécharmant** is a good place to aim for. It stands in the thick of the vines with views across to Monbazillac, and produces a typically full-bodied, aromatic wine, which ages well. The domaine is signed north off the D32 between Bergerac and Ste-Alvère.

Château de Tiregand

April–Oct Mon–Sat 9am–noon & 2–6pm; Nov–March Mon–Fri 9am–noon & 2–5.30pm • ☎ 05 53 23 21 08, ⓦ chateau-de-tiregand.com

Opposite the turning to Domaine du Haut-Pécharmant, at the end of a long alley, the much grander **Château de Tiregand** also offers free tastings and guided tours of the estate. Their star wine is the Cuvée Grand Millésime. Although not normally open to the public, if you phone ahead, you may be able to visit the seventeenth-century *chais* and its extensive gardens (€3).

South of Bergerac

South of Bergerac, you gradually leave the vines behind as you cross an area of high, rolling country, featuring several small towns, which are well off the beaten tourist track but all the more appealing for that. First stop is **Issigeac**, with its picturesque medieval centre situated on a tributary of the Dropt. From here you can follow quieter back roads southwest along the **Dropt valley** to **Eymet**, a particularly satisfying *bastide* with a well-preserved central square and an abandoned castle, and on to **Allemans-du-Dropt**, where the focus of interest is a remarkable series of frescoes in its otherwise unassuming church. Last but not least comes **Duras**, the town from which the twentieth-century novelist Margaret Duras took her pen-name after spending part of her childhood in the region. Duras's semi-ruined but still forbidding castle holds a commanding position on Périgord's southwestern border.

GETTING AROUND   SOUTH OF BERGERAC

Public transport is almost non-existent. Buses do link Bergerac with Eymet and Issigeac, and Eymet with Allemans, but there are only one or two in each direction daily, none of which allows for a day-trip from Bergerac.

Issigeac

An almost perfectly circular huddle of houses in the midst of pastureland and orchards 8km southeast of Colombier along the D14, **ISSIGEAC** owes its prosperity to the bishops of Sarlat who established a residence here in 1317. Only fragments of the outer walls remain, and in recent years the village has been considerably tarted up, but otherwise its core of half-timbered medieval buildings is largely unspoilt and the narrow streets mercifully traffic-free.

The seventeenth-century **bishop's palace**, now containing various administrative offices, and the **Maison des Dîmes**, the former tax office, with its immense roof, command the village's north entrance. Behind the palace, and not much larger, the Gothic **church of St-Félicien** contains little of interest beyond some polychrome statues. Better instead to wander the old streets, starting with the **Grand Rue**, leading south to Issigeac's most famous building known as the **Maison des Têtes** for its roughly carved, almost grotesque crowned and grimacing heads. It stands on the corner with rue Cardénal, at the east end of which a house with a half-timbered upper storey on a narrow stone pedestal – allowing carts to pass on either side – resembles nothing so much as a toadstool. From here, take rue Sauveterre circling southwest past more medieval houses and then cross over the southern end of the Grand Rue to find the rue de l'Ancienne Poste, which meanders generally back northwards to the Maison des Dîmes.

ARRIVAL AND INFORMATION   ISSIGEAC

By bus Buses from Bergerac stop on the main road on the southwest side of Issigeac.

Tourist office In a vaulted cellar beneath the bishop's palace (June–Sept Tues–Fri 10am–12.30pm & 2–6pm, Sat 2–6pm, Sun 10am–1pm; Oct–May Tues–Fri 10am–noon & 2–5pm; ☎05 53 58 79 62, ⓦissigeac.fr). As well as

holding temporary exhibitions, which allow you to explore a few rooms of the palace, the office can provide you with a walking guide to the village.

Market On Sunday mornings, the village fills with market stalls.

ACCOMMODATION AND EATING

La Brucelière Place Capelle ☎05 53 73 89 61, ⓦlabruceliere.com. Located by the roundabout on the road to Beaumont, the cheery, family-run *Brucelière* offers five light and airy rooms with polished floors, beige curtains and wicker chairs, and crisp white bed linen. Whether you're staying here or not, it'd be remiss not to give its handsome, yellow and cream stone restaurant a try. *Menus* (from €24) feature devilishly tempting dishes like crayfish and mushrooms in ravioli parcels with shellfish sauce, and hot chocolate biscuit with fruit sauce. Restaurant open noon–2pm & 7.30–10pm, closed Tues eve & Wed. **€55**

Chez Alain ☎05 53 58 06 03, ⓦchez-alain.com. Just across the ring road from the bishop's palace, the supremely classy *Chez Alain* boasts a log fire in winter and a very pretty courtyard with a stone fountain for alfresco dining in summer. The *menus* (starting at €19) contain a

number of seafood delights, such as tuna and shrimp carpaccio, and a heavy presence of crayfish and lobster, but for lunch on Sunday you should go for the delicious *grand buffet* (€29). May–Oct Tues–Sat noon–2pm & 7.30–10pm, Sun noon–2pm; Nov–Dec & March Thurs–Sat noon–2pm & 7.30–10pm, Sun noon–2pm; April Wed–Sat noon–2pm & 7.30–10pm, Sun noon–2pm. Closed Jan & Feb.

★ **Passé & Present** 14 Grand Rue ☎05 53 63 35 31, ⓦpasse-et-present.com. You could quite easily miss this wonderful *chambre d'hote*, such is the mass of pretty foliage enveloping its little grey door. The interior is similarly winsome, its three gorgeous, parquet-floored rooms possessing lots of homely detail: ornamented fireplaces, handmade textiles and linens, black and white wall prints and the like. All rooms, one of which sleeps four, offer views of the pretty garden below. **€48**

Eymet

In contrast to Issigeac's meandering medieval streets, **EYMET**, 15km to the southwest, is laid out on a typical *bastide* chequerboard plan around a well-preserved arcaded central square, **place Gambetta**. Founded in 1270 by Alphonse de Poitiers (see p.293), Eymet changed hands on several occasions – not always by force – during the Hundred Years War and later joined Bergerac as a bastion of Protestantism. Indeed, locals are still proud of the fact that in 1588 Henry of Navarre, the then leader of the Protestant armies and future King Henry IV, wrote a letter from Eymet to his mistress, Diane d'Andouins. With its distinctive sloping roof, corner tower and trefoil windows, the house in which he supposedly set pen to paper is the grandest on place Gambetta; it is naturally called the **Maison d'Amour**. Otherwise, the square – also known as place des Arcades – is a wonderful confection of rough-hewn stone buildings and timbered medieval houses, their thick beams creaking and curving with age. Three sides of the square shelter broad arcades, variously concealing cafés and shops – the only thing rather spoiling the whole ensemble is the proliferation of cars.

Once you've soaked up the atmosphere here – which will take longer if you chance to be here for the Thursday-morning **market** – head to Eymet's ruined castle, just north of the centre. The castle hasn't been developed as a tourist sight at all, so you're free to wander inside the curtain wall and right up to the largely intact thirteenth-century keep, built shortly before the *bastide* itself.

ARRIVAL AND INFORMATION   EYMET

By bus Buses from Bergerac and Issigeac stop on the main boulevard east of the central square.
Destinations Allemans-du-Dropt (school term Mon–Fri 1 daily; 15min); Bergerac (Mon–Sat 1–2 daily; 45min); Issigeac (Mon–Fri 1–2 daily; 25min).

Tourist office 45 place Gambetta, under the arcades on the square's southeastern corner (May–Sept Mon–Sat 10am–12.30pm & 2–6.30pm; July & Aug also Sun 10am–12.30pm; Oct–April Tues–Sat 10am–12.30pm & 2–5.30pm; ☎ 05 53 23 74 95, ⓦ eymet-perigord.fr).

ACCOMMODATION

Camping du Château Rue de la Sole ☎ 05 53 23 80 28, ⓦ eymetcamping.com. A modest, peaceful little site north of place Gambetta between the château and the river; facilities include decent shower blocks, laundry and wi-fi, plus bike and boat rental. Closed Oct–April. **€12**
Maison 20 20 rue Traversière ☎ 06 32 32 13 24, ⓦ maison20.com. On a quiet residential street one block west of place Gambetta and running parallel to Boulevard National, is this very stylish boutique hotel. The two rooms are, to all intents and purposes, self-contained apartments (one can sleep three, the other five), with their own

kitchen-cum-lounge area. The furnishings, meanwhile, are a cool mix of contemporary and antique, with quirky bits and pieces gathered from all over the world by the hotel's exuberant owner. **€90**
Les Vieilles Pierres ☎ 05 53 23 75 99, ⓦ lesvieillespierres.fr. Just off the D933 to the south of town, this small, comfortable hotel basically consists of several chalet-like buildings gathered around a couple of small courtyards, hence all but two of the rooms are at ground level. They're simple at best, some with shower, some with bath, and there's a pool too. Breakfast €8. **€50**

EATING

La Maison d'Amour 37 place Gambetta ☎ 05 53 22 34 64. Place Gambetta has plenty of places to eat, the best of which is this always-busy crêperie and *salon de thé* located on the bottom floor of the square's most appealing building. You'll have a tricky time choosing from a mouthwatering menu of stuffed *galettes* (€7–10), like *canard à la Royale* (duck breast with honey and vinegar) and *Normande* (chicken with mushrooms and cider), but there are also some decent veggie options and salad platters. The interior is nicely done, but you can't beat sitting out on the colourful terrace. Tues–Sun

noon–2pm & 7–9.30pm.
Les Pieds Sur Terre 41 bd National ☎ 05 53 27 53 49. The location, on the town's main through road, really couldn't be any less inviting, but don't let put you off. This smart, modern-looking restaurant specializes in fantastically tasty grills, which come with a choice of either rice, creamed potatoes or salad, and *moules-frites*, though there's plenty of other fishy stuff on the menu, like salmon fishcakes and seafood spaghetti. Mains from €10. Tues–Sun noon–2pm & 7.30–10pm.

2

Allemans-du-Dropt

Head 10km downstream from Eymet to the tiny village of **ALLEMANS-DU-DROPT**, not much more than a homely little central square and the **church of St-Eutrope** (daily 9am–6pm; free). The church's top-heavy lantern tower (topped with a carp as opposed to a cock) and grand west door – both nineteenth-century additions to the much-altered tenth-century building – are rather misleading. The interior, meanwhile, would be unremarkable were it not for some recently restored fifteenth-century **frescoes** depicting the Crucifixion and Last Judgement. A number of scenes have been lost or damaged over the years, but on the whole the paintings, which were only rediscovered in 1935, are unusually complete. They read from left to right as you enter, starting with the Last Supper and ending with a particularly graphic view of Hell. Despite the best efforts of St Michael, clad in medieval armour, a mere two souls seem bound for heaven while the damned are being carried off by the basket-load, or skewered on a spit, to be thrust into a boiling cauldron.

The village also boasts two fine old market halls; directly behind the church stands the **Old Covered Market**, which has also served as a town hall and a prison in its time – this version dates from 1732, as evidenced by its withered wooden columns. In a similar vein, but of somewhat sturdier proportions, is the **Prune Market Hall**, just around the corner from the tourist office. So named because it was traditionally the centre for the local prune markets, it was rebuilt following a fire in 1855.

Having seen these, take a stroll to Allemans' western outskirts. As you set off on the D211 out of the village towards Duras, you pass first an old *lavoir*, then a splendid **pigeonnier** standing in somebody's back garden. Such pigeon-houses, which only noblemen had the right to build, are fairly common throughout southwest France, but this elegant hexagonal brick and oak-framed structure, raised up on seven pillars, each capped to prevent rats climbing up, is a particularly fine example.

ARRIVAL AND DEPARTURE   ALLEMANS-DU-DROPT

By bus Buses stop on place de la Mairie, southwest of the church.

INFORMATION AND ACTIVITIES

Tourist office13 place de la Liberté (April–June, Sept & Oct Tues–Sat 2–5pm; July & Aug Tues–Sat 11am–1pm & 2–5pm; ☎05 53 20 25 59, ⓦallemansdudropt.com) opposite the church. Though Allemans is easy enough to find your way around, it's still worth picking up an English-language walking guide.

Canoe rental In July and August you can rent canoes at the campsite (☎06 33 65 42 24).

ACCOMMODATION AND EATING

Camping municipal ☎05 53 20 23 37. There's a tiny, low-key municipal campsite beside the river, north across the old stone bridge from the village. Closed Sept–April. **€10**

L'Étape Gasconne Place de la Mairie ☎05 53 20 23 55, ⓦwww.letapegasconne-hotel.com. Just across from the Prune Hall, a peaceful and good-value hotel whose comfortable rooms rather belie the dowdy, old-fashioned bar downstairs. Three rooms have balconies looking onto the hotel's outdoor pool, and in the absence of anywhere else to eat in the village, there's a reasonable restaurant serving traditional cuisine; *menus* from €15. Restaurant open daily noon–2pm & 7.30–10pm; Oct–April closed Sun eve, and Nov–March closed Fri eve. Breakfast €7. **€54**

Duras and around

From Allemans, the Dropt winds its way northwest for 10km to where the castle-town of **DURAS** lords it over the valley from its rocky outcrop. The château towers were truncated during the Revolution, but they still afford fine views beyond the Dropt to the country around, an enchanting region of rolling hills topped with windmills, of pasture, orchards, woods and, particularly to the north, of vines. The town of Duras sits at the heart of an interesting **wine region**, worthy of its own appellation. Sandwiched between Bergerac and the Entre-Deux-Mers region, Duras wines come in all shades: reds, dry whites, and some increasingly well-regarded sweet whites, lighter than those of Monbazillac.

Château des Ducs de Duras

Feb, March, Nov & Dec daily 2–6pm; April–June, Sept & Oct daily 10.30am–1pm & 2–6pm; July & Aug daily 10am–7pm • €6 • ☎ 05 53 83 77 32, Ⓦ chateau-de-duras.com

The chequered history of Duras is evident in the mix-and-match architecture of the Château des Ducs de Duras, which dominates the town. The château was founded in 1137, but then rebuilt after 1308 by Bertrand de Goth, nephew of Pope Clément V; it is said he used money confiscated from the Templars. Rebuilt again after the Hundred Years War, it was then extensively remodelled during the more peaceful and prosperous late sixteenth and seventeenth centuries. The finishing touches were added in 1741, just in time to be thoroughly ransacked during the Revolution, after which the château was left to crumble until the commune bought it in 1969. Since then, it has been thoroughly restored, allowing you to visit almost the whole building, from the basements, where the bakery is still recognizable, to the panoramic ramparts at the top. On your way round, look out for wells cut straight through the bedrock and freshwater tanks in case of siege, and a monstrous kitchen fireplace big enough to roast a whole ox. The dukes obviously liked to build on a grand scale – across a wide, open courtyard the entrance hall is impressive enough, and the ceremonial hall above has no fewer than eleven chimneys.

Moulin de Cocussotte

May–Sept Wed–Sun 2–6pm • €4 • ☎ 05 53 83 83 44

Three kilometres southeast of Duras, back on the banks of the river Dropt just north of the town of St-Pierre, the **Moulin de Cocussotte** and its surrounding garden are a haven of bucolic calm. As well as the ivy-covered thirteenth-century mill and its slowly turning waterwheel, the garden has a wide variety of trees and plants and a shop-cum-café selling some rustic local produce including wine and honey.

ARRIVAL AND INFORMATION   DURAS

By car Sadly, Duras is pretty much inaccessible without your own transport – the closest station is at Ste-Foy-la-Grande, but from there a taxi costs €30.

Tourist office 14 bd Jean-Brisseau (July & Aug Mon–Sat 9am–12.30pm & 2–6pm, Sun 10am–1pm; Sept–June Mon–Fri 9am–noon & 2–5.30pm; ☎ 05 53 83 63 06, Ⓦ paysdeduras.com).

Maison de Vins The best place to find out more about the local wines is the tremendously innovative Maison de Vins (June–Sept Mon–Fri 10am–1pm & 2–6.30pm; Oct–May Mon–Fri 9am–12.30pm & 2–5.30pm; ☎ 05 53 94 13 48, Ⓦ cotesduras.com), on the D668 just downhill from Duras to the south. As well as the standard opportunity to taste and buy, this showcase also has interactive displays on the history of the local wine region, and its own small sample vineyard, planted with different types of vine.

ACCOMMODATION AND EATING

Camping municipal ☎ 05 53 83 70 18, @ mairie-de-duras@wanadoo.fr. The only campsite in Duras itself is the extremely basic municipal site right under the château's north wall; the only facilities are showers and toilets. Closed Sept–June. **€10**

Le Cabri Rte de Savignac ☎ 05 53 83 81 03, Ⓦ lecabri.eu.com. Out on the D203 to Savignac, *Le Cabri* is a well-equipped campsite located on a former farm. There's a surprisingly good on-site restaurant here too, where you can tuck into inexpensive lunch and evening *menus* (€13–15) along with some decent local wines. Restaurant open daily noon–2pm & 7–10pm, closed Sat lunchtime & Wed. **€17**

Hostellerie des Ducs Bd Jean-Brisseau ☎ 05 53 83 74 58, Ⓦ hostellerieducs-duras.com. A few paces back along from the tourist office, this rather grand-looking building, complete with ostentatious turret hovering near the entrance, makes for a most comfortable stay; variously priced rooms are available, either with a shower or bath, and some with a/c. In addition to a pool, spa/sauna and flower-filled terrace, there's also an excellent conservatory restaurant serving upmarket regional cuisine; duck with Duras prunes and wine sauce, and saddle of lamb with cream of beans and *fougasse* are typically colourful dishes. Restaurant closed Sat lunch, Sun eve & Mon lunch. Breakfast €9.50. **€72**

2

West to Castillon-la-Bataille

Downstream from Bergerac, the steep north slopes of the Dordogne valley are once again clothed in vines all the way along to the more illustrious vineyards of St-Émilion. The valley here is flat and uninteresting, dominated by a major road and rail line, but there are a few diversions en route. First is **Ste-Foy-la-Grande**, which – with its excellent Saturday market and medieval traces – is by far the most rewarding town on this stretch, and certainly the best base, offering good transport links, hotels and restaurants. From here, you could make a couple of worthwhile excursions to see the well-preserved mosaics at Montcaret's Gallo-Roman villa, and the **Château de Montaigne**, where the influential Renaissance thinker and confirmed sceptic, Michel de Montaigne, wrote most of his famous *Essais*. **Castillon-la-Bataille**, the other main town on the river here, is where the Hundred Years War came to a spectacularly bloody end in 1453; today the battle is commemorated in a monumental summer spectacle. Other than that, the town seems rather down on its luck compared to Ste-Foy, and you won't want to linger except to sample the area's good-value red wines, produced on the border with St-Émilion.

GETTING AROUND   WEST TO CASTILLON-LA-BATAILLE

Public transport along this stretch of the Dordogne is limited to trains on the Sarlat–Bordeaux line. With just a couple of trains per day between some of these towns, it requires careful planning and a fair bit of walking to reach the area's more interesting sites.

Ste-Foy-la-Grande

Heading west from Bergerac along the River Dordogne, the first place you come to of any size is the prosperous town of **STE-FOY-LA-GRANDE**. The central **place Gambetta** retains some of its original arcades, now shading lively café terraces, while **rue de la République** also boasts several fine, timbered medieval houses, the most grandiose of which, with its corner tower, now houses the tourist office. However, it's the soaring, jagged spire of the **church of Notre-Dame** that marks this particular building out as the street's most prominent edifice. The bulk of this present incarnation dates from the mid-seventeenth century, its beautifully proportioned interior pure Gothic, with tall, slender pillars reaching upwards to a fine rib-vaulted ceiling. Take a look, too, at the stained glass windows, depicting characters from the Old and New Testaments.

Also worth a wander is the riverside esplanade a short walk to the north, from where you can cross the river via the pont Michel Montaigne to visit Ste-Foy's modest museum, the **Maison du Fleuve et du Vin** (June–Sept Tues–Sun 2–5.30pm; Oct–May Mon, Thurs & Fri 2.30–4.30pm; €3), covering the role played by river trade in the town's history and providing information on the wine produced around Ste-Foy. Even if that doesn't tempt you, it's definitely worth timing your visit to Ste-Foy to catch the Saturday-morning **market**, one of the region's biggest and most important, when the whole town centre is closed to traffic.

ARRIVAL AND DEPARTURE   STE-FOY-LA-GRANDE

By train The *gare SNCF* lies five minutes' walk south of town; from the station, turn left along avenue de la Gare then walk north along avenue Paul Broca and then rue Victor Hugo, Ste-Foy's major shopping street.

Destinations Bergerac (5–12 daily; 20min); Bordeaux (6–12 daily; 1hr); Castillon-la-Bataille (6–12 daily; 15–20min); Lamothe-Montravel (1–3 daily; 15–20min); St-Émilion (4–7 daily; 35min).

2

INFORMATION AND ACTIVITIES

Tourist office 102 rue de la République (June & Sept Mon–Sat 9.30am–12.30pm & 2.30–6pm; July & Aug Mon–Sat 9.30am–1pm & 2.30–6.30pm, Sun 10am–1pm; Oct–May Tues–Sat 9.30am–12.30pm & 2.30–5.30pm; ☎ 05 57 46 03 00, ⓦ tourisme-dordogne-paysfoyen.com).

Canoe rental In July and August you can rent canoes from Canoe Kayak (☎ 05 53 24 86 12, ⓦ canoe-kayak-port-ste -foy.com) on the north side of the river opposite *Camping*

de la Bastide (see below).

Bike rental Available close by from Rando-Cyclo (☎ 05 53 24 86 12; €8 half day, €12 full day).

Boat trips In July and August Bateau de Promenade Rivesdor offer 45min riverboat trips (€5) along the Dordogne; departures take place from Quai de la Brèche, a short walk down from the tourist office.

ACCOMMODATION

Camping de la Bastide Allée du Camping ☎ 05 57 46 13 84, ⓦ camping-bastide.com. Anyone with a tent should head about 500m east along the river's south bank on avenue Georges Clemenceau – the extension of rue de la République – to this very comfortable three-star site, which has modern shower blocks, a laundry, play area, games room and pool. Closed Oct–April. **€22**

Escapade ☎ 05 53 24 22 79, ⓦ escapade-dordogne .com. With your own transport, there's the option of the *Escapade*, four kilometres west of Ste-Foy, just south of the D936. This country hotel offers twelve unfussy rooms in a converted tobacco-drying barn as well as sports facilities and a restaurant serving generous Périgord cooking (*menus* from €20; eve and Sun lunch only). Closed

Nov–Jan. Breakfast €7. **€54**

Grand Hôtel 117 rue de la République ☎ 05 57 46 00 08, ⓦ grandhotelstefoy.com. Not nearly as grand as its name implies, this is nevertheless a decent enough hotel, with airy, high-ceilinged rooms, albeit just a touch old-fashioned and slightly frayed around the edges. Still, it's handily located smack bang in the centre and fairly priced. Closed two weeks in both Dec & Feb. Breakfast €6. **€52**

Le Grain de Sel 101 rue Victor Hugo ☎ 05 57 41 35 43, ⓦ hotel-restaurant-dordogne.fr. Just on the edge of the old centre as you're coming in from the train station, the ten spotlessly clean, generously sized rooms here are painted in warm, predominantly burgundy, colours and come with beautifully styled wood-carved furnishings. Breakfast €6. **€63**

EATING AND DRINKING

★ **Au Fil de l'Eau** 3 rue de la Rouquette ☎ 05 53 24 72 60, ⓦ restaurantaufildeleau.com. On the north side of Pont Michel Montaigne, the super smart *Au Fil de l'Eau* is one of the best regarded fish restaurants in the region, serving delectable dishes like monkfish fried in red wine, and fillet of mackerel in orange sauce (*menus* from €28). Be sure to grab a table out in the conservatory, which affords marvellous views across the water. Daily noon–

2pm & 7.30–10pm, closed Sun eve & Mon.

Les Sarments 36 rue J-J Rousseau ☎ 05 57 46 00 22. One block down from the tourist office, *Les Sarments* is a homely little street corner restaurant set around a pretty stone fireplace. The menu is particularly strong on pasta and fish, for example swordfish with lemon butter, with *menus* from €20. Thurs–Mon noon–2pm & 7–10pm.

Around Ste-Foy-la-Grande

The area **around Ste-Foy-la-Grande** holds several worthwhile excursions, though in order to reach any of them, you will require your own wheels. One attractive option, particularly if you don't have a car, would be to rent a bike in Ste-Foy (see above) and then follow the flat, quiet side roads running parallel to the D936.

Jardins de Sardy

April–Oct daily 10am–6pm • €6 • ☎ 05 53 27 51 45

Travelling west on the D936 from Ste-Foy, garden-lovers might like to make a brief detour after about ten kilometres up into the hills north of the river to visit the **Jardins de Sardy** in Vélines. Though not huge, the gardens – a combination of English and Italian style – occupy a pretty, sheltered spot overlooking the Dordogne. The centrepiece is an informal pond garden set against the wisteria-covered farmhouse, where it's tempting to linger on the terrace over a cold drink or a light lunch, surrounded by the heady scents of aromatic plants.

Montcaret Roman villa

June–Sept daily 9.45am–12.30pm & 2–6.30pm; Oct–May daily except Sat 10am–12.30pm & 2–5.30pm • €3 • ☎ 05 53 58 50 18

Three kilometres further along the main road, another right turn brings you to **MONTCARET** and the remains of a fourth-century **Gallo-Roman villa**, most of which lies randomly scattered around the village church. The first mosaic was discovered in 1827, but it wasn't until the early twentieth century that major excavation works took place, carried out by local villager, Pierre-Martial Tauziac. Still, only about one-tenth of the villa has been fully excavated, but it's more than enough to demonstrate the occupants' affluent lifestyle, from underfloor heating and a variety of hot and cold baths to a grand reception room measuring 350 square metres. The floors, baths and covered walkways were laid with elaborate mosaics, of which large areas have survived relatively intact, most notably in the cold bath, which is superbly decorated with shellfish, dolphins and octopuses – the only figurative decorations remaining. No less impressive is the "dining room", or Cruciform Room, housed within a glass building adjoining the reception; here, you can see the more abstract pattern of shields and fish scales, alongside a couple of skeletons; note, however, that from mid-November to mid-April those mosaics outdoors are covered to protect them from frosts and are therefore not on view. Back next to the reception area is a small museum displaying some of the many objects found on the site, such as pottery fragments, bits of axes, amphorae and oil lamps.

Château de Montaigne

Feb–April, Nov & Dec Wed–Sun 10am–noon & 2–5.30pm; May–June, Sept & Oct Wed–Sun 10am–noon & 2–6.30pm; July & Aug daily 10am–6.30pm; closed Jan • €7 • ☎ 05 53 58 63 93, ⓦ chateau-montaigne.com

Back lanes lead another three kilometres northwest to the sleepy village of **ST-MICHEL-DE-MONTAIGNE**, where Montaigne (1533–92) wrote many of his chatty, digressive and influential essays on the nature of life and humankind. Even if you haven't read any of his works, it's worth making the pilgrimage to the **Château de Montaigne**, just beyond the village to the north, to learn more about this engaging, if somewhat quirky and complex, character.

Montaigne's castle residence burned down in 1885, and its modern reconstruction is now closed to the public. You can, however, go on a guided tour (45min; in French only) of the fourteenth-century **tower** where Montaigne closeted himself away after

---

MONTAIGNE

The third son of a Catholic father and a mother from a wealthy Spanish-Portuguese Jewish family, Michel Eyquem, **Lord of Montaigne**, had an unusual education which involved everyone, including the servants, speaking to him in Latin, and being woken by a musician to ensure "his brain not be damaged". It certainly seems to have caused no harm, since Montaigne went on to become a councillor and later mayor of Bordeaux and was highly respected for his tolerance, wisdom and diplomacy. There is evidence that he also possessed a mischievous sense of humour – throughout the bitter Religious Wars, the Catholic Montaigne apparently took pleasure in ringing his chapel bell as loudly and as often as possible to annoy his Protestant neighbours. On the other hand, it must also be said that Montaigne, who held the Protestant leader Henry of Navarre in great esteem, played an important role in resolving the conflict, though he didn't live to see peace restored in 1598.

Though he attended Mass regularly before his death, and received the last sacrament, Montaigne's writings are renowned for their scepticism; in a typical outburst he declares, "Man is insane. He wouldn't know how to create a maggot, and he creates Gods by the dozen." His philosophical standpoint was essentially an argument for introspection – "if man does not know himself, then what can he know?" While it is criticized as being inconclusive, his legacy is rather his great originality of thought and his essays' wide-ranging questioning of generally accepted truths.

1571 to work on his three volumes of essays. On the ground floor was his private chapel, the first floor is the room where he died and the final storey held the library. Unfortunately his priceless collection of more than a thousand books, all carefully annotated, was dispersed immediately after his death, but some traces of his thought can still be found in the Greek and Latin maxims he inscribed on the beams.

Castillon-la-Bataille

As you travel the final five kilometres west from Lamothe-Montravel to **CASTILLON-LA-BATAILLE** you'd be forgiven for not noticing as you cross the Lidoire valley. In 1453 this is where the French routed the English in the last major **battle** of the Hundred Years War (see box below). There's nothing to mark the site, save an uninspiring monument to the English general Talbot on the spot where he supposedly died close to the River Dordogne, two kilometres east of Castillon, but every summer the local citizenry stage a spectacular floodlit re-enactment (see box below).

The **town** itself is run-down and instantly forgettable, and there's very little by way of practicalities. But if do find yourself with a bit of time to kill here, you could wander down to the river east of town, where there are a few blades of grass and some picnic tables, taking in on your way the thirteenth-century Porte de Fer – all that remains of the medieval walls – and the eighteenth-century church of St-Symphorien, a rare example of Baroque architecture in the region, though it has the feel of a municipal building rather than a church.

Château Cap de Faugères

Visits and tastings by appointment • ☎ 05 57 40 34 99, ⓦ chateau-faugeres.com

One of the more prestigious names in this area is **Château Cap de Faugères**, a couple of kilometres northwest from Castillon outside the village of Ste-Colombe. The red wines here are of lower quality, but similar in spirit to those of neighbouring St-Émilion – but they come in a lot cheaper, usually at under €10 per bottle. One of the taller stories told locally is that the English defeat at Castillan was partly due to their troops discovering a stash of the local hooch one evening and developing such a taste for it that it affected their performance on the battlefield the next day.

THE BATTLE OF CASTILLON

What is now known as the **Hundred Years War** had been rumbling back and forth through southwest France from 1337, but in the 1440s the French, led by the great military commander Bertrand du Guesclin, began to push the English armies back. In reply, the English despatched the equally renowned **Sir John Talbot**, Earl of Shrewsbury, with orders to regain the lost territory. He took Bordeaux in 1452 and had swept through to Castillon by July 1453.

Here a large French force, camped beyond the town, was waiting for him, but when the Castillon garrison withdrew without much of a fight, Talbot believed it would be an easy battle. Instead he was walking straight into a trap. The French had gathered three hundred pieces of artillery – a relatively new development – and ranged them in the hills either side of the valley. On **July 17**, after Talbot had heard Mass, a messenger reported mistakenly that the French were breaking camp and retreating when all they were doing was moving the baggage to the rear. Talbot hastily rallied his men and led them in pursuit straight into the mouth of the valley and a murderous crossfire. Talbot and four thousand of his men were killed – if not immediately, then by the pursuing archers or simply drowning as they attempted to flee across the Dordogne. As news of the carnage spread, other English-held towns quickly capitulated, until more than a century of warfare finally came to an end.

The event is evoked each summer in the superb Bataille de Castillon (☎ 05 57 40 14 53, ⓦ batailledecastillon.com), which takes place 2km north of town and stars around 450 actors, some 300 more volunteers and 50 horses. Shows take place on roughly twelve dates from mid-July to mid-August, with tickets costing around €22.

ARRIVAL AND DEPARTURE

By train Castillon's *gare SNCF* is located on the northeast side of town about five minutes' walk along rue Gambetta. Destinations Bergerac (5–12 daily; 40min); Bordeaux

(6–12 daily; 30–40min); Lamothe-Montravel (Mon–Sat 1–4 daily; 5min); St-Émilion (4–7 daily; 8min); Ste-Foy-La-Grande (5–12 daily; 15–20min).

INFORMATION

Tourist office Place Marcel Paul (Mon–Sat 9.30am–noon & 2–6pm; ☎ 05 57 40 27 58, ✉ otcastillonpujols@wanadoo.fr); it's a five-minute walk west from place de Gaulle along rue Victor-Hugo. The tourist office keeps lists of *chambres d'hôtes* in the vicinity.

Maison du Vin Place de Gaulle (Mon–Fri 9am–6pm; ☎ 05 57 40 00 88, ⓦ cotes-de-castillon.com). They stock a representative sample of wines and can advise on visiting vineyards in the area.

ACCOMMODATION AND EATING

La Fontaine de Manon 57 rue Victor-Hugo ☎ 05 57 40 24 48. Fifty metres along from the tourist office, this is just about the best restaurant in town; though it doesn't quite qualify as *haute cuisine*, it does offer an agreeable atmosphere to enjoy some French classics, like duck paté or *moules-frites* (*menus* €12 at lunchtime, €18 eves). Daily noon–2pm & 7.30–10pm, closed Sun eve & Wed.
La Pelouse ☎ 05 57 40 04 22. A small two-star municipal

campsite with limited facilities, but its location by the river to the east of Castillon compensates somewhat. Closed mid-Oct to May. €15
Le Phénix 24 place Pierre Orus ☎ 05 57 40 00 14. If you do need to stay in Castillon, then just about your only option in the town itself is *Le Phénix*, which has dull but reasonable-value rooms above its bar-restaurant – all have bathrooms, televisions and a/c. Breakfast €5. €50

East to Le Buisson

The Dordogne River begins to get more interesting upstream from Bergerac, thanks largely to the two great meanders it makes near **Trémolat** and **Limeuil** before the hills begin to close in. The castles, abbeys and villages south of the river are also worth exploring, giving the option of two routes: along the Dordogne itself, or looping inland up the heavily wooded Couze valley to the village of **Cadouin**, with its austere abbey church and elaborately carved cloister.

GETTING AROUND

Transport along the Dordogne valley is provided by trains on the Bergerac–Sarlat line, with the stations at Lalinde, Trémolat and Le Buisson served fairly regularly. To get to the towns and churches on the inland route, you need your own car or bike – though it's hilly country for cycling.

Along the Dordogne

Following the Dordogne east from Bergerac, the first sight of any interest is the half-completed **Château de Lanquais**, as much for the story behind its architecture as for its somewhat dilapidated interiors. The working paper mills at **Couze-et-St-Front** also merit a quick stop, while **Lalinde** provides hotels, transport and other tourist facilities, before you meet the first of the Dordogne's great loops, the **Cingle de Trémolat**. At the top of the second meander, the feudal village of **Limeuil** marks where the River Vézère flows into the Dordogne and where you pass into the Périgord Noir, while the final destination, **Le Buisson-de-Cadouin**, sits on an important rail junction on the Bergerac–Sarlat and Agen–Périgueux lines.

Château de Lanquais

April–June & Sept–Oct daily except Tues 2.30–6pm; July & Aug daily 10am–7pm • €8 • ☎ 05 53 61 24 24, ⓦ chateaudelanquais.fr

The **Château de Lanquais**, 15km east of Bergerac and just outside the village of the same name, is described in tourist literature as "Périgord's unfinished Louvre". It is one of the region's more expensive châteaux to visit, but its isolation and rugged

2

charm make for an enjoyable little excursion. The story goes that in the mid-sixteenth century, when Bergerac and much of the surrounding country was under Protestant sway, Lanquais was owned by a Catholic, Isabeau de Limeuil, cousin to Catherine de Médicis. In a brave – or foolhardy – move, Isabeau commissioned the architects of the Louvre in Catholic Paris to add a wing in similar style to her castle. Before the work could be completed, however, the Protestant armies besieged the château in 1577 and left the facade pitted with cannonballs.

They didn't destroy it, though, and you can still discern the change in styles where the Renaissance wing, with its dormer windows and ornamentation, was grafted onto the medieval fortress. It's an imposing rather than an attractive building and some of the interiors are in need of restoration, but there are one or two rooms worth a peep. As in many Périgord châteaux, it's the fireplaces that steal the show, notably that occupying one whole wall of the "blue salon" with its two enigmatic bulls'-skull carvings. The difference between medieval and Renaissance styles is perhaps most discernible in the kitchen, where the large stone slabs of the former give way to the Italian *pisé* style of mosaic flooring, whereby stones are dug into the earth. Underneath the kitchen are the extensive cellars, part of which once functioned as a prison – as evidenced by the one remaining gloomy cell. The adjoining pavilion, meanwhile, was a nineteenth-century addition by a local abbot.

Below the castle is a small **lake** offering children-focused activities including supervised swimming (July & Aug daily 1.30–7.30pm; €2.50) and the hiring out of miniature novelty motorboats – including a trawler, cruise liner, and police boat – on which to chug slowly around the lake (April–Oct daily; €4 for 15min).

Couze-et-St-Front

Two kilometres from Lanquais you drop down to the Dordogne again at what was once an important paper-making centre, **COUZE-ET-ST-FRONT**. Head down a side street in the northwest corner of the town to see a series of beautiful old mill buildings, some cut into the cliff face itself, all profiting from the source of power provided by the River Couze. During the industry's heyday in the late fifteenth century – when some thirteen mills were in operation here – *gabares* would carry the paper along the river to Bordeaux, from where it would be exported abroad, principally the Netherlands.

Moulin de la Rouzique

April–June & Sept–Oct Mon–Fri 2–6pm; July & Aug daily 10am–7pm • Guided tour €7 • ☎ 05 53 24 36 16, ⓦ moulin-de-la
-rouzique.com

The only water-wheel still turning in Couze-et-St-Front is that of the fifteenth-century **Moulin de la Rouzique**, where you can see how paper is made in time-honoured fashion, using rags. Note that it is only possible to visit on a **guided tour**, for which there are no set times, so you'll just have to wait until there are enough people for a small group. Tours begin inside the *chiffonerie* (rags room), itself hewn into the rock face, where the rags were stored to make the paper pulp – a mix of plant fibres and water. Here, the crushing machine would set to work, its hammers crushing the rags, which would eventually soften and decompose following several weeks in large vats of water. Today, though, a far more efficient Dutch machine is used, which is able to convert around 30kg of rags into paper pulp in around ten hours, a process so powerful that it renders decomposition unnecessary. The metal water-wheel still turns at quite a lick, having replaced the old wooden wheel (still on view) some years ago. The tour concludes in the drying room, where you can examine a beautiful collection of beautiful antique watermarked papers.

Departing from Couze-et-St-Front, you have the choice either to continue east along the river to Lalinde or delve inland along the Couze valley to Beaumont (see p.112).

Lalinde

The only town of any size along this stretch of the Dordogne, **LALINDE** guards an important river-crossing 3km upstream from Couze and 23km from Bergerac. In 1267 Henry III of England chose the little settlement on the river's north bank to become the first English *bastide*. The central market square, grid plan and fragments of wall remain, but Lalinde's most attractive aspects are the church and gardens on its balustraded riverfront and a large canal basin immediately to the north. The canal was built in the nineteenth century to bypass a dangerous set of rapids, made more hazardous in legendary times by the presence of a dragon, La Coulobre, which lurked in a cave on the opposite bank. According to legend, St Front (see p.47) got rid of the monster in the fourth century by burning it on an enormous bonfire on the hill above its lair – grateful citizens later erected the tiny cliff-top **Chapelle de St-Front** in his honour. You can get to the chapel in ten minutes on foot by crossing the bridge and then scrambling up the steep marked path in the hillside.

Nowadays Lalinde is a bustling market town (Thursday is the main market day, and there's also a smaller farmers' market on Saturday) and prosperous commercial centre.

ARRIVAL AND DEPARTURE
LALINDE

By train The *gare SNCF* lies five minutes' walk across the canal on avenue du Général Leclerc.
By bus Buses to Bergerac depart from the central place de la Halle.

Destinations Bergerac (school term Mon–Sat 1–3 daily, school hols Tues–Thurs & Sat 1–2 daily; 40min); Port de Couze (as for Bergerac; 15min).

INFORMATION AND ACTIVITES

Tourist office In the Jardin public, by the old bridge (June & Sept Mon–Sat 10am–1pm & 2–6pm; July & Aug Mon–Sat 10am–1pm & 2–7pm, Sun 10am–1pm; Oct–May Mon–Fri 10am–1pm & 2–6pm; ☎05 53 61 08 55,

ⓦpays-des-bastides.com).
Bike rental You can rent bikes from the Centre VTT de Lalinde, Maison de l'Écluse (closed Nov–March; ☎05 53 24 12 31), beside the canal bridge.

ACCOMMODATION AND EATING

★ **Côté Rivage** Badefols-sur-Dordogne ☎05 53 23 65 00, ⓦcote-dordogne.com. Three kilometres east of Lalinde, on the south side of the river in Badefols-sur-Dordogne, this refined hotel offers seven beautifully thought-out rooms, each one styled according to a different theme, for example, the wine room, the chocolate room, the games room and the songs room. The restaurant is a joy too; it not only looks superb, with fantastic view, across the river, but the food is first class; *cèpe* mushroom terrine with duck confit and truffle-flavoured salad shoots, and roasted cod with aubergine caviar and mango sauce are typically tantalizing dishes. Restaurant open daily 7.30–10pm. Closed Jan. Breakfast €7. **€52**
Le Forêt 2 place Victor-Hugo ☎05 53 27 98 30, ⓦleforet-hotel-dordogne.com. This refined little hotel, located west of town at the end of rue des Martyrs, boasts considerable charm, from its range of good-looking rooms – a couple have four-poster beds, while those on the top

floor have retained their original beams – to the plethora of paintings and antiques dotted around. The *salon de thé* on the ground floor is by far the best place in town to grab a cup of coffee and a pastry. *Salon de thé* open daily 8am–7pm. Breakfast €9.50. **€52**
Moulin de la Guillou ☎05 53 61 02 91, ⊜la-guillou @wanadoo.fr. The *Moulin*, 1.5km east of town, is a relaxed and spacious two-star campsite, which offers canoeing and kayaking, archery and a large swimming pool among its many facilities. Closed Sept–May. **€14**
Le Périgord 1 place du 14-Juillet ☎05 53 61 19 86, ⓦhotelduperigord.com. A short walk down from the station, the distinctive, sandy-coloured exterior of this smallish hotel conceals sixteen fairly run-of-the-mill rooms, though they certainly don't want for colour, with green carpets, burgundy walls and orange bedspreads. Breakfast €7. **€52**

Trémolat

Some 8km upstream from Lalinde the Dordogne snakes its way through two huge meanders, of which the first you come to, the **Cingle de Trémolat**, is the tighter and therefore more impressive. The best views are from the limestone cliffs to the north – follow signs to the Panorama de Trémolat, or on upwards to the Bélvèdere de Rocamadour – from where the whole meander is visible. Over to the east, a heavily fortified church tower pinpoints the picturesque village of **TRÉMOLAT**. Trémolat has a boulangerie and small supermarket for stocking up on picnic supplies.

ARRIVAL AND INFORMATION   TRÉMOLAT

By train The *gare SNCF* is located just over a kilometre to the south of the village.

Tourist office Tucked away in one corner just behind the

church (Mon–Fri 9am–noon & 2–6pm; July & Aug daily 10am–1pm & 3–6pm; ☎05 53 22 89 33, ⓦtourisme -tremolat.fr).

ACCOMMODATION AND EATING

Bistrot d'En Face ☎05 53 22 80 06. Owned by the Vieux *Logis* hotel (see below), the sprightly *Bistrot d'en Face* restaurant, just on the corner of the main square, makes a good pit-stop, with lunch *menus* from €14.50 and evening *menus* from €20; expect dishes like melon, avocado and crab cocktail, and duck foie gras with fig compote. Daily noon–1.30pm & 7–9.30pm; closed Mon & Tues mid-Oct to mid-April.

Camping de Tremolat ☎05 53 22 81 18. On the banks of the Dordogne, a good-sized campsite with a restaurant/ bar, pool and some excellent sports facilities, including

canoeing and kayaking. Closed Oct–April. €17

Vieux Logis ☎05 53 22 80 06, ⓦvieux-logis.com. A luxury, top-dollar hotel in a former priory with all the sophistication you'd expect from a *Relais & Châteaux* residence; twenty utterly swish rooms – all leather seating and marble tiles – in addition to two cosy lounges, a smoking room, large pool surrounded by formal gardens and a lovely terrace for summer dining at the hotel's gastronomic restaurant (*menus* from €40). Restaurant open daily noon–1.30pm & 7–9.30pm; closed Wed & Thurs mid-Oct to mid-April. Breakfast €18. €190

Limeuil

The D31 east from Trémolat takes you over the ridge for a bird's-eye view of the second meander in the Dordogne, the **Cingle de Limeuil**. The road then drops down to the honey-stoned village of **LIMEUIL**, on the confluence of the Vézère and Dordogne rivers and an attractive sight, straggling down the steep hillside. Limeuil reached its first peak in the Middle Ages, thanks to its strategic location, and then another in the nineteenth century when local craftsmen built boats for the booming river trade. Today, the village retains its medieval character, as you'll soon discover if you wander under the old gate and up narrow, central rue du Port on the way to the hilltop **park** (Easter–June, Sept & Oct daily except Sat 10am–12.30pm & 2–6pm; July & Aug daily 10am–8pm; €7), where the feudal château once stood. The park is pleasantly leafy, with some pretty water features, and does monopolize the best views from here, but since the entry fee is about as steep as the hill it's on, you might prefer to head for the classic viewpoint near Trémolat.

Back at the bottom of the hill, the willow-shaded riverbank makes a good picnic spot, and also has a pebbly **beach** from which you can go for a dip in the river, though it's too shallow and fast-flowing to allow serious swimming. This is also the base for all canoeing and kayaking trips on the river.

INFORMATION AND ACTIVITIES   LIMEUIL

Tourist office Jardin de la Mairie, just up rue de Port and through the little gateway on your left (June–Sept Mon–Fri 10am–12.30pm & 2–6pm, Sat 10am–12.30pm; Oct–May 9am–noon & 1.30–5.30pm; ☎05 53 63 38 90, ⓦlimeuil-en-perigord.com). Pick up one of their informative walking leaflets, which guide you around the village in about an hour and a half.

Canoe, kayak and bike rental From Canoës Rivières Loisirs (☎05 53 63 38 73, ⓦcanoes-rivieres-loisirs.com) based on Limeuil's beach. A one-hour trip along the

Dordogne river to Buisson (6km) costs €8.50 in a canoe and €11 in a kayak, while a trip up the Vézère River to Le Bugue (8km) costs €10.50 and €13 respectively; though you can rent for longer periods. Bikes costs €12 for half a day and €17 for a full day.

Riding There's an excellent riding centre, La Haute Yerle, in Alles-sur-Dordogne (☎05 53 63 35 85, ⓦrando-equestre -hauteyerle.com), which offers treks from half a day up to a week's circuit of the Périgord Noir.

ACCOMMODATION AND EATING

Au Bon Accueil Rue du Port ☎05 53 63 30 97, ⓦau-bon-accueil-limeuil.com.   Small,   friendly

hotel-restaurant positioned towards the top end of this pretty cobbled street. The hotel has five tidy, violet- and mauve-coloured rooms, though they're rather on the sparse side, with smallish beds and boxy little bathrooms. The restaurant, meanwhile, not only looks great – one room has bright orange walls, the other exposed stone walls, plus there's a vine-covered terrace with views along the valley – but the food is outstanding; sublime dishes like rabbit in a rich mustard sauce, and sautéed pork in a home-brewed Limeuil beer, in addition to half a dozen daily home-made desserts chalked up on a board. Menus start at just €12 for lunch and €19 in the evening. Restaurant open daily noon–2pm & 7–10pm. Hotel and restaurant both closed Nov–March. €75

Port de Limeuil ☎ 05 53 63 29 76, ⊛ leportdelimeuil .com. Campers are extremely well catered for at this excellent three-star site just across the river. Facilities include well-shaded pitches, laundry, restaurant/snack bar, lots of sporting activities including pool, plus bike and canoe hire. Closed Sept – May. €28

Chapelle St-Martin
Daily 9am–7pm • Free

One kilometre northeast of Limeuil on the Le Bugue road is the **Chapelle St-Martin**; if it's locked, you can get the key from the house opposite. A Latin inscription inside this dumpy little Romanesque chapel records that it was dedicated to St Thomas à Becket, the archbishop of Canterbury murdered by Henry II's courtiers in 1170 after the king famously asked who would rid him of "this turbulent priest". The inscription goes on to relate that the chapel was founded in 1194 by Henry's son and successor, Richard the Lionheart, together with Philippe II (Philippe Auguste) of France on their return from the Third Crusade, "to beseech the pardon of God". There are also the remnants of fifteenth-century frescoes in the choir: to the right a Crucifixion scene and the Descent from the Cross; to the left the Flight from Egypt. Note also the *pisé* floor – giving the appearance of pebbles, but actually made of long, narrow stones placed upright – and the roof of stone slates, *lauzes*, over the choir. You'll meet these architectural features again and again as you penetrate deeper into the Périgord Noir.

Le Buisson-de-Cadouin

LE BUISSON-DE-CADOUIN, 5km south of Limeuil, is the last stop on this stretch of river. The town has nothing in the way of sights, or indeed much of a practical nature, but 1km southeast are the **Grottes de Maxange** (April–June, Sept & Oct daily 10am–noon & 2–5pm; July & Aug daily 9am–7pm; €7.50; ☎ 05 53 23 42 80, ⊛ lesgrottesdemaxange .com), which were discovered completely by chance in 2000 by the owner of the quarry in which they are located. The caves were then opened in 2003, while a newly discovered and equally impressive gallery was revealed to the public in 2009; tours last forty minutes and take in around 350 metres. These caves are particularly unusual in that they hide

---

CUSSAC CAVE

In September 2000, great excitement broke out among art historians and archeologists when a speleologist nosing around Cussac, near Le Buisson-de-Cadouin, stumbled on a previously unknown decorated cave containing more than one hundred **prehistoric engravings**. So important is Marc Delluc's discovery that it's been dubbed the "Lascaux of engraving", in reference to the famous Vézère-valley cavern (see p.149).

Cussac cave is particularly significant because of the number and size of the engravings. The biggest is a four-metre-long bison, while some scenes comprise as many as forty figures. They are also unusually well preserved, the outlines etched deep into the clay by artists sometime between 25,000 and 30,000 years ago. **Horses**, **bison**, **mammoths**, **rhino** (rhinos) and **deer** all feature strongly, but there are also very rare representations of **birds**, as well as **female silhouettes**, **fertility symbols** and a strange long-snouted animal that has yet to be identified.

Because of the vulnerability of these caves (see p.149), it is unlikely that Cussac will ever be opened to the public. The local authorities, however, are keen to capitalize on the tourist potential. There's talk of creating a replica as at Lascaux, but in the meantime you can get a glimpse of what all the fuss is about at ⊛ www.culture.fr/culture/arcnat/cussac/en.

unusually extensive displays of *excentriques*. These delicate limestone formations, some looping round on themselves, others suddenly veering off in a different direction, are believed to occur where water evaporates from extremely fine fissures in the rock. Here and there the walls glitter with star-like formations known as *aragonites*. Look out, too, for the cave-bear scratches on the walls. Maxange is also one of the more accessible caves in the region, with no stairs or narrow passages to negotiate.

2

ARRIVAL AND INFORMATION
LE BUISSON-DE-CADOUIN

By train Le Buisson is a junction on the Bordeaux–Sarlat and Agen–Périgueux train lines, and its *gare SNCF*, to the north of the town centre, is also the closest station to Cadouin; for a taxi call Taxi Morante on ☎ 05 53 22 06 51.
Destinations Agen (2–5 daily; 1hr 30min); Bergerac (6 daily; 30–40min); Le Bugue (4–6 daily; 8min); Couze (2–3 daily; 25min); Les Eyzies (4–6 daily; 15min); Lalinde

(6 daily; 20min); Périgueux (4–6 daily; 50min); Sarlat (5–7 daily; 40min); Trémolat (5 daily; 10min).
Tourist office Place André Boissière, 150m down from the train station (July & Aug Mon–Fri 10am–1pm & 2–5.30pm, Sat 10am–1pm; Sept–June Mon–Fri 10am–1pm & 2–5.30pm; ☎ 05 53 22 06 09, ⓦ dordogne-vezere.com).

ACCOMMODATION AND EATING

Manoir de Bellerive ☎ 05 53 22 16 16, ⓦ bellerive hotel.com. Less than two kilometres east of town on the road to Siorac, the *Manoir de Bellerive* is an elegant little château built on the orders of Louis-Napoleon in 1830. It now contains a charming luxury hotel set in an English-style park on the banks of the Dordogne. Some of the rooms in the original manor house have river views, while those in the quieter *orangerie* annexe have private terraces. There's also a tennis court, pool and a perfect breakfast spot on the terrace overlooking the Dordogne. Its refined, Michelin-starred restaurant serves delicacies such as

sturgeon with foie gras followed by roast veal with a mushroom and artichoke sauce (*menus* €55–85). Restaurant open daily noon–1.30pm & 7.15–9.30pm, closed Sun eve & Mon. Breakfast €15. **€145**
Le Pont de Vicq Av de la Dordogne ☎ 05 53 22 01 73, ⓦ campinglepontdevicq.com. Around 2km beyond the train station, on the road to Le Bugue, this large and tidy three-star campsite has a heated pool, as well as a long beach for bathing, and canoe and kayak hire on site; in summer there's also a snack bar where you can drink and eat barbecued food till late. Closed Oct–April. **€15**

The Couze valley

The **Couze valley**, striking southeast of the paper-making town of Couze-et-St-Front, has provided an important thoroughfare since Gallo-Roman times. It's a region of thickly wooded hills and pastoral valleys, interspersed with comely villages, such as Beaumont, and hilltop churches, none finer than those at St-Avit-Sénieur and Montferrand-du-Périgord.

Beaumont

Part of Edward's I's motivation for founding **BEAUMONT** in 1272, on a dominant spur 10km upstream, was to guard the route. As in many such *bastides*, the fourteenth-century **church of St-Front** was built for military as well as religious reasons – a final outpost of defence in times of attack – hence the two bulky towers either side of the entrance, and the well inside. The north tower, to the left of the entrance, is the old clocktower; it is lower by some thirty metres than the south tower, a brooding presence complete with battlements. The largely Gothic interior is a hollow, single-nave structure, and is fairly ordinary save for its impressive vaulted ceiling. There are one or two other interesting aspects, notably a couple of fading fifteenth-century frescoes in the choir, one of a man, the other of a woman, though neither identified.

The main focus of the town, however, is the attractive **Place Centrale**, which once held sixteen arcades, of which seven now remain. The square's most notable building is **Maison Lafitte**, a fine timbered house on the south side, which used to sit above a covered market; note the cross of St Andrew set between the windows. The modern-day market takes place here on Tuesdays and Saturdays. Off to the west of the square stands the Porte de Luzier, one of the original sixteen town gates.

INFORMATION

Tourist office Place Centrale (July & Aug Mon–Sat 10am–12.30pm & 2–6pm, Sun 10am–1pm; Sept–June Mon–Fri 10am–noon & 2–5pm; ☎05 53 22 39 12, ⓦpays-des-bastides.com). They stock an impressive selection of English-language history and architecture leaflets on Beaumont, St-Avit and Montferrand.

ACCOMMODATION AND EATING

Hostellerie de St-Front 3 rue Romieu ☎05 53 22 30 11, ⓦhostellerie-de-saint-front.com. A short walk along from the church, the very hospitable *Hostellerie* has six pleasant rooms, some with shared bathroom facilities; those at the back have private terraces with good views over the countryside. The restaurant here is very commendable, excelling with traditional recipes and home-made products. Restaurant open daily except Tues noon–1.45pm & 7–10pm. Breakfast €6. **€49**

St-Avit-Sénieur

On the other side of the valley, roughly 4km by road, the semi-ruined abbey of **ST-AVIT-SÉNIEUR** stares across at Beaumont from another rocky knoll. It grew up around the burial place of a fifth-century hermit, Avitus, who was born at Lanquais and later served in the Visigoth army until taken prisoner in 507 by the Frankish king Clovis, a recent convert to Christianity. At some point during his fourteen years' captivity in Paris, Avitus followed suit, and was then instructed in a vision to return to Périgord, where he lived as a hermit until his death in 570. Tales of his miracles soon attracted pilgrims and the simple chapel grew into a monastery; the present **church** (daily 10am–noon & 2–6pm; free) was founded in the early twelfth century, and an inscription records that the saint's bones were brought here in 1117.

Montferrand-du-Périgord

The D26 continues southeast up the narrowing valley for another 8km to the seemingly forgotten village of **MONTFERRAND-DU-PÉRIGORD**, where a clutch of typical Périgord houses shelters beneath the semi-ruined château. A single street leads up past a superb sixteenth-century market hall – bigger, and sturdier it seems, than some of the surrounding houses – to where a path takes off west through the woods. Roughly a kilometre later it comes out near the hilltop **church of St-Christophe**, standing on its own in a cemetery. It used to be the parish church but has gradually been diminished over the years to little more than a stocky bell tower so it's surprising to find that the twelfth- and fifteenth-century frescoes have survived. There's some wonderful detail to admire, not least on the north wall (to your left as you enter), where you can just about make out a sea monster, mouth agape readying itself to swallow the damned, next to which is a woman riding a lion, supposedly the symbol of lust. The oldest painting is on the north wall of the choir, portraying St Leonard releasing prisoners (the little building below symbolizing the prison), while St Christopher himself makes an appearance on the west wall, carrying the Infant Jesus upon his shoulder.

ACCOMMODATION AND EATING

Lou Peyrol ☎05 53 63 24 45, ⓦhotel-loupeyrol -dordogne.com. Owned by a young, friendly English– French couple, the *Lou Peyrol* is a small, creeper-covered country hotel down on the main road, with five rustic rooms (think wrought-iron beds with floral-patterned bedspreads) and a restaurant serving traditional Perigordin cooking, such as smoked duck salad, and foie gras in Montbazillac wine; *menus* from €20. Closed Oct–Easter. Breakfast €8. **€45**

Cadouin

At the same time that Augustinian monks were busy building their church in honour of St Avit (see above), the Cistercians founded a typically austere **abbey** in what is now the village of **CADOUIN**, 8km to the northeast of Montferrand-du-Perigord, up the D25. The abbey aside, Cadouin's handsome confection of honey- and

2

gold-coloured stone buildings is a big draw for many tourists. Moreover, there's no shortage of terrific places to sleep and eat here, most of which are on or just off **place de l'Abbaye**, the pretty main square. Leaving Cadouin, most people drop straight down to the Dordogne at Le Buisson, from where the caves around Les Eyzies (see p.131) are within easy striking distance.

The abbey

Place de l'Abbaye • **Cloister** April–June, Sept & Oct daily except Tues 10am–1pm & 2–6pm; July & Aug daily 9am–7pm; Nov, Dec, Feb & March Mon–Thurs & Sun 10am–12.30pm & 2–5pm • €6 • ☎ 05 53 63 36 28, ⊛ semitour.com

The efforts of the Cistercians were given a boost when, in 1117, crusaders returning from the Holy Land brought them a piece of cloth believed to have been part of Christ's shroud. For eight hundred years it drew flocks of pilgrims – including Eleanor of Aquitaine, Richard the Lionheart and King Louis IX – until in 1935 the two bands of embroidery at either end were shown to contain an Arabic text from the early eleventh century.

The cloth is usually displayed in the flamboyant Gothic **cloister**, accessed via a separate entrance to the north of the church door, though at the time of writing it was removed for restoration work. In any case, it plays second fiddle to the finely sculpted but badly damaged capitals around the cloister, most of which are concentrated along the north wall; the first one you come to is of two monks opening a book, beyond which are two merchants squabbling over a goose. Next to this, above the abbot's seat, is a superb bas-relief, showing Jesus carrying the cross while two soldiers dice for his tunic, and a procession of monks alongside a prostrate Mary Magdalene – the remains of a Crucifixion scene. A little further along you can just make out the traces of a fifteenth-century fresco, the only one remaining. Scattered along the east side of the cloister, meanwhile, are some twenty-five pendants, representing prophets and evangelists.

Adjacent to the cloister stands the contrastingly austere Romanesque **church** (free), with its stark, monumental west wall and unusual double-tier belfry roofed with chestnut shingles. Inside, the triple nave is equally spartan and so high that the pillars appear to bulge outwards. You can still see the chains above the altar where the shroud was suspended in its casket, but the main point of interest is the stained glass in the north aisle, installed around a century ago, which recounts the story of the shroud's journey from Jerusalem.

ARRIVAL AND INFORMATION
CADOUIN

By train The only way to get here by public transport is to take the train to Le Buisson (see p.112) and then a taxi for the final 6km (count on around €10); otherwise it's a long hike up the steep hill.

Tourist office The village has its own summer-only tourist office (May–Sept Mon–Fri 9am–1pm & 2–6pm, Sun 2–6pm, closed Sat; ☎ 05 53 57 52 64, ⊛ dordogne-vezere .com), which doubles as a boutique selling local produce.

ACCOMMODATION

★ **L'Ancienne Gendarmerie** Rte de Beaumont ☎ 05 53 58 39 84, ⊛ anciennegendarmerie.com. Situated some 300m from the main square on the Beaumont road, the name of this fabulous *chambre d'hôte* is a bit of a giveaway, for this is the Cadouin's erstwhile police station. There are four lovely en-suite rooms, each possessing warm stone walls, exposed beams and colourful floor tiling; two have their own balcony overlooking the garden. If you fancy lounging elsewhere, then take yourself off into the elegant communal sitting room, with its open hearth, books aplenty and a DVD player complete with a selection of films. The price includes an excellent Dutch-French breakfast. Closed mid-Dec to mid-Jan. **€65**

★ **Auberge de Jeunesse** Abbaye de Cadouin ☎ 05 53 73 28 78, ⊛ fuaj.org/Cadouin. Adjacent to the cloister, the monks' dormitories have been turned into an excellent and very friendly HI youth hostel, with five-, seven- and ten bedded dorms, as well as private rooms with shower, basin and mezzanine-floor sleeping area. There's also a well-equipped kitchen and laundry facilities (€3). Picnics and hot evening meals can be provided upon request, though breakfast is included in the price. Closed mid-Dec to end Jan. Dorm beds **€20.80**, doubles **€23.80**

Les Jardins de l'Abbaye Rte de Monpazier ☎ 05 53 61 89 30, ⊛ jardinsabbaye.com. Out on the Montferrand road just above the village, this is a calm, shady site which also has some attractive mobile homes set above the camping area on a series of picturesque ridges. Snack bar and outdoor pool. Closed Oct–April. €15, Mobile homes from €360 per week

De Salvatat Rte de Belvès ☎05 53 63 42 70, ⓦlasalvetat.com. Located around 4km south of Cadouin in lovely open countryside, the family-friendly *Salvatat* provides the most restful option hereabouts. The hotel keeps a range of rooms, from those in the main building to more private rooms in the secluded garden area a short walk away, each with its own terrace, table and chairs; all rooms have tea- and coffee-making facilities, while those with a/c are slightly more expensive. Moreover, there's a large, clean pool, extensive grounds for strolling and a very commendable restaurant. Closed mid-Oct to Jan. Breakfast €11. €100

★ **Les Songes de l'Abbaye** Place de l'Abbaye ☎05 53 63 94 18, ⓦsongesdelabbaye.com. Situated plum on the main square, this spanking new *hotel de charme* has four exceptionally cool, gloriously colourful rooms (yellow, salmon, mauve and grey), all furnished in gorgeous French oak and chestnut wood. The bathrooms are similarly snappy, featuring huge showers, glass basins and wood-framed mirrors, as is the dining area with its red-painted wooden beams running across the ceiling. €80

EATING AND DRINKING

Chez Cathy et Paulo Place de l'Abbaye ☎05 53 63 42 79. If you've had enough duck and foie gras, this informal café-cum-restaurant, perfectly positioned on Cadouin's sunny main square, serves generous salads, pizzas and omelettes for around €8. It also seems to be the place where most people congregate for an evening drink. The service, however, can be painfully slow. Daily 10am–10pm.

Restaurant de l'Abbaye Place de l'Abbaye ☎05 53 63 40 93, ✉delpech@wanadoo.fr. Cadouin's best restaurant offers tasty, traditional *menus* from €13, with rabbit terrine with chestnuts, and a terrific chocolate nut pie among the dishes. The predominantly bare brick interior, with a beautiful stone fireplace at its centrepiece, looks fabulous, though dining alfresco looking across to the abbey is no less inviting. April–Oct daily except Mon noon–2pm & 7.30–10pm; Nov–March open daily for lunch and Sat eve.

Un Air de Campagne Av Republique ☎05 53 27 37 66. A short walk up the main road from place de l'Abbaye, *Un Air* is an utterly charming restaurant, in so much as there's a menu at all; it consists of not much more than a few crêpes, omelettes and salads, though there is a cracking little two-course *menu* (€11.50) of duck with home-made potato fritters, followed by a bowl of Périgordin ice cream (vanilla and walnut) – best enjoyed with a carafe of wine. Eating takes place at dinky wooden tables topped with red and white checked clothes surrounded by bales of hay: delightful. Daily 11am–10pm.

Sarlat and the Périgord Noir

CANOEING NEAR LA ROQUE-GAGEAC

Sarlat and the Périgord Noir

The central part of the Dordogne valley and its tributary, the valley of the Vézère, form the heart of the Périgord Noir. This is distinctive Dordogne country: rivers meandering through deep-cut valleys framed by limestone cliffs; dense, dark oak woods; orchards of walnut trees; and flocks of ducks and low-slung grey geese. This rich, fertile land has provided food and shelter since the earliest times, and the first settlers left behind them the world's greatest concentration of prehistoric sites. Later generations built the beetling medieval castles and huddled villages that now provide the region's iconic images. It is rich fare, best taken at a gentle pace and concentrating on a few sites rather than trying to see everything.

3

The focal point of the Périgord Noir region is its capital, **Sarlat-la-Canéda**. Though this medieval town boasts no great monuments, the warren of old lanes, hidden courtyards and fine architecture, the background for many a period drama, not to mention its excellent weekly markets, are not to be missed.

Sarlat is within spitting distance of the two iconic river valleys, which have come to define the whole region. First up is the **Vézère valley**, cutting diagonally across the region from the northeast. The valley's immense, overhanging cliffs have been worn away by frost action over the millennia to create natural rock shelters where humans have sought refuge for thousands of years, leaving an incredible wealth of archeological and artistic evidence from the late Paleolithic era. The two unmissable highlights are the outstandingly preserved polychrome paintings of the **Grotte de Font-de-Gaume**, which you can still visit in the original, and the reproduction at **Lascaux**, near Montignac. The valley has more than cave paintings to offer, however: several sites show how cliff shelters were lived in throughout the Middle Ages up until relatively recently, while some breathtaking chasms like the **Gouffre de Proumeyssac** are the work of nature alone.

In the **Dordogne valley**, it's the region's medieval, feudal history that's most palpable in this sublime, château-studded stretch. **Beynac** and **Castelnaud**, two semi-ruined fortresses on either side of the river, are without doubt the most spectacular. Closer to river level, **La Roque-Gageac** presents a more homely scene. From a distance, save for its red-tiled roofs, the village is barely distinguishable from the vertical cliff into which it nestles. This is also one of the best spots in the whole country to hop on a **canoe** and take a leisurely trip downstream.

With so many first-class sights in such a compact area, it's not surprising that this is one of the most heavily visited inland areas of France, and as a result has all the concomitant problems of crowds, high prices and tat. If you can't come out of season, seek accommodation away from the main centres, visit places first thing in the morning and always drive along the back roads even when there is a more direct route available.

Highlights

❶ Sarlat Wander the cobbled lanes of this beautifully preserved medieval town, which hosts one of the region's best markets. See p.121

❷ Manoir d'Eyrignac The formal gardens, with their manicured hornbeam hedges and trompe-l'oeil parterre, are as much a work of art as of nature. **See p.128**

❸ Vézère valley Prehistoric artists left moving testimony of their skill in myriad decorated caves here, among them the magnificent friezes of Lascaux and Font-de-Gaume, the bas-reliefs of the Abri du Cap-Blanc and the drawings of the Grotte de Rouffignac. **See p.130**

❹ La Roque-St-Christophe Multistorey living medieval-style in these dozens of rock shelters cut into the limestone cliffs. See p.143

❺ Château de Castelnaud This archetypal feudal fortress lording it over the Dordogne valley contains a superb museum of medieval warfare. **See p.160**

❻ La Roque-Gageac Very touristy, but nevertheless one of the region's most picturesque villages, with its jumble of roofs and the towering cliffs above mirrored in the Dordogne's slow-moving waters. **See p.162**

HIGHLIGHTS ARE MARKED ON THE MAP ON P.120

THE BEST PREHISTORIC CAVES (FOR ART)

Lascaux II Superb replica of the summit of Cro-Magnon art. See p.149
Grotte de Font-de-Gaume Beautifully preserved paintings and engravings in a narrow tunnel. See p.134
Abri du Cap Blanc Sculpted frieze of life-size horses and bisons. See p.137
Grotte de Pech-Merle "The chapel of mammoths" stands out among more than five hundred drawings. See p.219
Grotte de Rouffignac Hop on an electric train to view drawings of mammoths and woolly rhinos in a kilometre-long cave. See p.138
Grotte de Sorcier Mystifying engraving of a human – the "Sorcier" – among many animals. See p.141

GETTING AROUND

By train Though you'll need your own transport for exploring much of the Périgord Noir, two train lines cut through the area. Sarlat is the terminus of a line from Bordeaux via Bergerac, while trains between Agen and Périgueux stop at Le Bugue and Les Eyzies; the best place to

THE PÉRIGORD NORD

change between the two lines is Le Buisson (see p.112). In addition, the northern Vézère valley can be accessed from Terrasson, on the Brive–Bordeaux main line.
By bus The region is served by a minimal smattering of bus routes, though even these early-morning school services

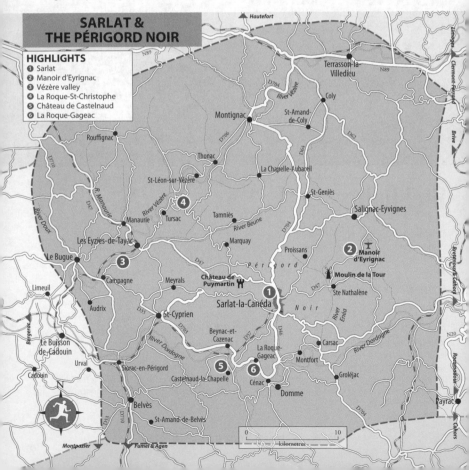

SARLAT & THE PÉRIGORD NOIR

HIGHLIGHTS
❶ Sarlat
❷ Manoir d'Eyrignac
❸ Vézère valley
❹ La Roque-St-Christophe
❺ Château de Castelnaud
❻ La Roque-Gageac

can fizzle out entirely in the school holidays.
By bike In addition to bike rental outfits in Sarlat, Les Eyzies and Montignac (see town accounts for details), you can also rent bikes through Bike Bus, based at Castelnaud (☎06 08 94 42 01, ⓦbike-bus.com). They offer a range of bikes, including mountain bikes, tourers and children's

bikes, with prices starting at €20 per day. They deliver free to Sarlat, Beynac, La Roque-Gageac, Vitrac and Daglan and charge €2/km for deliveries elsewhere. Aquitaine Bike is also based in the Périgord Noir, at Le Coux-et-Bigaroque, and offers free deliveries free within 30km, or further afield for a fee.

Sarlat-la-Canéda and around

Very picturesque and very touristy, **SARLAT-LA-CANÉDA** (usually known just as Sarlat) sits in a green hollow between hills 10km or so north of the River Dordogne. You hardly notice the modern suburbs, as it is the mainly fifteenth- and sixteenth-century houses of the old town in mellow, pale ochre-coloured stone that draw the attention. Unless you are here for the Saturday market, it won't take more than half a day to explore. There's a large range of **accommodation**, both in and just outside the town, making it the most natural base for exploring the Périgord Noir.

The ramparts surrounding old Sarlat were torn down in the late 1800s, at about the same time that the north–south **rue de la République** was cut through the centre to create its main thoroughfare. The streets to the west remain relatively quiet; the east side is where you'll find the majority of sights.

The hills above Sarlat contain a number of sights, from the **Moulin de la Tour**, a water mill making walnut oil by traditional methods, to the topiary gardens

3

FESTIVALS AND EVENTS

Where we haven't given a specific information number contact the relevant tourist office.

Late March, April or early May Sarlat: La Ringueta (ⓦringueta-sarlat.fr). At Pentecôte (Whit Sunday) in even-numbered years, place de la Grande-Rigaudie is the venue for traditional games and sports of the Périgord.

Mid-July to early August Sarlat: Festival des Jeux du Théâtre (☎05 53 31 10 83, ⓦfestival-theatre-sarlat.com). One of France's most important theatre fests, covering a wide range of material from Shakespeare to the avant-garde Theatre of the Absurd, as well as several productions for children. The open-air performances take place over two to three weeks in various venues around town.

Mid- to late July Montignac: Festival de Montignac (☎05 53 50 14 00, ⓦwww.festivaldemontignac.assoo.org). Major arts festival featuring local and international folk groups from as far afield as South America and China. As well as ticket-only events, there are street performances, food stalls, exhibitions and crafts demonstrations during the week.

August to early October St-Léon-sur-Vézère and around: Festival du Périgord Noir (☎05 53 51 95 17, ⓦfestivalduperigordnoir.fr). Baroque and classical music concerts in the atmospheric churches of St-Léon,

St-Amand-de-Coly, Sarlat and other venues throughout the region.

Early August Les Eyzies and around: Festival Musique en Périgord (ⓦmusiqueenperigord.fr). Interesting mix of medieval and classical works alongside jazz and traditional music from around the world. Concerts take place over ten days in the Romanesque churches of Les Eyzies, Campagne and Audrix, among other venues.

First fortnight in August Belvès and Cadouin: Festival Bach (ⓦfestivalbach.fr). Dedicated to the composer and comprising a handful of concerts generally held in Belvès church and the abbey at Cadouin.

Early November Sarlat: Festival du Film (☎05 53 29 18 13, ⓦville-sarlat.fr/festival). One-week festival previewing films from around the world, including special screenings of student productions.

MARKETS

The main markets in this region are at Belvès (Sat); Le Bugue (Tues & Sat); Domme (Thurs); Les Eyzies (April–Oct Mon); Montignac (Wed & Sat); St-Cyprien (Sun); St-Geniès (Sun); Sarlat (Wed & Sat); and Terrasson (Thurs).

of the **Manoir d'Eyrignac**, with perhaps a detour to the picturesque village of
St-Geniès. Heading westwards, the still-occupied **Château de Puymartin** tends to be
overshadowed by the more famous castles along the Dordogne, but contains some
unusual interior decorations, while the nearby **Cabanes de Breuil**, a harmonious
group of what were probably shepherds' huts, represent a completely different
architectural tradition. With the exception of St-Geniès, which, with an early start, is
accessible on the Sarlat–Périgueux bus route, you'll need your own **transport** to reach
any of these places.

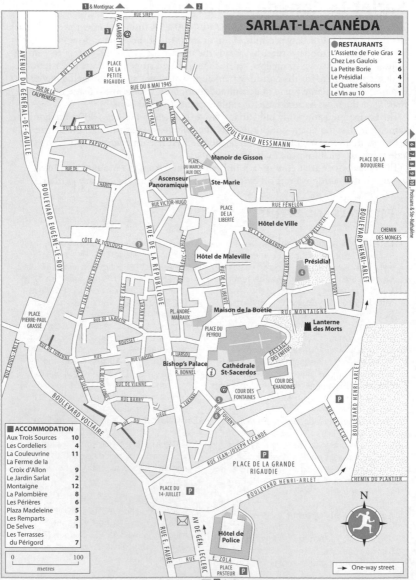

Brief history

Though it started life as a Gallo-Roman settlement, Sarlat really came to prominence in the late eighth century when Benedictine monks established an **abbey** here, later dedicated to a former bishop of Limoges, St Sacerdos. In 1147 **Bernard of Clairvaux** also left his mark when he preached the Second Crusade – according to legend he miraculously cured the sick by offering them bread he had blessed. In spite of this, the townspeople were keen to gain independence from Church rule, and in 1298 were eventually granted the right to elect their own consuls by Louis VIII. In return, they remained loyal to the French Crown during the Hundred Years War and staunchly Catholic in the Wars of Religion, when the town suffered considerably at the hands of the Protestants. The fine **Renaissance** facades visible today date from a period of prosperity in between these two wars. That they are so well preserved is largely due to the fact that the town went into slow decline after the late 1700s. By the early twentieth century the centre was in a pretty poor state, but was saved from further decay by the vision of **André Malraux**, the novelist, Resistance hero and politician who launched the concept of the *secteur sauvegardé* ("protected area") in 1962. Sarlat's town centre was a pilot for this initiative, saving it from excessive postwar renovation and providing funds for a huge restoration project. Today, the 65 protected monuments in the medieval centre make it the most popular tourist destination in the whole of Dordogne, packed to the gunwales in summer, though still relatively undisturbed during the winter months.

Place de la Liberté

Sarlat's labyrinthine lanes fan out from **place de la Liberté**, the central square where the big Saturday **market** spreads its stands of flowers, foie gras, truffles, walnuts and mushrooms according to the season; it's mostly foodstuffs in the morning and general goods after lunch.

Hôtel de Maleville

Place de la Liberté • Closed to the public

The finest building on place de la Liberté is the **Hôtel de Maleville**, tucked into its southwest corner. The facade facing onto the square consists of a tall, narrow building in French Renaissance style with ornate window surrounds; turn down the lane beside it to see its more classical Italianate frontage, with a balustraded terrace and two medallions above the door representing Henry IV and, according to popular belief, his mistress Gabrielle d'Estrée.

Maison de La Boétie

Place du Peyrou • Ground floor occasionally open for art exhibitions

The lane beside the Hôtel de Maleville continues through a series of passages and geranium-filled courtyards to emerge beneath Sarlat's most famous house, the **Maison de La Boétie**. Though its prominent gables and tiers of mullion windows, each within a sculpted frame, are certainly eye-catching, much of the building's renown derives from the fact that the poet and humanist Étienne de La Boétie, a close friend of Michel de Montaigne (see p.105), was born here in 1530. He went on to study law in Orléans, where he wrote his most famous work, *Discourse on Voluntary Servitude*, though it wasn't published until after his premature death at the age of 33. A treatise on the tyranny of power, and thus a very early expression of anarchism, the *Discourse* later struck a cord with Rousseau and other radical thinkers in the run-up to the Revolution.

Cathédrale St-Sacerdos and around

The former bishop's palace, opposite the Maison de La Boétie, sports a Renaissance gallery and windows, while the large and unexciting **Cathédrale St-Sacerdos** (daily 9am–6pm) to which it is attached mostly dates from a seventeenth-century renovation. More interesting are the two pretty courtyards to the south of the cathedral – **cour des Fontaines**, filled with the sound of playing water, and **cour des Chanoines**, surrounded by a pleasing assembly of buildings – and the passage around the chevet where Sarlat's nobles were laid to rest in arched niches, *enfeux*, let into the wall. Less illustrious mortals were buried in the cemetery above, presided over by a curious bullet-shaped tower, the **Lanterne des Morts**, built in the twelfth century. Its exact purpose remains a mystery. Local tradition maintains that it commemorates St Bernard's visit in 1147 (see p.123).

Further north along the same slope you come to the **Présidial**, the former seat of royal justice, now a restaurant (see p.127).

Ascenseur Panoramique

April–Dec daily 9am–9pm, though check with the tourist office (see opposite) for the latest hours; closed in wet weather • April–Oct €5, Nov–March €4 • Tickets available at the tourist office, or on-site by credit card only • ☎ 05 53 31 45 45

From the Présidial, drop back down to place de la Liberté and pass behind the back of the church of Ste-Marie (now a covered market accessed through massive, and ugly, metal doors) to find the entrance to the **Ascenseur Panoramique**, a lift built into the church tower. The glass-sided lift takes you up 35 metres to peer out of the top of the tower, which was never roofed, for ten minutes, while the guide points out Sarlat's more famous monuments, including some of its 22 towers and remnants of the medieval walls. From up here you also get a bird's-eye view of the town's many *lauze* roofs (see box, p.127).

Manoir de Gisson

Place du Marché-aux-Oies • Daily: mid-Feb to end March & Oct to mid-Jan 11am–5pm, April–June & Sept 10am–7pm, July & Aug 10am–8pm; closed mid-Jan to mid-Feb • €7 • ☎ 05 53 28 70 55, ⓦ manoirdegisson.com

Dominating the north side of the place du Marché-aux-Oies – a delightful corner decorated by three bronze geese – stands the **Manoir de Gisson**. This impressive building, with its hexagonal tower and stone-mullion windows, offers a rare chance to see inside one of Sarlat's noble houses. It dates from the thirteenth century, though was considerably enlarged in the fifteenth, by the Gisson family, whose members most famously served as consuls in charge of the town's public order. You'll find their portraits inside, presiding over rooms decked out with furniture from medieval times to the seventeenth century, much of it fashioned in local walnut. At the top of the lovely circular, stone staircase don't miss the chance to admire the internal structure of the heavy *lauze* roof (see box, p.127).

West of rue de la République

If time allows, it's worth crossing over rue de la République to wander the western sector, particularly rue Jean-Jacques Rousseau. There's nothing particular to see, beyond more cobbled lanes and ornate doorways or the odd defensive tower, but this side of Sarlat is less touristy and quieter.

Gorodka

La Canéda • July & Aug daily 10am–midnight, Sept–June daily 2–6pm • €8 • ☎ 05 53 31 02 00, ⓦ gorodka.com

Just outside Sarlat, 4km south off the D704 to Gourdon, **Gorodka**, the home and gallery of conceptual artist Pierre Shasmoukine, provides a complete break from Sarlat's medieval monuments. This is a rambling place with various galleries crammed full of inventive pieces of art, enlivened by a strong dose of irony. The extensive grounds serve as an offbeat gallery of the weird and wonderful, including a giant dragonfly made from the body of a helicopter and bizarre, sinister-faced plastic totems that glow in the dark.

ARRIVAL AND DEPARTURE
SARLAT

By train Sarlat's *gare SNCF* is just over 1km south of the old town on the road to Souillac.
Destinations Bergerac (5–7 daily; 1hr–1hr 50min); Bordeaux (5–7 daily; 2hr 20min–3hr 20min); Le Buisson (5–7 daily; 30min); Castillon-la-Bataille (5–7 daily; 1hr 40min–2hr); Lalinde (5–7 daily; 45min–1hr 30min); St-Cyprien (5–7 daily; 15min); Ste-Foy-la-Grande (5–7 daily; 1hr 20min–2hr 10min); Siorac-en-Périgord (2–3 daily; 20min); Trémolat (5–6 daily; 20–50min).
By bus Buses from Périgueux (Périgord Voyages; ☎ 05 53 59 01 48) and Souillac (Belmon Voyages; ☎ 05 65 37 81 15) pull into place Pasteur, immediately south of the centre. Souillac buses also call at the train station.
Destinations Carsac (2–4 daily; 20min); Montignac (July & Aug Wed only, other school hols Mon–Fri 1 daily, school

term Mon–Fri 1–2 daily; 30min); Périgueux (July & Aug Wed only, other school hols Mon–Fri 1 daily, school term Mon–Fri 1–2 daily; 1hr 40min); St-Geniès (July & Aug Wed only, other school hols Mon–Fri 1 daily, school term Mon–Fri 1–2 daily; 20min); Souillac (2–4 daily; 50min–1hr).
By car It's normally easy to find a parking space in Sarlat, though more difficult on market days and in July and August. Paid parking is available all around Sarlat's ring road, the most convenient being on place de la Grande-Rigaudie. Prices and the maximum stay vary by season; check the instructions on the meter. Note that Sarlat's medieval core is mostly closed to traffic in July and August (daily 11am–6am) and at weekends from mid-April to end June & Sept (8pm Sat to 6am Mon).

GETTING AROUND

Car rental Europcar (☎ 05 53 30 30 40, ⓦ europcar.co.uk), on place de Lattre-de-Tassigny, near the train station.
Taxis Call Allo Philippe Taxi (☎ 05 53 59 39 65 or ☎ 06 08 57 30 10, ⓦ allophilippetaxi.monsite-orange.fr), or Brajot Taxi (☎ 05 53 59 41 13).
Bike and scooter rental Bikes are available from

Cycleo, 44 rue des Cordeliers (from €15 per day; ☎ 05 53 31 90 05 or ☎ 06 32 21 61 10, ⓦ cycleo.fr), while MC Moto, 4 av de Selves (☎ 05 53 59 06 11, ⓦ mcmoto24.com) rents out scooters (from €38 per day) and 125cc motorbikes (€56 per day).

INFORMATION AND ACTIVITIES

Tourist office In the heart of the old centre at 3 rue Tourny (April Mon–Sat 9am–noon & 2–6pm, Sun 10am–1pm & 2–5pm; May & June Mon–Sat 9am–6pm, Sun 10am–1pm & 2–5pm; July & Aug Mon–Sat 9am–7pm, Sun 10am–noon & 2–6pm; Sept Mon–Sat 9am–1pm & 2–6pm, Sun 10am–1pm & 2–5pm; Oct to mid-Nov Mon–Sat 9am–noon & 2–5pm, Sun 10am–1pm; mid-Nov to March Mon–Sat 9am–noon & 2–5pm; ☎ 05 53 31 45 45, ⓦ sarlat-tourisme.com). The tourist office also sells maps of hiking and mountain-bike trails around the Périgord Noir (€1.50 per map; €14.90 for all 27 maps). While here, pick up the leaflet *Sortir à Sarlat*, a run-down of the town's

cultural calendar, including its excellent theatre and film festivals (see box, p.121).
Guided tours Available April to October (1–3 daily; 1hr 30min; €5.50), with English-language tours weekly in summer (mid-May to July & Sept to mid-Oct Wed 11am; 1hr; €5.50). Alternatively, you can rent an English-language audio guide (2hr; €5).
Canoe rental Head to Vitrac, 7km south of Sarlat, where two well-rated canoe companies set up either side of the bridge: Canoë Loisirs (☎ 05 53 28 23 43, ⓦ canoes-loisirs .com) and Copeyre Canoë (☎ 05 53 28 23 82, ⓦ canoe -copeyre.com).

ACCOMMODATION

Note that during the peak holiday season (June–Sept) it's advisable to book several weeks in advance and to consider the quieter places outside the town centre. If you arrive without a reservation, the tourist office will do what they can to assist, for a nominal fee of €2, but they can't guarantee to find anything.

IN SARLAT
★ **Les Cordeliers** 51 rue des Cordeliers ☎ 05 53 31 94 66, ⓦ hotelsarlat.com. You'll need to book early for this excellent English-run *chambre d'hôte* in an elegant eighteenth-century townhouse decked out with period furnishings just outside the historic centre. Spacious rooms

are equipped with a/c and impeccable bathrooms. Those on the top floor are tucked under the eaves, and one boasts its own roof terrace. Both the rooms and the copious breakfast (€7.50) offer excellent value for money. Two nights' minimum stay required, though it's worth double-checking. Closed Nov–Feb. **€95**

La Couleuvrine 1 place de la Bouquerie ☎ 05 53 59 27 80, ⓦ la-couleuvrine.com. One of Sarlat's more atmospheric hotels, *La Couleuvrine* partly occupies one of the town's defensive towers, with exposed stone walls and big fireplaces downstairs. It contains 28 comfortable rooms, though the cheapest are small – it's worth upgrading to "superior" (€75). Best of all is the tower room with views across town (€85). There's also a good restaurant (*menus* from €21) and a lunchtime bistro (*formules* at €15 and €22). Breakfast €9.50. **€65**

Le Jardin Sarlat 14 rue du Jardin-de-Madame ☎ 05 53 29 22 67, ⓦ lejardin-sarlat.com. A highly rated English-owned *chambre d'hôte* tucked down a quiet backstreet a short walk from the town centre. It's set in a lush garden with a vine-covered terrace, fruit trees and a splash-pool. Inside is a residents' lounge and four airy, en-suite bedrooms. The generous breakfast (€8) will set you up for the day. Closed mid-Dec to Feb. **€80**

Montaigne Place Pasteur ☎ 05 53 31 93 88, ⓦ hotelmontaigne.fr. This two-star hotel occupies an imposing building just south of centre. The rooms, in cool creams, have less character but are well equipped for the price, including double-glazing and a/c. Breakfast €9. Closed mid-Nov to mid-Feb. **€55**

Les Périères Rue Jean-Gabin ☎ 05 53 59 05 84, ⓦ lesperieres.com. Sarlat's closest campsite is on a terraced hillside 1km northeast of the centre up rue Jean-Jaurès. It's spacious and well equipped – facilities include heated indoor pool, outdoor pool, washing machines, tennis courts and grocery shop – but for two people, including electricity, in high season it costs almost as much as a cheap hotel (€33). Closed Oct–March. **€29**

Plaza Madeleine 1 place de la Petite-Rigaudie ☎ 05 53 59 10 41, ⓦ hoteldelamadeleine-sarlat.com. Sarlat's oldest and once grandest hotel, located just outside the medieval centre, has lost some of its charm with its recent makeover, heavy on the greys. But the rooms are still as attractive, with their blend of traditional and modern styling, and well equipped. The four-star facilities include a bar, business centre, heated pool, jacuzzi and spa (free to guests) and secure parking (€12). Breakfast €12.50. **€121**

Les Remparts 48 av Gambetta ☎ 05 53 59 40 00, ⓦ hotel-lesremparts-sarlat.com. Cheap and cheerful little hotel in a convenient location offering 25 fuss-free rooms. Though lacking somewhat in decor, all rooms come with bathroom, TV and a/c. Secure parking available (€8.50). Breakfast €8.50. Closed Dec–Feb. **€68**

De Selves 93 av Gambetta ☎ 05 53 31 50 00, ⓦ selves-sarlat.com. Modern four-star benefiting from a small garden and free use of a covered and heated pool, sauna and jacuzzi shared with the adjacent – and much more expensive – sister hotel. The well-kept rooms have modern, if unexciting decor and a/c. Garage €12. Breakfast €12. Closed Jan to mid-Feb. **€98**

AROUND SARLAT

Aux Trois Sources Pech-Lafaille ☎ 05 53 59 08 19, ⓦ hebergement-sarlat.com. A very well-priced *chambre d'hôte* in a handsome seventeenth-century manor house 3km east of Sarlat on the road to Ste-Nathalène. Four charming, rustic, en-suite rooms, with wooden floors, rugs and original hearths, are squeezed into a converted barn, and there's a fifth – more spacious – in the main house (€50). It's surrounded by an attractive park, with chestnut trees and pond, not to mention the three springs. Breakfast included. **€45**

La Ferme de la Croix d'Allon La Croix-d'Allon ☎ 05 53 59 08 44, ⓦ location-gites-sarlat.com. Five unpretentious *chambres d'hôtes* on a working cattle farm 2km from Sarlat on the road to Proissans. All rooms have private bathrooms and there's a heated pool and also a fully equipped kitchen and barbecue available for guests. Breakfast included. Closed mid-Nov to Feb. **€60**

★ **La Palombière** Ste-Nathalène ☎ 05 53 59 42 34, ⓦ lapalombiere.fr. A five-star job, this is one of the region's best campsites, roughly 10km east of Sarlat on the D47. It's in a lovely, peaceful location in an extensive area of mature woodland, is very well equipped – including restaurant, bar, grocery store, pools and tennis courts – and puts on all sorts of kids' events in summer. Closed mid-Sept to April. **€29**

Les Terrasses du Périgord Pech-d'Orance ☎ 05 53 59 02 25, ⓦ terrasses-du-perigord.com. Welcoming, well-tended campsite in a superb hilltop position 2.5km north of Sarlat on the Proissans road. Plenty of flowers and spacious pitches surrounded by thick hedges make this one of the nicest sites around. Facilities include pools, snack bar, grocery store and bike hire. Closed mid-Sept to mid-April. **€19**

EATING AND DRINKING

During the main tourist season Sarlat is chock-a-block with restaurants. In winter pickings are thinner, but those that do stay open tend to be the better quality places patronized by locals. You'll find foie gras, duck and walnuts in various guises everywhere, alongside another local staple: *pommes sarladaises*, potatoes crispy-fried in duck fat with lashings of garlic, parsley and, sometimes, mushrooms.

L'Assiette de Foie Gras 4 rue Landry ☎ 06 17 66 47 91. Don't expect rapid service, but it's worth the wait to sample the delights of this little restaurant run by a young Argentinian chef who adds an international twist to top-quality local produce. On the *menus* (around €20–33), which change frequently, you might find sushi made with foie gras or tuna grilled with sesame and yakitori sauce. Reservations recommended. Jan–May & Oct–Dec noon–2pm & 7–9pm; June–Sept noon–2pm & 7–10pm; closed at least one day per week.

★ **Chez Les Gaulois** 1 rue Tourny ☎ 05 53 59 50 64. Charcuterie addicts will love this authentic and welcoming restaurant where cured Savoy, Corsican and Spanish hams and sausages hang from the ceiling. They're served, along with Savoy cheeses, on a choice of platters and in salads (around €10–14) or you can buy to take away. July, Aug & school hols daily noon–2pm & 7–9pm; April–June & Sept–Feb Tues–Sat noon–2pm & 7–8.30pm.

La Petite Borie 4 rue Tourny ☎ 05 53 31 23 69. Friendly and consistently reliable restaurant offering good service and classic Périgord cuisine at affordable prices. The majority of ingredients are sourced locally, with home-made foie gras featuring strongly. The fixed-price *menus* (€12.50–€26.50) offer excellent value for money, each starting with a traditional garlic soup. July & Aug daily noon–2.30pm & 7–9.30pm; Sept–June Tues–Sat noon–2.30pm & 7–9.30pm, Sun noon–2.30pm. Closed two weeks in Nov or Jan.

Le Présidial 6 rue Landry ☎ 05 53 28 92 47. Classy restaurant to the east of the centre in the former tribunal with a walled garden and airy, elegant rooms. While the

setting is more spectacular than the food, especially when floodlit on a summer's evening, it's a reliable choice, offering dishes such as delicately spiced salmon tartare and iced ginger nougat. *Menus* €19–42. April–June, Sept & Oct Mon & Thurs 7–9pm, Tues, Wed, Fri & Sat noon–2pm & 7–9pm; July & Aug Mon 7–9pm, Tues–Sat noon–2pm & 7–9pm.

Le Quatre Saisons 2 Côte de Toulouse ☎ 05 53 29 48 59, ⓦ 4salsons-sarlat-perigord.com. Escape the hubbub of central Sarlat to this small, refined restaurant on the west side of rue de la République and up a steep flight of stairs. The cooking is creative, with dishes such as lamb tenderloin on a bed of dry rosemary flambéed at the table, and luscious deserts. *Menus* €15–36. April–June & Sept–Nov Thurs–Mon noon–1.30pm & 7–8.30pm; July & Aug daily noon–1.30pm & 7–8.30pm.

Le Vin au 10 10 rue Fénelon ☎ 05 53 29 47 80, ⓦ levinau10.com. Get there early or reserve for this stylish wine bar with a handful of tables on a quiet street leading up from Sarlat's main square. They serve a carefully selected range of wines from the region and further afield, with inventive and tasty food to accompany them. Try nems (Vietnamese spring rolls) filled with confit de canard (preserved duck) and iced soufflé with walnuts to follow. Lunch menu €16, dinner €33, or feast on the truffle menu in summer €60. April–June, Sept & Oct daily except Sun noon–2pm & 7–9pm; July & Aug daily noon–2pm & 7–9pm.

DIRECTORY

Hospital The Centre Hospitalier is on rue Jean-Leclaire (☎ 05 53 31 75 75) to the northeast of the centre.

Newspapers You'll find English papers and the *International Herald Tribune* on sale around Sarlat. Try the Maison de la Presse at 34 rue de la République and 31 av Gambetta.

Internet access Both the gallery-café *L'Oeuil de la Gazelle*, 9 cours des Fontaines (daily: Easter–June, Sept & Oct 10am–6.30pm; July & Aug 10am–1am), and the *French Coffee Shop*, 35 av Gambetta (Mon–Sat 8am–7.30pm), offer wi-fi access or use of a computer free to customers.

Police Sarlat's Gendarmerie is at 1 bd Henri-Arlet

(☎ 05 53 31 71 10).

Post office The main post office is at Place du 14-Juillet, 24200 Sarlat.

Shopping While the markets are the best place to buy foie gras, walnuts, walnut oil, prunes and other local foods straight from the farmer, place de la Liberté, rue de la Liberté and rue des Consuls are full of speciality shops. On place de la Liberté, the Distillerie du Périgord (☎ 05 53 59 31 10, ⓦ distillerie-perigord.com) makes delectable liqueurs from walnut and plum, as well as fruits in alcohol – try their Guinettes, containing local morello cherries.

BUILDING BLOCKS

The hallmarks of the Périgord region are the primitive-looking stone huts called *bories*, and the mottled-grey roofs made of limestone slabs (*lauzes*) used on cottage and château alike. Although they are now protected, the cost of maintaining these roofs – the stones weigh on average 500kg per square metre – means that many have been replaced with terracotta tiles. A floor made out of *lauzes* is called *pisé*, and is commonly found in châteaux and chapels, the stones inserted upright into a bed of clay and lime. While you'll find *lauze* roofs and, to a lesser extent, *pisé* floors in evidence throughout the region, *bories* are less common. The best examples are at Les Cabanes du Breuil, near Sarlat (p.129).

Moulin de la Tour

30min guided visits: April & May Wed & Fri 9am–noon & 2–6pm; June & Sept also open Sat 2–6pm; July & Aug Mon, Wed, Fri 9am–noon & 2–6pm, Sat 2–6pm; Oct–March Fri 9am–noon & 2–6pm • €4.60 • ☎ 05 53 59 22 08, ⓦ moulindelatour.com

On the banks of the River Enéa, 9km east of Sarlat and 2km north of **Ste- Nathalène** on the Proissans road, a sixteenth-century water mill still grinds out walnut oil in time-honoured fashion. The pressing room of the **Moulin de la Tour**, where creaking cog-wheels drive a cylindrical grinding stone set at right angles to the flat base, is dark, cosy and full of the most delicious aromas. Here the nuts – ready-shelled by local pensioners – are ground to a paste, heated gently over a wood fire and then pressed to extract the oil; an average pressing gives roughly fifteen litres of oil from thirty kilos of nuts.

At the end of the guided visit, you get the opportunity to taste some of the produce. If you come on a day when the grinding room is not operating, only the shop (Mon–Sat 9am–noon & 2–7pm) will be open, selling the mill's own walnut, hazelnut and almond oils.

3

Manoir d'Eyrignac

House not open to the public; gardens daily: April 10am–7pm; May–Sept 9.30am–7pm; Oct 10am–dusk; Nov–March 10.30am–12.30pm & 2.30pm–dusk • March to mid-Nov €12; Mid-Nov to Feb €9.50 • ☎ 05 53 28 99 71, ⓦ eyrignac.com

The River Enéa rises among oak woods on a plateau to the north of Ste-Nathalène. Though the hills appear scrubby and dry, one of the Enéa's tributaries is fed by seven springs, the same springs that prompted a seventeenth-century noble, Antoine de Costes de la Calprenède, to build a manor house here, the **Manoir d'Eyrignac**, and which now sustain his descendants' glorious **gardens**, signed to the northeast along back roads from Ste-Nathalène.

The gardens aren't huge, but, consisting of lush evergreens – mainly hornbeam, box, cypress and yew – clipped and arranged in formal patterns of alleys and borders, achieve remarkable effects with almost no colour. The regimented lines are softened by the occasional pavilion or fountain and by informal stands of trees framing the countryside around. The original formal garden was laid out by an eighteenth-century Italian landscaper, and later converted to an English romantic garden according to the fashion of the times. What you see today is the work of the last forty years, the creation of the present owner's father in a combination of Italian and French styles.

The complex also contains a small **exhibition hall** next to the ticket office, where you can watch a video about the garden and its history, and a restaurant-cum-snack bar. You can also bring your own food and take advantage of their picnic tables.

St-Geniès

With time to spare, the cluster of buildings some 14km north of Sarlat known as **ST-GENIÈS** is worth a detour. It's a typical Périgord Noir village, with its partly ruined château and fortress-like church all constructed from the same warm-yellow stone under heavy *lauze* roofs. Unless it's market day (Sunday morning), it won't take long to explore, the only sight being the **Chapelle de Cheylard**, standing on its own on a small knoll to the east. The fourteenth-century frescoes inside have suffered over the years – at one time the chapel served as a dance hall – but a number remain visible, including a particularly manic bunch pelting St Stephen with stones.

Château de Puymartin

45min guided visits: April–June & Sept 10am–noon & 2–6pm; July & Aug 10am–6.30pm; Oct to mid-Nov 2–5.30pm • €7.50 • ☎ 05 53 59 29 97, ⓦ chateau-de-puymartin.com

Eight kilometres northwest of Sarlat on the D47, the **Château de Puymartin** stands guard over the headwaters of the Petite Beune River, which flows down to join the

Vézère at Les Eyzies (see p.131). The castle, which underwent extensive remodelling in the seventeenth and nineteenth centuries, has been in the same family since 1450 and is remarkably well preserved.

Among a large collection of family heirlooms, most noteworthy are the **tapestries**, particularly those in the grand hall, depicting the Siege of Troy. The Classical theme continues in the seventeenth-century trompe-l'oeil paintings on the chimneypiece here and in the guest bedroom, where Zeus visits Danaë in a shower of gold – presumably he would have been surprised to find her clothed and holding a cross, a liberty taken in the more puritanical 1800s.

The same sensibilities demanded that a number of naked figures in the **mythological room** also be dressed. To preserve the original, visitors now only see a replica, but it is still an extraordinary sight. The room, though not large, is completely covered in monochrome scenes from mythology: snake-haired Medusa, Argus with his hundred eyes and Althaea murdering her son Meleager by burning a brand. The general consensus is that the room was a place of meditation, though surprisingly it also served as a children's nursery for some time.

Like all good castles, Puymartin also has its ghost, in this case La Dame Blanche, who supposedly haunts the north tower. In real life she was Thérèse de St-Clar, the lady of the household during the sixteenth century, who, on being surprised in the arms of a lover, was walled up in the tower until she died fifteen years later. More prosaically, it's worth climbing up into the roof here to admire the elaborate timber framework supporting the *lauzes*.

Cabanes du Breuil

April–Oct daily 10am–7pm; Nov–March Sat & Sun 2–6pm • €5 • ☎ 06 80 72 38 59, 🌐 cabanes-du-breuil.com

At the opposite end of the architectural scale to Puymartin are the **Cabanes du Breuil**, a couple of kilometres up in the hills to the northwest of the château. You'll find these dry-stone circular huts under conical *lauze* roofs scattered throughout the region, but none so picturesque as this group belonging to a small, working farm. Known locally as *bories*, the huts were originally used for human habitation, then for animals or storage.

PÉRIGORD WALNUTS

According to archeological evidence, **walnuts** have formed part of the Périgordin diet for more than 17,000 years. In medieval times, walnut oil was so valuable that it was sometimes used as a form of currency, and in the seventeenth century it was exported by river (via Bordeaux) to Britain, Holland and Germany. Walnuts are still central to the local economy today: rich in polyunsaturated fats, potassium, magnesium and vitamin E, both nuts and oil are marketed for their health-giving properties – they're said to help reduce cholesterol, stimulate the memory and protect against the effects of ageing. The nuts are also incorporated into bread, cakes, tarts and ice cream, or served whole with salads and the local *Cabécou* cheese. Green walnuts are often pickled in vinegar, but can also be made into jam or used to flavour wines and liqueurs. Not even the leaves are wasted: picked young, they give a distinctive tang to walnut apéritif.

In recognition of the walnut's importance to the economy – and indeed culture – of the region, four varieties (Grandjean, Marbot, Corne and Franquette) were granted an **Appellation d'Origine Contrôlée** (AOC) in 2002, to guarantee that you're buying only premium-quality, locally grown produce. Walnuts are grown in the Lot, Corrèze and Charente *départements*, but the heart of the industry is the Dordogne, with more than 4000 hectares (40 square kilometres) of orchards. To capitalize on the AOC label, the local authorities have put together a **Route de la Noix**, along the Dordogne valley from Argentat to Beynac and north to Hautefort. Free leaflets outlining the suggested itineraries are available from tourist offices, indicating producers and traditional oil mills open for visits as well as specialist patisseries and restaurants serving dishes with a nutty theme.

In season (June–Sept) there's a video presentation explaining how the huts are made, but really these beautiful structures speak for themselves.

The Vézère valley and around

Billed as the "Vallée de l'Homme", the **Vézère valley** is home to the greatest concentration of **prehistoric sites** in Europe. They are by no means the oldest, but the sheer wealth and variety are quite stunning. It was here also that many important discoveries were made in the nineteenth and early twentieth centuries.

The valley, now listed by UNESCO as a World Heritage site, draws more than two million visitors a year. The epicentre of all this activity is **Les Eyzies-de-Tayac**, where the National Museum of Prehistory contains many important finds and gives a good overview of what's on offer. The choice of sites nearby is bewildering, but at the very least you should visit the **Grotte de Font-de-Gaume** and the **Abri du Cap Blanc**, both in the Beune valley to the east of Les Eyzies and harbouring the best cave paintings and bas-relief sculptures still open to the public. Also within striking distance of Les Eyzies, this time to the north, are the **Grotte de Rouffignac**, one of the area's largest caves, with a breathtaking array of animal engravings accessible only by an underground electric train, and the **Château de l'Herm**, an evocative ruined castle with literary associations.

Back on the River Vézère, the market town of **Le Bugue** is a good place to base yourself, less dominated by tourism than Les Eyzies. It also gives access to the **Grotte du Sorcier**, with its highly significant human image, and to a different kind of cave, the stunning chasm of the **Gouffre de Proumeyssac**.

Alternatively, you can head north along the river from Les Eyzies to reach a more diverse collection of sights, ranging from the semi-troglodytic settlements at **La Madeleine** and **La Roque St-Christophe** – where a whole town was built into the cliff face – to prehistoric theme parks and the appealing Renaissance castle, the **Château de Losse**. Finally you come to the pretty town of **Montignac**, just a couple of kilometres from the valley's biggest name, the cave of **Lascaux**. Lascaux itself has been closed to the

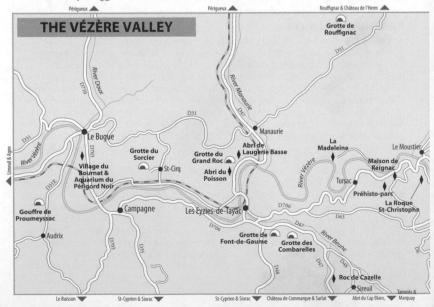

VISITING THE PREHISTORIC CAVES

Visitor numbers to most caves are severely restricted, either for conservation reasons or, in the case of Lascaux II (see p.149), simply because the site can only hold up to forty people at a time. At the most popular, including Lascaux II, the Grotte de Font-de-Gaume (see p.134) and Grotte des Combarelles (see p.136), you have to buy **tickets** in advance by phoning the ticket office or visiting in person, though in some cases it's now also possible by email. If you can, buy your tickets several weeks in advance, sometimes longer during peak periods.

In all cases you have to join a **guided tour**, which usually lasts around 45min. Some are offered in English, while others provide a translated text, but they are tiring — and the talks get repetitive. Unless you're a real prehistory buff, limit yourself to just two or three sites, rather than risk losing that sense of magic.

The remote location of the caves makes them hard to access for **travellers with disabilities**. As a reconstruction, Lascaux II is more accessible, as are the copies at Le Thot. But if you're in doubt, it's best to ask.

3

public since 1963, but its legendary paintings – with all their exceptional detail, colour and realism – have been faithfully reproduced in nearby **Lascaux II**.

GETTING AROUND   THE VÉZÈRE VALLEY

As far as transport is concerned, Le Bugue, Les Eyzies and Terrasson, the northern gateway to the valley, are all accessible by train, while you can get to Montignac by bus from Sarlat and Brive (via Terrasson) if you plan carefully. Most sights are at least a couple of kilometres away from these centres, though, so without your own vehicle you'll rely heavily on walking or taxis.

Les Eyzies-de-Tayac and around

The principal base for visiting the Vézère valley is **LES EYZIES-DE-TAYAC**, 20km northwest of Sarlat. Its location, between the river and a towering cliff, is dramatic, but the town consists of only one street and boasts little of interest apart from its Musée National, home to the largest collection of Paleolithic art in France. While out of season it offers a good choice of hotels and restaurants, Les Eyzies gets completely overrun in summer.

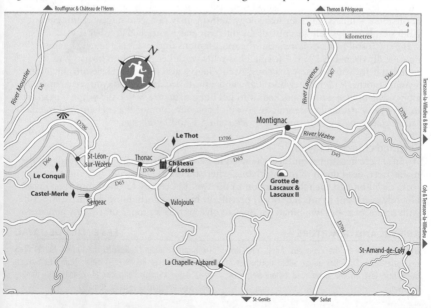

Pôle International de la Préhistoire

Feb to mid-May & Oct–Dec daily except Sat 10am–5pm; mid-May to Sept daily 10am–6pm • Free • ☎ 05 53 06 06 97, ⓦ pole-prehistoire.com

Before tackling the Vézère-valley sites, you might want to pop by this documentary centre, on the east side of town, for a quick introduction to what's on offer. All the prehistoric sites are marked on a 3-D model, with interactive displays, and two slide presentations show how the area has evolved over the last 400,000 years. Knowledgeable staff are available to answer questions and can help plan an itinerary. They also organize various events and temporary exhibitions.

Musée National de la Préhistoire

June & Sept daily except Tues 9.30am–6pm; July & Aug daily 9.30am–6.30pm; Oct–May daily except Tues 9.30am–12.30pm & 2–5.30pm • €5 • Free to under-25s from the European Union & the first Sunday of each month • ☎ 05 53 06 45 65, ⓦ www.musee-prehistoire-eyzies.fr

Under the jutting limestone cliff that dominates Les Eyzies, Paul Dardé's 1930 statue of Neanderthal man, portrayed as an ape-like hunk, stands staring out over the Vézère. Beside him, the **Musée National de la Préhistoire** occupies the remains of a castle built into the rock as well as a striking new building constructed around it. The museum contains a vast array of increasingly sophisticated stone tools of the Paleolithic era (two million to 10,000 years ago). The first floor is devoted to blades found at various archeological sites, accompanied by some rather more engaging short films showing how these blades were made and then used. Upstairs are some good recreations (and the odd original) of engravings and sculptures from the era.

Musée de l'Abri Pataud

45min guided visit: April–June & Sept to mid-Oct Mon–Fri 10am–noon & 2–6pm; July & Aug daily 10am–noon & 1–6pm; closed mid-Oct to March • €5 • ☎ 05 53 06 92 46

In the late nineteenth century, local farmer Martial Pataud discovered prehistoric remains when he was cutting a new road beside what is now the Musée National. The rock shelter (*abri*), which had been occupied for over 15,000 years before the roof collapsed around 20,000 years ago, yielded a rich hoard of finds, a selection of which are now on display in the next-door **Musée de l'Abri Pataud**, occupying what was previously the Patauds' wine cellar. Much of the excavation was carried out in the late 1950s and early 1960s, one of the first "modern" digs which enabled unusually precise analysis of the successive human occupations – unless you're an archeology buff this may not seem hugely exciting, but the guide's explanations help sort out all the different eras mentioned at other sites.

The site is still being explored, but the most famous find so far is a female "Venus" figurine discovered in 1958. The small bas-relief, with her pendulous breasts and rounded belly, you see today is a copy. Archeologists also found six skeletons, including a young mother with her newborn baby and a pearl necklace; again, you see a copy here alongside a bronze statue modelled from her bone structure, while the original pearls are in Les Eyzies' national museum (see above). Look out, too, for the enchanting little ibex (*bouquetin*) carved on the museum's rock ceiling 17,000 years ago.

Fortified church of Tayac

If you're here in summer and feel the need to get a bit of space from the crowds on the main street, head down to the riverbank, where there's a nice picnic area and riverside path, or 500m past the railway station to the twelfth-century **fortified church** of Tayac. Nobody ever went to much effort to prettify it, but it's a forbidding defensive structure, with no steeples, but two broad parapets to give archers a proper shot at any attackers.

ARRIVAL AND DEPARTURE	**LES EYZIES-DE-TAYAC**
By train A stop on the Périgueux–Agen train line, Les Eyzies' *gare SNCF* lies about 500m northwest of the centre just off the main road before you cross the river.	Destinations Agen (2–5 daily; 1hr 40min); Belvès (2–5 daily; 30min); Le Bugue (2–7 daily; 7min); Le Buisson (2–7 daily; 15min); Périgueux (4–7 daily; 30–40min); Siorac-en-Périgord (2–5 daily; 30min).

GETTING AROUND

Taxis Taxi Tardieu (☎05.53.06.93.06).

Car rental You can rent cars at the tourist office through Avis (see p.26).

INFORMATION AND ACTIVITIES

Tourist office On the main road right in the town centre (April to mid-June Mon–Sat 9am–noon & 2–6pm, Sun 10am–noon & 2–5pm; mid-June to mid-Sept Mon–Sat 9am–7pm, Sun 10am–noon & 2–6pm; mid-Sept to Oct Mon–Sat 9am–noon & 2–6pm; Nov–March Mon–Fri 9am–noon & 2–6pm, Sat 10am–noon & 2–5pm; ☎05 53 06 97 05, ⓦtourisme-vezere.com). In addition to plentiful information on local sights and *chambres d'hôtes*, they also offer free wi-fi access, and there's a 24hr ATM outside.

Bike rental You can rent bikes at the tourist office (€20 per day). It's best to reserve in advance, particularly in high season.

Canoe rental Les Eyzies is the main base for canoeing trips on the Vézère. Three companies cluster around the bridge just north of the town centre from Easter to late September, depending on the weather: Canoës Vallée

Vézère (☎05 53 05 10 11, ⓦcanoesvalleevezere.com), AVCK (☎05 53 06 92 92, ⓦvezere-canoe.com) and Les 3 Drapeaux (☎05 53 06 91 89, ⓦcanoes-3drapeaux.fr). All operate by driving you upstream to Tursac (10km) or St-Léon (20km) to canoe back down to Les Eyzies. The Vézère is narrower and quieter than the Dordogne, cutting a thin channel between high cliffs and wooded banks. The scenery is perhaps less dramatic than the château-studded stretch of the Dordogne around Beynac (see p.157), but you do pass beneath several of the troglodytic forts and dwellings lining the valley.

Hiking The tourist office sells hiking maps of the area (€2.50) and gives out a leaflet describing the "Chemins de la Préhistoire", two hikes up the valley to Laugerie-Basse (8km round trip) and beyond to Le Madeleine (15km round trip). Along the route you'll find information panels in English.

ACCOMMODATION

While there are some great places to stay in Les Eyzies, they can be pricey, especially in high season, when it's better to stay out of the main centre or in one of the villages around. Note that most places close in winter, so it's wise to book ahead if you're visiting between October and April.

IN LES EYZIES

Le Cro-Magnon 54 av de la Préhistoire ☎05 53 06 97 06, ⓦhostellerie-cro-magnon.com. The *Cro-Magnon* is a sunny, inviting building with yellow shutters and vine-covered walls built into the cliff on the north side of town. Rooms are bright with all the necessary comforts and there are good communal areas, with open hearths, armchairs and a small library, as well as a pool. The restaurant serves one daily *menu* (€25) with a choice of seasonal dishes. Breakfast €10. Closed mid-Nov to mid-March. **€86**

Des Falaises 35 av de la Préhistoire ☎05 53 06 97 35, ⓦhotel_des_falaises.monsite-orange.fr. The best-value rooms in Les Eyzies are located behind a central café-bar run by a friendly owner. They're bright and cheerful, clean and well kept. All are en suite (though there's no TV) and the marginally more expensive ones (€42) on the back of the building have their own balconies. Breakfast €5. Open all year on reservation. **€38**

★ **La Ferme de Tayac** 14 rue de Tayac ☎05 53 06 04 61, ⓦfermedetayac.com. Though only 1km from Les Eyzies, this welcoming *chambre d'hôte* in twelfth-century buildings beside Tayac church is a real haven. The five beautifully appointed rooms and spacious communal areas are full of artistic touches, as are the flower-filled gardens. There's a pool and bikes you can borrow to ride into town. Three-night minimum stay required, though it's always worth checking. Price includes breakfast. Closed Nov–March. **€90**

★ **Les Glycines** 4 av de Laugerie ☎05 53 06 97 07, ⓦles-glycines-dordogne.com. Les Eyzies' most beguiling hotel by some distance stands on the main road just north of the centre. It's a romantic place, with light, airy rooms, full of drapes and frills, and a beautiful garden behind, criss-crossed by shady paths, with a swimming pool in the middle. The nicest rooms open directly onto the garden (€165). There are plans to open a spa centre and a bistro in addition to the main restaurant (see p.134). Breakfast €15. Closed mid-Oct to May, though is considering opening year round. **€115**

Hostellerie du Passeur Place de la Mairie ☎05 53 06 97 13, ⓦhostellerie-du-passeur.com. The vine-covered *Du Passeur* is in a prime spot right in the centre beside the tourist office, but set back from the road. The rooms are pleasant enough, many decked out in rich ochre hues, and have three-star comforts. Downstairs is a smart restaurant (lunch *menu* €17; eves €37–49; closed for lunch on Tues & Sat) with a super terrace by the river. Breakfast €13. Closed Nov–March. **€92**

★ **Le Moulin de la Beune** Rue du Moulin-Bas ☎05 53 06 94 33, ⓦmoulindelabeune.com. A pretty, converted mill building on the southern edge of Les Eyzies, this old-fashioned hotel has simple, spacious and well-priced rooms, some looking out onto its peaceful garden and the rushing stream. There is also a lovely restaurant, *Au Vieux Moulin* (see p.134), so it's well worth considering the half-board option. Breakfast €8. Closed Nov–March. **€64**

La Rivière 3 rte du Sorcier ☎ 05 53 06 97 14, ⓦ lariviereleseyzies.com. A good, inexpensive choice about 1km from Les Eyzies on the Périgueux road. There are just six unfussy rooms, all en suite, in a typical Périgord farmhouse with access to a pool, bar, laundry and a simple restaurant. There's also a well-tended, four-star campsite, which shares the same facilities as the hotel. Breakfast €9. Closed Nov–March. Camping €24, rooms €49

AROUND LES EYZIES-DE-TAYAC

La Grange du Mas Le Mas-de-Sireuil ☎ 05 53 29 66 07, ⓦ grange-du-mas.com. Welcoming *chambre d'hôte* with five simple rooms on a working farm just outside the village of Sireuil, 5km east of Les Eyzies. They only offer half-board, but it's good value, comprising produce from the farm and including drinks. There's also a pool and tennis court. Closed Oct–March. Half-board for two adults €104

Laborderie Tamniès ☎ 05 53 29 68 59, ⓦ hotel-laborderie.com. Perched 13km up the Beune valley, northeast of Les Eyzies, this geranium-decked hotel occupies four separate buildings, with a big choice of rooms – the best are those in the newer blocks with balconies or terraces overlooking the extensive garden and pool (from €66) – and a good restaurant (see below). Early booking is advisable in summer. Breakfast €9.80. Closed Nov–March. €64

EATING AND DRINKING

IN LES EYZIES

Au Coup de Silex 4 rue du Musée ☎ 05 53 05 14 29. This is one of the better non-hotel restaurants in Les Eyzies and makes a handy place for a pit-stop opposite the Musée National. It's open all day for drinks and ices, and also serves varied and well-priced meals, ranging from omelettes and salads to tiramisu with local strawberries. Efficient service and generous portions make it a popular spot, though its opening hours can be a bit erratic. Lunch *menus* from €12.90 and €19 in the evening. April–June & Sept–Oct Mon & Thurs–Sun 11.30am–2.30pm & 6.30–9.30pm, Tues 11.30am–2.30pm; July & Aug Mon–Fri & Sun 11.30am–2.30pm & 6.30–9.30pm, Sat 6.30–9.30pm.

Les Glycines ☎ 05 53 06 97 07, ⓦ les-glycines-dordogne.com. For a gastronomic treat try the restaurant at the hotel *Les Glycines* (see p.133). There is a strong emphasis on local and seasonal produce, including vegetables and salads from the hotel garden. The weekday lunch *menu* (Wed–Sat) at €28 offers excellent value for money, while dinner *menus* start at €55 – or you can splash out on the tremendous truffle *menu* at €95. Reservations highly recommended. Mon & Tues 7.30–9pm; Wed–Sun 12.15–1.30pm & 7.30–9pm; July & Aug daily 12.15–1.30pm & 7.30–9pm. Closed mid-Oct to May, though is considering opening year round.

★ **Au Vieux Moulin** ☎ 05 53 06 94 33, ⓦ moulindelabeune.com. One of Les Eyzies' best restaurants is the *Au Vieux Moulin*, attached to the *Moulin de la Beune* hotel (see p.133), where you can enjoy great dishes like foie gras ravioli or squab casserole (young pigeon) sitting either in the old-fashioned, stone-walled dining room, or outside in the garden where the tiny River Beune rushes past. The prices are great too, with full *menus* costing €19–48. Mon, Thurs, Fri & Sun noon–1.30pm & 7–8.30pm; Tues, Wed & Sat 7–8.30pm. Closed Nov–March.

AROUND LES EYZIES-DE-TAYAC

Auberge de Layotte Tursac ☎ 05 53 06 95 91, ⓦ aubergelayotte.com. It's worth searching out this rustic *auberge* lost in the middle of nowhere – signed off the D47 north of Les Eyzies, at the end of a dirt track – for a taste of old-style country cooking. Run by an extrovert and enthusiastic young couple, there's just one, five-course *menu* (€30 including drinks) offering such delights as nettle soup, home-cured hams, beef stew and walnut cake. Everything but the wine, bread and cheese is home-made. By reservation only. March–June & Sept–Dec Thurs–Sat noon–1pm & 7–8pm, Sun noon–1pm; July & Aug Tues–Sat noon–1pm & 7–8pm, Sun noon–1pm.

Laborderie Tamniès ☎ 05 53 29 68 59, ⓦ hotel-laborderie.com. This hotel restaurant is equally popular for its pretty country setting and its good-value *menu*, a cut above the standard local fare. Choose between Aquitaine sturgeon in truffle cream and duck breast laced with blackberry sauce, followed perhaps by iced walnut soufflé. *Menus* €20–48, or count on around €45–50 à la carte. April–Oct Mon–Wed 7–8.30pm, Thurs–Sun noon–1.30pm & 7–8.30pm.

Grotte de Font-de-Gaume

1hr guided visits daily except Sat: mid-May to mid-Sept 9.30am–5.30pm; mid-Sept to mid-May 9.30am–12.30pm & 2–5.30pm • €7.50, combined ticket with Grotte des Combarelles & Abri du Cap Blanc €21 • ☎ 05 53 06 86 00, ⓦ eyzies.monuments-nationaux.fr

Since they were first discovered in 1901, over two hundred Magdalenian-era (18,000–10,000 years old) polychrome paintings and engravings have been found in the narrow tunnel of the **Grotte de Font-de-Gaume**, just over a kilometre east of Les Eyzies along the D47 to Sarlat. In order to preserve them, only 96 people are allowed to enter the cave each day, in groups of twelve, and they may restrict the numbers even further.

OPPOSITE CAVE ART, LASCAUX II (SEE P.149)>

CAVE ART

Thousands of years ago early inhabitants of the Dordogne and Lot region created some of the most expressive and moving prehistoric paintings, engravings and reliefs seen anywhere in the world. While these stunning works of art lie scattered throughout the area, hidden deep within limestone caves and on cliff walls, by far the greatest concentration is in the **Vézère valley** in the heart of the Dordogne.

The **Cro-Magnon people** people who swept across Europe 40,000 or so years ago are responsible for the earliest cave art in the region. Named after a rock shelter near Les Fyzies, where the first skeletons were discovered, they were a nomadic people, who tracked herds of reindeer across what was then steppe, occasionally settling in riverside rock shelters under overhanging cliffs. They developed increasingly sophisticated tools using bone, ivory and antlers and later crafted ornaments such as necklaces. Some 20,000 years ago, the Cro-Magnon had honed their artistic skills sufficiently to depict supremely realistic animals on the walls of their rock shelters, by means of engraving and sculpting with flints or painting with dyes made from charcoal, manganese dioxide and red ochre.

Approximately 17,000 years ago, during what is now known as the **Magdalenian** period, named after another site in the Vézère valley, there was a real explosion in the quantity and level of sophistication of prehistoric art. It was prompted by the use of the tallow lamp, fuelled with reindeer fat, which allowed artists to penetrate deep within the limestone caves. They covered the walls of passages and cavern ceilings with hundreds of drawings, paintings and engravings. In some places artists used the natural contours of the rock to produce supremely realistic, almost 3-D representations of horses, bison and other animals. Some of the drawings are almost like caricatures, in which mammoths are portrayed by just a couple of lines. Occasional human figures also appear, most spectacularly in the Grotte du Sorcier (see p.141).

Why exactly did these cave-dwellers dedicate such skill and time to their art? It's a question that evokes endless debate. While it's likely that the significance of the caves was in some way spiritual, the exact nature of the relationship between Cro-Magnon people and their art remains opaque. Some scholars believe that the paintings and engravings were some form of **ritual practice** or **magic** to evoke a successful hunt, while others think they have a **shamanistic role**, with the animals advancing into the caves as into the afterlife.

You'll often hear guides at the sites lament the fact that we know so little, but perhaps the desire for categorical meaning misses the point – that the paintings and engravings reveal a desire to capture elusive, transcendent beauty – or in other words, "art for art's sake". Whatever the truth, not knowing certainly adds to the wonder and magic of these caves.

The cave mouth is no more than a fissure concealed by rocks and trees above a small, lush valley. Inside is a narrow twisting passage of irregular height over 100m long, where you quickly lose your bearings in the dark. The majority of the **paintings** depict bison, but also horses, mammoths, reindeer and wild cats, and many unexplained signs such as the so-called "**tectiforms**", comprising a very gently inclined, upside down "V" with vertical lines beneath.

The first painting you come to is a frieze of bison at about eye level: reddish-brown in colour, massive, full of movement and an almost palpable force. Further on, a horse stands with one hoof slightly raised, resting; another appears to be galloping or jumping, and, in a breathtakingly tender depiction, one reindeer gently licks another's nose.

But the most miraculous painting of all is a frieze of five bison discovered in 1966. The colour, remarkably sharp and vivid, is preserved by a protective layer of calcite. Shading under the belly and down the thighs is used to add volume with a sophistication that seems utterly modern.

Another panel consists of **superimposed drawings**, a fairly common phenomenon in cave-painting, sometimes the result of work by successive generations, but here an obviously deliberate technique: a reindeer in the foreground shares legs with a large bison to indicate perspective.

Grotte des Combarelles

1hr guided visits daily except Sat: mid-May to mid-Sept 9.30am–5.30pm; mid-Sept to mid-May 9.30am–12.30pm & 2–5.30pm • €7.50, combined ticket with Grotte de Font-de-Gaume & Abri du Cap Blanc €21 • Tickets available from Font-de-Gaume booking office (see box below) • ☎ 05 53 06 86 00, ⓦ eyzies.monuments-nationaux.fr

The myriad engravings of the **Grotte des Combarelles**, a short distance further along the D47 from Font-de-Gaume, were discovered a few days before the latter in 1901. Only five decorated caves had been discovered prior to this, and with the jury still out on primitive man's artistic abilities, they were an incredibly significant find. As with Font-de-Gaume, visitor numbers are restricted (there's a maximum of six people per tour) and booking is highly recommended, especially in peak season.

You make your way down a long, claustrophobic tunnel, stopping every now and then while the guide picks out a tiny selection of the six-hundred-plus **engravings** identified so far. It is a veritable Magdalenian menagerie: mostly horses, but also bison, reindeer, mammoths, rhinos, bears, ibex, aurochs and wild cats; stylized human figures and geometric symbols also feature.

A good deal of imagination is required to recognize some of the fainter outlines, often superimposed one upon another, while others are astounding in their simplicity and realistic treatment – among the finest are the heads of a horse and a lioness, where the dips and projections in the rock provide eyes, nostrils and even bone structure.

TICKETS FOR THE GROTTES DE FONT-DE-GAUME AND LES COMBARELLES

Because of the limit on visitor numbers allowed to enter the caves of Font-de-Gaume and des Combarelles, it is essential to book ahead by phone (☎ 05 53 06 86 00) or email (ⓔ fontdegaume@monuments-nationaux.fr) several weeks in advance at any time of year and as early as possible for July and August, especially for Font-de-Gaume. Tickets go on sale in January for the coming year. Note that you have to pay for your tickets by credit card at least 15 days in advance, including a €1.50 booking fee. If you haven't got a ticket, you can try queuing up at the ticket office first thing in the morning for one of the 50 tickets sold on the day, but you'll need to get there early.

Roc de Cazelle

Daily: March & Oct to mid-Nov 10am–6pm; April–June & Sept 10am–7pm; July & Aug 10am–8pm; mid-Nov to Feb 11am–5pm • €7 • ☎ 05 53 59 46 09, ⊛ rocdecazelle.com

Continue along the D47 for another couple of kilometres from the Grotte des Combarelles (see opposite)and you'll be greeted by mammoths roaring and the sound of people chipping flints at **Roc de Cazelle**, a theme park that reconstructs life 12,000 years ago. It's really best for children, but the imaginative design helps bring the surrounding caves to life. Various scenes – from hunting and gathering to painting and sculpting – are scattered around a wooded valley once occupied by prehistoric man, culminating in a real troglodyte fortress and a troglodyte farm that was inhabited up to the 1960s.

Abri du Cap Blanc

45min guided visits daily except Sat: mid-May to mid-Sept 9.30am–5.30pm; Sept 16–May 14 9.30am–12.30pm & 2–5.30pm • €7.50 • ☎ 05 53 06 86 00, ⊛ eyzies.monuments-nationaux.fr

Not a cave but a natural rock shelter, the **Abri du Cap Blanc** lies on a steep wooded hillside above the River Beune about 7km east of Les Eyzies; it's signed left off the D47 shortly after the Grotte des Combarelles. The shelter contains a superb **sculpted frieze** of horses and bison dating from the middle Magdalenian period (16,000–13,000 years ago), discovered in 1909 behind thick layers of sediment.

Unfortunately, the excavation was carried out in such a hurry that the frieze had been badly damaged before anyone realized it was there. Even so, it is quite remarkable, mainly for its scale – the middle horse, which closely resembles the wild Przewalski horse of Central Asia, is virtually life-size – but also the depth of some of the sculptures. The bodies were obviously polished to set them off against the rough background, while traces of ochre and manganese pigments indicate that they were also painted at one time.

Château de Commarque

Daily: April 10am–6pm; May, June & Sept 10am–7pm; July & Aug 10am–8pm • €6.50 • ☎ 05 53 59 00 25, ⊛ commarque.com

Continuing up the Beune valley from Abri du Cap Blanc (see above) you come to the elegant sixteenth-century Château de Laussel (closed to the public) and, on the opposite side, the romantic ruins of the **Château de Commarque**. Dating from the twelfth century, Commarque was a **castrum** – a fortified village made up of six separate fortresses, each belonging to a different noble family, of which the best preserved is that built by the powerful Beynac clan in the fourteenth century. The site was abandoned some 200 years later, then left to moulder until the late 1960s when the present owner, Hubert de Commarque, came to the rescue.

The ruins have now been made structurally sound and it's possible once again to climb the Beynac's 30m-high tower for views over the surrounding countryside. In summer, the site makes a spectacular setting for concerts, plays and other events.

To reach Commarque, cars have to approach from the south, following signs from the D47 Sarlat road. Note that it's about a 600m walk from the car park to the entrance, though anyone with reduced mobility can drive down to the site.

Grotte du Grand Roc

40min guided visits: Feb–Easter & mid-Nov to end Dec Mon–Thurs & Sun 10am–noon & 2–5pm; Easter–June & Sept to mid-Nov daily 10am–6pm; July & Aug daily 10am–7pm • €7.20, combined ticket with Laugerie Basse €9.50 • ☎ 05 53 06 92 70, ⊛ semitour.com

Two kilometres north of Les Eyzies on the D47 to Périgueux, the entrance to the **Grotte du Grand Roc** lies under the cliffs that line much of the Vézère valley. There's a great view from the mouth of the cave, which was discovered in 1924 in the continuing search for prehistoric art. Instead, they found a fantastic array of **rock formations** along some 80m of tunnel. Most unusual are the still-unexplained *excentriques* growing in all directions, and triangles formed by calcite crystallizing in still, shallow pools.

Abri de Laugerie Basse

Feb–Easter & mid-Nov to end Dec Mon–Thurs & Sun 10am–noon & 2–5pm; Easter–June & Sept to mid-Nov daily 10am–6pm; July & Aug daily 10am–7pm • €6.20, combined ticket with Grotte du Grand Roc €9.50 • ☎ 05 53 06 92 70

Sixty years before the discovery of the Grotte de Grand Roc, Edouard Lartet and Henry Christy had identified a rock shelter further along the same cliff. The **Abri de Laugerie Basse** was inhabited almost constantly over the last 15,000 years – most recently in the form of farmhouses built against the rock – and yielded hundreds of **engravings** and **sculptures**, not on the rock face but on pieces of bone or fashioned out of individual stones. The majority date from the late Magdalenian period (13,000–10,000 years ago) when prehistoric art reached its peak.

They include a mysterious engraving of a very pregnant woman lying under a reindeer, and a sculpted female torso, the first so-called "Venus figure" – obviously symbols of fertility, though it's not known whether they relate to fertility rites – discovered in France. These and other important finds are presented in a short film before visiting the shelter; there's little to see otherwise, though during the visit you learn a lot about the history of the excavations and what conditions were like during the Magdalenian era.

Abri du Poisson

1hr guided visits daily except Sat, by appointment only via the Font-de-Gaume ticket office (see box, p.136), or by phone or email • €3 • ☎ 05 53 06 86 00, ✉ fontdegaume@monuments-nationaux.fr

More interesting than the Abri de Laugerie Basse is the **Abri du Poisson**, which lies on the road from Les Eyzies just before the Grotte du Grand Roc. The rock shelter – one of many along a side valley – contains one of the very few sculpted fish in prehistoric art. It's a real beauty too, a metre-long male salmon, complete with gills and beak, probably carved about 25,000 years ago. The deep-cut rectangular outline is not a prehistoric picture-frame, however, but the remains of an abortive attempt by a Berlin museum to acquire the salmon soon after it was discovered in 1912. Since then the shelter has been kept sealed up and can now be visited by a maximum of twenty people per day.

Grotte de Rouffignac

1hr guided visits daily: April–June, Sept & Oct 10–11.30am & 2–5pm; July & Aug 9–11.30am & 2–6pm • €6.50, English-language audio guide €1.50 • ☎ 05 53 05 41 71, ⊕ www.grottederouffignac.fr

Soon after Grand Roc, the D47 turns northwest to follow the Manaurie valley. Seven kilometres beyond the village of **Manaurie**, you'll pass a right turn signed to the **Grotte de Rouffignac**, another 7km uphill among dense woods.

The visit starts with a 1km ride on a little electric train along the bed of an underground river that dried up about three million years ago. On the way the guide points out where hibernating bears scratched their nests and human visitors left their mark in the form of graffiti – including a priest, Abbé de la Tour, in 1808. In fact records show that the cave was known about in the sixteenth century, but it took until 1956 before the 13,000-year-old monochromatic drawings and engravings were recognized.

Over 260 animal figures have been identified so far, the vast majority of which are mammoths, including a superb patriarch, his great tusks arcing under a piercing eye. Most dramatic is the final chamber, when you descend from the train to wander around beneath a ceiling covered with mammoths, woolly rhinos, horses, bison and ibex. When these drawings were done, the cave here was less than a metre high – proof that the authors were prepared to suffer for their art, and of their mysterious obsession with penetrating as deep into these caves as possible.

Rouffignac

The Grotte de Rouffignac is located about 5km south of **ROUFFIGNAC** town, which was destroyed by German troops in 1944 and subsequently rebuilt. They drove everyone out before torching it; the only buildings to survive were the church, with its carved portal and unusual, twisted columns inside, and the adjacent house.

Château de l'Herm

April, May & July–Sept daily 10am–7pm • €6 • ☎ 05 53 05 46 61, ⓦ chateaudelherm.com

Four kilometres north of Rouffignac town, the **Château de l'Herm** also has an unhappy history, in this case a complicated tale of murders, forced marriages and disputed inheritance rights. In the end the castle was abandoned and left to crumble away for more than three centuries to leave an atmospheric ruin engulfed by trees. Since 2000, however, a massive restoration project is under way, initially to protect the existing structure from further decay.

Two big round towers and some decorative touches from the fifteenth and sixteenth centuries remain: a late Gothic doorway opens onto a spiral stone staircase, at the top of which is a beautifully worked palm-tree vault, while three sculpted fireplaces cling one above the other to the wall of an otherwise empty shell. At the bottom of the keep, you can still distinguish the castle's grim-looking dungeons. It was these evocative ruins, looking out over the thickly wooded country where rural rebels thrived, which inspired Eugène Le Roy for his novel *Jacquou le Croquant* (see p.304), in which a nineteenth-century rebellion culminates in the Château de l'Herm being burned to the ground.

Le Bugue and around

LE BUGUE lies on the north bank of a meander in the Vézère 11km downstream from Les Eyzies, and is a good alternative base. It's not only less crowded in season but is also a more attractive town, with a riverfront setting and scattering of old houses along the River Doux, which flows into the Vézère here. On Tuesdays and Saturdays, the town comes alive with one of the better markets in the area.

The heart of Le Bugue is place de la Mairie, the town centre and market square, from where there are good views in both directions along the river. From here, rue de Paris, the main shopping street, heads north towards Le Bugue's old quarter around the generously named Grande Rue, while the D703, heading southeast along the river, takes you out past the town's two rather second-tier sights.

Village du Bournat

Daily: April–June & Sept 10am–6pm; July & Aug 10am–7pm • €12.90 • ☎ 05 53 08 41 99, ⓦ lebournat.fr

The more interesting of Le Bugue's two sights, particularly for younger children, is the **Village du Bournat**. This is a fair recreation of a Périgord village in the early 1900s complete with *lauze*-roofed cottages, chapel, schoolhouse, baker, flour-mill, fairground rides and so forth. The entry price seems expensive, but there's a lot to see, including demonstrations of local crafts, such as clog- and barrel-making, potting and basketry, and you can come and go as you please within a day. There's also a restaurant and snack bar on site.

Aquarium du Périgord Noir

Mid-Feb to March & Oct to mid-Nov Mon–Sat 2–6pm, Sun 10am–6pm; April, May & Sept daily 10am–6pm; June daily 10am–7pm; July & Aug daily 9am–7pm • €10.90 • ☎ 05 53 07 10 74, ⓦ aquariumperigordnoir.com

Next door to the Village du Bournat, the **Aquarium du Périgord Noir** has a large collection of freshwater fish – kept for the most part in open tanks, some of which you can walk under. At set times each day you can watch – and children can assist with – the feeding of the more benign species. The aquarium also has a collection of caimans and an indoor reptile zone, full of coils of snakes and bored-looking iguanas.

ARRIVAL AND DEPARTURE	LE BUGUE

By train Trains on the Périgueux–Agen line pull into Le Bugue's *gare SNCF*, roughly 2km southeast on the D703; call Taxis Sourbier (☎ 05 53 07 41 35) if you need a taxi. Note that the station is unstaffed, so you'll need to buy your tickets on the train.

Destinations Agen (3–6 daily; 1hr 30min); Belvès (3–6 daily; 25min); Le Buisson (3–7 daily; 8min); Les Eyzies (4–7 daily; 7min); Périgueux (4–7 daily; 45min); Siorac-en-Périgord (3–6 daily; 20min).

INFORMATION AND ACTIVITIES

Tourist office On the riverbank a short walk west of place de la Mairie along rue du Jardin-Public (April to mid-June Mon–Sat 9.30am–12.30pm & 2–6pm, Sun 10am–noon & 2–5pm; mid-June to mid-Sept Mon–Sat 9.30am–1pm & 2–6.30pm, Sun 10am–1pm & 2–5pm; mid-Sept to mid-Nov Mon–Fri 9.30am–12.30pm & 2–6pm, Sat 10am–noon & 2–5pm; mid-Nov to March Tues–Fri 9.30am–12.30pm & 2–6pm, Sat 10am–noon & 2–5pm; ☎ 05 53 07 20 48, ⊛ tourisme-vezere.com).

Canoe rental Canoëric (☎ 05 53 03 51 99, ⊛ canoe -perigord.com), beside the Village du Bournat.

ACCOMMODATION

IN LE BUGUE

Le Cygne 2 rue du Cingle ☎ 05 53 06 01 16, ⊛ lecygne -perigord.com. Though it's on the main road, the nicest hotel in Le Bugue is this friendly, good-value place opposite the tourist office. It offers comfortable, bright and spacious rooms, most of them with double-glazed windows. There's also an excellent restaurant (see below). Breakfast €8.50. Closed mid-Dec to mid-Jan. **€53**

Le Royal Vézère Place de l'Hôtel-de-Ville ☎ 05 53 07 20 01, ⊛ hotel-royal-vezere.com. Once Le Bugue's grandest hotel, this three-star occupies a prime position on the river right in the town centre. Its other main draws are a roof-top swimming pool and recommended restaurant (see below). Cheaper rooms face onto the road (€55) or the square (€70), but it's worth upgrading to one with river views (€85). And ask for a renovated room, too; the rest are showing their age. Garage €7. Breakfast €9.50. Closed mid-Oct to March. **€55**

Les Trois Caupain Le Port ☎ 05 53 07 24 60, ⊛ camping-des-trois-caupain.com. A welcoming and well-equipped three-star campsite located on the riverbank 1km east of town. Among its facilities, it boasts two pools, one of them heated, and a bar-restaurant in season (mid-April to mid-Sept). Closed Nov–March. **€19**

Vézère Lodge 10 rte de Campagne ☎ 05 53 09 58 05, ⊛ vezere-lodge.com. Set slightly back from the D703 1.5km southeast of Le Bugue, this is a cheap-and-cheerful option run by a friendly young couple. It has just six simple en-suite rooms, a pool and a decent restaurant (*menus* from €15; closed Mon, Tues & Wed lunchtime). Breakfast €7. Closed Oct to mid-March. **€39**

AROUND LE BUGUE

★ **L'Auberge Médiévale** Audrix ☎ 05 53 07 24 02, ⊛ auberge-medievale.fr. In the tiny, picturesque hamlet of Audrix, 6km from Le Bugue past the Gouffre de Proumeyssac, is this hidden gem of a traditional country hotel. With its eight simple but pretty rooms, all with en-suite facilities and views either of the Romanesque church or the valley below, it really is one of the most peaceful and idyllic spots in the region. Breakfast €7. Closed Nov to mid-March. **€45**

Brin d'Amour St-Cirq ☎ 05 53 07 23 73, ⊛ brindamourcamping.com. Up in the hills north of St-Cirq, midway between Le Bugue and Les Eyzies, this three-star campsite is an excellent choice if you've got your own transport: small, friendly, well-run and lacking the regimented feel of so many sites. Facilities include a heated pool, tennis court, grocery store (April–Sept) and restaurant (July & Aug). Closed mid-Oct to Easter. **€19.50**

La Maison Oléa La Combe-de-Leygue ☎ 05 53 08 48 93, ⊛ olea-dordogne.com. Two kilometres out of town, signed off the D703 to Sarlat, this *chambre d'hôte* has three pretty rooms and two suites for families. Four have private balconies with good views of the surrounding countryside (from €105), and there's a heated salt-water swimming pool. Breakfast included. Closed mid-Dec to mid-Jan. **€95**

EATING AND DRINKING

IN LE BUGUE

Le Cygne 2 rue du Cingle ☎ 05 53 06 01 16, ⊛ lecygne -perigord.com. While this hotel-restaurant is lacking in atmosphere, it serves decent food, with a choice of regional *menus* (weekday lunch €16, eves and weekends €25) or the "Menu du Cygne" if you want a change from foie gras and duck (€32). Alternatively, you can eat from the limited *carte*. Mid-Jan to mid-Dec Tues–Sat noon–1.30pm & 7.30–9pm, Sun noon–1.30pm.

Le Pha 25 rue du Jardin-Public ☎ 05 53 08 96 96, ⊛ lepha.fr. In fine weather, get here early or phone ahead to reserve a table overlooking the river at this friendly little place beside the tourist office. It serves an unusual mix of Asian and French dishes: everything from the regular *magret* (duck breast) and local salads to duck with pineapple, beef and ginger soup or *banh bao* (Vietnamese steamed dumplings). *Menus* €15–28. Daily: Feb–June & Sept to mid-Dec noon–1.30pm & 6.30–8.15pm; July & Aug noon–2.30pm & 6.30–9.30pm. Closed one day a week off-season.

Le Royal Vézère Place de l'Hôtel-de-Ville ☎ 05 53 07 20 01, ⊛ hotel-royal-vezere.com. The restaurant at the *Royal Vézère* hotel is in a prime position in the town centre with a terrace jutting out over the river. It offers nicely presented traditional cuisine on a wide choice of *menus* (€18–37) or expect to pay around €30–45 à la carte. April to mid-Oct daily noon–2pm & 7–9pm; Closes two days a week in April and may close one or two weekday lunchtimes from May to mid-Oct.

AROUND LE BUGUE

Du Château Campagne ☎05 53 07 23 50, ⓦhotelcampagne24.fr. If you're looking for somewhere to eat between Le Bugue and Les Eyzies, try this traditional hotel-restaurant in the attractive village of Campagne. You can opt for the bistro (Mon–Sat noon–2pm; *menu* at €12), or the more formal restaurant (*menus* €22–39) serving Périgordin cuisine, plus a choice of fish dishes. Easter to mid-Oct daily noon–2pm & 7–9.30.

★**La Vieille Treille** Audrix ☎05 53 07 24 02,

ⓦauberge-medievale.fr. The restaurant of Audrix's charming hotel (see opposite) serves delicious and well-priced regional cuisine from a broad range of *menus* of four-to-five courses from €14.50 to €30. House specialities include warm Camembert cheese with truffles and langoustine raviolis. In summer you can sit out in the shade of a vine-draped trellis. Mid-March to June, Sept & Oct daily except Wed noon–2pm & 7–9pm; July & Aug daily noon–7pm & 7–9pm.

Gouffre de Proumeyssac

45min guided visits daily: Feb, Nov & Dec 2–5pm; March & mid-Sept to end Oct 9.30am–noon & 2–5.30pm; April–June & Sept 1–15 9.30am–6pm; July & Aug 9am–7pm • €9.30; €17.50 descent in basket; €0.90 per audio guide • ☎ 05 53 07 27 47, or ☎ 05 53 07 85 85 for reservations, ⓦ gouffre-proumeyssac.com • In July & Aug reserve well in advance by phone or internet to save queuing. To descend in the basket, phone ahead at any time of the year (internet reservations not accepted)

High-tech has hit the Vézère in a big way at the **Gouffre de Proumeyssac**, a vast and spectacular limestone cave 5km south of Le Bugue on the D31E2. Its 40m-high vault dripping with multicoloured stalactites, ranging from fine needles to massive petrified waterfalls, is dubbed the "crystal cathedral". To heighten the sense of atmosphere you enter in the dark, then the music builds as lights pick out various formations before revealing the whole chamber in a grand finale.

It's cleverly done, though some will find it too commercialized, even down to stacks of calcite-coated pottery souvenirs, and a far cry from when the cave was first opened in 1907. At that time the only way in was via a basket lowered through a hole in the roof under flickering torchlight – you can still make the descent by eleven-person basket, which rotates as it makes its way down.

Even before the chasm was fully explored and its size and beauty discovered, it had a gruesome notoriety in local folklore: it gets a mention in Eugène Le Roy's 1899 work *Jacquou le Croquant* as the "*Trou de Pomeissac*" near Le Bugue, into which so many people had been thrown after being murdered on the neighbouring highway, that the hole had to be blocked up..."

Grotte du Sorcier

30min guided visits daily: April & Sept to mid-Nov 10am–6pm; May & June 10am–6.30pm; July & Aug 10am–7.30pm • €6.50 • ☎ 05 53 07 14 37, ⓦ grottedusorcier.com

If you take the D703 south from Le Bugue and turn left down a quiet back road just before crossing the train line, you eventually come to the village of **St-Cirq**, halfway to Les Eyzies. St-Cirq is known above all for the **Grotte du Sorcier**, a shallow cave with some thirty engravings dating from between 17,000 and 19,000 years ago.

The majority of engravings depict animals (look at the tremendous image of the horse turning its head back towards the entrance), but the most significant is the "Sorcerer" himself, a rare image of a human being in Magdalenian cave art. The enigmatic figure has been interpreted in countless ways: as a fertility symbol, half man and half pregnant woman; as a shaman or spiritual leader, with his musical instrument and dancing legs; or indeed as a man's head with the body of a horse. However you choose to see him, he makes a fascinating counterpoint to the supremely realistic animals you see elsewhere: the Sorcerer is compelling evidence of ancient cave art's figurative or metaphorical purpose.

After the guided tour of the cave, have a quick look around the site's **museum**, a collection of blades and fossils dating from different eras in which it was occupied. Then, if you're feeling athletic, climb up to explore the vestiges of a **medieval fortress** and look-out posts in the rock face beyond the museum.

3

The Vézère between Les Eyzies and Montignac

To the northeast of Les Eyzies, the D706 follows the River Vézère all the way to Montignac, taking you past a range of sights appealing to all ages, from the rock-shelters of **La Madeleine** and **La Roque St-Christophe** to the Renaissance splendour of the **Château de Losse** and **Le Thot**, a wildlife park with a prehistoric theme. On the way, you'll pass the prettiest village in the whole valley – **St-Léon-sur-Vézère**.

Tursac

The village of **Tursac** sits astride the main road 5km upstream from Les Eyzies. Though there's nothing remarkable to see here, it boasts a recommended restaurant and makes a good base for campers exploring this stretch of valley.

ACCOMMODATION AND EATING TURSAC

La Ferme du Pelou ☎ 05 53 06 98 17, ��laferme dupelou.com. Of the two good campsites near Tursac, this two-star site signed off the D706 to the south of the village is the more basic but spectacularly located, perched on the hilltop overlooking La Madeleine (see below) and its meander from the east. Pitches are spacious, grouped around an old Périgordin farmhouse with chickens running around amid the flowers. There are two pools and lots of walks around. No internet access. Closed mid-Nov to mid-March. **€12**

★ **La Source** ☎ 05 53 06 98 00, ⓦrestaurant-la-source .fr. Tursac's central square, just off the main road, is home to this well-regarded restaurant with a pleasant garden and imaginative daily specials, including home-smoked fish and

duck breast and produce from their organic garden. There's a two-course *menu* at €18.50, three courses at €22.50 and a popular four-course *menu surprise* at €24.50. They'll also provide vegetarian options if you phone a day ahead. Reservations recommended. March–June & Sept–Dec Mon & Thurs–Sun noon–2pm & 7–9pm; July & Aug daily except Wed noon–2pm & 7–9pm.

Le Vézère Périgord ☎ 05 53 06 96 31, ⓦlevezere perigord.com. North of Tursac, this is a well-run, spacious and good-value campsite set back from the main road among trees. Facilities include a decent-sized pool with water slides, tennis court and fitness room. There's also a bar, restaurant and grocery store in season (May–Sept). Closed mid-Nov to Easter. **€20**

La Madeleine

Daily: Easter–June, Sept & Oct 10am–6pm; July & Aug 10am–8pm; Nov–Easter 11am–5pm • €6 • ☎ 05 53 46 36 88, ⓦla-madeleine -perigord.com

On the far side of the river from Tursac, 3km by road, is the semi-troglodytic medieval settlement of **La Madeleine**. It lies near the neck of a huge meander, where the Vézère takes a 3km loop to cover less than 100m as the crow flies.

The cliffs here have been inhabited on and off for the last 15,000 years. Indeed, the prehistoric rock shelter down by the water's edge yielded such a wealth of late-Paleolithic tools and engravings that archeologists named the period Magdalenian; one of the more intriguing finds was a carving of a man with a bestial head, believed to be a mask, now on display at Les Eyzies' museum (see p.132). There's a copy here, too, along with copies of other important finds, such as a bison with its finely engraved head looking back over a powerful shoulder.

Further up the cliff subsequent settlers constructed a whole village complete with fortress, drawbridge, village square and chapel, all dating back to the tenth century. La Madeleine was inhabited until 1920, and the Resistance (see p.300) used it as a hideout, but now the chapel is the only building completely intact. Nevertheless, enough remains to give a good sense of what such cliff-dwellings were like.

Préhisto-parc

Daily: Feb, March, Oct & Nov 10am–5.30pm; April–June & Sept 10am–6.30pm; July & Aug 10am–7.30pm • €6.80 • ☎ 05 53 50 73 19, ⓦ prehistoparc.fr

Plastic Neanderthals hunting mock mammoths to an accompanying soundtrack won't be everyone's cup of tea, but the **Préhisto-parc**, just beyond the turning to La Madeleine on the D706, is another attempt to recreate the daily life of prehistoric man. If you've already visited the more varied Roc de Cazelle (see p.137), you can give this a miss, but otherwise it's fun to take in, especially if you've got children in tow. A woodland walk takes you past tableaux of encampments, people making flints, painting, sculpting and generally being busy in a prehistoric sort of way.

Maison Forte de Reignac

Daily: Feb, March, Oct, Nov & during Christmas school hols 10am–6pm; April 10am–6.30pm; May, June & Sept 10am–7pm; July & Aug 10am–8pm • €7 • ☎ 05 53 50 69 54, ⓦ maison-forte-reignac.com

Next door to the Préhisto-parc (see opposite), the cliffs were occupied throughout the Middle Ages and into the twentieth century at the Maison Forte de Reignac, a fortified, semi-troglodytic feudal residence whose knights owed allegiance to the superior lord at St-Christophe (see below). It presents an intriguing combination of primitive cave-dwelling (some of the rooms occupy the old rock shelters) and medieval opulence.

The three storeys of the house are furnished with items from different periods of its occupation and contain interesting displays on the feudal system (pick up the English leaflet at the entrance for full translations). The most interesting rooms are the grand reception room on the ground floor, with its authentic *pisé* floor, monolithic washbasin and smoking wood fire, and the last room you see, the former bedroom of the countess of Reignac, which is very elegantly furnished. Above the house, you can climb to higher rock shelters to appreciate the defensive nature of the site, and admire the views along the valley. The visit ends with rather a gruesome display of instruments of torture and punishment.

La Roque St-Christophe

Daily: Jan 2–5pm; Feb, March & Oct to mid-Nov 10am–6pm; April–June & Sept 10am–6.30pm; July & Aug 10am–8pm; mid-Nov to Dec 10am–5.30pm • €7.80 • ☎ 05 53 50 70 45, ⓦ roque-st-christophe.com

The enormous natural refuge of **La Roque St-Christophe**, 3km upriver from Tursac, is made up of about one hundred **rock shelters** on five levels hollowed out of the limestone cliffs. The whole complex is nearly 1km long and up to 80m above ground level, where the River Vézère once flowed.

The earliest traces of occupation go back over 50,000 years, although permanent settlement dates from around the ninth century when the site's natural defences really came into their own. At its peak during the Middle Ages, the settlement had grown into a veritable town clinging to the rock face – with its own marketplace, church, prison, abattoir, baker and artisans' workshops – and was able to shelter over one thousand people in times of trouble. And there was no shortage of those, culminating in the Wars of Religion when Protestant sympathizers took refuge here. After they were kicked out in 1588, Henri III ordered the town and fortress demolished – which means you need a good imagination to recreate the scene from the various nooks and crannies hacked into the rock.

In summer, there are frequent **guided visits** (in French only). Although instructive they can get a bit tedious – better to take one of their English-language leaflets and wander at your own pace.

St-Léon-sur-Vézère and around

ST-LÉON-SUR-VÉZÈRE, 6km above Tursac, is by far the most attractive village along the whole Vézère valley. It sits off the main road in a quiet bend of the river guarded by two châteaux – one topped by a fairy-tale array of turrets – and boasts one of the region's most harmonious Romanesque churches. In summer the church serves as one of the principal venues, along with St-Amand-de-Coly (see p.150), for classical music concerts during the **Festival du Périgord Noir** (see box, p.121). For the best views of the village, walk over the iron-girder bridge and turn left along a footpath on the opposite bank.

3

Le Conquil

Daily: April–June 10am–6pm; July & Aug 10am–7.30pm; Sept & Oct 2–5pm • €7.80 • Includes tree-top adventure course: children (under 1m 10cm) €11, junior (1m 10cm to 1m 40cm) €14, adult (over 1m 40cm) €19 • ⓦ parc-aux-dinosaures.com

If you head up the hill on the far side of the bridge from St-Léon, you come to **Le Conquil**, an attraction largely aimed at families with its "dinosaur park" and a nicely situated tree-top obstacle course, with **zip-wires** running along the bank of the Vézère. It also includes a series of shallow **troglodytic shelters**, the most interesting of which contains dozens of niches in the rock, used for housing pigeons in the Middle Ages. Otherwise the caves don't have much to see, but children might enjoy wandering through the woods trying to spot the full-size model dinosaurs and other animals lurking in the trees, before you get up to the clifftop belvedere. Overall, Le Conquil can't really compare to some of the other attractions in the valley, but it's a good bet if you're after something of interest to suit all ages.

ARRIVAL AND DEPARTURE   ST-LÉON-SUR-VÉZÈRE

By bus Buses from Terrasson via Montignac stop near the campsite at the entrance to St-Léon.
Destinations Montignac (Mon–Fri 1 daily during school term only; 25min); Terrasson (Mon–Fri 1 daily during school term only; 1hr).

INFORMATION AND ACTIVITIES

Tourist office In summer a tourist office opens opposite the campsite at the entrance to St-Léon (May, June & Sept Tues–Sat 10am–noon & 4–6pm; July & Aug Tues–Sun 10am–1pm & 2–7pm; ☎ 05 53 51 08 42, ⓦ saint-leon-sur-vezere.com). It offers a computer for internet access (€1 for 15min).

Canoe rental APA (☎ 05 53 50 67 71, ⓦ canoevezere .com), by the bridge in St-Léon from Easter to mid-November depending on the weather. A popular option is to do the whole descent in two days: Montignac to St-Léon and then St-Léon to Les Eyzies.

ACCOMMODATION AND EATING

IN ST-LÉON-SUR-VÉZÈRE

Auberge du Pont ☎ 05 53 50 73 07. A lovely wisteria-covered restaurant with a shady summer terrace beside the bridge. It serves a wide choice of dishes in generous portions, including fresh salads, local trout, Limousin beef and a selection of vegetarian options. It also serves wood-fired pizzas and a wicked array of home-made ice creams and sorbets. *Menus* start at €15 at lunchtime and €20 in the evening. Mid-March to mid-Nov & school hols Mon & Thurs–Sun noon–2.30pm & 7–9pm, Tues &Wed noon–2.30pm.

★ **Déjeuner sur l'Herbe** ☎ 05 53 50 69 17. Tucked down beside the church you'll find this tiny shop selling top-notch local produce to eat at picnic tables along the riverbank or to take away. A platter of cheese or charcuterie, for example, with a hunk of country bread, costs around €12.50 and a salad €7, while an open toasted sandwich comes in at €9.50. To round things off, try a slice of walnut cake (€3). March–June & Sept–Nov Mon–Fri & Sun 10.30am–6.30pm; July & Aug daily 9am–9pm.

Municipal campsite ☎ 05 53 51 08 42 or ☎ 05 53 50 7316. St-Léon's small municipal campsite, with just 26 pitches, is right on the river beside the bridge. There are no frills, but it is beautifully quiet and well maintained. No wi-fi, but you can use the computer at the tourist office (see above), which doubles as the campsite reception. May–Sept. €9

Le Paradis ☎ 05 53 50 72 64, ⓦ le-paradis.fr. Excellent five-star campsite 3km south of St-Léon on the D706, where thick hedges separate the pitches. Facilities include three nicely designed pools, with plans for a fourth, set among luxuriant vegetation; a restaurant, bar and shop; wi-fi (€5 for 3hr); and a communal herb garden. You can rent bikes and canoes here and they also organize canoe trips. Not surprisingly, you need to book early for the summer season. April–Oct. €29

AROUND ST-LÉON-SUR-VÉZÈRE

Auberge de Castel-Merle Sergeac ☎ 05 53 50 70 08, ⓦ hotelcastelmerle.com. A handsome country inn perched on the hill above the prehistoric rock shelters at Sergeac (see p.146) and still run by the descendants of Marcel Castanet, who first excavated the site. The rooms are cheerful, but its main attribute is its clifftop terrace where on fine evenings you can eat dinner – traditional, home cooking – overlooking the Vézère (*menus* from €17; daily except Sun; restaurant open to residents only). The friendly, English-speaking owners can also provide a wealth of information about the area. Price includes breakfast. Closed Oct–March. €73

CLOCKWISE FROM TOP THE DOMME VALLEY (P.163); SARLAT MARKET (P.121); LA ROQUE-ST-CHRISTOPHE (P.143)>

L'Auberge du Peyrol Sergeac ☎05 53 50 72 91. Also known as "Chez Jeannine", this *auberge* just north of Sergeac, about 6km from St-Léon, is popular for its consistently good country cooking served in attractive, rustic surroundings or under the trees in summer. It's not expensive either, with lunch *menus* starting at €14 and €18 in the evenings. You could try foie gras lightly fried with apples, venison terrine or *anchaud de porc confit* (rolled pork joint with herbs cooked slowly in goose fat). Credit cards not accepted. Reservation recommended. March–June & Sept–Dec Tues–Thurs & Sun 12.30–2pm, Fri & Sat 12.30–2pm & 7.30–9pm; July & Aug Mon 7.30–9pm, Tues–Sun 12.30–2pm & 7.30–9pm.

Castel-Merle

Sergeac • Guided tours: mid-April to Sept daily except Sat 10–6pm • €6.50 • ☎05 53 50 79 70, ⊛castel-merle.com

Southeast across the Vézère from St-Léon, just beyond the village of **SERGEAC**, the rock shelters of **Castel-Merle** are unusual in that excavation activities are still going on here, carried out by a joint Franco-American team. If you're lucky, you can watch them at work in June and July. The site has yielded a terrific number of flints, bones and beads over the years, including a necklace of shells from the Atlantic, presumably obtained by trade. In 2007, the teams also discovered the earliest evidence so far of mural wall art, a series of animal engravings dating from around 37,000 years ago, during the early Aurignacian period.

Descendants of Marcel Castanet, who first excavated the site, take you on a fascinating guided tour (thorough English-language booklet available) visiting five of the ten shelters. Only one of these still contains any **cave art**, including three rather poorly preserved bison sculptures, but you learn a lot about the history and significance of the site, and the lives of the people who once lived here. You can also try throwing a spear using a prehistoric propelling device – it's not easy.

Château de Losse

Thonac • 40min guided visits daily: May–Sept daily except Sat noon–6pm • €9 • ☎05 53 50 80 08, ⊛chateaudelosse.com

Of several castles along the Vézère valley, the Renaissance **Château de Losse** stands out as the most striking. It occupies a rocky bluff 4km upstream from St-Léon on the main D706, though the best views are from the opposite bank, where the D65 provides a quiet and picturesque back road from St-Léon to Montignac (see opposite).

The present castle was constructed in the 1570s by Jean II de Losse, royal tutor and the governor of Guyenne, on medieval foundations. It has changed little since then, a well-proportioned L-shaped building surrounded by dry moats and watchtowers. Inside, the château's present owners have established an impressive collection of sixteenth- and seventeenth-century **furniture** and **tapestries**. Among the latter, the Florentine *Return of the Courtesan* is particularly successful in its use of perspective, while the colours of this and the Flemish rendition of knights preparing for a tournament remain exceptionally vibrant. There's also a rare, tulip-decorated tapestry dating from around the time of the Dutch tulipomania in 1634, when tulips cost more than gold.

On your way out, note the inscription over the unusually imposing gatehouse which quotes one of Jean II's favourite maxims: "When I thought the end was in sight, I was only beginning." His perhaps jaundiced view is forgivable – of his five sons, four were killed in war and the fifth had no heirs to inherit the family estates. After the tour you are free to wander the beautifully tended gardens, including beds of lavender and rosemary and a charming little "knot garden".

Le Thot

Thonac • Feb to mid-April, Nov & Dec Tues–Sun 10am–12.30pm & 2–5.30pm; mid-April to June, Sept & Oct daily 10am–6pm; July & Aug daily 10am–7pm; • €7.20, or €13.40 combined ticket with Lascaux II (see p.149) • ☎05 53 50 70 44, ⊛semitour.com

It's back to prehistory at **Le Thot**, 1km into the hills west of the Château de Losse. The combined museum and animal park focuses on prehistoric art, not only the technical aspects but also some of the **wildlife** that provided inspiration: Przewalski horses with their erect manes, ibex, deer and European bison are all resident here. You'll also see **aurochs**, though these primitive wild cattle really died out in the 1600s – the beasts here are a close approximation achieved through selective breeding in the early twentieth century.

The **museum** explains the different techniques and styles of cave art, and allows you to appreciate how skilfully the artists depicted these same animals. But the most interesting aspect is the reproduction of four friezes from the Lascaux caves, which you won't see at Lascaux II (see p.149), including a rotund black cow, who seems almost to be dancing on her slender legs, and two powerful bison back-to-back. Experts then explore the paintings and speculate on their meaning in three video presentations, unfortunately in French only.

Montignac and around

Some 26km upstream from Les Eyzies, **MONTIGNAC** is an attractive town, with a vibrant annual **arts festival** in July (see box, p.121). The town serves as the main base for exploring the Vézère valley's northern sights, foremost of which is **Lascaux**'s painted cave, though the Romanesque abbey church of **St-Amand-de-Coly** is also worth a visit.

Montignac straddles the Vézère, with the **old town**, home to numerous timbered fourteenth- to sixteenth-century houses, to the north of the river, and the tourist office and most hotels to the south along rue du 4-Septembre.

The old town centres on pretty place d'Armes, a harmonious square of warm, sun-bathed stone, adorned with hanging creepers and smart blue shutters. Nearby is place Carnot, where a **market** is held on Wednesday and Saturday mornings, beneath the dominant spire of the square's somewhat unexciting twentieth-century church. To the west of the two squares, a narrow alleyway called rue des Jardins leads uphill to give a view of the town's abandoned feudal castle (not open to the public), which was the abode of the once powerful counts of Périgord (see p.290).

South of the river is the Faubourg, with more elegant buildings, including the galleried former hospice where the town's municipal offices are now housed, and a number of older timbered structures on rue de la Pégerie.

ARRIVAL AND DEPARTURE   MONTIGNAC

By bus Buses from Périgueux, Sarlat and Brive via Terrasson stop on place Carnot and place Tourny, at the north end of rue du 4-Septembre. Those serving St-Léon only stop on place Tourny.

Destinations Brive (Mon–Fri 1 daily during school term only; 1hr 15min); Périgueux (school term Mon–Fri 1–2 daily, July & Aug Wed only; Christmas & Easter school hols Mon–Fri 1–2 daily; 1hr); St-Geniès (school term time Mon–Fri 1–2 daily; Christmas & Easter school hols Mon–Fri 1–2 daily; 10min); Sarlat (school term time Mon–Fri 1–2 daily; Christmas & Easter school hols Mon–Fri 1–2 daily; 30–40min); St-Léon-sur-Vézère (Mon–Fri 1 daily during school term only; 25min); Terrasson (Mon–Fri 2 daily during school term only; 30–40min).

INFORMATION AND ACTIVITIES

Tourist office On place Bertran-de-Born, rue du 4-Septembre (Jan Mon–Fri 10am–12.30pm; Feb & March Mon–Sat 10.30am–12.30pm & 2–5pm; April Mon–Sat 10am–12.30pm & 2–6pm; May & June Mon–Sat 9.30am–12.30pm & 2–6pm; July & Aug daily 9am–7pm; Sept Mon–Sat 9.30am–12.30pm & 2–5pm; Oct–Dec Mon–Sat 10am–noon & 2–4pm; ☎ 05 53 51 82 60, ⓦ tourisme-vezere.com). They sell a map detailing 31 walking routes around Montignac (€2.50) and offer free wi-fi and one computer for internet access. Behind the tourist office you'll find the summer ticket office for Lascaux II (see box, p.150); April to mid-Sept daily 9am–6pm).

Bike rental Monti'Bike (☎ 07 77 08 29 63), behind the tourist office on place Bertran-de-Born, with prices starting at €14 per day.

Canoe rental Montignac has two canoe rental outlets, both open roughly June to September: Les 7 Rives (☎ 05 53 50 19 26) beside the more northerly Pont de la Paix; and Kanoak (☎ 06 75 48 60 47; ⓦ c.farache.free.fr, ✉ kanoak @sfr.fr) below the old bridge.

3

ACCOMMODATION

IN MONTIGNAC

De la Grotte 63 rue du 4-Septembre ☎ 05 53 51 80 48, ⒲ hoteldelagrotte.fr. A quirky, old-fashioned place with a fair amount of charm and an attractive garden, while its cheap-and-cheerful rooms are in a more modern annexe. It also offers a traditional restaurant serving meals either in the garden or among a riot of frills and flounces in the dining room (*menus* €19–34). Breakfast €8.50. Closed two weeks in Jan & one in Feb. **€52**

★ **Hostellerie la Roseraie** Place d'Armes ☎ 05 53 50 53 92, ⒲ laroseraie-hotel.com. In a characterful ivy- and wisteria-clad building on a quiet square, this is the nicest place to stay in Montignac. The 14 rooms are prettily decorated with period furniture and floral touches, while the spacious garden has a landscaped, spring-water pool and an abundance of roses. *La Roseraie* is also home to one of Montignac's best restaurants (see below) – if you're staying here, it's well worth considering the *demi-pension* option. Breakfast €14. Closed Nov–March. **€95**

Le Lascaux 109 av Jean-Jaurès ☎ 05 53 51 82 81, ⒲ hotel-lascaux.com. This welcoming three-star about 300m out of Montignac on the Sarlat road offers bright, modern rooms, not huge at the cheaper end but equipped with nice touches such as a tea-maker and music station. There's a sizeable garden and a restaurant (*menus* €24–34), in addition to secure parking. Breakfast €9.50. Closed mid-Nov to mid-Feb. **€69**

Le Moulin du Bleufond Av Aristide Briand ☎ 05 53 51 83 95, ⒲ bleufond.com. A well-tended three-star campsite on the riverbank 500m downstream from Montignac, where each pitch is scheduled behind a good, thick hedge. Facilities include a heated pool, tennis court

and sauna. There's also a snack bar in season (April–Sept). Wi-fi €3 for 30min. Closed early Oct to March. **€23**

Le P'tit Monde 54 rue du 4-Septembre ☎ 05 53 51 32 76, ⒲ hotellepetitmonde.com. A short walk from the centre along the Sarlat road, this is the cheapest option in town, offering simple, well-priced rooms with TV and either shared or en-suite facilities. It also has a small garden, mostly taken up by a plunge-pool, and a restaurant (*menus* €13–20). Breakfast €8. **€45**

Relais du Soleil d'Or 16 rue du 4-Septembre ☎ 05 53 51 80 22, ⒲ le-soleil-dor.com. A three-star hotel with comfortable, fully equipped rooms – those in the main block are now slightly worn. The best are situated in a more modern annexe at the back (€107), in one corner of the hotel's pretty park overlooking a pool. Other facilities include a spa (€8–30), restaurant (*menus* from €27) and bistro (*menus* from €12). Breakfast €13.40. Closed Jan. **€83**

AROUND MONTIGNAC

★ **La Licorne** Valojoulx ☎ 05 53 50 77 77, ⒲ licorne-lascaux.com. In the picturesque village of Valojoulx, 7km south of Montignac on the way to St-Léon, you'll find this attractive and welcoming *chambre d'hôte*. It offers five homely rooms in buildings dating from the thirteenth century overlooking a garden and pool. The best are "Mélilots", a huge room complete with four-poster bed (€99), and "Les Templiers", which opens onto the garden (€85). It also offers excellent home cooking (Mon, Thurs & Sat evening on request; €27), including a copious breakfast (included in the price). **€72**

EATING AND DRINKING

For consistent quality and gracious surroundings, you can't beat the hotel-restaurant at *La Roseraie*, but if your priority is the setting, head to the northern riverbank where a number of places to eat – with not a lot to choose between them – have outside seating right on the river, beneath medieval timbered supports.

La Chaumière 53 rue 4-Septembre ☎ 05 53 50 14 24. In cold weather or if you're looking for something different, head for this cosy little place serving hearty meat and cheese specialities of the Savoie. Try chiffonnade (ultra-thin slices of ham), raclette (melted cheese served with boiled potatoes and cold meats) or tartiflette (potatoes cooked with onions, bacon and lashings of cheese). Portions are generous and everything is home-produced. There is one *menu* at €18. Otherwise, you can eat from the *carte* for around €20–25. July & Aug daily noon–2pm & 7–9pm; Sept–June Tues–Sat 7–9pm.

Hostellerie la Roseraie Place d'Armes ☎ 05 53 50 53 92, ⒲ laroseraie-hotel.com. The restaurant of this aptly named hotel, with its rose-flanked terrace, serves a daily *menu du marché* (€23) or various options from the seasonal menu, starting at two courses for €29. Dishes might

include local asparagus, *cèpes*, Quercy lamb or strawberries from Les Eyzies. April–Oct daily except Tues noon–1.30pm & 7.30–9.30pm.

Lou Cantou La Coste ☎ 05 53 51 86 92. Don't be put off by the setting, set back off the main D706 2km south of Montignac: *Lou Cantou* is forging a reputation for itself with its refined and inventive cuisine, where locals and tourists rub shoulders in the rustic if somewhat cavernous dining hall or on the terrace in fine weather. There's a choice of good-value seasonal *menus* (€18–32), including such delights as lightly fried foie gras on a slice of pear or *fondant de chocolat façon after eight*. Mid-April to Oct daily except Tues noon–1.30pm & 7.30–9.30pm; Nov to mid-April Tues–Sat noon–1.30pm & 7.30–9.30pm, Sun noon–1.30pm.

Grotte de Lascaux

The **Grotte de Lascaux** was discovered in 1940 by four teenagers in search of their dog, which had fallen into a deep cavern on a hill just south of Montignac. The cave was found to be decorated with marvellously preserved animal paintings, executed by Cro-Magnon people some 17,000 years ago, which are among the finest examples of prehistoric art in existence. Lascaux was opened to the public in 1948 and over the next fifteen years the humidity created by more than a million visitors caused algae and then an opaque layer of calcite to form over the paintings. The algae was cured by disinfection, but the "white disease" was a more serious problem, and in 1963 the authorities decided to close the cave and build a replica (known as Lascaux II) some 200m from the original cave. The problems persist, however, and the plan is now to close the hillside completely to human access (see box below).

Lascaux II

45min guided visits: Feb to mid-April & Nov & Dec Tues–Sun 10am–12.30pm & 2–5.30pm; mid-April to end June, Sept & Oct daily 9.30am–6pm; July & Aug daily 9am–8pm; closed Jan • €9.70, combined ticket with Le Thot €13.40 (see p.146) • ☎ 05 53 51 95 03, ⓦ lascaux.culture.fr or ⓦ semitour.fr

Opened in 1983, **Lascaux II**, signed 2km south of Montignac, was the result of ten years' painstaking work by twenty artists and sculptors using the same methods and materials as the original cave painters. The almost perfect facsimile comprises ninety percent of the Lascaux paintings concentrated in the Hall of Bulls and the Axial (or Painted) Gallery, a distance of less than 100m. While it can't offer the excitement of the real thing, the reproduction is still breathtaking.

In the **Hall of Bulls,** five huge aurochs – one 5.5m long with an astonishingly expressive head and face – dominate the ceiling, while the **Axial (Painted) Gallery** is covered with more cattle surrounded by deer, bison and horses rendered in distinctive Lascaux style with pot-bellies and narrow heads. Some are shaded or spotted with different coloured pigments, while others, like the bulls, are drawn in black outline. One particularly dynamic series is of three horses appearing to be in the different

---

SAVING LASCAUX

Even though access to **Lascaux cave** has been strictly controlled since 1963, limited only to scientists and others with special permission, **fungal contamination** continues to threaten the paintings. In 2001, feather-shaped patches of white mould, later identified as *Fusarium solani*, common in agricultural areas, began spreading rapidly throughout the cave. In a controversial emergency measure, the authorities sprayed it with antibiotics and fungicides and, when they failed to halt the spread of the mould, covered the floors with quicklime. This controlled the contamination, but soon created other problems in this incredibly fragile environment. It was eventually removed in 2004.

Then, while attempts to formulate a global conservation programme were proceeding, in 2006 new **black stains** were discovered on the ceilings. By 2007 they had spread to some of the paintings, most notably the Black Cow. The stains appear to be a complex contamination which is not yet fully understood. This time the Scientific Committee authorized localized chemical treatment, after which the cave was sealed off for three months. According to the latest surveys, the contamination seems at least to be stabilized. Experts hope the new climate-control system installed in spring 2012 will help stop further degradation.

As to what is causing these contaminations, no one yet knows for sure. Various theories put forward include global warming, rising humidity, badly designed or inadequate climate-control systems and the presence of humans. To complicate matters further, these prehistoric caves are very poorly understood. Every treatment so far has led to unexpected side-effects.

One thing is sure, though: that the proximity of Lascaux II is contributing to the problem. So another Lascaux revolution is planned, and the authorities hope to open **Lascaux IV** in 2015. IV will be a facsimile of the entire cave, at an estimated cost of around €60 million, and will be located a safe distance from the original, down in the valley below.

TICKETS FOR LASCAUX II

Up to two thousand **tickets** for Lascaux II are on sale each day. However, these go fast during the peak holiday periods, when it's best to buy in advance either by going to the ticket office in person or making a credit-card booking over the phone (☎ 05 53 5 95 03); bookings can be made up to seven days in advance.

Note also that in winter (mid-Sept to April) tickets are normally on sale at the site, while in season (April to mid-Sept) they are available only from a ticket booth behind Montignac tourist office – the system varies from year to year, so check in Montignac first before heading up to the site.

It's also worth knowing that you can buy tickets for Lascaux II at Le Thot (see p.146), thereby avoiding the queues in peak season.

3

phases of breaking into a gallop. You don't have to be an expert to appreciate the incredible skill employed by the prehistoric artists, who would have painted these animals from memory by the light of flickering oil lamps, nor to appreciate their sense of perspective and movement, and the sheer energy they manage to convey.

St-Amand-de-Coly

Nine kilometres east of Montignac, the village of **ST-AMAND-DE-COLY** boasts a superb fortified Romanesque **church**. Despite its size and bristling military architecture, the twelfth-century abbey church manages to combine great delicacy and spirituality. It is supposedly built over the burial place of the sixth-century St Amand, who gave up soldiering to become a hermit. Despite a promising start, however, the abbey never really prospered and had largely been abandoned by the late 1400s. In 1575 a Protestant garrison withstood a heavy siege here for six days, after which the building continued to crumble until 1868, when it was classified as a historic monument; since then it has been entirely restored.

With its purity of line and simple decoration, the church is at its most evocative in the low sun of late afternoon or early evening. Its **defences**, added in the fourteenth century, left nothing to chance: the church is encircled by ramparts, its walls are 4m thick, and a passage once skirted the eaves, with numerous positions for archers to rain down arrows and blind stairways to mislead attackers. Walk up the hill behind the church to admire its vast *lauze* roof and defensive elements.

If you're lucky enough to be here in the autumn you might catch a classical music concert in the church during the **Festival du Périgord Noir** (Aug to early Oct).

ACCOMMODATION AND EATING   **ST-AMAND-DE-COLY**

Gardette ☎ 05 53 51 68 50, ⊚ hotel-gardette.fr. This small, simple and spotless hotel sits near the church. It has just ten rooms in two separate buildings; try to get one of the two rooms with balconies overlooking the church. They all come with TV and immaculate bathrooms. The restaurant serves decent country cooking, with *menus* from €20 to €27. No wi-fi or internet access. Breakfast €7. Closed mid-Oct to March. **€55**

Manoir d'Hautegente Coly ☎ 05 53 51 68 03, ⊚ manoir-hautegente.com. A very grand – but not sniffy – creeper-clad manor house some 3km north of St-Amand, beyond the village of Coly. Set in its own grounds well back from the road, the hotel has a pool, sumptuous rooms overlooking the grounds to the river and one of the region's best restaurants. In fine weather, tables are set up on the terrace, overlooking the water; it's magical at night. *Menus* start at €35, rising to €75 for the *menu dégustation*. Dishes

include eggs with truffles, rabbit stuffed with dried tomatoes and basil or inside-out lemon meringue pie. Restaurant open May to mid-Oct Mon–Fri 7–9pm, Sat & Sun noon–1.45pm & 7–9pm. Breakfast €15. Closed mid-Oct to April. **€95**

Table de Jean Coly ☎ 05 53 51 68 08. Beside the road in the village of Coly, the same team behind the *Manoir d'Hautegente* (see above) have opened a convivial bistro, popular with locals and tourists for its well-presented but fresh, affordable dishes. There's a lunch *menu* at €14.50, which changes daily, and two more elaborate options at €20 and €30, or you can eat from the *carte* for around €30. Old photos and exposed stone walls set the scene. May to mid-July & mid-Aug to early Oct Tues–Fri noon–2pm & 7–9pm, Sat 7–9pm, Sun noon–2pm; mid-July to mid-Aug daily noon–2pm & 7–9pm.

Terrasson-la-Villedieu

Beyond Montignac the prehistoric sites die out and the Vézère valley becomes busier and more industrialized as it opens out towards **TERRASSON-LA-VILLEDIEU**, 15km upstream, and Brive (see p.74). The old part of Terrasson, a knot of lanes on the river's south bank, merits a quick wander, leading from the arched stone bridge up to the ramparts for panoramic views and to the sixteenth-century abbey church beyond. But the main reason for coming here is to visit its resolutely contemporary garden, **Les Jardins de l'Imaginaire** on a terraced hillside to the west of the church.

Les Jardins de l'Imaginaire

1hr 15min guided visits: April–June, Sept & Oct daily except Tues 10–11.30am & 2–5pm; July & Aug daily 10am–6pm • €7.50 from the ticket office on place de Genouillac, below the garden entrance; ticket office open daily except Tues 9.30–11.30am & 1.30–5pm; July & Aug daily 9.30am–6pm • ☎ 05 53 50 86 82, ⓦ jardins-imaginaire.com

Opened in 1996, the **Jardins de l'Imaginaire** were designed by American landscaper Kathryn Gustafson. In them she explores common themes found in gardens throughout history and among different cultures, from the Romans' sacred groves and the Hanging Gardens of Babylon to moss, water and rose gardens, the last a magnificent display of nearly two thousand varieties. In this respect it is much more than "just" a garden, which is why they insist you go with a guide to explain the complicated symbolism; English-language texts are available. It's full of imaginative touches: a forest of wind chimes, a stark line of weather-vanes and, above all, the use of water to splendid effect.

ARRIVAL AND INFORMATION   TERRASSON-LA-VILLEDIEU

If you're travelling by public transport, you might find yourself passing through Terrasson since it lies on the Brive–Bordeaux train line and has regular bus links to Brive. During school term time there is also a bus service to Montignac on weekdays. While the new Brive-Vallée de la Dordogne airport is not that far away (see p.78), there is no direct public transport to Terrasson; you have to travel via Brive.

By train Terrasson's *gare SNCF* lies on the north side of town at the far end of avenue Jean-Jaurès.
Destinations Bordeaux (1–2 daily; 2hr–2hr 30min); Brive (3–7 daily; 15–20min); Périgueux (4–7 daily; 35–50min).
By bus Buses stop on place de la Libération, on the main west–east Brive road, near the old bridge, and some services also at the train station.

Destinations Brive (school term Mon–Fri 3 daily; school hols Mon–Fri 1 daily; 45min); Montignac (school term Mon–Fri 1 daily; 40min).
Tourist office Rue Jean-Rouby, immediately west of place de la Libération (July & Aug Mon–Sat 9.30am–12.30pm & 2–6pm, Sun 9.30am–12.30pm & 2–5.30pm; Sept–June Mon–Sat 9am–noon & 2–6pm; ☎ 05 5350 37 56, ⓦ ot-terrasson.com).

ACCOMMODATION AND EATING

Les Agapes Rue de la Halle ☎ 05 53 50 14 75, ⓦ lesagapesterrasson.fr. A good eating option, on an attractive square below the west door of the abbey church, with a pretty courtyard at the back for warm weather. It serves tasty seasonal cuisine, a cut above the local competition, with options such as *taboulé* of langoustines cooked in orange oil or calf's kidneys laced with balsamic vinegar. Weekday lunch *menus* start at €12.50, or at €17.50 on weekends and evenings, or you could simply opt for a large salad. July & Aug daily noon–2pm & 7–9.30pm; Sept–June Mon & Tues noon–2pm, Thurs–Sun noon–2pm & 7–9.30pm. Closed two weeks in Feb/March & two weeks in Oct/Nov.

L'Imaginaire Place du Foirail ☎ 05 53 51 37 27, ⓦ l-imaginaire.com. Just seven large, plush rooms, including one suite, in this classy hotel near the Jardins de l'Imaginaire. The rooms are equipped with three-star comforts and decked out in cool creams, with wooden floors and minimalist bathrooms with roomy showers or baths. There's also a well-rated through rather expensive restaurant (*menus* €25–69; July & Aug closed Mon lunchtime; Sept–June closed Sun eve, Mon & lunchtime Tues). Secure parking €5. Breakfast €13. Closed mid-Nov to early Dec. **€125**
★ **La Mandragore** Place de l'Abbaye ☎ 05 53 51 34 17. The best place to eat in Terrasson. Perched above the

3

river near the abbey church, this restaurant has unbeatable views from its terrace. The chef cooks up unusual takes on local produce, such as Chinese-style duck with bamboo shoots and glass noodles, and early strawberries with basil-flavoured *fromage blanc*, all beautifully presented and often garnished with flowers. In addition to a short *carte* (around €40 for three courses), it offers three good-value *menus*, from a €15 weekday lunch, presented on a single platter, or a €20 *menu* which changes every day, up to the €55 *menu dégustation*. Mon & Thurs–Sun noon–2pm & 7–9pm, Tues noon–2pm.

The middle Dordogne

The stretch of river to the south of Sarlat sees the Dordogne at its most appealing, forming great loops between rich fields, wooded hills and craggy outcrops. This is also castle country, where great medieval fortresses eyeball each other across the valley. Most date from the Hundred Years War, when the river marked a frontier of sorts between French-held land to the north and English territory to the south.

For the visitor today, things start slowly in the west with the service town of **St-Cyprien** and nearby **Belvès**, now a sleepy little place where people once lived in troglodyte houses beneath its streets, but châteaux come thick and fast thereafter. The first you reach on the river's north bank is **Beynac**, a stunning village of russet-hued, stone-roofed cottages cascading to the river. A short distance further upstream, the **Jardins Suspendus de Marqueyssac** provide respite among Italian-style terraced gardens and woodland promenades, with views of both Beynac and its archrival over on the south bank, the craggy **Château de Castelnaud**. Then a brief diversion westwards brings you to the far-from-militaristic castle of **Les Milandes**, once owned by the cabaret artist Josephine Baker and now set up as a museum in her honour.

Heading back upstream, the next stop is **La Roque-Gageac**. This lovely village caught between the river and the rock face is up there with Beynac and Castelnaud as one of the Dordogne's most photographed – and visited – sights. Across on the south bank,

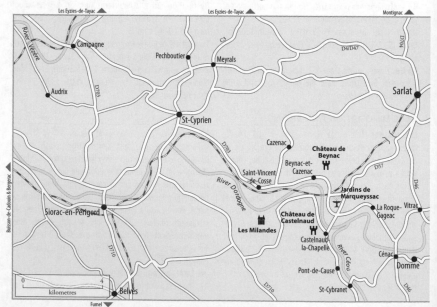

Domme, a fortified *bastide* town perched on the cliff edge, is no pushover on either the tourist stakes or as regards its views. From up here you can take in a 10km sweep of the river, giving you a foretaste of the **Cingle de Montfort**, a particularly picturesque meander set off by yet another glorious château to the east. Before you cross from the Dordogne *département* into the Lot, there's just one more castle to go, the **Château de Fénelon**, an attractive blend of medieval and Renaissance architecture with good collections of furniture and weaponry.

GETTING AROUND   THE MIDDLE DORDOGNE

You can just about forget about public transport in this area. St-Cyprien, Siorac-en-Périgord and Belvès are accessible by train, but the picturesque Sarlat line runs past all the prime sights around Beynac without stopping. The only place accessible by bus is Carsac, a village with a pretty church just east of Montfort, which is a stop on the Sarlat–Souillac bus route.

St-Cyprien and around

Despite its location, just 20km west of Sarlat and 10km south from Les Eyzies, **ST-CYPRIEN** remains a refreshingly workaday place set back from the busy D703. Admittedly, it hasn't got much in the way of sights, but the whole place really comes to life on Sunday mornings for one of the area's best **markets**. The hillside setting is also attractive and, although the town itself has few accommodation options, hotels and *chambres d'hôtes* in neighbouring villages make it a possible base. The old centre's narrow lanes of medieval houses and labourers' cottages, a good number still unprettified, hold the greatest interest. They zigzag up from the modern, lower town towards the austere **abbey church** founded by twelfth-century Augustinian monks. You certainly can't accuse the church of being pretty either, though there's a certain robust grandeur about its Romanesque tower and the echoing nave. The interior is worth a look for some fine eighteenth-century sculpted wooden statues on its retables, and is an evocative setting for classical music concerts in summer.

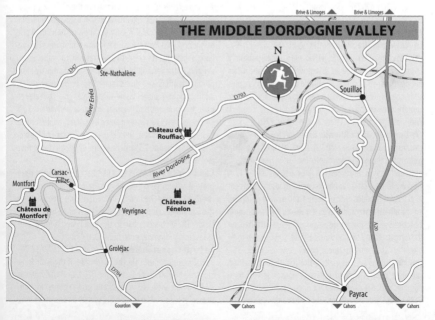

ARRIVAL AND INFORMATION

By train St-Cyprien's train station, on the Bordeaux–Sarlat line, is located about 1km south of the centre. There's no ticket office, so buy your tickets on the train.

Destinations Bergerac (4–6 daily; 1hr–1hr 30min); Bordeaux (3–6 daily; 2hr 15min); Le Buisson (4–6 daily; 15min); Sarlat (4–6 daily; 25min); Siorac-en-Périgord (1–2 daily; 8min).

Tourist office On place Charles-de-Gaulle, in the centre of the lower town. The office produces a good walking map of

ST-CYPRIEN

St-Cyprien and coordinates an active programme of concerts, events and activities in summer (May Mon–Fri 9.30am–12.30pm & 1.30–5.30pm, Sat 10am–12.30pm & 2.30–5.30pm, Sun 10am–12.30pm; Jun–Sept Mon–Fri 9.30am–12.30pm & 1.30–6pm, Sat 9.30am–12.30pm & 2.30–6pm, Sun 10am–12.30pm; Oct–April Mon–Fri 9.30am–12.30pm & 1.30–5.30pm, Sat 9.30am–12.30pm; ☎ 05 53 30 36 09, ⓦ tourismevalleedordogne.com).

ACCOMMODATION AND EATING

There are no particularly good accommodation options in St-Cyprien, but you'll find plenty of choice scattered in the hills and villages around. There is a cluster near the typical Périgord village of Meyrals, 5km north of St-Cyprien. The other option is to head 8km downstream to Siorac-en-Périgord – a junction, albeit infrequently served, on the Sarlat–Bordeaux and Agen–Périgueux train lines. Across the river from Siorac, the village of Le Coux-et-Bigaroque also has a good place to stay.

ST-CYPRIEN

★ **Le Cro-Marin** Rue Gambetta ☎ 05 53 29 43 62. On St-Cyprien's high street, just along from the tourist office, this fishmonger doubles up as a restaurant, with a few tables inside, spreading onto the pavement in summer. The menu changes daily, but seafood platters are a popular choice (around €16 and €32), or you could opt for something along the lines of tomato and haddock salad, followed by fish couscous or moules-frites. There's a two-course lunch *formule* at €12.50 (Tues–Sat). Otherwise, a three-course meal will cost around €25–30. Reservations recommended. Mid-June to Sept Tues–Sat 12.15–1.30pm & 7.15–9.30pm, Sun 12.15–1.30pm; Oct to mid-June Tues–Thurs & Sun 12.15–1.30pm, Fri & Sat 12.15–1.30pm & 7.15–9.30pm.

MEYRALS

Le Chèvrefeuille Pechboutier ☎ 05 53 59 47 97, ⓦ lechevrefeuille.com. English-owned, family-friendly *chambre d'hôte* in a hamlet 2.5km west of Meyrals. It has five pretty, en-suite rooms, a pool and spacious garden, plus additional facilities including a well-equipped kitchenette, laundry room and bikes. Two nights' minimum stay required. Prices include breakfast. Closed Nov to Easter. **€70**

★ **Domaine de la Rhonie** Boyer ☎ 05 53 29 29 07, ⓦ domainedelarhonie.com. You are assured a warm welcome at this beguiling country inn lost in the middle of nowhere, 3.5km northeast of Meyrals, off the C3. A working farm, it offers twelve cheerful, modern rooms set in extensive grounds with a covered and heated pool, and an excellent restaurant, which focuses on traditional Périgord cuisine. Expect dishes using geese fattened on the farm itself and their walnuts, in addition to other local produce. This means meat-heavy *menus* (€23–35), featuring dishes such as melt-in-the-mouth foie gras and succulent magret (grilled breast of goose) served with pommes sarladaises. Restaurant open Easter to mid-Nov daily except Sun 7.30–8pm. Guests have the option of a

well-priced half-board *menu* at €20.50. Breakfast €10. Closed mid-Nov to Easter. **€74**

La Ferme Lamy Boyer ☎ 05 53 29 62 46, ⓦ ferme-lamy.com. You'll need to book early to get one of the 12 stylish rooms at this three-star hotel surrounded by woods and fields, on the road just before you reach the *Domaine de la Rhonie* (see above). The whole place is immaculate, from the en-suite bathrooms to the big infinity pool and flower-filled garden, not to mention the breakfast-spread of home-made jams and breads. Meals provided on request. Breakfast €13. Closed early Nov to March. **€118**

SIORAC-EN-PÉRIGORD

Auberge du Trèfle à Quatre Feuilles ☎ 05 53 31 60 26, ⓦ letrefle4feuilles.com. In the centre of Siorac, you'll find seven good-value rooms located in a separate building at the rear of a popular restaurant. They are functional but bright and well kept, all with en-suite bathrooms, TV and double-glazing. It's wise to book ahead to sample the delights of the restaurant. Working with fresh, mostly local produce, it offers well-priced four-course *menus* (€21–€37), which might feature home-made foie gras, tartare of pollock with lemon and beetroot smoothie, and rounded off with strawberry tart accompanied by a green-apple sorbet. Restaurant open: Mon, Tues, Thurs & Sun noon–1.30pm & 7–9pm; Sat noon–1.30pm. Breakfast €7. Hotel closed first two weeks of Jan. **€46**

Camping du Port ☎ 05 53 31 63 81, ⓦ campingduport.net. A cheap and relaxed two-star campsite on the riverbank beside the bridge; to reach it, turn down behind the Carrefour supermarket. Mature trees provide plenty of shade. There's a snack bar on site in July and August, and plans for a swimming pool. April–Oct. **€12**

Le Petit Chaperon Rouge La Faval ☎ 05 53 29 37 79, ⓦ chaperonrouge.fr. On the north side of the river from Siorac, set on a hillside just off the D703, *Le Petit Chaperon Rouge* is an inexpensive, peaceful country inn. In high season you'll need to book early to stay in one of its nine homely rooms, nothing fancy but impeccably maintained. Their restaurant is authentic and good value, with a summer terrace shaded by lime trees. In winter, meals are served in an old-fashioned, floral dining room among gleaming tableware. The fixed-price *menus* start at €12 for weekday lunches, and at €20 for four courses weekends and evenings. Alternatively, you can expect to pay around €40 from the carte. Restaurant open: July & Aug daily 12.30–1.30pm & 7.30–9pm, Dec–June & Sept to mid-Oct Mon & Thurs–Sun 12.30–1.30pm & 7.30–9pm, Wed 7.30–9pm. Breakfast €6.50. Closed mid-Oct to end Nov. **€50**

LE COUX-ET-BIGAROQUE

Manoir de la Brunie ☎05 53 31 95 62, ⓦmanoirdelabrunie.com. *Chambre-d'hôte* accommodation oozing character in a fifteenth-century manor house 1km northwest of Le Coux-et-Bigaroque, signed off the D703. The more expensive rooms (€86–99) are huge, with high ceilings and decked out with period furniture. There's a salt-water pool and extensive parkland with splendid views over the Dordogne valley. Evening meals provided on request (€27). Breakfast €8–12. Closed Dec & Jan. **€75**

Belvès

Accessible by public transport, and a possible base before you reach the most touristy stretch of the Dordogne valley, is the picturesque hilltop town of **BELVÈS**, 12km south of St-Cyprien. There's no mistaking the town's strategic importance, encircled by ramparts on a promontory above the Nauze valley and bristling with seven towers – even the central square is called place d'Armes. These days, however, the only battles likely to take place here involve haggling over prices at the Saturday-morning **market** under the old *halle*, or a hotly disputed game of *boules*.

Several fine streets, lined with handsome houses from various eras, lead off place d'Armes: **rue Rubigan**, reached under the old stone gateway, is a narrow, winding medieval street, while on **rue des Filhols** you can see the imposing tower of the Maison des Consuls and further up a battered ornate Renaissance facade slapped on the twelfth-century Hôtel Bontemps.

Rue Jacques-Manchotte, on the other side of the square, leads past shops and cafés towards the imposing thirteenth-century **church of Notre-Dame**, an interesting example of early, undecorative Gothic architecture, where recently discovered medieval frescoes are currently being restored.

On the way, if it's open, you could also pop into the **Organistrum** at 14 rue Jacques-Manchotte (no fixed hours; free; ☎05 53 29 10 93), a combined museum and workshop producing medieval instruments. Music-lovers might also be interested in Belvès' principal annual event, the **Festival Bach**, dedicated to the composer, with at least one concert in the church during the first fortnight of August (see box, p.121).

Troglodyte houses

35min guided tours (minimum of four persons required): mid-June to mid-Sept eight visits daily (three in English) 10.30am–6pm; mid-Sept to mid-June Mon–Sat bilingual visits at 11am & 3.30pm, but confirm times with the tourist office (see p.156) • €4, tickets on sale at the tourist office • ☎05 53 29 10 20

In 1907 the wheel of a cart crossing place d'Armes broke through the roof of a warren of **troglodyte houses**. Hollowed into the rampart wall, these damp, dark and insalubrious dwellings were inhabited from the twelfth century up to the mid-1700s, after which they were blocked up and forgotten. So far eight "houses" have been opened, consisting of single rooms averaging a mere 20 square metres apiece for a family plus animals. It's hard to imagine what they must have been like to live in, even if the more sophisticated dwellings boast chimneys, raised sleeping areas and shelves cut into the soft rock.

Filature de Belvès

Fongauffier • 45min guided visits April–June, Sept & Oct daily except Sat 2–4pm; July & Aug daily 10am–7pm • €7 • ☎05 53 57 52 64, ⓦfilaturedebelves.com

In the Nauze valley just below Belvès, on the D710, this former **woollen mill** produced top-quality yarn for the Aubusson tapestry workshops until the 1990s. It has now been opened as a museum, where you learn about the history of wool in the area and how the raw fleeces were processed into various grades of yarn.

The machines you see today date from the late 1940s, when electricity replaced water-power. Though none of them is working, films of similar machines in action give the general idea. The visit ends with the chance to try felt-making, weaving or using vegetable dyes. It makes a fun visit, particularly if you have children in tow.

ARRIVAL AND INFORMATION   BELVÈS

By train Belvès lies on the Agen–Périgueux line, with the *gare SNCF* down on the main road below the town.
Destinations Agen (3–5 daily; 1hr–1hr 15min); Le Bugue (3–5 daily; 25min); Le Buisson (3–5 daily; 15min); Les Eyzies (3–5 daily; 30–40min); Périgueux (3–5 daily; 1hr–1hr 15min); Siorac-en-Périgord (3–5 daily; 6min).
Tourist office On the ground floor of the fifteenth-century Maison des Consuls, just off the market square at 1 rue des Filhols (May–June & Sept 1–15 daily 10am–12.30pm & 2.30–6pm; July & Aug daily 10am–1pm & 2.30–7.30pm; mid-Sept to April Mon–Sat 10am–12.30pm & 2.30–5.30pm; ☎05 53 29 10 20, ⓦ tourisme-belves.com). They provide a computer terminal for free internet access.

ACCOMMODATION AND EATING

Le Belvédère 1 av Paul-Crampet ☎05 53 31 51 41, ⓦ hotel-restaurant-perigord.com. The slightly more upmarket of two hotels next door to each other at the far west end of rue Jacques-Manchotte. The rooms don't quite live up to the smart, blue-shuttered exterior, particularly the smaller rooms at the cheaper end, but they are clean and provide all the two-star comforts you'd expect, including en-suite bathroom, TV and telephone. It also has an attractive terrace and a decent restaurant (*menus* €22–31). Restaurant open Oct–April closed Wed & Thurs. Breakfast €7.50. €48

Le Home 3 place de la Croix-des-Frères ☎05 53 29 01 65, ⓦ lehomedebelves.fr. Next to *Le Belvédère*, this friendly, one-star hotel offers ten old-fashioned, no-frills rooms, with tiny bathrooms at the bottom price range; room 5 is the largest available, with a small salon (€52). The restaurant is popular for its good-value traditional cuisine, with four-course *menus* starting at €14 on weekdays and €20 on Saturday evenings and Sundays.

Restaurant open daily April–Sept; Oct–March closed Fri eve & Sun. Breakfast €6.50. €42

Manoir de la Moissie Bd de la Moissie ☎05 53 29 93 49, ⓦ lamoissie.fr. On the western edge of Belvès, signed off the D53 Monpazier road, by the municipal tennis courts, this sixteenth-century manor house now provides stylish *chambre-d'hôte* accommodation. Four beautifully decorated and spacious rooms sit under the eaves, while guests also have access to an enormous communal room downstairs, a TV room and washing machine, as well as the surrounding park. Secure parking available. Breakfast €6. €48

Les Nauves Le Bos Rouge ☎05 53 29 12 64, ⓦ lesnauves.com. Belvès' nearest campsite, in a quiet spot 4km southwest off the D53 Monpazier road. They offer good-size plots and a pool, and organize various kids' activities in July and August. From June to September and at weekends they also open a grocery store, bar and restaurant. April–Oct. €23

Beynac-et-Cazenac and around

Clearly visible on an impregnable cliff edge on the Dordogne's north bank, its clifftop **castle** soaring above the valley, the eye-catching village of **BEYNAC-ET-CAZENAC** was built in the days when the river was the only route open to traders and invaders. Now the busy main road squeezes between the cliffs and the water, creating a horrible bottleneck from June to mid-September. At this time you're best advised to arrive first thing in the morning to escape the worst of the crowds.

Château de Beynac

1hr guided tours daily: April–Sept 10am–6.30pm; Oct to mid-Nov & mid-Dec to March 10am–dusk, though it's best to check; closed five weeks mid-Nov to mid-Dec • Guided tours are in French only; alternatively, you can buy a rather basic summary in English (€0.15) and go it alone • €7.50 • ☎05 53 29 50 40

It's three kilometres by road from the waterfront to the **Château de Beynac** or, alternatively, it takes fifteen minutes to walk up the steep lane among the *lauze*-roofed cottages. The lichenous-grey castle is protected on the landward side by double walls and ditches; elsewhere the sheer drop of almost 150m does the job. The redoubtable Richard the Lionheart nevertheless took and held Beynac for a decade,

THE LIGHTER SIDE OF BEYNAC

Particularly in summer, the tiny village of Beynac, cramped between road and cliff-face, can get oppressively crowded. Thankfully there are a number of ways to escape and enjoy a more peaceful perspective on the countless castles in the area.

River trips Gabarres de Beynac (April–Oct 10am–12.30pm & 2–6pm; €7.50; ☎05 53 28 51 15, ⓦgabarre-beynac.com), based on a jetty next to the riverside car park, offer 50-minute river cruises on their replica *gabarres*, the traditional wooden river-craft, affording excellent views of castle and village.

Canoeing The stretch of the Dordogne between Vitrac and Beynac, taking you past a breathtaking parade of castles, is the most stunning canoe-trip in the region. If you hire a canoe in Beynac, the company will drive you upriver before you canoe back down to your vehicle. In town, you'll find Copeyre Canoë (☎05 53 28 23 82, ⓦcanoe-copeyre.com; May–Sept), while Canoës Roquegeoffre (☎05 53 29 54 20, ⓦcanoe-rougeoffre.com), based 3km downstream near St-Vincent-de-Cosse, offers the best value around and is open all year.

Hot-air ballooning The ultimate slow-paced activity is also a possibility here: if you phone ahead, Montgolfière et Châteaux (☎06 71 14 3496, ⓦwww.montgolfiere-chateaux .com; from €180 per adult) will collect you from Beynac's riverside car park to take you to the launch site.

Walking The cheapest way to get away from the crowds around Beynac's port and castle is to walk inland away from the river; the tourist office (see below) sells maps for €1.50. It details five suggested routes around Beynac from 4km to 10km, with the longer itineraries taking you to the beautifully unspoilt fifteenth-century church of Cazenac, where some unusual modern stained-glass windows depict scenes from daily life in this area in the nineteenth century.

until a gangrenous wound ended his term of blood-letting in 1189; apparently the heart-shaped keys and keyholes were fashioned in his memory. Though the English regained the castle briefly – thanks to the Treaty of Brétigny rather than any military prowess – in essence Beynac remained loyal to the French Crown during the Hundred Years War.

The buildings are in surprisingly good condition thanks to a mammoth restoration project over the last forty years, which is scheduled to continue until at least 2030. You enter into a **guardroom**, one of the castle's more atmospheric rooms along with the **great hall**, where the nobles of Beynac, Biron, Mareuil and Bourdeilles – the four baronies of Périgord (see p.290) – met; note the unusual ox-skull motif over the fireplace, previously found at the Château de Lanquais (see p.107). Also good are the twelfth-century **kitchens**, complete with a cobbled ramp allowing horses access to the central courtyard, and kitted out with no-nonsense tables, vats, meat-hooks and great pulleys. If it looks familiar, that's because it featured in Luc Besson's epic, *Jeanne d'Arc*.

For most people, however, it's the **views** that steal the show, notably from the top of the keep, where you get a stupendous – and vertiginous – sweep over the surrounding châteaux: Marqueyssac (see p.158), Fayrac (see p.161) and Castelnaud (see p.160).

ARRIVAL AND INFORMATION   BEYNAC-ET-CAZENAC

By car You need your own vehicle to get to Beynac. Parking is available down by the river, in a string of three car parks on the road up to the castle and beside the castle itself. It is all paid parking (daily 9am–noon & 2–7pm), except for the last of the three on the road to the castle. Once you've bought a ticket (€2.50 for two hours, €4 for a day), you are free to move to another car park if you choose.

Tourist office At the bottom of the road up to the château (☎05 53 29 43 08; Feb, March & Oct–Dec Fri 2–5pm, Sat 9am–12.30pm & 1.30–5pm, Sun 9am–12.30pm; April–June & Sept Mon–Wed & Fri–Sun 9am–12.30pm & 1.30–5pm, Thurs 10am–12.30pm & 1.30–5pm; July & Aug Mon–Wed 9.30am–12.30pm & 1.30–6pm, Thurs 10am–12.30pm & 1.30–6pm, Fri & Sat 9.30am–12.30pm & 1.30–7pm, Sun 9.30am–12.20pm & 1.30–5pm).

ACCOMMODATION AND EATING

IN BEYNAC

Le Capeyrou ☏ 05 53 29 54 95, ⓦ campinglecapeyrou
.com. A three-star campsite on the riverbank immediately
east of Beynac, with unbeatable views up to the château.
The best plots are those lined up along the river, though
they could do with more hedges around. There's a good-
size heated pool and well-equipped children's play area,
plus a bar. Closed Oct to mid-April. **€16**

Du Château ☏ 05 53 29 19 20, ⓦ hotel-beynac
-dordogne.com. A two-star hotel on a bit of a busy
junction, where the road heads up to the castle; those on
the front have double-glazing and a shared terrace with
river views – best appreciated in the quiet of the evening.
The rooms are bright and impeccably clean, equipped with
satellite TV. There's a tiny pool and wi-fi access in the
communal areas, plus a computer terminal, and one of
Beynac's better restaurants, which has a broad range of
menus, ranging from a €15.50 weekday lunch *menu* to €39
for a four-course extravaganza. House specialities include
tourin (the local garlic soup), eggs baked with truffles and
sturgeon in a Monbazillac sauce. They also offer large
salads, omelettes and a few vegetarian dishes. Restaurant
open daily noon–2pm & 7.30–9.30pm. Breakfast €8. **€69**

La Petite Tonnelle ☏ 05 53 29 95 18. This well-
respected restaurant is surprisingly relaxed, despite its
location on the road up to the château, opposite *Pontet*. In
addition to daily specials, it offers an array of *formules* and
menus, starting at €16 for two courses and €32 for four,
plus a fine choice of local wines to wash it down. Everything
is home-made, including home-smoked duck breast and
Scottish salmon. Or try the guinea-fowl with fennel and
lemon, or herb-roasted Quercy lamb. Reservations
recommended. Daily noon–2pm & 7–9pm.

Pontet ☏ 05 53 29 50 06, ⓦ hostellerie-maleville.com.
With the benefit of being off the main drag, on the road
leading up to the château, this little place offers thirteen
comfortable rooms, all a/c, with en-suite bathrooms and
TV, but wi-fi is only available in the communal areas.
Breakfast €7. Closed Jan. **€50**

AROUND BEYNAC

Balcon en Fôret Tral-Pech ☏ 05 53 28 24 01, ⓦ www
.ladordogne.info. If you're looking for a treat well away
from the madding crowds, try this welcoming *chambre
d'hôte* perched among woods just off the road to Cazenac
– and only five minutes to Beynac by footpath. They offer
two huge and beautifully appointed rooms, with plans for
a third, so you'll need to book early. Evening meals
available on request (€32 including drinks). Prices include
breakfast. **€135**

Jardins Suspendus de Marqueyssac

Daily: Feb, March & Oct to mid-Nov 10am–6pm; April–June & Sept 10am–7pm; July & Aug 9am–8pm; mid-Nov to Jan 10am–5pm •
€7.40, or €14 with Château de Castelnaud (see p.160) • Candlelit evenings July & Aug Thurs 7pm–midnight, €12 • ☏ 05 53 31 36 36,
ⓦ marqueyssac.com

Three kilometres east of Beynac, the Dordogne loops south round a long and narrow
wooded promontory, at the tip of which the **Château de Marqueyssac** presides over its
terraced "hanging" **gardens**. A few rooms of the château, a typically mellow Périgord
mansion of the late eighteenth century, are now open to the public, but it is the
surrounding gardens and the **views**, encompassing the châteaux of Beynac, Fayrac and
Castelnaud, that are the star attractions.

The gardens were first laid out in the 1600s by the then owner, Bertrand Vernet de
Marqueyssac, under the inspiration of Le Nôtre, the landscaper responsible for Versailles.
However, most of the features you see today were added two centuries later when the
500m long Grande Allée was established – thousands of box trees clipped into plump
cushions – and 6km of woodland walks opened up along the ridge to the east. In recent
years, landscape gardeners have added more modern touches, including sculptures and
the "boxwood chaos" resembling angular stone blocks. All paths lead to a 130m-high
belvedere from where you can see La Roque-Gageac nestling under its cliff (see p.162).

For those not so interested in gardens, there's the Via Ferrata, an exhilarating
cliff-walk suspended 100m up along a narrow path and a series of ropes, beams and
brackets attached to the rock face, to which you are secured by a safety line. It is
restricted to those over 8 years old and 1m 30 in height. Phone ahead or check the
website for the current schedule.

Between Easter and mid-November, the **restaurant-salon de thé** serves meals and light
refreshments (noon–7pm), and on Thursday evenings in July and August thousands of
candles and fairy lights give the gardens a magical touch.

Castelnaud-la-Chapelle

Rivals for centuries, the feudal fortresses of Beynac and **CASTELNAUD-LA-CHAPELLE**, on the Dordogne's south bank, now vie over visitor numbers. There's no question that Beynac has the edge with its more dramatic location and arguably the better views, but the **Château de Castelnaud** provides the more entertaining visit – and more informative; allow at least a couple of hours.

Château de Castelnaud

Daily: Feb–March & Oct to mid-Nov 10am–6pm; April–June & Sept 10am–7pm; July & Aug 9am–8pm; mid-Nov to Jan 2–5pm; Christmas hols 10am–5pm • €8.20, or €14 with Jardins Suspendus de Marqueyssac • ☎ 05 53 31 30 00, ⊛ castelnaud.com

Like Beynac, **Castelnaud** was founded in the twelfth century and bitterly fought over on many occasions, starting with the bellicose Simon de Montfort, who seized it as early as 1214 during his Cathar crusades (see p.292). During the Hundred Years War the lords of Castelnaud sided with the English, slugging it out for nearly four decades with the French at Beynac until Charles VII besieged Castelnaud in 1442. After holding out for three weeks, a treacherous English captain handed over the keys in return for his life and the princely sum of four hundred crowns.

Heavily restored in the last decades, the château now houses an excellent **museum of medieval warfare**. Its core is an extensive collection of original weaponry, including all sorts of bizarre contraptions, such as an "organ" which sprayed lead balls from its multiple barrels, and a fine assortment of armour.

Throughout the year, but particularly during school holidays, staff give demonstrations of iron forging, weaponry and firing the trebuchet siege engine. Evening visits led by guides in period costume are also on offer (mid-July to end Aug Mon–Fri at 8.15pm; €11; in French only).

Note that there's a charge of €3 to leave your car in the upper car park, closest to the château, from where it's still a fair walk down. Alternatively, you can park for free in the lower car park, on the main road, and then walk up.

Eco-musée de la Noix du Périgord

April to mid-Nov daily 10am–7pm • €4.50 • ☎ 05 53 59 69 63, ⊛ ecomuseedelanoix.site.voila.fr

On the D57 south of Castelnaud, by the turning up to the château, it's worth stopping briefly at the **Eco-musée de la Noix du Périgord** for everything you ever wanted to know about nuts – **walnuts**, specifically. As well as detailing oil pressing, the exhibition reveals historical gems such as the fact that Louis XI's beard was trimmed using heated walnut shells, and that walnuts were used in the insulation of American spaceships. It also points out the nuts' many health benefits, before you're shepherded through to the well-stocked shop. If you're lucky the mill itself will be working (July & Aug Tues, Wed & Thurs afternoons), but otherwise there's a self-explanatory video featuring Ste-Nathalène's more authentic Moulin de la Tour (see p.128). The adjacent orchard, spattered with giant cement walnuts and picnic tables, will appeal to young children.

ACTIVITIES
CASTELNAUD-LA-CHAPELLE

Bike rental Bike Bus ☎ 06 08 94 42 01, ⊛ bike-bus .com). From here you can follow a quiet cycle route along the lovely Céou valley to Daglan and L'Abbaye-Nouvelle, in the Lot.

Canoe rental On the riverfront, beside the bridge, you can rent canoes at the Base Municipale Canoë-Kayak (☎ 05 53 29 40 07; open all year).

ACCOMMODATION

Lou Castel ☎ 05 53 29 89 24, ⊛ loucastel.com. While there are no hotels in Castelnaud, you'll find this lively four-star campsite set among oak woods on the plateau roughly 3km to the south. It has several pools, water slides, a grocery store, bar and restaurant, as well as children's

activities in July and August. Closed Oct–March. €27

★ **La Tour de Cause** Pont-de-Cause ☎ 05 53 30 30 51, ⊛ latourdecause.com. High-quality *chambre-d'hôte* accommodation in a lovely Périgordin manor house in the hamlet of Pont-de-Cause, a couple of kilometres south of

JOSEPHINE BAKER AND THE RAINBOW TRIBE

Born on June 3, 1906, in the black ghetto of East St Louis, Illinois, **Josephine Baker** was one of the most remarkable women of the twentieth century. Her mother washed clothes for a living and her father was a drummer who soon deserted his family, yet by the late 1920s Baker was the most celebrated cabaret star in France, primarily due to her role in the legendary **Folies Bergère** show in Paris. On her first night, de Gaulle, Hemingway, Piaf and Stravinsky were among the audience, and her notoriety was further enhanced by her long line of illustrious husbands and lovers, which included the crown prince of Sweden and the crime novelist Georges Simenon. She also mixed with the likes of Le Corbusier and Adolf Loos, and kept a pet cheetah, with whom she used to walk around Paris. During the war, she was active in the **Resistance**, for which she was awarded the Croix de Guerre. Later on, she became involved in the civil rights movement in North America, where she insisted on playing to non-segregated audiences, a stance that got her arrested in Canada and tailed by the FBI in the US.

By far her most bizarre and expensive project was the château of **Les Milandes**, which she rented from 1938 and then bought in 1947, including 300 hectares (3 square kilometres) of land, after her marriage to the French orchestra leader Jo Bouillon. Having equipped the place with two hotels, three restaurants, a mini-golf course, tennis court and an autobiographical wax museum, Baker opened the château to the general public as a model multicultural community, popularly dubbed the "village du monde". Unable to have children of her own, in the course of the 1950s she adopted babies (mostly orphans) of different ethnic and religious backgrounds from around the world. By the end of the decade, she had brought twelve children to Les Milandes, including a black Catholic Colombian and a Buddhist Korean, along with her own mother, brother and sister from East St Louis.

Over 300,000 people a year visited the château in the 1950s, but her more conservative neighbours were never very happy about Les Milandes and the "Rainbow Tribe". In the 1960s, Baker's financial problems, divorce and two heart attacks spelt the end of the project, and despite a sit-in protest by Baker herself (by then in her sixties), the château and its contents were auctioned off in 1968. Still performing and as glamorous as ever, Josephine died of a stroke in 1975 and was given a grand state funeral at La Madeleine in Paris, mourned by thousands of her adopted countryfolk.

Castelnaud on the D57. There's a choice of three rooms downstairs and two up in the eaves, all with their own charm. Guests also have access to a salon and kitchen area, a computer and a salt-water pool. The American owners go out of their way to make you comfortable. Two-night minimum stay required, though it's always worth checking. Price include a copious breakfast. Closed mid-Oct to May. **€92**

Les Milandes

Daily: April & May 10am–6.30pm; June to mid-July & Sept 10am–7pm; mid-July to Aug 9.30am–7.30pm; Oct 10am–6.15pm • €9 • ☎ 05 53 59 31 21, ⓦ milandes.com

From Castelnaud it's a scenic drive 5km west along the river past **Château de Fayrac** (not open to the public) with its slated pepper-pot towers – an English forward position in the Hundred Years War, built to watch over Beynac – to **Les Milandes**. Built in the late 1400s, the château was the property of the Caumont family (the lords of Castelnaud) until the Revolution, but its most famous owner was the Folies Bergère star, **Josephine Baker** (see box above), who fell in love with it while visiting friends in the area in 1937.

It's easy to see why. The Renaissance château, sitting high above the Dordogne, has all the necessary romantic ingredients: towers, machicolations, balustrades, gargoyles, ornate dormer windows and terraced gardens shaded by great, glossy-leafed magnolias. After she bought Les Milandes in 1947, Josephine set about modernizing it, adding creature comforts such as the en-suite bathrooms, whose decor was inspired by her favourite perfumes – Arpège-style black tiles with gold taps and ceiling in one, Dioresque pink marble with silver-leaf in another. But it's really the stories surrounding

Josephine and Les Milandes that are more intriguing than the château itself. Her roller-coaster life story is enough to fill a book, but you can trace the broad outlines from the collection of photos and posters. The few costumes that escaped the auctioneer's hammer in 1968 are also on display, though these are somewhat moth-eaten after mouldering in the cellar for 25 years.

After visiting the château, you can explore the gardens, where they hold **falconry demonstrations** every afternoon and mornings from June to September. From the terrace, there are views down on the J-shaped swimming pool belonging to one of the many fun-parks Josephine established in the area.

La Roque-Gageac

The village of **LA ROQUE-GAGEAC**, on the river's north bank 5km east of Beynac, is almost too perfect, its ochre-coloured houses sheltering under dramatically overhanging cliffs. Regular winner of France's prettiest village contest, it inevitably pulls in the tourist buses, and since here again the main road separates the village from the river, the noise and fumes of the traffic can become oppressive. The best way to escape is to slip away through the lanes and alleyways that wind up through the terraced houses. The other option is to rent a canoe and paddle over to the opposite bank, where you can picnic and enjoy a much better view of La Roque than from among the crowds milling around beneath the village, at its best in the burnt-orange glow of the evening sun.

INFORMATION AND ACTIVITES · LA ROQUE-GAGEAC

Tourist office Occupies a hut by the main car park on the Sarlat side of town (Easter to June & Sept daily 10am–1pm & 2–5pm; July & Aug Mon & Fri–Sun 10am–1pm & 2–7pm, Tues–Thurs 10am–1pm & 2–6pm; ☎ 05 53 29 17 01).

Boat trips From April to October two companies offer one-hour round-trips in a *gabarre* (the traditional river craft) down to Castelnaud, leaving from beside the main car park on the east side of La Roque: Gabares Norbert (☎ 05 53 29 40 44, ⍟ gabarres.com; €9) and Gabarres Caminades (☎ 05 53 29 40 95, ⍟ gabarrecaminade.com; €9). There's nothing to choose between the two companies; both offer live commentary in French, or a pre-recorded English version on a headset.

Canoe rental Canoë Dordogne (☎ 05 53 29 58 50, ⍟ canoesdordogne.fr) and Canoë Vacances (☎ 05 53 28 17 07, ⍟ canoevacances.com), both east of La Roque in the direction of Vitrac and Sarlat.

ACCOMMODATION AND EATING

La Belle Étoile ☎ 05 53 29 51 44, ⍟ belleetoile.fr. Nicest of the town's hotels is the family-run *La Belle Étoile*, on the main road below the fort, with fifteen elegant, airy rooms, all double-glazed and boasting a/c. It's worth paying extra for a room on the front with river views (€75). The hotel also boasts La Roque's best restaurant which, with its shady terrace and river views, makes a great place for a splurge, though you'll need to book ahead. It offers a varied selection of regional specialities, with three-courses *menus* starting at €30, all beautifully presented, and attentive service. Restaurant open April–Oct Tues & Thurs–Sun 12.30–1.30pm & 7.15–9pm, Wed 7.15–9pm. Breakfast €10. Closed Nov–March. €55

La Ferme Fleurie Le Colombier ☎ 05 53 28 33 39, ⍟ perigord.com/la-ferme-fleurie. For a more peaceful place to stay, head 5km northeast of La Roque on the road to Sarlat to this *auberge* surrounded by flower-filled gardens. The floral theme is continued in the eight simple but perfectly comfortable en-suite bedrooms.

They also offer more basic accommodation in shared dorms in their *gîte d'étape* (€24 per person, including breakfast) and a good-value restaurant serving dishes incorporating ingredients produced on the farm, including everything duck related. There's just one *menu* at €17 (or €23 including foie gras), for which you get five courses including aperitifs and coffee. Meals are served evenings only at communal tables. Reservations are a must. Restaurant closed Wed. Breakfast included. Closed Nov–March. €54

Manoir de la Malartrie Vézac ☎ 05 53 29 03 51, ⍟ chambresdhotes-lamalartrie.com. This belle-époque château offers luxurious chambre-d'hôte accommodation on the D703 just west of La Roque. Even if the faux-medieval exterior isn't quite your cup of tea, the interiors are sumptuous and it's in a perfect setting, with a heated pool, garden and terraces overlooking the river. The only slight hiccup is the proximity of the road. Breakfast €16. Closed Jan & Feb. €128

Domme and around

High on the scarp on the south bank of the river, 5km southeast from La Roque-Gageac and 10km due south of Sarlat, **DOMME** is an exceptionally well-preserved, terribly pretty *bastide*, now wholly given over to tourism. Its foremost attraction, however, is its position. From the chestnut-shaded **Esplanade du Belvédère** at the town's northern edge, you look out over a wide sweep of river country encompassing everything from Beynac to the Cingle de Montfort (see p.164). The drop here is so precipitous that fortifications were deemed unnecessary when the *bastide* was founded in 1281. They lived to regret it: in 1588 a small band of Protestants scaled the cliffs at dawn to take the town completely by surprise. The intruders stayed four years, during which time they destroyed the church amongst other buildings, before they were forced to abandon the town again to Catholic control.

Once you've admired the view and wandered the quiet backstreets, there's nothing much really to detain you in Domme unless it happens to be market day (Thursday mornings), when stalls spill out of the central square south down the main commercial street, the Grande-Rue, itself lined with souvenir shops.

Porte des Tours

Guided tours March–Oct; by appointment only – apply to the tourist office (see below) • €6.60

Much of Domme's thirteenth-century walls and three of the gateways they skirted remain. Of the latter, the best-preserved and most interesting is easterly **Porte des Tours**, flanked by two round bastions. In 1307 a group of Templar knights was imprisoned here for eleven years. You can still see traces of the graffiti they carved on the walls depicting Crucifixion scenes, the Virgin Mary, angels and various secret signs. Alternatively, you can see photos of the carvings in the town's museum of traditional arts and crafts (see below).

Musée des Arts et Traditions Populaires

Place de la Halle • April–June & Sept daily 10.30am–12.30pm & 2.30–6pm; July & Aug Mon–Fri & Sun 10.30am–7pm, Sat 10.30am–12.30pm & 2.30–7pm • €4

On the town's central square, the **Musée des Arts et Traditions Populaires** focuses on local life in the nineteenth and twentieth centuries. The displays are nicely done, if not wildly interesting.

Grotte de Domme

Place de la Halle • Daily: mid-Feb to March, Oct, Nov & winter school hols 2.30–4.30pm; April & May 10.15am–noon & 2.30–5.30pm; June & Sept 10.15am–noon & 2.15–6pm; July & Aug 10.15am–6.30pm • €8 including museum; tickets available at the tourist office

The **caves** of Domme, which extend hundreds of metres under the village from beneath the timbered market hall, can definitely be given a miss. The concretions are badly discoloured with algae and can't compare with any of the area's other limestone caverns; the only good point is the exit onto the cliff face with a panoramic lift up to the top and a pleasant stroll back along the promenade de la Falaise.

Cénac

On the way to – or from – Domme, it's worth making a brief stop in **CÉNAC**, down by the river, to admire its Romanesque **church**, the chapelle St-Julien, located a short distance along the D50 to St-Cybranet. Apart from a lovely *lauze* roof, its main draw is the remarkably distinct carving on the capitals, featuring various animals and demons, including Daniel taming the lions.

INFORMATION AND ACTIVITITES   **DOMME AND AROUND**

Tourist office On place de la Halle (mid-Feb to April & Sept daily 10am–noon & 2–6pm; May & June daily 10am–12.30pm & 1.30–6pm; July & Aug daily 10am–7pm; Oct to mid-Nov & Christmas hols daily 10am–noon & 2–5pm; mid-Nov to mid-Feb Mon–Fri 10am–noon & 2–4.30pm; ☎ 05 53 31 71 00, ⊛ ot-domme.com).

3

Canoe rental Cénac Périgord Loisirs (☎ 05 53 29 99 69, ⓦ canoedordogne.pro), beside the bridge below Domme, offers canoe rental all year.

ACCOMMODATION AND EATING

Le Belvédère Esplanade de la Belvédère ☎ 05 53 31 12 01. This café-restaurant has unbeatable views from its terrace, located on the very cliff edge. Your best bet is to come for a drink or ice cream, served all day, though it also offers standard brasserie fare, such as omelettes, salads and regional dishes, with *menus* starting at €15 and main dishes priced at between €10 and €15. April–Sept daily 11.30am–3.30pm & 6–9.30pm.

Cabanoix et Châtaigne 3 rue Geoffroy-de-Vivans ☎ 05 53 31 07 11, ⓦ restaurantcabanoix.com. Cosy little restaurant just off the Grande-Rue with a well-deserved reputation for its creative takes on traditional local cuisine. Foie gras features strongly, though there are always a couple of fish and vegetarian dishes. There's a broad range of *formules* and *menus* to choose from, with three-course options at €29 and €32. No views, but a quiet courtyard or tables by the fire in winter. Reservations recommended. Mid-Feb to June & Sept to mid-Dec daily except Wed & Sat noon–2.30pm & 7.30–9.30pm; July & Aug Mon–Fri & Sun noon–2.30pm & 7.30–9.30pm, Sat 7.30–9.30pm. Closed mid-Dec to mid-Feb.

Côté Figue 1 porte Delbos ☎ 05 53 31 82 87, ⓦ cotefigue.fr. Just outside the walls on the southwest side of Domme, this handsome mansion offers comfortable *chambre-d'hôte* accommodation in five large, cool rooms. It's perched on the hillside looking south, with lovely views from its terraced gardens and a large, heated pool. The generous buffet breakfast (€7.50) of home-made breads and cakes will set you up for the day. Evening meals available on request (€18.50). **€79**

L'Esplanade Esplanade de la Belvédère ☎ 05 53 28 31 41, ⓦ esplanade-perigord.com. The smartest place to stay in Domme, right on the cliff edge, though you'll pay a hefty premium for a room with a view, decked out with period furniture (€160). The rest are not huge, but equipped with three-star comforts and prettily decorated in soft pastels. It has an excellent restaurant, where you won't find any confit or magret in sight. Instead, the chef dishes up delights such as guinea-fowl stuffed with *cèpes*, scrambled eggs with truffles and even truffle ice cream, with *menus* costing from €35 to €70. In winter, truffle enthusiasts are treated to a sublime *menu de truffes* costing €100. In summer, cheaper midday meals are available on the terrace. Restaurant open mid-Feb to Nov & mid-Dec to mid-Jan Mon 7.15–9pm, Tues–Sun 12.15–2pm & 7.15–9pm. Note that opening days can vary, especially in winter – phone ahead to be sure. Hotel and restaurant closed Nov to mid-Dec & mid-Jan to mid-Feb. Breakfast €13. **€108**

Le Nouvel Hôtel 1 Grande-Rue ☎ 05 53 28 36 81, ⓦ domme-nouvel-hotel.com. Simple, reasonably priced if slightly old-fashioned en-suite rooms in this little hotel just down from Domme's central square. The rooms are above a restaurant serving regional dishes (*menus* from €14). Breakfast €8.30. Closed mid-Nov to mid-Dec & Jan. **€59**

Upstream towards Souillac

If you're taking the prettier north bank of the Dordogne from Domme, the spectacular, white-walled **Château de Montfort** (not open to the public) soon comes into view atop its well-defended promontory. The distinctive, Disneyesque turrets date from its nineteenth-century reconstruction. To complete the picture it overlooks the almost perfect curve of the **Cingle de Montfort**, not the biggest but certainly the tightest of the Dordogne's many meanders.

Carsac-Aillac

Two kilometres further on from Château de Montfort, another inviting little Romanesque **church** below the village of **CARSAC-AILLAC** makes a good place to pause. Though the meadow setting is delightful, the church's **carvings** are the main point of interest: in this case Arabic-influenced capitals around the choir and some later keystones. Note, too, the Stations of the Cross made by Russian abstract artist Léon Zack, who was a refugee here during World War II. Carsac also has some decent **accommodation** options, which could be used as a base for Sarlat, only 10km to the northwest.

ARRIVAL AND DEPARTURE — CARSAC-AILLAC

By bus Buses on the Sarlat–Souillac route stop outside the post office in Carsac-Aillac. Destinations Sarlat (1–3 daily; 15–20min); Souillac (2 daily; 30–40min).

ACCOMMODATION AND EATING

Delpeyrat ☎ 05 53 28 10 43, ✉ philippe.delpeyrat @wanadoo.fr. In the centre of Carsac, the family-run *Delpeyrat* is a charmingly old-fashioned place offering well-priced rooms, most of them set back from the road overlooking a small garden, and equally homely cooking (*menus* from €13; restaurant closed Sun eve & Sat midday). Breakfast €6.50. Closed mid-Oct to mid-Dec. **€38**

L'Ombrière Montfort ☎ 05 53 28 11 38, ✇ lombriere .com. You'll need to book early for this hospitable, Italian-owned *chambre d'hôte* in an eighteenth-century manor house perched above the Cingle de Montfort, a couple of kilometres west of Carsac and only five from Sarlat. Its four

light, airy rooms are tastefully decorated and very reasonably priced, including a copious breakfast. There's also a cosy lounge and fine views from the terrace. Evening meals – with an Italian twist – are available on request in the low season (Oct–May). Price includes breakfast. **€92**

Le Relais du Touron Le Touron ☎ 05 53 28 16 70, ✇ lerelaisdutouron.com. Set in extensive grounds 500m along the Sarlat road from Carsac, the *Relais* makes a peaceful place to stay. The rooms are fairly functional but spacious and well kept, occupying a modern block beside an outdoor pool. Restaurant meals also available (*menus* from €19.50). Breakfast €9.50. Closed Nov to Easter. **€88**

Château de Fénelon

Ste-Mondane • Easter–June & Sept Mon, Wed–Fri & Sun 10.30am–12.30pm & 2.30–6.30pm, Sat 2.30–6.30pm; July & Aug daily 10.30am–7pm; Oct to mid-Nov daily except Tues 2.30–5pm; closed mid-Nov to Easter • €8 • ☎ 05 53 29 81 45, ✉ chateau.fenelon @wanadoo.fr

From Carsac you need to cross south over the Dordogne and continue along eastwards for some 5km to find the **Château de Fénelon**, clamped to its own rocky outcrop. With its triple walls and great round towers topped with *lauzes*, the castle exudes all the might of the original medieval fortress. As you get closer, however, the Renaissance-era additions and other, later embellishments become more apparent – the large mullion windows and the gallery closing the interior courtyard, for example.

The castle's most illustrious occupant was **François de Salignac de la Mothe-Fénelon**, who was born here in 1651. Private tutor to the heir to the throne and later archbishop of Cambrai, he fell from grace when King Louis XIV interpreted his work *Télémaque* – which recounts the adventures of Ulysses' son – as a thinly veiled attack on the Crown. His intention had been to teach the young prince the finer points of kinghood, but for his pains Fénelon was banished to Cambrai where he died in 1715. He is remembered with much pride at Fénelon today. There's a mock-up of his study and numerous portraits, but the present owners have also amassed a worthwhile collection of period furniture, tapestries and medieval weaponry. The ornate walnut chimneypieces are also eye-catching.

From the Château de Fénelon the route continues east along the Dordogne, past one of its main rivals, the Château de Rouffillac (not open to the public), on the opposite bank, before finally reaching Souillac (see p.170) 17km later.

3

The Upper Dordogne valley and Rocamadour

ROCAMADOUR

The Upper Dordogne valley and Rocamadour

In its upper reaches the River Dordogne cuts a green swathe through the rocky limestone plateau of Haut-Quercy, as the northern sector of the Lot *département* is traditionally known. It is a land of walnut orchards and strawberry fields and although the cliffs rise to considerable heights in places, the valley here lacks the drama of the perched castles and towns immediately downstream. Instead, away from the main towns, it offers a slow, lazy river and a pace of life to match, quieter lanes, more modest castles and a succession of unspoilt riverside villages, such as Autoire, Cressensac and Carennac that proudly proclaim their status as amongst the most beautiful in France.

The main gateway to the Upper Dordogne valley is **Souillac**, a busy little town whose major attraction is its domed abbey church. A short distance upstream, an attractive back road strikes off along the River Ouysse, a minor tributary of the Dordogne, heading southeast to the spectacular pilgrimage town of **Rocamadour**, whose seven religious sanctuaries are built almost vertically into a rocky backdrop.

Back on the Dordogne, near the little village of **Lacave**, the river meanders in a north-easterly direction through walnut orchards and dozing villages to the dramatic crags around **Gluges**, where it has carved the **Cirque de Montvalent** out of the plateau. North of here, the market town of **Martel** sees surprisingly few tourists, given its medieval centre full of turreted mansions, while, to the east, **Carennac** merits a stop for its picturesque lanes and the twelfth-century carved portal adorning its church. Carennac also lies within striking distance of the **Gouffre de Padirac**, where a collapsed cavern has left a gaping hole in the limestone plateau. Upstream of Carennac the Dordogne valley begins to open out to form a broad plain around its confluence with the Cère. **Bretenoux**, the main town guarding the Cère valley, isn't itself a particularly engaging place, but it's more than compensated for by the nearby **Château de Castelnau**, which still dominates the country for miles around. North of Bretenoux is the pleasing town of **Beaulieu-sur-Dordogne,** while south is **St-Céré**, which provides a good base for exploring the region, and beneath the brooding towers of its ruined château, a scattering of stone and half-timbered townhouses attests to the town's fifteenth- and sixteenth-century heyday. There's more Renaissance architecture on show on the facade and in the superb stone staircase of the **Château de Montal**, a few kilometres to the west. The nearby villages of **Autoire** and **Loubressac**, meanwhile, are rooted firmly in the Quercy soil, their houses sporting little pigeon-lofts and the red-tiled roofs splayed gently above the eaves, which are typical of the region.

Festivals, events and markets p.171
Walk with the animals p.178

The Tale of Young King Henry p.182
"La Môme Piaf" and Gluges church p.184

CHÂTEAU DE CASTELNAU

Highlights

❶ **Souillac** In the abbey church of Ste-Marie the image of the prophet Isaiah is a masterpiece of Romanesque art. **See p.170**

❷ **Rocamadour** One of France's top pilgrimage sites defies gravity in its spectacular cliff-edge location. **See p.174**

❸ **Carennac** Wander the lanes of this typical Quercy village and then peek inside its quiet cloister. **See p.184**

❹ **Gouffre de Padirac** Take a boat trip on an underground river accessed via an immense cavern. **See p.186**

❺ **Château de Castelnau** Fans of military architecture shouldn't miss this brooding fortress. **See p.187**

❻ **Beaulieu-sur-Dordogne** Laidback market town on the banks of the Dordogne that sees fewer tourists than it deserves. **See p.188**

❼ **Château de Montal** Admire some of the region's finest Renaissance carvings on the facade and staircase of this stately home. **See p.192**

❽ **Autoire** Picture-perfect village encircled by limestone cliffs. There are good views from the top, as well. **See p.194**

HIGHLIGHTS ARE MARKED ON THE MAP ON P.170

GETTING AROUND

THE UPPER DORDOGNE VALLEY

By train Souillac, Rocamadour, St-Denis-lès-Martel (for Martel) and Bretenoux can be reached by train. Cressensac/Gignac is also on the train line, and is just 5km from the new Brive-Vallée de la Dordogne airport (ⓦ aeroport-brive-vallee-dordogne.com).

By bus Souillac, St-Denis-lès-Martel (for Martel) and Bretenoux are connected by fairly regular bus services.

There are less regular buses to Martel, Carennac, Beaulieu and St-Céré, while connections between the area's smaller towns are not particularly good. If you plan to do a lot of bus journeys, it would be worth getting hold of the comprehensive timetable, *Les Bus du Lot*; tourist offices in larger towns such as Souillac and Bretenoux should have copies.

Souillac and around

Traffic-ridden **Souillac** suffers from being the major gateway to both Sarlat and the Périgord Noir to the west and to the upper reaches of the Dordogne valley to the east, and though the nearby A20 *autoroute* brings some relief, it will never be a particularly pretty place. The town's main attraction is the **Église Ste-Marie**, with its exquisite carvings, but it also has a small enclave of old streets, which are worth a quick wander. A handy landmark to aim for is the semi-ruined **belfry** of St-Martin church, partially destroyed in the Wars of Religion, on the southeast corner of the old centre.

Immediately upstream from Souillac, the valley is dominated by the A20 road-bridge, but a few meanders of the river later and you're back among quiet lanes and unspoilt scenery. One place to head for is **Lacave**, a village on the south bank with some passably interesting limestone caves. From Lacave you can take an attractive detour south along a tributary river, the Ouysse, as it cuts its way through a mini-gorge in the

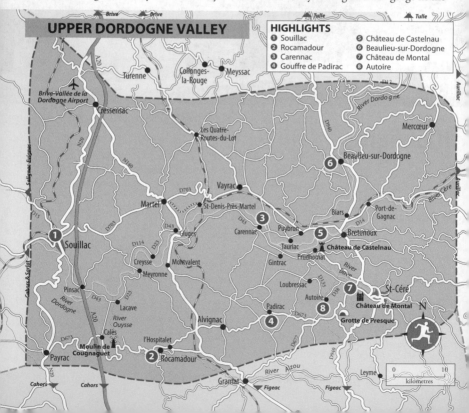

UPPER DORDOGNE VALLEY

HIGHLIGHTS
❶ Souillac ❺ Château de Castelnau
❷ Rocamadour ❻ Beaulieu-sur-Dordogne
❸ Carennac ❼ Château de Montal
❹ Gouffre de Padirac ❽ Autoire

FESTIVALS, EVENTS AND MARKETS

Second Sunday in May Beaulieu-sur-Dordogne: Fête de la Fraise. France's strawberry capital gets down to some serious baking with an 800-kilo strawberry tart. There's a great strawberry market, too.

Late May or early June Rocamadour: Fête des Fromages Fermiers. At Pentecôte (Whit Sunday) artisan cheese producers gather above the town at L'Hospitalet to show off their wares. In addition to the cheeses, there are folk concerts.

Mid-July Rocamadour: Les Éclectiques de Rocamadour. This week-long music festival ranges from classical ballet to Eastern European folk groups. Ticket only concerts take place in the Basilique St-Sauveur and the château.

Mid-July to mid-August St-Céré and around: Festival de St-Céré et du Haut-Quercy (☎05 65 38 28 08, ⓦfestival-saint-cere.com.). Three weeks of opera, recitals, orchestral works and chamber music in St-Céré (including the châteaux of Montal and Castelnau), Beaulieu, Martel, Cahors and Souillac. Tickets required.

Third week in August Rocamadour: Cantica Sacra (ⓦcantica-sacra.fr). One-week sacred singing course open to members of the public wishing to improve their singing technique in an exceptional setting.

Third weekend in July Souillac: Souillac en Jazz (☎05 65 37 81 56, ⓦsouillacenjazz.net). International jazz acts let rip in the streets of Souillac for six days of concerts, films, exhibitions and a feast on the final night. The big-name, ticket-only events take place outdoors next to the abbey church.

July 23 Martel: Foire à la Laine. A wool fair, in which the best fleeces are judged under the market hall.

Second weekend in August Souillac: Festival du Mime Automate (☎05 65 37 07 07). About fifteen groups of mime artists give performances (mostly free) in the streets of Souillac on the Friday and Saturday.

Early September Rocamadour: Semaine Mariale. The week dedicated to the Virgin Mary is celebrated with pilgrimages, prayers and Masses, including torchlight processions to the Chapelle Notre-Dame.

Last weekend in September Rocamadour: Rassemblement Européen de Montgolfières. Hot-air balloons take off from the valley below Rocamadour; for the best views, take up position early on the Belvédère in L'Hospitalet.

MARKETS

The main **markets** in this region are at: Beaulieu-sur-Dordogne (Wed & Sat); Bretenoux (Tues & Sat); Martel (Wed & Sat); St-Céré (Sat & first and third Wed of month); and Souillac (Fri). In addition to the weekly market, an annual truffle market takes place in Martel between mid-December and the end of January.

limestone plateau, to visit a 600-year-old working flour mill. Continue on this route and you will eventually find yourself in Rocamadour (see p.174).

Sainte-Marie

Walk one block west of the belfry of St-Martin and you come to a wide, open space dominated by the beautiful Romanesque **abbey church of Ste-Marie**. Its Byzantine domes are reminiscent of the cathedrals of Périgueux and Cahors, though on a smaller scale, while its largely unadorned interior conveys a far greater sense of antiquity. The first church on this site belonged to a priory founded in the tenth century, which became an abbey five hundred years later. Badly damaged during both the Hundred Years War and Wars of Religion, the church was restored in the seventeenth century before being abandoned during the Revolution. Sadly, only fragments of the **Romanesque sculptures** that once graced the main, west, portal have survived, but those that do remain – now reassembled inside the west door – are superb. Those on the tympanum tell the story of a local monk, Théophile, who was dismissed from the treasury for corruption. Desperate to regain his position, he is said to have made a pact with the Devil, but then fell seriously ill and, full of remorse, besought the Virgin Mary for forgiveness. His luck was in – the final scene depicts Théophile's dream of the Virgin accompanied by St Michael driving the Devil away. The greatest piece of craftsmanship is the bas-relief of the prophet Isaiah to the right of the door. Fluid and supple, it appears that the elongated, bearded figure clutching his parchment and with one leg extended is dancing for joy as he proclaims news of the coming of the Messiah.

Musée de l'Automate

Place de l'Abbaye • Jan–March, Nov & Dec Wed–Sun 2.30pm–5.30pm; April, May & Oct Tues–Sun 10am–noon & 3–6pm; June & Sept daily 10am–noon & 3–6pm; July & Aug daily 10am–7pm • €5.50 • ☎ 05 65 37 07 07, ⓦ musee-automate.fr

Behind the Ste-Marie church, to the west, the **Musée de l'Automate** contains an impressive collection of nineteenth- and twentieth-century mechanical dolls and animals that dance, juggle and perform magical tricks. Most come from the once-famous Rouillet-Decamps workshops in Paris and include such pieces as a life-size 1920s jazz band, Charlie Chaplin and a woman doing the twist.

ARRIVAL AND DEPARTURE
SOUILLAC

By air Brive-Vallée de la Dordogne airport is 25 minutes north of Souillac, offering twice-weekly flights from London (☎ 05 55 22 40 00, ⓦ aeroport-brive-vallee -dordogne). The nearest train station is Cressensac/Gignac (see p.170), or car hire is available at the airport.

By train Getting to Souillac by public transport is not a problem since it lies on the main Paris–Toulouse train line. The *gare SNCF* lies just over a kilometre northwest of town; take av Jean Jaurès and then av Martin-Malvy, which will bring you out at the west end of av Gambetta, the old quarter's main east–west artery.

Destinations Brive (6–9 daily; 25min); Cahors (6–9 daily; 40min–1hr); Cressensac/Gignac (6–9 daily; 20min); Gourdon (6–9 daily; 15min); Montauban (6–8 daily; 1hr 30min); Paris (5–6 daily; 4hr 30min); Toulouse (6–8 daily; 1hr 55min).

By bus Buses from Sarlat, Brive, Gourdon and St-Denis-lès-Martel (on the Brive–Figeac train line) mostly stop at the train station or the Sarlat road, while Eurolines buses (tickets from Voyages Belmon, av de Sarlat; ☎ 05 65 37 81 15, ⓦ eurolines .fr), en route between Toulouse and London, Brussels, Hanover and Amsterdam, stop in central Souillac on the place du Foirail, a large square to the east of the main N20.

Destinations Brive (school term Mon–Sat 1–2 daily, rest of year Tues–Thurs & Sat 1–2 daily; 1hr–1hr 15min); Martel (Mon–Sat 1 daily; 20–30min); St-Denis-lès-Martel (Mon–Sat 1 daily; 35–45min); Sarlat (3–5 daily; 50min).

By car Place du Foirail provides the most convenient car parking for the centre.

GETTING AROUND

Car rental A.C. Loc'46, 22 av du Général-de-Gaulle (☎ 05 65 32 68 74, ⓦ acloc46.fr).

Bike rental Carrefour du Cycle, 23 av Général-de-Gaulle (☎ 05 65 37 07 52), the northern extension of bd

Louis-Jean Malvy.

Canoe rental Copeyre Canoë (☎ 05 65 32 72 61, ⓦ copeyre.com), next to *Les Ondines* campsite (see opposite). They also have bikes for rent here.

INFORMATION

Tourist office Bd Louis-Jean Malvy, across the road from place du Foirail (July & Aug Mon–Sat 9.30am–12.30pm & 2–7pm, Sun 10am–noon & 3–6pm; Sept–June Mon–Sat 10am–noon & 2–6pm; ☎ 05 65 37 81 56, ⓦ tourisme-vallee -dordogne.com). From inside the office, a window gives a view down into the nave of the disused church of St-Martin.

Internet Available at the Point Information Jeunes (Cyberbase), av de Sarlat (Tues–Fri 10am–noon & 3–6pm, Sat 10am–noon; ☎ 05 65 37 89 58).

Market Souillac's main market takes place on Friday mornings.

ACCOMMODATION

Chastrusse Nadaillac-de-Rouge, 10km southwest of Souillac ☎ 05 65 37 60 08, ⓦ hotel-restaurant -chastrusse.com. Delightfully unpretentious place with rooms either in the old block – the nicer option – or modern bungalows around the pool, with an excellent restaurant

serving such earthy delights as *pastis aux pigeons* and *tarte aux noix* – they expect you to have a hearty appetite. Restaurant open Feb to mid-Oct daily (except Sat lunch) noon–2.30pm & 7.30–9pm. Breakfast €7. **€45**

Domaine de la Paille Basse 9km northwest of

Souillac ☎ 05 65 37 85 48, ⓦ lapaillebasse.com. Friendly four-star campsite that's the place to head for if you've got your own transport. It's set on a lovely, high spot, signed off the D15 to Salvignac. Closed mid-Sept to mid-May. **€29.90**

Grand Hotel 1 allée de Verninac ☎ 05 65 32 78 30, ⓦ grandhotel-souillac.com. A friendly hotel decked out in a contemporary style, located next to the tourist office. Some rooms have private balconies, while their shady terrace on the main street is ideal for a light lunch, and their elegant restaurant, *L'Imprévu*, offers *menus* in the range €17.90–33.00. Restaurant open noon–2.30pm & 7–9pm. Breakfast €8.50. **€50**

Les Ondines ☎ 05 65 37 86 44, ⓦ camping-lesondines .com. Large, three-star campsite down by the river to the south of town with a heated pool plus separate pool for children, in a secluded location. Wi-fi throughout. Closed Oct–April. **€19.80**

★ **Le Pavillon Saint-Martin** 5 place St-Martin ☎ 05 65 32 63 45, ⓦ hotel-saint-martin-souillac.com. Housed in a sixteenth-century notary's mansion, *Le Pavillon Saint-Martin* has a lovely stone-flagged entrance hall and a spectacular staircase, and is furnished with a variety of bright, comfortable rooms, ranging from old-fashioned floral to eye-assaulting reds and oranges. Breakfast includes fresh strawberries in season and is served in a vaulted cellar. Private parking €5. Breakfast €9.50. **€77**

La Vieille Auberge 1 rue de la Recège ☎ 05 65 32 79 43, ⓦ la-vieille-auberge.com. Across the old quarter at the west end of avenue Gambetta, this is Souillac's most upmarket hotel. The rooms in the main building are well equipped but rather functional. The good but pricey restaurant (Tues–Sun noon–2pm & 7–9pm plus mid-Feb to mid-Nov) offers *menus* from €25. Breakfast €11. **€75**

EATING

Along with those listed below, don't forget the hotel restaurants (see above), which are all worth trying. There are also several delightful cafés offering more basic food. Head west into the old quarter, well away from the traffic-ridden centre, where the streets are cobbled and the town pump still works; you may see Souillac in a new light.

Le Beffroi 6 place St-Martin ☎ 05 65 37 80 33. This restaurant sits at the southern end of the *place* and is particularly lovely in summer, when it's warm enough to eat out on the terrace under the wisteria. Simple *plats du jour* are around €8 and there are very good *menus* from €12 to 25.50. Daily noon–2.30pm & 7–9pm.

Lycée d'Hôtellerie Av Roger Couderc ☎ 05 65 27 03 00. If you fancy a slightly different eating experience, head for the *Lycée*, situated on a hill to the west of the old quarter, where you can act as a guinea-pig for trainee chefs and waiters/waitresses. Don't be put off, though – the food is generally excellent and advance reservations are required.

Menus are under €25 at lunchtime for four courses, and €35 in the evening for a five-course meal. Mon–Fri noon & from 7pm.

Le Redouillé 28 av de Toulouse ☎ 05 65 37 87 25. Despite its inconvenient location about 1km south of the centre along boulevard Louis-Jean Malvy, this may be the best place to eat in Souillac. *Menus* range from €21 and make innovative use of local produce to create such mouth-watering dishes as calves' sweetbreads with *sauce aux morilles,* duck wings in kumquat sauce or *charlotte de confit de canard*. Feb–Dec Tues–Sat noon–2pm & 7–9.30pm, Sun noon–2pm.

Lacave and around

Following the Dordogne upstream along the D43 you soon leave the *autoroute* behind as you crest the hill and drop down to **LACAVE**, on the river's south bank 14km southeast of Souillac.

Grottes de Lacave

Guided tours (1hr 15min) daily: mid- to end March & Oct 10am–noon & 2–5pm; April–June 9.30am–noon & 2–6pm; July to mid-Aug 9.30am–6pm; mid-Aug to end Sept 9.30am–noon & 2–5.30pm • Adults €9.20, children €6 • ⓦ grottes-de-lacave.com

A cavernous hole in the limestone cliffs overshadowing the village marks the entrance to a series of underground lakes, together making up the **Grottes de Lacave**, which can be visited on guided tours. You travel the first few hundred metres by electric train, after which there's a lift up to the kilometre-long gallery resplendent with all manner of stalactites and stalagmites, from petrified "waterfalls" to great organ pipes. But the highlight here is the magical reflections in the lakes' mirrored surfaces – at one point they also use ultraviolet light to reveal the glittering fluorescence of the "living" water-filled formations while the older, dry deposits remain lost in the darkness.

Ferme-Auberge Calvel ☎ 05 65 37 87 20. Just 2km out of Lacave on the D23 northeast to Meyronne, this friendly little place offers basic *camping à la ferme* with space for just a handful of tents. The restaurant serves up rustic, cuisine (*menus* €6). Closed mid-Sept to April; reservations preferred. No credit cards. **€9**

Le Pont de l'Ouysse ☎ 05 65 37 87 04, ⓦ lepontdelouysse.fr. A stylish country hotel with Michelin-starred restaurant and a lovely terrace overlooking the river. It has fourteen immaculate rooms and lies in an idyllic spot about a kilometre west of Lacave on the Souillac road. Restaurant open April–Oct Tues 7.30–9pm, Wed–Sun noon–2pm & 7.30–9pm. *Plats* from €26, *menus* from €60; reservation advisable for non-residents. Breakfast €16. **€130**

Calès

From where the River Ouysse empties into the Dordogne just west of Lacave, a minor road heads south along the tributary, winding its way up the valley side to the plateau near the village of **CALÈS**, 5km later. The village is a neat and tidy place with little more than a couple of decent hotels in its centre.

Le Petit Relais ☎ 05 65 37 96 09, ⓦ hotel-petitrelais.fr. This well-kept little hotel has a pleasingly rustic atmosphere, spick-and-span rooms and a pretty, flowery terrace where you can enjoy a good-value *menu* from €23. They also have a surprisingly extensive wine list. Restaurant open May–Sept daily noon–1.30pm & 7–8.30pm; weekends only Oct to mid-Feb & mid-March to April. Breakfast €9. **€63**

Moulin de Cougnaguet

Visit by guided tour (30min) April to mid-Oct daily 10am–noon & 2–6pm • Adults €4, children €2 • ☎ 05 65 38 73 56, ⓦ cougnaguet.com

At Calès the road from Lacave joins the D673 and turns east before dropping back down to the river, which has here carved out a mini-gorge. For an interesting diversion, turn left just after crossing the river and about a kilometre later you'll reach the **Moulin de Cougnaguet**, a fourteenth-century fortified mill, which ceased working commercially only in 1959. During the tour, the enthusiastic owner points out its many defensive features – including arrow slits and sluice gates which, when opened from inside the mill, unleashed a torrent of water to sweep away anyone attempting to ford the millrace – and also puts the mill through its paces. Standing close to 1.5 tonnes of stone spinning at eighty revolutions per minute you get a real feel for the pent-up power of the water waiting calmly upstream.

On to Rocamadour

From the Moulin de Cougnaguet it's 12km to Rocamadour. The D673 takes you back up onto the plateau and into Rocamadour from the north, but for a more dramatic approach follow the footpath (the GR6) along the valley. It runs alongside the River Ouysse past another mill – this was once big wheat country and even in high summer the Ouysse, part of which flows underground, never dries up – before turning eastwards along the River Alzou. Gradually the valley closes in until you round a bend and see the pilgrimage town of Rocamadour clinging to the cliff like a lost city.

Rocamadour and around

Halfway up the northern cliff face of the deep and abrupt canyon of the River Alzou, the spectacular setting of **ROCAMADOUR** is hard to beat, with the turrets and spires of the **Cité Religieuse** at its heart, sandwiched between the jumbled roofs of the medieval town and the château's crenellated walls above. However, as you draw closer the spell is broken by the constant stream of pilgrims and more secular-minded visitors, particularly in summer, who fill lanes lined with shops peddling incongruous souvenirs. The main reason for Rocamadour's popularity – going back centuries – is the supposed miraculous properties of the statue of the **Black Madonna**, enshrined in the Cité's smoke-blackened **Chapelle Notre-Dame**. Modern tourists are also courted with a number of secondary attractions, including two wildlife parks, scattered on the plateau to the north and east of town. Even if those don't appeal, it's worth venturing up to the hamlet of **L'Hospitalet**, on the cliff (1.5km by road) east of Rocamadour, for the finest views of the town.

Brief history

The first mention of Rocamadour's Chapelle Notre-Dame dates from 1105, although evidence suggests pilgrims started coming here as early as the ninth century. However, things really got going when a perfectly preserved body was discovered in a rock-hewn tomb beside the chapel in 1166. It was promptly declared to be that of Zacchaeus, later **St Amadour**; according to one legend, Zacchaeus – a tax-collector in Jericho at the time of Christ – was advised by the Virgin Mary to come to France and lived out his years in Rocamadour as a hermit. As tales of the saint and associated miracles spread, the faithful began to arrive in droves from all over Europe. St Bernard, numerous kings – including Henry II of England and Louis IX of France (St Louis) – and thousands of ordinary mortals crawled up the **Grand Escalier** (the pilgrims' staircase) on their knees to pay their respects and to seek forgiveness or cures. Others came simply to plunder the shrine – among them the Young King Henry (see box, p.182) – but they were easily outclassed by the Huguenots, who, in 1562, tried in vain to burn St Amadour's corpse and finally resigned themselves to hacking it to bits instead. In the meantime, centuries of warfare and plague led to a decline in the number of pilgrims. The buildings gradually fell into ruin until the bishops of Cahors, hoping to revive the flagging pilgrimage, financed a massive reconstruction in the early nineteenth century and so gave us the Rocamadour we see today.

Old Town

The **old town** is easy enough to find your way around since there's just one street, pedestrianized rue de la Couronnerie, which runs west from Porte du Figuier – one of Rocamadour's four medieval gateways – to the wide stone staircase leading up to the sanctuaries roughly 300m later. Follow the main road east from Porte du Figuier, on the other hand, and it will take you winding up the valley side to L'Hospitalet (see p.177); pedestrians can use the quieter Voie Sainte, a narrow lane which branches off left after a couple of hundred metres.

La Cité Religieuse

The steep hillside above rue de la Couronnerie supports no fewer than seven chapels, known collectively as "Les Sanctuaires", or the **Cité Religieuse**. There's a lift dug into the rock-face (see p.179), but it's far better to climb the 216 worn and pitted steps of the **Grand Escalier**, up which the devout once dragged themselves on their knees to the doors of the Cité. Inside lies a small square, the parvis, completely hemmed in by the various chapels.

Basilique St-Sauveur

Daily: July & Aug 8am–9pm; Sept–June 8.30am–6.30pm, though these times can vary

The largest chapel in the Cité Religieuse is the **Basilique St-Sauveur**, a vaulted Romanesque-Gothic hall which up until 1900 provided lodgings for pilgrims who couldn't afford anything better. An unusual and rather rickety-looking twentieth-century wooden gallery covers the rock-face wall and there are several paintings of notable visitors on the other walls. The slightly sparse altar has a fine bronze frontal of the Ascension, surmounted by a rather gruesome sixteenth-century Christ on the Cross.

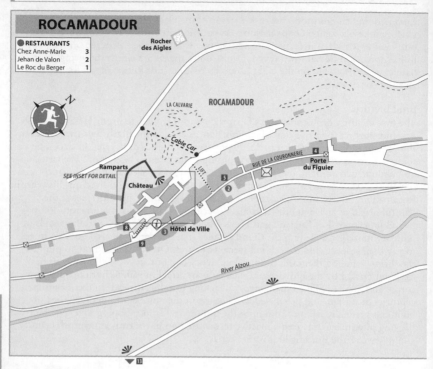

Chapelle Notre-Dame

Daily: July & Aug 8am–9pm, Sept–June 8.30am–6.30pm, though these times can vary

The little **Chapelle Notre-Dame** is nestled against the rock and the wall of the Basilique St-Sauveur, and is where the miracle-working twelfth-century **Black Madonna** resides. The crudely carved statue, less than 70cm tall, still wears a faint smile despite her mutilated state, though the adult-featured Jesus balanced on her knee looks decidedly out of sorts. The rest of the chapel is unremarkable, but note the empty recess in the rock outside, where St Amadour's body was found, and a rusty sword protruding from the cliff above. According to local tradition this is Durandal, the trusty blade of the legendary Roland whose heroic exploits are recorded in the twelfth-century *Chanson de Roland* (*The Song of Roland*), though it's not revealed exactly how it got here from northern Spain, where Roland supposedly died in battle against the Moors in 778. Beside the chapel's ornately carved door there are also some faded fifteenth-century frescoes depicting a macabre fight between the Living and the Dead.

Chapelle St-Michel

Accessible only by guided tours of the Cité (see p.179)

Opposite the Chapelle Notre-Dame, tucked tightly into a corner of the place Parvis with one long wall of overhanging rock, the twelfth-century **Chapelle St-Michel** is home to two incredibly well-preserved twelfth-century polychrome paintings of the Annunciation and the Visitation.

The château

Ramparts daily 8am–8pm • €2

East of the Cité Religieuse there's a sandy esplanade and the cable car (see p.179) that will take you to the top of the cliff. Alternatively, you can walk up the shady zig-zag

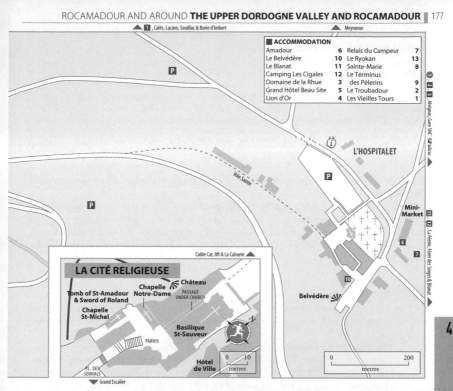

path, *La Calvarie*, past tableaux depicting the Stations of the Cross, or take a more direct and steeper path to come out near the **château**, a full 150m above the river below. While the château itself, a mostly nineteenth-century reconstruction, is private, you can walk round the **ramparts** for vertiginous views.

Rocher des Aigles

April, May & Sept Tues–Sun 2–5pm; June Tues–Sun 1–6pm; July & Aug daily 1–7pm; Oct Tues, Thurs, Fri & Sun 2.30pm–5pm; closed Nov–March • Flying demonstrations April, May & Sept Tues–Sun 2.30pm & 4pm; June Tues–Fri 1.30pm, 3 & 4.30pm; July & Aug daily 1–5.30pm roughly every hour; Oct Tues, Thurs, Fri & Sun 3pm • €9.50 • ☎ 05 65 33 65 45, ⊛ rocherdesaigles.com

The road leading west from the château brings you almost immediately to the first of Rocamadour's two wildlife parks, the **Rocher des Aigles**, a breeding centre for birds of prey. The cages seem uncomfortably small, but with a production rate of nearly a hundred chicks a year the birds can't be overly stressed about it. There's a film explaining the breeding programme, which aims to reintroduce a number of rare species to the wild, and you can also see the hatching room where scrawny chicks warm themselves under sun lamps. Best, though, are the thirty-minute flying demonstrations, in which a dozen or so condors, fish eagles and other such majestic birds are allowed to soar free over the valley.

L'Hospitalet

It's worth coming up to **L'Hospitalet** for the tremendous views of the medieval Cité from the cliff-edge belvedere. It's stunning at any time, but particularly magical at night when the buildings are illuminated (March–Nov & Christmas hols).

To get there, head about 700m east from the top of the lifts along the cliff edge to join the main road, the D673 from Calès (see p.174). After another 150m you reach

> ## WALK WITH THE ANIMALS
>
> If you're a keen walker and happen to be in the area in the last week of April, you might like to join in the **Transhumance**, a five-day, seventy-kilometre walk spearheaded by a flock of sheep. Open to the public, the route starts off in Rocamadour and heads to Luzech (see p.232), via narrow country lanes and rolling fields. Unlike in mountainous regions in France, transhumance is not yet a tradition in the Lot, but local associations, as well as the Conseil Général (◍lot.fr), are actively promoting it in the hope that it will become so. There's a practical side to the idea, too: as the sheep traverse fields lent by local landowners, they will eat down the grass, in a demonstration of ecological land maintenance.

the modern, plate-glass **tourist office** (see opposite), which marks the western extent of **L'Hospitalet**.

L'Hospitalet's name refers to a pilgrims' hospital founded on the clifftop here in the thirteenth century, of which only a few ruined walls and a chapel containing a copy of the Black Madonna remain. A crossroads lying immediately to the northeast of the chapel represents the centre of modern L'Hospitalet, which consists of a scattering of hotels, cafés and shops.

Forêt des Singes

April & Sept 1–15 daily 10am–noon & 1–5.30pm; May & June daily 10am–noon & 1–6pm; July & Aug daily 9.30am–6.30pm; mid-Sept to Oct Mon–Fri 1–5pm, Sat & Sun 10am–noon & 1–5pm; Nov Sat & Sun 10am–noon & 1–5pm • Adults €8.50, children €5 • ◍ la-foret -des-singes.com

About 300m east of L'Hospitalet is the second of the wildlife parks, the **Forêt des Singes**; it's one of the better such parks, with some 130 Barbary apes roaming twenty hectares of oak and scrubland in relative freedom. The aim is conservation – so far around six hundred young monkeys have been reintroduced to North Africa. The best time to visit is during the cool of the early morning or evening and in early summer when the youngsters are frolicking about.

La Borie d'Imbert

Daily mid-March to Sept 10am–6.30pm • Adults €5, children €3, some parts free • ◍ rocamadourlaboriedimbert.com

An attraction worth visiting, particularly for those with children, is **La Borie d'Imbert**, situated on the D247 in the direction of Souillac. The old farmhouse, La Maison de Justine, has countrified rooms complete with traditional cookware and furniture, while the baby farm animals are a sure winner for the very young. The goats are milked every day from 5.30–7pm, and in the farm shop you can taste and buy the Rocamadour goats' cheese (see p.180) and home-produced charcuterie.

ARRIVAL AND DEPARTURE   ROCAMADOUR

Getting to Rocamadour by public transport is awkward. There are no buses, and Rocamadour-Padirac *gare SNCF*, on the Brive–Figeac line, lies 3km away to the northeast. If you don't want to trek into town alongside the main road, you can call a taxi (Taxi Herbert ☎ 06 73 44 79 98 or ☎ 06 81 60 14 60). Note that the station is rarely staffed, and there's no ticket machine, so check the times of return trains carefully on arrival and buy a return ticket beforehand.

By car Since Rocamadour is pedestrianized, if you arrive by car you'll have to park in L'Hospitalet, where there is a large, free car park at the top of the cable car; this is your best bet if you're staying at one of the hotels with no parking facilities in the centre of the town. Otherwise you can park in the valley several hundred metres below, and rather than walking into town from the valley car park, you could take Le Petit Train (April–Sept departures every 15min; €2.50 one way, €3.50 return); they also do two 30min evening tours with a commentary (9.30pm or 10pm; €5).

GETTING AROUND

By lift In the village centre, a lift (daily: April & Oct 9am–6pm; May, June & Sept 9am–7pm; July & Aug 8am–8pm; Feb, March, Nov 1–15 & Christmas school hols, 9am–6pm; closed mid-Nov to Jan, except the school hols; every 3min; €2 one way, €3 return) links the town's main street, rue de la Couronnerie, with the Cité Religieuse above.

By cable car A cable car (daily: April & Oct 9am–6pm; May, June & Sept 9am–7pm; July & Aug 8am–10pm; Nov–March 10am–12.30pm & 2–5.30pm; every 3min; €2.50 one way, €4.10 return) departs from just east of the Cité to emerge on the clifftop near the château and the upper car parks.

INFORMATION

Tourist office Rocamadour has two tourist offices sharing the same phone number and website: the main one is located on the western outskirts of L'Hospitalet (April daily 10am–12.30pm & 2–6pm; May, June & Sept daily 10am–12.30pm & 2–7pm; July & Aug daily 10am–7pm; Oct Mon–Fri 10am–noon & 2–5pm, Sat & Sun 2–5.30pm; Nov–March Mon–Fri 10am–noon & 2–5pm; ☎ 05 65 33 22 00, ⊕ tourisme-vallee-dordogne.com). The second is on rue de la Couronnerie next to the Hôtel de Ville (daily: April, June & Sept 10am–12.30pm & 1.30–6pm; July & Aug 9.30am–7pm; Oct 10am–12.30pm & 2–5.30pm; Nov–March 2–5pm).

Guided tours The tourist office puts on daily guided tours of the Cité for a group of 5–20 people for €89 (French- English- and Spanish-language options available). If you're by yourself then the office will slot you into a group. Pre-book via the tourist office at least the day before. The tours might not always run in the winter months/low season.

Money There's a 24hr ATM outside the L'Hospitalet tourist office.

Supermarket The mini-market in l'Hospitalet sells basic provisions (see p.177), but otherwise the nearest food shops and a pharmacy are in Alvignac, 7km northeast.

ACCOMMODATION

One of the benefits of staying over in Rocamadour is that you can enjoy the town at its quietest in the early morning and late evening, and the hotels here are not too expensive. The downside is that everywhere is completely booked up in summer for miles around, and most places close during the winter months. Outside these periods, there are some good options, with a choice between central Rocamadour, the modern places in L'Hospitalet or somewhere in the surrounding countryside.

OLD TOWN

Grand Hôtel Beau Site Rue de la Couronnerie ☎ 05 65 33 63 08, ⊕ bestwestern-rocamadour.com. Rocamadour's top hotel occupies a lovely old mansion – its entrance all flagstone floors and oak beams – right in the centre, with more modern rooms in an annexe across the road. It has an excellent restaurant, the *Jehan de Valon* (see p.180), and a pool 2km away. Hotel closed mid-Nov to mid-Feb. Breakfast €12.50. **€80**

Lion d'Or Porte Figuier ☎ 05 65 33 62 04, ⊕ liondor -rocamadour.com. Just inside the old city gate at the east end of rue de la Couronnerie, this old-fashioned, family-run hotel is one of the cheaper options in the old quarter, offering small but adequate en-suite rooms. Their restaurant is right across the street with good but equally no-nonsense food. Hotel closed mid-Dec to March. Breakfast €8. **€53.50**

Sainte-Marie Place des Senhals ☎ 05 65 33 63 07, ⊕ hotel-sainte-marie.fr. This friendly place halfway up the Grand Escalier is extremely popular. The rooms are simple and some quite small, but the location and restaurant with tasty food and superb views down into the valley make up for it. The restaurant is open April–Oct noon–2.30pm & 7–9.45pm, and serves a *plat du jour* at €10.50, with *menus* at €14–28. Breakfast €8. **€45**

Le Terminus des Pèlerins Place de la Carreta ☎ 05 65 33 62 14, ⊕ terminus-des-pelerins.com. A good option

on rue de la Couronnerie, at the bottom of the Grand Escalier. Some rooms have terraces overlooking the valley, while all are painted in fresh, modern colours and have spacious bathrooms. Their restaurant is popular for its traditional and regional cuisine, with a *plat du jour* at €10 and *menus* from €17.50. Restaurant open April to mid-Nov noon–2.30pm & 7–9.30pm. Breakfast €8. **€55**

L'HOSPITALET AND AROUND

Amadour Place de l'Europe, L'Hospitalet ☎ 05 65 33 73 50, ⊕ amadour-hotel.com. No views from this newly refurbished modern hotel a hundred metres north of the *Belvédère* (see below), but acceptable rooms – some with a small terrace – friendly service and a swimming pool. Hotel closed mid-Oct to March. Breakfast €5. **€46**

Le Belvédère L'Hospitalet ☎ 05 65 33 63 25, ⊕ hotel -le-belvedere.fr. Not the most beautiful hotel, but the rooms are decent and the location, on the cliff edge as you come into L'Hospitalet from Rocamadour, is superb. Note that only the more expensive rooms enjoy prime views, though you can also enjoy them from the excellent restaurant's big picture windows. *Plat du jour* €12, *menus* from €18. Restaurant open Feb–Dec daily noon–2pm & 7–9pm. Breakfast €8.50. **€55**

Le Blanat Blanat, 4km east of Rocamadour just across the N140 ☎ 05 65 33 68 27, ⊕ gite-blanat-rocamadour .com. In a tiny hamlet, this is a useful place to find in this area,

4

as unlike most options it remains open all year (reservations are required out of season). Set in a pretty garden, it offers five simple *chambre d'hôte* rooms and four self-catering rooms equipped with corner kitchen and barbecue. No credit cards. The GR6 runs close by. B&B and self-catering **€46**

Camping Les Cigales ☏ 05 65 33 64 44, ⓦ camping -cigales.com. Three-star campsite east of the *Amadour* (see p.179). It has a couple of large pools and plenty of space for activities including volleyball, mini-golf and table tennis. It also has a useful restaurant and snack bar. Camping closed Sept–June. **€20.80**

Domaine de la Rhue 6km northeast of Rocamadour, off the D840 ☏ 05 65 33 71 50, ⓦ domainedelarhue .com. This is a delightful *chambre d'hôte* in the converted stable block of a small château. The beautiful rooms have wooden flooring and mosquito nets, while there's also a pool and large garden. Keen walkers might like to try the trail to Rocamadour (60min); for the less keen it's 10min by car. **€95**

Relais du Campeur ☏ 05 65 33 63 28, ⓦ lerelaisdu campeur.com. Leafy but fairly basic two-star campsite situated next to the *Amadour* (see p.179). It offers a heated pool and children's playground. Closed Sept–April. **€17.80**

Le Ryokan Mages, just south of Rocamadour and signed off the D32 ☏ 05 65 11 63 67, ⓦ leryokan.fr. Meaning "Japanese country inn", this charming *chambre d'hôte* occupies a converted stone barn decked out in a Japanese theme, furnished with objects collected during the hosts' travels in Asia. They also use renewable energy sources to heat the barn. All rooms are non-smoking. Closed Nov–March. **€58**

Le Troubadour Belveyre, 1km north of L'Hospitalet on the D673 ☏ 05 65 33 70 27, ⓦ www.hotel-troubadour .com. A small and delightful hotel with flowery, en-suite rooms, where you can truly get away from the crowds. There's a pool and bikes, and a residents-only restaurant (*menus* from €28). Restaurant open mid-Feb to mid-Nov daily 7–9pm. Breakfast €11. **€65**

Les Vieilles Tours Lafage, 3km west of L'Hospitalet just off the D673 ☏ 05 65 33 68 01, ⓦ vtrocamadour .com. A surprisingly affordable country-house hotel that offers a spot of luxury. Set in large grounds, the buildings have been beautifully restored – one room incorporates a mini tower – and there are splendid views all around, as well as a pool and an excellent restaurant, which is open April to mid-Nov & Christmas 7.30–9.30pm. *Menus* from €29. Half-board obligatory July & Aug. Breakfast €12. **€73**

EATING AND DRINKING

Eating in Rocamadour is a mixed bag and there are a good few greasy fast-food joints and tourist traps. In general, the best restaurants are those attached to the hotels (see p.179), along with a few more everyday recommendations; note that most places are closed in winter. The local speciality, which you'll find on most menus, is *Rocamadour*, a round disc of goat's cheese, often served on toast or with a walnut salad, or occasionally flambéed in brandy or drizzled with honey. Elsewhere in the region it is known as *Cabécou*, but cheeses produced around Rocamadour warrant their own special *appellation* – and even their own festival (see box, p.171). You can buy it at shops selling the inevitable foie gras and other regional produce, but for other picnic fare the only proper food shop hereabouts is the mini-market (April to mid-Oct) beside the *Amadour* (see p.179) in L'Hospitalet.

Chez Anne-Marie Rue de la Couronnerie ☏ 05 65 33 65 81. A jolly little place that's popular for its cheap-and-cheerful mix of grills, omelettes and salads in addition to regional dishes. They also serve a vegetarian *menu* at €19; *menus* from €17.50 with lots of choice. Daily noon–2.30pm & 7–9.30pm; closed second half of Jan.

★ **Jehan de Valon** Rue de la Couronnerie ☏ 05 65 33 63 08. You need to book ahead for a table in this elegant restaurant, with panoramic views over the Alzou valley. Their seasonal *menus* include a good variety of fresh fish as well as local specialities, with prices starting at €26; count on at least €40 for á la carte. Simpler fare is on offer in their adjoining brasserie where a *plat du jour* will set you back around €12 and a three-course *menu* €19.60. Mid-Feb to Nov daily 12.30–1.30pm & 7.30–9pm (9.30pm in July & Aug).

Le Roc du Berger Bois de Belvyre, 1.5km from Rocamadour in the direction of Pauillac ☏ 05 65 33 19 99, ⓦ rocduberger.fr. A wooden country inn situated in the middle of a truffle orchard, where traditional dishes such as *confit de canard* and lamb steaks are given extra flavour by being cooked over an open fire; *menus* €19–25.50. Reservation strongly advised in high season. April–Sept daily noon–2.30pm & 7.15–9pm; Sat & Sun only in Oct.

Martel and around

Fifteen kilometres east of Souillac, **MARTEL**'s medieval centre is built in a pale, almost white, stone, offset by warm reddish-brown roofs. A Turenne-administered town (see p.81), its heyday was during the thirteenth and fourteenth centuries when the viscounts granted certain freedoms, including the right to mint money, and established

a royal court of appeal here. The good times ceased, however, when the wars showed up: Martel was occupied briefly by English forces during the Hundred Years War and suffered again at the hands of the Huguenots in the sixteenth century.

Despite the town's rather turbulent past, on the whole the compact old centre has survived remarkably intact, with the exception of the ramparts, which have been dismantled to make way for the wide boulevard that now rings Martel's pedestrianized centre. Take any of the lanes leading inwards and you will soon find yourself in the cobbled main square, **place des Consuls**. It is mostly taken up by the eighteenth-century *halle*, scene of a busy market on Wednesday and Saturday mornings, but on every side there are reminders of the town's illustrious past, most notably the grand Gothic **Palais de la Raymondie** on the square's east side, now occupied by the *mairie*. Begun in 1280, it served as both the Turenne law courts and fortress, hence the large square tower – one of seven that gave the town its epithet, *la ville aux sept tours*. On the square's south side is another of the towers – a circular five-storey turret belonging to the **Maison Fabri**. According to tradition, this striking building is where Young King Henry, son of Henry II, died in 1183 (see box below).

One block south of here, rue Droite leads east to the town's main church, **St-Maur**, built in a fiercely defensive, mostly Gothic style, with a finely carved Romanesque tympanum depicting the Last Judgement above the west door.

ARRIVAL AND INFORMATION   MARTEL

By train The *gare SNCF* is at St-Denis-lès-Martel, 7km to the east of Martel, on the Brive–Figeac and Brive-Aurillac lines. Destinations Figeac (5–6 daily; 1hr); Gramat (5–6 daily; 20–30min); Rocamadour-Padirac (4–5 daily; 15–20min); Souillac (4–5 daily; 25min); Vayrac (2 daily; 5min).

By bus Without your own transport, the best way to get to Martel is via one of two bus services, both of which stop on the ring road to the southwest of the centre. One route comes from Brive and the second from Souillac. The bus from Souillac passes through Martel on its way to the *gare SNCF* at St-Denis-lès-Martel; if there's no convenient bus heading back from St-Denis to Martel, call Mme Daubet (☏ 05 65 37 34 87) for a taxi. Destinations Brive (school hols Tues & Sat 1 daily; rest of year Tues 1 daily; 1hr); St-Denis-lès-Martel (Mon–Sat 1–2 daily; 10–15min); Souillac (Mon–Sat 2 daily; 35min).

By tourist train In season, a tourist train runs along a splendid stretch of decommissioned line from Martel towards St-Denis and back – but not as far as St-Denis station – along cliffs 80m above the Dordogne (departures by diesel train: April–June & Sept Tues & Thurs 2.30pm; July & Aug Mon, Tues, Thurs & Fri 11am, 2.30pm & 4pm, Sat 2.30pm; €7 return; departures by steam train: April–Sept Sun & hols 11am, 2.30pm & 4pm, also mid-July to end-Aug Mon–Thurs same times; €9.50 return; ☏ 05 65 37 35 81, ⓦ trainduhautquercy.info). It departs from the otherwise disused station two hundred metres south of town; reservations are recommended.

Tourist office Palais de la Raymondie on place des Consuls (April–June, Sept & Oct Mon–Sat 9am–noon & 2–6pm; July & Aug daily 9am–7pm; Nov–March Mon–Fri 9am–noon & 2–5pm; ☏ 05 65 37 43 44, ⓦ martel.fr) can provide further information about the train and about Martel's festivals, including the annual wool fair (see box, p.171 for more).

THE TALE OF YOUNG KING HENRY

At the end of the twelfth century, Martel provided the stage for one of the tragic events in the internecine conflicts of the Plantagenet family. When Henry Plantagenet (King Henry II of England) imprisoned his estranged wife Eleanor of Aquitaine, his sons took up arms against their father. The eldest son, also **Henry** (nicknamed the Young King since he was crowned while his father was still on the throne), even went so far as to plunder the viscountcy of Turenne and Quercy. Furious, Henry II immediately stopped his allowance and handed over his lands to the third son, Richard the Lionheart. Financially insecure, and with a considerable army to maintain, Young King Henry began looting the treasures of every abbey and shrine in the region. Finally, he decided to sack the shrine at Rocamadour (see p.175). This last act was to mark his downfall, for shortly afterwards he fled to Martel and fell ill with a fever. Guilt-ridden and fearing for his life, he confessed his crimes and asked his father for forgiveness. Henry II was busy besieging Limoges, but sent a messenger to convey his pardon. On the messenger's arrival in Martel, Young Henry died, leaving Richard the Lionheart heir to the English throne.

ACCOMMODATION

Auberge des 7 Tours Av de Turenne ☎ 05 65 37 30 16, ⓦ auberge7tours.com. Rather small and simply furnished rooms are compensated for by the shaded terrace with views of the town, or over the countryside from the restaurant's picture windows. The restaurant is open July & Aug daily; April–June & Sept–Oct Mon–Fri lunch & Sat eve; Nov–March Mon–Fri lunch. Breakfast €7.50. **€44**

Relais Ste-Anne Rue du Pourtanel ☎ 05 65 37 40 56, ⓦ relais-sainte-anne.com. If you have money to spare, this expensive but absolutely gorgeous hotel

occupies a former girls' boarding school and is set in immaculate gardens with its own chapel, pool and beautifully appointed rooms. There is an excellent restaurant where chef Rimet-Mignon tempts the appetite with delectable dishes such a lobster with foie gras ravioli; and for pudding armagnac and orange macaroons. Menus from €25. Restaurant open Fri, Sat & Sun 12.30–1.30pm plus evenings daily 7.30–8.30pm; note it's reservation only. Hotel closed mid-Nov to mid-March. Breakfast €13 (€15 if served in room). **€95**

EATING AND DRINKING

Au Hazard Balthazar Rue Tournemire ☎ 05 65 37 42 01, ⓦ lesbouriettes.com. You can eat outside or upstairs in the cheerily rustic restaurant above the shop selling home-made local produce such as foie gras, wholesome lamb stew and walnut oil. Menus from €17.80. Easter to Sept daily noon–1.45pm & 7–9pm.

Ferme Auberge Moulin à Huile de Noix ☎ 05 65 37 40 69. This restaurant is attached to a working walnut-oil mill, 3km east off the D703 to St-Denis and Bretenoux. Don't be put off by the modern concrete exterior; the dining rooms upstairs have a bit of character and the food – all regional dishes with

a strong preference for duck and walnuts – is both excellent and plentiful; menus from €15. Reservations essential. Easter to mid-Oct Tues–Sun 12.30–2pm & 7.30–9pm.

La Mère Michèle Rue Senlis ☎ 05 65 37 35 66. Well liked for its nicely presented dishes at prices that won't break the bank; plat du jour €7.50 and menus from €11. Feb–Nov Thurs–Tues noon–2pm & 7–9pm.

Plein Sud Place des Consuls ☎ 05 65 37 37 77. This little place has a surprisingly wide menu, a selection of good pizzas from €8, regional specialities and a choice of salads (from €12). April–Sept Tues–Sun noon–2.30pm & 7–9.30pm.

Meyronne

Roughly 8km south of Martel as the crow flies, the sleepy hilltop village of **MEYRONNE**, is certainly worth a lunchtime stop. In the eleventh century the bishops of Tulle, northeast of Brive, built a château here to defend what was then an important bridging point over the River Dordogne.

ACCOMMODATION AND EATING   MEYRONNE

★ La Terrasse ☎ 05 65 32 21 60, ⓦ hotel-la-terrasse .com. Housed in the town's château, La Terrasse is a splendid hotel complete with spiral stairs, old chimneys and an

excellent restaurant with wonderful views and menus from €20. Restaurant open mid-March to Oct daily except Wed lunch 12.15–1.15pm & 7.15–9pm. Breakfast €13. **€90**

Creysse

CREYSSE, some 3km from Meyronne, is an idyllic hamlet – with a dinky market hall and fast-running stream – that sits in the lee of a knuckle of rock, where a fortified gate and scraps of wall are all that remain of a château once owned by the viscounts of Turenne (see p.81). Their twelfth-century **chapel**, standing immediately above the village, has fared rather better (it's currently undergoing restoration but is normally open to visitors; ask for the key at the *mairie*), and is worth a look for its *pisé* floor and unique arrangement of two apsidal chapels.

ACTIVITIES   CREYSSE

Bike and canoe rental Port Loisirs (☎ 05 65 32 20 82, ⓦ portloisirs.com).

ACCOMMODATION AND EATING

Auberge de L'Île ☎ 05 65 32 22 01, ⓦ auberge -de-lile.com. This is a fairly simple but very appealing hotel, straddling the stream in the village centre whose plane-tree-shaded terrace is hard to resist;

they offer a brasserie menu in addition to full meals (menus from €13.50). Restaurant open mid-March to Nov daily 12.15–1.30pm & 7.30–8.30pm. Breakfast €9. **€50**

Camping du Port ☎ 05 65 32 20 82, �🖥 campingduport .com. Excellent three-star campsite beside the Dordogne a hundred metres east of Creysse. In addition to the river beach it offers a lovely pool and a small restaurant. Closed Sept– June. **€14.80**

Gluges

The cliffs lining the Dordogne valley are more dramatic upstream from Creysse. For the most impressive scenery, follow the D23 northeast for a good two kilometres and then branch off right along the D43. The road quickly narrows down to a single track – with passing spaces – cut into the rock. You emerge two kilometres later at another huddle of houses, **GLUGES**, whose prime attraction is its location under the cliffs and its views south to the **Cirque de Montvalent**, where the meandering river has carved a great semicircle out of the cliffs; for a sweeping panorama, climb up to the hilltop Belvédère de Copeyre, signed off the main road one kilometre above Gluges to the east. In the lee of the great cliff you can still see the ruined troglodyte chapel of **Saint-Pierre-és-Liens**, founded by Gaillard Mirandol on his return from the First Crusade in 1095. It was eventually superseded by the little village **church**, which is worth a quick peek on its own account, as there's a fascinating tale attached to it (see box below).

ACTIVITIES   GLUGES

Bike and canoe rental Copeyre Canoë (☎ 05 65 37 33 51, �🖥 copeyre.com), down by the campsite (see below).

ACCOMMODATION AND EATING

Les Falaises ☎ 05 65 37 37 78, �🖥 camping-lesfalaises .com. A well-kept three-star riverside campsite opposite the village, with canoe rental facilities and a small bar/ shop (open July & Aug). Closed mid-Sept to mid-June. **€13**

Carennac and around

CARENNAC is without doubt one of the most beautiful villages along this part of the Dordogne valley. It sits on a terrace above the river's south bank 16km or so east of Martel; backtrack to Gluges and then head upstream on the D43 for the prettiest route. It is best known for its typical Quercy architecture and the richly carved

---

"LA MÔME PIAF" AND GLUGES CHURCH

Édith Giovanna Gassion was one of the most enigmatic figures of twentieth-century France. Born in 1916 in the backstreets of Paris, she rose to fame and became a cultural icon. She was nicknamed "La Môme Piaf", a colloquialism meaning "the little sparrow", in reference to her diminutive size – she was 142cm – by nightclub owner, Louis Leplée, who first discovered her in the Pigalle area of Paris in 1935. Despite her subsequent success, Piaf led a troubled and turbulent life, gradually becoming more and more reclusive. She liked to escape whenever possible to the peaceful atmosphere of the Dordogne valley, and the tiny troglodyte village of Gluges became one of her favourite spots; she would come here to wander the lanes and pray in the little church. One evening as the curé, Monsieur Delbos, was locking the doors he turned to find Piaf standing behind him. He told her that he would soon have to close the church permanently, as the repair bills were more than the congregation could afford – the two stained-glass windows particularly were badly damaged and no longer safe. Piaf offered to fund the replacement windows on condition that the donation would remain anonymous until after her death. The windows were duly replaced and the curé kept his promise. In 1963, after Piaf's untimely death at the age of 47, he finally revealed her secret to his congregation. A special Mass was held for her, and the tiny *place* in front of the church was renamed place Edith Piaf in her honour.

tympanum of its Romanesque priory church. Founded in the eleventh century by Benedictine monks, the priory grew rich from pilgrims en route to Santiago de Compostela. Sacked during the Hundred Years War (see p.293), it then enjoyed a second renaissance in the late fifteenth and sixteenth centuries, when the church was restored and a château built alongside. But by the 1700s the rot had set in as the monks became lazy and corrupt, and the priory was finally closed after the Revolution.

Église St-Pierre

Jan–March & Oct Mon–Sat 10am–noon & 2–5pm; April–June & Sept Mon–Sat 10am–noon & 2–6pm; July & Aug daily 10am–1pm & 2–7pm; Nov–Dec Mon–Fri 10am–noon & 2–5pm, Sat 2–5pm • €2

You get one of the best views of the village's towers and higgledy-piggledy russet-tiled roofs as you approach from the west. The houses cluster so tightly round the priory buildings that it's hard to tell them apart, but if you follow the road along the river bank, you'll soon find a gateway leading to a cobbled courtyard and the **Église St-Pierre**. Straight ahead of you the church's twelfth-century tympanum – in the style of Moissac and Cahors – dominates its recessed west door, with its carvings in exceptionally good condition.

South of the church, still inside the courtyard, you gain access to the **cloister and chapter house**. The cloister's Romanesque and flamboyant Gothic galleries were somewhat mutilated during the Revolution, but they are in any case overshadowed by the late-fifteenth-century, life-size *Mise au Tombeau* (*Entombment of Christ*) on display in the chapterhouse. So supremely detailed is the sculpture that you can even see the veins in Christ's hands and legs. Joseph of Arimathea and Nicodemus, holding either end of the shroud, are richly attired as a fifteenth-century nobleman and pilgrim respectively, while behind them Mary Magdalene, her hair a mass of ringlets, ostentatiously wipes away a tear.

The château

Espace Patrimoine Easter to June & Oct Tues–Fri 10am–noon & 2–6pm; July–Sept daily 10am–noon & 2–6pm • Free

In the sixteenth century the *doyens* (deans) in charge of the priory and its dependent churches built themselves a grand residence, referred to nowadays as the **château**, abutting the church's north wall. A few stone chimneypieces and the great hall's painted ceiling remain from this era, but little else, since the building has been partially modernized to serve as an **Espace Patrimoine**. Displays cover the geography, history, architecture and economy of the Dordogne valley from Bretenoux downstream to Souillac; it provides a good overview of what the region has to offer. Staff here also organize a broad range of guided visits (to Carennac, Martel and Souillac, for example, some in English) and workshops based on the art and history of the Dordogne valley; contact the Service Animation du Patrimoine (☎05 65 33 81 36, ⓦpays-vallee -dordogne.com) for further information.

ARRIVAL AND DEPARTURE CARENNAC

By train Carennac's nearest *gare SNCF* is at Vayrac, 8km northwest on the other side of the river, on the Brive–Aurillac line; note that there are no ticket sales at this station but you can buy tickets from the conductor on board the train. Call ☎05 65 32 40 32 if you need a taxi. However, services are more frequent to St-Denis-lès-Martel, 10km to the west (see p.182), on the Brive–Figeac line.

By bus Buses from Gramat, St-Céré and Vayrac (with connections to Brive, St-Denis and Biars-Bretenoux) will drop you beside the *mairie* on the south side of town.

Destinations Gramat (school term Wed 1 daily; 30min); St-Céré (school term Mon–Fri 1 daily, rest of year Wed 1 daily; 20min); Vayrac (school term Mon–Fri 1 daily, rest of year Wed 1 daily; 10min).

INFORMATION AND ACTIVITIES

Tourist office In the priory courtyard (Jan–March & Oct Mon–Sat 10am–noon & 2–5pm; April–June & Sept Mon–Sat 10am–noon & 2–6pm; July & Aug daily 10am–1pm & 2–7pm; Nov–Dec Mon–Fri 10am–noon & 2–5pm, Sat 2–5pm; ☎05 65 10 97 01,

ⓦ tourisme-vallee-dordogne.com).
Canoe rental You can also rent canoes, at the *L'Eau Vive* campsite, in season from Saga Team (☎05 55 28 84 84, ⓦ dordogne-soleil.com).

ACCOMMODATION

L'Eau Vive ☎05 65 10 97 39, ⓦ camping-lot-eauvive .com. A good municipal campsite beside the river 1km east of Carennac, with a pool and snack bar open daily. Closed Nov–April. **€20.80**

Hostellerie Fénelon ☎05 65 10 96 46, ⓦ hotel -fenelon.com. The village has just one hotel, on the main street to the east of the château. Comfortable and reasonably priced, it has a pool and good restaurant specializing in traditional regional cuisine. *Menus* begin at

€19. Restaurant open daily noon–1.30pm & 7.15–9.30pm. Breakfast €10 (children €5). **€71**

La Petite Vigne ☎05 65 50 25 84, ⓦ lapetitevigne -carennac.com. A small English-run *chambre d'hôte* at the entrance to the village, with three immaculate bedrooms, a cosy dining room (for guests' use only) and a pretty flower-filled terrace, open for a bite of lunch for residents and non-residents alike (daily 12.30–2pm; *menus* from €13.50). Hotel closed Sept–April. **€65**

EATING AND DRINKING

Relais de Gintrac Gintrac ☎05 65 38 49 41. A very popular if isolated place – about 3km from Carennac southeast along the D30 – offering wholesome country

cooking washed down with well-priced wines. *Menus* from €14. Mid-Nov to end-Oct Wed–Sun noon–1.45pm & 7–9pm.

The Gouffre de Padirac

1hr 30min guided tours daily: April–June 9.30am–5pm; July 9.30am–6pm; Aug 8.30am–6.30pm; Sept & Oct 10am–5pm • Adult €9.60, child €6.60, child under 4 free • ⓦ gouffre-de-padirac.com

Local legend holds the Devil responsible for opening the gaping mouth of the **Gouffre de Padirac** in the middle of the limestone plateau 10km south of Carennac. The hole is over 30m wide and 75m deep, its sides festooned with dripping ferns and creepers, though the sense of mystery is somewhat diminished these days by the presence of a lift-cage built against the side. Rather than the Devil, the chasm was probably formed by a cave roof collapsing centuries ago; locals took refuge here during the Hundred Years War and probably long before. The cave system was not properly explored, however, until 1889 when spectacular stalactites – the biggest a staggering 75m tall – and lakes were discovered. Even today teams are still exploring the caves and passages.

The visit starts with a **boat trip** along an underground river, after which you walk on past barrages and massive cascades formed by calcite deposits over the millennia. The lakes are pretty, but the most notable feature here is the sheer scale of the formations and the height of the passages carved out of the rock, reaching nearly 100m at their highest. Be warned, though: it is very, very touristy and best avoided at peak periods, when you'll wait ages for tickets. And in wet weather you'll need a waterproof jacket.

ARRIVAL AND DEPARTURE   THE GOUFFRE DE PADIRAC

By train The nearest *gare SNCF* is Rocamadour-Padirac, more than 10km to the west, from where you could take a taxi (☎05 65 33 63 10).
Tourist office In Padirac village (July & Aug Mon–Sat

10am–12.30pm & 2–7pm; mid- to end June & early to mid-Sept Mon–Fri 2–6pm; ☎05 65 33 47 17, ⓦ tourisme -vallee-dordogne.com), a couple of kilometres south of the *gouffre*.

ACCOMMODATION AND EATING

Giscard Le Bourg, Thegra ☎05 65 38 77 31, ⓦ hotel -giscard.com. About 2km back towards Rocamadour in the medieval village of Thegra, this simple but friendly little hotel-restaurant has a cool terrace and a pool (July & Aug). *Menus*

from €12.50 at lunch and €18.50 in the evening. Restaurant open May–Sept daily noon–2pm & 7–9pm & Oct–April Sun–Fri noon–2pm & 7–9pm. It's reservation only in the evenings. Breakfast €6.80. **€47**

Bretenoux and around

Some 10km east of Carennac, the *bastide* town of **BRETENOUX**, founded in 1277 by the barons of Castelnau, sits on the south bank of the River Cère just upstream from where it joins the Dordogne. It was obviously a pretty little place at one time – the cobbled and arcaded **place des Consuls** behind the tourist office is a delight, especially on **market** days (Tues & Sat mornings) – but these days the town suffers from a busy main road and modern development. With its transport connections, however, Bretenoux is a useful staging post for the nearby towns of St-Céré and Beaulieu-sur-Dordogne (see p.190 & p.188). And east of here, the journey to Aurillac takes you through a very picturesque and otherwise inaccessible landscape, popular with walkers and cyclists.

ARRIVAL AND DEPARTURE   BRETENOUX

By train Bretenoux's *gare SNCF*, on the Brive–Aurillac line, is officially known as Bretenoux-Biars since it is located some 2km north of the River Cère in the town of Biars. Taxis wait outside the station, or call ☎ 05 65 10 90 90.
Destinations Aurillac (3–4 daily; 45min–1hr); Brive (3–4 daily; 35–40min); St-Denis-lès-Martel (3–4 daily; 15min); Vayrac (1–2 daily; 10min).

By bus There are buses (#11, operated by Delbos; ☎ 05 65 38 24 19) from here to Bretenoux and St-Céré, but only on Wednesday, Thursday and Saturday; in Bretenoux the bus stop is on the main road, avenue de la Libération, near the post office a couple of hundred metres south of the river.
Destinations Bretenoux (Wed, Thurs & Sat 1–3 daily; 5min); St-Céré (Wed & Sat 2 daily; 15min).

INFORMATION AND ACTIVITIES

Tourist office Avenue de la Libération, just south of the bridge (July & Aug Mon–Sat 9.30am–7pm, Sun 10am–1pm; Sept–June Mon–Sat 10am–noon & 2–6pm; ☎ 05 65 38 59 53, ⓦ tourisme-vallee-dordogne.com).
Bike rental Cycles Bladier on avenue de la Libération

(☎ 05 65 38 41 56), where you can rent bikes for a trip out to the Château de Castelnau.
Canoe rental Available in July and August at the *Bourgnatelle* campsite down by the river at Bretenoux (☎ 05 65 10 89 04).

ACCOMMODATION AND EATING

There are no hotels in Bretenoux itself. Best look in the countryside around the village, and also in Port-de-Gagnac, 6km northeast on the D14 in the village of Port-de-Gagnac, on the north bank of the Cère.

BRETENOUX
La Bourgnatelle ☎ 05 65 10 89 04, ⓦ dordogne -vacances.fr/camping_bretenoux. A leafy three-star campsite located on an island just across the bridge on the north side of Bretenoux. It has a pool, table tennis and snack bar open July & Aug. Closed Oct–April. €19
★ **Domaine de Granval** ☎ 05 65 11 24 55, ⓦ domaine degranval.com. A charming *chambre d'hôte*, 2km south of Bretenoux on the D803, with five lovely rooms, all at ground level. There's also a pool, flowery terrace and evening meals at €25. Closed mid-Oct to April. €80
Les Saveurs ☎ 05 65 39 72 39. A pretty restaurant on the sunny side of place des Consuls with good-value *menus* from €11. A lovely place to sit and admire the architecture. March– Oct Mon–Thurs 12.30–2pm, Fri & Sat 7.30–9.30pm.

PORT-DE-GAGNAC
Auberge du Vieux Port ☎ 05 65 38 50 05, ⓦ www .auberge-vieuxport.com. Homely and cosy, the *Vieux Port* has very well-kept rooms and most have views of the river. The restaurant (Mon eve to Sun eve) serves very good-value regional cuisine; *menus* from €15.50. Breakfast €8.50. €60
Hostellerie Belle Rive ☎ 05 65 38 50 04, ⓦ bellerive -dordogne-lot.com. The *Hostellerie Belle Rive* is a touch more upmarket than the *Vieux Port*. It has ten delightful rooms and the chef is a local celebrity. Restaurant open Easter to mid-Oct daily noon–1.30pm & 7.30–9pm; mid-Oct to Easter Mon–Sun lunch only. Breakfast €9. €75

Château de Castelnau

April & Sept daily 10am–12.30pm & 2–5.30pm; May–Aug daily 10am–12.30pm & 2–6.30pm; Oct–March Wed–Sun 10am–12.30pm & 2–5.30pm • Adults €7.50, under 18 years free (guided tour included in entry price) • ⓦ castelnau-bretenoux.monuments-nationaux.fr

Bretenoux lies within striking distance of the **Château de Castelnau**, 2.5km to the southwest – one of this region's most outstanding examples of medieval military architecture. The great fortress dominates an abrupt knoll to the east of the village, its sturdy towers and machicolated red-brown walls visible for miles around. It dates from the mid-tenth century, but took on its present form – a triangular fort with a massive square keep and three round towers, the whole lot surrounded by ramparts and dry moats – during the Hundred Years War under the ownership of the powerful barons of Castelnau. By the early eighteenth century, however, the Castelnau family had died out. Their abandoned château was sacked during the Revolution, sustained even greater damage in a fire in 1851 and was left to rot until it was salvaged, somewhat bizarrely, in 1896 by a celebrated tenor of the Parisian Comic Opera, Jean Mouliérat. He threw his fortune into its restoration and into amassing the valuable but rather dry collection of religious art and furniture from the fifteenth to eighteenth centuries, which populates the handful of rooms you see on the guided tour. The views from the ramparts, though, are extremely impressive; on a clear day you can just make out the towers of Turenne, nearly thirty kilometres to the north (see p.81).

As you exit the castle's inner enclosure, turn left along the walls to take a quick look in the **Collégiale St-Louis**. Built of the same red stone and with powerful buttresses, this little Gothic church contains a fine fifteenth-century polychrome statue of the Baptism of Christ – note the startled expression of the angel holding his clothes – and a macabre treasure in the form of a bone from the arm of St Louis (alias King Louis IX of France). In 1970 the relic was taken to St Louis in America to commemorate the founding of the city.

4

Beaulieu-sur-Dordogne and around

At Bretenoux the River Dordogne turns northwards to Biars; the valley here is wide and industrial – with factories such as Andros churning out enough jam to make this the "jam capital" of Europe. Aspects improve 8km north of Biars at **BEAULIEU-SUR-DORDOGNE**, beautifully situated on a wide bend in the river. It's a perfectly proportioned town, with an abbey church that boasts another of the great masterpieces of Romanesque sculpture, and yet is refreshingly untouristy.

Arriving from Bretenoux, the main road skirts south of Beaulieu's compact and semi-pedestrianized core of old streets. On its way it passes through a large square, **place Marbot**, which represents the town's modern centre, off which rue de la République leads north to **place du Marché**. Here, you'll find some nicely faded stone and half-timbered buildings, along with the twelfth-century **abbey church of St-Pierre**, a surprisingly large building, whose architecture reflects its position on the border between Limousin and Languedoc. The pairs of rounded arches piercing the belfry, for example, are typical Limousin styling, while the subject matter and style of carving on the magnificent **south portal** belongs firmly to the south. The tympanum is presided over by an oriental-looking Christ with one arm extended to welcome the chosen on the Judgement Day. Around him a mass of angels and apostles, even the dead rising from their graves below, seem ready to burst with vitality.

It won't take long to cover the rest of Beaulieu, but it's worth devoting half an hour or so to wandering its maze of lanes. In particular, there are a number of half-timbered houses along **rue Ste-Catherine**, running east from place du Marché, while if you head northwest along **rue de la République** and **rue de la Chapelle** you'll pass some handsome sculpted facades before emerging beside the **Chapelle des Pénitents** in an attractive spot on the riverbank. This twelfth-century chapel now makes a splendid venue for the occasional art exhibition or concert; if it's open, it's worth popping in to see the collection of religious art.

ARRIVAL AND DEPARTURE | BEAULIEU

By train It's just over 6km from Beaulieu to the Bretenoux-Biars *gare SNCF* (see p.187). Unfortunately there are no connecting buses. If you need a taxi in Beaulieu, call ☎05 55 91 02 83.

By bus You can get to Beaulieu by bus from Brive; services stop on place du Champs-de-Mars, a large shady square just west of place Marbot, which marks the modern centre. Destinations Argentat (July & Aug Mon–Sat 3 daily; 40min); Brive (school term Mon–Sat 1–3 daily, July & Aug Mon–Sat 1–2 daily, rest of year Tues, Thurs & Sat 1 daily; 1hr).

INFORMATION

Tourist office On the south side of place Marbot (April–June & Sept–Oct Mon–Sat 9.30am–12.30pm & 2.30pm–6pm, Sun 9.30am–12.30pm; July & Aug daily 9.30am–1pm & 2.30pm–7pm; Nov–March Mon–Sat 10am–12.30pm & 2.30pm–5pm; ☎05 55 91 09 94, ⒲tourisme-vallee-dordogne.com).

Bike rental Aventures Dordogne Nature (☎05 55 28 86 45, ⒲adndordogne.org), at the *base nautique* on the other side of the river; you can drive round or get there via a footbridge to the north of the town centre.

Boat trips From May to October traditional wooden *gabares* depart from the riverbank near the Chapelle des Pénitents for a one-hour jaunt upstream – contact the tourist office (see above).

ACCOMMODATION

★ **Auberge de Jeunesse** Rue de la Chapelle ☎05 55 91 13 82. Welcoming hostel set in a magnificent half-timbered and turreted building, with surprisingly modern dorms inside and a well-equipped kitchen. Meals are available on request for groups of ten or more. Hostel closed mid-Oct to Easter. Breakfast €4.50. Dorms **€14.50**

Camping des Iles On the island to the north of the main road-bridge ☎05 55 91 02 65, ⒲camping-des-iles.com. Well-kept and shady three-star site with a solar-heated pool, pétanque and snack bar (July & Aug). Closed mid-Sept to mid-April. **€23.50**

Les Charmilles 20 bd St Rodolphe de Turenne ☎05 55 91 29 29, ⒲auberge-charmilles.com. The most appealing option in Beaulieu, this bright, clean, riverside hotel is on the northeast side of town. It has just eight rooms, each named after a variety of strawberry. It also boasts an attractive terrace where you'll eat well; *menus* start at €14 for lunch, €19 in the evening. Restaurant open Jan–Nov Mon–Sat noon–2pm & 7–9pm. Breakfast included. **€120**

Les Flots Bleus Place du Monturu ☎05 55 91 06 21, ⒲hotel-flotsbleus.com. A lovely riverside hotel with seven well-decorated rooms (those overlooking the river are more expensive) and an atmospheric restaurant (see below). Hotel closed mid-Nov to March. Breakfast €9. **€69**

★ **Relais de Vellinus** Place du Champ-de-Mars ☎05 55 91 11 04, ⒲vellinus.com. Comfortable hotel imaginatively decorated in warm, contemporary colours. It also has a good restaurant, where you can enjoy elegantly presented dishes that combine regional products with original flavourings – spiced scallops or walnut soufflé accompanied by walnut liqueur for example. *Menus* start at €18; the restaurant is open Easter to Oct daily noon–1.30pm & 7–8.30pm; Nov to Easter Mon–Thurs noon–1.30pm & 7–8.30pm. Breakfast €10. **€59**

Le Turenne 1 bd St Rodolphe de Turenne ☎05 55 91 94 72, ⒲www.leturenne.com. Perhaps the most upmarket hotel in town, housed in a thirteenth-century former abbey and stylishly decorated in bold contemporary colours. The restaurant offers innovative cuisine and *menus* from €22.50. Restaurant open daily noon–2pm & 7–9pm. Breakfast included. **€105**

EATING AND DRINKING

★ **Café Douceur** 34 rue du Général-de-Gaulle ☎05 55 28 67 05. This delightful café serves a wide choice of teas and coffees as well as innovative lunchtime platters (all €9) such as *pissaladière* with onions, thyme, tomatoes and olives, to eat in or take away. The atmosphere is pleasant and relaxed, with armchairs for lounging in. Sun–Tues & Thurs–Fri 9am–7pm, Wed 9am–2pm.

Les Flots Bleus Place du Monturu ☎05 55 91 06 21, ⒲hotel-flotsbleus.com. This restaurant has the perfect riverside setting, with a summer terrace that faces Beaulieu's Chapelle des Pénitents, creating a unique ambience, while creative and beautifully presented dishes using the best local produce make it extremely popular. Reservations advised in season. July & Aug Mon eve to Sun 12.15–2pm & 7–8.30pm; March–June & Sept to mid-Nov Tues–Sun 12.15–2pm.

Velouté Rue de la Bridolle ☎05 55 91 14 51. The hotel restaurants are good places to eat, but for a change it's well worth seeking out this little place, set beside the church in rue de la Bridolle. Both the decor and cuisine are appealingly modern, the latter changing inventively according to season. *Menus* from €14.50 at lunch, €18 in the evenings. March–July & Sept to mid-Dec Wed–Fri noon–2.30pm & 7–10pm, Sat noon–2.30pm; Aug daily except Sun eve.

Argentat

Upstream from Beaulieu, the Dordogne valley becomes wilder as you enter the first forest-covered foothills of the Massif Central. It makes for a lovely drive along the D12 as far as **Argentat**, the last town of any size on the river, where it's easy to while away an hour or so sitting at one of the waterside cafés. Beyond Argentat, however, the Dordogne changes character entirely, due to a series of hydroelectric dams that turn the river into a succession of huge reservoirs.

St-Céré and around

About 9km south of Bretenoux on the River Bave, a minor tributary of the Dordogne, you come to the medieval town of **St-Céré**, dominated by the brooding ruins of the **Château de St-Laurent-les-Tours**. The château is now home to an engaging museum dedicated to tapestry designer Jean Lurçat, who revitalized contemporary French tapestry, but the town's prime attraction is its old centre peppered with picturesque half-timbered houses.

St-Céré makes a useful base for exploring the surrounding area. The town lies on the border between the empty but glorious wooded hills of the Ségala to the east and south, and the dry limestone *causse* to the west. However, the region's most impressive sight, and one not to be missed, is the Renaissance **Château de Montal**, 2km west of St-Céré, with its sculpted facade and grand staircase. From here you can loop south via the **Grottes de Presque** – a limestone cave with a tremendous variety of unusually colourful concretions – to arrive at the lip of the Cirque d'Autoire for dramatic views over the russet-red roofs of **Autoire** village, which provide a splash of colour in the valley far below. On the way back to St-Céré the route passes through another captivating little village, **Loubressac**, which can hardly have changed for centuries.

Place de la République

Arriving in St-Céré from the north, the first things you see are the two powerful keeps of the Château de St-Laurent-les-Tours, once part of a fortress belonging to the viscounts of Turenne (see p.81). The town itself sits in the valley to the southwest where the old houses cluster round place du Mercadial and place de l'Église. These two squares lie north and south respectively of rue de la République, the main shopping street cutting through the old centre which, at its southeast end, comes out into **place de la République**. This big, open square is where you'll find car parks, cafés and the town's main tourist facilities.

The noble houses

St-Céré owes its existence to the martyrdom of **Ste Spérie** in 780. Born the daughter of the then lord of St-Laurent, Sérenus, Spérie pledged her life to God at an early age, and when later she refused to marry a local nobleman, she was beheaded by her brother and buried on the riverbank. Later a chapel was erected on the spot around which the town began to develop in the tenth century. It lay initially under the jurisdiction of the counts of Auvergne, but was transferred to the Turenne viscounts in 1178. They beefed up the fortress and, as usual, granted the town a certain degree of autonomy. Its heyday didn't arrive, however, until after the fifteenth century when St-Céré's wealthy merchants began investing in the noble houses that can still be seen today.

The best of the townhouses lie in the streets to the north of rue de la République, notably around **place du Mercadial**, which is particularly appealing; to find it, walk one block north from rue de la République and turn left along rue du Mazel. You come out opposite the town's most eye-catching building, the **Maison des Consuls**, where the administrative council used to meet – it now hosts various free art exhibitions in summer. Beneath the pitched tile roof, the building's most striking feature is the slightly overhanging upper storey of neatly layered brick in a timber frame. The same design is echoed in the **Maison Arnoud**, on the north side of the square, whose ground floor is a mere three metres wide. Rue St-Cyr, the lane to the right of this house, takes you east and then south past several elegant Renaissance buildings and into a recently renovated area of courtyards and alleys.

Church of Sainte-Spérie

There's not much of interest on the south side of rue de la République, though the church of Sainte-Spérie, largely rebuilt after the Wars of Religion, is worth a quick peek for its eighteenth-century altarpiece with a statue of St Spérie standing on the left. It was carved by a local monk who received 240 *livres* and, for some reason, four handkerchiefs for his pains.

Galerie d'Art Le Casino

Av Jean Mouliérat • July–Sept daily 9.30am–noon & 2.30pm–6.30pm; Feb–June daily except Tues 9.30am–noon & 2.30pm–6.30pm; Oct–Jan closed Mon & Tues • Free • ☎ 05 65 38 19 60

St-Céré is proud of local artist, **Jean Lurçat** (1892–1966), who first came to the Lot to join the Resistance in 1941, then decided to settle in Château St-Laurent after the war. He is best known for his big, bold tapestries, of which the most famous is the eighty-metre-long *Chant du Monde* (*Song of the World*), which portrays the vagaries of human existence and our inherent power for both good and evil. The tapestry is now on display in Angers, but you can get an idea of Lurçat's distinctive style – typically incorporating animals and birds, both real and fantastic, against dark blue or black backgrounds – by visiting the **Galerie d'Art Le Casino**, 100m northeast of the old town; from place de la République walk north on boulevard Lurçat a short distance before turning right down avenue Jean Mouliérat.

Château de St-Laurent-les-Tours

Atelier-Musée Jean Lurçat Mid-July to Sept daily 9.30am–noon & 2.30pm–6.30pm; plus two weeks at Easter 9.30am–noon & 2.30pm–6.30pm • €2.50 • ☎ 05 65 38 28 21, ⓦ musees.lot.fr

The **Château de St-Laurent-les-Tours** sits a kilometre or so above St-Céré – take avenue du Docteur Roux heading northeast past the hospital and then follow the signs winding uphill. Of the Turenne fortress only the ramparts and two square towers remain, the smaller one dating from the late twelfth century and the taller, eastern tower from the 1300s. The rest of the castle was destroyed during the Wars of Religion, but around 1895 the then owner built himself a neo-Gothic mansion between the two towers. It is this building in which Jean Lurçat (see opposite) set up his studio in 1945 and which is now the **Atelier-Musée Jean Lurçat**. Alongside his sketches and illustrations, a slide show of the *Chant du Monde* and a short biographical film, the museum's most interesting feature is the artist's unmistakable paintings covering the ceilings and doors.

ARRIVAL AND DEPARTURE   ST-CÉRÉ

It's possible to reach St-Céré by bus from Bretenoux, Cahors and Figeac, but you'll need your own transport to explore the rest of the area. If you've got the energy to tackle some of the local hills, you can always rent a bike in St-Céré (see p.192).

By train The nearest *gare SNCF* to St-Céré is Bretenoux-Biars (see p.187), a good 10km to the north, from where there are buses on two days a week (Wed & Sat; Delbos ☎ 05 65 38 24 19) on to St-Céré.

By bus You can reach St-Céré by bus from Cahors via Gramat, and from Figeac (both also operated by Delbos). All these services drop you on place de la République.

Destinations Bretenoux (Wed & Sat 2 daily; 5min); Bretenoux-Biars (Wed & Sat 2 daily; 10min); Cahors (Mon & Wed–Sat 1 daily; 1hr 45min); Carennac (school term Mon–Fri 1 daily, rest of year Wed 1 daily; 20min); Figeac (3–4 weekly; 1hr); Gramat (school term Mon–Sat 1–2 daily, rest of year Mon & Wed–Sat 1 daily; 30–40min).

4

INFORMATION AND ACTIVITIES

Tourist office On the north side of place de la République (July & Aug Mon–Sat 9am–7pm, Sun 10am–1pm; Sept–June Mon–Sat 10am–noon & 2–6pm; ☎ 05 65 38 11 85, ⓦ tourisme-vallee-dordogne.com).

Bike rental Cycles St-Chamant, 45 rue Faidherbe (☎ 05 65 38 03 23), to the west of place de la République.

ACCOMMODATION

De France 139 av François-de-Maynard ☎ 05 65 38 02 16, ⓦ lefrance-hotel.com. Modern, upmarket place east off place de la République, with well-priced en-suite rooms, a pool and a flowery garden where you can eat out under a huge chestnut tree. *Menus* from €15.50. Restaurant open mid-Jan to mid-Dec daily 12.15–1.15pm & 7.30–9.30pm. Breakfast €9.50. **€47**

Le Soulhol Quai Salesses ☎ 05 65 33 47 81, ⓦ campinglesoulhol.com. Three-star campsite beside the river a short walk east of the *Victor-Hugo*, offering a heated pool, BBQ area, bike rental and free wi-fi throughout the site. Closed mid-Sept to May. **€16.20**

★ **Les Trois Soleils de Montal** Les Prés de Montal ☎ 05 65 10 16 16, ⓦ 3soleils.fr. This fantastic hotel is the most luxurious in St-Céré and boasts a Michelin-starred restaurant (see below) – it's also graced with beautifully appointed rooms and is set in extensive gardens. Closed Nov–Feb. Breakfast €14. **€119**

★ **Victor-Hugo** 7 av des Maquis ☎ 05 65 38 16 15, ⓦ hotel-victor-hugo.fr. You'll get a warm welcome from the young owners at this hotel beside the old bridge in the southeast corner of place de la République. There are three family rooms with balconies and four others that open directly onto a sunny terrace overlooking the river. The chef uses fresh local produce in the restaurant. *Menus* from €13.10 for lunch and €28.10 in the evening. Restaurant open daily (except three weeks in Oct and two weeks in March) noon–2.30pm & 7–9.30pm. Private garaging is €5. Breakfast €9. **€55**

EATING AND DRINKING

The best places to eat in St-Céré are the restaurants at the *De France* (see above) and *Victor-Hugo* (see above). Otherwise, try the cafés and brasseries around place de la République and place du Mercadial. For picnic fodder, there's a small market on Sunday mornings on place de la République and a much larger affair spreading throughout the old town on the first and third Wednesdays of the month.

L'Instant 3 place du Mercadial ☎ 05 65 10 66 82. Serves delicious quiches and salads on its covered terrace and courtyard. In the afternoons from May–Sept it turns into a cosy tearoom. *Menus* are from €11 at lunch and €19.50 in the evening. July & Aug Mon–Sat lunch & dinner; Sept–June Mon–Thurs & Sun lunch, plus Fri & Sat dinner; rest of year Mon–Sat lunch only.

Pizzeria du Mercadial 4 place du Mercadial ☎ 05 65 38 35 77. This is a lovely little place, with a rustic setting and a terrace, serving pizzas (€12), as well as pasta (€12) and grills (€15). *Menus* from €12.50 at lunch; in the evenings it's à la carte. Feb–Dec Tues–Sun noon–2pm & 7–9.30pm.

★ **Les Trois Soleils de Montal** Les Prés de Montal ☎ 05 65 10 16 16, ⓦ 3soleils.fr. A Michelin-starred treat: *Les Trois Soleils'* lunchtime weekday *menu* at €30 is a bargain for such a tranquil setting among immaculate gardens. The *menus* (others from €42) feature fresh, locally produced ingredients with a creative twist – try the pig's trotter stuffed with preserved duck meat served with a *galette* and sauce of *cèpes*, for instance. April–Sept daily except Mon lunch noon–1.45pm & 7.30–9pm; Oct, Nov, Feb & March Tues eve to Sun lunch.

Château de Montal

April & Sept daily 10am–12.30pm & 2–5.30pm; May–Aug daily 10am–12.30pm & 2–6.30pm; Oct–March Wed–Sun 10am–12.30pm & 2–5.30pm • Adult €7.50, minors and disabled card-holders free • ⓦ montal.monuments-nationaux.fr

Two kilometres west of St-Céré, the **Château de Montal** is a superb example of French Renaissance architecture. Its interesting history began in 1523 when Jeanne Balzac d'Entraygues, the widow of Amaury de Montal, started transforming the medieval fortress into a Renaissance palace, as was all the rage. But then came news that her eldest son, Robert, had been killed in Italy and poor Jeanne lost the heart to continue. Nevertheless the de Montal family continued to own the château up to the Revolution, after which it was bought by a certain Monsieur Macaire who gradually sold off the chimneypieces, sculptures and even the carved window surrounds. Rescue was at hand, however, in the form of Maurice Fenaille, a rich industrialist and patron of the arts,

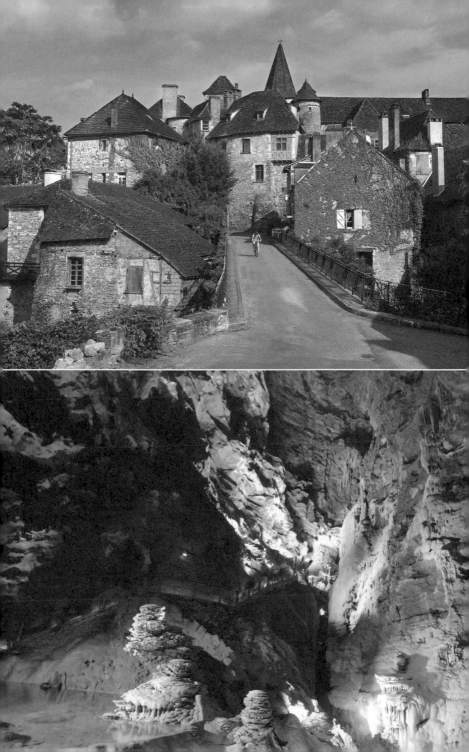

who bought the château in 1908 and began to restore it to its former glory. In just five years he managed to track down nearly everything that had been sold, including some of the original wall-coverings, and also filled the rooms with a fine collection of Renaissance and Louis XIII furnishings, before giving the whole caboodle to the state in 1913. Later, during World War II, Montal was chosen as a hiding place for thousands of paintings from the Louvre, including the *Mona Lisa*, which were moved from Paris for safekeeping.

The inner courtyard

The rear of the château, which you see first on approach, still exudes a thoroughly medieval air with its small windows, steep *lauze* roof and pepper-pot towers, but turn the corner into the **inner courtyard** and you're immediately transported to sunny Italy. The lovely pale stone of the two facades is worked into delicate carvings, including a frieze of mermaid-like sibyls and, above, busts representing three generations of the de Montal family: Jeanne is flanked by her husband and son Robert on the west wing, while her parents take pride of place over the front door.

The interior

The craftsmen went to work inside as well as on the outside, particularly on a magnificent **staircase** made from the same local limestone. As you climb up, notice the carving on the panels above, each bearing a different design, which gets finer and more elaborate towards the top. The rest of the interior can't quite compare, but there are some massive old oak tables, a good, homely kitchen and an excellent collection of tapestries, including a rare example featuring a pastoral scene with descriptive boxes of text, like an early cartoon.

Grottes de Presque

45min guided tours daily: mid-Feb to June & Sept–mid-Nov 9.30am–noon & 2–6pm; July & Aug 9.30am–6.30pm • Adults €7, children €3.50 • ⓦ grottesdepresque.com

About 3km southwest along the D673 from the Château de Montal the road cuts through a hillside as it climbs up onto the *causse*. When they were digging this road in 1825, engineers discovered the entrance to the **Grottes de Presque**. The cave system is not only unusually accessible, with a few stairs, but it also contains a marvellous variety of stalactites and stalagmites, some up to 10m high, as well as columns, semi-translucent curtains and glistening crystalline cascades. The other notable feature is the sheer amount of colour, from pure white to grey, yellow and deep orange. This is the result of rainwater picking up iron, manganese and other minerals as it percolates through the 90m of rock above, minerals that are then deposited along with the calcite, drip by drip, inside the cave.

Autoire

Eight kilometres, by road, west of the Grottes de Presque (follow the D673 southwest for another 4km and then turn right on the D38), the River Autoire has carved an impressive canyon, the **Cirque d'Autoire**, into the limestone plateau. The D38 brings you in above the *cirque* – for the best views, walk west from the car park for about five minutes, following the footpath across a bridge and up onto the opposite hillside. In the valley bottom, some 2km below you, lies the extremely pretty little village of **AUTOIRE** where the ochre-hued houses, including several rather grand piles built by nobles from St-Céré in the fifteenth and sixteenth centuries, snuggle round a very plain, solid Romanesque church.

ACCOMMODATION AND EATING AUTOIRE

Auberge de la Fontaine ❶ 05 65 10 85 40, ⓦ auberge
-de-la-fontaine.com. This lovely little hotel is on the main
street opposite the church. It's a simple country inn offering
basic but well-kept rooms and good regional country cooking
washed down with local Coteaux de Glanes wines; *menus*
from €12.50 at lunch and €19.80 in the evenings. Restaurant
open July & Aug daily noon–1.30pm & 7.30–9pm; March–
June & Sept–Dec Tues–Sat noon–1.30pm & 7.30–9pm. Sun

noon–1.30pm. No wi-fi. Breakfast €7.50. **€46**
La Cascade ❶ 05 65 38 20 02. Just across the road is the
place to go for a good lunch, serving crêpes, salads and
regional dishes in a cheerful stone-walled room or on a
terrace with wonderful views up to the *cirque; menus* from
around €15. March–June & Sept to mid-Dec Wed–Mon
12.10–1.30pm; July & Aug daily 12.10–1.30pm &
7.30–9pm.

Loubressac

It's 8km back to St-Céré from Autoire, but it's worth taking a short diversion 6km
northwest along the D135, little more than a country lane, to **LOUBRESSAC**. The
narrow lanes of this fortified hilltop village are full of flowers and typical Quercy
houses. You can't visit the château standing on the cliff edge, but there are grand views
from the lookout point immediately to the east of the village, taking in the whole
sweep of the Dordogne, Bave and Cère valleys across to St-Céré and the châteaux of
Castelnau and Montal.

INFORMATION LOUBRESSAC

Tourist office In season a tourist office opens up just
outside Loubressac's southern gateway (April Mon–Sat
2–6pm; May, June & Sept Mon 2.30pm–6.30pm, Tues–Sat

10am–12.30pm & 3–6.30pm; July & Aug Mon–Sat
9am–1pm & 3–7pm, Sun 4–7pm; ⓦ tourisme-vallee
-dordogne.com).

ACCOMMODATION AND EATING

La Garrigue ❶ 05 65 38 34 88, ⓦ camping-lagarrigue
.com. Very pleasant little three-star campsite with a pool
and snack bar among fields a couple of hundred metres
south of the village. Closed Sept–April. **€15.70**
Lou Cantou La Place ❶ 05 65 38 20 58, ⓦ loucantou
.com. Simple hotel with good views from its front rooms.
There's a restaurant with *menus* from €13.50 at lunch, and
from €21.50 in the evenings. Restaurant open April to mid-
Nov daily 12.15–2pm & 7.30–8.30pm; Dec–March Tues–
Thurs & Sat 12.15–2pm & 7.30–8.30pm, Fri 12.15–2pm.

Breakfast €8.50. **€56**
Relais de Castelnau Rte de Padirac ❶ 05 65 10 80 90,
ⓦ relaisdecastelnau.com. The modern *Relais de Castelnau*
sits just outside the village on the main road west to
Padirac. It enjoys splendid views and also boasts a pool and
a highly rated restaurant. *Menus* from €18.50. Restaurant
open Easter to end April & Oct Tues–Sat 7.30–8.45pm;
May–Sept daily 7.30–8.45pm. Hotel closed Nov to Easter.
Breakfast €9.50. **€95**

The Lot Valley and around

PONT VALENTRÉ, CAHORS

5

The Lot Valley and around

Like the Dordogne, the River Lot rises in the foothills of the Massif Central and is dammed in its upper reaches to form huge reservoirs. It begins to get more interesting, however, where it enters the Lot département, the boundaries of which roughly coincide with the old province of Quercy. Here the serpentine river carves its way through the immense limestone plateau – encompassed by the Parc naturel régional des Causses du Quercy – that characterizes the region.

The largest town in the Lot valley, and capital of the *département*, is **Cahors**. It may lack the higgledy-piggledy charm of Sarlat or Bergerac, but compensates for this with a pleasingly workaday atmosphere and a wonderful location in the middle of a meander. It also boasts the best example of a fortified medieval bridge left in France, the **Pont Valentré**, while the country round about produces an extremely distinctive dark, almost peppery red **wine**.

The Lot valley is at its most picturesque upstream from Cahors. The scenery may not be as dramatic as the middle reaches of the Dordogne, but the sheer cliffs here host their fair share of perched fortresses and feudal villages. Foremost among these is spectacular **St-Cirq Lapopie**, while the nearby **Grotte de Pech-Merle**, with its glittering rock formations and prehistoric cave art, draws almost as many visitors. Pech-Merle lies in the hills above the wild and pretty **Célé valley**, which leads northeast to lovely, medieval **Figeac**, the Lot's second largest town.

North and west of Figeac stretches the **Causse de Gramat**, the biggest and wildest of the region's limestone *causses*. With its huge vistas, it makes a welcome change from the confining valleys and a great place for walking or cycling, though it has few notable sights beyond the village of **Assier**, in the far southeast, with its extraordinary church. On its western edge the Causse de Gramat suddenly gives way to a lovely area of gentle wooded hills known as the **Bouriane**. Again, there are no must-see sights, though its capital, **Gourdon**, a once-prosperous town built of butter-coloured stone, is worth a stop-off, and the nearby **Grottes de Cougnac**, with a smattering of prehistoric cave paintings and some exceptionally delicate limestone concretions, repay a visit.

Returning to the Lot valley, the river south of Cahors wriggles its way westwards through vineyards and past ancient towns and villages. By far the most striking of these is **Puy-l'Évêque**. An outpost of the bishops of Cahors, the town's medieval and Renaissance houses jostle for space on a steep incline, reaching upwards like trees for light, though none is equal to the bishop's thirteenth-century keep towering above. An even more dramatic sight lies in store in the country northwest of Puy-l'Évêque where the **Château de Bonaguil** is an outstanding example of late-fifteenth-century military architecture, its great bulk silhouetted against the wooded hillside.

Further downstream things begin to quieten down again as the valley flattens out towards **Villeneuve-sur-Lot**. Despite unattractive modern suburbs, the town has a decent supply of hotels and restaurants, and with the river sliding through an old centre built of stone and warm red brick, it's a pleasant and convenient place to stay. Villeneuve – as its name indicates – was also one of the many "new towns", or *bastides*, founded in this area in the thirteenth and fourteenth centuries. You'll find the best examples of *bastide*

Highlights

❶ Pont Valentré Cahors' signature sight is the fortified medieval bridge guarding the town's western approaches. **See p.207**

❷ St-Cirq Lapopie Perched high above the River Lot, this former feudal stronghold boasts stunning views and lovely, labyrinthine alleys to explore. **See p.212**

❸ Grotte de Pech-Merle The combination of dazzling limestone formations and more than five hundred prehistoric drawings make this cave unmissable. **See p.219**

❹ Figeac A laid-back riverside town with plenty of medieval architecture and a fascinating museum of writing. **See p.220**

❺ Château de Bonaguil One of the last medieval fortresses built in France, and now a magnificent ruin. **See p.238**

❻ Bastides Monpazier provides an almost perfect example of the region's myriad fortified towns. **See p.246**

HIGHLIGHTS ARE MARKED ON THE MAP ON PP.200–201

5

architecture in the hills to the north, where the villages of **Monflanquin** and **Monpazier** seem hardly to have changed since the Middle Ages. The same can't be said for the **Château de Biron**, lying between the two, which was altered and expanded extensively during the Renaissance, but its superb hilltop location makes it hard to resist.

GETTING AROUND	THE LOT VALLEY AND AROUND

Travelling by public transport is not that easy, and many bus services to smaller towns only run at school times, if at all. You'll need your own transport for exploring the Célé valley, the Bouriane and other places off the beaten track.

By bus Bus services run along the Lot valley from Cahors east to Figeac and west to Fumel. Other buses head north from Cahors and Figeac to Gramat, while Gramat and Gourdon are served by trains from Brive. Future cuts to the network are likely, so for any public transport it's wise to get information from the relevant tourist offices before you travel. All the buses to places listed in this chapter are covered in a useful booklet, *Les Bus du Lot*, available at tourist offices; otherwise

contact the transport information desk of the Conseil Général du Lot (☎ 05 65 53 43 91, ⓦ lot.fr).

On foot Look out for the free walking map, *Carte de la Randonnée*, and the series of booklets *Promenades et Randonnées* (€7) available from local tourist offices or from the departmental office (see p.40).

By houseboat A leisurely possibility is to rent a houseboat and pootle along the Lot (see p.27).

Cahors

A sunny southern backwater built in a tight meander of the River Lot, **CAHORS** was the chief town of the old province of Quercy and is now the modern capital of the Lot *département*. Its somewhat troubled history has left a warren of dark medieval lanes, a

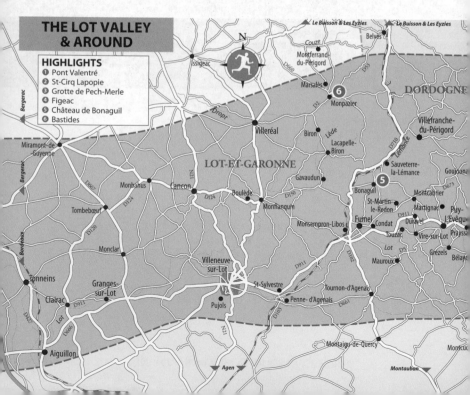

THE LOT VALLEY & AROUND

HIGHLIGHTS
1. Pont Valentré
2. St-Cirq Lapopie
3. Grotte de Pech-Merle
4. Figeac
5. Château de Bonaguil
6. Bastides

rather knocked-about cathedral and impressive fortifications, among them Cahors' famous landmark, the turreted **Pont Valentré**. Another reason to come here is to sample the local **wines**, heady and black but dry to the taste (see box, p.204).

Compact and easily walkable, Cahors is surrounded on three sides by the River Lot and protected to the north by a series of fourteenth-century fortifications. Most sights of interest lie within the cramped confines of the medieval streets on the peninsula's eastern edge, focused around the twin domes of the **Cathédrale St-Étienne**. From here, **rue Nationale** leads south past the former homes of wealthy merchants to the flood-prone artisans' quarter, while north of the cathedral the land continues to slope gently upwards along **rue du Château-du-Roi**, where bankers and aristocrats once lived, towards the old town gate with its guardhouse and tower. Of medieval Cahors' three fortified bridges, only westerly **Pont Valentré** remains – one of the finest surviving bridges of its time. More recent history is commemorated in a couple of passably interesting **museums** and, on a fine day, there are good views from the summit of **Mont St-Cyr**, which overlooks the town from the southeast.

Brief history

Both the names Quercy and Cahors derive from the area's first-known inhabitants, the local Gaulish tribe known as the **Cadurci**. At some time between the seventh and fifth centuries BC they founded their settlement near a sacred spring, immediately across the river to the southwest of modern Cahors, which the Romans, who arrived in overwhelming force in 51BC, later called **Divona Cadurcorum**. Following successive Vandal and Frankish invasions after the fifth century, only a few fragments of Roman stonework remain, as well as the spring, which continues to supply Cahors' drinking water.

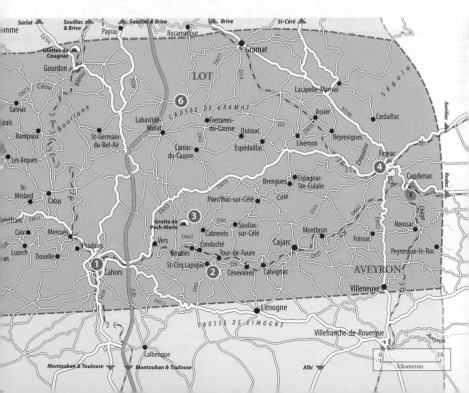

5

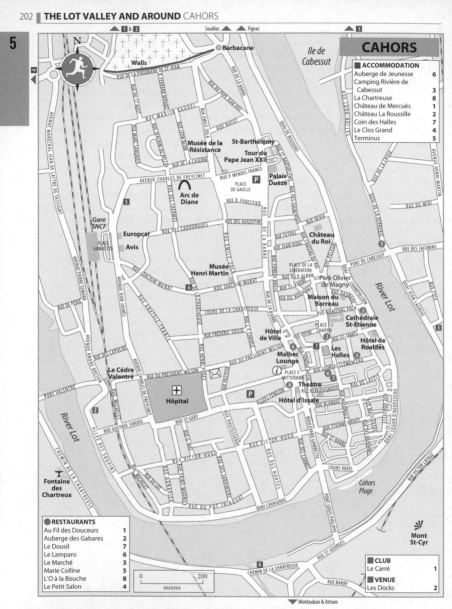

CAHORS

ACCOMMODATION

Auberge de Jeunesse	6
Camping Rivière de Cabessut	3
La Chartreuse	8
Château de Mercuès	1
Château La Roussille	2
Coin des Halles	7
Le Clos Grand	4
Terminus	5

RESTAURANTS

Au Fil des Douceurs	1
Auberge des Gabares	2
Le Dousil	7
Le Lamparo	6
Le Marché	3
Marie Colline	5
L'O à la Bouche	8
Le Petit Salon	4

CLUB

Le Carré	1

VENUE

Les Docks	2

It wasn't until the seventh century that the then Bishop (later Saint) Didier finally erected a wall to protect the nascent town and his rapidly growing cathedral.

The **bishops of Cahors** gradually spread their net until they not only ruled over a vast area extending down the Lot as far as Puy-l'Évêque but also controlled the all-important river trade. By the early thirteenth century Cahors was entering its **golden age**, as powerful local merchants known as Caorsins, together with Lombard bankers fleeing the Cathar crusades, turned the town into Europe's chief banking centre – a wealth that was reflected in the gentrification of various townhouses, bridges and cathedral. When the local bishop, Jacques Duèze, was named **Pope John XXII** in

1316, Cahors had reached its apogee. His greatest legacy was a university, which remained one of the most important in France for the next four centuries.

By now, however, the English and French armies were at loggerheads. Cahors was never attacked during the Hundred Years War, but the end result was the same: under the Treaty of Brétigny (1360) it succumbed reluctantly to **English occupation**. When French rule was eventually restored around 1440, the Caduciens set about rebuilding their ravaged town, adding a few Italianate flourishes and developing a distinctive decorative style comprising carved or moulded rose blossoms, flaming suns and the so-called "*bâtons écotés*" ("pruned branches"), which is still in evidence today.

Unlike several of its neighbours, Cahors remained staunchly Catholic during the **Wars of Religion**. As a consequence it was sacked by the Protestant Henry of Navarre, the future King Henry IV of France, when he seized it after a brief battle in 1580. Later the same year, however, one of many peace treaties saw the town returned to the Catholic fold. By way of recompense, Henry later donated six thousand *livres*, half of which went towards restoring the cathedral.

FESTIVALS, EVENTS AND MARKETS

Late March to early April Figeac: Le Chaînon Manquant (☎05 34 51 48 88, ⓦreseau -chainon.com). Five days of contemporary performance art introducing up-and-coming talent from France and around the world. Mix of street performances and ticketed events.

Mid-July Monpazier: Fête Médiévale (☎05 53 22 68 59, ⓦpays-des-bastides.com). In addition to its many small summer events, Monpazier steps back in time for five days, with banquets, concerts and equestrian displays.

Mid-July Cahors: Blues Festival (☎05 65 35 99 99, ⓦcahorsbluesfestival.com). A week of blues, jazz and rock, French and international artists bare their souls in the streets, Les Docks and the Théâtre de Verdure, rue Wilson and Boulevard Gambetta. The early performances are free, later ones are ticketed. The tourist office has a leaflet with all details.

Mid-July Assier: Assier dans tous ses États (☎05 65 40 42 42, ⓦfestivalassier.com). Jazz and theatre festival with events taking place in local gardens, the village square, the church and the château courtyard. Some free events.

Mid-July to mid-August Cahors: Festival de St-Céré et du Haut-Quercy (☎05 65 38 28 08, ⓦfestival-saint-cere.com). Three-week festival of opera, orchestral works and chamber music, with ticketed concerts in Cahors' cathedral and Musée Henri-Martin.

Late July Cajarc: Africajarc (ⓦafricajarc.com). Cajarc moves to an African beat during three days of concerts, exhibitions, craft displays, markets and food stalls. Tickets required for the main concerts.

First weekend in August Gourdon: Grande Fête Médiévale. Gourdon lets rip with two days of junketing complete with jugglers, fire-eaters, musicians and the works. Entry €3.50.

Early August Puy-l'Évêque: Fête Votive. One of the area's most important local fêtes, lasting five days with a free dance every night, a funfair and a fireworks spectacular with music on the Sunday.

Early to mid-August Château de Bonaguil: Festival du Théâtre (☎05 53 71 17 17, ⓦbonaguil .org). The inner court and moats make a spectacular venue for this festival of French theatre held over eight or nine days. There's a play or musical event every night (tickets required), as well as workshops, street theatre and lectures.

Mid-August Monflanquin: Journées Médiévales. Two days of mead, minstrels and merry japes as Monflanquin goes medieval. Jousting, banquets, siege engines – you name it. You can even rent costumes.

First weekend in September Peyrusse-le-Roc: Spectacle Pyrosymphonique. The ruined towers of Peyrusse make a spectacular setting for a *son-et-lumière*-cum-fireworks display, complete with banquet (€15–20 including dinner).

MARKETS

The region's main markets take place at Aiguillon (Tues & Fri); Cahors (Wed & Sat); Cajarc (Sat); Duravel (Sat); Figeac (Sat); Fumel (Sun); Gourdon (Tues & Sat, also Thurs in July & Aug); Gramat (Tues & Fri); Luzech (Wed); Monflanquin (Thurs); Monpazier (Thurs); Monsempron-Libos (Thurs); Prayssac (Fri) and Villeneuve-sur-Lot (Tues, Wed, Sat & Sun).

5

Over the years Cahors gradually expanded to fill the entire peninsula, though it was not until the nineteenth century that Bishop Didier's ramparts were finally razed. They were replaced by a tree-lined boulevard that was later named after Cahors' most famous son, the politician **Léon Gambetta** (see box opposite). The heart of present-day Cahors is place François Mitterand, named after yet another politician, a recently renovated wide open square. During the renovation process, and excavation of the car park housed underneath, a staggering amount of ancient ruins were uncovered. Work was stopped, archeologists called in and part of a Roman amphitheatre emerged. The much-needed car park was still built, but it contains a semi-circle of the amphitheatre (the rest is under the old college), carefully lit for public display, a parking facility and a day out in one.

The cathedral

The oldest and simplest of the Périgord-style Romanesque churches, the **Cathédrale St-Étienne** dates largely from the early twelfth century, when Bishop Didier's original cathedral was rebuilt in part to house the relic of the Holy Coif. According to local legend, this cloth, said to have covered Christ's head in the tomb, was brought back from the Holy Land around this time by Bishop Géraud de Cardaillac.

THE WINES OF CAHORS

So dark that they're often referred to as "black wines", the red **wines of Cahors** are by far the most distinctive of the southwestern wines, full-bodied with lots of tannin, and they generally need long ageing to bring out their best – the accepted period is about ten years; longer than that and many are past their best. The dominant **grape variety** is Malbec (also known as Auxerrois or Cot), which gives the wine its rich tannin content, its colour and its ability to age. Up to thirty percent of another grape variety is permitted for AOC Cahors, usually Merlot and Tanat – Merlot for roundness and aroma, Tanat to help the ageing process. However, most of the very best wines are 100% Malbec. The distinctive bite of a young Cahors wine goes well with charcuterie and stews, while the more aromatic older wines usually accompany red meats, game and the local goat's cheese, *Cabécou*.

VINEYARDS

There are approximately 43 square kilometres under vines in the *appellation*, which stretches from Cahors west along the Lot for 30km to Soturac, producing on average 240,000 hectolitres (roughly 32 million bottles) per annum. Before **visiting the vineyards**, pick up a copy of the free *Le Vignoble de Cahors, Châteaux et Domaines*, which details the two hundred or so producers in the *appellation*; it's available from the tourist office (see p.208) and from wine merchants in Cahors (see p.210), or from the Maison du Vin de Cahors, 430 av Jean-Jaurès (Mon–Fri; ☎05 65 23 22 24), opposite the station; note that the Maison du Vin does not otherwise cater to individuals.

SAMPLING AND BUYING WINE

For an introduction to what's on offer, head for the imposing **Château Lagrézette** (daily 10am–7pm; ☎05 65 20 07 42, ⊛chateau-lagrezette.tm.fr), 10km northwest of Cahors on the D12 midway between Douelle and Mercuès. In addition to sampling their award-winning wines you can visit the magnificent, state-of-the-art *chais* dug into the hillside, though it's best to call in advance to arrange this. Also worth a visit for its reliably good wines – if not for its ambience – is the **Côtes d'Olt** co-operative (April–Oct Mon–Sat 8am–noon & 2–6pm; July & Aug also Sun 10am–12.30pm & 2–6pm; Nov–March Mon–Sat 8am–noon & 2–6pm; ☎05 65 30 71 86) on the river's south bank about 17km west of Cahors on the D8 in the commune of Parnac. In general you can expect to pay between €10 and €20 for a very decent Cahors, although some of the region's prestige wines fetch €70 or more.

LÉON GAMBETTA

Heralded as the "father of the Republic", **Léon Gambetta** was born in Cahors in 1838. After graduating as a lawyer, he specialized in defending republican sympathizers accused of political crimes against Emperor Napoléon III. The republicans soon rallied around Gambetta – a charismatic man and great orator – and, when Napoléon was forced to surrender to an invading Prussian army in 1870, he was among those who quickly proclaimed the **Third Republic**, the regime which continued to govern France until 1940. It had a rocky start, however. With the Prussians besieging Paris, Gambetta fled the capital by balloon to organize the war effort in the provinces. While he opposed the armistice signed in 1871, Gambetta and his band of moderate republicans, or "Opportunists", were able to keep the Republic afloat despite constant attacks from both the monarchist majority and the radical Left. He served as president of the National Assembly from 1879 to 1882, but later that year his career was cut short when he accidentally shot himself with a revolver, and died soon after.

Numerous reconstructions have been carried out over the centuries, meaning St-Étienne's exterior is rather unexciting, with the notable exception of the elaborately decorated portal above the **north door**. Carved in around 1140, it depicts Christ's Ascension. Side panels show scenes from the life of St Stephen (St Étienne), the first Christian martyr who was stoned to death around 35 AD, while the outer arch portrays people being stabbed and sliced with axes.

Inside, the cathedral is much like Périgueux's St-Étienne (see p.53), with a nave lacking aisles and transepts, roofed with two monumental domes. High in the west dome, original fourteenth-century frescoes again depict the stoning of St Stephen, encircled by eight giant prophets. In 1988 further paintings from the same era were discovered behind layers of plaster just inside and above the west door. They consist of faded but beautiful Creation scenes, including Adam and Eve in the Garden of Eden and many finely observed birds and animals.

To the right of the choir, the aptly named **Deep Chapel** bears scars from the Wars of Religion, when Protestant armies hacked away at its carvings. They also caused irreparable damage to the **cloister**, accessed by a door next to the Deep Chapel, though the flamboyant Gothic colonnades still retain some intricate craftsmanship. The door surrounds are also beautifully carved, if rather battered; that on the northeast wall leads into **St Gausbert's Chapel** (only accessible as part of the guided tours run by the tourist office; see p.208), which holds the **Holy Coif** – a decidedly unimpressive, rather grubby looking piece of padded cloth – among chalices, gilded statues and other treasures.

Place Jean-Jacques Chapou

The square on which the cathedral stands, **place Jean-Jacques Chapou**, commemorates a local Resistance leader killed in a German ambush in July 1944. On its west side, look for a sign above what is now a bank announcing *Bazar Génois: Gambetta Jeune et Cie*. This is where **Léon Gambetta** (see box above), the son of an Italian grocer, spent his childhood. At its southern end the square extends into place Galdemar, popularly known as place de la Halle. The covered **market hall** at its centre, built as a corn exchange in 1865, provides the focus for Cahors' lively markets. There's a fresh food **market** in the *halle* here (daily except Sun pm & Mon), and a more extensive market on Wednesday and Saturday mornings spreading north into the cathedral square; in winter (Nov to mid-March), the *halle* plays host to a Saturday morning *marché au gras*, selling all manner of duck and goose products. Nearby place François Mitterrand also hosts an antiques fair-cum-flea market on the first and third Saturdays of the month.

5

> ### JACQUES DUÈZE AND CHÂTEAUNEUF-DU-PÂPE
>
> Cahors' home-grown cleric, **Jacques Duèze**, was immensely fond of his native town, and no less fond of its powerful black wines. So much so that when elected to the papacy, as John XXII, and forced to move his episcopal seat from Cahors to the Holy See in Avignon, he devised a wheeze for continuing to imbibe his favourite tipple. Rather than having the wine transported 400 kilometres from the Cahors vineyards to the papal palace, he built a new summer palace on the banks of the Rhône and planted his beloved Malbec vine-stock around it. Thus a new wine was born, which the locals christened Châteauneuf-du-Pâpe. In essence a Cahors wine in all but name.

The medieval streets

A warren of narrow lanes and alleys fills the area between boulevard Gambetta and the eastern riverbank, where the majority of houses, turreted and built with flat, thin southern brick, have been handsomely restored during recent decades. From the market square, **rue Nationale** cuts almost due south through the heart of medieval Cahors to where the old Roman bridge once stood – the foundations are still just visible when the water level is low. Other roads worth exploring in the area are canyon-like rue Bergougnioux and its easterly extension rue Lastié, which comes out among a pretty group of brick and timber buildings around place St-Urcisse.

One of Cahors' most attractive corners lies just north of the cathedral along **rue Daurade**, where a lovely row of buildings overlooks a little park named after the sixteenth-century poet Olivier de Magny, who lived at no. 12. His house is overshadowed, though, by the thirteenth-century **Maison du Bourreau**, the "executioner's house", with its big arched openings and line of double windows above. The name dates from the Revolution, when the public executioner lived here; naturally, the building is said to be haunted.

Continuing north along rue Daurade you reach the southern end of **rue Château-du-Roi** and its extension, **rue des Soubirous**. This is the "upper town", where the houses become distinctly grander. One of the most imposing is the fourteenth-century **Château du Roi** itself, built by cousins of Pope John XXII but later taken over by the king's emissary when the bishops lost their stranglehold on Cahors in the fifteenth century. Its massive, featureless walls can be easily seen from the eastern riverbank.

Wealthy Cadurciens were very fond of adding turrets to their homes and there are a number of examples scattered through the Soubirous quarter. To see them properly it's best to head down to the river – rue du Four-Ste-Catherine provides the most interesting route – to a vantage point across Pont de Cabessut. Cahors' skyline stretches in front of you from the cathedral domes in the south via Collège Pélegry, with its crenellated hexagonal turret, and the square, solid tower of the Château du Roi. In the far distance the **Tour du Pape Jean XXII** and the **Tour des Pendus** pinpoint Cahors' northern ramparts, which still stretch partway across the peninsula.

Musée de la Résistance

Place Bessières • Daily 2–6pm • Free

Cahors' two museums deserve a brief stop. The first, in a small building on the north side of place Charles-de-Gaulle, is the **Musée de la Résistance**, which documents the history of the local Resistance movement against the broader context of German occupation, deportations and, finally, Liberation in 1945. The most interesting section, on the ground floor, deals with local history, where you can read about Jean-Jacques Chapou, after whom the cathedral square is named (see p.205), and about the *Mona Lisa*'s sojourn in the area (see p.194).

Musée Henri Martin

792 rue Émile-Zola • Mon & Wed–Sat 11am–6pm, Sun & public holidays 2–6pm; closed when changing temporary exhibitions • €3 •
☎ 05 65 20 88 66

Musée Henri Martin is housed in a seventeenth-century former episcopal palace. Exhibits range from Gallo-Roman pots to works by nineteenth- and twentieth-century artists such as Dufy, Vlaminck and Utrillo. However, pride of place goes to seventeen oil paintings by local artist **Henri Martin** (1860–1943), whose mix of Impressionism and Pointillism perfectly evokes the lazy sun-filled landscapes of this part of France, and an important collection dedicated to **Léon Gambetta**. With over two thousand documents, photographs, sculptures and paintings, only a fraction is on show at any one time.

Pont Valentré

The top reason most people venture to Cahors is to see the dramatic **Pont Valentré**, which guards the western river crossing. Its three powerful towers, originally closed by portcullises and gates, made it an independent fortress, which was so imposing, in fact, that the bridge was never attacked. Building it was a problem, however: work started in 1308, but the bridge was not completed for another seventy years. According to legend, the Devil was to blame – at least in part. The story goes that the architect, exasperated at the slow progress, sold his soul in exchange for the Devil's assistance. As the bridge was nearing completion, he tried to wriggle out of the deal by giving the Devil a sieve with which to carry water for the masons. The Devil took revenge by creeping up the central tower every night to remove the last stone, thus ensuring that the bridge would never be finished. If you look carefully at the top of the tower's east face, you'll see a little devil, which was added when Pont Valentré was renovated in 1879. On the far side of the river, the old pumping station of **Cabazat** now houses a **museum** (June–Aug daily 10am–1pm & 3–7pm; Sept–Dec Fri–Mon 11am–1pm & 3–6pm; ☎05 65 53 04 99) detailing the bridge's history. Most of the information is in French, but you can pick up a leaflet that has the basics in English. Glass floors show off the pumping mechanism below, while the café makes for a pleasant, if a little pricey, riverside spot.

Mont St-Cyr

All around Cahors rise the dry, scrubby uplands of the *causse*. These valley sides were carpeted with vines from Roman times until the nineteenth century when phylloxera set in, after which the land was used for grazing sheep; now, however, only the lines of tumbled-down stone walls and abandoned farmhouses remain. One of the few landmarks around is the red-and-white TV mast on the summit of **Mont St-Cyr**, overlooking Cahors to the southeast. At 264m, this is the place to head for bird's-eye views of the town: the division between medieval and seventeenth-century Cahors becomes very apparent from the summit, particularly in summer when tree-lined boulevard Gambetta picks out the former course of the ramparts.

It's a stiff but straightforward climb to the summit of Mont St-Cyr. From the southern end of boulevard Gambetta, cross Pont Louis-Philippe, then take the steps behind the Virgin's statue and keep going up for about twenty to thirty minutes. Though you can drive, it takes almost as long, as the road winds for about 5km among

---

LES JARDINS SECRETS

A quirky way to unearth Cahors' history is to find the **Jardins Secrets**, a series of around thirty gardens making use of otherwise vacant patches of land dotted around the old town and the river. Medicinal herbs, vines and fruit orchards all feature, laid out as they would have been by monks or local gardeners. Pick up a map of the garden locations from the tourist office (see p.208) or at the boat tour ticket booths near Pont Valentré; all the descriptions are in English.

5

stunted oaks and pines across the plateau. Apart from the views, there are picnic tables at the top and a café-bar, which also serves food till 7pm from June (closed Mon & Tues) till the end of summer.

Cahors Plage

If you attempt Mont St Cyr in high season you can cool off at the free riverside **beach** (first week of July to third week of Aug daily 11am–8pm), on place de l'Acacias beside Pont Louis Philippe, when you come down. The lively, sandy beach comes complete with straw parasols, beach bars, picnic tables and a bouncy castle.

ARRIVAL AND DEPARTURE

CAHORS

By train The *gare SNCF* sits 500m away from the centre of town, on place Jouinot Gambetta.

Destinations Brive (7 daily; 1hr–1hr 10min); Gourdon (6 daily; 30min); Montauban (6 daily; 40–50min); Paris-Austerlitz (6 daily; 4–5hr); Souillac (6 daily; 45min); Toulouse (7 daily; 1hr–1hr 20min).

By bus The *gare SNCF* is the terminus for many buses, while others stop on place de Charles-de-Gaulle at the north end of the main boulevard. The tourist office stocks bus timetables, or phone the Conseil Général's central information desk (☎ 05 65 53 43 91). Tickets for Eurolines buses are available from Voyages Belmon, 2 bd Gambetta (☎ 05 65 35 59 30), at the north end of bd Gambetta.

Destinations Albas (4–10 daily; 30min); Bouziès (3–5 daily; 30min); Cajarc (3–5 daily; 1hr); Figeac (3–5 daily; 1hr 45min); Fumel (4–8 daily; 1hr–1hr 15min); Gramat (Mon, Weds, Thurs & Sat 1 daily; 1hr 10min); Luzech (4–10 daily; 20min); Monsempron-Libos (4–8 daily; 1hr 15min–1hr 30min); Puy-l'Évêque (4–10 daily; 45min); St-Céré (Mon, Wed, Thurs & Sat 1 daily; 1hr 45min); St-Martin-Labouval (3–5 daily; 45min); Tour-de-Faure (3–5 daily; 40min); Vers (4–8 daily; 15–20min); Villefranche-de-Rouergue (weekdays 1 daily; 1hr 15min).

By car The most convenient place to park is in the Parking de l'Amphithéatre under the allées Fénelon.

GETTING AROUND AND INFORMATION

Car rental Avis, opposite the train station on place Jouinot-Gambetta ☎ 05 65 30 13 10.

Taxis There are taxi stands outside the train station and on bd Gambetta, or call Allo Taxi (☎ 05 65 22 19 42).

Tourist office Cahors' tourist office (Mon–Sat 9am–12.30pm & 1.30–6pm; July & Aug plus Sun 10am–noon; ☎ 05 65 53 20 65, ✇ tourisme-lot.fr) occupies a handsome building on the north side of place François Mitterrand. It provides detailed

walking maps of the town, and also organizes guided tours (some in English) in season, covering a variety of themes (various dates throughout the year; €6.50). In addition to the tourist office there is a small information office (mid-April to Oct daily 11am–6pm) in the old toll booth on Pont Louis-Philippe, on the southern tip of the peninsula, dedicated to the route de St Jacques. They are a mine of information for walkers and will even book accommodation.

ACTIVITIES

Bike rental The nearest outlets are in Douelle, about 10km west of Cahors, where you'll find Antinéa Loisirs (July & Aug only; ☎ 05 65 30 95 79), who also rent kayaks. Made in Douelle (☎ 05 65 30 78 20, ✇ madeindouelle.com) is open all year.

Boat tours Safaraid (April–Oct; 1hr 15min; €9; ☎ 05 65 35 98 88, ✇ canoe-kayak-dordogne.com) offers

tours with English commentary round the Cahors meander from the jetty below Pont Valentré. Les Croisières Fénelon (day-trip to St-Cirq Lapopie €55, includes a meal; ☎ 05 65 30 16 55, ✇ bateau-cahors .com) also puts on a varied programme of excursions. There are ticket booths for both companies beside the Pont Valentré jetty.

ACCOMMODATION

Cahors has a broad range of hotels, though the choice, particularly in the middle price categories, is not particularly inspiring. Instead, there's better value for money in the surrounding region, though you'll need your own transport to get there.

HOTELS IN CAHORS

La Chartreuse Saint Georges ☎ 05 65 35 17 37, ✇ hotel-la-chartreuse.com. This modern hotel is in an excellent position on the south bank, a five-minute walk from the city centre. Rooms are a little plain, but a spacious

restaurant serving good food (*menus* from €14 lunch and €25 in the evening), with wonderful river views, more than makes up for them. There's also a pool and a terrace. Restaurant open daily noon–2pm & 7.30–10pm. Breakfast €9.50. **€95**

Coin des Halles 30 place St-Maurice ☎ 05 65 30 24 27, ⓦ lecoindeshalles.com. Right in the heart of the old town, this hotel, situated, as its name implies, in the corner of the market square, offers clean, bright rooms, though some are on the small side. The bar-restaurant teems with life all day long (*plat du jour* €9.50, *menu* €16). Restaurant open July–Sept daily noon–2pm & 7–10pm; Oct–June Tues–Sun noon–2pm & 7–10pm. Breakfast 8. **€67**

Terminus 5 av Charles de Freycinet ☎ 05 65 53 32 00, ⓦ balandre.com. Cahors' most opulent hotel occupies a nineteenth-century bourgeois residence near the station. The grandeur has faded somewhat, but quirky touches such as pianos on the landing help make it nostalgic rather than shabby. Breakfast €10. **€79**

HOTELS AROUND CAHORS

Château de Mercuès Mercuès ☎ 05 65 20 00 01, ⓦ chateaudemercues.com. High on its promontory 6km to the northwest of Cahors, for centuries this was the humble residence of the bishops of Cahors. It is now a luxury hotel with pool, tennis courts, excellent wine cellars (tastings available July & Aug; free) and a restaurant serving such delicacies as roast turbot with asparagus and local truffle oil. Restaurant open Tues–Thurs for dinner, Fri–Sun lunch and dinner. Closed mid-Oct to Easter. Breakfast €26. **€250**

Château La Roussille Chemin du Moulin, Labéraudie ☎ 05 65 22 84 74, ⓦ chateauroussille.com. A welcoming *chambre d'hôte* five minutes' drive from Cahors centre; take the D8 in the direction of Moulin de Labéraudie. It has one room and two suites, all with their own individual character, a lounge and a billiard room and is set in a large park complete with solar-heated pool. Evening meals (€27) are by request. May–Oct. **€80**

Le Clos Grand 12 rue des Claux Grands, Labéraudie, Pradines ☎ 05 65 35 04 39. In Pradines, a suburb 5km northwest of Cahors, this welcoming hotel looks out over fields and has a pleasant, shady garden. Most rooms occupy a purpose-built annexe beside the pool, each with a little terrace or balcony and en-suite bathroom. Locals come here for the good-value food (*menus* €17 at lunch, €26.50 in the evening). Restaurant open July–Sept daily 12.15–1.30pm & 7.30–8.45pm; Sept to mid-Dec & Jan–June Tues to Sat 12.15–1.30pm & 7.30–8.45pm, Sun 12.15–1.30pm. Breakfast 8. **€55**

HOSTEL AND CAMPSITE

Auberge de Jeunesse 222 rue Joachim Murat ☎ 05 65 35 64 71, ⓦ fuaj.org/cahors. Pleasantly situated in a quiet building behind a park, this hostel is not far from the *gare SNCF*. Washing and drying facilities and a large garden make this a perfect place for walkers. Evening meal €10. Breakfast €4. **€14.30**

Camping Rivière de Cabessut Rue de la Rivière ☎ 05 65 30 06 30, ⓦ cabessut.com. Three-star campsite in a quiet spot beside the river just over 1km from Cahors across Pont de Cabessut; facilities include a shop, snack bar, small pool and canoe rental. Closed Sept–April. **€18.80**

EATING AND DRINKING

Cahors has no shortage of good places to eat, many of which make full use of the excellent local produce. Most are concentrated in the streets of the medieval town, though you'll also find brasseries, pizzerias and cafés along boulevard Gambetta. There are also plenty of boulangeries and patisseries. The *halles* has three very good boucheries and a splendid fromagerie.

★ **Au Fil des Douceurs** 90 quai de la Verrerie ☎ 05 65 22 13 04. A floating restaurant and much-loved local institution, moored on the far side of Pont de Cabessut. The food is haute cuisine, with typical regional dishes making excellent use of fresh market produce. But the pièce de résistance is the outstanding view, the crenellated towers of medieval Cahors painted against a setting sun. *Menus* are €14.50 at lunch and €25–60 in the evening. Reservations recommended – ask for a table with a riverside view. Tues–Sat noon–1.30pm & 7.30–9pm.

★ **Auberge des Gabares** 24 place Champollion ☎ 05 65 53 91 47. This sort of traditional, single-*menu* restaurant is usually found in the depths of the country rather than in the middle of a town, albeit on a wisteria-covered terrace overlooking the Lot. The food, like the decor, is simple and unfussy, and it's good value, too, with five courses for a mere €15 including wine. There's more choice on Saturday evenings, when they stretch to another €22 *menu*. Either way you'll need a good appetite. Tues–Sat noon–1.30pm & 7.30–8.30pm.

Le Dousil 124 rue Nationale ☎ 05 65 53 19 67. This wine bar is a great place to sample local reds before setting off on the wine trail. They dish up good food, too, including cheese or charcuterie platters, open sandwiches and more substantial mains such as *cassoulet*. *Menus* from €11.50 lunch; à la carte in the evening. Wine is sold by the glass or bottle. July & Aug daily 11am–3pm & 6pm–1am; Sept–June Tues–Sat 11am–3pm & 6pm–1am.

★ **Le Lamparo** 76 rue Georges Clemenceau ☎ 05 65 35 25 93, ⓦ lelamparo.com. Large, bustling restaurant that spills out onto the square in summer. It's justifiably popular for its generous portions, slick service and very reasonable prices. Though the speciality is pizza (from €8.50), there's plenty of variety, including mountainous salads and local dishes such as *confit de canard*, plus enticing desserts to follow – try the *café gourmand*. *Menus* from €17.50. Mon–Sat noon–2.15pm & 7–10.30pm.

Le Marché 27 place Chapou ☎ 05 65 35 27 27, ⓦ restaurantlemarche.com. This elegant restaurant on the market square serves delicate dishes made from fresh local produce. *Menus* are €19 at lunch, €35 in the evening. Mid-May to Oct & mid-Nov to April Tues–Sat noon– 2pm & 7.30–9pm.

Marie Colline 173 rue Georges Clemenceau ☎ 05 65 35 59 96. You need to reserve or wait till around 1pm to find space at this bright, airy vegetarian restaurant run by two sisters. The choice is limited – two entrées and two main dishes (*plat du jour* €8.50) which change daily – but it's all freshly made, using locally produced vegetables. Save room for one of their scrumptious desserts. Lunch only: July–Aug Mon–Sat; Sept–June Mon–Fri.

★ **L'O à la Bouche** 56 allées Fénelon ☎ 05 65 35 65 69. Cahors' favourite fine-diner has moved from its traditional location to a chic open-plan restaurant in the centre of town. Here you can watch chef Dive conjure up such delectable treats as smoked duck with marinated courgettes and ratatouille terrine. The lunchtime *plat du jour* is incredible value at €13.50, while evening *menus* are from €27. The restaurant tables billow out onto place François Mitterrand in summer. April–Oct & mid-Nov to mid-March Tues–Sat noon–1.30pm & 7–9.30pm.

★ **Le Petit Salon** 79 bd Gambetta ☎ 05 65 21 28 73. The best of the street cafés lining the sunny side of the boulevard, this tiny salon has two tricks up its sleeve: an enticing window full of home-made cakes – the macaroons are to die for – and a short but delicious vegetarian lunch *menu*. To be sure of a choice be there by noon. *Plat du jour* €7.80, *menu* €11.80. Tues–Sat 10am–6pm (lunch served noon–2pm).

NIGHTLIFE AND ENTERTAINMENT

Cahors is not exactly a hub for nightlife, but there's more here than meets the eye, especially in season. For events, ask at the tourist office, which publishes lists of the many festivals (see box, p.203), exhibitions, concerts and plays taking place in Cahors. Classical concerts are also held in the cathedral. *Le Dousil* (see p.209) is a great place to start the evening, as are the many bars along the boulevard.

Le Carré Quai Lagrive ☎ 90 80 44 48 72, ⓦ carre -club.com. This little nightclub on the east bank of the river has great music. On Fridays the entrance fee for men is €5, while girls get in free; on Saturdays it's €10 for all. €2 compulsory bag check. Fri & Sat 11.30pm–6.30am.

Les Docks 430 allées des Soupirs ☎ 06 65 22 36 38, ⓦ myspace.com/lesdocks. Down on the waterfront, *Les*

Docks serves as a youth venue and events space, with bands every Friday. Office open and tickets available Tues–Fri 9am–noon & 2–6pm, Sat 2–6pm.

Théâtre Place François Mitterrand ☎ 05 65 20 88 60, ⓦ mairie-cahors.fr. For plays, the principal venue is the Neoclassical – and very plush – Municipal Theatre Dionysus, which puts on a varied programme of theatre, dance, concerts and opera.

DIRECTORY

Books and newspapers The Maison de la Presse, 73 bd Gambetta, stocks the main English-language papers and magazines as well as local guides and quite a few light reading books, while Librairie Calligramme, 75 rue du Maréchal Joffre, is a more serious bookshop carrying a few heavyweight English-language titles.

Cinema Cahors has two cinemas, the three-screen ABC, 24 rue des Augustins (☎ 05 65 35 03 11, ⓦ abc-cahors.fr) and Le Quercy, 871 rue Émile-Zola (☎ 05 65 22 20 05, ⓦ lequercy.fr), near the Musée Henri-Martin.

Hospital Centre Hospitalier Jean Rougier, 449–335 rue du Président Wilson (☎ 05 65 20 50 50). Emergencies should head round the back of the building.

Internet access There's an internet café (Mon–Sat 10am–8pm, Sun 2–8pm), opposite the north entrance to the cathedral. Alternatively, *Les Docks* by the Pont Valentré also has internet access (Tues–Fri 9am–noon & 2–6pm).

Police Commissariat de Police, 1 rue de l'Ancienne Gendarmerie ☎ 05 65 23 17 17.

Wine Malbec Lounge (mid-June to Sept) is a plush wine bar/cum promotional centre adjoining the tourist office on the place François Mitterrand. You can taste three different wines from the hundreds on display for just €3, and absorb a vast amount of information from the knowledgeable waitresses. Atrium (ⓦ g-vigouroux.fr), on the N20, as you come into town from the south, is a good place to buy wines from the châteaux de Mercuès, de Haute-Serre, Caïx and Leret Monpezat at close to château prices; it also offers tastings and advises on vineyard visits. Le Cèdre Valentré, 32 av André Breton (ⓦ www.cedrevalentre.com), has a boutique at the east end of Pont Valentré, which also sells local produce and souvenirs.

East along the Lot

5

Upstream from Cahors the Lot valley becomes narrower and the cliffs higher. The river is confined to ever-tighter meanders and castles sprout from inaccessible knuckles of rock, often with red-tiled villages clinging to their flanks. Delightful **St-Cirq Lapopie**, 30km or so east of Cahors, perched precariously on the edge of a 100m drop, is the most dramatic sight in the whole valley. Further along the river's south bank on the D8, the Renaissance **Château de Cénevières** boasts an interesting history, as well as some unusual frescoes and a good collection of period furniture. The only major settlement along this stretch of river is **Cajarc**, an important market town with an incongruous modern art gallery; the town is also a stop on the pilgrims' road to Santiago de Compostela. Upstream, the scenery takes over once again as the Lot winds its way past more medieval villages and castles, and beneath a 300-metre-high belvedere, the **Saut de la Mounine**, on the valley's southern lip. There's nothing particular to stop for along the last stretch of river heading northeast to **Capdenac**, near **Figeac** (see p.220). Instead, you could take a diversion south across the *causse* to where the **Grotte de Foissac** harbours some prehistoric remains alongside a varied and colourful array of stalactites and stalagmites, and then continue on across country to the atmospheric ruins of **Peyrusse-le-Roc**.

GETTING AROUND   **THE LOT VALLEY**

The Lot valley is unusually well served by public transport, with an SNCF bus running along the river's north bank from Cahors via Figeac to Capdenac. It stops at almost every village en route, though you'll have to walk across to those south of the river, and will need your own transport to explore the high country on either side.

Vers

Immediately east of Cahors, the Lot valley is taken up with a busy main road, train tracks and scattered modern developments, above which soars the bridge for the A20 *autoroute*. However, things improve dramatically after the village of **VERS**, some 15km upstream, where the main D653 to Figeac strikes off northeastwards. Vers itself doesn't merit a stop, unless you are in search of overnight **accommodation**.

ARRIVAL AND GETTING AROUND   **VERS**

By bus Buses stop near *La Truite Dorée* hotel.
Bike rental La Roue Libre, place du Communal

(☎ 05 65 31 45 57, ⓦ larouelibre.net), in the centre of the village near the church.

ACCOMMODATION AND EATING

La Truite Dorée ☎ 05 65 31 41 51, ⓦ latruitedoree.fr.
La Truite Dorée, at the entrance to the village overlooking the River Vers where it flows into the Lot from the north, is the most attractive accommodation option; rooms in the modern annexe have balconies over the river. There's an

excellent restaurant, much patronized by locals, offering *menus* from €13 at lunch and €23 in the evenings. Restaurant open daily March to mid-Nov noon–1.30pm & 7.30–9pm. Breakfast €9. **€74**

Bouziès

East of Vers, the D662 hugs the north bank of the Lot as it meanders back and forth beneath cliffs that loom ever higher as you near **BOUZIÈS**, located on the south bank across a narrow suspension bridge. The main reason for coming here is to walk along the **chemin de halage**, a towpath cut into the cliff just above water level on the river's south bank. In pre-railway days it was used by men hauling produce-laden *gabares* boats upstream. It now forms part of the GR36 long-distance footpath, indicated by red and white markers, which you can join at the car park on the east side of Bouziès. The rock-hewn section starts after about 500m and extends for some 300m; if you're feeling energetic, you can then continue on to St-Cirq Lapopie (see p.212).

5

Another way of exploring the riverbank is to take to the water. Bouziès is a **boating** and **canoeing** centre, with several companies setting up shop on the south side of the bridge in the summer.

ARRIVAL AND DEPARTURE   BOUZIÈS

By bus SNCF buses stop on the main road near the bridge. Destinations Cahors (3–5 daily; 45–50min); Cajarc (3–5 daily; 40min); Capendac (3–5 daily; 1hr 50min); St Cirq Lapopie; (3–5 daily; 10min).

ACTIVITIES

Boat rental You can rent canoes by the river, while Lot Navigation (☎05 65 24 32 20, ⍟lot-navigation.com) has "picnic boats" for rental from April to October. Four-person boats are €30 per hour, €110 for the full day, twelve-person boats cost €190 for the full day; reservations are recommended at least one week in advance. If you don't want to pilot your own vessel, Bateaux Safaraid (☎06 65 35 98 88, ⍟safaraid -croisieres.com), runs excursions to St-Cirq Lapopie and back (April–Oct 3–5 trips daily; 1hr 30min; €10). Finally, you can rent houseboats here through Nicols (see p.27).

ACCOMMODATION AND EATING

Les Falaises Le Bourg ☎05 65 31 26 83, ⍟hotel -falaises-bouzies.federal-hotel.com. Bouziès has a decent hotel, with its own restaurant (*menus* from €16), in the village centre. Note that the rooms in the main building overlooking the pool and gardens are preferable to those in the older block behind. Restaurant open April–Oct daily noon–2pm & 7–9pm. Breakfast €9. **€74**

St-Cirq Lapopie

The cliff-edge village of **ST-CIRQ LAPOPIE** sits 5km east of Bouziès, high above the south bank of the Lot. With its cobbled lanes, half-timbered houses and gardens virtually unspoilt by modern intrusions, the village is an irresistible draw for the tour buses, but it's still worth the trouble, especially if you visit early or late in the day.

St-Cirq today consists of one main street running steeply downhill for 500m from Porte de la Peyrolerie in the west to easterly Porte de Pélissaria; in between which it's variously known as rue de la Peyrolerie, **rue Droite** – between the central market square, place du Sombral, and the church – and rue de la Pélissaria. All along are stone and half-timbered houses, under steeply pitched and gabled Quercy roofs.

Brief history

There has been a **castle** on this rocky protuberance, known as La Popie, since Gallo-Roman times, if not before. It was such a strategically important site that in the Middle Ages it was owned by not only the viscount of St-Cirq but also the other three viscounts of Quercy (Gourdon, Cardaillac and Castelnau). A feudal town soon grew up within the protection of its walls, although it wasn't a particularly safe haven: St-Cirq took a battering from the English during the Hundred Years War, while in the Wars of Religion it was seized by the Protestant Henry of Navarre, who ordered the castle to be destroyed in 1580 to keep it from the Catholics. Undaunted by these events, local craftsmen built up a reputation for their skill in **wood turning**, specifically of boxwood, which they fashioned into goblets, furniture and taps for casks. They continued to ply their craft into the nineteenth century, but following industrialization St-Cirq went into steep decline until it was rediscovered in the early twentieth century by the artistic fraternity, most famously **Henri Martin** (see p.207), **Man Ray** and the surrealist poet **André Breton**, who came to live here in the 1950s. The fame of St Cirq has been spreading ever since, and in 2012 it was voted the "most popular village" in France.

Château and church of St-Cirq

The first place to head for is the ruined **château** to the north of place du Sombral. Precious little remains of the castle, but the site is fantastic, plunging down to the river 100m below. Further east along the cliff edge, the fortified **church of St-Cirq** is now the village's dominant building. It's in a pretty sorry state itself, though you can still make out faint traces of thirteenth-century murals where the original Romanesque chapel was incorporated into a larger church three hundred years later.

Musée Rignault

Le Bourg • Late March to end Sept daily except Tues 10am–12.30pm & 2.30–6pm; July & Aug open until 7pm; closed two weeks in May or June to change exhibitions • €1.50

Below the church of St-Cirq, to the east, the Musée Rignault occupies a lovely fortified mansion with a romantic little rock garden and various other embellishments added by an art dealer who came to live here in 1922. A few pieces of his wide-ranging art collection are on display, while the rest of the space is given over to temporary exhibitions.

Maison Daura

Le Bourg • ☎ 05 65 40 78 19, ⓦ magp.fr

Maison Daura, near the entrance to the village, was once the home of Catalan painter **Pierre Daura**. It's an exceptionally beautiful example of Gothic architecture, with archetypal windows and perfectly preserved doors, a fit setting for the purpose it now serves – a residence for international artists. It hosts frequent modern art exhibitions, which are open to the public and well worth a look; the tourist office (see below) will have all details.

ARRIVAL AND INFORMATION   ST-CIRQ LAPOPIE

By bus Buses on the Cahors–Figeac route drop you across the river in the hamlet of Tour-de-Faure; from here you can call a taxi (Philippe Merle; ☎ 06 15 23 61 61) or leg it up the steep hill for the last 2km.

By car There are three car parks for St-Cirq: the lowest, 800m below the village, is free, the one closest to the village centre charges €3.50, including entry to the two museums, and the third sits 300m above the village and costs €2.

Tourist office Place du Sombral (daily 10am–1pm & 2–6pm; ☎ 05 65 31 29 06, ⓦ tourisme-lot.com), can furnish you with a handy English-language walking guide to St-Cirq.

Market In July and August there's a small market on place du Sombral on Wednesday mornings.

ACCOMMODATION

There are various accommodation options in the village itself, all of which get booked up weeks ahead in summer. The best bet is to look in Tour-de-Faure, on the other side of the river.

Auberge du Sombral Place du Sombral ☎ 05 65 31 26 08, ⓦ lesombral.com. Very pleasantly located hostel in the heart of the village, though this does mean parking some distance away. It offers plain but perfectly adequate rooms and a good restaurant (*menus* from €16 lunch and €22 in the evening). Restaurant open April to mid-Nov Mon–Wed, Fri & Sat noon–2pm & 7.30–9pm. Public parking €3.50. Breakfast €8.50. **€66**

Les Gabarres Tour-de-Faure ☎ 05 65 30 24 57, ⓦ hotellesgabarres.com. A good-value hotel in Tour-de-Faure with plain rooms that are more than compensated for by friendly welcoming staff, a pool, flower-filled terrace and garden. Breakfast €8.80. **€61**

Gîte d'Étape Le Bourg ☎ 05 65 31 21 51. A perfectly adequate stop-over housed in the old Musée de la Memoire, now closed. It has washing and kitchen facilities; no meals are offered, but restaurants and snacks are available in the village. **€13.20**

Maison Redon La Combe, Tour-de-Faure ☎ 05 65 30 24 13, ⓦ maisonredon.com. Wonderfully peaceful *chambre d'hôte* in an ivy-covered house, with five spacious, well-appointed rooms and a lovely garden. Closed Sept–May. **€74**

La Pelisseria ☎ 05 65 30 25 52, ⓦ hoteldelapelisseria .pagesperso-orange.fr. A splendid hotel-cum-chambres d'hôte in the centre of the village, straddling two of the oldest houses. Only open six weeks of the year, from around July 20. It features a small pool and leafy garden. Book well in advance. Breakfast included. **€80**

★ **St Cirq** Tour-de-Faure ☎ 05 65 30 30 30, ⓦ hotel -lestcirq.com. Enjoy the spectacular views of St Cirq itself from this gorgeous hotel. Rooms are spacious and beautifully appointed, and there's a large garden and heated pool. Feb to mid-Nov and 2 weeks at Christmas. Breakfast €12.50. **€88**

CAMPSITES

Camping de la Plage Down by the bridge ☎ 05 65 30 29 51, ⓦ campingplage.com. Well-run three-star campsite, offering a restaurant/snack bar and canoe and bike rental as well as all sorts of other activities, including guided walks, rock climbing and pot-holing, through Kalapca loisirs (☎ 05 65 30 29 51, ⓦ kalapca.com). Closed mid-Oct to April. **€20.90**

5

La Truffière ☎ 05 65 30 20 22, ⓦ camping-truffiere .com. A spacious, well-managed campsite on the plateau 3km southeast of St-Cirq via the D42. Their restaurant is open in high season, and there's a heated pool and children's play area. Closed Sept to mid-April. €17.90

EATING AND DRINKING

The nearest food shop is a small grocer down in Tour-de-Faure. If you're self-catering you might like to head 12km south to the charming little town of Limogne-en-Quercy where you'll find everything you need, including a Sunday morning market.

Le Gourmet Quercynois Rue de la Peyrolerie ☎ 05 65 31 21 20, ⓦ restaurant-legourmetquercynois.com. Sit out on the shady terrace at this quaint restaurant and enjoy dishes such as pork with honey and herbs or duck with truffles; *menus* are from €14.80. Feb–Nov daily noon– 2pm & 7–9pm.

★ **Lou Bolat** Just inside Porte de la Peyrolerie ☎ 05 65 30 29 04, ⓦ loubolat.com. A choice of crêpes, salads and regional dishes are on offer here, with dishes starting at €8.50 and *menus* at €12.50. July & Aug daily noon– 9pm; Sept–June Wed–Mon noon–2pm.

L'Oustal Rue de la Pélissaria ☎ 05 65 31 20 17. A tiny little place tucked into a corner at the top end of rue de la Pélissaria just south of the church, serving only organic food. Midday *menus* €12.50, from €16 in the evenings. Easter–June & Sept to mid-Oct Thurs–Mon noon–2pm & 7–9pm, Tues noon–2pm; July & Aug daily noon–2pm & 7–9pm.

Château de Cénevières

Guided tours daily except Sun morning, April–Sept 10am–noon & 2–6pm, Oct & Nov daily 2pm–5pm • Adults €6, children €3 • ⓦ chateau-cenevieres.com • The nearest bus stop is in St-Martin-Labouval, a good kilometre downstream and across on the north bank

Seven kilometres out of St-Cirq, along the quiet D8 road (avoid the main D662), you reach the **Château de Cénevières**, perched on a rocky spur just beyond Cénevières village. The château, which largely dates from the sixteenth century in its present form, belonged to the **de Gourdon** family for nine hundred years until the line petered out in 1616. The last in line, Antoine de Gourdon, was a fervent supporter of the Reformation, so much so that the Protestant leader Henry of Navarre stayed here before attacking Cahors in 1580. Antoine brought back a rich haul that included the cathedral's principal altar – the boat carrying it, however, capsized and the altar is now somewhere at the bottom of the Lot. The château was saved from being torched during the Revolution by a quick-thinking overseer who opened the wine cellars to the mob, though he couldn't save the library, nor the coat of arms and other carvings on the facade. Cénevières was sold only once during its long history, to the ancestors of the present owners in 1793. Over the years they have uncovered several unusual Renaissance-era **frescoes**: notably, a frieze of the Istanbul skyline in the grand salon, and scenes from Greek mythology alongside what is believed to be a representation of an alchemist's fire and the philosopher's stone adorning a little vaulted chamber.

Cajarc

CAJARC, which lies on the river's north bank 9km upstream from Calvignac, is the biggest town on the Lot between Cahors and Capdenac. It consists of a small core of old lanes encircled by the boulevard du Tour-de-Ville, where you'll find facilities such as banks, food shops and a post office as well as cafés and brasseries. The town's only sight as such is the **Maison des Arts Georges-Pompidou** (open during exhibitions daily except Mon 2–6pm; ☎ 05 65 40 78 19, ⓦ magp.fr; free), on the northeastern outskirts on the D19 Figeac road. The gallery is named in honour of the former French prime minister, who bought a holiday home near here in 1963, and hosts three or four major contemporary art exhibitions a year.

FROM TOP CHÂTEAU DE BONAGUIL (P.238); CAFÉ IN ST-CIRQUE LAPOPIE (P.212)>

5

ARRIVAL AND INFORMATION

By bus SNCF buses stop on the north side of town on place du Foirail.

Tourist office Tour-de-Ville (April–June & Sept Mon–Sat 3–6pm, Sun 10am–12.30pm; July & Aug daily 10am–12.30pm & 2.30–7pm; ☎ 05 65 40 72 89), housed in a converted chapel.

Market A market takes place on Saturday afternoons on place du Foirail, with larger *foires* on the 10th and 25th of every month.

ACCOMMODATION

Gîte d'Étape Place du Foirail ☎ 06 14 66 54 89. Each floor here has individual shower and kitchen facilities. No wi-fi or meals served but restaurants are within walking distance. **€12.30**

Mas de Garrigue La Garrigue, Calvignac ☎ 05 65 53 93 31, ⓦ masdegarrigue.com. A few kilometres back towards Cahors lies this delightful *chambre d'hôte*, set in a restored fifteenth-century hunting lodge. It offers five beautifully appointed bedrooms. Evening meals (€35) available on Mon, Wed and Sat by reservation only. **€110**

La Peyrade Rte de Cahors ☎ 05 65 10 42 03, ⓦ hotel-lapeyrade.fr. A simply furnished, welcoming hotel offering rooms and apartments at a budget price. The restaurant also has good-value *menus* from €12. Restaurant open April–Sept Mon–Sat 7–9pm, Sun 12.30–2pm; Oct–March Thurs–Tues 7–9pm. Breakfast €6. **€56**

La Ségalière 380 av François Mitterand ☎ 05 65 40 65 35, ⓦ lasegaliere.com. The smartest hotel in town, around 400m east on the D662 to Capdenac. It's a modern, concrete building – not beautiful, but airy and with nicely decorated rooms, some with a small balcony overlooking the pool and spacious gardens. There's also a good restaurant with *menus* from €22. Restaurant open April–Oct daily 7–9.15pm, plus Sat & Sun noon–2.30pm. Breakfast €10. **€85**

Le Terriol ☎ 05 65 40 72 74. A basic two-star municipal campsite beside the river roughly 200m southwest of the centre. It offers laundry facilities and a communal freezer; the municipal swimming pool is next door. Closed Sept–May **€11.50**

EATING AND DRINKING

Brasserie du Tour de Ville 7 bd du Tour-de-Ville ☎ 05 65 40 67 09. The *Brasserie du Tour de Ville,* on the eastern side of the town, is a good place to watch the world go by, though it can get busy in summer. *Plat du jour* €8.50, *menu* €18. June–Oct daily noon–3pm & 7–10pm; Nov–May daily noon–2.30pm & 7–9pm.

Cajarc Gourmand Place de L'Église ☎ 05 65 40 69 50, ⓦ cajarcgourmand.com. It's worth trying *Cajarc Gourmand*, on a quiet square beside the church, for its inventive and well-presented cuisine, such as foie gras ravioli with vegetables. They have various *formules* and *menus* ranging from €11.50 up to €26. March–June & Sept–Nov Fri–Wed noon–2pm & 7.30–9.30pm; July & Aug daily noon–2pm & 7.30–9.30pm.

QUERCY SAFFRON

Saffron was originally introduced to the region by returning crusaders in the twelfth century, and quickly became a major source of income. However, production of the spice declined drastically in the eighteenth century, largely due to the significant manpower requirements. Obtained from the dried stigmas of the saffron crocus, the spice can only be picked by hand early on autumn mornings. It takes 200,000 flowers and over forty hours' labour to obtain a kilogram of dried saffron, and pound for pound it's more expensive than gold. Historically the spice has been used in sweet and savoury dishes, particularly in central Asia, as well as for dyeing cloths, as a hangover remedy and to cure tuberculosis and measles. It's also supposed to have cancer-suppressing properties.

Around seventy farms in the Lot valley area now produce saffron commercially, and many of them can be visited, particularly around harvest time in **October**. Their organization's website, ⓦ safran-du-quercy.com, details recipes using saffron, and they host two major **saffron fairs**, at St-Céré (see p.190) in mid-July to mark the planting season, and at Cajarc (see p.214) at the end of October to celebrate the harvest – the latter is larger and offers more opportunities for tasting and buying.

On to Capdenac

5

Upstream from Cajarc, the Lot twists through one more giant meander and then straightens out until you reach the next big loop at Capdenac. Buses follow the northerly route past a succession of picturesque villages and castles, but if you've got your own transport, the less-travelled roads along the river's south bank make for a more interesting journey through walnut orchards and past weathered farm buildings, then up on to the flat, empty *causse* with little sign of habitation, save for the occasional dolmen or *cabane*, the traditional, stone-built shepherds' huts.

Where the D127 first climbs up from the river, /km from Cajarc, it skirts along the edge of a 300-metre high cliff formed by the meander. The spot is known as the **Saut de la Mounine** ("Monkey's Leap"), after a legend concerning a local lord who ordered his daughter to be thrown off the cliff when she fell in love with a boy he disapproved of. A hermit took pity on the girl and secretly dressed a monkey in her clothes instead. When the poor beast was chucked over the edge, the lord repented, of course, and was only too relieved to discover he'd been outwitted. He apparently forgave his daughter, but history doesn't relate whom she married. Whatever the outcome, it's a marvellous view from up here, taking in the meander filled with patchwork fields and the ruined Château de Montbrun on the far hillside where the lord and his fortunate daughter once lived.

A few kilometres further on you drop back down to the river along tiny lanes that wend their way northeastwards for about 15km before hitting the main D922. Turn left here and you'll be in Figeac (see p.220) in about ten minutes. Alternatively, if you cross over and follow the D86 along the river, another 7km will bring you to **CAPDENAC**, a major railway town on the south bank of the River Lot. There's a great view from the high ridge above the town and river to the north, but otherwise Capdenac is of little interest.

Grotte de Foissac

1hr guided tours: April, May & Oct daily except Sat 2–5pm; June & Sept daily 10–11.30am & 2–6pm; July & Aug daily 10am–6pm • €7.60 • ☎ 05 65 64 77 04, ⓦ grotte-de-foissac.com

One of the area's less-frequented caves, the **Grotte de Foissac** lies about 3km west across the *causse* from Foissac village. The cave was discovered in 1959 by a local pot-holing club, who found not only a huge cavern of colourful and varied concretions, including delicate needles, some bulging out into onion shapes, but also evidence of human activity going back at least four thousand years. From the number of **skeletons** and their positions, it seems that, unusually, the cave was used as a cemetery. It was also a source of clay – you can still see where people dug it out with their hands, and they also left large and beautifully fashioned pots, probably for storing grain. But the most moving evidence is the lone footprint left by a child deep inside the cave.

Peyrusse-le-Roc

Twenty kilometres east of Foissac village, via beautiful back lanes through Naussac and along the Roselle, the ruined towers of **PEYRUSSE-LE-ROC** are well worth a look. The "modern" village, a tiny weatherworn huddle of half-timbered houses gathered round a seventeenth-century church, sits above a narrow valley. On the valley sides, hidden in the steep woods, lie the scattered remains of a fortified medieval town which once sheltered some 4500 people – a sizeable population in those days – who were seeking their fortunes in the local silver mines. But their luck ran out in the early sixteenth century, when silver from the recently discovered Americas began to flood the market, and the town was eventually abandoned around 1700. The site is gradually being tidied up and some of the buildings restored, but it still remains an atmospheric place.

A path leads from the northwest corner of the church square to a pinnacle of rock crowned by **twin towers**, all that's left of the medieval fortress that protected the town. If you've got a head for heights, you can scramble up the iron ladders for a vertiginous

5

view of the gorge. From here a cobbled mule trail leads steeply down through the woods, where the stones of a Gothic church, synagogue and hospital stand roofless, to the river and a little thirteenth-century chapel, complete but not open to the public. To return to the modern village, follow the river downstream and pick up another path, which takes you past the old market hall to the village gate. It's possible to do shorter circuits simply by following the signs, or you can buy a guidebook and map (€3.50) from the **tourist office** (see below).

INFORMATION   PEYRUSSE-LE-ROC

Tourist office Beside the church (Mon–Sat 10am–noon; ☎ 05 65 80 49 33).

The Célé valley

Instead of following the River Lot east from Cahors, you can take an alternative route to Figeac along the wilder and narrower **Célé valley**, which joins the Lot a kilometre or so upstream from Bouziès (see p.211). A single road winds through the luxuriant canyon-like valley, frequented mainly by canoeists and walkers on the GR65 footpath, which runs sometimes close to the river, sometimes on the edge of the *causse* on the north bank. The major settlement along here is **Cabrerets**, a village not far upstream from the Célé's confluence with the Lot, which serves as a base for the nearby cave system of **Grotte de Pech-Merle**. Continuing northeast, the valley is punctuated by a succession of villages and hamlets built against the cliff face. Of these, two in particular stand out: **Marcilhac-sur-Célé**, about halfway along the valley, for the atmospheric ruins of its abbey; and the tiny hamlet of **Espagnac-Ste-Eulalie** in the north, where another, more substantial church sports a delightfully whimsical belfry.

GETTING AROUND   THE CÉLÉ VALLEY

By bike There's no public transport along the Célé, but you can rent bicycles at Conduché, where the Célé joins the Lot, at Bureau des Sports Nature (☎ 05 65 24 21 01, ⓦ perso .orange.fr/bureau-sports-nature).

By canoe It's possible to descend the Célé by canoe; rental outlets in St-Cirq, Figeac and near Cabrerets will organize the necessary transport.

Cabrerets

CABRERETS lies 4km up the Célé from its confluence with the Lot, the approach guarded by the sturdy **Château de Gontaut-Biron** (not open to the public), on a small flood plain where the River Sagne joins the Célé. It's a pretty enough spot, but the only real reason to linger here is to take advantage of its tourist amenities.

INFORMATION   CABRERETS

Tourist office There's a small summer-only tourist office in the village centre (June Wed–Sat 11am–1pm & 2–6pm, July Mon–Sat 10am–1pm & 2–6pm, Aug Mon–Sat 10am–1pm & 3–7pm; ☎ 05 65 31 27 12) that sells handy guides detailing walks in the area.

ACCOMMODATION AND EATING

Auberge de la Sagne ☎ 05 65 31 26 62, ⓦ hotel -auberge-cabrerets.com. The small, smart and absolutely spotless *Auberge de la Sagne*, 1km west of the village on the road to the Grotte de Pech-Merle, is perhaps the best of the accommodation options. There's a pool, well-tended garden and a restaurant offering good-quality home cooking and *menus* for €18. Restaurant open mid-April to mid-Oct daily noon–1.30pm & 7–9pm. Breakfast €7. **€55**

Le Cantal Cabrerets ☎ 05 65 31 26 61. Petite and very

basic two-star campsite immediately north of Cabrerets on the other side of the Célé. Closed mid-Oct to mid-April. **€9.50**

Des Grottes Le Bourg ☎ 05 65 31 27 02, ⓦ hoteldesgrottes.com. In the village itself, overlooking the Célé, *Des Grottes* is a welcoming place with functional rooms, some with and some without en-suite, a good restaurant (*menus* from €13.50) and a pretty terrace and a pool. Breakfast €7. **€60**

Grotte de Pech-Merle

1hr guided visits, English written commentary available: April–Nov daily 9.30am–noon & 1.30–5pm • Adults €9, children €5 • ☎ 05 65 31 27 05, Ⓦ pechmerle.com

Up in the hills 3km west of Cabrerets by road, or 1km via the footpath from beside the *mairie*, the **Grotte de Pech-Merle** takes some beating. Discovered in 1922 by two local boys, the galleries are not only full of the most spectacular limestone formations – structures tiered like wedding cakes, hanging like curtains, or shaped like discs or "cave pearls" – but also contain an equally dazzling display of more than five hundred **prehistoric drawings**. To protect the drawings, tickets are restricted to seven hundred per day (it's advisable to book four or five days ahead in July and August and at least one day ahead at other times; internet bookings must be made at least a week in advance), and the guides make sure you're processed through in the allotted time. If possible, it's worth allowing yourself time to visit the **museum**, located beside the ticket office (same hours; same ticket), before your scheduled tour. A twenty-minute film, subtitled in English, provides an excellent overview of Pech-Merle and its prehistoric art.

Chapelle des Mammouths

The Grotte de Pech-Merle's drawings date mostly from the early Magdalenian era (around 10,000–17,000 years ago), contemporaneous with much of the cave art in the Vézère valley (see p.130), with which they share many similarities. The first drawings you come to are in the so-called **Chapelle des Mammouths**, executed on a white calcite panel that looks as if it's been specially prepared for the purpose; note how the artists used the contour and relief of the rock to do the work, producing utterly convincing mammoths with just two lines. In addition to the mammoths, there are horses, oxen and bison charging head down with tiny rumps and arched tails; the guide will point out where St-Cirq's André Breton (see p.212) added his own mammoth – he was fined but the damage was done.

The horse frieze

After the Chapelle des Mammouths comes a vast chamber containing the glorious **horse frieze**, the oldest of the drawings (at around 25,000 years). Two large horses stand back to back, the head of one formed by a natural protuberance of rock, and their hindquarters superimposed to provide perspective. The surface is spattered with black dots of some unknown symbolic significance and silhouettes of hands, while the ceiling is covered with finger marks preserved in the soft clay. On the way you pass the skeletons of cave-hyena and bears that have been lying there for thousands of years, and, finally, the footprints of an adolescent preserved in a muddy pool some eight thousand years ago.

Musée de l'Insolite

Lieu dit Liauzu, Cabrerets. April–Sept 9am–1pm & 2–8pm; rest of year by appointment • €2, €5 if you want to take photos • ☎ 05 65 30 21 01, Ⓦ museedelinsolite.com

Don't miss the gloriously eccentric **Musée de l'Insolite** (Museum of the Quirky), situated on the D41 heading up the Célé from Cabrerets. After about 3km you emerge from a tunnel and are suddenly confronted by old bikes, mannequins and even the shells of cars hanging from the rock face. They belong to a sculptor with an engaging sense of humour, and are mostly based on wordplay and puns in French. Both his garden and gallery are full of bizarre montages fashioned out of tree stumps, old machines and other bits of scrap.

Marcilhac

MARCILHAC 16km upstream from Cabrerets, has a partly ruined Benedictine **abbey** (call ☎ 05 65 40 65 52 for guided tours; July to mid-Sept 2–4.30pm; €3). Founded some time prior to the ninth century, the abbey had the good fortune to be in charge of the modest sanctuary at Rocamadour (see p.174), in which St Amadour's body was

5

discovered in 1166. The subsequent revenue from pilgrims and benefactors led to a brief golden age, which came to an end when English troops laid waste to the building in the Hundred Years War. It never really recovered and was abandoned after the Reformation. Entering the abbey from the south, a rather primitive and badly damaged ninth-century Christ in Majesty decorates the tympanum over the ruined door. In the damp interior of the church itself are late-fifteenth-century frescoes of the Apostles and another Christ in Majesty, with the local nobility's coats of arms below. The few religious treasures that survived – such as a seventeenth-century polychrome pietà and a nicely rendered statue of a pilgrim – are now on display in the small **Musée d'Art Sacré** (mid-June to mid-Sept 10.30am–12.30pm & 2.30–5.30pm; free) in a handsome half-timbered house immediately west of the abbey church.

INFORMATION AND ACTIVITIES	MARCILHAC
Tourist office The Musée d'Art Sacré (see above) doubles as a summer tourist office (mid-June to mid-Sept 10.30am–12.30pm & 2.30–5.30pm; ☏05 65 40 68 44, ⊛marcilhac.fr).	**Bike and boat rental** Passion Aventure (☏06 10 73 73 12, ⊛location-canoe-cele.com). Along the river by the bridge, they rent canoes and organize descents of the Célé and rock-climbing and pot-holing outings.

ACCOMMODATION

Le Pré de Monsieur ☏05 65 40 77 88, ⊛camping -marcilhac.com. Two-star municipal campsite just north	of the village, with a pool, tennis, volleyball, badminton and its own restaurant. Closed Oct–April. **€12**

Espagnac-Ste-Eulalie

The tiny and beautiful hamlet of **ESPAGNAC-STE-EULALIE** lies about 12km upriver from Marcilhac and is reached via an old stone bridge. Immediately across the bridge, an eye-catching octagonal lantern crowns the belfry of the priory **church of Notre-Dame-du-Val-Paradis** (1hr guided tours: daily 10.30am & 4.30pm, with extra visits at 6pm for walkers; by appointment only, call Mme Bonzani on ☏05 65 40 06 17). The building itself is strangely ill-proportioned, a result of the nave being truncated in the Hundred Years War, which somehow adds to its charm. Inside, apart from a typically over-the-top altarpiece from the Counter-Reformation, the most interesting features are the ornate tombs of the church's thirteenth-century benefactor, Aymeric d'Hébrard de St-Sulpice, a local man who became bishop of Coimbra in Portugal, and those of the duke of Cardaillac and his wife, who financed the rebuilding of the choir in the fourteenth century.

ACCOMMODATION AND EATING	ESPAGNAC-STE-EULALIE
Gîte d'Étape ☏05 65 11 42 66. An ancient fortified gateway south of the church now houses a *gîte d'étape* offering very good-value accommodation. Kitchen and dining facilities available, no meals, but *L'Hôte Paysan* (see below) is nearby. Closed Oct–March. Singles **€11.20**, doubles **€30.40**	Reservations are essential as opening hours vary accordingly out of season. At least July & Aug daily noon–3pm & 7–9pm, but open at other times (call before turning up).
L'Hôte Paysan ☏05 65 11 41 50. Simple but excellent-quality food in this little restaurant in the row of houses next to the church. *Menus* at lunch are €10, €12 in the evening.	**Le Moulin Vieux** ☏05 65 40 00 41, ⊛camping -lemoulinvieux.com. A good three-star campsite in Brengues, 3km back downstream from Espagnac. Facilities include a restaurant (daily July & Aug), pool, mini-golf and canoe hire. **€14.10**

Figeac

Situated on the River Célé some 70km east of Cahors, **FIGEAC** is a very appealing town with an unspoilt medieval centre that's, surprisingly, not encumbered by tourism. Its principal church, the **Église St-Sauveur**, contains a sumptuous rendition of the Passion of Christ in a side chapel, and there's an excellent **museum** devoted to famed locally born Egyptologist Jean-François Champollion. Apart from these two sights, it's a

5

pleasure just to wander the narrow lanes, lined with a delightful array of houses, both stone and half-timbered, adorned with carvings, ornate colonnaded windows and elaborate ironwork.

Figeac's old quarter sits on the north bank of the River Célé, its ramparts and ditches now replaced with a ring of boulevards. From the southern boulevard, the town's main artery and principal shopping street, pedestrianized **rue Gambetta**, leads north from the old stone bridge, **Pont Gambetta**, to place Carnot, with its market hall, and to neighbouring place Champollion.

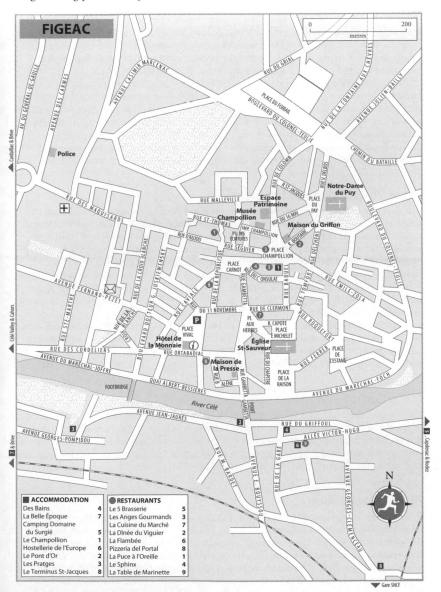

5

Brief history

Like many other provincial towns hereabouts, Figeac owes its beginnings to the foundation of an **abbey** in the early days of Christianity, one which quickly became wealthy thanks to its position on the pilgrim roads to both Rocamadour (see p.174) and Compostela (see p.290). In the Middle Ages the town flourished as a trading centre, exporting wine and woollen fabrics throughout Europe, so much so that the wealthy merchants began to challenge the abbey's authority. In 1302 King Philip IV (the Fair) resolved the issue by sending his representative, the Viguier, to bring Figeac directly under royal control. At the same time he granted the town the all-important right to mint money. Figeac's fortunes declined during the Hundred Years War, then revived at the time of the Renaissance, but it was the Wars of Religion that pushed it into eclipse. The town threw in its lot with the Protestants in 1576, providing them with an important safe-haven, until it was brought forcefully back into line in 1622. Figeac later became an important centre for tanning hides, and received a further boost with the arrival of the railway in 1862.

During **World War II** the Germans converted Figeac's Ratier metal workshop into a factory churning out propellers for Luftwaffe bombers. When the Resistance destroyed the plant in 1944, more than five hundred local men were carted off to concentration and labour camps, from which at least 120 failed to return at the end of the war. By the 1960s the town's old quarter had declined to such an extent that the majority of buildings were declared uninhabitable. It was designated a preservation zone in 1986, since when the authorities have put a lot of effort into restoring the medieval and Renaissance buildings.

Place Vival and the old quarter

The best place to start your explorations is on **place Vival** to the west of rue Gambetta, where the tourist office occupies the eye-catching **Hôtel de la Monnaie**. The building's origins go back to the thirteenth century when the city's mint was located in this district, and it's typical of Figeac's medieval merchants' houses, starting off with arcaded openings on the ground floor, while the colonnaded and sculpted windows above indicate the living quarters. These are now home to a none-too-exciting **museum** (May, June & Sept Mon–Sat 10am–12.30pm & 2.30–6pm, Sun 10am–1pm; July & Aug daily 10am–7pm; Oct–April Mon–Sat 10am–noon & 2.30–6pm; €2) of old coins and archeological bits and pieces found in the surrounding area.

On the eastern side of rue Gambetta you'll find the much-altered **Église St-Sauveur** on a big, gravelled square overlooking the river. Its lofty yet restrained nave provides a striking contrast to the intimate **Notre-Dame de la Pitié** chapel, to the south of the choir, decorated with heavily gilded but dramatically realistic seventeenth-century carved wood panels.

Place Carnot

Cafés spread their tables under the nineteenth-century *halle* in the middle of **place Carnot**, at the top of rue Gambetta, surrounded by a delightful range of stone and half-timbered houses. Some sport open wooden galleries at the top; another typical feature of this region, these *solelhos* were used for drying and storing foodstuffs. On the eastern side lies *Le Sphinx* café, where the father of Jean-François Champollion (see opposite) had his bookshop.

Place Champollion

Place Carnot opens into the grander but equally alluring **place Champollion**, named after **Jean-François Champollion**, who finally cracked Egyptian hieroglyphics by deciphering the Rosetta Stone (see box opposite). The square's south side is dominated by a stunning, white-stone Gothic mansion with a row of handsome ornamental windows, filled with lacy trefoil stonework. Opposite, the **Maison du Griffon** on the corner with rue de Colomb is far less ostentatious, but this is Figeac's oldest house, built in the twelfth century and named after a barely visible griffin carved on the left-hand window arch (now blocked up) on the third floor.

Musée Champollion

Place Champollion • April–June Tues–Sun 10.30am–12.30pm & 2–6pm, July–Aug daily 10.30am–6pm, Sept & Oct–March Tues–Sun 2–5.30pm • Adults €5, 13–18 years €2.50, under 12 years free • ☎ 05 65 50 31 08, ⓦ musee-champollion.fr

Champollion was born nearby in a house off place Champollion, to the northwest of the square, which now contains the fascinating **Musée Champollion**, dedicated not only to Champollion's life and work but also to the history of writing, with displays on Egyptian, Chinese, Mayan and Hebraic systems. In addition to many beautiful examples of hieroglyphic script, the museum houses an excellent collection of Egyptian funerary objects from the sixth and seventh centuries BC – sarcophagi, amulets and statues of the gods and goddesses, such as Bastet, a superb bronze cat, and an exquisitely crafted head of the god-king Osiris.

Place des Écritures

At the west end of impasse Champollion, a gigantic reproduction of the Rosetta Stone – the work of American artist Joseph Kossuth – forms the floor of the tiny **place des Écritures**, above which is a little garden with medicinal herbs and tufts of papyrus in pots. If it's open, you can cut through the **Espace Patrimoine** (April to early July & late Sept to end Oct Tues–Sun 2–6pm; early July to late Sept daily 10am–12.30pm & 3–7pm; free), a one-room exhibition illustrating Figeac's history and architecture, to rue de Colomb.

Notre-Dame du Puy

Round the corner on rue Delzhens, the large square tower looming over the street is the last vestige of the Viguier's fourteenth-century residence. You'll get a better view of it if you continue on up the hill to the **church of Notre-Dame du Puy**. Transformed into a veritable fortress by the Protestants in the late 1500s, then partially destroyed by Catholic reprisals, it now contains little of interest, but its cedar-shaded terrace is a peaceful spot from which to look down on the roofs of Figeac. When you're done, take cobbled rue St-Jacques twisting and turning down the hillside back to rue de Colomb and place Champollion.

CHAMPOLLION AND THE ROSETTA STONE

Jean-François Champollion was born in Figeac in 1790, the son of a bookseller who opened a shop on place Carnot, in what is now *Le Sphinx* café. His interest in Egypt was first sparked by news coming back from Napoleon Bonaparte's 1798 Egyptian adventures, and when an acquaintance showed him the ancient Egyptians' so-far indecipherable script two years later, he became hooked. Declaring that he would solve the puzzle, Champollion set about studying ancient and Middle Eastern languages – he eventually mastered a mind-boggling total of twenty – and poring over hieroglyphs. One of the most important resources available was the **Rosetta Stone**. A slab of black basalt measuring around 120cm in height and 80cm wide, the stone was discovered in 1799 by French soldiers building fortifications around the town of Rosetta in the Nile delta; three years later it fell into British hands when they seized Egypt from the French, and it now resides in London's British Museum.

The crucial significance of the Rosetta Stone is that the same text – a decree issued in 196 BC recording the honours to be accorded to the young Pharaoh Ptolemy – is repeated in three different scripts: **hieroglyphics**, demotic (an abbreviated, cursive form of hieroglyphics used for everyday affairs) and Greek. By being able to translate the Greek, scholars then had fresh clues, but it took until 1822 before Champollion made the final breakthrough when he realized that hieroglyphs were, broadly, not pictograms but phonetic characters – within two years he had identified the majority of symbols, and all this without having set foot in Egypt. He made his one and only voyage to the country in 1828, but died of a stroke four years later at the age of 41.

5

ARRIVAL AND DEPARTURE

FIGEAC

By train Figeac's *gare SNCF* – on the Toulouse–Clermont-Ferrand and Toulouse–Figeac–Brive lines – lies about 600m south of the town centre.

Destinations Assier (4–7 daily; 25min); Brive (5–6 daily; 1hr 10min); Cordes (4–5 daily; 1hr 20min); Gramat (4–7 daily; 50min); Laguépie (3–6 daily; 1hr); Najac (3–6 daily; 1hr 10min); Paris-Austerlitz (1 overnight; 7hr); Rocamadour (4–6 daily; 40min); St-Denis-lès-Martel (5–7 daily; 55min); Toulouse (3–5 daily; 2hr 20min); Villefranche-de-Rouergue (3–5 daily; 45min).

By bus SNCF buses from Cahors, Gramat and Villefranche -de-Rouergue stop at the train station. For details of all bus routes, call the central information desk on ☎ 05 65 53 43 91.

Destinations Assier (Mon–Thurs 1 daily; 25min); Cahors (3–5 daily; 1hr 45min); Cajarc (3–5 daily; 30–35min); Gramat (Mon–Thurs 1 daily; 50min); St-Céré (school term Tues–Fri 1 daily, school hols Tues, Thurs & Sat 1 daily; 50min–1hr 10min); Tour-de-Faure (3–5 daily; 1hr); Villefranche-de-Rouergue (1–2 daily; 40min).

By car If you're arriving by car, note that the old quarter is largely pedestrianized. The most convenient parking is along the riverbank, where it's free, or on place Vival.

GETTING AROUND AND INFORMATION

Bike rental Office Intercommunal du Sport du Pays de Figeac/Cajarc, 2 av du Général-de-Gaulle (☎ 05 65 34 52 54, ⓦ ois-figeac-cajarc.com).

Car rental ADA, on the road west to Cahors (☎ 05 65 11 62 92); Avis, 1 av Georges-Pompidou (☎ 05 65 34 10 28). Both offer station pick-ups on request.

Taxis Call Bernard Taxis on ☎ 05 65 50 00 20, or Didier Escribano on ☎ 05 65 50 01 73.

Tourist office Place Vival, in the very striking Hôtel de la Monnaie building (May, June & Sept Mon–Sat 10am–12.30pm & 2.30–6pm, Sun 10am–1pm; July & Aug daily 10am–7pm; Oct–April Mon–Sat 10am–noon & 2.30–6pm; ☎ 05 65 50 04 58, ⓦ tourisme-figeac.com or ⓦ tourism-figeac.com in English). They supply a useful do-it-yourself guide to Figeac and sell various booklets outlining walks in the surrounding area, while in summer you can sign up for one of their excellent guided tours (in French only), of which "*À la découverte de Figeac*" provides the best general introduction (April, May & Sept Sat 4.30pm; July & Aug Tues–Thurs, Sat & Sun 4.30pm; 1hr 30min; €5.50).

Market The main weekly food market is on place Carnot on Saturdays, while dry goods are sold on place Vival.

ACCOMMODATION

★ **Des Bains** 1 rue du Griffoul ☎ 05 65 34 10 89, ⓦ hoteldesbains.fr. Just across from the old town, this hotel is one of the nicest places to stay in Figeac. Rooms are spotless and the more expensive ones have a/c and balconies. What makes the hotel special though, is the friendly and energetic hosts, who are a mine of information about the local area. Breakfast €7.50. **€59**

★ **La Belle Époque** Le Coustal, Camboulit, 7km southwest of Figeac, off the D19 ☎ 05 65 40 04 42, ⓦ domainelabelleepoque.com. A fabulous *chambre d'hôte*, restaurant and campsite, centred around a restored seventeenth-century farm, buried deep in the heart of the countryside. Restaurant open July & Aug daily noon–1pm & 7–8.30pm; Sept–June Thurs–Mon noon–1pm & 7–8.30pm (*menu* €24). Camping **€13.60**, rooms **€85**

Camping Domaine du Surgié ☎ 05 65 34 83 76 or ☎ 05 61 64 88 54, ⓦ domainedusurgie.com. Well-equipped four-star campsite 2km north of Figeac that has a restaurant (open daily), a good shop, several pools and a leisure programme in high season. Closed Sept–April. **€26.50**

Le Champollion 3 place Champollion ☎ 05 65 34 04 37. This welcoming place offers ten surprisingly modern en-suite rooms above a popular café right in the centre. Try and get one of the two rooms overlooking the square. Breakfast €7. **€52**

Hostellerie de l'Europe 51 allée Victor-Hugo ☎ 05 65 34 10 16, ⓦ hotel-europe-figeac.com. One block behind the *Des Bains*, on a busy main road, this 1930s hotel is better than it looks from the outside. The rooms come with a/c and other two-star comforts, and there's a small pool and a restaurant (*menus* from €12 at lunch, €16 in the evenings). Restaurant open daily 12.30–1.30pm & 7.30–9pm. Breakfast €8.50. **€67**

Le Pont d'Or 2 av Jean-Jaurès ☎ 05 65 50 95 00, ⓦ hotelpontdor.com. Modern riverside hotel offering spick-and-span rooms with good-sized bathrooms, those on the riverfront have balconies. Other facilities include a restaurant, bar, rooftop pool and gym. Restaurant open Feb–Nov daily noon–2.30pm & 7.30–9.30pm. *Menus* from €12.50 at lunch, €22 in the evenings. Breakfast €12. **€91**

Les Pratges 6 av Jean-Jaurès ☎ 05 65 50 01 42, ⓦ lesmaisonsdemarie.com. Lovely quiet *chambre d'hôte* offering four beautifully decorated rooms, all en-suite, in a large old house just across the river from the town centre; there's also a pool, and a small park on the doorstep. Breakfast €5. **€80**

Le Terminus St-Jacques 27 av Georges-Clemenceau ☎ 05 65 34 00 43, ⓦ hotel-terminus.fr. This small family-run hotel is handy for the train station and a favourite with walkers. Rooms are nothing special, but are comfortable enough and the restaurant (*menu* €24.50) is open Mon–Sat 7.30–10pm. Breakfast €8.50. **€61**

EATING AND DRINKING

Figeac's old centre is well provided with restaurants, offering everything from pizza to haute cuisine. For picnic food, there's a handy supermarket on the corner of rue Gambetta and rue de Clermont, and the charcuterie at 20 quai Bessières sells a wide range of salads as well as meats.

Le 5 Brasserie 5 place Champollion ⊙05 65 50 10 81, ⓦrestaurant-le5.fr. Stylish place with comfortable interior furniture, vaulted ceilings, and huge windows. It serves up tasty French food with a regional flavour, menus from €12.50 at lunch and €21.50 in the evenings. July & Aug daily noon–2pm & 7.30–9.30pm; Sept–June Mon & Tues noon–2pm, Wed–Sat noon–2pm & 7.30–9.30pm.

★ **Les Anges Gourmands** 4 rue Séguier ⊙05 65 34 08 01, ⓦlesangesgourmands.com. A charming little restaurant squeezed between place Carnot and place Champollion; there are only twenty covers and it's first come first served, so get there early. The cooking is regional and hearty, dishes such as chou farci and canard parmentier are given a slight twist and in the evenings the atmosphere vibrates to the sound of jazz. Lunch menus €12.50, evening menus €15.50. July & Aug daily from 11.30am for lunch & 6pm for dinner; Sept–June Tues–Thurs lunch only, Fri & Sat from 11.30am for lunch & from 6.30pm for dinner.

La Cuisine du Marché 15 rue Clermont ⊙05 65 50 18 55, ⓦlacuisinedumarchefigeac.com. One of Figeac's most popular fine-dining establishments, serving fresh local produce, as the name suggests, with delicious menus from €17 for midweek lunch and €28 in the evenings and at the weekend. Mon 7–9.30pm, Tues–Sun noon–1.45pm & 7–9.30pm.

★ **La Dînée du Viguier** 4 rue Boutaric ⊙05 65 50 08 08, ⓦladineeduviguier.fr. This restaurant is housed in one of the most luxurious buildings in Figeac, and it's not as expensive as one might expect for such rarefied cuisine: there's a good-value midday menu from €19 and evening menus start from €29, though you're looking at around €60 eating à la carte. There are only a handful of tables in its elegant stone-walled room, so reservations are essential. Mid-Feb to mid-Jan Tues–Fri & Sat eve to Sun noon–2pm & 7.30–9.30pm.

La Flambeé 28 rue Caviale ⊙05 65 34 72 12, ⓦrestaurant-flambee-figeac.fr. Join the locals in this excellent little restaurant specializing in chargrilled meats and pastas. Menus from €13 at lunch to €16.50 in the evenings, but beware it gets very busy. Mon–Sat noon–2pm & 7–9pm.

Pizzeria del Portel 9 rue Ortabadial ⊙05 65 34 53 60. A good-value and convivial place serving tasty pizzas, big salad platters and no fewer than seven varieties of moules-frites including pesto and Roquefort. It also has the benefit of an outside terrace. Most dishes are around €12. Easter–Oct Mon–Sat noon–2pm & 7.30–9.45pm; Oct to Easter Tues–Sat noon–2pm & 7.30–9.45pm.

★ **La Puce à l'Oreille** 5 rue St-Thomas ⊙05 65 34 33 08. Located north of place Carnot in a handsome fifteenth-century residence with an interior court for fine weather, and walls adorned with work by local artists, this place serves rich Quercy fare – make sure you leave room for one of their scrumptious desserts. Menus from €15 at lunch and €24.50 in the evenings, and there's an extensive regional wine list. Mid-Dec to mid-Nov Tues–Sun noon–1.30pm & 7–9.30pm.

Le Sphinx 7 place Carnot ⊙05 65 14 05 81. This cocktail bar is just around the corner from the Musée Champollion, on the market square. It also serves good traditional food (menus €13) under the old covered market. April–June Mon–Sat noon–3pm & 7–9.30pm; July & Aug daily noon–3pm & 7–9.30pm; Sept–March Mon–Sat noon–3pm.

La Table de Marinette 51 allée Victor-Hugo ⊙05 65 50 06 07, ⓦlatabledemarinette.fr. It's worth venturing south across the river for the well-priced menus in this stylish Art Deco restaurant. The choice isn't huge but it's all good, and they offer a wide range of pricing – from €12 for lunch, €15 in the evenings, while eating à la carte will set you back upwards of €35. Sat–Thurs noon–2pm & 7–9pm.

DIRECTORY

Books and newspapers For local guides and English newspapers, try Maison de la Presse, down by the river at 2 rue Gambetta.

Hospital Centre Hospitalier, 33 rue des Maquisards

⊙05 65 50 65 50.

Police Commissariat de Police, Cité Administrative, place des Carmes ⊙05 65 50 73 73.

The Causse de Gramat

After the intimate beauty of the Lot and Célé valleys, the wide horizons of the **Causse de Gramat** to the north make a refreshing change. It's an empty land with few people or villages, filled only with the sound of sheep bells and the cicadas' persistent clamour during the tinder-box-dry summers. Across the gently undulating landscape of scrubby

5

pines and oaks, and close-cropped grass spattered with orchids and aromatic plants, you'll come across dolmens, shepherds' dry-stone huts and strange *lacs de St-Namphaise* – water holes hacked out of the rock – but little else to make you want to stop. The exceptions are mostly along the *causse*'s southern boundary, starting off in the far southeast with **Assier**, a small village put on the map by a vainglorious military man who built a château and church here. From Assier the route tracks westward through a series of picturesque villages to the even more diminutive **Caniac-du-Causse**, last resting place of the hermit St Namphaise. At Caniac the route turns northwards into the wildest part of the *causse* towards the busy market town of **Gramat**, home to an above-average wildlife park.

GETTING AROUND   CAUSSE DE GRAMAT

The main towns in this area are well served by public transport. Assier and Gramat both lie on main train lines and are also accessible by bus. However, to do the *causse* justice you really do need your own means of getting about. With few roads and only a sprinkling of villages, this is a great area for walking or mountain biking; most tourist offices have maps of recommended routes.

Assier

If it weren't for the immoderate – and immodest – nature of Galiot de Genouillac, **ASSIER**, some 17km northwest of Figeac, would probably have remained an insignificant village. Chief of artillery under François I and an inspired tactician, de Genouillac earned his stripes during the decisive French victory at Marignano in 1515 during the Italian wars, after which he returned to his native village bathed in glory to erect a **château** befitting his status (May–June & Sept daily except Tues 10am–12.30pm & 2–6.45pm; July & Aug daily 10am–12.30pm & 2–6.45pm; Oct–April daily except Tues 10am–12.30pm & 2–5.30pm; €3; ⍟assier.monuments -nationaux.fr). Built in the latest Renaissance style, it was said to rival the châteaux of the Loire, with its vast interior courtyard flanked by four round towers, its galleries, loggias and carved friezes – and liberal repetition of de Genouillac's motto: *J'aime fortune* ("In love with chance/success"). After 1768, however, the château and its contents were sold off lock, stock and barrel to raise money, leaving only part of the west wing – and even that is in a pretty poor state.

You can get a better idea of de Genouillac's decorative tastes from the **church** he also had built in the village square. It's an extraordinary edifice, not just because of its size and the feeling that it was built to the glory of de Genouillac rather than God, but mainly due to a frieze running round the exterior depicting Roman centurions, guns being hauled across the Alps, flame-spewing cannon and cities under siege – all beautifully realized but hardly normal church ornamentation. Less surprisingly, the most interesting feature inside is the great man's tomb in an intricately vaulted chapel near the west door. He appears twice: as a bearded man lying with his feet on powder sacks, and as a soldier leaning nonchalantly against a cannon.

ARRIVAL AND INFORMATION   ASSIER

By train Assier is a stop on the main Figeac–Brive train line. The *gare SNCF* lies nearly 1km west of the village.
By bus All buses running between Figeac and Gramat stop at the *gare*, and some also stop on the church square.

Tourist office On place de l'Église's, northeast corner (mid-June to mid-Sept Mon–Sat 10am–12.30pm & 3–6pm; ☎05 65 40 50 60, ⍟otivalleecausse.com).

ACCOMMODATION AND EATING

L'Assiérois ☎05 65 40 56 27, ⍟lassierois.com. Accommodating hotel-restaurant with six small but immaculate rooms, all en-suite, just opposite the church. The restaurant offers traditional family cuisine (lunch menus from €13, evening *menus* €28). Restaurant open June–Aug Tues–Sat noon–1pm & 7–9.30pm, Sun noon–1pm; Sept–May Tues–Sat noon–1pm & 7–9.30pm, Sun noon–1pm; closed Wed eve. Breakfast €6.50. **€42**

The southern causse

With your own transport, you can take a circuitous route from Assier through **the southern causse** before cutting northeast to Gramat. There are a few scattered sights to aim for, but on the whole it's the scenery that takes precedence in this high, open country with its grand vistas.

Five kilometres southwest of Assier on the D653, **LIVERNON** is the first of a string of attractive villages, in this case distinguished by a particularly appealing Romanesque belfry, with its rhythmically spaced arches. The route then meanders further south via **ESPÉDAILLAC** – a cluster of crumbling towers and pigeon-lofts – to **QUISSAC**, roughly 10km from Livernon. The main claim to fame of this tiny village is that the ninth-century soldier-turned-hermit **St Namphaise** lived in a nearby grotto. He's a very important person on the *causse*, since it was he who, according to legend, dug the shallow ponds in the rock that are characteristic of this region, thus providing water for the flocks of sheep; ironically, he is said to have been killed by an irate bull. There's a statue of Namphaise dressed as a soldier in Quissac church, and you can see one of his famous *lacs* about 1km south of the village beside the Coursac road.

The dying Namphaise supposedly threw away his hammer – with which he presumably created the ponds – and declared that he would be buried wherever it came to rest; it landed 8km away in what is now the village of **CANIAC-DU-CAUSSE**. It's a sleepy, flowery place, undisturbed by the trickle of visitors coming to view Namphaise's small, unadorned sarcophagus lying in a diminutive twelfth-century crypt beneath the village church.

From Caniac cut north across country on the D42, keeping a lookout on the right for signs down a dirt track to the Site de Planagrèze, a couple of kilometres later. At the end of the track various footpaths and biking trails strike out across the *causse*, while one of the more accessible dolmens stands a short walk south. On the way you pass a fenced-off area, in the middle of which is another typical feature of the *causse*, a limestone sinkhole, the **Igue de Planagrèze**; in this particular case pot-holers have so far explored 800m of tunnels.

From here the D42 continues north to Fontanes-du-Causse, where there's a choice of routes to Gramat: you can either stick to the back lanes, or cut west to the faster D677.

Gramat

The biggest town on the *causse*, and its capital, **GRAMAT** developed at the junction of two major Roman roads. Its fortunes increased further when pilgrims started passing through en route to Rocamadour (see p.174), and it received another boost when the railway came here in 1863. Even today it's an important market town, with two weekly **markets** (Tues & Fri morn) and bigger *foires* on the second and fourth Thursdays of each month. Though a few vestiges of the medieval town remain, Gramat is mostly of interest as somewhere to base yourself for a day or so; as well as being an ideal starting point for exploring the *causse*, it's within easy striking distance of Rocamadour, only 9km away to the northwest, and fairly convenient for sights in the upper Dordogne valley (see p.168).

Gramat would be more appealing if it weren't for the busy N140 and D677 funnelling through **place de la République**, a big square on the east side of town. If you walk west from here along the **Grande Rue**, though, you'll suddenly find yourself among the narrow lanes of the old quarter. There's not a lot to see here, but both the place de l'Hôtel de Ville, at the top of the Grande Rue, and the market square, south of the Grande Rue down rue Notre-Dame, are attractive corners.

Jardins du Grand Couvent

Daily: June, Sept & Oct 2–6pm; July & Aug 10am–7pm; private visits available in May • €5 • ⓦ jardinsgrandcouvent.com

South out of town, head to the flourishing **Jardins du Grand Couvent**, behind a convent complex, you can also see the lovely old wash house and bread ovens used by the nuns until fairly recently; they also run a small shop and tea room.

5

Parc Animalier de Gramat

Daily: Easter to Sept 9.30am–7pm; Oct to Easter 2–6pm, Sun in Oct plus school hols 9.30am–6pm • €9.50, children €5.50 •
☎ 05 65 38 81 22, ⓦ gramat-parc-animalier.com

The main reason for most people's visit to this area is the **Parc Animalier de Gramat**, a couple of kilometres further south of the Jardins du Grand Couvent, on the D14. Encompassing half a square kilometre of the *causse*, the park is home to an unusually varied selection of animals: the 150 mostly European species include wolves, otters, bears, ibex – with their magnificent curved horns – and *mouflon*, a type of goat crowned with four horns. Allow at least two hours if you want to cover the whole park.

ARRIVAL AND INFORMATION   GRAMAT

By train The *gare SNCF* is 1km south of the centre; if no taxis are waiting, call Adgié on ☎ 05 65 38 75 07 or ☎ 05 65 38 0 54.
Destinations Assier (3–7 daily; 10–15min); Brive (6 daily; 45min); Figeac (4–8 daily; 30min); Paris-Austerlitz (1 overnight; 7hr); Rocamadour (4–6 daily; 8min); St-Denis-lès-Martel (4–6 daily; 25min); Toulouse (1 daily; 3hr).
By bus Some buses call at the train station but most drop you on place de la République.

Destinations Assier (Mon–Sat 1 daily; 25min); Cahors (Mon, Wed, Thurs & Sat 1 daily; 1hr 10min); Figeac (Mon–Sat 1 daily; 50min); St-Céré (school term Mon–Fri 1 daily, school hols Tues, Thurs & Sat 1 daily; 1hr 15min).
Tourist office Place de la République (April–June & Sept–Nov Mon–Sat 10am–12.30pm & 2–6pm; July & Aug Mon–Sat 10am–12.30pm & 2–7pm, Sun 10am–12.30pm; Nov–March Mon–Sat 10am–12.30pm & 2–5.30pm; ☎ 05 65 38 73 60, ⓦ rocamadour.com).

ACCOMMODATION AND EATING

Le Centre Place de la République ☎ 05 65 38 73 37, ⓦ lecentre.fr. On the square's east side, you can't miss the electric-green shades of *Le Centre*, which is equally cheerful inside, with good-value, brightly decorated en-suite rooms. Restaurant open March–Oct daily noon–2pm & 7.15–9pm; Nov–Feb Mon–Thurs noon–2pm & 7.15–9pm, Fri & Sun noon–2pm. Lunch *menus* cost from €14 and are €19 in the evening. Breakfast €8.50. **€61**

La Cuisine d'Alain 2 rue de la Liberté ☎ 05 65 38 87 87. In addition to the hotel restaurants, *La Cuisine d'Alain*, in the old town, makes a good pit-stop. You'll need to get here early – or reserve – at lunchtime, when locals swarm in to fill the two small rooms and pavement tables between scurrying serving staff. There's a bewildering choice of *formules* and *menus*, starting at €10 for lunch and €13 in the evenings. Mon–Sat noon–2pm & 7–9pm.

Lion d'Or Place de la République ☎ 05 65 10 46 10,

ⓦ liondorhotel.fr. The refined *Lion d'Or* is on the north side of the square; its rooms are modern, smart and comfortable, while the restaurant (*menu* €21) offers top-quality cooking. Restaurant open July–Sept daily noon–1.15pm & 7.30–8.30pm; Oct–June Tues–Sat noon–1.15pm & 7.30–8.30pm, Sun noon–1.15pm. Breakfast €9. **€61**

★ **Relais des Gourmands** ☎ 05 65 38 83 92, ⓦ relais-des-gourmands.fr. The nicest place to stay in Gramat, though unpromisingly situated opposite the train station. Despite the location, it's a delightful, flowery spot, with airy rooms, a pool and an excellent restaurant serving all the classics as well as lighter versions of regional cuisine. Evening *menus* from €18.50. Restaurant open daily July & Aug 12.30–2pm & 7.30–9pm; Sept–June Tues–Sat 12.30–2pm & 7.30–9pm, Sun 12.30–2pm. Hotel closed Jan–March. Breakfast €8.50. **€62**

Gourdon

Thirty-five kilometres west of Gramat, **GOURDON** is an attractive town, its medieval centre of butter-coloured stone houses attached to a prominent hilltop, neatly ringed by shady modern boulevards, known collectively as the **Tour-de-Ville**. While it has no outstanding sights, Gourdon makes a quiet, pleasant base, not only for the nearby **Grottes de Cougnac**, with their prehistoric paintings, but also for the **Bouriane** (see p.230) to the south.

The town

Where the ramparts once stood, Gourdon's medieval centre is now entirely surrounded by the **Tour-de-Ville**. The best-preserved gateway into the centre is southwesterly Porte du Majou, which stands guard over the old town's main street, **rue du Majou**, lined with mellow stone-built houses, some, like the **Maison d'Anglars** at no. 17, with its ogive arches and mullion windows, dating back as far as the thirteenth century; look out on the right, as you go up, for the delightfully – and accurately – named rue Zig-Zag.

At its upper end, rue du Majou opens onto a lovely cobbled square beneath the twin towers of the massive fourteenth-century **church of St-Pierre**. Note the traces of fortifications, in the form of machicolations, over the west door, but you'll find nothing of particular interest inside, beyond some seventeenth-century gilded bas-reliefs by a local sculptor depicting the life of the Virgin Mary. The **Hôtel de Ville** – a handsome if unpretentious building whose arcaded ground floor once served as the market hall – stands on the west side of the square, while east of the church in place des Marronniers an ornately carved door marks the home of the Cavaignac family, who supplied the nation with numerous prominent public figures in the eighteenth and nineteenth centuries.

From the north side of the church, a path leads to the top of the hill where Gourdon's castle stood until it was razed in the early seventeenth century in the wake of the Wars of Religion. At 264m in height, it affords superb views over the wooded country stretching north to the Dordogne valley.

ARRIVAL AND DEPARTURE   GOURDON

By train The *gare SNCF* is located roughly 1km northeast of the old centre. From the station, walk south on avenue de la Gare, then turn right onto avenue Gambetta to come out on the south side of the Tour-de-Ville. If you want a taxi, call Taxi Brice (☎ 06 99 52 56 16).
Destinations Brive (6 daily; 40min); Cahors (6 daily; 30min); Montauban (3 daily; 1hr 30min); Paris-Austerlitz

(2 daily; 4hr 30min); Souillac (6 daily; 15min); Toulouse (6 daily; 1hr 45min).
By bus All services terminate on place de la Libération on the southwest side of the Tour-de-Ville.
Destinations Souillac (school term Mon–Fri 1 daily, school hols Tues 1 daily; 1hr).

GETTING AROUND AND INFORMATION

Car rental ADA 101 av Gambetta (☎ 05 65 41 40 08).
Bike rental Nature Evasion, 73 av Cavignac (☎ 05 65 37 65 12), out on the west side of town.
Tourist office 24 rue du Majou (March–May & Oct Mon–Sat 10am–noon & 2–6pm; June & Sept Mon–Sat 10am–noon & 2–6pm, Sun 10am–noon; July & Aug

Mon–Sat 10am–7pm, Sun 10am–noon; Nov–Jan Mon–Sat 10am–noon & 2–5pm; ☎ 05 65 27 52 50, ⓦ tourisme-gourdon.com). They dispense details of Gourdon's festivities (see box, p.203) and also offer guided tours at 5pm on Thursdays in July & August (€4).

ACCOMMODATION AND EATING

In addition to the hotels (see below), you'll find cafés and restaurants scattered around Tour-de-Ville. For picnic fare, there are fresh-food markets on Tuesdays beside the church in place St-Pierre, and on Saturdays beside the post office. In July and August an important farmers' market takes place on Thursday mornings in place St-Pierre, while the Tour-de-Ville is closed off on the first and third Tuesdays of each month for a traditional country fair.

Domaine le Quercy Gourdon ☎ 05 65 41 06 19, ⓦ domainequercy.com. Well-equipped three-star campsite with pool and restaurant open in high season, 1.5km north on the D704 Périgueux road beside a leisure lake. Closed Sept–April. **€27.40**
Hostellerie de la Bouriane Place du Foirail ☎ 05 65 41 16 37, ⓦ hotellabouriane.fr. The smartest option in town, with elegant decor and a good traditional restaurant serving *menus* from €28. Restaurant open May to mid-Oct

daily 7–9pm & Sun 12.15–1.30pm; mid-Oct to April Tues–Sat 7–8.30pm. Breakfast €13. **€87**
De la Promenade 48 bd Galiot-de-Genouillac ☎ 05 65 41 41 44, ⓦ lapromenadegourdon.fr. Basic, cheerful and very reasonably priced with immaculate rooms and a pub-style restaurant (*menus* from €12 at lunch and evening *menus* at €19). Restaurant open Easter to Sept daily noon–2pm & 7–9.30pm; Oct to Easter Mon–Sat noon–2pm & 7–9.30pm. Breakfast €6.50. **€57**

5

The Grottes de Cougnac

1hr guided tours daily: April–June & Sept 10–11.30am & 2.30–5pm; July & Aug 10am–6pm; Oct 2–4pm • €7.50, children €5.50 • In-depth 2hr-long tours Wed at 9am • €12 • ☎ 05 65 41 47 54, ⓦ grottesdecougnac.com

Signed off the Sarlat road a couple of kilometres north of Gourdon, the **Grottes de Cougnac** were discovered in 1949 by a local water-diviner. To begin with, all the subsequent explorers found were rock formations – notably ceilings festooned with ice-white needles like some glitzy ballroom decoration – but three years later they hit gold when they came across **prehistoric paintings**. These date from between 25,000 and 19,000 years ago, when Cro-Magnon people ventured deep inside the caves to paint panels of ibex, reindeer and mammoths in elegant outline, using the rock's undulating surface to provide a sense of form and movement. They also left hundreds of mysterious signs – mostly dots and pairs of short lines – in addition to two human figures seemingly pierced by spears, a motif also found in Pech-Merle (see p.219). The temperature inside is 13°C, so take a coat.

The Bouriane

The tranquil **Bouriane** region lies south of Gourdon, a large and very pretty area of luxuriant woods and valleys merging into neighbouring Périgord, a striking contrast to the sparse upland causses to the east. It's primarily a place to wander, with no particular destination in mind, but anyone interested in twentieth-century art should visit **Les Arques**, in the south of the region, where a number of powerful, sometimes disturbing, sculptures by Russian exile Ossip Zadkine are on display.

Salviac

The first place of any size you come to along the D673, 14km from Gourdon, is the fortified village of **SALVIAC**, whose Gothic church (known as the Abbaye Nouvelle) was built in the late thirteenth century by Jacques Duèze of Cahors, the future Pope John XXII (see p.202), and still contains fine stained-glass windows from that era. It's worth a brief stop for the location as much as anything, but is sadly rarely open to the public; call ☎ 05 65 41 25 24 to arrange a visit.

Cazals

Seven kilometres further on from Salviac, the *bastide* town of **CAZALS** has seen better days: its feudal château and ramparts were largely destroyed during the Hundred Years War, though its big central square remains, giving the town character and hosting a splendid Sunday market. On the southern outskirts there is a small multi-sport leisure lake which doubles as a pleasant spot for a picnic.

Rampoux

From Cazals, you can work your way 9km eastwards through enticing back lanes to **RAMPOUX**. This unusually scattered hamlet is home to a Romanesque priory church in which one of the original frescoes can still be seen – a very faded Christ in Majesty in the apse. Better preserved are those from the fifteenth century in the south chapel, portraying the life of Jesus.

Les Arques

LES ARQUES sits buried in the countryside 10km southwest of Rampoux and 6km south of Cazals. It's a higgledy-piggledy village on a hillock above the River Masse, but its main draw is the Romanesque **church** and the neighbouring **Musée Zadkine** (April–Oct Tues–Sun 10am–1pm & 3–7pm; Nov–March Tues–Sun 2–6pm; adult €3, under 13 years old free). A Russian émigré and well-known sculptor, **Ossip Zadkine** set up a studio in Les Arques in 1934 and worked on and off in the village until his death in 1967, producing big, powerful statues full of restless energy. Many are on a mythological or musical theme, such as those of Orpheus and Diana, the latter metamorphosing from tree to woman, and there's a strong Cubist influence, although his works grew more abstract towards the end of his life. Some of his most compelling pieces are displayed inside the church opposite the museum, whose cool stone interior provides the perfect foil for a passionate rendering of Christ on the Cross and, in the crypt, the *Pietà*. During his time in Les Arques, Zadkine also discovered some twelfth-century frescoes in the nearby église St-André – you can get a key from the museum.

Goujounac

A good place for an overnight stay or tasty meal is charming little **Goujounac**, with its butter-coloured stone houses, 5km southwest of Les Arques, whose **church** has rather worn Romanesque carvings of Christ in Majesty and the four Evangelists over the south door.

St Médard

About 7km southeast of Goujounac, the picturesque medieval hamlet of **St Médard** sits pillowed against a forested hill. Apart from a renowned restaurant and the twelfth-century church, with its particularly decorative stone stoup, there is little to see, unless you should bump into Leon the peacock – the village pet, and a lordly bird that struts the narrow streets in a regal fashion.

ACCOMMODATION AND EATING   **THE BOURIANE**

CAZALS

⭐ **La Caminade** ☎ 05 65 21 66 63, ⓦ lacaminade .com. Part of the old ramparts now house this lovely *chambre d'hôte* signed off the main road to Cahors. The beautiful rooms are peaceful, and there's a salt-water pool and barbecue terrace. **€98**

LES ARQUES

⭐ **La Récréation** ☎ 05 65 22 88 08, ⓦ restaurant -traiteur-lot.com. In season, it's worth timing your visit to the Zadkine museum in order to have lunch in the old schoolhouse at the entrance to the village, now home to an attractive restaurant. *Menus* start from €26 for lunch (July & Aug), €35 in the evening and for some lunches (Sept–Oct & March–June) – a snip for five splendid courses. On Thursday eve in season they knock up delicious tapas dishes. Reservations essential. March–June & Sept–Oct noon–1.30pm & 7.30–9.30pm; July & Aug daily except Wed noon–1.30pm & 7.30–9.30pm.

GOUJOUNAC

Camping La Pinède ☎ 05 65 36 61 84, ⓦ camping -goujounac.com. Lovely three-star camp site immediately west of Goujounac on the D660 Villefranche road. Facilities include a pool with water slides, tennis, and children's play area, so it's an ideal site for families

with young children. Restaurant due to open May 2013. Closed Oct–April. **€15**

Hostellerie de Goujounac ☎ 05 65 36 68 67, ⓦ goujounac.com. Opposite the church, this Dutch-owned hotel with five simple rooms offers honest country cooking. Their signature Indonesian buffets (€24.50) are held on the last Sun of the month all year. Restaurant open April–Sept Tues to Sat noon–2pm & 7–8.30pm, Sun noon–2pm; Oct–March Wed–Sat noon–2pm & 7–8.30pm. Reservations advised. Breakfast €9. **€59**

ST MÉDARD

⭐ **Le Gindreau** ☎ 05 65 36 22 27, ⓦ legindreau .com. If you're looking for somewhere special to eat in the area, head east to St-Médard, where you'll find one of the Lot's most distinguished restaurants, the Michelin-starred *Gindreau*, serving up such delights as seafood bisque with a gratin of crustaceans or local lamb with Rocamadour cheese, potatoes and pickled pork rind; the desserts in particular are real works of art and include cherries soaked in Cahors wine. *Menus* start at an affordable €39, rising to a gastronomic €160. In summer, tables are laid out under the chestnut trees. Reservations advised in high season. April–May & Nov to mid-March Wed–Sat noon–2pm & 7.30–9.3pm, Sun noon–2pm; May–Sept Wed–Sun noon–2pm & 7.30–9.30pm.

5

West along the Lot from Cahors

The Bouriane's southern boundary is marked by the River Lot, which follows a particularly convoluted course downstream of Cahors as it doubles back on itself again and again between cliffs that gradually diminish towards the west. Standing guard over one of the larger meanders is **Luzech**, whose main claim to fame is the scant remains of a Roman encampment on the hill above the town. Continuing downstream, the route winds through a series of villages perched above the river, culminating in one of the most beautiful along the entire Lot valley, **Puy-l'Évêque**. A castle-town built on a terraced cliff, it dominates the last of the river's meanders, and its wandering lanes, tunnels, staircases and fountains together compensate for the lack of any first-rate sights. The area around **Duravel** and **Touzac**, further west again, with its fine selection of hotels and restaurants, provides a good base for visiting the impressive **Château de Bonaguil** in the hills to the north of the Lot. The last of the medieval castles to be constructed in France, and now partially in ruins, it still bristles with sophisticated defensive devices. Back on the Lot, **Fumel** is a major transport hub and service centre, though otherwise contains nothing to make you dally – better to hurry on downriver to where **Penne-d'Agenais**, with its striking basilica, lords it over the valley.

GETTING AROUND   **WEST ALONG THE LOT**

Public transport along this stretch of the river consists of an SNCF bus that threads along the valley from Cahors via Luzech, Prayssac, Puy-l'Évêque and Fumel to terminate at Monsempron-Libos, on the Agen–Périgueux train line. On the way it also passes through or close by most of the smaller villages cited below, but you'll need your own transport to reach the Château de Bonaguil and Grezels.

Luzech

Twenty kilometres downriver from Cahors, **LUZECH** is situated on the narrow neck of a particularly large meander, overlooked by a twelfth-century **keep**. Little remains of the fortress beyond a few foundation stones, but it's worth trekking up for a splendid view over the Luzech meander. It's 1.5km by road, or you can walk up in about ten minutes: from the north end of rue de la Ville; follow signs for the GR36 footpath, past the castle keep and then just keep climbing. For a less strenuous jaunt, head south for about 2km to visit a tiny chapel, **Notre-Dame de l'Isle**, surrounded by vines and walnut trees on the very tip of the meander.

The town itself has a small area of picturesque alleys to the north of **place du Canal**, the central square spanning the isthmus.

Maison des Consuls

Grande Rue de la Ville • **Ammonite collection** June–Sept Mon–Fri 10am–1pm & 3–7pm, Sat 3–7pm • €3, or €5 with Ichnospace
Ichnospace June–Sept, Mon–Fri 10am–1pm & 3–7pm, Sat 10am–1pm & 2–6pm • €3, or €5 with the Musée Armand Viré **Musée Armand Viré** Same hours as tourist office – see below

In the centre of town, you'll find the **Maison des Consuls**, built in 1270. The building is home to the tourist office, as well as two of Luzech's three museums. The first houses a collection of ammonites, and you can continue in the prehistoric vein with a trip to the **Ichnospace** also on Grande Rue de la Ville in the *médiathèque*. Inside you'll find 140-million-year-old dinosaur footprints from nearby Crayssac, displayed over an area of sixty square metres.

Back in the Maison des Consuls, the **Musée Armand Viré**, displays archeological finds from around Luzech. The majority of items come from the fortress above the town, which has been occupied since the early Iron Age; the Romans reinforced it and erected a temple on the site, which is now known as the Oppidum d'Impernal. Though there are some delicate Gaulish safety-pins and needles, the exhibits in the museum demonstrate

5

the huge leap in craftsmanship ushered in by the Romans in the first century BC: look out for the unusual folding spoon and the coins chopped in half for small change.

ARRIVAL AND DEPARTURE
LUZECH

By bus Buses from Cahors pull in beside a roundabout at the east end of place du Canal.
Destinations Albas (4–10 daily; 10min); Cahors

(4–10 daily; 25min); Monsempron-Libos (4–10 daily; 1hr); Prayssac (4–10 daily; 25min); Puy-l'Évêque (4–10 daily; 30min).

INFORMATION AND ACTIVITIES

Tourist office Maison des Consuls (Feb–March & Oct Mon–Thurs 10am–1pm & 2–5pm, Fri 10am–noon; May–Sept Mon–Sat 10am–1pm & 2pm–6pm; winter opening times restricted to three days a week, and variable; ☏ 05 65 20 17 27, ⓦ ville-luzech.fr).
Boat rental Luzech marks the end of the navigable river descending from St-Cirq Lapopie (although it is currently

undergoing works to make it fully navigable again). Nautic rents houseboats and Naviglot (mid-May to mid-Sept; ☏ 05 65 20 18 19) rents pleasure boats, canoes and bikes and organizes river-trips with wine-tasting (1hr 30min; €8). Both Nautic and Naviglot are based a couple of kilometres north of Luzech near the village of Caix.

ACCOMMODATION AND EATING

Gîte d'Étape Luzech ☏ 05 65 30 72 32. A good bet for a stopover if you're walking, this *gîte d'étape* is located just before the western bridge. It offers washing facilities, kitchen and living area. <u>€10.50</u>
Le Vinois Caillac ☏ 05 65 30 53 60, ⓦ levinois.com. If you fancy a little sophistication, head 5km north along the river to the small village of Caillac where this lovely hotel has a pool, a pretty garden, ten bedrooms and an airy dining room, all decorated in a minimalist Japanese style. Chef Jean-Claude

Voisin will tickle your palate with delectable dishes (*menus* from €17.50 at lunch, €35 for dinner) concocted from the best local ingredients. Restaurant open April–Oct Tues–Sun noon–2pm & 7.30–9pm. Breakfast €13.50. <u>€96</u>
Zotier ☏ 05 65 30 54 22, ⓦ zotier.com. This welcoming *chambre d'hôte* is on the western edge of town, with five very prettily decorated bedrooms, a shady garden and delicious evening *menus* (€21) using local produce and fruit from the orchard. <u>€78</u>

Albas

The prettiest route downstream from Luzech – which is followed by the bus – is the D8 along the river's south bank. It's especially beguiling in summer when the intense green of the vines and walnut trees in the valley bottom is offset against the dark grey cliffs. The river loops back and forth across the flood plain, with a village at the bottom of each meander. The first you come to, and the most attractive, is **ALBAS**, 5km from Luzech, instantly recognizable by its tall church spire. The church is nineteenth-century and otherwise uninteresting, but the steep lanes below retain a few noble fourteenth- and fifteenth-century facades, a reminder of when the bishops of Cahors maintained a residence here. Look out for the arched double doors of the houses lining the street, they conceal deep cellars, reminders of the days when the Lot was fully navigable and Albas was the main port for Cahors wine; hundreds of barrels were stored here to be shipped downstream to Bordeaux and onwards to the world. As you reach the esplanade you can see the spot where the boats were loaded, and where every other May, at the biennial **fête du vin** (ⓦ feteduvin-cahors.fr), a barrel is brought downstream, unloaded and ceremoniously paraded through the village; it signals the start of the largest wine festival in the area (next due 2013, 2015; €12 including wine). Cross the river by the narrow bridge and look back up at the village for a view that graces a million postcards.

EATING AND DRINKING
ALBAS

Auberge d'Imhotep ☏ 05 65 30 70 91. Two kilometres east of Albas, the *Auberge d'Imhotep* is a friendly little restaurant named after the ancient Egyptian who supposedly discovered the art of *gavage* – the process of force-feeding ducks for foie gras – in 2600 BC. Naturally,

duck features strongly and they also offer an excellent Cahors wine list and a generous helping of jazz. *Menus* from €16. Reservations advised in season. April–Oct Tues–Sun noon–1.30pm & 7.30pm–3.30am.

Castelfranc

Three kilometres west of Albas, at the little hamlet Le Mayne, the bus turns north to cross the river at engaging little Castelfranc. It's a riverside *bastide* village built on a grid pattern around a pretty central *place* by the indefatigable bishops of Cahors. On the northern side lies its main attraction, the thirteenth-century church with its four-bell *clocher mur*, whilst on the southern side there's a good little restaurant (see below). Wander a couple of hundred metres further south and you'll find yourself back at the river where Castelfranc has another surprise attraction, a river beach complete with picnic tables.

EATING AND DRINKING
CASTELFRANC

Du Pont 3 av Pont du Fer ☎ 05 65 21 80 92. Unsurprisingly, this delightful little restaurant is located right next to the bridge. The location isn't quite as beguiling as it sounds, as a line of cottages shields the view from the river, but the bistro makes up for it with a charming courtyard garden, shaded by a huge vine. *Menus* €13 for mid-week lunch, €20.50 in the evenings. The Cahors–Montsempron bus stops right outside. Daily noon–1.45pm; July & Aug Mon–Sat 7–9.30pm; Sept–June

Thurs–Sat 7–8.30pm.
La Vigne Haute 1 av Tonneliers ☎ 05 65 53 08 45, ⊛ restaurant-la-vigne-haute.com. A comfortable, traditionally furnished eatery known for its soufflés and grills, which are executed over a charcoal fire in the dining room itself. The chef is Vietnamese, so there is likely to be an exotic kick in the *menu du jour*. Lunch *menu* from €12, from €24.50 in the evening. Thurs–Tues noon–2pm & 7–10pm; closed Christmas and two weeks in Feb.

Prayssac

Heading west from Castelfranc the road hugs the cliff, affording ravishing glimpses of the fertile Lot valley. After a scant couple of kilometres you roll into the bustling little town of Prayssac. It isn't the prettiest town in the valley, nor the most historically interesting, but in summer there's a real buzz about it. The plane-tree-lined place d'Istrie has great cafés, spilling out over shady pavements. Outside the tourist office is a stern statue of Marechál Bessières, Prayssac's most famous son, born here in August 1768. Bessières was a brilliant commander and a great friend of Napoleon Bonaparte. He died in 1813 after a direct hit from a cannonball, which turned out to be a lucky stroke for Wellington and the allies; Napoleon reputedly asserted that had Bessières been with him he would have prevailed at Waterloo.

The real reason for visiting Prayssac is its main **market**, the best in the area, filling the centre around the place de l'Église and spreading into neighbouring streets every Friday morning. In high summer it's difficult to get anywhere near it – it's best to leave your car at the side of the road, along with five hundred others, walk in and soak up the atmosphere.

ARRIVAL AND INFORMATION
PRAYSSAC

By bus SNCF buses from Cahors stop in the rue Colonel Pardes in front of the place d'Istrie. From Monsempron-Libos they stop in front of the post office.
Destinations Albas (4–10 daily; 15min); Cahors (4–10 daily; 55min); Duravel (4–8 daily; 15min); Fumel (4–8 daily; 25min); Luzech (4–10 daily; 25min); Monsempron-Libos (4–8 daily; 35min); Touzac (2–3 daily; 15–20min); Puy L'Eveque (4–8 daily; 10min).
Tourist office 1 bd de la Paix (Mon 9am–1pm, Tues–Fri 9am–1pm & 2.30–6pm, Sat 9am–12.30pm & 2–5pm, Sun

9am–12.30pm; ☎ 05 65 22 40 57, ⊛ tourisme-prayssac .com).
Canoe hire At the small base at Floiras ☎ 05 65 32 72 61, on the south bank of the river opposite the *Hostellerie Clau del Loup*.
River walk There's a lovely riverside walk between Castelfranc and Prayssac, also useful if you're on foot and want to visit the Castelfranc restaurants from Prayssac, as you can't easily walk along the main road.

ACCOMMODATION AND EATING

Prayssac has several options for eating. For picnic food there are two good supermarkets, one on the western outskirts towards Puy L'Eveque, the other on the southern side opposite the pompiers. Boulangeries abound, the best of the bunch is Lasjournias, on the place d'Istrie. There is also a very good fromagerie and delicatessen, next door. But if you happen to be here on market day you'll be utterly seduced by an overwhelming assault on your senses, and rightly so.

5

Le 14 14 place d'Istrie ☎05 65 36 04 86. Possibly the best of the cafés around the *place*, the courtyard has been decorated in mellow terracotta and lavished with Mediterranean plants, while the interior is extremely stylish and mostly for sale, as it doubles as a boutique. The tables burst out through the gates on market days, so get there early or be prepared for a wait. *Menus* €14 at lunch and €27 in the evening. Café open Tues–Sat 9am to late afternoon for drinks. Daily noon–2.30pm & 7–9.30pm.

Clau del Loup Mètairie haute, Juillac, 2km south of Prayssac on the D8 ☎05 65 36 76 20, ⓦclaudelloup .com. A beautifully renovated hotel among walnut orchards in the hamlet of Juillac. They have a charming garden, a pool and a stylish restaurant serving excellent regional dishes. *Menus* from €20. Restaurant open daily noon–1.30pm & 7–9pm. Breakfast €12. €125

O Plaisir des Sens 50 bd Aristide Briand ☎05 65 22 47 12, ⓦo-plaisir-des-sens.com. This is a quirky little restaurant in a corner of place de la Liberté that delivers an unexpectedly elegant platter. *Menus* €13.50 at lunch, €26.50 in the evening. Tues 7–9pm, Wed–Sat noon–1.30pm & 7–9pm.

La Vènus Square La Vènus ☎05 65 22 47 10, ⓦrestaurant-la-venus.com. A reliably good little eatery with an Italian flavour, situated on the eastern side of town. The chef is French and the waitress English making the restaurant extremely popular with both French locals and British visitors. *Menus* from €13 at lunch, €22.50 in the evening. Wed–Sat noon–1.30pm & 7–9pm, Sun noon–1.30pm.

Grézels and around

Around 5km south of Prayssac, just off the D8, lies the hamlet of Belaye; it's worth a quick trip to this perched medieval village for the stunning views of the Lot valley alone. Some 4km further west you arrive at the little village of **GRÉZELS**, another episcopal seat, though in this case its château – a very sober affair – has survived thanks to a seventeenth-century rebuild. The prime attraction here, on the main road through the village, is the restaurant (see below).

EATING AND DRINKING   GRÉZELS

La Terrasse ☎05 65 21 34 03. Renowned for its jovial host and no-nonsense cuisine; there's only one *menu* (€18, including wine) that changes daily. Make sure you've got a healthy appetite as portions are huge and the owner likes to see clean plates. Reservations recommended. Oct to mid-Sept Tues–Sun 12.30–1pm.

Puy-l'Évêque and around

Back on the north bank, and a mere five kilometres from Prayssac, **PUY-L'ÉVÊQUE** contends with St-Cirq Lapopie (see p.212) as the Lot valley's prettiest village. After 1227 it marked the western extremity of the Cahors bishops' domains and it's the remains of their thirteenth-century **château**, a big square keep like that at Luzech, that provides the town's focal point. Puy-l'Évêque changed hands any number of times during the Hundred Years War, but then withstood a prolonged Protestant siege in 1580 during the Wars of Religion. Ardent anti-clerics tried to change the name to Puy-Libre during the Revolution, then Puy-sur-Lot, but the locals weren't convinced and it soon reverted to Puy-l'Évêque.

There are no great sights to speak of, just lanes of medieval and Renaissance houses built in honey-coloured stone. Beside the castle keep at the top of the town, the **place de la Truffière** is the venue for the main weekly **market** (Tues morning); in summer a small farmers' market also takes place on Saturdays in the lower town on place Georges Henry, at the west end of rue des Platanes. From place de la Truffière, **rue du Fort** leads steeply down then flattens out beneath an imposing fourteenth-century building distinguished by its Gothic windows, which served as the bishops' audience chamber. As it curves round the hill, rue du Fort becomes rue Bovila and then peters out beside a staircase descending to rue des Capucins. This road heads back east along the hillside to **place Guillaume-de-Cardaillac** and then **place de la Halle**, the town's two most picturesque corners. Downhill from place de la Halle again, you come to rue de la Cale, with the dark alleys of the artisans' quarter off to the left, and the old **port**. For the best **view** of the whole ensemble walk out onto the modern bridge which crosses the Lot here. Alternatively, head for the belvedere in front of the **church of St-Sauveur** that guards Puy-l'Évêque's northeast quarter – literally, since it once formed an integral part of the fortifications; look carefully and you can still see where cannonballs found their target during the siege of 1580.

ARRIVAL AND INFORMATION

PUY-L'ÉVÊQUE

By bus SNCF buses from Cahors stop in front of the church on place du Rampeau and down on rue des Platanes to the southeast of the old centre.
Destinations Albas (4–10 daily; 15min); Cahors (4–10 daily; 1hr); Duravel (4–8 daily; 5–10min); Fumel (4–8 daily; 15–20min); Luzech (4–10 daily; 25–30min); Monsempron-Libos (4–8 daily; 20–25min); Prayssac

(4–10 daily; 10min); Touzac (2–3 daily; 10–15min).
Tourist office 12 Grand Rue (July & Aug Mon–Sat 9.30am–6.30pm, Sun 9am–12.30pm; Sept–June Mon & Sat 9am–12.30pm, Tues, Thurs & Fri 9am–noon & 2–5.30pm, Wed 9am–12.30pm & 3–5.30pm; ☎05 65 21 37 63, ⓦ puy-leveque.fr).

ACCOMMODATION AND EATING

Belle Vue Place de la Truffière ☎05 65 36 06 60, ⓦ hotelbellevue-puyleveque.com. Perched on the edge of a cliff, this refurbished place has very stylish rooms, all with highly contemporary decor and fine views, and with a restaurant to match. For more laid-back dining they also have a brasserie at the front. *Menus* from €18 lunch and €32 in the evening, while it's around €12 for a *plat* in the brasserie. Restaurant open Feb–June & Sept–Dec Wed–Sat noon–1.45pm & 7.30–9.30pm; July & Aug Tues–Sat noon–1.45pm & 7.30–9.30pm. Breakfast €10 (€12 in room). **€76**
★ **Camping Les Vignes** ☎05 65 30 81 72, ⓦ camping-les-vignes.net. Three kilometre south along the river on the D28; signed off the road to the bridge from town, you'll find this superb, spick-and-span three-star campsite, with exceptionally friendly owners. There's also a small shop, and activities for children such as sports and games in the summer you can rent canoes on the supervised river beach, and to top it all off they'll give you a discount if you produce *The Rough Guide*. **€15.05**

Franck Tonel 49 rue Ernest Marcouly ☎05 65 21 32 56. If you would like to try a true local speciality *Franck Tonel* is the place to go. He's an artisan boulanger and patissier, renowned throughout the region for his delicious tarte aux noix. Tues–Sat 9am–12.30pm & 2.30–6pm, Sun 9am–noon.
Henry 23 rue du Docteur Rouma ☎05 65 21 32 24, ⓦ hotel-henry.com. Pleasant rooms at a budget price, though you should try and get one at the back to avoid road noise. The restaurant serves large quantities of local cuisine. *Menus* from €13 lunch and €17 in the evenings. Restaurant open mid-April to mid-Sept daily noon–2pm & 7–10pm; mid-Sept to mid-April Sun–Thurs noon–2pm & 7–10pm, Fri noon–2pm. Breakfast €6. **€44**
Le Pigeonnier ☎05 65 21 37 77. A great café-cum-bistro on the south bank of the river offering huge salads, grills and *galettes*, with an unbeatable view of the village thrown in. *Plats* from €6.80. May–Oct Tues–Sat noon–2pm & 7–9.30pm; in July & Aug also 2–6pm for ice creams and drinks.

Martignac

One of the best excursions from Puy-l'Évêque is to the hamlet of **MARTIGNAC**, 2.5km north, where the much-altered Romanesque **church of St-Pierre-ès-Liens** contains some remarkable late-fifteenth- and early-sixteenth-century frescoes; hidden under plaster until 1938, they are reasonably well preserved. Characters on the north wall represent the Seven Deadly Sins being escorted to the mouth of Hell, each mounted on a different animal: Lust on a billy goat, Gluttony scoffing ham and wine and riding a pig, and scruffy Sloth on a donkey bringing up the tail. The Seven Virtues surround the apse, their grey robes tumbling about them, with Courage and Temperance being the easiest to recognize – the former holds a serpent, while Temperance carefully waters down her wine.

Duravel and around

Downstream of Puy-l'Évêque, the Lot valley begins to open out as the hills along the southern bank fade away. Those to the north continue a while longer, providing a green backdrop for the pretty eleventh-century **church** at **DURAVEL**, 6km from Puy-l'Évêque. Its crypt contains the remains of no fewer than three saints – Poémon, Agathon and Hilarion, their bodies having been brought back from the Holy Land in the eleventh century – but the village is unfortunately spoilt by the busy main road passing through its centre.

Aux Dodus d'Audhuy 3km northeast of Duravel ☎05 65 22 91 82. It's worth making the effort to arrange a meal at this welcoming *chambre d'hôte* signed just off the D911; their excellent cooking is available to all if booked in advance. *Menus* from €11 at lunch and €22 in the evenings. Restaurant open Tues–Sat noon–3pm & 7–9pm. **€100**

Le Clos Bouyssac ☎05 65 36 52 21, ⓦcampingbytheriver.eu. This is a shady two-star campsite a short distance south along the riverbank. Facilities include a small shop and snack bar (July & Aug only), pool, river beach, canoe hire and volleyball. Closed Sept–April. **€17**

Montcabrier

With your own transport, you can cut northwest across country from Duravel to visit the magnificent ruined castle of Bonaguil. On the way it's worth taking a short detour to **MONTCABRIER**, just over 5km north of Duravel, if for no other reason than because this tiny *bastide* seems to have been forgotten by the renovators and tourist authorities. There's a clutch of once-noble residences around the chestnut-shaded main square, but the village is best known for a diminutive statue lodged in the north nave of its quietly crumbling **church of St-Louis**. It is one of the first stone representations of the saint, formerly King Louis IX, showing him as a bearded figure wearing a painted crown. It's also slightly macabre: when Louis died on a crusade in 1270, his body was immediately chopped into pieces and dispatched around Europe to meet the demand for relics. Apparently, one unspecified piece of the king now resides inside this little statue.

Château de Bonaguil

Daily: March, April & Oct 10.30am–12.30pm & 2–5.30pm; June 10am–12.30pm & 2–6pm; July & Aug 10am–7pm; Sept 10.30am–12.30pm & 2–6.30pm; Nov Sun, bank hols & school hols 2–5pm; Dec & Feb school hols 2–5pm • €7 adults, €4 children • Guided tours 1hr 30min; English tours available in July & Aug • ☎ 05 53 71 90 33, ⓦ bonaguil.org

From Montcabrier take the D673 from below the village heading southwest, then turn west through the delightful hamlet of St-Martin-Le-Redon and start climbing. As the road crests the ridge you get a stunning view of the **Château de Bonaguil**, 7km from Montcabrier, perched at the end of a wooded spur. The castle dates largely from the fifteenth and sixteenth centuries when Bérenger de Roquefeuil, from a powerful Languedoc family and by all accounts a nasty piece of work, inherited the partially ruined castle. Fearing revolts by his vassals, he decided to transform it into an impregnable fortress, just as his contemporaries were abandoning such elaborate fortifications. It took him around forty years to do so, constructing a double ring of walls, six huge towers, a highly unusual, narrow boat-shaped keep and sophisticated loopholes with overlapping lines of fire. Perhaps because of such elaborate precautions, Bonaguil was never attacked, and although some demolition occurred during the Revolution, the castle still stands, bloodied but unbowed.

The site attracts up to two thousand tourists per day in July and August. It's best to arrive first thing in the morning to avoid the worst of the crush, and rather than joining the **guided tours**, which get tedious when it's very busy, it's preferable to buy a guidebook from the ticket gate and do it yourself. The château provides the backdrop for a **firework** extravaganza on the Friday following July 14, and then in early August makes a stunning venue for a **festival** of theatre (see p.203).

Auberge les Bons Enfants ☎05 65 71 23 52, ⓦlesbonsenfants-bonaguil.com. There are a couple of eating places below the castle, including this English-run restaurant, which serves drinks and snacks all day in high season, as well as a more substantial regional *menu* at €16.80. Feb–June days vary (check website or phone in winter) noon–2.30pm & 7–9pm; July, Aug & Sept–Oct daily noon–2.30pm & 7–9pm.

Fumel

Eight kilometres southwest of Bonaguil and 12km west of Duravel, **FUMEL** – an important stronghold in medieval times – is now a busy industrial town, which holds little of interest beyond its transport facilities and a decent hotel. It lies on the north bank of the Lot, spilling along the main road from its old centre – focused around **place du Postel** – in the east, past a huge factory making car parts, and then merges 4km later with the western suburb of **MONSEMPRON-LIBOS**. There is little to say about Monsempron either, except that it happens to be a terminal for both trains and buses. Perhaps for that reason it also hosts a huge rambling – and best-value – market, on the place du Marché, every Thursday.

ARRIVAL AND DEPARTURE
FUMEL

By train You'll find the *gare SNCF* in Monsempron-Libos, set back from the river near the new road-bridge at the end of avenue de la Gare.

Destinations Agen (up to 8 daily; 40–55min); Le Bugue (4–6 daily; 50min–1hr); Les Eyzies (4–6 daily; 55min–1hr 10min); Penne-d'Agenais (6–7 daily; 15–20min); Périgueux (4–6 daily; 1hr 30min).

By bus SNCF buses from Cahors terminate at the *gare SNCF*, having first called in Fumel at place du Postel. Destinations from Monsempron-Libos: Cahors (4–8 daily; 1hr 15min); Duravel (4–8 daily; 20min); Fumel (4–8 daily; 6–10min); Luzech (4–8 daily; 50min–1hr); Prayssac (4–8 daily; 35min); Puy-l'Évêque (4–8 daily; 30min); Touzac (2–3 daily; 25min).

GETTING AROUND AND INFORMATION

Bike rental AJF Cycles, 8 place du Postel ☎ 05 53 71 14 57.
Taxis Fumélois ☎ 05 53 71 39 50.
Tourist office Place Georges Escandes (July & Aug

Mon–Sat 9am–1pm & 2.30–6.30pm, Sun 9am–1pm; Sept–June Tues–Sat 10am–noon & 3–6pm; ☎ 05 53 71 13 70, ⓦ tourisme-fumelois.fr).

ACCOMMODATION AND EATING

Camping les Catalpas ☎ 05 53 71 11 99, ⓦ les -catalpas.com For a campsite nearby, head 3.5km east through the village of Condat to this friendly little place. Facilities include a restaurant/bar (open daily May–Sept), pool, river beach and pétanque. SNCF buses stop 1.5km up the road in Condat itself. Closed mid-Nov to March. **€18**
La Ferme de Myriam ☎ 05 65 70 49 83, ⓦ laferme demyriam.com. A lovely *chambre d'hôte* 5km from Fumel, and an equal distance from the *gare SNCF* at Monsempron-Libos, just off the D431. It's a splendid old stone farmhouse, with comfortable bedrooms and

good home cooking. *Table d'hôte* is offered 3–4 times a week on demand and costs €24 including aperitif and wine. **€66**
Hostellerie Le Vert 9km southeast of Fumel, on the D5 ☎ 05 65 36 51 36, ⓦ hotellevert.com. Lovely old farm set in fields just east of Mauroux, off the Puy-l'Évêque road. It boasts a heated pool, a handful of charmingly refurbished rooms and an excellent restaurant serving upmarket regional cuisine. *Menu* €36. Restaurant open April–June Fri–Wed 7.30–8.30pm; July, Aug & Sept–Oct daily 7.30–8.30pm;. Breakfast €10. **€110**

Penne-d'Agenais

The last stop along the valley before Villeneuve-sur-Lot is the beautiful but touristy old fortress-town of **PENNE-D'AGENAIS**, 15km downstream from Fumel on the river's south bank, where a silver-domed **basilica** teeters on the cliff edge. **Notre-Dame-de-Peyragude** dates back to 1000, but had the misfortune to be built on a particularly strategic pinnacle of rock. After Richard the Lionheart erected a castle right next door in 1182, the chapel found itself in the crossfire on any number of occasions; in 1412 Penne changed hands no fewer than four times. The most recent construction was only completed in 1949; there's nothing particular to see inside, and the neighbouring castle was razed during the Wars of Religion, but the climb is rewarded with panoramic views.

From **place Gambetta**, the main square immediately south of the old town, **rue du 14-Juillet** ducks under a medieval gate. From here just follow your fancy uphill along narrow lanes lined with an alluring mix of brick and stone houses – all incredibly spick and span. A few twists and turns later you emerge beside the basilica.

By train Penne lies on the Agen–Paris main line, its *gare SNCF* a couple of kilometres southeast down the D103 to Agen.
Taxi Andrée Garcia ☎ 06 15 27 05 91.

Tourist office Rue du 14-Juillet just inside the medieval gate (Mon–Sat 9am–12.30pm & 2–6pm, Sun 2–6pm; ☎ 05 53 41 37 80, ⓦ penne-tourisme.com). They supply comprehensive lists of *chambres d'hôtes* and *gîtes* in the area.

ACCOMMODATION

Camping Municipal Les Berges du Lot ☎ 05 53 41 22 23. A small, two-star riverside campsite near the bridge over the Lot in St-Sylvestre-sur-Lot; facilities include a pool and a children's play area. Closed Sept to mid-May. **€8.50**

Camping Municipal Lac Férrié ☎ 05 53 41 30 97. A three-star campsite beside a lake just north of Penne's *gare SNCF*, it offers a pool, children's play area and pétanque. Closed Sept–June. **€16.08**

EATING AND DRINKING

Le Bombecul Place Paul Fromet ☎ 05 53 71 11 76, ⓦ bombecul.free.fr. Offers casual dining with a Moroccan twist, as well as a wide selection of locally made ice cream. *Menus* from €15 at lunch, €26 in the evenings. March, Oct & Nov Fri & Sat noon–2pm & 7.30–9pm, Sun noon–2pm; April–June & Sept Wed–Sat noon–2pm & 7.30–9pm, Sun noon–2pm; July & Aug, daily noon–2pm & 7.30–9pm.

La Maison sur la Place ☎ 05 53 01 29 18, ⓦ lamaisonsurlaplace.com. A lovely restaurant by the entrance to the village, offering sophisticated country cooking in elegant surroundings. *Menus* from €24 for two dishes, €31 for three. June–Sept Tues–Sat noon–1.30pm & 7.30–9.15pm, Sun noon–1.30pm; mid-Oct to May Thurs–Sat noon–1.3pm & 7.30–9.15pm, Sun noon–1.30pm.

Villeneuve-sur-Lot and around

Straddling the river 10km west of Penne-d'Agenais, **VILLENEUVE-SUR-LOT** is a pleasant, workaday sort of town. It has no terribly compelling sights, but the handful of attractive timbered houses in the old centre goes some way to compensate. Founded in 1251 by Alphonse de Poitiers, Villeneuve was one of the region's earliest *bastide* towns (see box, p.244), and in no time it developed into an important commercial centre, which it remains to this day. As elsewhere, its ramparts have given way to encircling boulevards, but the distinctive chequerboard street plan survives, along with two medieval gates and the old, arched bridge.

As for excursions further afield, the nearby hilltop village of **Pujols** makes for an enjoyable trip while further down the Garonne, **Aiguillon** provides a clutch of picturesque medieval lanes perfect for a wander.

Porte de Paris

The *bastide*'s principal entrance was northerly **Porte de Paris**, also the prison – one of whose occupants was an unfortunate, and incompetent, baker incarcerated for the heinous crime of turning out substandard bread. From here the semi-pedestrianized rue de Paris leads south to Villeneuve's main square, **place Lafayette**; surrounded by arcaded townhouses in brick and stone, it bursts into life on market days (Tues & Sat).

Église Ste-Catherine

The town's most striking landmark is the 55-metre-tall, octagonal red-brick tower of the **Église Ste-Catherine**, east of rue de Paris. The church was founded at the same time as the *bastide*, but then rebuilt in the late nineteenth century when it was in danger of collapse. In addition to an unusual north–south axis, the new architects chose a dramatic neo-Byzantine style, with a line of three domes above the nave, mosaic portraits of the six St Catherines – including St Catherine of Alexandria, to whom the church is dedicated, third from the left – and a multitude of saints on a frieze inspired

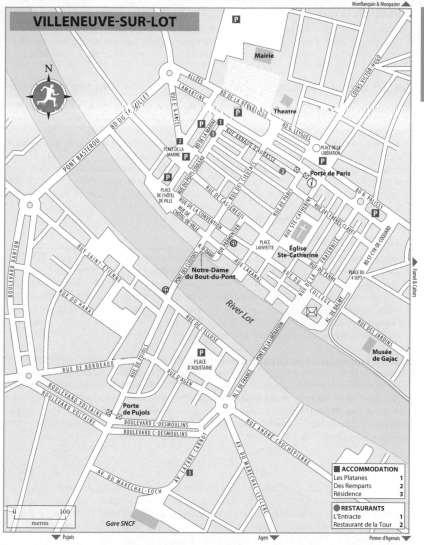

by early Christian art. A few relics of the old church remain, notably some attractive stained-glass windows, the oldest dating from the fourteenth century.

Pont des Cieutats and around

The road running parallel to rue de Paris to the west, **rue des Cieutats**, leads to the thirteenth-century **Pont des Cieutats**, originally topped with three towers reminiscent of Cahors' Pont Valentré (see p.207), and, just beside it on the north bank, a tiny chapel full of candles and votive plaques. The sixteenth-century **Notre-Dame du Bout-du-Pont** enshrines a small wooden statue of the Virgin holding Jesus gingerly in her arms. It was found in the river here by a sixteenth-century boatman when his craft mysteriously stopped midstream – or so the legend goes.

5

Musée de Gajac

2 rue des Jardins • Mon–Fri 10am–noon & 2–6pm, Sat & Sun 2–6pm • €3 • ☎ 05 53 40 48 00, ⓦ ville-villeneuve-sur-lot.fr

It's worth checking what's on at the **Musée de Gajac**, which has interesting temporary exhibitions and will give guided tours if booked in advance – ask at the tourist office (see below) for details.

ARRIVAL AND INFORMATION   VILLENEUVE-SUR-LOT

By bus SNCF runs regular bus services from Agen calling at Villeneuve's former *gare SNCF* (where there's an SNCF ticket office), five minutes' walk south of the centre, and terminating at the Hôtel de Ville.
Also buses to Pujols, Société Beyris ☎ 05 53 41 74 85, but timetables change frequently, so call for information or ask at the tourist office.
Destinations Agen (8–10 daily; 45–50min); Monflanquin (school term Mon–Fri 1 daily).
Tourist office 3 place de la Libération (July & Aug

Mon–Sat 9.30am–12.30pm & 2.30-6.30pm; Sept–June Mon–Sat 9am–noon & 2–6pm; ☎ 05 53 36 17 30, ⓦ tourisme-villeneuve-sur-lot.com).
Internet Cyberphone.com, at the corner of rue Parmentier and rue du Collège.
Market The main markets take place on Tuesday and Saturday mornings on place Lafayette, with an organic market on Wednesday mornings on place d'Aquitaine, south of the river.

ACCOMMODATION

Les Platanes 40 bd de la Marine ☎ 05 53 40 11 40, ⓦ hoteldesplatanes.com. Located on the old quarter's northwest corner, this is an old-fashioned hotel with very well-priced rooms and all spotlessly clean. Closed late-Dec to mid-Jan. Breakfast €7.50. **€52**
Des Remparts 1 rue Etienne Marcel ☎ 05 53 70 71 63, ⓦ hotel-des-remparts.eu. Welcoming, bright and very

popular, this hotel is great value. Breakfast €6. **€50**
★ **Résidence** 17 av Lazare Carnot ☎ 05 53 40 17 03, ⓦ hotellaresidence47.com. This friendly place offers unbeatable value for money, and there's a restaurant next door. Closed Christmas to mid-Jan. Garage €5. Breakfast €7.50. **€48**

EATING

L'Entracte 30 bd de la Marine ☎ 05 53 49 25 50. This elegant place caters for more traditional tastes. Their seafood in particular is highly recommended; the desserts are excellent. *Menus* from €13.90 at lunch, €23.50 in the evening including wine. Easter–Oct and mid-Nov to Easter except school hols Fri–Tues noon–1.30pm & 7.15–9pm.

Restaurant de la Tour 5 rue Arnaud d'Aubasse ☎ 05 53 71 89 70. Good little restaurant, popular with locals, which serves a lovely crêpe as well as more traditional cuisine. *Menus* from €15.90. April–Sept Sat–Thurs noon–2pm & 7–9.30pm; Oct–March Mon–Thurs noon–2pm & 7–9.30pm.

Pujols

Three kilometres south of Villeneuve, the two-street village of **PUJOLS** stands high above the plain behind its thirteenth-century ramparts. The town is a popular excursion destination, partly because it's a beguiling little place with its flowery nooks and crannies, and partly for views over the surrounding country – for locals, though, the main reason to come to Pujols is gastronomic.

Immediately inside Pujols' main north gate, it's hard to tell where the fortifications end and the Gothic **church of St-Nicolas** begins. It contains nothing of particular note, whereas the **Église Ste-Foy** (open during temporary exhibitions, which take place most of the time between April and October; free), on the far side of the market square, is decorated with fifteenth- and sixteenth-century frescoes. Though faded, many are still visible, such as St George poised over the dragon and St Catherine with her wheel of torture, both around the apse. And look out, too, for a painting in the baptismal chapel (first on the left as you enter), depicting the old bridge at Villeneuve-sur-Lot sporting its three towers.

EATING AND DRINKING   PUJOLS

Aux Délices du Puits Rue de la Citadelle ☎ 05 53 71 61 66. For somewhere smaller and less formal, try this little

place next to the well. It serves salads from €8.50 and good pizzas from €7.50. Hot food served noon–2.30pm &

6.15–9.30pm. Reservation required for evenings in off season. June–Aug daily 10.30am–10pm; Sept–May Mon & Thurs–Sat 10.30am–10pm.
La Toque Blanche ☎ 05 53 49 00 30, ⊛ la-toque -blanche.com. Top of the restaurant list for miles around is this Michelin-starred jewel, just south of Pujols with views back to the village. Dishes include lobster, truffle and foie gras salad, and stuffed pigs' trotters, but it's not outrageously expensive; weekday lunch *menus* start at €23, rising to €39 in the evenings. Mid-July to end-Oct & mid-Nov to end-June Tues–Sat noon–2pm & 7.30–9pm.

Aiguillon

Around thirty kilometres west of Pujols, the hilltop town of **AIGUILLON** stands guard over the confluence of the Lot and Garonne rivers as it has done at least since Roman times. Nowadays Aiguillon's most imposing building is the eighteenth-century, Neoclassical **Château des Ducs** – now a school – which dominates the western approach to the town. It was built by the duc d'Aiguillon who, having served as an army chief and governor of Brittany under Louis XV, returned to transform his medieval château into a mini-Versailles, though the grand balls and other festivities were soon cut short by the Revolution. The small area of medieval lanes with their half-timbered houses to the north of the château is worth a wander, and the church next to the château boasts a lovely, delicate organ.

ARRIVAL AND INFORMATION   AIGUILLON

By train Aiguillon's *gare* SNCF, on the Agen–Bordeaux train line, lies a couple of minutes' walk below the château to the southwest along avenue de la Gare.
Tourist office Beside the château on the central place du 14-Juillet (Tues–Fri 9am–noon & 2–6pm; plus June–Aug Sat 10am–noon; ☎ 05 53 79 62 58, ⊛ ville-aiguillon.eu).
Market Aiguillon's bustling markets take place on Tuesdays and Fridays.

ACCOMMODATION

La Terrasse de l'Étoile 8 cours Alsace-Lorraine ☎ 05 53 79 64 64, ⊛ hotel-restaurant.laterrassedeletoile .com. Handsome stone and brick hotel at the east end of place du 14-Juillet; they have a small pool and a good traditional restaurant. Restaurant open Mon–Thurs 12.30–2pm & 7.30pm, Fri 12.30–2pm. Breakfast €6. **€54**

The bastide country

Although *bastides*, or medieval new towns (see box, p.244), are by no means unique to this stretch of country north of the Lot, it's here that you'll find the two finest examples. The more southerly of the pair is **Monflanquin**, which makes a good place to start because of its museum outlining the history, architecture and daily life of the *bastides*. The route then heads northeast, skirting round the flanks of the imposing **Château de Biron**, before reaching **Monpazier**. This is the most typical of the *bastides*, with virtually no modern development around. There's a small museum here, too, but Monpazier's prime attraction is its atmosphere, "like a drowsy yellow cat, slumbering in the sun" as Freda White so aptly describes it in *Three Rivers of France* (see p.304).

Nevertheless, some effort is required to reach it. Neither the Château de Biron nor Monpazier is accessible by **public transport**. The best on offer is the **bus** from Villeneuve to Monflanquin, but even that is aimed at the school run.

Monflanquin

Some 17km north of Villeneuve-sur-Lot, pretty **MONFLANQUIN**, founded in 1252 by Alphonse de Poitiers, is nearly as perfectly preserved as Monpazier, though less touristy and impressively positioned on top of a hill that rises sharply from the surrounding country, visible for miles. Despite being constructed on a steep slope, it conforms to the regular pattern of right-angled streets leading from a central square to the four town

5

gates. The ramparts themselves were demolished on Richelieu's orders in 1630, but otherwise Monflanquin has experienced few radical changes since the thirteenth century.

The main square, tree-shaded **place des Arcades** – where the **market** still takes place on Thursdays as decreed in the *bastide*'s founding charter – derives a special charm from being on a slope. Its grandest building is the Gothic **Maison du Prince Noir** in the northeast corner, where the Black Prince is said to have stayed. On this north side you'll also find the high-tech **Musée des Bastides**, above the tourist office (mid-May to June & mid-Sept to Oct Mon–Sat 10am–noon & 2–6pm, Sun 3–5pm; July to mid-Sept daily 10am–7pm; Nov–April Mon–Sat 10am–noon & 2–5pm, early May also Sun 3–5pm ⓦmonflanquin-museedesbastides.jimdo.com; €4, students €1.50, under-12s free). A treasure trove of information about the life and history of *bastides*; most of the text is translated into English, but unfortunately not the audio-tapes. Then, after a quick wander through Monflanquin's old centre, it's worth heading north past the **church**, which took on its pseudo-medieval look in the early twentieth century, to end up on a terrace with expansive views northeast to the next stop, Château de Biron (see opposite).

ARRIVAL AND INFORMATION MONFLANQUIN

By bus Buses from Villeneuve-sur-Lot stop on the main road below the *bastide* in modern Monflanquin; simply walk uphill until you hit rue St-Pierre heading north to place des Arcades. **Tourist office** Place des Arcades (mid-May to June & mid-Sept to Oct Mon–Sat 10am–noon & 2–6pm, Sun 3–5pm; July to mid-Sept daily 10am–7pm; Nov–April Mon–Sat 10am–noon & 2–5pm, early May also Sun 3–5pm; ❼05 53 36 40 19, ⓦmonflanquin-tourisme.com). They can furnish you with details of the many events taking place here in summer (see box, p.203). In summer, regular tours are led by the costumed jester Janouille la Fripouille. The tours are in French only, but it's worth following along for the antics.

BASTIDES

From the Occitan *bastida*, meaning a group of buildings, **bastides** were the new towns of the thirteenth and fourteenth centuries. Although they are found all over southwest France, from the Dordogne to the foothills of the Pyrenees, there is a particularly high concentration in the area between the Dordogne and Lot rivers, which at that time formed the disputed "frontier" region between English-held Aquitaine and Capetian France.

That said, the earliest *bastides* were founded largely for **economic and political** reasons. They were a means of bringing new land into production – this was a period of rapid population growth and technological innovation – and thus extending the power of the local lord. But as tensions between the French and English forces intensified during the late thirteenth century, so the motive became increasingly **military**. The *bastides* now provided a handy way of securing the land along the frontier, and it was generally at this point that they were fortified.

As an incentive, anyone who was prepared to build, inhabit and defend the *bastide* was granted various perks and concessions in a founding **charter**. All new residents were allocated a building plot, garden and cultivable land outside the town. The charter might also offer asylum to certain types of criminal or grant exemption from military service, and would allow the election of **consuls** charged with day-to-day administration – a measure of self-government remarkable in feudal times. Taxes and judicial affairs, meanwhile, remained the preserve of the representative of the king or local lord under whose ultimate authority the *bastide* lay.

The other defining feature of a *bastide* is its **layout**. They are nearly always square or rectangular in shape, depending on the nature of the terrain, and are divided by streets at right angles to each other to produce a chequerboard pattern. The focal point is the market square, often missing its covered *halle* nowadays, but generally still surrounded by arcades, while the church is relegated to one side, or may even form part of the town walls.

The busiest *bastide* founders were **Alphonse de Poitiers** (1249–71), on behalf of the French Crown, after he became count of Toulouse in 1249, and **King Edward I of England**, Edward Plantagenet (1272–1307), who wished to consolidate his hold on the northern borders of his duchy of Aquitaine. The former chalked up a total of 57 *bastides*, including Villeneuve-sur-Lot (1251), Monflanquin (1252), Ste-Foy-la-Grande (1255) and Eymet (1270), while Edward was responsible for Beaumont (1272), Monpazier and Molières (both 1284), among others.

ACCOMMODATION

Moulin de Boulède Boulède ☎05 53 36 16 49, ⓦlemoulindeboulede.com. This is a lovely little hotel just west of Monflanquin on the D124 to Cancon, which has a handful of pleasant rooms, all en-suite. The owner's real passion, though, is his restaurant, where he specializes in fish dishes such as *filet de sole aux épinards et raviolis*. *Menus* start from a very reasonable €14 including wine and coffee (€23 in the evenings). Restaurant open Mon–Sat noon–2pm & 7.30–9pm, Sun noon–2pm. Breakfast €7.50. **€55**

EATING AND DRINKING

The best place for picnic fodder is the Thursday-morning market on place des Arcades, though you can also buy provisions at the supermarket on the main road immediately south of town. The neighbouring wine cooperative, the Cave des 7 Monts (☎05 53 36 33 40; closed Mon morn, Sat pm & Sun), represents some two hundred local vineyards producing some very palatable and reasonably priced wines; tastings are available free of charge.

La Bastide ☎05 53 36 77 05. A good option on the square, this British-run crêperie serves salads and crêpes on their lovely terrace with splendid views down the length of rue Ste-Marie. *Menus* from €12 and crêpes from €6.50. July & Aug daily noon–2pm & 7.30–9pm; rest of year Tues–Sat noon–2pm & 7.30–9pm, Sun noon–2pm.

Le Bistrot du Prince Noir ☎05 53 36 63 00. A welcoming wine bar/restaurant in the southwest corner of the square that's the pick of the village's bunch. It boasts an excellent choice of local wines (€2 a glass) and *menus* from

€15 at lunch and €27 in the evenings. May Thurs–Mon noon–2pm & 7–9pm; June & Sept Thurs–Tues noon–2pm & 7–9pm; July & Aug daily noon–2pm & 7–9pm.

Le Café de Gavaudun Gavaudun, 10km east of Monflanquin ☎05 53 40 99 34. Unassuming but extremely popular little place on the main road, serving delicious local cuisine. There is no menu, as all food is bought fresh, in local markets. An average *plat du jour* is about €14. Mid-Jan to Christmas Thurs–Tues noon–2pm & 7.30–9pm.

Château de Biron

Feb, March & Nov to mid-Dec Tues–Thurs & Sun 10am–12.30pm & 2–5.30pm; April–June & Sept to mid-Nov daily except Mon 10am–12.30pm & 2–6pm; July & Aug daily 10am–7pm • €6 • ☎05 53 05 65 65, ⓦsemitour.com

Twenty-two kilometres northeast of Monflanquin, via a picturesque route along the River Lède, the vast **Château de Biron** dominates the countryside for miles around. It was begun in the eleventh century and added to piecemeal over the years by the Gontaut-Biron family, who occupied the castle right up to the early twentieth century. The biggest alterations were made in the fifteenth and early sixteenth centuries, when Pons de Gontaut-Biron started reconstructing the eastern wing. The result is an architectural primer, from the medieval keep through flamboyant Gothic and Renaissance to an eighteenth-century loggia in the style of Versailles.

Rather than the guided tour (in French only; 45min–1hr), at busy times it's better to borrow the English-language text from the ticket desk and wander at will. The most striking building in the grassy **lower court** is the Renaissance chapel, where the sarcophagi of Pons and his brother Armand, bishop of Sarlat, lie. Though their statues were hacked about during the Revolution, the Italianate biblical scenes and three Virtues carved on the sides still show fine craftsmanship. On entering the cobbled and confined **inner courtyard** around its twelfth-century keep, the route takes you to a dungeon and through the lord's apartments, with their Renaissance chimney and wood-panelled hall, to a vast reception room and an equally capacious stone-vaulted refectory. If the rooms decked out as a tannery, torture chamber and weavers' workshop make you feel as though you're walking through a film set, you are – Biron is a favourite for period dramas, the most recent being *Le Pacte des Loups* in 2000.

ACCOMMODATION AND EATING   CHÂTEAU DE BIRON

Auberge du Château Château de Biron ☎05 53 63 13 33. Beside the path up to the castle, the *Auberge* has a good midweek lunch *menu* at €13 (€26 in the evenings). March–Oct daily noon–2pm & 7–9pm.

Le Moulinal Lacapelle-Biron ☎05 53 40 84 60, ⓦlemoulinal.com. Lacapelle-Biron boasts one of the region's best campsites beside a leisure lake. It has two pools, a shop, an internet café and a good restaurant and

5

bar (daily 2–9pm). Closed mid-Sept to April. **€8.50**
Le Palissy Place du Monument aux Morts, Lacapelle-Biron. Head southeast 5km – by road or on the GR36 footpath – to Lacapelle-Biron and you'll find this friendly little place on the main road. It has a Dutch chef and consequently rather a

polyglot atmosphere. It also caters for vegetarians and is extremely popular with locals. The excellent-value regional *menus* start from €11 at lunch and €18 in the evenings. Daily noon–2pm, plus April–Sept daily 7.30–9.30pm & Oct–March Wed & Fri–Mon 7.30–9.30pm.

Monpazier

From the Château de Biron it's only another 8km north to **MONPAZIER**, the finest and most complete of the surviving *bastides*, made up of a lovely warm-coloured stone on a hill above the River Dropt. Founded in 1284 by King Edward I of England on land granted by Pierre de Gontaut-Biron, and picturesque and placid though it is today, Monpazier has a hard and bitter history, being twice – in 1594 and 1637 – the centre of **peasant rebellions** provoked by the misery that followed the Wars of Religion (see p.295). Both uprisings were brutally suppressed: the 1637 peasants' leader was broken on the wheel in the square and his head paraded around the countryside. In an earlier episode, Sully, the Protestant general, describes a rare moment of light relief in the terrible **Wars of Religion**, when the men of Catholic Villefranche-de-Périgord planned to capture Monpazier on the same night as the men of Monpazier were headed for Villefranche. By chance, the two sides took different routes, met no resistance, looted to their hearts' content and returned congratulating themselves on their luck and skill, only to find that things were rather different at home. The peace terms were that everything should be returned to its proper place.

Place des Cornières

After such a turbulent past, it comes as something of a surprise to find Monpazier has survived so well. Three of its six **medieval gates** are still intact and its central square, **place des Cornières**, couldn't be more perfect with its oak-pillared *halle* and time-worn, stone-built houses, no two the same. Deep, shady arcades pass beneath all the houses, which are separated from each other by a small gap to reduce fire risk; at the corners the buttresses are cut away to allow the passage of laden pack animals. On Thursday mornings the square comes to life for the weekly **market**, which expands on the third Thursday of each month into a fair. In mushroom season (roughly Aug & Sept depending on the weather) people also come here in the afternoons to sell their pickings, while in December there's a truffle market.

Monpazier's main north–south axis is **rue Notre-Dame**, which brings you into the northeast corner of place des Cornières, past the much-altered **church**. The thirteenth-century building opposite is a bit battered, but this is Monpazier's oldest house, where the tax collector received his share of the harvest.

Ateliers des Bastides

May–Oct Wed–Mon 10am–12.30pm & 2.30–7pm • Free

The local museum, the **Ateliers des Bastides**, sits west of place des Cornières along rue Jean-Galmot, and boasts a few prehistoric remains and other historical bits and pieces. However, it is largely devoted to local adventurer Jean Galmot, who was born here in 1879 and was assassinated in 1928 in French Guiana, then a penal colony, where he was aiding its fledgling independence movement. There is, however, no information in English.

During the summer months the museum also hosts a number of temporary **art exhibitions**, and the town puts on all sorts of other events to draw the tourists, from book fairs to medieval jamborees (see box, p.203). Outside these occasions, however, there's not much else to do in Monpazier beyond soak up the sun at a café on the market square.

5

INFORMATION

MONPAZIER

Tourist office Place des Cornières (July & Aug daily 10am–12.30pm & 2–7pm; Sept–June Tues–Sat 10am–12.30pm & 2–6.30pm, Sun 2–5pm; ☎ 05 53 22 68 59, ⊛ pays-des-bastides.com). Among all sorts of useful information, they produce a free DIY tour of the town, with information in English and games for children, and a book of eleven way-marked walks in the area (€2.50).

ACCOMMODATION

Camping de Véronne 3km northwest in Marsalès ☎ 05 53 22 65 50. Pleasantly located next to a lake, this small campsite has two sailboats for children (free) and a restaurant/bar. Closed mid-Sept to mid-June. €35

Edward 1er ☎ 05 53 22 44 00, ⊛ hoteledward1er.com. Housed in a nineteenth-century château, these luxurious rooms offer peace and quiet, while the restaurant downstairs is extremely popular and reservation is essential in high season. *Menus* from €30. Restaurant open March–June & Sept to mid-Nov Thurs–Tues 7.30–9pm; July & Aug daily 7.30–9pm. Breakfast €12. €104

De France 21 rue St-Jacques ☎ 05 53 22 60 06, ⊛ hoteldefrancemonpazier.fr. Occupies a lovely medieval building on the southwest corner of place des Cornières. It has a fine regional restaurant serving *menus* from €18, while in summer it also offers lighter brasserie-style fare. Restaurant open Easter to mid-Oct Mon–Thurs noon–2pm & 7–9pm, Fri noon–2pm, Sat noon–2pm & 7–9pm, Sun noon–2pm. Breakfast €9. €55

Le Moulin de David ☎ 05 53 22 65 25, ⊛ moulin-de-david.com. Luxurious four-star campsite in the Dropt valley that's a favourite with tourists, so reserve well in advance. Facilities include a lovely pool, two restaurants and bar, shop and children's play area. Closed Oct–March. €24

EATING AND DRINKING

You'll eat very well in the two hotel restaurants (see above). Alternatively the cafés and bars around place des Cornières are perfect for a sunny lunch or cool afternoon drink. You could also turn north and wander along rue Notre-Dame.

Bistrot 2 ☎ 05 53 22 60 64, ⊛ bistrot2.fr. Just outside the town walls, this little bistro is owned by the same people as the *Edward 1er* (see above) and you can sit out on the terrace watching the world go by as you sample their local ingredients. *Menu* €30. June–Sept daily noon–2pm & 7.30–9pm; Oct–May Mon noon–2pm, Tues–Thurs noon–2pm & 7.30–9pm, Sat 7.30–9pm.

Le Privilège du Périgord 58 rue Notre-Dame ☎ 05 53 22 43 98, ⊛ privilegeperigord.com. A good bet, comprising a number of cosy dining rooms plus tables in the courtyard. *Menus* from €19.50 lunch and €24.50 eves. April–Oct Tues–Sun noon–2.30pm & 7.30–9.30pm.

South of the River Lot

NAJAC

South of the River Lot

The southern border of the Dordogne and Lot region is defined by the River Garonne in the west and by the Tarn and Aveyron in the east. On the whole this area to the south of the Lot offers less dramatic scenery than further north, but by the same token it sees fewer tourists. It is a fertile land, full of sunflowers and fruit orchards, particularly along the Garonne and spreading over the hills to the north: plums, pears, peaches, cherries, apples, apricots and nectarines all grow here, as well as melons, strawberries and the succulent chasselas grapes.

The first of the region's two gateways is **Agen**, the only major town on the Garonne between Bordeaux and Toulouse and more pleasant than it first appears, with an old centre built of pink-mottled brick and a fine local museum. Southwest of Agen, what's left of **Nérac**'s castle and its riverside pleasure gardens – where King Henry IV misspent his youth – still exudes a slightly decadent air. The river here is the Baïse, which flows north to join the Garonne near **Buzet-sur-Baïse**, in the centre of a small wine region.

Upstream from Agen, the region's unmissable sight is the abbey church at **Moissac**, with its wonderful carvings. The Garonne valley here is at its flattest and most featureless, but north of Moissac things improve as you climb up onto the low, rolling plateau of the **Quercy Blanc**, which stretches north almost to Cahors. It's a region of white-stone farmhouses, sun-drenched hilltop villages, windmills and *pigeonniers* – pigeon houses, often raised on stilts – by the hundred. Of these, the prettiest village is **Lauzerte**, but **Montpezat-de-Quercy** also merits a visit for its display of religious art, including a series of superb tapestries.

Near Montpezat the N20 and the A20 *autoroute* mark the eastern extent of the Quercy Blanc and funnel traffic south to **Montauban**. This brick-red city, not far north of Toulouse and on the Paris main line, is the region's second gateway, and justifies a few hours' exploration thanks to its art museum and central square surrounded by elegant townhouses. It sits on the banks of the Tarn in the midst of an alluvial plain, which, in the east, gives way abruptly to hills. Running through them, the stunning **Gorges de l'Aveyron** are punctuated with ancient villages perched high above the river, while **St-Antonin-Noble-Val**, with its core of medieval lanes, lies in the valley bottom caught between soaring limestone crags. Beyond St-Antonin, it's worth making a short detour south across the plateau to the aptly named **Cordes-sur-Ciel**, where noble facades line the steeply cobbled lanes, before rejoining the Aveyron beneath **Najac**'s much-contested fortress. The gorge opens out to the north of Najac, but it's worth continuing the last few kilometres to **Villefranche-de-Rouergue**, in the centre of which, in the monstrous shadow of its church tower, lies a perfectly preserved arcaded market square.

CLOISTER AT THE ÉGLISE ABBATIALE ST-PIERRE, MOISSAC

Highlights

❶ Moissac The carvings decorating the south porch and cloister of Moissac's abbey church are masterpieces of Romanesque art. **See p.261**

❷ Quercy Blanc Take time to savour the bucolic countryside between the Garonne and Lot valleys, dotted with vines, sunflowers and sleepy hilltop villages. **See p.266**

❸ Lauzerte Set on a hilltop amid the fruitful fields of the Quercy Blanc, this perfectly preserved bastide village offers outstanding views. **See p.266**

❹ St-Antonin-Noble-Val A compact and charming medieval town set against the limestone cliffs of the Gorges de l'Aveyron. **See p.277**

❺ Cordes-sur-Ciel Perched on its knuckle of rock, this fortified town is the jewel of the Tarn and a favourite haunt of artists and artisans. **See p.280**

❻ Château de Najac Climb the tower of Alphonse de Poitier's erstwhile stronghold for vertiginous views over the Aveyron valley. **See p.282**

❼ Villefranche-de-Rouergue The arcaded and sloping central square makes a superb setting for the weekly market. **See p.283**

HIGHLIGHTS ARE MARKED ON THE MAP ON PP.252–253

6

By train Three major train lines fan out across this region from Toulouse: along the Garonne valley to Montauban, Moissac and Agen; north via Montpezat to Cahors; and northeast through Cordes, Najac and Villefranche en route to Figeac.

By bus Bus services in the region are limited and patchy, often running only at school times. There is one regular service between Agen and Nérac, while Montcuq,

Montauban and Villefranche-de-Rouergue all link up with Cahors.

By boat A good way to get about is by boat on the Canal de Garonne, which shadows the Garonne for nearly 200km from near Langon in the east, passing through Buzet, Agen and Moissac, among other places, to Toulouse, where it joins the Canal du Midi.

Agen and around

AGEN, capital of the Lot-et-Garonne *département*, lies on the broad, powerful River Garonne halfway between Bordeaux and Toulouse. Close to the A62 *autoroute* and connected to both cities by fast and frequent train services, and to Paris by train and plane, it provides a useful gateway to the southern reaches of the Dordogne and Lot region. However, Agen is more than just a transport hub. Inside the ring of hypermarkets and industrial estates lies a core of old lanes lined with handsome brick houses, several churches worth a look and a surprisingly good fine arts museum. Add to that a number of excellent restaurants and a good choice of hotels. Make sure you try some prunes while you're there – pruneaux d'Agen are world famous and the basis for many local desserts.

Agen makes for a pleasant half-day's exploration, or a base from which to cover the surrounding country. The most interesting jaunts take you southwest to **Nérac**, where kings and queens disported themselves on the Baïse's wooded banks, and west to the wine town of **Buzet-sur-Baïse**.

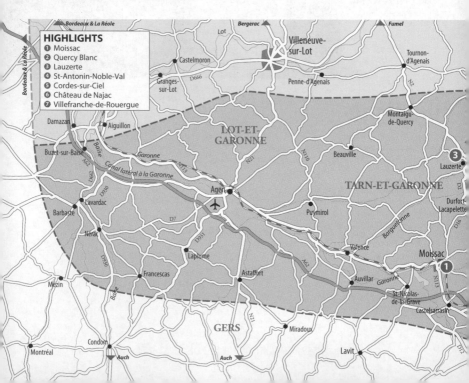

The old centre

The old centre of Agen lies on the east bank of the Garonne. It is quartered by two nineteenth-century boulevards – **boulevard de la République**, running east–west, and north–south **boulevard du Président-Carnot** – which intersect at place Goya and make for easy navigation. To the northeast stands **Cathédrale St-Caprais**, somewhat misshapen but worth a look for its finely proportioned Romanesque apse and radiating chapels.

6

Musée des Beaux-Arts

Daily except Tues: May–Sept 10am–6pm, Oct–April 10am–12.30pm & 1.30–6pm • €4.40 • ☎ 05 53 69 47 23, ⓦ agen.fr

Agen's foremost sight lies southwest on place Dr-Esquirol: beside the exuberant, Italianate municipal theatre, the **Musée des Beaux-Arts** is magnificently housed in four adjacent sixteenth- and seventeenth-century mansions adorned with stair turrets and Renaissance window details. Inside you'll find a rich variety of archeological exhibits, furniture and paintings – among the latter, a number of Goyas and a Tintoretto rediscovered during an inventory in 1997. Best, though, are the basement's Roman finds, which include intricate jewellery and a superb white-marble Venus.

Église des Jacobins and around

Temporary art exhibitions daily except Tues 2–6pm • Prices vary

To the west of place Dr-Esquirol, a clutch of brick and timber houses – the bricks forming neat zigzags within the timber frame – represent Agen's most attractive corner. From here a short and narrow alley, **rue Beauville**, cuts through to rue Richard-Coeur-de-Lion, with more eye-catching facades and the **Église des Jacobins**. This big, brick Dominican church was founded by Dominican monks in the thirteenth century, then

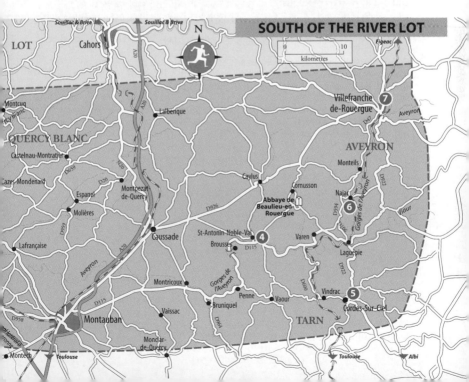

6

FESTIVALS, EVENTS AND MARKETS

Mid-May Montauban: Alors, Chante! (☎05 63 63 66 77, ⓦalorschante.com). Over Ascension weekend various well-known, and not-so-well-known, artists take part in this festival of French song (tickets required).

Late May or early June Moissac: Fêtes de Pentecôte (☎05 63 04 63 63). A traditional fair on the banks of the Tarn over the Whitsun weekend, with fireworks on the Monday night.

July and August Moissac: Les Soirs de Moissac (☎05 63 04 06 81). Varied programme of concerts, choral works and recitals, including world music, held in the cloister or the church of St-Pierre (tickets required).

Mid-July Villefranche-de-Rouergue: VISA Francophone (☎05 65 45 41 12, ⓦvisa-francophone .com). A one-week competition of French song held in the streets of Villefranche. Some ticket-only events, proceeds go to charity.

Mid-July Cordes-sur-Ciel: Fête du Grand Fauconnier (☎05 65 56 34 63, ⓦgrandfauconnier .com). This two-day medieval festival converts the town into a costumed extravaganza, complete with exhibitions on medieval crafts and falconry. Daily admission to the old town is €9, and you can hire medieval costumes for the occasion.

Early July to early August Montauban and around: Jazz à Montauban (☎05 63 63 56 56, ⓦjazzmontauban.com). International jazz and blues artists play in Montauban and various other towns around the *département* (tickets required for most events). There's also a "festival off" with free concerts in the cafés and streets of Montauban.

Late July Cordes-sur-Ciel: Musique sur Ciel (☎05 63 56 00 75, ⓦfestivalmusiquesurciel.fr). Ten days of classical concerts, some by featured contemporary composers, in the church of St-Michel.

Late July to mid-August Lauzerte and around: Festival du Quercy Blanc (☎05 65 31 83 12). Concerts of classical and chamber music held mostly in churches around the region, including Lauzerte, Montcuq, Montpezat-de-Quercy and Castelnau-Montratier. Tickets available from local tourist offices.

End of July or start of August Lauzerte: Les Nuits de Lauzerte (☎05 63 94 61 94, ⓦnuitsdelauzerte.free.fr). Over the space of a weekend, Lauzerte becomes an art installation and performance space, through which you walk at night, taking your time and wandering at your own pace past street theatre, contemporary dance, music and projections. Tickets from the tourist office (€10).

Early August Villefranche-de-Rouergue and around: Festival en Bastides (☎05 65 45 76 74, ⓦespaces-culturels.fr). Five days of contemporary theatre and performance art animate the streets of Villefranche and Najac, amongst other places. Some ticketed events, information from any participating tourist office.

Third weekend in September Moissac: Fête du Chasselas and Fête des Fruits et des Légumes (☎05 63 04 63 63). Every year the Fête du Chasselas celebrates the local grape, with tastings on offer and a competition to find the pick of the bunch; the event takes place in the market hall. Every two years (in the odd years) the whole range of local fruits plus vegetables are also on display and there are all manner of related events throughout the town.

Second weekend in October Auvillar: Marché Potier (☎05 63 39 57 33). Some forty exhibitors take part in this important pottery fair held on the place de la Halle.

MARKETS

The main **markets** in the region are at Agen (Sat & Sun); Cordes (Sat); Laguépie (Wed & Sun); Lauzerte (Wed & Sat); Moissac (Sat & Sun); Montauban (Weds & Sat); Montcuq (Sun); Nérac (Sat); St-Antonin-Noble-Val (Sun); St-Nicolas-de-la-Grave (Mon); and Villefranche-de-Rouergue (Thurs).

served as the Protestants' headquarters before being used as a prison during the Revolution. It now forms an annexe of the Musée des Beaux-Arts and hosts temporary art exhibitions. Inside, you can see unusual Gothic frescoes of leaves and geometric patterns in trompe-l'oeil on the walls and ceiling.

West of the church is the river and the public gardens of **Esplanade du Gravier**, where a footbridge crosses the Garonne – from it you can see a 550-metre **canal bridge** dating from 1843 further downstream.

ARRIVAL AND DEPARTURE   AGEN

By plane Flights from Paris arrive at Agen's La Garenne airport, around 3km southwest of town; a taxi into the centre costs roughly €20. Airlinair (⚙airlinair.com) operates flights to Paris Orly from Agen's La Garenne airport.
Destinations Paris Orly (3 daily Mon–Fri, 1 on Sun; 1hr 30min).

By train The gare SNCF is located on the north side of town. From in front of the station, boulevard du Président-Carnot leads south to place Goya, where it crosses the town's other main thoroughfare, the east–west boulevard de la République.

Destinations Bordeaux (up to 19 daily; 1hr–1hr 20min); Moissac (5–9 daily; 25–45min); Monsempron-Libos (4–8 daily; 35–45min); Montauban (6–9 daily; 40–50min); Périgueux (3–5 daily; 7hr–7hr 20min); La Réole (7–9 daily; 50min); Toulouse (12–14 daily; 1hr–1hr 15min).

By bus The gare routière is next to the gare SNCF. For up-to-date bus schedules ask at the tourist office or phone the transport desk of the Conseil Général on ☎ 05 53 69 42 03.
Destinations Nérac (Mon–Fri 4 daily, 5 in school times; 40min); Villeneuve-sur-Lot (5–10 daily; 45min).

By car Free car parking can be found along the riverbank and on place du 14-Juillet.

GETTING AROUND AND INFORMATION

Bike rental Méca Plus, 18–20 av du Général-de-Gaulle (☎ 05 53 47 76 76, ⚙ comptoir-du-deux-roues.fr; closed Sun).

Car rental Avis, 12 bd Sylvain Dumon, near the train station and at the airport (☎ 05 53 47 76 47); Europcar, 120 bd du Président-Carnot and near the train station (☎ 05 53 47 37 40).

Taxis There is a taxi stand at the train station, or call Agen Taxis 9 (☎ 06 09 37 07 74).

Tourist office 38 rue Garonne (July & Aug Mon–Sat 9am–7pm, Sun 9.30am–12.30pm; Sept–June Mon–Sat 9am–12.30pm & 2–6.30pm ☎ 05 53 47 36 09, ⚙ ot-agen .org).

ACCOMMODATION

Agen has some good hotel options scattered around its centre, especially at the budget end, though you'll also find four-star luxury at a reasonable price. There's a clutch of chain hotels at the exit from the autoroute.

★ **Des Ambans** 59 rue des Ambans ☎ 05 53 66 28 60. The best value of the budget hotels, with nine small, tidy rooms; note that all but the most expensive lack an en-suite toilet. It's clean, friendly and central, which means you need to book well ahead for the summer season. Oct–March occasionally closed weekends. Breakfast €6. **€40**

Camping Moulin de Mellet ☎ 05 53 87 50 98, ⚙ camping-moulin-mellet.com. Eight kilometres west of Agen in St Hilaire de Lusignan lies this friendly campsite, boasting two swimming pools and a small restaurant. At the time of writing the campsite was changing ownership; check the website for the most up-to-date prices and opening seasons.

Des Îles 25 rue Baudin ☎ 05 53 47 11 33, ⚙ hotel-des -iles.fr. This family-run hotel boasts ten lovely, individually decorated rooms, some with a small balcony and all en suite. Breakfast €6.90. **€47**

★ **Des Jacobins** 1 place des Jacobins ☎ 05 53 47 03 31, ⚙ chateau-des-jacobins.com. Oozing character, Agen's top hotel occupies an elegant nineteenth-century town house swathed in greenery beside the Jacobins church, and its rooms are decked out with antique furniture, gilt mirrors and plush fabrics. Breakfast €10. **€130**

Le Périgord 42 cours du 14-Juillet ☎ 05 53 77 55 77, ⚙ leperigord47.com. This large hotel is stuck in a bit of a traffic island; however, the rooms, decked out in country

---

BOAT TRIPS ALONG THE CANAL DE GARONNE

The Canal de Garonne (formerly known as the Canal latéral à la Garonne) was once part of a heaving artery of commerce, forming part of the great Canal de Deux Mers, linking the Canal du Midi at Toulouse with the Garonne River. This in turn finally connected the Mediterranean to the Atlantic. Today the peaceful waterways are given over to pleasure, the canal is clean and overhung with trees, and flotillas of ducks replace the commercial barges. **Locaboat Plaisance** (☎ 05 53 66 00 74, ⚙ locaboat.com) offers cruises along the canal from March to October; prices vary from €860–1600 per week for a 3–5 person boat, depending on the season and the level of comfort.

6

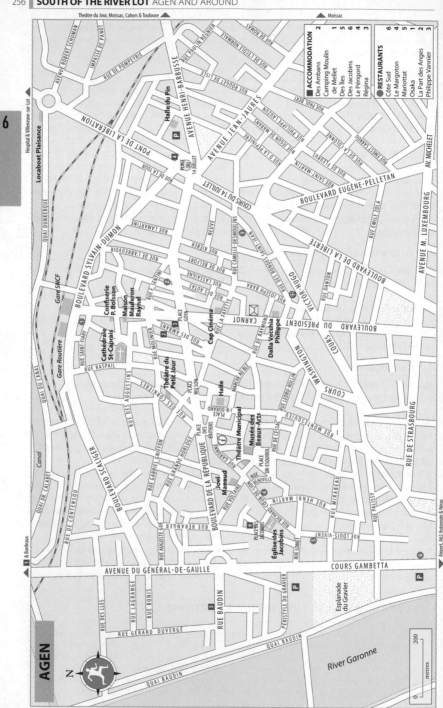

AGEN

N

0   200
metres

River Garonne

Theatre du Jour, Moissac, Cahors & Toulouse

Moissac

Hospital & Villeneuve-sur-Lot

Locaboat Plaisance

1 & Bordeaux

Airport, A62 Autoroute & Nérac

■ ACCOMMODATION	
Des Ambans	2
Camping Moulin de Mellet	1
Des Iles	5
Des Jacobins	6
Le Périgord	4
Regina	3

● RESTAURANTS	
Côte Sud	6
Le Margoton	4
Mariottat	5
Osaka	1
La Part des Anges	2
Philippe Vannier	3

PRUNEAUX D'AGEN

Agen grew rich at first on the trade of manufactured goods, such as cloth and leather, flowing through its river port, but the industrial revolution put paid to all that and since then the town's prosperity has been based on agriculture – in particular, its famous **prunes** and **plums**. Plums (*prunes* in French) were introduced to France by crusaders returning from Syria in the eleventh century. It is believed that Benedictine monks at Clairac, near the confluence of the Lot and Garonne, were the first to cultivate the fruit, a variety known as *prune d'Ente*, which thrives on sun, high humidity and chalky soils and is also excellent for drying thanks to its size and high sugar content. Though plums now grow throughout the region, the dried fruit (*pruneaux*) were originally exported via the port at Agen – and are thus known as **pruneaux d'Agen**.

Nowadays **prunes** are one of the region's principal money-spinners and in late August the orchards are a hive of activity as the ripe fruit are shaken from the trees. They are dried slowly in hot-air ovens to retain the flavour – during which process they lose three-quarters of their weight. Even so, the biggest prunes weigh in at 20g.

You can learn more facts and figures about prune production in the specialist *confiseries* of Agen (see p.258) and also at an enjoyable **farm-museum**, Au Pruneau Gourmand (mid-March to mid-Oct daily 9am–noon & 2–7pm, Sun 3–7pm; mid-Oct to mid-March Mon–Sat 9am–noon & 2–6.30pm, Sun 2–6.30pm; closed last 2 weeks in Jan; adults €3.80, under-12s free; ℗musee -du-pruneau.com), near the village of Granges-sur-Lot, 10km northeast of Aiguillon (see p.243). In mid-September, nearby St-Aubin hosts a fair devoted to the prune, lasting several days. Call Monflanquin tourist office (☎05 53 49 55 80) for information.

---

florals, are spacious, comfortable and reasonably priced and the restaurant serves good local fare (*menus* €17.50 at lunch, €23.50 in the evenings). Restaurant open daily noon–2pm & 7–9.45pm. Breakfast €8. **€56**

Régina 139 bd du Président-Carnot ☎05 53 47 07 97, ℗hotelreginagen.com. Rambling and welcoming hotel on the main road south of the station; ask for a quieter room at the back. The cheaper rooms don't have toilets, but the rest have good-sized bathrooms and modern, pale-wood furnishings, and the buffet breakfast is better than most. If you are arriving outside reception opening hours (4–8pm weekdays, variable at weekends), call in advance to get the door code. Breakfast €6.50. **€68**

EATING AND DRINKING

The best place to look for somewhere to eat in Agen is within the rough semi-circle between boulevard de la République, rue des Cornières and rue Emile Sentini, plus along rue La Fayette and its extension rue Camille Desmoulins running east from boulevard Carnot. Ethnic restaurants and fast-food outlets sit on rue Voltaire and rue Garonne further west, while there are a couple of decent cafés on boulevard de la République and at its western junction with avenue du Général-de-Gaulle.

Côte Sud 36 cours Gambetta ☎05 53 96 16 67, ℗restau-cotesud.com. A modern take on a traditional family restaurant, stylishly decorated in subdued mauves with comfortable seating and down-lighting. *Menus* feature local cuisine from €12 at lunch, along with €22 for a market *menu* rising to about €35 to eat á la carte. Mon–Sat noon–1.30pm & 7.30–9pm, Sun 7.30–9pm.

Le Margoton 52 rue Richard-Cœur-de-Lion ☎05 53 48 11 55, ℗lemargoton.com. Stylish little place near the Jacobins church, serving a good range of seafood in addition to rich game dishes such as guinea fowl, pigeon and venison. Menus start at €16.50 for lunch and go up to €35 in the evening. Early Jan to mid-July & Aug to mid-Dec Tues–Fri & Sat eve noon–1.30pm & 7.45–9.45pm.

Mariottat 25 rue Louis Vivent ☎05 53 77 99 77, ℗restaurant-mariottat.com. Agen's most elegant restaurant occupies a grand old villa with a sumptuous interior. It concentrates on mostly local produce, including duck in all its guises, with beautifully presented *menus* starting at a very reasonable €26 for lunch and rising to €48 and above in the evenings and at weekends. Eating à la carte will set you back about €70. Tues–Fri noon–1.15pm & 8–9.15pm, Sat 8–9.15pm, Sun noon–1.15pm.

Osaka 38 bd Sylvain Dumon ☎05 53 66 31 76, ℗osaka -agen.fr. Japanese place opposite the station serving good sushi, *teppanyaki* and noodle soups. There is a €15 evening *menu*, though à la carte is pricey. July tomid-June, Tues–Sat noon–2pm & 7–10pm.

La Part des Anges 14 rue Emile Sentini ☎05 53 68 31 00, ℗lapartdesanges.eu. This refined little restaurant is the place to go for well-prepared and presented local dishes, such as black Gascon pork, beef from Duras and

6

cheeses aged on the premises. In summer they put a few tables outside in the pedestrian-only street; *menus* from €21. Jan to mid-Feb, March–Aug & mid-Sept to mid-Dec Tues–Sat noon–1pm & 7–9.30pm.

Philippe Vannier 66 rue Camille Desmoulins ☎ 05 53 66 63 70, ⊕ philippe-vannier.com. A stylish restaurant with a cool, art-lined dining room. There's a good-value lunchtime *formule* for €22, rising to €42 in the evenings; the inventive menu includes langoustines marinated in lime, and a range of indulgent desserts such as chocolate mousse with orange and mango jam. Note that reservations are essential on Sundays. Mon 7.45–9pm, Tues–Sat noon–1pm & 7.45–9pm, Sun noon–1pm.

ENTERTAINMENT

Agen has a reputation for its thespian activities; there are several theatre groups that perform in the open air, both in Agen and nearby towns; ask at the tourist office (see p.255). If you prefer the big screen there is a large multi-screen cinema on boulevard Carnot.

Théâtre du Jour 21 rue Paulin-Régnier ☎ 05 53 47 82 08, ⊕ theatredujour.fr. Stages innovative works and doubles as a drama school.

Théâtre Municipal Place Dr-Esquirol ☎ 05 53 66 26 60, ⊕ agen.fr. Puts on a varied programme of theatre, dance, concerts and opera by local, national and international artists.

Cap cinema d'Agen 78 bd du Président-Carnot ☎ 05 53 47 06 95, ⊕ capcimema.com. A huge multi-screen cinema in the centre of town; tickets from €5.80.

MARKETS AND SHOPPING

The main shopping streets are boulevard de la République and boulevard du Président-Carnot, while pedestrianized rue Molinier, south of the cathedral, has a few smarter boutiques. The thing to buy in Agen is prunes (see box, p.257). You'll find them in the markets and at a number of specialist shops (see below).

Markets A fresh produce market takes place daily except Mon in the covered market on place Jean-Baptiste Durand. There is also a large farmers' market held on Wednesday and Sunday mornings in the Halle du Pin, beside place du 14-Juillet, as well as a smaller one on Saturday mornings on the Esplanade du Gravier, and an organic market, also on Saturdays, on place des Laitiers, off boulevard de la République. The most interesting of several agricultural fairs are the *foire de la prune* (first or second Mon after Sept 15), devoted to plums and prunes, and the *foire aux oies et canards gras* (second Sun in Dec) for foie gras and all manner of products made from duck and goose. The fairs take place in varying locations around the town centre; contact the tourist office (see p.255) for further information.

Maison Mauferon Raynal 165 bd du Président-Carnot ☎ 05 53 66 37 65. For picnic supplies try this lovely bakery at the junction of boulevard du Président-Carnot and cours Washington.

Dalla Vecchia Philippe 62 bd du Président-Carnot ☎ 05 53 66 28 82. A good *boucherie*, a few doors down from the bakery; if you're looking for barbecue fodder this would be a good bet.

Joel Manaud 37 rue Voltaire ☎ 05 53 66 67 63. The place to go for charcuterie; they also stock a wide range of tempting salad options.

Confiserie P. Boisson 20 rue Grande-Horloge ☎ 05 53 66 20 61. Opened in 1835 and still using traditional methods to produce chocolate prunes, truffle prunes, prunes in armagnac and stuffed prunes, among other delicacies. You can also ask to see a short explanatory film in English.

DIRECTORY

Hospital Centre Hospitalier, rte de Villeneuve (☎ 05 53 69 70 71), located 1.5km northeast of central Agen on the N21 to Villeneuve-sur-Lot.

Internet The library on place Armand Fallières has wi-fi facilities, though opening hours are limited especially in July & Aug.

Police Commissariat de Police, 4 rue Palissy (☎ 05 53 68 17 00), situated to the south of the old quarter.

Post office 72 bd du Président-Carnot.

Nérac

Thirty kilometres across high, rolling hills to the southwest of Agen, you come to the castle town of **NÉRAC** on the banks of the River Baïse. It's hard to believe that this drowsy backwater, seat of the **d'Albret** family, once matched the Parisian court in its splendour and extravagance, or that the bitter rivalries between Protestant and Catholic were played out here. Nowadays, it's an attractive and prosperous little place, where you can happily spend a few hours wandering the riverbanks and what's left of the d'Albrets' **castle**.

The d'Albrets first came to Nérac around 1150 and over the next three centuries grew to become one of Aquitaine's most powerful dynasties – largely through a talent for marrying well. First they gained the Pyrenean kingdom of Navarre by marriage, and then in 1527 Henry II d'Albret wed **Marguerite d'Angoulême**, sister to King Francis I of France. Intelligent and cultured, Marguerite filled her Nérac court with scholars and proponents of the new Protestant faith, including Jean Chauvin (John Calvin), who stayed here briefly in 1534. Neither Henry nor Marguerite converted, but their determined and ambitious daughter, **Jeanne d'Albret**, did so in 1560, thus making Nérac an important Protestant stronghold. Jeanne's son, also Henry, for his part married the young and beautiful **Marguerite de Valois**, sister of the king of France and Catherine de Médicis, in 1572 and so ushered in Nérac's golden era. Their court glittered with eminent writers, diplomats and nobles, poets and musicians, while Henry indulged in the innumerable amorous conquests that earned him the nickname *Le Vert Galant*; Queen Margot, as she was called, was no retiring violet either, and the marriage was eventually annulled in 1599, by which time Henry had become **Henry IV** of France and removed his court to Paris.

The château

April–Sept daily 10am–6pm; Oct–March Tues–Thurs 10am–6pm, Sat & Sun 2–6pm • €4, under-12s free

Throughout their glory days, the d'Albrets added to their **château** on the river's west bank, at the far end of the bridge coming into Nérac from Agen. By the sixteenth century they had made it into a comfortable palace, of which only the north wing with its Renaissance gallery still exists, the other three having been partially destroyed in 1621 and finished off during the Revolution. It now houses a local history museum, of which the most interesting displays relate to Henry, Queen Margot and their larger-than-life relatives.

Église St-Nicolas

North of the château stands the Neoclassical **Église St-Nicolas,** which was built in the mid-eighteenth century and contains some attractive nineteenth-century stained-glass windows, depicting scenes from the Old and New Testaments. From the terrace here you get good views of the triple-arched **Pont-Vieux** and the ancient roofs of the area known as **Petit-Nérac** on the opposite side of the river. It's worth wandering over the bridge and turning right along rue Séderie, where the wooden balconies of old tanneries overhang the river, to come out beside Nérac "port", now bustling with cruise boats in summer, below the Pont-Neuf.

La Garenne

South from the port across the main road, avenue Georges Clemenceau, a shady woodland path, leads 1.5km along the riverbank. **La Garenne**, as the area is known, was laid out as a royal pleasure park in the sixteenth century. The aviaries of exotic birds, the arbours and minstrels have long gone, but it's still a pleasant place to stroll or picnic. Not far from the entrance, look out for the **Fontaine de Fleurette**, marked by a statue of a prostrate and scantily clad young woman. According to legend, Fleurette was a gardener's daughter who had the misfortune to be seduced by *Le Vert Galant* and, when his attentions drifted elsewhere, drowned herself in the river. The inscription reads: "She gave him all her life. He gave her but one day."

Cap Cauderoue

April, May & Oct Wed, Sat & Sun 1.30–6pm; June & Sept Wed, Sat & Sun 11am–6pm; July & Aug daily 9.30am–8pm • €16, under 20 years old €8 • ☎ 05 53 65 52 74, ⟨w⟩ cap-cauderoue.com

Cap Cauderoue, 5km west of Nérac, is a treetop adventure playground, where visitors make their way, via ropes and swings, around an obstacle course high above the ground. The site also offers **mountain biking** and archery. It is popular with older children and teens; a little muscle is required.

ARRIVAL AND DEPARTURE   NÉRAC

By bus Citram buses (☎ 05 56 43 68 43) from Agen stop on the central place de la Libération, next to the château.

INFORMATION AND ACTIVITIES

Tourist office Avenue Mondenard (May, June & Sept Tues–Sat 9am–noon & 2–6pm, Sun 10am–noon & 3–5pm; July & Aug Mon–Sat 9am–7pm, Sun 10am–12.30pm & 3–5.30pm; Oct–April Tues–Fri 9am–noon & 2–6pm, Sat 9am–noon & 2–5pm; ☎ 05 53 65 27 75, ⓦ albret-tourisme.com).

Internet There's internet access in the Espace d'Albret overlooking the quay.

Boat rental In summer you can rent pleasure boats at the port through Les Croisières du Prince Henry (☎ 05 53 65 66, ⓦ croisieresduprincehenry.com; €90 for half a day or €130 for a whole day for 2–7 people). If you don't want to captain, take a cruise with commentary on a traditional *gabare* a short distance up the Baïse to the first lock and back (April–Oct; 1hr; €7.50).

ACCOMMODATION

D'Albret 40 allée d'Albret ☎ 05 53 97 41 10, ⓦ restaurant-albret.fr. On the wide boulevard a couple of minutes' walk southwest of the centre of town, this welcoming, family-run place has a good choice of rooms and a cheerful restaurant serving well-priced regional *menus* from €12. Restaurant open Mon–Thurs & Sat noon–2pm & 7.30–9.30pm, Fri & Sun noon–2pm. Breakfast €6.50. **€49.20**

Auberge du Pont Vieux 19 rue Séderie ☎ 05 53 97 51 04, ⓦ vieux-pont.com. Comfortable, old-fashioned rooms with wooden shutters and flower-draped balconies overlooking the river, as well as a restaurant with very good-value *menus* (€11 at lunch, €19.50 in the evenings). Restaurant open Tues–Sun noon–1.30pm & 7–9pm. Breakfast €7. **€68**

EATING AND DRINKING

Chocolaterie Artisanale la Cigale 2 rue Calvin ☎ 05 53 65 15 73, ⓦ chocolaterie-la-cigale.fr. For delicious, beautifully made chocolatey goodies, head for this splendid chocolaterie, a couple of minutes' walk south of the *gare SNCF*. Tues–Sat 9am–noon & 2–6pm; closed second half of July.

L'Escadron Volant 7 rue Henri IV ☎ 05 53 97 19 04. Salads and sweet crêpes in addition to the standard duck-based dishes, in a prime spot facing the château entrance. *Menus* from 11.90 at lunch and €18 in the evenings. May–Aug Mon–Sat noon–2pm & 7–9.30pm; Sept–April Tues–Sat noon–2pm & 7–9.30pm.

★ **Le Relais de la Hire** Francescas ☎ 05 53 65 41 59, ⓦ la-hire.com. *Le Relais* is 10km southeast of Nérac in the lovely village of Francescas, and is probably the best place to eat in the area. You can feast on such dishes as roast spiced turbot with caramelized onions in an elegant eighteenth-century house or its flower-filled garden. You can eat à la carte for around €50 or there are *menus* at €14.50 and €30. It's worth allowing the time to wander round the village. Mid-Nov to end-Oct Tues–Sat noon–2pm & 7.30–10pm, Sun noon–2pm & 7.30–10pm.

★ **Le Vert Galant** 11 rue Séderie ☎ 05 53 65 31 99. Does a nice line in *tartines* – toasted bread with a huge range of things to pile on top – accompanied by regional products. Their speciality is a delicious duck confit, pear and bacon *tartine*. It also serves over fifty flavours of ice cream (available all day), including tomato and basil and the very interesting Camembert and pumpkin. There is a lunchtime *menu* for €11.90 and in the evening it's à la carte. April–June & Sept–Oct Tues 7.30–9.30pm, Wed–Mon noon–2pm & 7.30–9.30pm; July & Aug daily noon–2pm & 7.30–9.30pm.

Buzet-sur-Baïse

BUZET-SUR-BAÏSE lies roughly 30km west of Agen, in the shadow of the Château de Buzet (not open to the public), which stands high on the green hillside, now separated from its village by the *autoroute*. Buzet itself is rather dull, but as the vines on this south bank of the Garonne indicate, you're in wine country and you shouldn't miss the chance to visit the local **wine cooperative**, Les Vignerons de Buzet (July & Aug Mon–Sat 9am–12.30pm & 2–7pm; Sept–June Mon–Sat 9am–noon & 2–6pm; ☎ 05 53 84 74 30, ⓦ vignerons-buzet.fr), east of the village on the D642. Founded in 1953, this is France's largest wine cooperative, with around three hundred growers producing fourteen million bottles on average per year. The majority are strong red wines which benefit from ageing – Grande Réserve, Baron d'Ardeuil and Château de Gueyze stand out among the many award-winning wines produced by the cooperative which also offers free tastings. It's also well worth arranging for one of their exceptionally informative **guided tours** of the vinification plant and **chais** (July & Aug daily 10am & 3pm; Sept–June by appointment only; visits in English on request ☎05 53 84 17 16).

ACTIVITIES
BUZET-SUR-BAÏSE

Boat trips Aside from wine, the other reason to visit Buzet is to rent a boat for a trip along the Canal de Garonne, the Baïse or the Lot. Aquitaine Navigation (☎05 53 84 72 50, ⓦaquitaine-navigation.com), based at the *halte nautique*

on the canal below Buzet village, has small pleasure boats for rent hourly (€30 for a 4-person boat) and by the half-day or day, as well as houseboats for longer excursions (from €775 for a 2–3-person boat, but prices vary seasonally).

EATING AND DRINKING

★ **Le Vigneron** ☎05 53 84 73 46. The nicest eating option in Buzet is on the broad main street and offers a four-course *menu du jour* (€14.80) and a special Sunday lunch *menu* (€24) including an hors-d'oeuvre buffet and a trolley stacked with delectable home-made desserts. The

house speciality is a confection of crêpes layered with *crème patissière*, coated in meringue and baked. Tues–Sat noon–2pm & 7.30–9.45pm, Sun noon–2pm; closed two weeks in Feb.

Moissac and around

There is little of historical interest left in the modern town of **MOISSAC**, some 40km southeast of Agen, largely because of the terrible damage wreaked by the flood of 1930, when the Tarn, swollen by a sudden thaw in the Massif Central, burst its banks, destroying 617 houses and killing more than a hundred people. The cloister and porch of the Benedictine **abbey church of St-Pierre**, a masterpiece of Romanesque sculpture and model for dozens of churches throughout the region, survived to make Moissac a household name in the history of art. The flat plains to the south and west of Moissac are less exciting, not least because of the looming presence of a nuclear power plant, but there are, nevertheless, a couple of places worth visiting along the banks of the Garonne: **St-Nicolas-de-la-Grave**, for its nature reserve and little museum devoted to the founder of Detroit, after whom Cadillac cars were named, and **Auvillar**, for its exquisite market square.

Moissac sits with its back to the old river cliffs on the north bank of the Tarn just before its confluence with the Garonne. The town's compact centre is bordered to the south by the Canal de Garonne, to the east by boulevard Camille Delthil and to the west by boulevard Lakanal, at the south end of which Pont-Napoléon carries road traffic over the Tarn. Moissac's main east–west thoroughfare, named rue Gambetta in the west, rue Ste-Catherine and then rue Malaveille, brings you into the central market square, **place des Récollets**, where you'll find the most convenient car park.

Église Abbatiale St-Pierre

Church daily **Cloister** daily: April–June & Oct 9am–noon & 2–6pm; July & Aug 9am–7pm; Sept 9am–6pm; Nov–March 10am–noon & 2–5pm • €5; tickets are available from the tourist office (see p.263) and allow entry to the Musée d'Arts et Traditions Populaire (see p.263)
From place des Récollets, rue de la République leads north towards the red-brick belfry of the **Église Abbatiale St-Pierre**. Legend has it that Clovis first founded a church here in 506, though it seems more probable that its origins belong to the seventh century, which saw the foundation of so many monasteries throughout Aquitaine. The first Romanesque church on the site was consecrated in 1063 and enlarged the following century when Moissac became a stop on the Santiago de Compostela pilgrim route. Since then the church has survived countless wars, including siege and sack by Simon

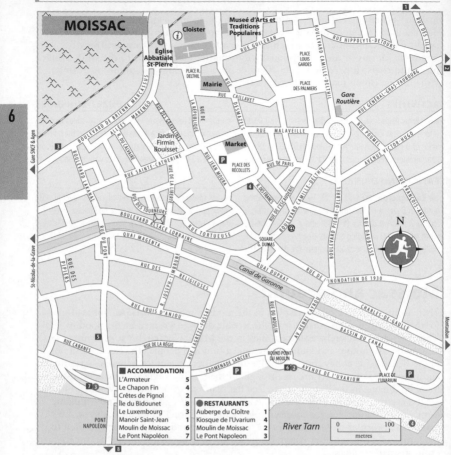

de Montfort in 1212, during the crusade against the Cathars. Indeed, the fact that it is still standing at all is something of a miracle. During the Revolution the cloister was used as a gunpowder factory and billet for soldiers, who damaged many of the carvings, while in the 1850s it only escaped demolition to make way for the Bordeaux–Toulouse train line by a whisker.

The south porch

Apart from the dumpy, red-brick belfry, the first thing you see approaching the church from the town centre is the great stone arc of the **south porch**, with its magnificent tympanum, completed in 1130. It depicts Christ in Majesty, right hand raised in benediction, the Scriptures resting on his knee, surrounded by the Evangelists and the 24 elders of the Apocalypse – every one different – as described by St John in the Book of Revelation. Below, the central pillar bears the figures of St Paul and St Jeremiah, the latter with the most beautifully doleful face imaginable, in the same elongated style as at Souillac (see p.170).

The interior

There is fine carving on the capitals inside the porch, and the **interior** of the church, which was remodelled in the fifteenth century, is painted with intricate patterns and filled with interesting wood and stone statuary. The most outstanding are those in the second chapel on the right as you enter: a lovely stone *Pietà* in which Mary, enveloped in pastel blue, holds her son gently in her arms, and an equally compelling statue of Mary Magdalene with one arm outstretched and a thick tress of hair falling round her knees.

The cloister

The **cloister** is accessed through the tourist office, behind the church to the west, where you can see a ten-minute video (in English on request) describing its main features. The cloister surrounds a garden shaded by a majestic cedar, and its pantile roof is supported by 76 alternating single and double marble columns. Each column supports a single inverted wedge-shaped block of stone, on which are carved, with extraordinary delicacy, all manner of animals and plant motifs, as well as 46 scenes from the Bible and the lives of the saints, among them Daniel in the lions' den, the Evangelists, fishermen on Lake Galilee, St Peter being crucified upside down and the decapitation of John the Baptist. Despite the damage done during the Revolution, they are in amazingly good shape. An inscription on the middle pillar on the west side explains that the cloister was constructed in the time of the Abbot Ansquitil in the year of Our Lord 1100.

Musée d'Arts et Traditions Populaires

June–Oct daily 2–6pm; July & Aug also 10am–1pm • €2, or €5 combined ticket with Église Abbatiale St-Pierre

The same ticket for the church gains you entry to the rather less interesting **Musée Marguerite Vidal d'Arts et Traditions Populaires**, housed in the former abbots' palace on rue de l'Abbaye immediately northeast of the church. Apart from a good collection of local ceramics, including faïence from Auvillar (see p.265), it contains a hotchpotch of furniture, ecclesiastical robes and religious treasures, portraits of old Moissac residents and a mock-up of a Quercy farmhouse interior.

ARRIVAL AND DEPARTURE   MOISSAC

Moissac is well served by public transport, with train connections to Toulouse and Agen. For the rest of the region you'll be reliant on your own transport or taxis.

By train Moissac's *gare SNCF* lies about 500m west of the centre along avenue Pierre Chabrié; from the station follow this road east and, where it curves northwards, you'll see steps leading down to the church square.
Destinations Agen (6–8 daily; 30min); Bordeaux (1 daily; 1hr 50min); Montauban (5–8 daily; 20min); Toulouse (4–5 daily; 45min).

By bus Run by Bus Gerla (☎05 63 04 55 50); the bus stops outside the Tribunal and services are limited – you need to book in advance. Gerla runs a special service for pilgrims and will also arrange other services to Cahors, Montauban and Toulouse airport on request; call for details.
Destinations Lauzerte (Wed & Sat 1–2 daily; 30min).

INFORMATION AND ACTIVITIES

Tourist office 6 place Durand-de-Bredon (daily: April–June & Oct 9am–noon & 2–6pm; July & Aug 9am–7pm; Sept 9am–6pm; Nov–March 10am–noon & 2–5pm; ☎05 63 04 01 85, ⓦmoissac.fr). Situated at the west end of the church it has details of Moissac's festivals (see box, p.254) and of concerts taking place in the church

and cloister in the summer months.
Bike rental Moissac-Loisirs, 29 rue Malaveille ☎05 63 04 03 48, on the north side of the market square.
Internet Video Pilote, 8 rue Camille Delthil (Tues–Fri 3–8pm; Sat 10.30am–noon & 3–8pm).

ACCOMMODATION

L'Armateur 22 rue du Pont ☎05 63 32 85 10, ⓦhotelarmateur.fr. This chic hotel is housed in an eighteenth-century mansion with a long walled garden,

complete with pool. It also boasts a fine restaurant with *menus* from €17 for lunch, heading up to €45 for the evening *dégustation*. Restaurant open Mon eve to Fri and

6

Sat eve to Sun lunch, 12.30–2pm & 7.30–9pm. Breakfast €11. The more expensive, garden-side rooms cost up to €130. **€110**

Le Chapon Fin 3 place des Récollets ☎05 63 04 04 22, ⓦhotelchaponfin.fr. Situated on the south side of the market square, this comfortable hotel offers clean, simple rooms and a good location. Private parking by prior reservation only, €6.50. Breakfast €8.50. **€65**

Crêtes de Pignols 1167 chemin de Lacapalette ☎05 63 04 04 04, ⓦcretesdepignols.com. Charming little hotel that exudes a warm and friendly vibe about 4km northeast of Moissac off the D927, close to the river. It boasts a pool and a good restaurant with *menus* in the range €15–26. Restaurant open daily 7.30–9pm (lunch available only on reservation for parties of ten or more). Breakfast €8. **€56**

Île du Bidounet ☎05 63 32 52 52, ⓦcamping -moissac.com. A good-value, shady three-star campsite on a little island 2km from central Moissac across the Pont-Napoléon. Facilities include pool, bar and children's play area. Closed Sept–April. **€17.20**

Le Luxembourg 2 av Pierre Chabrié ☎05 63 04 00 27, ⓦhoteluxembourg82.com. A nicely old-fashioned place halfway along the road to the station, though it suffers slightly from road noise and the train tracks running behind, despite double-glazing. Even if you're not staying here, the restaurant is worth a visit for its good-value traditional meals. *Menus* are €12 at lunch, and €16 in the

evenings and Saturday. Restaurant open mid-Jan to mid-Dec Tues–Sat noon–2pm & 7.30–9pm. Private parking €4. Breakfast €7. **€49**

Manoir Saint Jean Saint-Paul d'Espis ☎05 63 05 02 34, ⓦmanoirsaintjean.com. Nine kilometres north of Moissac, the manor is set in its own attractive grounds and offers nine suites, all individually decorated with plush furnishings, paintings and chandeliers. There is also a first-rate restaurant serving delicious seasonal produce – organic wines, meat and wild fish with fresh herbs from the garden. *Menus* at €30 for lunch and €38 in the evening. Restaurant open June–Sept daily noon–1.15pm & 7.30–9.15pm; Oct–May Tues to Sat noon–1.15pm & 7.30–9.15pm, Sun noon–1.15pm. Breakfast €13. **€140**

★ **Le Moulin de Moissac** Esplanade du Moulin ☎05 63 32 88 88, ⓦlemoulindemoissac.com. Occupying a former water-mill just east of the Pont-Napoléon, this is the nicest hotel in town. It's a large, imposing building, but the inside has been beautifully refurbished and the rooms have very comfortable beds, swish bathrooms and mod cons such as DVD players. It also boasts a spa and a gorgeous restaurant (see below). Breakfast €13.50. **€96**

Le Pont Napoléon 2 allée Montebello ☎05 63 04 01 55, ⓦle-pont-napoleon.com. A few very classy rooms above a fine restaurant (see below). The hotel overlooks a busy road beside the bridge, but inside it is a haven of tranquillity and the prices are extremely reasonable. Breakfast €8. **€59**

EATING AND DRINKING

The square outside the abbey boasts a variety of restaurants, though most are only open at lunchtimes. For picnic fodder, there's a small fresh-produce market in the covered hall on place des Récollets (Tues–Sun) while on Saturday and Sunday mornings farmers' stalls fill the whole square. You'll also find a boulangerie and boucherie at the bottom of rue Jean Moura, near place G. Dumas.

★ **Auberge du Cloître** Place Durand-de-Bredon. In fine weather, eat at the magnolia-shaded *Auberge du Cloître*, beside the tourist office, serving incredibly fresh local produce, some from the chef's own garden. *Menus* from €12.50 lunch and €20 eves. Mid-May to mid-Sept Tues–Sun 12.15–2pm & 7.30–9.30pm; mid-Sept to mid-May Tues, Thurs–Sat 12.15pm & 7.30–9.30pm, Wed & Sun 12.15–2pm.

Kiosque de L'Uvarium Av de L'Uvarium ☎05 63 94 88 14. A casual place with a large terrace that serves grills, salads and pastas, all at around €12.50. The adjoining outdoor entertainment space hosts a variety of events on summer evenings, such as theatre, Latin dance displays and even hip-hop. May–Sept Wed–Mon noon–3pm & 6.30–10pm.

★ **Le Moulin de Moissac** Esplanade du Moulin ☎05 63 32 88 88, ⓦlemoulindemoissac.com. Occupying a former water-mill just east of the Pont-Napoléon, this sumptuous restaurant is one of the best in the area, tempting the palate with dishes such as local farm guinea fowl simmered in ginger and teamed with a mushroom risotto. Evening *menus* at €37. Mon–Fri noon–2pm & 7.30–9.30pm, Sat & Sun 7.30–9.30pm.

Le Pont Napoléon 2 allée Montebello ☎05 63 04 01 55, ⓦle-pont-napoleon.com. This is the excellent restaurant attached to *Le Pont Napoléon* (see above) and it's worth eating here at least once, just for a treat. *Menus* start at €28 for lunch and €35 in the evening, or around €46 à la carte. Daily noon–2pm & 7.30–9.30pm.

St-Nicolas-de-la-Grave

Eight kilometres southwest of Moissac, the small *bastide* of **ST-NICOLAS-DE-LA-GRAVE** is dominated by a four-square château atop a low rise on the south bank of the

Garonne. Its oldest tower – the fattest of the four, on the northeast corner – is attributed to Richard the Lionheart, who passed through here on his return from the Third Crusade in the late 1100s. Nowadays, however, it houses the *mairie*, and there's nothing to see inside.

Musée Lamothe-Cadillac

July & Aug daily 10am–12.30pm & 3–6.30pm; Sept–June ask the tourist office (see below) • Free

St Nicolas is prouder of its second claim to fame as the home town of **Antoine Laumet**, founder of Detroit in America, who was born here in 1658. His birthplace, just southwest of the central square, now contains the **Musée Lamothe-Cadillac**, worth a quick look in passing as much for the story of Laumet's life as for any of the exhibits, which comprise mock-ups of a period bedroom and kitchen, and masses of documentation, some of it in English. Laumet was an adventurer who, on leaving for Canada in 1683, adopted the upper-crust name of de Lamothe-Cadillac. He later turned up in America in the service of King Louis XIV, where he founded a number of forts, among them a cavalry outpost called *le détroit* between lakes Erie and Huron in 1701. Two hundred years later, a Detroit car company was looking for a name at the same time as the city was celebrating its anniversary. They decided to honour Detroit's founding father, and thus were Cadillacs born.

INFORMATION   ST-NICOLAS-DE-LA-GRAVE

Tourist office Place du Platane (July & Aug daily 10am–12.30pm & 3–6.30pm; Sept–June Mon 8am–12.30pm, Tues–Fri 2–6pm; ☎05 63 94 82 81, Ⓦstnicolasdelag.online.fr; outside these hours the *mairie* on rue du Champs de l'Église will provide information).

ACCOMMODATION

St-Nicolas has no hotels, but there is a *chambre d'hôte* and the tourist office has details of others.

Camping Plan D'Eau ☎05 63 95 50 00. Decent two-star campsite 2km north of the village, where the Garonne and Tarn rivers form a large lake; the campsite is part of a leisure complex with snack bar and canoe and bike rental among other facilities, and you can also go bird-watching in the adjacent nature reserve. Closed mid-Dec to mid-June. €10.70

Chambres d'hôte au Château 1 bd des fossés de Raoul ☎05 63 95 96 82, Ⓦau-chateau-stn.com. A lovely *chambre d'hôte* in an old *maison de maître*. Bedrooms are spacious and calming, and there is a private pool. €64

Auvillar

AUVILLAR, 14km west of St-Nicolas, is perched on a cliff on the Garonne's south bank. Its feudal château and ramparts were demolished in the eighteenth and nineteenth centuries, but thankfully the wonderful old village centre remains. From the main road skirting south of the village, you duck under the seventeenth-century **Tour de l'Horloge** to find yourself in the gently sloping triangular-shaped **place de la Halle** surrounded by a harmonious ensemble of brick and timber buildings with arcades running all around. At the square's cobbled centre stands a pleasing circular stone-pillared market hall, built in the early nineteenth century.

Musée du Vieil Auvillar

Place de la Halle • Mid-April to mid-Oct daily except Tues 2.30–6.30pm; mid-Oct to mid-April Sat & Sun 2.30–5.30pm • €2

It's worth poking your nose into the **Musée du Vieil Auvillar**, on the square's north side, for its collection of local pottery. Auvillar was already known for its pottery production in the sixteenth century, but in the following century they began making *faïence* of sufficiently high quality to rival that imported from Holland and Italy. Local potters still have a good reputation, as witnessed by the big pottery fair held every October (see box, p.254).

Tourist office Place de la Halle (April to mid-Oct daily 10am–12.30pm & 2–5.30pm, mid-June to mid-Oct till 7pm; mid-Oct to March Tues–Sun 2–5.30pm; ☎ 05 63 39 89 82, ⓦ auvillar.com).

ACCOMMODATION AND EATING

De l'Horloge ☎ 05 63 39 91 61 ⓦ horlogeauvillar .monsite-orange.fr. For somewhere to stay or eat, head for *De l'Horloge* beside the gate tower: in addition to a clutch of spacious en-suite rooms, they run a restaurant with *menus* from €14 at lunch and €24 in the eves. On a sunny day you can sit on their shady terrace overlooking the main street. Restaurant open mid-Jan to mid-Dec Sat 8–9.30pm, Sun–Thurs noon–1.45pm & 8–9.30pm. Hotel closed mid-Oct to mid-April. Buffet breakfast €11. **€59**

Quercy Blanc

As you head north from Moissac, the land gradually rises to gently undulating, green and woody country, cut through by parallel valleys running down to meet the Garonne and planted with vines, sunflowers and maize, as well as apple and cherry orchards. It's a very soft landscape, the villages are small and widely scattered, and the pace of life seems about equal with that of a turning sunflower. This is the **Quercy Blanc**, named after the area's grey-white soils and building stone, a region with few sights, but one which lives up to the image of deepest rural France. The single most interesting place to head for is **Lauzerte**, atop a river bluff 25km north of Moissac. Further north again, **Montcuq** distinguishes itself with its solid square keep, the remnants of a twelfth-century fortress, standing guard over the medieval village, while way over to the southeast, **Montpezat-de-Quercy** is home to a Gothic church with a surprising collection of art treasures, including a beautiful and complete set of Flemish tapestries. Further east still, **Lalbenque** is a name that reverberates around the high temples of gastronomy, the truffle centre of the south.

GETTING AROUND   **QUERCY BLANC**

Public transport around Quercy Blanc consists of three separate bus services: the first enables you to reach Lauzerte from Moissac, the second runs to Montcuq and Lalbenque from Cahors, and finally Montpezat is a stop on the route between Cahors and Montauban.

Lauzerte

The first of the sleepy hilltop villages that you reach travelling north from Moissac is **LAUZERTE**. It stands on a promontory between two rivers, a press of white-walled houses contained within its medieval ramparts, with the "new" town spilling down the south and eastern slopes. The site's strategic importance was not lost on the counts of Toulouse, who took control of Lauzerte in the late twelfth century and granted it the status of a *bastide*, with all the rights and privileges that entailed, in 1241. The other notable event in its history took place fifty years later, when the townspeople threw out the English occupiers. By way of reward the French king, Philip IV, elevated Lauzerte to capital of the Bas Quercy (Lower Quercy) region and seat of the royal seneschal (the king's representative). However, its heyday came to an end in the late sixteenth century when Lauzerte was demoted to a mere district capital in the aftermath of the Wars of Religion.

Nevertheless, a few vestiges of its glory days remain in the old town, which lies clustered around the pretty, arcaded central square, **place des Cornières**, and the church of **St-Barthélémy**. The church's origins go back to the thirteenth century, but it was largely rebuilt after the Protestants wreaked their havoc, and its main point of interest nowadays is the gilded Baroque altarpiece, dedicated to the Virgin Mary and depicting scenes from her life, which fills the north chapel. Behind the church, there are good views of the patchwork landscape all around from the **place du Château**, where the castle once stood on the promontory's northern tip. From here **rue de la Garrigue**, and its extension **rue de la Gendarmerie**, double back south of the church, running along the ridge past a number of thirteenth- and fourteenth-century merchants' houses with their big ground-floor arches and colonnaded windows above.

ARRIVAL AND INFORMATION   LAUZERTE

By bus There is a bus service run by Bus Gerla (☎ 05 63 04 55 50) to Lauzerte from Moissac, but it only runs on Wednesdays and Saturdays, returning to Moissac at 2pm; reservation is necessary. Buses leave from outside the Crédit Agricole bank.

By car There is car parking in the lower section of the

town, from where you can walk up to the medieval town via a series of steps, or you can drive to the top and park just outside the ramparts, where there is a large car park.

Tourist office Place des Cornières (July & Aug daily 9am–7pm; Sept–June Mon–Sat 9am–noon & 2–6pm; ☎ 05 63 94 61 94, ⓦ lauzerte-tourisme.fr).

ACCOMMODATION AND EATING

Aube Nouvelle Durfort-Lacapellete ☎ 05 63 04 50 33, ⓦ aubenouvelle.com. Belgian-run manor house in the countryside 9km south of Lauzerte on the D2. The restaurant serves *menus* from €14 at lunch and €21 in the evenings. Restaurant open mid-Jan to mid-Dec Sat 7.30–9pm, Sun–Fri noon–1.30pm & 7.30–9pm. Breakfast €8. **€61**

★ **Le Belvedere** Montagudet ☎ 05 63 95 51 10, ⓦ lebelvedere.biz. A lovely hotel a couple of kilometres west of Lauzerte towards Montagudet. Rooms are spacious and airy, there is an infinity pool with splendid views across the valley to Lauzerte, a spa and an excellent restaurant with lunch *menus* from €20, evening *menus* €35. Restaurant open daily noon–2pm & 7–9pm. Breakfast €10. **€79**

Du Quercy Faubourg d'Auriac ☎ 05 63 94 66 36,

ⓦ hotel-du-quercy.fr. A handful of old-fashioned but perfectly comfortable rooms, with a renowned restaurant to boot. In addition to traditional local dishes, such as *cassoulet*, farm chicken cooked in Cahors wine and *confit de canard* – the latter stuffed with foie gras – they serve a good range of fish and seafood dishes and game in season; *menus* start at €12.50 at lunch and €25 in the evenings. Reserve a table in advance. Restaurant open Tues–Sat 12.15–1.30pm & 7.30–9pm, Sun 12.15–1.30pm. Breakfast €7. **€46**

La Table des Trois Chevaliers Place des Cornières ☎ 05 63 95 32 69 11. Situated in the beautiful central *place*, this is a good place for a relaxed lunch or dinner. Dishes €7–18. Tues–Sun noon–2pm & 7.30–9pm.

Musée Yvan Quercy

Opening times vary, so phone to check • €5 • ☎ 05 63 95 84 02

Once you've explored Lauzerte's compact centre, it's worth venturing 8km southeast to visit a quirky museum near **CAZES-MONDENARD**, a village with a pretty Gothic church.

The core of the **Musée Yvan Quercy**, at the end of a long lane signed off the D16 Molières road 2km east of the village, is its collection of hearses, which was kick-started in 1970 when Monsieur Quercy was given an old hearse. Once he'd acquired a second one, word spread, and nearby parishes rushed to offer him theirs. By the time of his death, he had amassed nearly a hundred different models, some horse-drawn, others pulled by hand, from the seventeenth century up to the first motorized model manufactured by Peugeot in 1949. His family now continue his work. The collection also includes a large number of regular carriages, all in excellent condition, and some early farm machinery. After the tour, you are offered tastings of wine, pâtés and other local produce, and in season they also serve regional meals if you book in advance.

Montcuq

Thirteen kilometres northeast of Lauzerte along the Petite-Barguelonne valley, **MONTCUQ** – pronounce the "q" if you don't want to be saying "my arse" – is built around the flanks of a conical hill, on top of which stands a huge square keep. Like

6

> ### MONTCUQ MONOPOLY
>
> In 2007, Hasbro, makers of **Monopoly**, opened an internet voting site to decide which towns would feature on a new French version of the game. As a joke, web users started a campaign to feature Montcuq, reasoning that most foreigners would rudely mispronounce the name. It took off, and Montcuq won – but Hasbro decided to overrule the popular vote and use Dunkerque instead. The outcry was, predictably, huge. To make up for the lack of democratic compliance, Hasbro agreed to issue a special Montcuq version of Monopoly. The town was allowed to choose which streets would be used, and a local artist provided images. Look out for this unusual souvenir in shops around town.

Lauzerte, Montcuq guarded the ancient road to Cahors and lies on the Santiago de Compostela pilgrim route, but it seems to have had the knack of picking the wrong cause: it sided with the Cathars, was condemned for collaborating with the English and later became a Protestant stronghold. As a result, there's not much in the way of sights, though it's an attractive little place and has a very good Sunday morning market.

The tower
July & Aug 10am–noon & 4–7pm • €3, under-12s free

To get the lie of the land the best thing to do is climb up the **tower**. Any of the lanes leading uphill from rue de la Promenade, the wide boulevard to the south of the old town, will take you there. It was built at the turn of the eleventh century as part of a larger fortress, and although Louis IX ordered the ramparts destroyed, the ditches filled in and the tower's top knocked off in the aftermath of the Cathar crusades, at 24m, it's still a fair climb. The effort is rewarded with all-round views; even when the tower is closed, the pinnacle of rock it stands on is high enough to give a good panorama. As you wander back down the slope through the maze of stone and half-timbered houses, the church of **St-Hilaire** stands out with its octagonal brick tower, though there's nothing of particular interest inside.

ARRIVAL AND INFORMATION
MONTCUQ

By bus Buses run by Raynal Voyages (☎ 05 65 23 28 28) stop on rue de la Promenade near the tourist office. Destinations Cahors (school term Mon–Fri 1 daily; school hols Wed & Sat 1 daily; 35–45min).

Tourist office 8 rue de la Promenade (July & Aug Mon–Sat 9am–12.30pm & 3–6pm, Sun 10.30am–1pm; Sept–June Mon–Sat 9am–noon & variable afternoons; ☎ 05 65 22 94 04, ⓦ tourisme-montcuq.com).

ACCOMMODATION AND EATING

Du Parc ☎ 05 65 31 81 82, ⓦ hotel-restaurant-du-parc .fr. Welcoming hotel, 500m west of Montcuq on the Belmont road, with old-fashioned but comfortable rooms, a big, quiet garden and a decent, residents-only restaurant.

Restaurant open April–Oct (but will take reservations for groups outside this period); *menus* from €16.50. Breakfast €6.10. **€58.50**

SHOPPING

Chiméra 13 rue du Faubourg Saint-Pierre ☎ 05 65 22 97 01. Should you need a new supply of reading matter, Montcuq is also home to Chiméra, an English-owned

bookshop selling new and second-hand French and English titles. Opening hours vary; call to check.

Castelnau-Montratier

The route southeast of Montcuq takes you on a roller-coaster ride across the valleys and intervening hills, on one of which stands **CASTELNAU-MONTRATIER**, 20km from Montcuq, with its incongruous neo-Byzantine church and spacious market square.

CLOCKWISE FROM TOP DOVECOTE, LAUZERTE (P.266); HOUSE DETAIL IN CORDES-SUR-CIEL (P.280); CHAPEL IN THE QUERY BLANC COUNTRYSIDE>

6

Lalbenque

If you happen to be in the Quercy Blanc on a Tuesday between December and March head east along the D19 from Castelnau-Montratier to the village of **LALBENQUE**. Its eleventh-century church deserves more than a passing glance for its gilded wooden altarpiece, said to have been purchased in the late eighteenth century by a local carter from revolutionaries in Cahors for the paltry sum of 50 francs. Knowing he'd purchased a looted sacred treasure at a bargain price, he began to suffer twinges of conscience and confessed to his local priest, who immediately absolved the penitent and claimed the prize for his church, where it's been ever since.

At any other time of year, once you've inspected the church, that's just about it – Lalbenque is a sleepy little white-stone town, barely distinguishable from all the others in the Quercy Blanc. However, if you pull in at around 2pm on a winter afternoon you will witness a market like no other: trestle tables laden with **black truffles** line the main street, and a long rope stretches the length of them, holding back a seething mass of buyers, locals and tourists. At 2.30pm sharp, a bell rings and the rope is hauled away as buyers from all over France surge forward to begin negotiations. A price per kilo has been announced for the day, but that's just a guide, with some pretty sharp bargaining being necessary before all parties are satisfied. Truffles are rare and capricious, resisting every effort at widespread cultivation – the majority are still found in the wild. It's therefore the intrepid hunters who have the advantage; and before long only a few small specimens remain for the tourists to savour in a sumptuous truffle omelette that night.

INFORMATION

LALBENQUE

Tourist office A part-time summer office is situated on place de la Bascule (July & Aug Mon–Sat 9am–12.30pm & 2–6pm and Sun 10am–12.30pm; ☎05 65 31 50 08, ⓦ lalbenque.net). If the tourist office is closed, try the mairie on rue du Marché aux Truffes (Mon–Sat 9.30am–noon, plus Tues–Thurs 2–4pm; ☎05 65 31 61 17, ⓦ lalbenque.fr).

ACCOMMODATION AND EATING

If you prefer somebody else to cook your truffle for you, both restaurants in town offer a truffle-laden *menu* every market Tuesday, in addition to more everyday fare.

Lion d'Or 104 rue du Marché aux Truffes ☎05 65 31 60 19, ⓦ liondor-hotel-restaurant.fr. A modest little restaurant/café that nevertheless can perform wonders with a truffle. Lunch *menus* from €10.50, and they go up to €34 and €64 for truffle-studded *menus*. Daily noon–2pm & 7.30–9pm.

Le Logis de Reyjade Place de République, Montdumerc ☎05 65 22 89 56, ⓦwww.lelogisdereyjade.com. A lovely *chambre d'hôte* a few kilometres southwest of Lalbenque just off the D10. It is lavishly furnished with eighteenth-century antiques and set in a pretty garden. Table d'hôte €28 (reservation only). **€90**

Montpezat-de-Quercy

Ten kilometres southwest of Lalbenque through twisty country lanes you come to an interesting hilltop village, **MONTPEZAT-DE-QUERCY**. Traces of its medieval heyday remain in the arcaded central square and lanes of half-timbered houses, but the main reason to stop here is the **Collégiale St-Martin**, with its unusually rich hoard of treasures, standing at the southeast end of the promontory on which the village is built.

Collégiale St-Martin

Montpezat's church was founded in the early fourteenth century by Cardinal Pierre des Prés (1281–1361), a local who grew wealthy in the service of the Avignon popes. With its high and severe single nave, the interior is unexciting, at least in comparison with the fourteenth- to sixteenth-century artworks arrayed in the side chapels. Best are the battered but still lovely *Vierge aux Colombes*, her face framed by golden ringlets, in the second chapel on the left; a polychrome *Pietà* in the first on the right; and, next door, an English alabaster triptych depicting the Birth, Resurrection and Ascension of Christ – in the last only his feet are visible as he's whisked heavenwards. The church's finest treasures, though, are the five Flemish **tapestries** grouped around the choir. They were made especially for the church in the early sixteenth century, a gift from Jean IV des Prés, bishop of Montauban, and portray events from the life of St Martin de Tours, to whom the church is consecrated. The most famous scene is that in the first panel, where the future saint – at the time in the service of the Roman army – shares his cloak with a crippled beggar. The workmanship throughout is of superb quality, while the colours remain amazingly vibrant. Also in remarkably good condition is the white-marble sarcophagus and statue of Pierre des Prés, to the right of the choir, with his feet resting on a lion while his well-fed face is bathed in a contented grin.

INFORMATION

Tourist office Bd des Fossés (April & Oct Tues–Fri 10.30am–12.30pm & 1.30–5.30pm; May Tues–Fri 10am–1pm & 2–7pm; June & Sept Tues–Thurs & Sun 10am–1pm & 2–7pm; July & Aug Mon 2–6pm, Tues–Sun 10am–1pm & 2–7pm; Nov–March Tues, Thurs & Sun

MONTPEZAT-DE-QUERCY

11am–5pm; ☎05 63 02 05 55, ⓦtourisme-montpezat -de-quercy.com). The office doubles as a Maison des Vins where you can buy the local Côteaux du Quercy wines and pick up a brochure listing vineyards to visit, though they don't offer tastings.

ACCOMMODATION AND EATING

Camping Révéa le Faillal ☎05 63 02 07 08, ⓦrevea-vacances.fr. A well-tended two-star municipal campsite, in a leisure park on Montpezat's northern outskirts. Facilities include a pool, tennis, mini-golf, basketand volleyball. Closed Sept–April. **€6.53**

Ferme-Auberge de Coutié ☎05 63 67 73 51. You'll eat

very well at this atmospheric *ferme-auberge* – on the D20, 9km southwest of Montpezat and signed to the east of Espanel hamlet – on a Quercy farm surrounded by ducks and orchards. *Menus* €19–35, including wine. Reservations essential. Daily 12.30–1pm & 7–8pm.

Montauban

Lying 20km east of Moissac and 50km north of Toulouse, **MONTAUBAN** is a prosperous middle-sized provincial city, the capital of the largely agricultural *département* of Tarn-et-Garonne. Its beautiful old centre sits on the north bank of the River Tarn, a harmonious ensemble of warm, pink brick which looks its best at sunset, or at night when the steeples, massive old bridge and riverside facades are illuminated. The layout follows the typical *bastide* pattern: a regular grid of streets around an arcaded market square, the glorious **place Nationale**, but between the main streets lie enticing alleys, covered passages and interior courtyards. The greatest delight is simply to wander – the centre is only a ten-minute stroll from end to end – taking in the scattered sights as you go, of which the highlight is the **Musée Ingres**, dedicated to Montauban's most famous son.

The city's origins go back to 1144 when Alphonse Jourdain, count of Toulouse, decided to create a *bastide* here as a bulwark against English and French royal power. Indeed, it is generally regarded as the first *bastide*, the model for the medieval new towns found throughout this region (see box, p.244). Montauban has enjoyed various periods of great prosperity (as one can guess from the proliferation of fine houses), mainly based on trade in silk and other textiles. The first followed the suppression of the Cathar heresy and the final submission of the counts of Toulouse in 1229 and was greatly enhanced by the building of the Pont-Vieux in 1335, making it the best crossing point on the Tarn for miles. The Hundred Years War did its share of damage, as did Montauban's opting for the Protestant cause in the Wars of Religion, but by the time of the Revolution it had become once more one of the richest cities in the southwest.

Montauban couldn't be easier to find your way around. The most interesting area is the small kernel of streets based on the original *bastide*, enclosed within an inner ring of boulevards between **allée de l'Empereur** to the east and the river to the west. The main shopping streets are pedestrianized **rue de la Résistance** and **rue de la République**, which intersect in the *bastide*'s southern corner.

Place Nationale

In the centre lies the city's finest point, **place Nationale**, the hub of the city's social life. Rebuilt after a fire in the seventeenth century, it is surrounded on all sides by a double row of arcades beneath two- and three-storeyed townhouses, their uniformity tempered by the square's irregular shape.

Église St-Jacques

The distinctive octagonal belfry of the **Église St-Jacques**, a couple of minutes' walk away from place Nationale, shows above the southwestern rooftops. First built in the thirteenth century on the pilgrim route to Santiago de Compostela, the church bears the scars of Montauban's troubled history, not only in its mix of architectural styles, but in the holes gouged out of the belfry's fortified base by cannonballs during an unsuccessful siege by twenty thousand Catholic troops – held off by just six thousand locals – in 1621.

Musée Ingres

Daily : July–Oct 10am–6pm; Nov–June 10am–noon & 2–6pm • €5, or €7 during exhibitions

On the banks of the river south of the church stands a massive half-palace, half-fortress, begun by the counts of Toulouse, then continued by the Black Prince in 1363. He left it unfinished when the English lost control of the town, and so it remained until 1664 when the bishop of Montauban chose this very prominent spot for his residence. It is now the **Musée Ingres**, which houses paintings and more than four thousand drawings left to the city by locally born **Jean-Auguste-Dominique Ingres** (1780–1867). The collection includes several of the supremely realistic, luminous portraits of women, which are the artist's trademark. It also contains a substantial collection of works by another native, **Émile-Antoine Bourdelle** (1861–1929), the ubiquitous monumental sculptor and student of Rodin, alongside a hotchpotch of other exhibits, from Gallo-Roman mosaics to fifteenth- and sixteenth-century European fine art. In the early days of World War II, the museum hosted more illustrious visitors when the Louvre dispatched over three thousand works of art to Montauban for safe-keeping prior to the German invasion. When southern France was occupied in 1942, however, they were moved again to more remote locations, including the Château de Montal (see p.192).

Cathédrale Notre-Dame

Providing a stark exception to Montauban's red-brick homogeneity is a cold, sore-thumb of a building, the **Cathédrale Notre-Dame**, ten minutes' walk southeast up rue de l'Hôtel-de-Ville. It was erected on the city's highest spot at the end of the seventeenth century as part of the triumphalist campaign to reassert the Catholic faith, following the defeat and harsh repression of the Protestants. Inside the dazzling white Classical facade lies an echoing nave, whose main point of interest is another Ingres painting, *Le Voeu de Louis XIII*, hanging in the north aisle. Specially

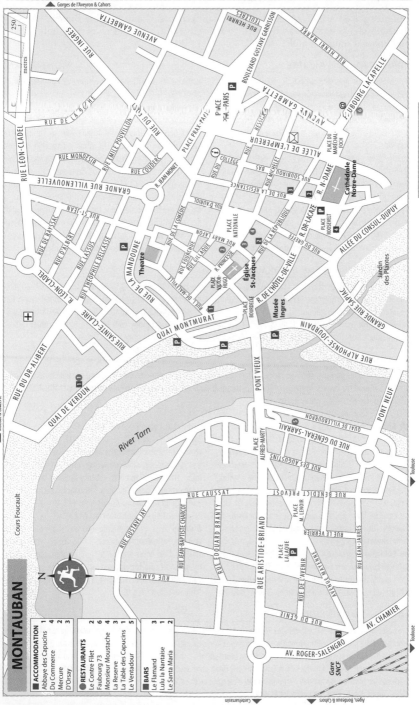

6

commissioned for the cathedral, the vast canvas depicts Louis offering France, symbolized by his crown and sword, to a Virgin and Child, and is strongly influenced by Raphael's romantic style.

ARRIVAL AND DEPARTURE   MONTAUBAN

By plane The nearest airport is Toulouse-Blagnac (☎ 08 25 38 00 00, ⓦ toulouse.aeroport.fr), 40km south of Montauban, straight down the A62 *autoroute*.

By train Montauban's *gare SNCF* lies roughly 1km west of centre across the Pont-Vieux at the far end of avenue Mayenne.

Destinations Agen (10–12 daily; 45–50min); Brive (2–5 daily; 1hr 50min); Cahors (3–8 daily; 40–50min); Moissac (7 daily Mon–Sat, 1 on Sun; 20min); Toulouse (every 30min or less; 25min).

By bus There's no central *gare routière*, so you'll need to ask at the tourist office (see below) for information about buses. While central Montauban is eminently walkable, you might want to hop on a city bus from the train station

to the centre (line A), stopping on allée de l'Empereur near place Prax-Paris, on the northeast side of town; tickets can be bought on the bus.

Destinations Bruniquel (school term Mon–Fri 4 daily; school hols Tues, Thurs & Sat 1 daily; 40min–1hr 10min); Cahors (Mon–Fri 1 daily; 1hr 15min); Laguépie (school term Mon–Fri 1 daily, school hols Tues, Thurs & Sat 1 daily; 1hr 40min); Montricoux (as for Bruniquel; 35–45min); St-Antonin-Noble-Val (as for Laguépie; 1hr 10min); Villefranche-de-Rouergue (Mon–Sat 1 daily; 1hr 45min).

By car The most convenient car park is the underground pay parking on place Prax-Paris or place Roosevelt. Free parking is available along the riverbanks beneath the Pont-Vieux and north of the theatre on rue de la Mandoune.

GETTING AROUND AND INFORMATION

Car rental Avis, 23 av Mayenne (☎ 05 63 20 45 73); Europcar, 21 av Roger Salengro (☎ 05 63 20 29 00). Both are located near the train station.

Tourist office Rue du Collège (July & Aug Mon–Sat 9am–6.30pm, Sun 10am–12.30pm; Sept–June Mon–Sat

9.30am–12.30pm & 2–6.30pm; ☎ 05 63 63 60 60, ⓦ montauban-tourisme.com). Staff will phone round for accommodation for you, at a charge of €1.60. This may still be time and money well spent in high summer, when rooms are hard to come by.

ACCOMMODATION

Montauban has a surprisingly limited range of hotels, a few family-sized options and a great many chain hotels, mainly clustered around the bypass. In the last few years things have been looking up in the luxurious guise of the *Abbaye des Capucins*, purse-pinchingly pricey but worth it.

★ **Abbaye des Capucins** 6–8 quai de Verdun ☎ 05 63 22 00 00, ⓦ abbayedescapucins.fr. A large and beautifully renovated hotel in a seventeenth-century monastery with a Michelin-starred restaurant attached, this is the last word in urban luxury. Rooms are spacious and well appointed, and there is a spa, a pool and bike rental (€4). It also owns two excellent restaurants, *La Table des Capucins* (see opposite) and the less formal *Bistro des Capucins* (daily 11am–11pm), which serves a great €26 *menu*. Breakfast €15. **€132**

Du Commerce 9 place Roosevelt ☎ 05 63 66 31 32, ⓦ hotel-commerce-montauban.com. This attractive hotel beside the cathedral offers the best deal in the centre. It boasts en-suite facilities in all its rooms. Closed Christmas

to mid-Jan. Parking €4–8. Breakfast €5–9. **€61**

Mercure 12 rue Notre-Dame ☎ 05 63 63 17 23, ⓦ mercure.com. Part of the nationwide *Mercure* chain of hotels, this is nevertheless a very good option as it's housed in an attractive eighteenth-century building right in the town centre. It boasts modern, reasonably spacious rooms and a good restaurant (*menus* from €13.40; daily noon–2.30pm & 7.30–10pm). Breakfast €12. **€107**

D'Orsay 29 rue Roger Salengro ☎ 05 63 66 06 66, ⓦ hotel-restaurant-orsay.com. Opposite the train station, this hotel has dated but comfortable enough rooms and a surprisingly good restaurant with *menus* from €25. Restaurant open Sat eve to Fri noon–1.30pm & 7.30–9pm. Breakfast €7. **€70**

EATING AND DRINKING

The best place for a picnic is the Jardin des Plantes, a pleasant green space south of the cathedral along the banks of a small tributary of the Tarn. You can buy provisions at pâtisseries and delicatessens on rue de la République and rue d'Auriol. While you're at it, keep an eye open for the local speciality, Montauriols, a chocolate-coated cherry preserved in armagnac; you'll find them at pâtisseries all over town. A few stalls sell fresh produce every day on place Nationale, but the main farmers' markets take place on Wednesday morning on place Lalaque on the station side of the river, and on Saturday mornings on allées Consul Dupuy, near the Jardin des Plantes.

RESTAURANTS

⭐ **Le Contre Filet** 4 rue des Princesses ☎ 05 63 20 19 75. Superb French cooking with a twist at this small restaurant. They are known for their beef in its signature sauce, but you can also feast on a kilo of mussels. *Menus* from €18. Reservations recommended. Mon, Tues, Thurs–Sat noon–2pm & 7–10pm, Sun noon–2pm.

Faubourg 73 73 Faubourg Lacapelle ☎ 05 63 93 55 54, ⓦ faubourg73.fr. Popular place offering tasty, good-value traditional meals and some more modern alternatives. Lunch *menu* €12.50, while in the evenings it's à la carte. Sept to Christmas & mid-Jan to mid-Aug Mon–Fri noon–2pm plus Thurs–Sat 7.30–10pm.

Monsieur Moustache 22 place Nationale ☎ 05 63 63 54 56. Sit on the *terrasse* under the arches at this informal family friendly place and watch the world go by on Montauban's famous square. *Menus* from €15. Daily noon–2pm & 7.30–9pm.

La Reserve 27 place Nationale ☎ 05 63 63 50 33. A lovely, upmarket little restaurant serving a good *menu* (from €15), including fish, in smart surroundings. Tues–Sat noon–2pm & 7–10pm.

⭐ **La Table des Capucins** 6–8 quai de Verdun ☎ 05 63 22 00 00, ⓦ abbayedescapucins.fr. The Michelin starred restaurant attached to *Abbaye des Capucins* (see opposite) has raced into the upper echelons of haute cuisine in just a few short years. Try the chef's signature starter, a delicate pâté of pressed leeks, sea bream tartare, smoked salmon and oysters in a velvety vinaigrette, which, as the menu points out, is not only delicious, but low calorie. *Menus* €32–65. Tues, Thurs, Fri & Sun 12.30–2pm plus Tues–Sun 8–10pm.

Le Ventadour 23 quai Villebourbon ☎ 05 63 63 34 58. This is one of Montauban's top restaurants, magnificently sited in an old house on the west bank near the Pont-Vieux. *Menus* in the range €22–40. Mid-Jan to mid-Aug & Sept–Dec daily 8–9.30pm plus Tues–Fri noon–1.30pm & 8–9.30pm.

BARS

Le Flamand 8 rue de la République ☎ 05 63 66 12 20, ⓦ cafeflamand.com. This cheery bar-café is the place to go for a beer – they serve a huge selection and have pretty extensive *menus* (€7–17) to go with it, with dishes including home-made pizzas, grills and salads as well as more local fare such as *tartiflette* and *cassoulet*. Mon–Sat noon–midnight.

Lulu la Nantaise 46 rue de la République ☎ 05 63 63 00 99. Busy brasserie cum bar, frequented by a large number of locals. With chairs and tables spilling out over the cobbles, this is a great place for lunch on a sunny day and is equally good in the early evening for tapas. Lunch *menus* €10–15. Mon–Sat 8am–8pm (Fri 2–8pm).

Le Santa Maria 2 place Léon Bourjade ☎ 05 63 91 99 09. Sip your drinks on a terrace overlooking the Tarn; they also serve numerous tapas and more substantial Tex Mex meals at about €20, including wine and coffee. Tues & Wed 7pm–2am, Thurs & Fri 7pm–3am, Sat 7pm–5.30am; closed two weeks in Sept.

DIRECTORY

Hospital Centre Hospitalier, rue Léon Cladel ☎ 05 63 92 82 82, to the north of the old quarter.
Police Commissariat de Police, 50 bd Alsace-Lorraine (☎ 05 63 66 76 50), northeast of the centre.

Post office Allée de l'Empereur, 82000 Montauban.
Taxis There are taxi stands at the station and the north end of allée de l'Empereur, or call ☎ 05 63 66 99 99.

The Gorges de l'Aveyron and around

In its lower course the Aveyron glides across the dull flood plain surrounding Montauban, offering little reason to stop other than the village of **Montricoux**, with its museum dedicated to a forgotten artist. The scenery becomes more interesting, however, about 30km east of Montauban where the river has sliced a narrow defile through the hills. The entrance to the **Gorges de l'Aveyron** is guarded by the fortress village of **Bruniquel**, its ancient houses assembled higgledy-piggledy on steep cobbled streets, while further east **Penne** perches beneath a crumbling castle. From here on the gorge gets increasingly dramatic as you work your way upriver to **St-Antonin-Noble-Val**, an excellent base for exploring the gorge and surrounding sights. The most compelling of these is the partially ruined **Abbaye de Beaulieu-en-Rouergue**, located 14km northwest, where the Gothic church has been converted into a contemporary art gallery. Beyond St-Antonin, **Laguépie** is less interesting but provides another possible base, from where you can hop south to the beguiling – if very touristy – hilltop town of **Cordes-sur-Ciel**. At Laguépie the Aveyron valley turns

6

abruptly north, and its sides close in again to form a second, increasingly deep, thickly wooded gorge, dominated by the ruins of **Najac**'s mighty fortress. It stands guard over the frontier of the former province of Rouergue, now the Aveyron *département*, and the southern approach to the refreshingly unprettified *bastide* of **Villefranche-de-Rouergue**.

<table>
<tr><td>

GETTING AROUND

</td><td>

THE GORGES DE L'AVEYRON

</td></tr>
<tr><td>

Buses Several buses – run by GAU Autocars (☎ 05 63 30 44 45) run along the Aveyron between Montauban and Laguépie, though they cater mostly to schoolchildren, which means they don't necessarily run every day and tend

</td><td>

to be at inconvenient times.
By train The best way of travelling between Laguépie, Najac and Villefranche is the Toulouse–Brive train line; these trains also stop at Cordes, further south.

</td></tr>
</table>

Montricoux

Just before you leave the flat alluvial plains, 25km west of Montauban, **MONTRICOUX** would hardly be worth the stop if it weren't for its intriguing art museum, the **Musée Marcel-Lenoir** (May–Oct daily except Tues 10am–6pm; €5; ⓦ marcel-lenoir.com), on the west side of the village.

Like Ingres (see p.272), Marcel Lenoir was another prolific local artist, who was born in Montauban in 1872 and died in Montricoux in 1931. He was much fêted during his early years, when he was at the forefront of Pointillism and Cubism, and he even presaged Art Deco as he searched for new means of expression. But Lenoir was also an irascible character and managed to offend so many critics, dealers and galleries that he was eventually cast into oblivion. And there he stays, despite the best efforts of the owner of this collection of 140 works spanning Lenoir's whole career. One of the most revealing is the *Kiss of Judas*, in which you see Picasso profiled in blue and Van Gogh cutting off Gauguin's ear, while Judas is portrayed as a well-known art critic of the time.

<table>
<tr><td>

ARRIVAL AND DEPARTURE

</td><td>

MONTRICOUX

</td></tr>
<tr><td colspan="2">

By bus Buses from Montauban and Laguépie stop on the main road across from the village on the river's south bank.

</td></tr>
</table>

ACCOMMODATION AND EATING

Aicí sèm pla ☎ 05 63 30 98 01, ⓦ www.aicisempla .com. This is a delightfully friendly campsite on a farm in Revel, 2km from Vaïssac. Facilities include a communal BBQ, boules court, bike hire and free wi-fi. Closed mid-to late-Dec. €16

Chez Terrassier ☎ 05 63 30 94 60, ⓦ chezterrassier .net. For comfortable accommodation, head 8km southwest of Montricoux to this pretty, modern spot, with a pool, in the middle of Vaïssac. Their restaurant serves *menus* from €13 at lunch and €21 in the evenings.

Restaurant open Mon–Fri noon–1.30pm & 7.30–9pm, Sat noon–1.30pm. Breakfast €9.50. €80

Les Gorges de l'Aveyron Le Bugarel ☎ 05 63 24 50 50, ⓦ gorges-aveyron.com. As you walk into the village, you'll pass the entrance to this very swish riverside hotel-restaurant along a lane beside the bridge, and it's as good as it looks. Evening *menus* €29 (lunch €19). Restaurant open May–Aug daily noon–2pm & 7.30–9pm; Sept–April Wed–Sun noon–2pm & 7.30–9pm. Breakfast €13. €100

Bruniquel

East of Montricoux the hills rise suddenly and 5km later the **Gorges de l'Aveyron** really get into their stride as you catch sight of the first of several fortified villages along these rocky crags. Once a Protestant stronghold, **BRUNIQUEL** shelters in the lee of its **castle** (daily: March–June & Sept–Oct 10am–6pm, July & Aug 10am–7pm, Nov 10am–5pm; closed mid-Nov to March; €2.50, or €3.50 for guided tour), teetering on the edge of a hundred-metre cliff. In fact there are two adjacent castles, since the original twelfth-century fortress had to be divided between rival cousins in 1484, but both are rather knocked about, although there is an impressive carved wooden fireplace in the "new" castle.

More engaging is the **Maison des Comtes de Payrol** (April–Sept daily 10am–6pm, July & Aug till 7pm; Oct Sat & Sun 10am–5pm; Nov–Feb by appointment only; ☎05 63 67 26 42; €3) to the west of the castle entrance. The thirteenth-century home of a wealthy merchant family, its vaulted cellars and panelled and frescoed rooms now house an unusually good local history museum, including an interesting collection of oil lamps and candle holders.

ARRIVAL AND INFORMATION

By bus Buses stop about 250m below Bruniquel to the south, beside a road leading up to the church.

Tourist offfice At the entrance to the village (April–Sept daily 10am–1pm & 2–6pm; Oct–March same hours but variable closing days; ☎05 63 67 29 84, ⓦ bruniquel.fr). All practical information, including accommodation details, is listed outside.

ACCOMMODATION AND EATING

Cornelia ☎05 63 67 75 68, ⓦcornelia-bruniquel .com. The swanky, Dutch-run *Cornelia*, located 200m from the tourist office, has four rooms, including the "Romantique" with a round bed, and the hammock-strewn attic. *Table d'hôte* is €25 (24hr notice required; daily March–Oct). €69

L'Étape du Château Promenade du Ravelin ☎05 63 67 25 00, ⓦetapeduchateau.com. This *étape* is a little more upmarket than most, featuring a spa and a sauna. *Table d'hôte* €25 – available daily but must be reserved a day in advance. Closed Christmas to mid-Jan. Breakfast included. €48

Penne and around

Six kilometres upriver from Bruniquel you come to the even more beautiful ridge-top village of **PENNE**, once a Cathar stronghold, with its ruined **castle** perched on an impregnable pinnacle. Everything is old and leaning and bulging, but holding together nonetheless, with a harmony that would be impossible to create purposely. There's just one cobbled street leading from an arch under the church belfry and through a second gate – where ancient grain measures are cut into the wall – to a footpath scrambling among the castle ruins. There's not much left, although restoration work is being undertaken, and it's an atmospheric spot, the piles of stones overrun with dog-roses, clematis and honeysuckle, with a panorama taking in the village roofs and the wooded country beyond.

Beyond Penne the gorge becomes deeper and more dramatic. To appreciate it at its best, turn off the main road just after Cazals, 6km from Penne, following signs for the **Corniche**, a single-track road which climbs steeply for a kilometre or so up to the cliff's edge. You'll be rewarded with tremendous views and, a little further on, a superbly sited **restaurant**, *La Corniche* (see below). Six kilometres later, you drop down to the river again to the west of St-Antonin-Noble-Val.

EATING AND DRINKING

La Corniche Brousses ☎05 63 68 26 95. Generous country dishes in a friendly atmosphere. In summer tables are laid on the terrace, in order to enjoy the wide views over the lovely Aveyron valley. *Menus* from €22 at lunch, €29 in the evenings. March–Nov Tues–Sat noon–1.15pm & 7.30–9.30pm, Sun noon–1.15pm; Dec–Feb Fri–Sat noon–1.15pm & 7.30–9.30pm, Sun noon–1.15pm.

La Terrasse 13 rue Peyragude ☎05 63 56 35 03, ⓦla-terrasse-restaurant-tarn.com. A fabulously sited bar-restaurant at the north end of the village, from the back terrace of which you get a first-class view of the castle's airy crag. Lunch *menus* from €15 and evening *menus* at €23. June–Sept daily noon–2pm & 7.30–9pm; Sept–June Thurs–Sun noon–2pm & 7.30–9pm.

St-Antonin-Noble-Val and around

The finest and most substantial town in this lower stretch of the Aveyron valley is **ST-ANTONIN-NOBLE-VAL**, 16km northeast of Penne. It sits on the river's north bank beneath the beetling white cliffs of the **Roc d'Anglars**, where it developed in the ninth century around an abbey said to house the remains of the evangelizing **St Antonin**. According to legend, his body was carried here in a boat guided by two white eagles from Pamiers, in the Ariège, where the saint met his death. Since then the town has endured all the vicissitudes of this region's history: it sided with the Cathars, then the Protestants and each time was walloped by the alien power of the kings from the north, until it eventually sank into oblivion after the seventeenth century. Yet, in spite of it all, a marvellous heritage of houses endowed by wealthy merchants remains from its medieval glory days, when St-Antonin was an important commercial centre, manufacturing linen and leather goods.

The easiest landmark to head for is the spire of the large but uninteresting neo-Gothic **church**, towards the town's southeast corner. Along the church's west wall rue du Pont-de-l'Aveyron leads south to the bridge, while rue Guilhelm Peyre curves northeast to **place de la Halle**. This square is St-Antonin at its most picturesque, with its cafés and pint-sized *halle*, and the focus of an important Sunday-morning market.

Musée du Vieux St-Antonin

Place de la Halle • July & Aug Mon & Wed–Sat 3–8pm • €1, under-10s free – reservation only from the tourist office • ☎ 05 63 30 63 47

The town's finest building is the **Maison des Consuls**, whose origins go back to 1125. The facade is pierced with arcades, pairs of colonnaded openings and a contrastingly severe oblong window on the first floor, on one pillar of which Adam and Eve hide their modesty; the old man on the pillar to the left, holding some books and a staff, is Emperor Justinian (483–565), who codified Roman law. The building's most striking feature, however, is the tower with its top-heavy loggia and too-perfect machicolations added by the nineteenth-century architect Viollet-le-Duc – though he did save the building from collapse. It now houses the **Musée du Vieux St-Antonin**, with an uninspiring collection of objects to do with the former life of the place, including various prehistoric finds.

ARRIVAL AND DEPARTURE   **ST-ANTONIN-NOBLE-VAL**

By bus Buses on the Montauban–Laguépie route stop near the Crédit Agricole bank on avenue Paul-Benet, the boulevard to the north of the old centre.

INFORMATION AND ACTIVITIES

Tourist office In the *mairie* next to the church (March & Oct Mon 2–5.30pm; Tues–Sun 10am–12.30pm & 2–5.30pm; April–June & Sept daily 10am–12.30pm & 2–6pm; July & Aug daily 9.30am–12.30pm & 2–7pm; Nov–Feb Mon & Sat 2–5pm, Tues–Fri 10am–12.30pm & 2–5pm; ☎ 05 63 30 63 47, ⓦ saint-antonin-noble-val.com).

Outdoor activities St-Antonin is the starting point for canoeing down this lower stretch of the Aveyron.

Variation La Plage (☎ 05 63 68 25 25, ⓦ variation82.eu) offers canoe rental, rock climbing and pot-holing excursions.

The English Bookshop 12 rue de la Pélisserie (☎ 05 63 67 01 61, ⓦ theenglishbookshop.org). If you're looking for some holiday reading, this is the place – everything in this friendly little shop is in English. Opening times vary but they are generally open Fri–Sun in summer.

ACCOMMODATION

Gorges de l'Aveyron ☎ 05 63 30 69 76, ⓦ camping -gorges-aveyron.com. About 1.5km out of town on the Marsac road you'll find this friendly campsite next to the river, overlooked by the cliffs. Facilities include a pool, bar, restaurant and childrens' play area; they will also lend out BBQs. Closed Oct–April. **€22.90**

Le Ponget Ponget ☎ 05 63 68 21 13. Just out of town on the Caylus road you'll find this simple but peaceful and well-kept campsite with great views of the cliffs and river. Closed Sept–May. **€12**

La Résidence 37 rue Droite ☎ 05 63 67 37 56, ⓦ laresidence-france.com. Smart Dutch-German-run *chambre d'hôte* on the road leading northwest out of place de la Halle. The rooms are large and light, with tiles or wooden floorboards and high ceilings – one even has its own roof terrace. **€80**

Les Trois Cantons ☎ 05 63 31 98 57, ⓦ 3cantons.fr. Travel 6km north up onto the *causse* to this spacious and well-organized campsite with three-star facilities including a heated pool, shop and snack bar. Closed mid-Sept to mid-April. **€22.50**

EATING AND DRINKING

For picnic food there's an excellent boulangerie on place Buoc, with a boucherie opposite; and if you happen to be here on a Sunday morning there's a wonderful market that will supply all your culinary requirements.

Carré des Gourmands 13 bd des Thermes ☎ 05 63 30 65 49, ⓦ carredesgourmands.fr. The place to go for a good lunch. The building has been a spa, a hotel and is now a splendid restaurant with a terrace right on the river; menus from €17 at lunch and €28 in the evenings. July–Aug daily noon–1.30pm & 7.30–9.30pm; Sept–Dec &

Feb–June Fri–Tues noon–1.30pm & 7.30–9.30pm.
Gazpacho 25 av Paul Benet ☎ 05 63 30 63 85. For basic food, head to *Gazpacho*, which serves large portions of brasserie fare with *menus* from €12.50. It's very popular with local expats, and you're as likely to hear English spoken as French. Daily noon–2pm & 7–9pm.

Abbaye de Beaulieu-en-Rouergue

April–Oct daily: 10am–noon & 2–6pm • €5 • ☎ 05 63 24 60 00, ⓦ art-beaulieu-rouergue.com

Apart from exploring the gorge itself, the best excursion from St-Antonin takes you 14km northwest to the beautiful Cistercian **Abbaye de Beaulieu-en-Rouergue**, which lies deep among wooded hills. The abbey was founded in 1144, though the present buildings date from the thirteenth century, and are remarkably unscathed considering it was sacked and burnt during the Wars of Religion, looted again during the Revolution and then used as a barn until the late 1950s; in 1844 Viollet-le-Duc even wanted to rebuild the whole caboodle in St-Antonin but had to give up through lack of funds. The present owners have now restored the church to create a superb exhibition space for their collection of **contemporary art**; displays change several times a year, in combination with temporary exhibitions. The high, light nave with its clean lines and lack of ornamentation, save for the delicate rose windows and a few sculpted capitals, provides the perfect foil for works by Jean Dubuffet, Simon Hantaï and Henri Michaux, among others.

Varen

Upstream from St-Antonin, the Aveyron valley widens out for a while and is spoilt by stone quarries. The only reason to stop is the village of **VAREN**, 16km from St-Antonin on the river's north bank. Its Romanesque **church** and tiny area of old streets repay a quick wander, but the prime attraction is another excellent though fairly upmarket **restaurant** (see below).

EATING AND DRINKING   VAREN

Moulin de Varen ☎ 05 63 65 45 10. The choice of dishes at this charming restaurant is surprisingly wide and the food beautifully presented. Prices start at €12 for lunch, rising to €25 for dinner, and the owner prides himself on his

carefully selected wine list too – he's happy to discuss the required vintage at length. Reservations recommended. July & Aug Tues–Sun noon–2pm & 7–9pm; Sept–June Thurs to Sat noon–2pm & 7–9pm, Sun noon–2pm.

Laguépie

LAGUÉPIE, 9km east of Varen, where the cliffs begin to close in again, guards the confluence of the Viaur with the Aveyron. The village has nothing in the way of sights, but is pretty enough and provides a useful base, served both by occasional buses from Montauban and by trains on the Toulouse–Brive line. The **church** pinpoints the village centre occupying a spit of land between the two rivers.

ARRIVAL AND INFORMATION   LAGUÉPIE

By train The *gare SNCF* lies 500m northwest on the north bank of the Aveyron.
Destinations Cordes-sur-Ciel (4–6 daily; 20min); Figeac (4–6 daily; 1hr); Najac (4–6 daily; 10min); Toulouse

(3–5 daily; 1hr 20min); Villefranche-de-Rouergue (4–6 daily; 25min).
By bus Buses terminate either by the *gare SNCF* or beside the church.

Destinations Bruniquel (school term Mon–Fri 1 daily; school hols Tues, Thurs, Sat 1 daily; 1hr); Montauban (as for Bruniquel; 1hr 30min); St-Antonin-Noble-Val (as for Bruniquel; 25min); Villefranche-de-Rouergue (Mon–Sat 1 daily; 35min).

Tourist office Place du Foirail (daily 10am–noon & 3–5pm, closed Wed afternoon & Sun afternoon; ☎ 05 63 30 20 34, ⓦ laguepie-en-rouergue.fr).

ACCOMMODATION AND EATING

Les Deux Rivières ☎ 05 63 31 41 41, ⓦ logis-de-france .fr. Laguépie's one and only hotel is a friendly and well-priced place on the north side of the bridge across the Aveyron. It is also a good place to eat, offering a choice between a brasserie and a formal restaurant with *menus* from €12.50 (€22.50 in the evening). Restaurant June–Aug daily noon–1.45pm & 7.30–9pm; Sept–May Mon–Thurs noon–1.45pm & 7.30–9pm, Sat 7.30–9pm. Breakfast €9. **€46**

Les Tilleuls ☎ 05 63 30 22 32. Municipal campsite in a shady spot beside the Viaur, roughly 1km to the east of Laguépie. There's a snack bar, tennis courts and small pool with children's slides on site. Closed Sept–May. **€10.60**

Cordes-sur-Ciel

The traveller who, from the terrace of Cordes, watches the summer night knows that he has no need to go further and that, if he so wishes, the beauty of this place, day after day, will lift him from all solitude.

Albert Camus

While you're in this part of the world it would be a shame to miss out on the spectacularly sited fortified town of **CORDES-SUR-CIEL**, 15km south of Laguépie on the D922 (it's also accessible by train). The origins of the suffix *sur-ciel* ("in the sky") become obvious as you approach the foot of the sudden hill on which the town is built, girded by several concentric walls and endowed with a score of medieval houses. It is something of an open-air museum and artisan centre, hugely crowded during July and August, but otherwise an atmospheric place to spend a few hours.

Founded in 1222 by Count Raymond VII of Toulouse, Cordes grew rich on **leatherworking** and in the following century the walls had to be enlarged no fewer than seven times to contain the expanding population. Things took a downturn, however, with the arrival of the plague in the fifteenth century, but Cordes later recovered, and developed a notable lace industry in the nineteenth century. However, its real renaissance came in the 1970s, when hippies, including the **craftsmen** and **artisans** whose studios now cram the old town, arrived to put Cordes back on the map, attracted by its beauty and abandon.

Camus' words give some idea of the town's allure, and hard though it may be to achieve such a placid state when the streets are packed during summer days, in the evening or out of season the romance of Cordes returns. It's worth rising early to view the sunrise from the ramparts, and with every other building a medieval mansion, walking the town before the crowds arrive is a delight. Its layout is simple: the old citadelle – known as the **haut cité** – runs along and down the sides of the long and narrow ridge which juts up from the plain, while the modern part consists of a clump of streets at the foot of the old town's eastern tip. The best route to the *haut cité* is the knee-cracking Grande Rue de l'Horloge ascending from the tourist office (see opposite), although at busy times it is more pleasant to take one of the picturesque but less crowded side streets. Alternatively, a **petit train** (May–Sept; €3) makes frequent trips from outside the tourist office.

Maison de l'Art du Sucre et du Chocolat

April–June & Sept–Oct Wed–Sun 10.30am–12.30pm & 1.30–7pm; July & Aug daily 10.30am–12.30pm & 1.30–7pm • €3 • ☎ 05 63 56 02 40

The main sights are arranged along the old town's axis. Heading straight up from the tourist office, you'll pass through progressively older gateways towards the heart of the *cité*. En route, you'll come across the **Maison de l'Art du Sucre et du Chocolat**, an exhibition of sculptures made entirely out of sugar or chocolate. They have a couple on display in the shop, so it's worth sticking your head round the door even if you don't want to see the full museum.

Maison du Grand Fauconnier

About halfway along Grande Rue Raymond VII, the elegant and symmetrical arcaded face of the fourteenth-century **Maison du Grand Fauconnier** conceals the **Musée d'Art Moderne et Contemporain** (Feb–March & Nov–Dec 2–5pm; April–May & Oct 11.30am–12.30pm & 2–6.30pm; June–Sept 11am–12.30pm & 2–7pm; €3.50; ☎05 63 56 14 79), which features works by the figurative painter Yves Brayer, who lived in Cordes from 1940, a French-only audio presentation explaining the town's lace-making tradition and a motley collection of modern art, including minor pieces by Picasso, Miró and Klee.

Just across the street squats the ancient covered market, where you can peer down one of the town's famously deep wells.

Maison du Grand Veneur and the Musée Charles Portal

As you're strolling along Grande Rue Raymond VII, look out for the **Maison du Grand Veneur** ("House of the Great Hunter"), a wonderful Gothic pile whose otherwise plain stone facade is festooned with amusingly sculpted and extremely well-preserved medieval caricatures of beasts and hunters. A few doors down is the impressively carved frontage of Raymond of Toulouse's old palace. Carry on along the street to leave the cité via the **Porte des Ormeaux** ("Gate of the Elms"), where you'll find the **Musée Charles Portal** (July & Aug daily except Tues 2–6pm; June & Sept Sat & Sun 2–6pm; May & Oct Sat & Sun 2–5pm; €2.50; ☎musee-charles-portal.asso-web.com). The official entrance to the museum is off rue St-Michel, and it houses a display on the medieval wells that riddle the town, and which were used in time of siege for water supply or to store grain.

ARRIVAL AND INFORMATION

CORDES-SUR-CIEL

By train Trains stop 5km to the west of Cordes at Vindrac (☎05 63 56 05 64), from where it's a pleasant hour-long walk or short taxi ride (☎05 63 56 14 80; about €5, more at weekends).

Destinations (Cordes-Vindrac) to: Figeac (4–6 daily; 1hr 20min); Laguépie (4–6 daily; 20min); Najac (4–6 daily; 30min); Toulouse (3–5 daily; 1hr); Villefranche-de-Rouergue (4–6 daily; 50min).

By bus Buses from Albi arrive near the tourist office in the lower town.

Destinations Albi (Mon–Sat 1–2 daily; 40min–1hr).

By car Parking can be a challenge – in the summer months the area a few metres east of the tourist office soon

fills up and cars line the roads leading into town. Don't be tempted to drive into the *haut cité*, better to park at the bottom and take the tourist train (see opposite).

Tourist office Place Jeanne Ramel-Cals (April–June & Sept–Oct Mon–Sat 10.30am–12.30pm & 2–6pm, Sun till 5pm; July & Aug Mon–Sat 9.30am–1pm & 2–6.30pm, Sun 10am–1pm & 2–6pm; Nov–March Mon–Sat 10.30am–12.30pm & 2–6pm, Sun till 5pm ☎05 63 56 00 52, ☎cordessurciel.fr). There's also an information point in the *haut cité* in the Musée d'Art Moderne et Contemporain (Feb–March & Nov–Dec 2–5pm; April–May & Oct 11.30am–12.30pm & 2–6.30pm; June–Sept 11am–12.30pm & 2–7pm).

ACCOMMODATION AND EATING

There are numerous options for eating in Cordes. The best restaurants are in the town's hotels, but there are plenty of cheaper options around the central place de la Halle and adjacent place de la Bride – some also offer magnificent views over the valley.

De la Cité Haut cité ☎05 63 56 03 53, ☎hoteldelacite -cordessurciel.com. Very pleasant two-star option, with large, clean rooms; it's an annexe of the *Vieux Cordes* (see p.282) and shares the same restaurant. Closed mid-Oct to Easter. Breakfast €12.50. **€79**

L'Escuelle des Chevaliers 87 Grande Rue Raymond VII ☎05 63 87 14 40, ☎micheldemonsegur.free.fr. Fantastic hostelry in a fourteenth-century building, adorned with heraldic tapestries. The owner has tried to preserve the atmosphere of the age of chivalry. Suits of armour and

6

ancient swords stand against the walls whilst pewter candelabra adorn the tables. The restaurant offers medieval-inspired dishes, rich ragouts and sucking pig followed by roasted chestnuts. There are even costumes supplied for knights and their ladies to wear during the meal. Restaurant open noon–2pm & 7.30–9pm (residents only Nov–April); reservations essential. Breakfast included. **€62**

Le Garissou ☎ 05 63 56 27 14, ⓦ aquadis-loisirs.com. A good campsite located in Les Cabannes, on the west of town. Facilities include a snack bar and pool. Closed Sept–May. **€13.20**

Le Vieux Cordes Haut cité ☎ 05 63 53 79 20, ⓦ hostelleriehvc.com. Probably the most atmospheric of the town's hotels, with stone walls, spiral staircases and elegant rooms. The restaurant serves *menus* from €22.50 and in summer you can eat in the ancient, cobbled courtyard under a canopy of wisteria. Don't miss out on the delicious desserts. Restaurant open June–Sept Wed–Sun noon–1.30pm & 7.30–9pm; Oct–Dec & Feb–May Wed–Sat noon–1.30pm & 7.30–9pm. Breakfast €12.50. **€62**

SHOPPING

There are more than forty boutiques in Cordes, including some which are thinly disguised as "museums". If you would like to shop for leatherwork, metal and handicraft items and price is not an issue, you could easily spend an afternoon or two (and a considerable sum) here. Many of the stores double as workshops, so even window-shopping is quite interesting.

Najac

At Laguépie (see p.279), the Aveyron valley heads northwards and the river flows through a wooded defile. The most picturesque route along the valley bottom is either the train or the GR36 footpath, while road users should take the D106 and D594 along the western line of hills. Either way, you eventually arrive at a bridge – 15km by road and slightly less on foot – beneath the brooding towers of **NAJAC**'s semi-ruined **castle**.

The castle occupies an extraordinary site on the peak of a conical hill isolated in the river's wide meander – a site chosen in the mid-1200s by **Alphonse de Poitiers** who wanted to bring the area's Cathar sympathizers to heel. He enlarged the original fortress and laid out a new town to the east in an elongated version of a *bastide* with its arcades and central market square. For a short while Najac prospered as the region's capital, but the site proved too restrictive and by the end of the thirteenth century it had lost out to Villefranche-de-Rouergue (see opposite), leaving the castle to be fought over endlessly in the conflicts that ensued. The Protestants pillaged it in 1572 and the revolutionaries had their turn in 1793, but, in spite of all this, Najac survived.

The heart of modern Najac consists of a big, open square lying to the east of the medieval village, where grey-tiled houses tail out westwards in a single street along the narrow spur connecting the valley side to the castle hill.

The château

Daily: April, May, Sept & Oct 10am–1pm & 3–5.30pm; June 10.30am–1pm & 3–6.30pm; early July 10.30am–1.30pm & 3–6.30pm; end July & Aug 10.30am–7pm; last week in Aug 10.30am–1.30pm & 3–7pm • €4 • ☎ 05 65 29 71 65

Entering Najac from the east you come first to the **faubourg**, the elongated market square bordered by houses raised on pillars. It slopes gently downhill towards a cobbled street, overlooked by more ancient houses, which leads past a fountain to the **château**. The castle is a model of medieval defensive architecture: its curtain walls reach to over 20m in places, within which five round towers supplement the square twelfth-century turret, and the castle is equipped with unusual multi-storey loopholes for archers. However, the main reason to visit is for the magnificent all-round view from the top of the keep, a full 200m above the river.

Church of St-Jean

April–Sept daily 10am–noon & 2–6pm; Oct Sun only • Free

Just below the castle, in what was the original medieval village, stands the huge, very solid-looking and austere **church of St-Jean**, which the villagers were forced to build at their own expense in 1258 as a punishment for their conversion to Catharism. In addition to a collection of reliquaries and an extraordinary iron cage for holding candles, the church has one architectural oddity: its windows are solid panels of stone from which the lights have been cut out in trefoil form. Below the church, a surviving Roman road leads downhill to where a thirteenth-century bridge spans the Aveyron.

ARRIVAL AND INFORMATION   NAJAC

By train The *gare SNCF* lies on the north side of the old bridge, 2km by road below the village. If you need a taxi, call ☎ 05 65 81 12 92.

Destinations Cordes-sur-Ciel (4–6 daily; 30min); Figeac (4–6 daily; 50min); Laguépie (4–6 daily; 10min); Toulouse (3–5 daily; 1hr 30min); Villefranche-de-Rouergue (4–6 daily; 15min).

By bus The bus from Villefranche terminates on the square to the east of the village.

Destinations Villefranche-de-Rouergue (Mon–Sat 1 daily; 30min).

Tourist office On the south side of the *faubourg* (April–June & Sept Mon–Sat 9am–noon & 2–6pm; July & Aug daily 9am–noon & 2–6pm; Oct–March Mon–Fri 9am–noon & 2–5pm, Sat 9am–noon; ☎ 05 65 29 72 05, ⓦ tourismenajac.com).

ACCOMMODATION AND EATING

Le Belle Rive ☎ 05 65 29 73 90, ⓦ lebellerive.fr. This welcoming and old-fashioned hotel occupies a lovely riverside position near the train station. From the garden you get an ant's-eye view of the château towering above. They also run an excellent restaurant serving good-value regional cooking, with *menus* from €24. Restaurant open April–Sept daily 12.30–2pm & 7.30–9pm; Oct Mon–Sat 12.30–2pm & 7.30–9pm. Breakfast €9. **€65**

Gîte d'Étape ☎ 05 65 29 73 94, ⓦ aagac.com. Budget accommodation situated at the leisure centre adjacent to the campsite (see below). Sparse but clean rooms have from 2 to 6 beds, there is a communal kitchen and dining area and also a restaurant facility for groups of 15 and over, reserved in advance. Closed Oct–April. **€15.30**

L'Oustal del Barry 2 place Sol del Barry ☎ 05 65 29 74 32, ⓦ oustaldelbarry.com. At the *faubourg's* east entrance you'll find this very comfortable hotel, whose restaurant is renowned for its subtle and inventive

cuisine. *Menus* from €21. April to mid-Dec daily 12.30–2pm & 7.30–9pm. Reservations essential. Breakfast €9.80. **€62**

Le Païsserou ☎ 05 65 29 73 96, ⓦ lescledelles.com. Najac's four-star riverside campsite, to the southwest of the old bridge, is spacious and very well equipped. Facilities include a restaurant/snack bar and large pool. Closed Sept–May. **€18.50**

★ **Relais Mont Le Viaur** St Andre de Najac, 1km east of Najac ☎ 05 65 65 08 08, ⓦ montleviaur.fr. Lovely stone building boasting calm, simply decorated rooms with en-suite bathrooms. The highlight is its wonderful restaurant – *the* place to eat in the area. They serve beautifully presented food, combining traditional and modern cuisine, with *menus* at €13 and €19.90. Restaurant open daily noon–2pm & 7–10pm; closed two weeks in Dec. All products are market-fresh and reservations are essential. Breakfast €8.50. **€58**

Villefranche-de-Rouergue

The second stretch of the Aveyron gorge peters out about 10km north of Najac, but it's worth continuing upstream the same distance again to the laid-back market town of **VILLEFRANCHE-DE-ROUERGUE**, which boasts one of the most atmospheric central squares in the whole region. As its regular form and the die-straight streets indicate, this is a *bastide*, founded in 1252 by the ubiquitous **Alphonse de Poitiers**, as part of the royal policy of extending control over the recalcitrant lands of the south. Villefranche became rich on trade and on copper from the surrounding mines. In 1369 it was also made the seat of the seneschal, the king's representative, with the right to mint money. While its wealthy merchants built the ornate houses that grace the cobbled streets to this day, conditions in the surrounding countryside were so desperate that in 1643,

6

more than ten thousand peasants, known as **Croquants** (see p.297), besieged the town for a week. As elsewhere, the rebellion was harshly put down and the leaders strung up in the market square.

The medieval quarter

Villefranche's medieval quarter lies on the north bank of the Aveyron, accessed by a modern road-bridge beside its pedestrian fourteenth-century counterpart. From the old bridge, the town's main commercial street, pedestrianized **rue de la République**, runs northwards up a gentle incline into the heart of the *bastide*. It is attractive enough, but no preparation for the central square you come out into, **place Notre-Dame**. The square, too, is built on a slope and is surrounded by unusually tall houses, arcaded at ground-floor level, some of which display elaborate window surrounds. If possible, try to visit on a Thursday morning when local merchants and farmers spread out their produce at the weekly **market**, presided over by the colossal porch and bell tower – nearly 60m high and fortified – of the **Collégiale Notre-Dame**, which dominates the square's east side. The church was started in 1260 but wars and fires intervened and it was not finally completed until 1519. Behind the altar are two fine mid-fifteenth-century stained-glass windows: the one on the left depicts the Creation; that on the right portrays sixteen characters from the Old and New Testaments. Also worth noting are the oak choir stalls alive with a superb array of beasts and demons, as well as scenes from daily life – they took the craftsman, André Sulpice, fifteen years to complete in the late fifteenth century.

Chapelle des Pénitents-Noirs

April–June Tues–Sat 2–6pm; July–Sept daily 10am–noon & 2–6pm • €4

On boulevard Haute Guyenne, which forms the northern limit of the old town, the seventeenth-century **Chapelle des Pénitents-Noirs** boasts a splendidly Baroque painted ceiling and an enormous gilded retable – resplendent after its recent renovation.

Chartreuse St-Sauveur

April–June Tues–Sat 2–6pm; July–Sept daily 10am–noon & 2–6pm • €4

An ecclesiastical building worth the slight detour is the **Chartreuse St-Sauveur**, in the grounds of a hospital about 1km south of town on the main D922 to Najac and Laguépie. It was completed in the space of ten years from 1450, giving it a singular architectural harmony. The highlight is the second of the two cloisters, a minuscule quadrangle of white, sculpted stone, while the church itself contains more examples of André Sulpice's craftsmanship on the screen and choir stalls.

ARRIVAL AND INFORMATION   VILLEFRANCHE-DE-ROUERGUE

By train The *gare SNCF* is located a couple of minutes' walk south across the Aveyron from the old centre.

Destinations Cordes-sur-Ciel (4–6 daily; 50min); Figeac (4–6 daily; 45min); Laguépie (4–6 daily; 25min); Najac (4–6 daily; 15min); Toulouse (3–5 daily; 1hr 40min).

By bus The *gare routière* is next to the *gare SNCF* on the southern side of the river (see above).

Destinations Cahors (Mon–Fri 1 daily; 1hr 25min); Figeac (1–2 daily; 40min); Laguépie (school term Mon–Fri 1 daily;

40min); Montauban (Mon–Sat 1 daily; 1hr 45min); Najac (Mon–Sat 1 daily; 45min).

Car rental Location U av de Toulouse, on the north side of town (☎ 05 65 65 15 47).

Tourist office Promenade du Giraudet (May, June & Sept Mon–Fri 9am–noon & 2–7pm, Sat 9am–noon & 2–6pm; July & Aug also open Sun 10am–12.30pm; Oct–April Mon–Fri 9am–noon & 2–6pm, Sat 9am–noon; ☎ 05 65 45 13 18, ⓦ villefranche.com).

ACCOMMODATION

Given its size, Villefranche is rather lacking in accommodation options, although there are one or two a little way out of town. The reason seems to be that Villefranche is just that little bit too far off the beaten track, and although it's a beautiful town, tourism is still limited, which of course only adds to its attractions.

★ **Auberge de la Poste** 45 rue Prestat ☎ 05 65 45 13 91. Friendly, labyrinthine old place opposite the post office, with decent rooms, though the cheapest share bathrooms. If you can brave the stairs, room 23 is a portholed eyrie on the top floor with views over the town rooftops. Their restaurant is open daily noon–2pm & 7–9.30pm and serves *menus* at €16. Breakfast €6. €42

Camping du Rouergue ⓦ campingdurouergue.com. Huge but friendly three-star municipal campsite, 1.5km to the south of Villefranche, signed off the D47 to Monteils. Facilities include pool, table tennis and a *buvette* (bar) in July & Aug. Closed Sept–April. 14.62

Les Fleurines 17 bd Haute Guyenne ☎ 05 65 45 86 90, ⓦ lesfleurines.com. Beautifully converted old stone building, decorated in contemporary style and ideally situated opposite the Chapelle des Pénitents-Noirs (see opposite). Breakfast €9.80. €69

Foyer des Jeunes Travailleurs 23 rue Lapeyrade ☎ 05 65 81 44 32, ⓦ fjtvillefranche.fr. HI-affiliated hostel providing some of the best-value accommodation you'll find anywhere nearby, in a wood-faced building next to the train station. It offers individual, double or family en-suite rooms – some of which are huge, with mezzanine floors and separate seating areas – kitchen facilities and canteen meals. You must either be or become an HI member to stay here (€10 for membership). Meals must be reserved a day in advance. Dorms €17.50, doubles €22

Relais de Farrou Rte de Figeac ☎ 05 65 45 18 11, ⓦ relaisdefarrou.com. Smart hotel about 20min out of town on the Figeac road; guests have use of a small spa and gym, and the hotel also provides bicycles and other activities. Restaurant open July & Aug daily, Sept–June Tues–Sat noon–2pm & 7.30–9pm. Breakfast €10. €100

EATING AND DRINKING

L'Assiette Gourmande Place André Lescure ☎ 05 65 45 25 95. Smart restaurant one block north of the church serving traditional meals in a pleasant stone-vaulted room or out on the square in fine weather. *Menus* from €15.50 lunch and €19.50 in the evenings. July & Aug Mon–Sat noon–1.30 & 7.30–9pm; Sept to end Dec & mid-Jan to June Mon, Thurs–Sat noon–1.30pm & 7.30–9pm, Tues noon–1.30pm.

L'Epicurien 8bis rue Raymond Saint-Gilles ☎ 05 65 45 01 12, ⓦ restaurant-leepicurien-villefranche.fr. Just down the road from the train station, Villefranche's most upmarket option specializes in fish, with *menus* from €15 at lunch or €30 in the evenings. Tues–Sat noon–2.30pm &

7–9.30pm, Sun noon–2.30pm.

La Gabelle 10 rue Belle-Isle ☎ 05 65 45 57 13, ⓦ lagabelle-restaurant-rouergue.com. Cheap and cheerful place one block south of the church, where you can eat pizzas, home-made pastas and grills from around €7.50. Mid-Jan to mid-June & July to Christmas Tues–Sat noon–2.30 & 7–10.30pm.

Le Globe 1 place de la République ☎ 05 65 45 23 19. Bustling, modern and hugely popular brasserie just across the old bridge, serving simple but decent fare. *Menus* from €14 including wine. July & Aug daily 7am–1am; Sept–June Mon–Thurs 7am–9pm, Fri & Sat 7am–midnight.

CYRANO DE BERGERAC

Contexts

History

The history of the Dordogne and Lot region is a fascinating illustration of how the political entity that is now a unified France in fact consists of numerous components of entirely distinct historical character. The southwest's vigorously independent cultural identity was forged millennia ago in the artistic endeavours of mysterious but highly gifted cave-dwellers, and hundreds of years ago in the influence of English rule and in the poetry of the troubadours, written in a language now virtually extinct. Even from the fifteenth century onwards, when the region was officially part of metropolitan France, it remained a distant territory, at least a week's travel from Paris, and one where local interests and powerful families held far more sway than the voice of the king. To this political detachment must be added the entirely secluded nature of the life led by the vast majority of the region's population, barely 15 percent of whom lived in towns even as late as 1910. Communicating in myriad local dialects, worshipping the gods of local folklore and working on the land in the same manner as their ancestors had for centuries, the rural poor of the Dordogne and Lot, largely oblivious to the causes – though certainly not the devastating consequences – of the political and religious conflicts going on around them, were only in the twentieth century dragged into the familiar historical timeline.

The beginnings

Primitive flint tools found in the Dordogne indicate human presence dating back at least 400,000 years. However, the region's archeological treasure trove really gets going with the **Neanderthal** people, who arrived on the scene some 100,000 years ago. Despite their brutish image, evidence now suggests that Neanderthals were surprisingly sophisticated. They developed not only an increasingly elaborate range of stone tools but also complex burial rituals. This didn't, however, equip them to compete with the next wave of immigrants sweeping across Europe between 30,000 and 40,000 years ago, and Neanderthals gradually died out.

Early archeologists named the newcomers **Cro-Magnon** after a rock shelter near Les Eyzies where the first skeletons were identified. Now they are better known as *Homo sapiens sapiens* – in other words, our direct ancestors. While Cro-Magnons developed ever more sophisticated tools, they also began to scratch fertility symbols into the rock, made various pigments and then took the great leap into abstraction that led to drawing, painting and carving. The earliest evidence of **prehistoric art** dates from around 30,000 years ago, but reached its apogee during the **Magdalenian** era

400,000 BC	c.30,000 BC	200 BC	51 BC	c.15 AD
Evidence of human presence in the Dordogne	Cro-Magnons create the earliest cave art near Les Eyzies	Romans begin to colonize southern France	Julius Caesar wins the battle of Uxullodunum (Puy D'Issolud), crushing tribal rule in the area	Administrative centres created at Divona Cadurcorum (Cahors) and Vesunna (Périgueux)

(10,000–17,000 years ago) – also named after a shelter in the Dordogne's Vézère valley. It was during this era that Cro-Magnon people covered the walls and ceilings of the region's caves with art of a quality that would not be seen again for several millennia.

Around 10,000 BC the all-important reindeer herds, the Cro-Magnons' one-stop source of meat, fat, skin, bone and sinew, began to move north as the climate grew warmer and wetter. Over the next three thousand years these nomadic hunter-gatherers were gradually replaced by settled **farming and pastoral communities** who left hundreds of **dolmens** (megalithic stone tombs) scattered over the region. This Neolithic era in its turn made way for the great metal-working cultures, culminating in the Iron Age, from around 700 BC. About the same time **Celtic** people began to spread into the region from north and central Europe, establishing trade routes and building towns and hilltop fortresses. They were skilled manufacturers and had their own coinage, but instead of a cohesive entity, comprised individual or loosely allied clans, continuously fighting among themselves. It was these disunited tribes that the Roman legions encountered when they arrived in what they called **Gaul** – roughly equivalent to modern France – in the second century BC.

The Roman occupation

At first the **Romans** contented themselves with a colony along the Mediterranean coast, but in 59 BC the threat of a Germanic invasion and various Celtic uprisings prompted **Julius Caesar** to subjugate the entire area. It took him just eight years. By 56 BC he had pacified southwest Gaul and the only real opposition came from a young Arvenian (modern-day Auvergne) chieftain called **Vercingetorix** who managed to rally a united Gaulish opposition in 52 BC. The Gauls had some initial victories, but in the end were no match for Caesar's disciplined armies. Vercingetorix was taken back to Rome in chains in 52 BC and the following year the Gauls staged their final stand at **Uxellodunum**, under the command of Lucterius, leader of the Cadurci. Caesar himself took command of the siege and eventually cut off their water supply thus forcing the surrender. **Uxellodunum** is generally believed to be at Puy d'Issolud, to the east of Martel (see p.180).

The battle was one of the major turning points in the region's history. In 16 AD Emperor Augustus established the new Gallo-Roman province of **Aquitania**, stretching from Poitiers south to the Pyrenees. Its capital was Burdigala (Bordeaux), and regional administrative centres were set up in Vesunna (Périgueux) and Divona Cadurcorum (Cahors), each with its forum, amphitheatre, law courts and temples. During more than three centuries of peace – the **Pax Romana** – that followed, the Romans built roads, introduced new technologies, traded, planted vineyards and established an urbanized society administered by an educated, Latin-speaking elite. Today, the physical traces of this practically and culturally sophisticated society are most visible in the Roman ruins in Périgueux and Cahors. Just as durable, though, has been the linguistic impact: as well as being the language of the rulers, Latin penetrated rural areas and eventually fused with the local Celtic dialects to form two broad new language groups: the *langue d'Oïl* (where "yes" is *oïl* – later, *oui*), spoken north of the Loire, and the *langue d'Oc*, or *Occitan* (where "yes" is *oc*), to the south.

By the third century AD, Roman authority was starting to crack. Oppressive aristocratic rule and an economic crisis turned the destitute peasantry into gangs of

16 AD	360 AD	507 AD	c.650
Emperor Augustus establishes the Gallo-Roman province of Aquitania	Frankish tribes invade from the north	Clovis, king of the Franks, founds the Merovingian dynasty	St Didier, bishop of Cahors, founds the abbey of St Pierre, Moissac

marauding brigands, who were particularly rampant in the southwest. But more devastating were the incursions across the Rhine by various restless **Germanic tribes**, starting with the Alemanni and Franks, who pushed down as far as Spain, ravaging farmland and looting towns along the way. In response, urban centres such as Périgueux were hurriedly fortified while the nobles hot-footed it to their country villas, which became increasingly self-sufficient – economically, administratively and militarily.

The crunch came, however, in the fifth century when first the Vandals and then the **Visigoths** stormed through the region as the Roman empire crumbled. For nearly a hundred years the Visigoths ruled a huge territory extending across southern France and into Spain, with its capital at Toulouse.

Christianity and independence

The Visigoths' destructive and mercenary temperament did not conduce to sustained rule, and in 507 AD they were driven out of the region by the **Franks**, a northern tribe who gave their name to modern France. The end of the Visigoths marked the beginning of a long period of relative independence for Aquitaine and the southwest. Although the Frankish king, Clovis, was to found the **Merovingian dynasty** whose power technically extended to this region, he failed to re-establish the same over-arching authority as the Romans had had.

The power vacuum had been filled, in part, by representatives of the early Church. **Christianity** had arrived from Rome in the early fourth century and was spreading slowly through France, but the invasion of the Vandals and Visigoths had put its advance on hold. It fell to **bishop Chronope**, active in the region between 506 and 533 AD, to re-establish the faith by a prolific programme of church building, most notably the first cathedral of St-Etienne in Périgueux. Chronope is also thought to have played a role in the creation of the legend of St-Front, after whom Périgueux's modern cathedral is named. Clovis himself had embraced Christianity around 500 AD and thereafter was happy to devolve a great deal of everyday administration to local bishops, such as those at Cahors.

The Merovingian empire began to disintegrate in the late seventh century, leaving the way clear for their chancellors, the Pepin family, to take control. One of their most dynamic scions, **Charles Martel**, defeated the Spanish Moors when they swept up through the southwest as far as Poitiers in 732. His grandson, **Charlemagne**, continued the expansionist policy of the **Carolingian** dynasty – so called for their fondness for the name Charles, or "Carolus" – to create an empire which eventually stretched from the Baltic to the Pyrenees.

Charlemagne and his descendants, however, had no more genuine control over the southwest region than the Merovingians had, preferring, like them, to rule from a distance. In 781 Charlemagne created the quasi-independent **kingdom** of Aquitaine – an area extending from the Loire to the Cévennes and from the Rhône to the Pyrenees. Within the kingdom, the Carolingians delegated administrative power to royally appointed bishops, now joined by a growing number of counts – Quercy and Périgord for example – who had been awarded territory in exchange for their loyalty. In theory, the king retained feudal authority, but in reality the bishops and counts did largely as they pleased.

c.732	781	814	844
Charles Martel defeats the invading Moors and founds the Carolingian dynasty	Charlemagne creates the quasi-independent kingdom of Aquitaine	Death of Charlemagne	Plundering Vikings sail up the Lot, Garonne, Dordogne and Isle rivers

THE WAY OF ST JAMES

According to the Bible, **St James the Apostle** was decapitated in Jerusalem in 44 AD. There is nothing to suggest how his remains came to be buried in northwest Spain, but in 820 it was declared that they had been discovered there, and during the fervent religious revival of the Middle Ages millions of pilgrims began flocking to his supposed tomb in **Santiago de Compostela**. The route took on a life of its own: monasteries, churches and hospitals were founded and villages grew up along the way to cater for the pilgrims wearing their distinctive cockleshell badge.

The pilgrimage faded out during the sixteenth century, partly because of the wars sweeping France and partly because the cathedral canons rather carelessly lost the saint's remains; the relics were allegedly hidden to keep them out of the hands of Sir Francis Drake, who was then sniffing around Galicia, but later no one could remember where they'd put them. By another "miracle" they were rediscovered by archeologists in 1879, declared by the pope to be the genuine article, and the pilgrimage revived, though on a far more modest scale.

In 1998 the whole system of paths and associated buildings was inscribed on the UNESCO World Heritage list. As a result, to walk the **chemin de St-Jacques** (Way of St James) – or at least some of it – has become popular again, partly as a spiritual quest, but also simply as a walking holiday. Three of the four main routes – from Vézelay, Le Puy-en-Velay and Arles – have been waymarked as long-distance footpaths (*grandes randonnées*, or GRs). Of these the GR654 from Vézelay and the GR65 from Le Puy pass through the Dordogne and Lot region; booklets outlining the routes are available in the Topo-guide series (see p.304).

The royal position became weaker still in the ninth century, in part due to a long-drawn-out **battle of succession** following Charlemagne's death in 814, but also thanks to a series of extravagantly destructive raids by the **Vikings**, who sailed their longboats down from Scandinavia. They had been raiding coastal areas for decades, but in 844 they penetrated deep inland along the Garonne, Dordogne, Isle and Lot rivers, plundering towns and churches. Périgueux was razed in 849: the annals of one monastery recount matter-of-factly, "the devastating Normans put fire to Périgueux and, without further ado, got back on their boats."

In the face of these destabilizing invasions the Carolingians were obliged to delegate ever more autonomy to the provincial governors until these eventually grew more powerful than the king. So it was that when **Hugues Capet** succeeded to the French throne in 987, founding a 400-year dynasty that in theory ruled the whole of France, he in practice had authority only over a small area near Paris. Around the turn of the millennium, Aldebert I, one of the counts of Périgord, is supposed to have rebuked a royal demand for payment of feudal dues with the withering question "*Qui vous a fait roi?*" – "Who made you king, then?" By this point, the local aristocratic families were more embroiled in jostling for power with one another than with the king. In the tenth century Périgord was carved up into four **baronies** (Beynac, Mareuil, Bourdeilles and Biron), while Quercy was divided between five powerful families (Turenne, Gourdon, Cardaillac, Castelnau and St-Sulpice). At the same time, the counts of Poitou (based at Poitiers) and Toulouse were fighting for control of what was once again the **Duchy of Aquitaine**. The former emerged victorious, thus creating a vast territory that by the twelfth century reached from the Loire to the Pyrenees. The Poitou counts also ushered in a period of relative peace, rapid economic growth and renewed religious vigour,

849	987	c.990	1122
Vikings raze Périgueux	Hugues Capet crowned king of France and founds the Capetian dynasty	Counts of Poitou take control of Aquitaine and begin construction of the Romanesque churches	Birth of Eleanor of Aquitaine

demonstrated in a wave of church building. To them we owe the lovely Romanesque churches (see box, p.294) seen throughout the region to this day. At least some of this building activity was spurred and financed by the great procession of **pilgrims** passing along the route to Santiago de Compostela in Spain (see box opposite).

English rule

It was the huge kingdom created by the amalgamation of the territories of the counts of Poitou and the dukes of Aquitaine that indirectly allowed the whole of the Dordogne and Lot region to fall into the hands of the **English Crown**. The cause of this catastrophe for the French royal family, the Capetian dynasty, was the strong-willed **Eleanor of Aquitaine** (1122–1204; see box below), who inherited the domains of Aquitaine and Poitou in 1137 at the tender age of 15. Fifteen years later, she ditched

---

ELEANOR OF AQUITAINE

The life of **Eleanor of Aquitaine** (1122–1204) is an incredible tale of romance and tragedy, of high farce and low intrigue that rivals any modern-day pot-boiler. As duchess of Aquitaine and countess of Poitou she was already a key figure in twelfth-century Europe. She then married two kings and gave birth to two more, effectively ruled England for a time and died at the grand old age of 82.

In 1137, at the age of just 15, Eleanor inherited the domains of Aquitaine and Poitou. These assets, combined with her intelligence and beauty, gave her a healthy list of suitors, at the head of which was the future King Louis VII of France. They were married in Bordeaux's St-André cathedral, and just a week later, the death of Louis VI made the young couple king and queen of France. The marriage, however, was not a success: it bore no male heirs, and the vivacious Eleanor found her attentions wandering elsewhere. In March 1152, they were divorced.

Just two months later, Eleanor married the handsome, charismatic and extremely ambitious **Henry of Anjou**, who was eleven years her junior, but far closer in temperament. The following year she bore him the all-important heir, and, when Henry II succeeded to the English throne in 1154, Eleanor found herself queen of England.

Although Eleanor spent much of her time in France, she and Henry produced at least eight children. Of these both Richard and John became kings of England, while only two, John and Eleanor, outlived her. In the meantime, since Henry proved reluctant to delegate power, his sons rebelled against him in 1173, supported by both Eleanor and her former husband, Louis VII; the latter hoped to put a more compliant neighbour on the English throne – and was possibly also out for a spot of revenge.

But the rebellion soon collapsed and Henry placed his wife under house arrest. She remained closely guarded until his death in 1189, but her problems had by no means ended. Richard I (the Lionheart), Eleanor's favourite son, was next in line. All went well until he was captured in 1192 while returning from the Third Crusade. The indomitable seventy-year-old waded in as unofficial regent, while also keeping her French possessions under control, for the next two years.

Eleanor withdrew from public life after Richard's release, and even more so after his death in 1199. She retired to the abbey of Fontevraud, in the Loire valley, where she died almost unnoticed in 1204, to be remembered as a popular, shrewd and effective ruler, well able to control her notoriously hot-blooded southern vassals.

1137	c.1140	1152	1154
Eleanor becomes duchess of Aquitaine at the age of 15	The fortified Château de Beynac is constructed at Beynac-et-Cazenac	Henry Plantagenet, Duke of Anjou and Normandy, later Henry II, is united to Eleanor of Aquitaine in Poitiers cathedral	Henry Plantagenet succeeds to the English throne and the region comes under English rule, ushering in a golden age of prosperity

her first husband, the French king, to marry **Henry of Anjou**, thereby creating an empire comprising Anjou and Normandy in addition to Eleanor's possessions. This in itself was a disastrous blow to the Capetians, but it was compounded in 1154 when Henry succeeded to the English throne (as Henry II). As a result, almost half of France fell under English rule. Much of it would remain so for the next three hundred years.

For the southwest region itself, however, English rule ushered in a period of peace, stability and impressive economic progress. With the major exception of **Richard the Lionheart** (Richard Coeur de Lion), Eleanor's third son, who plundered the region ruthlessly, the **English overlords** proved to be popular. For the most part they ruled from a distance, often preferring to stay put in England, and ensured the loyalty of their southern subjects by granting a large degree of independence to many of Aquitaine's rapidly growing towns and their local lords. Peasants lived under relatively privileged feudal conditions, helped by the fact that local lords were often in competition for their services. An important factor here was the building of dozens of **new towns**, the *bastides*, designed to secure border areas and accommodate the rapidly expanding population. In order to attract peasants to inhabit the new towns and cultivate the surrounding land, feudal lords had to offer enticing terms and considerable freedom.

The region continued to produce wheat and oats, but the real sensation of the era of English rule was the transformation of **wine** production into a lucrative and international industry. Merchants exporting the beloved claret of the English to London and other British ports grew wealthy, and the proceeds filtered through to the whole region. **Urban life**, too, began to take off, with the towns of Périgueux, Bergerac and Sarlat growing to populations of around five thousand each.

As English rule was delivered from across the Channel and therefore somewhat removed, it did not mean any perceptible invasion by the English language. On the contrary, independence from northern France allowed local language and culture to flourish, creating perfect conditions for the high-culture phenomenon of the **troubadours** (see box opposite).

The Cathar crusades

While the English ruled in Aquitaine, an audacious bid for independence from the political and religious dictats of the French Crown was also being made over to the east, by the powerful **counts of Toulouse**. From the mid-twelfth century on, the so-called **Cathars** (also known as Albigensians) had won a great deal of support in the area, which extended as far as the Dordogne valley, by preaching that the material world was created by the Devil and the spiritual world by a benevolent God. They also believed in reincarnation and that the only way to escape the mortal coil was to lead a life of saintly self-denial – all of which completely undermined the role of the clergy. To put an end to such **heresy**, Pope Innocent III unleashed a **crusade** against the Cathars in 1209, starting off with a particularly murderous attack led by **Simon de Montfort** in which the entire population of the Mediterranean town of Béziers, estimated at twenty thousand people, was slaughtered; the papal legate in charge of the assault is famously supposed to have proclaimed, "Kill them all. God will know his own."

A series of crusading armies, composed largely of land-hungry northern nobles, then proceeded to rampage through the region on and off for the next twenty years. This was followed by an equally vicious **inquisition** designed to mop up any remaining

1166	June 11 1183	Mid 12th century
Perfectly preserved body discovered in a cave in the Quercy, declared to be St Amadour. Rocamadour sanctuary built around it	Death of Henry the Young King at Martel, days after ransacking the holy shrines at Rocamadour	Cathars begin to spread through the region

Cathars, which culminated in the siege of Montségur, in the eastern foothills of the Pyrenees, in 1244, when two hundred people were burnt alive.

As a result of the Cathar crusades, the French Crown now held sway over the whole of southwestern France, including Toulouse. The new count of Toulouse was **Alphonse de Poitiers**, brother of the future Louis IX, whose lands stretched north through Quercy into Périgord, and west along the Garonne as far as Agen. Like his English neighbours, Alphonse started establishing a rash of *bastides* in order to impose his authority over his new domains.

The Hundred Years War

Though the English had lost their possessions north of the Loire by the mid-thirteenth century, they remained a perpetual thorn in the side of the French kings thanks to their grip on Aquitaine. Skirmishes took place throughout the century, followed by various peace treaties, one of which, in 1259, took Quercy and Périgord back into the English domain. But the spark that ignited the ruinous – and misnamed – **Hundred Years War** (1337–1453) was a Capetian succession crisis. When the last of the line, Charles IV, died without an heir in 1328, the English king, **Edward III**, leapt in to claim the throne of France for himself. It went instead to Charles's cousin, **Philippe de Valois**. Edward acquiesced for a time, but when Philippe began whittling away at English possessions in Aquitaine, Edward renewed his claim and embarked on a war.

The major battles of the war were almost all fought in the northern half of the country, where Edward won an outright victory at **Crécy**, before his son, the **Black Prince**, took the French king, Jean le Bon, prisoner at the Battle of Poitiers in 1356 and

---

THE LANGUAGE OF LOVE

The **troubadours**, poets and musicians of the twelfth century, were early pioneers of Western Europe's cultural renaissance. Their love poetry, written in **Occitan**, elevated the vernacular of the rural peasantry to the status of high culture and, for the first time since Roman occupation, language was used for something other than essential, practical communication. Troubadour poems focus on courtly love, an idealized, noble emotion which might be romantic, tender, familiar, feudal, patriotic – or, in the best poems, a combination of all these. Thus the Troubadours not only reintroduced art to the region, they also gave it a linguistic and cultural identity – when troubadours talk about their *pays*, they do not mean France as a whole, just the southwest.

The aggressive campaign of unification and standardization waged by the state following the 1789 revolution outlawed the everyday use of the Occitan **language**, causing its gradual disappearance as a native tongue. It continued to inspire poets, however, most notably **Frédéric Mistral**, an early winner of the Nobel Prize for literature, who wrote in Occitan. Today, the language described in 1900 by the visionary politician Jean Jaurès as "a noble language of courtship, poetry and art", is being revived. Basing their strategy on the models for the revival of the Welsh and Irish languages, regional authorities have established a number of Occitan-speaking **schools**, known as *Calandretas*, including one in Périgueux. Local colleges (roughly equivalent to an English secondary school) also offer Occitan as one of their language options. The Toulouse-based newspaper *Dépêche du Midi* prints a regular column in Occitan.

1209	1244	1250
Simon de Montfort leads the first crusade against the Cathars	The siege and surrender of the last Cathar stronghold at Montségur, 200 people were burnt alive	Alphonse de Poitiers, count of Toulouse begins a massive *bastide* building programme, including Monflanquin, Cordes, Najac and Ste-Foy-la-Grande

CHURCHES AND CASTLES: THE VIEILLES PIERRES OF PÉRIGORD

In spite of the many conflicts that have ravaged the countryside since the Middle Ages, the Dordogne and Lot region has preserved an impressive wealth of medieval **churches**, at the heart of almost every village in some areas, and **castles**, which seem to crown the crest of every hill, especially along the golden stretch of the Dordogne valley.

CHURCHES

Few traces now remain of the earliest churches, one exception being in St-Front in Périgueux, where the enthusiastic nineteenth-century restoration conceals traces of the original chapel built by bishop Chronope (see p.289) in the early sixth century. The region's golden age for church-building, however, came in the twelfth and thirteenth centuries, when the style of architecture and sculpture known as **Romanesque** (or sometimes Norman, in England) was dominant. In terms of architecture, these churches are characterized by round arches, sometimes domes (particularly in the Périgord region) and simple, graceful lines, but the highlights are often the sculptures that adorn the key structural points: the tympanum above the main entrance, the capitals at the top of supporting pillars, the keystones in their vaults – these all formed a blank canvas for craftsman to forge the most beautifully humane and unglorified depictions of saints, prophets and biblical stories. In no other architectural style are religious teachings so organically integrated into the physical structure of the church. The best examples include the churches in Souillac (see p.171) and Beaulieu (see p.188), in the upper reaches of the Dordogne, and the world-famous cloister at Moissac (see p.263) in the Tarn valley, but it's the range and variety of styles, from the Byzantine touches in Périgueux and Souillac to the unembellished purity, almost austerity, of the church at Cadouin (see p.114), which make the region such a goldmine.

Rarer, but of all the more interest for that, are the region's **Gothic** edifices. While in Romanesque architecture the charm lies in the detail, evoking a humble down-to-earth spirituality, in Gothic buildings it's the soaring, awe-inspiring ensemble that appeals, embodying a sense of elevation to a higher realm.

CASTLES

While the Hundred Years War was raging, it was said that "towns were loyal to the king; castles were a law unto themselves." In both the conflict between the French and English and the later religious wars, the region's powerful families sought to strengthen their own positions and independence by fortifying their residences.

Invariably built on high ground, for strategic reasons, many castles would originally have covered a large area, with entire villages enclosed within their walls. In most cases, they were destroyed or dismantled when captured during various wars, so today it is often just a ruined keep that remains. From a military perspective, two of the most satisfying are those at Beynac (p.156) and Castelnaud (p.160), squaring up to each other across the Dordogne river and offering commanding views over the surrounding countryside. For romance, it's hard to beat the rugged keep of Najac (p.282) rising above the village, shrouded in mist. In more peaceful centuries, the region's aristocracy set about making their residences more comfortable, and places like the Chateau de Hautefort (p.72) combined impregnability with stately grandeur, lavish furnishings and extravagant interior design.

In many cases, buildings were designed to serve both a religious purpose and a military one. The churches at Rocamadour (p.175), St-Amand-de-Coly (p.150) and Beaumont (p.112), to name just three, are notable for their imposing, fortified walls and slit windows, revealing them as buildings designed not just for worship, but also to be defended.

June 17 1308	1332	October 25 1415	1429
Construction of the Pont Valentré begins in Cahors	Edward III of England claims the French throne and sparks the Hundred Years War	Henry V of England inflicts a crushing defeat on the French army at Agincourt	Jeanne d'Arques, the maid of Orléans, rallies the French troops

established a capital at Bordeaux. The resulting treaty appeared to give the English victory, but the French fought back, banishing the English entirely but for a toehold in Bordeaux. In 1415, though, the tables turned again as Henry V inflicted a crushing defeat on the French army, against all odds, at the legendary battle of **Agincourt**. Once again, France seemed on the verge of unravelling at the seams, until **Jeanne d'Arc** (Joan of Arc) arrived on the scene. In 1429 she rallied the demoralized French troops, broke the English siege at Orléans and tipped the scales against the invaders. The English were slowly but surely driven back to their southwest heartland until even that was lost at the **Battle of Castillon** in 1453 (see box, p 116). Within months, the English surrendered Bordeaux, and their centuries-long adventure in France came to an end.

Although Castillon was the only major battle fought in the southwest, the region did not spare itself from **bloodshed**. The region's powerful families, operating from their fortified bases (see box opposite), sought to take advantage of the general chaos by attacking their neighbours and trying to strengthen their own hands. Many nobles swapped sides repeatedly, fighting under English or French colours as it suited them. **Raymond de Montaut**, for example, a powerful baron based in Mussidan, initially swore allegiance to the French Crown, but then fought with the English in the sieges of Bourdeilles (1369) and Limoges (1370). Only when he was captured by the French did he conveniently rediscover his patriotic sentiment and transfer his allegiance back. Most towns and castles were attacked at some point and many changed hands on numerous occasions, either by treaty or force. By the end of the war, farms and villages lay abandoned and roving bands of **brigands** terrorized the countryside, having abandoned all pretence of fighting for one side or the other. The population had been reduced by roughly a half to under twelve million, partly by warfare, but largely through famine and disease; millions died as the bubonic **plague** repeatedly swept through France during the fourteenth and fifteenth centuries.

Gradually the nightmare ended. Though the south now had to kow-tow to the hated northerners – the counts of Périgord were particularly big losers, having their land and privileges confiscated by the Crown – Louis XI proved to be an astute ruler who allowed some of the privileges granted by the English to remain. Trade – particularly the wine trade – began to revive, towns were rebuilt and land brought back into production.

The Wars of Religion

In the early sixteenth century the ideas, art and architecture of the **Renaissance** began to penetrate France. As elsewhere in Europe, the Renaissance had a profound influence on every aspect of life, engendering a new optimism and spirit of enquiry that appealed in particular to the new class of wealthy merchants. At the same time, increased trade and improved communications, including the invention of the printing press, helped disseminate ideas throughout Europe. Among them came the new **Protestant** message espoused by Martin Luther and John Calvin that the individual was responsible to God alone and not to the Church.

Such ideas gained widespread adherence throughout France, partly feeding on resentment of Catholic clergy who were often seen as closely linked to the oppressive feudal regime, but mainly because a handful of powerful families converted and, where the feudal overlord led, his subjects were bound to follow. On the national scale, the

July 17 1453	February 28 1533	August 23 1572
The crucial battle of Castillon effectively ends the Hundred Years War and with it English rule in southwest France	Michel de Montaigne, influential "Father of the Essay", born in the Dordogne region	The St Bartholomew's Day massacre

most significant families to convert were those of the **Bourbon-d'Albret** royal dynasty. In the southwest, the first Protestant (also known as **Huguenot**) enclaves were at Ste-Foy-la-Grande and Bergerac in the 1540s, followed soon after by Nérac, the fief of the **d'Albret** family (see p.258). As the Protestant faith took hold and Catholics felt increasingly threatened, the sporadic brutal attempts to stamp out Protestantism, such as a massacre in Cahors in 1560, erupted two years later into a series of bitter civil wars. Interspersed with ineffective truces and accords, the **Wars of Religion** lasted for the next thirty years.

On the Catholic side, a powerful lobbying group of traditionalists, organized mainly by the **de Guise** family, led an army against the Huguenots, who were in turn marshalled by **Admiral de Coligny**. The two armies toured northern France, occasionally clashing directly, but more often capturing and converting towns that had taken one side or the other. The duc de Guise was murdered in 1563, an act for which his allies held Coligny responsible. And in 1572, Coligny was among the victims of the war's bloodiest and most notorious date: the **St Bartholomew's Day Massacre**, when some three thousand Protestants, gathered in Paris for the wedding of Protestant **Henri d'Albret** to Marguerite de Valois, the sister of Henry III of France, were slaughtered.

Just as in earlier conflicts, the nationwide dispute was used as a pretext by **powerful families** in the southwest to consolidate their positions. Once again, private armies roamed the region, vying with each other in their savagery, but with only vaguely religious motives. Before his death, Coligny famously complained of Huguenot generals in the southwest who took no interest in the wider struggle and "refused to fight unless they could turn around and see their own chimney". One such general was the impulsive and ingenious **Geoffroi de Vivans**, who even succeeded in briefly capturing the staunchly Catholic towns of Sarlat and Périgueux. One of his most daring exploits, in 1588, involved hiding out in the caves beneath the hilltop town of Domme (see p.163) before scaling the formidable cliffs at dawn and taking the town with only a handful of men.

Some towns were attacked and changed hands repeatedly, either in violence or as a result of various **truces**, by which they were nominally declared either Catholic or Protestant. In reality, the majority of ordinary people, though cruelly affected by the fighting, saw little impact on their **notions of religion**, which remained a hotch-potch of rural paganism and local folklore, with only hints of orthodox Christianity, until several centuries later.

A twist of fate signalled the beginning of the end of the conflicts, when Henri d'Albret – king of Navarre and leader of the Protestant army – became heir to the French throne when Henry III's son died in 1584. Five years later, Henry III himself was dead, leaving a tricky problem, since a Protestant could not be king. After trying to seize the crown by force, Henri d'Albret eventually abjured his faith and became **Henry IV** of France. "Paris is worth a Mass," he is reputed to have said.

Once on the throne Henry IV set about reconstructing and reconciling his kingdom. Under the visionary **Edict of Nantes** of 1598 the Protestants were accorded freedom of conscience, freedom of worship in specified places, the right to attend the same schools and hold the same offices as Catholics, their own courts and the possession of a number of fortresses, including Montauban, as a guarantee against renewed attack.

1589	May 1637	1643	July 14 1789
Protestant Henri Bourbon D'Albret abjures his faith – "Paris is worth a Mass" – and is crowned Henry IV of France	Peasant's revolt savagely crushed at La Sauvetat-du-Dropt	Louis XIV, the Sun King, begins his long reign, exerting increasing control over the southwest	Storming of the Bastille

The stirrings of discontent

The Dordogne and Lot region had barely drawn breath after the end of the Wars of Religion, when a different type of conflict erupted – this time one whose causes the ordinary peasantry could identify with all too easily. The countryside lay in ruins and the cost of the wars and rebuilding fell squarely on their shoulders. Ruinous taxes, a series of bad harvests, high prices and yet more outbreaks of the plague combined to push them over the edge in the late sixteenth century. There were **peasant rebellions** in Normandy and Brittany, but the worst of the "**Croquants'**" (yokels') uprisings broke out in the southwest. The first major revolt occurred in the winter of 1593, when a number of towns and castles, including Monpazier, Excideuil and Puy-l'Évêque, were attacked. After two years of skirmishes, nobles pulled together an army in 1595 and the rebellion was quickly and savagely put down by the allied forces of the local nobility. The same grievances resurfaced in more uprisings in May 1637, however, no doubt nourished in part by tales of the earlier failed rebellion, passed down by word of mouth from generation to generation. This time, the revolt was altogether more serious. In the face of one tax demand too many, a ten-thousand-strong **peasant army** tried unsuccessfully to seize Périgueux. Instead, they took Bergerac and then marched on Bordeaux. They were stopped, however, at Ste-Foy-la-Grande and the final show-down took place soon after against 3400 royal troops at La Sauvetat-du-Dropt, south of Bergerac, leaving at least a thousand Croquants dead. The leaders were executed, one in Monpazier (see p.246), while the surviving rebels returned to the land.

Thereafter, the long reign of **Louis XIV** (1643–1715) saw the French Crown and Catholic religion begin to reassert control over the southwest. With the exception of the **Frondes** (of 1648–52), when aristocrats joined the lower classes in rebelling against royal taxes and when the army had to be brought in to crush demonstrations in Bordeaux, the state successfully reinstated military and feudal control. At the same time, the bishops of Sarlat and Périgueux set about the "Vendange des Âmes", the **Harvesting of Souls**, an aggressive campaign designed to eradicate strongholds of the Protestant faith. Protestant towns such as Bergerac were seized by the Catholics and Protestant rights were gradually eroded until in 1685 Louis revoked the Edict of Nantes, forbade Protestant worship and set about trying to eliminate the faith completely. Orders were given for the destruction of Protestant churches and of the castles of its most fervent supporters. Thousands of Protestants fled the southwest for the safety of the Netherlands, Germany and England.

At the same time, France began to establish a **colonial empire** in North America, Africa, India and the Caribbean, and, as trade from these places started to grow in the early eighteenth century, so Bordeaux and the other Atlantic ports prospered, in a so-called **golden age.**

Revolution

For the majority of people, however, little had changed. The gap between rich and poor grew ever wider as the clergy and aristocracy clung onto their privileges and the peasants were squeezed for higher taxes. Their general misery was exacerbated by a catastrophic harvest in 1788, followed by a particularly severe winter. Bread prices rocketed and on July 14, 1789, a mob stormed the **Bastille** in Paris, a hated symbol of

1790	1792	1799	1808
Creation of the modern *départements* of Dordogne, Lot and Tarn and Garonne, named after their major rivers	Declaration of the First Republic	Napoleon Bonaparte seizes power	Napoleon invades Spain, sparking the Peninsular War

the oppressive regime. As the **Revolution** spread, similar insurrections occurred throughout the country, accompanied by widespread peasant attacks on landowners' châteaux and the destruction of tax and rent records. In August the new National Assembly abolished the feudal rights and privileges of the nobility and then went on to nationalize Church lands.

In these early stages the general population of the southwest supported the Revolution. However, as the Parisian revolutionaries grew increasingly radical and proposed ever more centralization of power they found themselves in bitter opposition. Towards the end of 1792, as the **First Republic** was being declared, they finally lost out to the extremists and in October the following year **the Terror** was unleashed as mass executions took place throughout France; estimates run to three thousand in Paris and 14,000 in the regions.

Though revolutionary bands wrought a fair amount of havoc in the southwest, looting and burning castles and churches, hacking away at coats of arms and religious statuary, on the whole the region escaped fairly lightly; many aristocrats simply fled and their possessions were sold off at knock-down prices. Among many administrative changes following the Revolution, one of the most significant was the creation of **départements** in 1790 to replace the old provinces. Thus began yet another attempt at national unification, accompanied by efforts to draw the traditionally independent southwest into mainstream France. The campaign continued in the nineteenth century with moves to stamp out Occitan and other regional dialects (see box, p.293).

From Napoleon I to the Third Republic

By the end of 1794, more moderate forces were in charge in Paris. However, continuous infighting left the way open for **Napoleon Bonaparte**, who had made a name for himself as commander of the Revolutionary armies in Italy and Egypt, to seize power in a coup d'état in 1799. Napoleon quickly restored order and continued the process of centralization, replacing the power of local institutions by appointing a *préfet* to each *département* answerable only to the **emperor**, as Napoleon declared himself in 1804. Nevertheless, the Dordogne and Lot *départements* supported the new regime by providing many military leaders – and more lowly troops – for Bonaparte's armies: the most notable examples were Périgueux's Baron Pierre Daumesnil (see box, p.53) and Joachim Murat (1767–1815), the son of a village innkeeper near Cahors, who was proclaimed king of Naples in reward for his numerous military successes. As elsewhere, however, it was the burden of the unceasing **Napoleonic wars** that cost the emperor his support. The economy of Bordeaux in particular and the southwest in general was hard hit when Napoleon banned commerce with Britain, to which Britain responded by blockading French ports in 1807.

Few tears were shed in the region when Napoleon was finally defeated in 1815. The subsequent restoration of the **monarchy**, on the other hand, saw opinions divided along predictable lines: the aristocracy and the emerging *bourgeoisie* (the middle classes) rallied to the king, while the working population supported the uprising in 1848 – a shorter and less virulent reprise of the 1789 Revolution – which ended in the declaration of the **Second Republic**. The new government started off well by

June 17–18 1815	**1822**	**1852**	**1852**	**1870**
Battle of Waterloo, Napoleon is narrowly defeated by Wellington	Jean-François Champollion translates the hieroglyphs on the Rosetta Stone	Opening of the Canal Garonne	Napoléon III declared emperor	Cahors-born statesman, Léon Gambetta, crafts the Third Republic

setting up national workshops to relieve unemployment and extending the vote to all adult males – an unprecedented move for its time. But in elections held later in 1848 the largely conservative vote of the newly enfranchised peasants was sufficient to outweigh the urban, working-class radicals. To everyone's surprise, Louis-Napoléon, nephew of the former emperor, romped home. In spite of his liberal reputation, he restricted the vote again, censored the press and pandered to the Catholic Church. In 1852, following a coup and further street fighting, he had himself proclaimed **Emperor Napoléon III**.

Like his uncle, Napoléon III pursued an expansionist military policy, both in France's colonial empire and in Europe. And also like his uncle, this brought about his downfall. Napoléon III declared war on Prussia in 1870 and was quickly and roundly defeated by the far superior Prussian army. When Napoléon was taken prisoner the politicians in Paris – Cahors' Léon Gambetta among them (see box, p.205) – quickly proclaimed the **Third Republic**. Though it experienced a difficult birth, the Third Republic survived until 1940.

Into the twentieth century

Napoléon was more successful on the economic front, however. From the 1850s on, France experienced rapid **industrial growth**, while foreign trade trebled. The effect on the Dordogne and Lot region, however, was mixed.

The towns along the region's great rivers benefited most from the economic recovery. Although the region had no coal or mineral resources to stimulate large-scale industrialization (beyond metalworking around Fumel), industries were established along the navigable rivers – tanneries, paper mills, textile and glass industries. At the same time, agricultural areas within easy access of the rivers grew wealthy from exporting wheat, wine and tobacco. Many towns were given a facelift as their ramparts were torn down, wide avenues sliced through the cramped medieval quarters and a start was made on improving sanitation and water supply. Transport was also modernized, although the **railways** came late to the Dordogne and Lot and were never very extensive. The region's first railway, the Bordeaux–Paris line, was completed in 1851, while the following year saw the opening of the **Canal latéral** (now the Garonne Canal), linking the Garonne with the Canal du Midi and thus the Mediterranean.

All this created pockets of economic growth, but the **rural areas** in between became increasingly marginalized. Local industries dwindled in the face of competition from cheap manufactured goods and imports, while the railways simply provided the means for people to quit the country for the cities.

But by far the biggest single crisis to hit the area's rural economy in the late nineteenth century was **phylloxera**. The parasite, which attacks the roots of vines, wiped out almost one third of the region's vineyards in the 1870s and 1880s. For a while growers tried all sorts of remedies, from flooding the fields to chemical fumigation, before it was discovered that vines in America, where phylloxera originated, were immune and that by grafting French vines onto American root-stock it was possible to produce resistant plants. The vineyards were slowly re-established, but over a much smaller area. Many farmers turned to alternative crops, such as tobacco around Bergerac and sheep-rearing on the *cause* above Cahors.

1870–85	1914	1926	1939
Phylloxera wipes out vast swathes of the region's vine stock	Outbreak of WWI, thousands of youths from the southwest march north to battle, losing their lives in Flanders fields	The caves of Pech-Merle open to the public	Outbreak of WWII

The world wars

Such problems paled into insignificance, however, when German troops marched into northern France following the outbreak of **World War I** in 1914. The French government fled south to Bordeaux while thousands of southern men trekked north to lose their lives in the mud and horror of Verdun and the Somme battlefields. By the time the Germans were forced to surrender in 1918, the cost to France was 1.3 million dead, a quarter of whom were under 25 years of age, and three million wounded. Every town and village in the Dordogne and Lot, as elsewhere in France, has its sad war memorial recording the loss of this generation of young men.

In the aftermath of the war, agricultural and industrial production declined and the birth rate plummeted, although this was offset to some extent in the southwest by an influx of land-hungry refugees from Spain in the late nineteenth century and from Italy in the first decades of the twentieth. The French government lurched from crisis to crisis while events across the border in Germany became increasingly menacing.

In April 1940, eight months after the outbreak of **World War II**, Hitler's western offensive began as he overran Belgium, Denmark and Holland. In June the French government retreated to Bordeaux again and millions of refugees poured south as Paris fell to the Germans. **Maréchal Pétain**, a conservative 84-year-old veteran of World War I, emerged from retirement to sign an armistice with Hitler and head the collaborationist **Vichy government**, based in the spa town of Vichy in the northern foothills of the Massif Central. France was now split in two. The Germans occupied the strategic regions north of the Loire and all along the Atlantic coast, including Bordeaux, while Vichy ostensibly governed the "Free Zone" comprising the majority of southern France. The frontier, with its customs points and guardposts, ran from the Pyrenees north through Langon and Castillon-la-Bataille to just south of Tours, and from there cut east to Geneva. Then, in 1942, German troops moved south to occupy the whole of France until they were driven out by Britain, America and their allies after 1944.

Resistance to the German occupation didn't really get going until 1943 when **General de Gaulle**, exiled leader of the "Free French", sent **Jean Moulin** to unify the disparate and often ideologically opposed Resistance groups. Moulin was soon captured by the Gestapo and tortured to death by Klaus Barbie – the infamous "Butcher of Lyon", who was convicted as recently as 1987 for his war crimes – but the network Moulin established became increasingly effective. Its members provided information to the Allies and blew up train tracks, bridges and factories. They undertook daring raids into enemy-held towns; the high, empty uplands of the Dordogne and the Lot *départements* afforded safe bases for many Resistance fighters. But for every action, the Germans hit back with savage **reprisals**. In May 1944 the SS Das Reich division, based at Montauban, set out to break the local resistance by massacring civilians and torching houses in some twenty towns and villages; the worst atrocities took place in Terrasson-la-Villedieu, Montpezat-de-Quercy, Mussidan and Frayssinet-le-Gélat.

Soon afterwards the Germans were being driven out, but the fighting didn't stop there. In the weeks following **liberation** thousands of **collaborators** were executed or publicly humiliated – women accused of consorting with the enemy had their heads shaved and were sometimes paraded naked through the streets. Not surprisingly, the issue of collaboration left deep scars in rural communities throughout the region, a bitterness which occasionally surfaces to this day in local disputes.

1940	September 12 1940	February 1956	1961
Josephine Baker moves to Château Milandes in the Dordogne	The prehistoric cave paintings at Lascaux discovered by four teenagers	Severe and prolonged frost devastates Cahors vineyards, necessitating a mass replanting	After centuries of mixed produce and livestock, the first market exclusively for truffles is established in Lalbenque

Into the new millennium

The new millennium sees the same issues that have dominated the last fifty years in the region remaining paramount. One of the main themes, as in much of rural France, is that of **depopulation**. On average there are now 25 percent fewer people living on the land than at the end of the nineteenth century, rising to thirty percent or more in the worst-hit areas, such as parts of Lot-et-Garonne. Once again this has been partly offset by immigration, in this case by *pieds noirs* – French colonialists forced to flee Algeria after independence in 1962 – many of whom settled on farms in the southwest, and by north Europeans in search of the good life. Agricultural production is in slow decline as the younger generation leave the land, though this has partly been offset by a massive push towards mechanization and the amalgamation of small farms into larger, more efficient holdings – albeit often propped up by subsidies from the European Union.

Agriculture remains the backbone of the region's economy, notably wine production but also poultry, maize, fruit, tobacco, fishing and forestry. Cahors alone has 4,200 hectares of AOP (recently changed from the old AOC status) vines. Agen is also known for pharmaceuticals, while other main towns such as Périgueux, Figeac, Montauban, Fumel and Villeneuve-sur-Lot boast modest industrial sectors.

Besides agriculture and industry, **tourism** plays an increasingly important role in the regional economy. In recent years an enormous effort has gone into improving facilities and marketing the region, not just the honeypot attractions of Sarlat, Les Ezyies and the Dordogne valley châteaux, but also in the successful promotion of "green holidays", tempting people away from the Mediterranean and Atlantic coasts to discover all that the countryside has to offer. One of the largest such projects was the reopening of the River Lot and the Garonne Canal to navigation, but at a local level almost every town and village now puts on a programme of summer events to lure visitors.

Across France, however, the economy continues to be hampered by the seemingly perpetual stand-off between advocates of economic reform to liberalize markets and stimulate growth, and uncompromising defenders of the "**French Model**", with generous social allowances and high job security. Almost every section of society seems to have seen this debate come its way in recent years: from teachers to car manufacturers, employees in all industries have taken action to block any reforms which might erode their privileges. Perhaps most emblematic of the battle lines was the controversy in 2006 surrounding the government's attempt to introduce the **CPE** or "First Employment Contract", aimed at encouraging the employment of young people by making them less costly to hire/employ (with fewer social security benefits and no guarantee that they would be kept on after two years). The intended beneficiaries, however, were less than grateful, and took to the streets in their thousands to protest against the new contract, arguing that it was the first step towards the hire-and-fire culture reviled in left-wing French circles.

In the **2007 presidential election**, it seemed as though momentum was swinging behind the arguments of the economic reformers, as former interior minister **Nicolas Sarkozy**, a member of the centre-right UMP party, was elected president having campaigned for a hard-line "rupture" with the French Model. In power, however, he only fitfully pursued a free-market agenda.

1971	1992	2004	2006	May 2007
Cahors wine is awarded AOC status	Treaty of Maastricht; the European Union is born	National Prehistoric Museum opens in Eyzies-de-Tayac	Roman amphitheatre excavated in Cahors during the building of a car park	Nicolas Sarkozy elected president of France

Economic crisis

The **financial crisis** of 2008–09 hit manufacturing across France very badly, and its effects in the Dordogne and Lot region were most strongly felt in the wine business, with a partial collapse of prices and plummeting export sales. Housing prices plummeted too, sending many up-and-coming estate agents to the wall. In the light of the general discrediting of liberal capitalism, Sarkozy shrewdly abandoned his rupturist rhetoric in favour of a new-found pride in the traditional French system. This impeccable tactical U-turn left the Socialist opposition lost for words and floundering in the polls: the **2009 European elections** saw Sarkozy's party come out on top with 28 percent of the vote, while across France, including in the southwest region, the Socialists were pushed into third place behind a green alliance – "Europe Ecologie" – led by Daniel Cohn-Bendit, familiar as the youthful leader of the 1968 student uprising. By 2012, however, the power pendulum had swung the other way, with the Socialists once again claiming massive victories in the polls and painting, the southwest in particular, a sea of red. **François Hollande** was elected president, having promised to beat the recession by taxing wealthier citizens and larger corporations while separating risky investment banking enterprises from retail. He also promised to lower the retirement age from 62 to 60 and create 60,000 new teaching posts.

A consequence of the world's economic woes has been to make the situation of the thousands of **British residents** of the Dordogne and Lot region more difficult. Since the 1960s, low property prices, coupled with beautiful scenery and an enviable lifestyle, had attracted Brits, Dutch and other north Europeans to settle here in search of the good life. Now, though, volatile exchange rates and devalued savings and investments have caused what some are calling the biggest British exodus from France since Dunkirk.

Many locals hope that this will only be a short-term trend, as the region is in constant need of new settlers to restore its derelict farmhouses and pump money into the local economy. The importance of tourism based on the outstanding cultural heritage and natural resources of the region has long been recognized, but in July 2012 the area won a resounding victory as UNESCO named the Dordogne basin a **biosphere reserve**. Both the Dordogne and Lot valleys have very low population densities, both are rich in wildlife and both rely heavily on tourism; but the Dordogne also has one of the largest hydro-electric systems in France and an enormous estuary, sufficient reasons for the award of this prestigious status.

British tourism, and indeed settlement has always been tolerated in the area, indeed welcomed, too, because even after all these centuries, there still exists a vague and undoubtedly romantic sentiment among the resolutely independent, anti-Parisian southwesterners that they were better off under English rule, when at least the economy boomed and their forebears enjoyed a high degree of autonomy. Down the intervening years the region's strong sense of identity has been tested on many occasions, but has survived to resurface these days as a deep-burning pride in the land, its produce and its traditions.

2008	June 2010	May 2012	July 2012
Financial crisis hits the region, property prices drop and exchange rates fluctuate, forcing many British residents to return to the UK	Brive-Vallée de la Dordogne airport opens for business	François Hollande elected president of France	The Dordogne valley named a UNESCO biosphere reserve

Books

There are few English-language history books specifically devoted to the Dordogne and Lot region, and a bit of a dearth of novels, whether in French or in translation. A few of those that do exist – and are worth recommending – are detailed below, along with a number of general history books and classic texts which provide the background to events that have occurred in the region. The best books in this selection are marked by a ★ symbol.

HISTORY & BIOGRAPHY

Marc Bloch *Strange Defeat*. Moving personal study of the reasons for France's defeat in 1940 and subsequent caving-in to Fascism. Found among the papers of this Sorbonne historian after his death at the hands of the Gestapo in 1942.

Lynn Haney *Naked at the Feast*. A lively warts-and-all biography of the cabaret star Josephine Baker (see box, p.161), which traces the many setbacks and comebacks of her rags to riches tale, getting across her amazing charisma and just why France took her to its heart.

Colin Jones *The Cambridge Illustrated History of France*. A political and social history of France from prehistoric times to the mid-1990s, concentrating on issues of regionalism, gender, race and class. Good illustrations and an easy, unacademic writing style.

★ **Don and Petie Kladstrup** *Wine & War*. The role of wine in World War II and the often courageous and ingenious strategies used to prevent the best wines from being plundered by the German army; fascinating reading.

Marion Meade *Eleanor of Aquitaine*. Highly accessible biography of one of the key characters in twelfth-century Europe. The author fleshes out the documented events until they read more like a historical novel.

Ian Ousby *Occupation: The Ordeal of France 1940–1944*.

Somewhat revisionist 1997 account looking at how widespread collaboration was and why it took so long for the Resistance to get organized.

★ **Graham Robb** *The Discovery of France*. A fascinating alternative history of France, in which Robb goes in search of the reality of life for the provincial, rural majority ignored by the currents of history, before recounting the way in which the nineteenth century saw this other France gradually discovered and "civilized". Contains some excellent sections on the southwest.

Anne-Marie Walters *Moondrop to Gascony*. An absorbing and spine-tingling account of the real life of a secret agent in World War II; written in the immediate aftermath of the war, it reveals the naked courage of the French Resistance.

★ **Alison Weir** *Eleanor of Aquitaine: By the wrath of God, Queen of England*. A magnificent medieval pot pourri of romantic events that vividly chronicles the extraordinary life of this fascinating woman. Contains some interesting photographs, including one of the effigy on Eleanor's tomb at Fontevrault abbey, the only verifiable image of her still in existence.

★ **Theodore Zeldin** *The French*. Urbane and witty survey of the French world view – chapter titles include "How to be chic" and "How to appreciate a grandmother".

TRAVEL, ART AND LITERATURE

Patricia Atkinson *The Ripening Sun*. The ultimately uplifting tale of an Englishwoman who struggles against all kinds of adversity to establish a well-respected vineyard near Bergerac.

★ **Michael Brown** *Down the Dordogne*. In the late 1980s, Michael Brown fulfilled a long-held ambition to follow the Dordogne from its source in the Massif Central to the Gironde estuary. The story of his journey – on foot, by canoe and bicycle – provides a lyrical introduction to the region.

Elizabeth Chadwick *Daughters of the Grail*. This compelling novel offers an insightful glimpse into the little-known world of the much persecuted Cathars. Set in thirteenth-century southwest France the succession of

heroines battle with their beliefs, Catholic prejudice and eventually with the merciless Simon de Montfort.

★ **André Chastel** *French Art*. Authoritative three-volume study by one of France's leading art historians. Discusses individual works of art – from architecture to tapestry, as well as painting – in detail in an attempt to locate the Frenchness of French art. With glossy photographs and serious-minded but readable text.

★ **Arthur Conan-Doyle** *The White Company*. A far cry from Sherlock Holmes, here Conan-Doyle turns his talents to historical fiction, depicting a Hundred Years War where the English have hearts of gold and all the rest are jolly rotters.

Eugène Le Roy *Jacquou le Croquant*. This novel is one of the most important chronicles of the hardship of rural life in nineteenth-century France. The action takes place in the forest and villages around Montignac, home of the hero Jacquou who leads a vengeful revolt against the tyrannical local feudal lord.

Amanda Lawrence *White Stone Black Wine*. A readable and light-hearted account of an Englishwoman's experiences in the Quercy countryside, as she throws herself with gusto into local traditions and activities.

Christian Signol *La Rivière Espérance*. Set in the 1830s, this French novel – which was made into a hugely successful TV film – follows the adventures of a young sailor working the *gabares* that then plied the Dordogne. This nostalgic tale commemorates the end of an era as the railways relentlessly destroy the romanticized river life.

Peter Strafford *Romanesque Churches of France*. This scholarly guide to a handful of France's best churches contains a healthy section on those of the southwest, with several pages devoted to Moissac and Souillac alone. Strafford gives a somewhat dry but detailed account of the architecture and history of the churches featured, and an almost stone-by-stone description of some of the most important sculpture.

Freda White *Three Rivers of France, Ways of Aquitaine*. Freda White's classic books portray France in the 1950s before tourism came along to the backwater communities that were her interest. They are evocative books, slipping in history and culture painlessly, if not always accurately, and still provide a valuable and vivid overview of the region.

GUIDES

Cicerone Walking Guides Neat, durable guides, with detailed route descriptions. Titles include *The Way of Saint James; A Walker's Guide* and *The Way of Saint James; A Cyclist's Guide*, both of which follow the route from Le Puy to Santiago (GR65), and *Walking in the Dordogne*.

Peter Knowles *White Water: Massif Central*. Don't be put off by the series title, this guide covers rivers suitable for a spot of gentle family canoeing and canoe touring, including parts of the Dordogne, Lot, Tarn, Vézère, Célé and Aveyron. Packed with good, practical advice.

★ **Joy Law** *Dordogne*. Erudite and accessible thematic guide-cum-history text written by a long-time resident of the *département*, packed with interesting anecdotes and local colour.

Helen Martin *Lot: Travels through a limestone landscape in southwest France*. It's well worth investing in this updated and expanded edition of Helen Martin's classic book about the Lot if you're going to be spending much time in the *département*. Her passion for the area, which she has known for more than forty years, comes across loud and clear.

Hugh McKnight *Cruising French Waterways*. Essential reading for anyone going boating in France. It's not only a practical guide on navigating French rivers and canals, but also covers historical aspects and general tourist information.

Victoria Pybus *Live and Work in France*. An invaluable guide, packed with ideas and advice on everything from job-hunting, tax and bureaucracy to health care.

Alain Roussot *Discovering Périgord Prehistory*. Translated into English, this guide provides a solid introduction to the prehistoric caves of the Périgord. It covers the most significant caves in chronological order, while the illustrations give a taste of what's on offer.

Topo-guides The best of the walking guides covering the long-distance paths, Topo-guides are widely available in France and not hard to follow with a working knowledge of French. The series includes guides to the GR65 St-Jacques pilgrimage routes, the *Tour des Gorges de l'Aveyron* (Topo-guide #323), the *Traversée du Périgord* (#321) and, for shorter walks, *Dordogne à Pied* (#D024) and *Lot à Pied* (#D046).

FOOD AND DRINK

Stephanie Alexander *Cooking and Travelling in South-West France*. Inspiring and lavishly illustrated, this is a book for foodies. Alexander is a well-known Australian cookery writer whose deep-rooted passion for this region's food is practically palpable on every page.

Elisabeth Luard *Truffle*. Of all the gourmet treats available in the southwest, a truffle must surely be the ultimate prize. Luard demystifies this unprepossessing but delicious lump of fungus, showing you not only where to buy it, but exactly what to do with it when you get it home.

Orlando Murrin *A Table in the Tarn*. A beautifully presented celebration of southern cuisine; the first half of this coffee-table book describes the author's move to a run-down manor and the subsequent transformation to luxury *chambres d'hôtes*. The second half is a rich hoard of recipes that will have you racing to the kitchen, book in hand.

Jeanne Strang *Goose Fat and Garlic, Country Recipes from South-West France*. A huge store of traditional gastronomy from the old southwest. Strang lived and worked in the area for more than forty years and shares her profound knowledge in this book, which is perhaps a little thin on illustrations but makes up for the lack with recipes that you will find nowhere else.

Paul Strang *Wines of South-West France*. A bit dated now, but still by far the best English-language guide to the region's wines. In addition to the history of viticulture and brief reviews of recommended producers in all the wine-producing areas from Figeac to Bergerac, the book gives a glimpse into local culture and traditions.

French

French can be a deceptively familiar language because of the number of words and structures it shares with English. Despite this, it's far from easy, though the bare essentials are not difficult to master and can make all the difference. Even just saying "Bonjour Madame/Monsieur" and then gesticulating will usually get you a smile and helpful service. People working in tourist offices, hotels and so on, almost always speak English, though, and tend to use it when you're struggling to speak French – be grateful, not insulted.

PHRASEBOOKS AND COURSES

Rough Guide French Phrasebook Mini dictionary-style phrasebook with both English–French and French–English sections, along with cultural tips, a menu reader and downloadable scenarios read by native speakers.

Breakthrough French One of the best teach-yourself courses, with three levels to choose from. Each comes with a book and CD-ROM.

The Complete Merde! The Real French You Were Never Taught at School. More than just a collection of swearwords, this book is a passkey into everyday French,

and a window into French culture.

Oxford Essential French Dictionary Very up-to-date French–English and English–French dictionary, with help on pronunciation and verbs, and links to free online products.

Michel Thomas A fast-paced and effective audio course that promises "No books. No writing. No memorising", with an emphasis on spoken French, rather than conjugating verbs and sentence construction. ⓦ michelthomas.com /learn-french.

PRONUNCIATION

One easy rule to remember is that consonants at the ends of words are usually silent. *Pas plus tard* (not later) is thus pronounced "pa-plu-tarr". But when the following word begins with a vowel, you run the two together: *les oranges* (the oranges) becomes "layzoronge". Vowels are the hardest sounds to get right. Roughly:

a	as in hat	in/im	like the **an** in **an**xious
e	as in get	an/am	like the **don** in
é	between get and gate	en/em	Doncaster when said
è	between get and gut		with a nasal accent
eu	like the **u** in hurt	on/om	like the **don** in
i	as in machine		Doncaster said by
o	as in hot		someone with a heavy
ô, au	as in over		cold
ou	as in food	un/um	like the **u** in understand
u	as in a pursed-lip version of use		

More awkward are the combinations *in/im*, *en/em*, *an/am*, *on/om*, *un/um* at the beginning and end of words, or followed by consonants other than *n* or *m*. Again, roughly:

Consonants are much as in English, except that: *ch* is always "sh", *h* is silent, *th* is the same as "t", *ll* is like the "y" in yes, *w* is "v", and *r* is growled.

Basic words and phrases

French nouns are divided into masculine and feminine. This causes difficulties with adjectives, whose endings have to change to suit the gender of the nouns they qualify. If you know some grammar, you will know what to do. If not, stick to the masculine form, which is the simplest – it's what we have done in this glossary.

BASICS

hello (morning or afternoon)	bonjour	closed	fermé
hello (evening)	bonsoir	big	grand
goodnight	bonne nuit	small	petit
goodbye	au revoir	more	plus
yes	oui	less	moins
no	non	a little	un peu
thank you	merci	a lot	beaucoup
please	s'il vous plaît	cheap	bon marché, pas cher
sorry	pardon/je m'excuse	expensive	cher
excuse me	pardon	good	bon
ok/agreed	d'accord	bad	mauvais
help!	au secours!	hot	chaud
here	ici	cold	froid
there	là	with	avec
this one	ceci	without	sans
that one	cela	man	un homme
open	ouvert	woman	une femme

NUMBERS

1	un	21	vingt-et-un
2	deux	22	vingt-deux
3	trois	30	trente
4	quatre	40	quarante
5	cinq	50	cinquante
6	six	60	soixante
7	sept	70	soixante-dix
8	huit	75	soixante-quinze
9	neuf	80	quatre-vingts
10	dix	90	quatre-vingt-dix
11	onze	95	quatre-vingt-quinze
12	douze	100	cent
13	treize	101	cent-et-un
14	quatorze	200	deux cents
15	quinze	300	trois cents
16	seize	500	cinq cents
17	dix-sept	1000	mille
18	dix-huit	2000	deux mille
19	dix-neuf	5000	cinq mille
20	vingt	1,000,000	un million

DAYS AND DATES

January	janvier	Sunday	dimanche
February	février	Monday	lundi
March	mars	Tuesday	mardi
April	avril	Wednesday	mercredi
May	mai	Thursday	jeudi
June	juin	Friday	vendredi
July	juillet	Saturday	samedi
August	août	August 1	le premier août
September	septembre	March 2	le deux mars
October	octobre	July 14	le quatorze juillet
November	novembre	November 23	le vingt-trois novembre
December	décembre	2013	deux mille treize

TIME

today	aujourd'hui	now	maintenant
yesterday	hier	later	plus tard
tomorrow	demain	at one o'clock	à une heure
in the morning	le matin	at three o'clock	à trois heures
in the afternoon	l'après-midi	at ten-thirty	à dix heures et demie
in the evening	le soir	at midday	à midi

TALKING TO PEOPLE

When addressing people you should always use *Monsieur* for a man, *Madame* for a woman, *Mademoiselle* for a young woman or girl. Plain *bonjour* by itself is not enough. This isn't as formal as it seems, and it has its uses when you've forgotten someone's name or want to attract someone's attention.

Do you speak English?	Parlez-vous anglais?	I understand	Je comprends
How do you say it in French?	Comment ça se dit en français?	I don't understand	Je ne comprends pas
What's your name?	Comment vous appelez-vous?	Can you speak more slowly?	S'il vous plaît, parlez moins vite
My name is...	Je m'appelle...	How are you?	Comment allez-vous?/Ça va?
I'm	Je suis	fine, thanks	Très bien, merci
...English	...anglais[e]	I don't know	Je ne sais pas
...Irish	...irlandais[e]	Let's go	Allons-y
...Scottish	...écossais[e]	See you tomorrow	À demain
...Welsh	...gallois[e]	See you later	À plus tard *or* À toute à l'heure
...American	...américain[e]		
...Canadian	...canadien[ne]	See you soon	À bientôt
...Australian	...australien[ne]	Leave me alone!	Fichez-moi la paix! (aggressive)
...a New Zealander	...néo-zélandais[e]	Please help me	Aidez-moi, s'il vous plaît

QUESTIONS AND REQUESTS

The simplest way of asking a question is to start with *s'il vous plaît* (please), then name the thing you want in an interrogative tone of voice. For example:

Where is there a bakery?	S'il vous plaît, la boulangerie?	where?	Où?
		how?	Comment?
Which way is it to Cirq-Lapopie?	S'il vous plaît, la route pour Cirq-Lapopie?	how many/how much?	Combien?
		when?	Quand?
Can we have a room for two?	S'il vous plaît, une chambre pour deux?	why?	Pourquoi?
		at what time?	À quelle heure?
Can I have a kilo of oranges?	S'il vous plaît, un kilo d'oranges?	what is/which is?	Quel est?

GETTING AROUND

bus	autobus/bus/car	single ticket	aller-simple
bus station	gare routière	return ticket	aller-retour
bus stop	arrêt de bus	validate your ticket	compostez votre billet
train/taxi/ferry	train/taxi/ferry	valid for	valable pour
boat	bâteau	ticket office	vente de billets
plane	avion	how many kilometres?	combien de kilomètres?
train station	gare (SNCF)	how many hours?	combien d'heures?
platform	quai	hitchhiking	autostop
What time does it leave?	Il part à quelle heure?	on foot	à pied
What time does it arrive?	Il arrive à quelle heure?	Where are you going?	Vous allez où?
a ticket to...	un billet pour...	I'm going to...	Je vais à...

I want to get off at the road to...	Je voudrais descendre à la route pour...	next to	à côté de
...near	... près/pas loin	behind	derrière
far	loin	in front of	devant
left	à gauche	before	avant
right	à droite	after	après
straight on	tout droit	under	sous
on the other side of	de l'autre côté de	to cross	traverser
on the corner of	à l'angle de	bridge	pont

ACCOMMODATION

a room for one/two people	une chambre pour une/deux personne(s)	blankets	couvertures
a twin room	une chambre à deux lits	quiet	calme
a double bed	un grand lit	noisy	bruyant
a room with a shower	une chambre avec douche	hot water	eau chaude
a room with a bath	une chambre avec salle de bains	cold water	eau froide
for one/two/three nights	pour une/deux/trios nuits	Is breakfast included?	Est-ce que le petit déjeuner est compris?
Can I see it?	Je peux la voir?	I would like breakfast	Je voudrais prendre le petit déjeuner
a room on the courtyard	une chambre sur la cour	I don't want breakfast	Je ne veux pas de petit déjeuner
a room over the street	une chambre sur la rue		
first floor	premier étage	Can we camp here?	On peut camper ici?
second floor	deuxième étage	campsite	un camping/terrain de camping
with a view	avec vue		
key	clef	tent	une tente
to iron	repasser	tent space	un emplacement
do laundry	faire la lessive	youth hostel	auberge de jeunesse
sheets	draps		

DRIVING

car	voiture	air line	ligne à air
service station	garage	put air in the tyres	gonfler les pneus
service	service	battery	batterie
to park the car	garer la voiture	the battery is dead	la batterie est morte
car park	un parking	plugs	bougies
no parking	défense de stationner/stationnement interdit	to break down	tomber en panne
		gas can	bidon
gas station	station service	insurance	assurance
petrol	essence	green card	carte verte
diesel	gazole/gasoil	traffic lights	feux
(to) fill it up	faire le plein	red light	feu rouge
oil	huile	green light	feu vert

HEALTH MATTERS

doctor	médecin	stomach ache	mal à l'estomac
dentist	dentiste	period	règles
I don't feel well	Je ne me sens pas bien	pain	douleur
medicines	médicaments	it hurts	ça fait mal
prescription	ordonnance	chemist	pharmacie
I feel sick	Je suis malade	hospital	hôpital
I have a headache	J'ai mal à la tête		

OTHER NEEDS

bakery	boulangerie	money	argent
food shop	alimentation	toilets	toilettes
supermarket	supermarché	police	police
to eat	manger	telephone	téléphone
to drink	boire	cinema	cinéma
camping gas	camping gaz	theatre	théâtre
stamps	timbres	to reserve/book	réserver
bank	banque		

Food and dishes

BASIC TERMS

l'addition	bill/check	le menu	menu
beurre	butter	moutarde	mustard
bouteille	bottle	oeuf	egg
chauffé	heated	offert	free
couteau	knife	pain	bread
cru	raw	poivre	pepper
cuillère	spoon	salé	salted/savoury
cuit	cooked	sel	salt
à emporter	takeaway	sucre	sugar
formule	lunchtime set menu	sucré	sweet
fourchette	fork	table	table
fumé	smoked	tisane	a flower or herb infusion or tea
huile	oil	verre	glass
lait	milk	vinaigre	vinegar

SNACKS AND STARTERS

un sandwich/une baguette	a sandwich	à la coque	boiled
au jambon	with ham	durs	hard-boiled
au fromage	with cheese	brouillés	scrambled
au saucisson	with sausage	pochés	poached
au poivre	with pepper	omelette	omelette
au pâté (de campagne)	with pâté (country style)	nature	plain
croque-monsieur	grilled cheese and ham sandwich	aux fines herbes	with herbs
		au fromage	with cheese
croque-madame	grilled cheese and bacon, sausage, chicken or egg sandwich	aux truffes	with truffles
		charcuterie	pâté and cold meats
		crudités	raw vegetables with dressings
panini	toasted Italian sandwich		
tartine	buttered bread or open sandwich	hors d'oeuvres	combination of charcuterie, crudités, smoked fish and other cold starters
oeufs	eggs		
au plat	fried		

PASTA (PÂTES), PANCAKES (CRÊPES) AND FLANS (TARTES)

nouilles	noodles	pissaladière	tart of fried onions with anchovies and black olives
pâtes fraîches	fresh pasta		
crêpe au sucre/aux oeufs	pancake with sugar/eggs	tarte flambée	thin pizza-like pastry topped with onion, cream and bacon or other combinations
galette (de sarrasin)	buckwheat pancake		

SOUPS (SOUPES)

bisque	shellfish soup	potage	thick soup, usually vegetable
bouillabaisse	Mediterranean fish soup	potée	thick vegetable and meat soup
bouillon	broth or stock	soupe à l'oignon	onion soup with a chunk of
consommé	clear soup		toasted bread and melted
garbure	potato, cabbage and meat soup		cheese topping
miques	dumplings of maize or wheat flour served in a thick soup or as a large dumpling in a stew, sliced	tourain, tourin	garlic soup made with duck or goose fat served over bread topped with cheese

FISH (POISSON), SEAFOOD (FRUITS DE MER) AND SHELLFISH (CRUSTACES OR COQUILLAGES)

alose	shad	flétan	halibut
anchois	anchovies	gambas	king prawns
anguilles	eels	hareng	herring
bigourneaux	periwinkles	homard	lobster
brandade de morue	puréed, salted cod with oil, milk, garlic and mashed potato	huîtres	oysters
		lamproie	lamprey
brème	bream	langoustines	saltwater crayfish
brochet	pike	limande	lemon sole
bulot	whelk	lotte de mer	monkfish
cabillaud	cod	loup de mer	sea bass
calmar	squid	maquereau	mackerel
carrelet	plaice	merlan	whiting
colin	hake	moules (marinière)	mussels (with shallots in white wine sauce)
coques	cockles		
coquilles St-Jacques	scallops	raie	skate
crabe	crab	rascasse	scorpion fish
crevettes grises	shrimp	rouget	red mullet
crevettes roses	prawns	saumon	salmon
daurade	sea bream	sole	sole
écrevisses	freshwater crayfish	thon	tuna
éperlan	smelt	truite	trout
escargots	snails	turbot	turbot
esturgeon	sturgeon		

FISH DISHES AND TERMS

aïoli	garlic mayonnaise served with salt cod and other fish	grillé	grilled
		hollandaise	butter and vinegar sauce
arête	fish bone	à la meunière	in a butter, lemon and parsley sauce
beignet	fritter		
darne	fillet or steak	mousse/ mousseline	mousse
la douzaine	a dozen	pané	breaded
frit	fried	quenelles	light dumplings
friture	deep-fried small fish	thermidor	lobster grilled in its shell with cream sauce
fumé	smoked		

MEAT (VIANDE) AND POULTRY (VOLAILLE)

agneau (de pré-salé)	lamb (grazed on salt marshes)	boudin blanc	sausage of white meats
		boudin noir	black pudding
andouille/andouillette	tripe sausage steak	caille	quail
bifteck		canard	duck
boeuf	beef	caneton	duckling

contrefilet	sirloin roast	oie	goose
dinde, dindon	turkey	onglet	cut of beef
entrecôte	rib steak	os	bone
faux filet	sirloin steak	poitrine	breast
foie	liver	porc	pork
foie gras	(duck/goose) liver	poulet	chicken
gibier	game	ris	sweetbreads
gigot (d'agneau)	leg (of lamb)	rognons	kidneys (usually lamb's)
grenouilles (cuisses de)	frogs (legs)	sanglier	wild boar
grillade	grilled meat	steak	steak
hâchis	chopped meat or mince	tête de veau	calf's head (in jelly)
	hamburger	tournedos	thick slices of fillet
langue	tongue	tripes	tripe
lapin, lapereau	rabbit, young rabbit	tripoux	mutton tripe
lard, lardons	bacon, diced bacon	veau	veal
lièvre	hare	venaison	venison
merguez	spicy, red sausage	volaille	poultry
mouton	mutton		

MEAT AND POULTRY DISHES AND TERMS

aiguillettes	thin, tender pieces of duck	cuisse	thigh or leg
aile	wing	en croûte	in pastry
au feu de bois	cooked over wood fire	épaule	shoulder
au four	baked	farci	stuffed
blanquette, daube, estouffade, navarin, ragoût	types of stew	garni	with vegetables
		gésier	gizzard
		gigot (d'agneau)	leg (of lamb)
blanquette de veau	veal in cream and mushroom sauce	grillé	grilled
		magret de canard	duck breast
boeuf bourguignon	beef stew with Burgundy, onions and mushrooms	marmite	casserole
		médaillon	round piece
brochette	kebab	noisettes	small, round fillets
canard de périgourdin	roast duck with prunes, pâté foie gras and truffles	pavé	thick slice
		poêlé	pan-fried
carré	best end of neck, chop or cutlet	poule au pot	chicken simmered with vegetables
choucroute	pickled cabbage with peppercorns, sausages, bacon and salami	rôti	roast
		sauté	lightly cooked in butter
		steak au poivre (vert/rouge)	steak in a black (green/red) peppercorn sauce
civet	game stew		
confit	meat preserve	steak tartare	raw chopped beef, topped with a raw egg yolk
coq au vin	chicken cooked until it falls off the bone with wine, onions and mushrooms		
		tournedos rossini	beef fillet with foie gras and truffles
		viennoise	fried in egg and breadcrumbs
côte	chop, cutlet or rib		
cou	neck		

TERMS FOR STEAKS

bleu	almost raw	bien cuit	well done
saignant	rare	très bien cuit	very well done
à point	medium		

GARNISHES AND SAUCES

américaine	white wine, cognac and tomato	diable	strong mustard seasoning
au porto	in port	forestière	with bacon and mushroom
béarnaise	sauce of egg yolks, white wine, shallots and vinegar	fricassée	rich, creamy sauce
		mornay	cheese sauce
beurre blanc	sauce of white wine and shallots, with butter	périgourdine/périgueux	rich wine sauce, possibly with truffles
bonne femme	with mushroom, bacon, potato and onions	provençale	tomatoes, garlic, olive oil and herbs
bordelaise	in a red wine, shallot and bone-marrow sauce	rouille	a mayonnaise of chillies and garlic
chasseur	white wine, mushrooms and shallots	savoyarde	with Gruyère cheese

VEGETABLES (LÉGUMES), HERBS (HERBES) AND SPICES (ÉPICES)

ail	garlic	fenouil	fennel
artichaut	artichoke	fèves	broad beans
asperge	asparagus	flageolets	white beans
avocat	avocado	haricots (verts, rouges, beurres)	beans (French/string, kidney, butter)
basilic	basil		
betterave	beetroot	lentilles	lentils
câpre	caper	mange-tout	snow peas
carotte	carrot	menthe	mint
céleri	celery	moutarde	mustard
champignon, cèpe, chanterelle, girolle, morille	types of mushrooms	oignon	onion
		persil	parsley
		piment	pimento
chou (rouge)	(red) cabbage	poireau	leek
choufleur	cauliflower	pois, petits pois	peas
ciboulette	chives	poivron (vert, rouge)	sweet pepper (green, red)
concombre	cucumber	pommes de terre	potatoes
cornichon	gherkin	radis	radish
échalotes	shallots	riz	rice
endive	chicory	salade verte	green salad
épinards	spinach	tomate	tomato
estragon	tarragon	truffes	truffles

VEGETABLE DISHES AND TERMS

à l'anglaise/ à l'eau	boiled	à la grecque	cooked in oil and lemon
beignet	fritter	jardinière	with mixed diced vegetables
biologique	organic	mousseline	mashed potato with cream and eggs
duxelles	fried mushrooms and shallots with cream		
		parmentier	with potatoes
farci	stuffed	pimenté	peppery hot
feuille	leaf	piquant	spicy
fines herbes	mixture of tarragon, parsley and chives	pistou	ground basil, olive oil, garlic and parmesan
garni	served with vegetables	râpée	grated or shredded
gratiné	browned with cheese or butter	sauté	lightly fried in butter
		à la vapeur	steamed

FRUIT (FRUITS) AND NUTS (NOIX)

abricot	apricot	melon	melon
amande	almond	melon d'eau	watermelon
ananas	pineapple	mirabelle	small yellow plum
banane	banana	mûre	blackberry
brugnon, nectarine	nectarine	myrtille	blueberry
cacahouète	peanut	noisette	hazelnut
cassis	blackcurrant	noix	nut, walnut
cérise	cherry	orange	orange
citron	lemon	pamplemousse	grapefruit
citron vert	lime	pastèque	watermelon
figue	fig	pêche	peach
fraise (de bois)	strawberry (wild)	pistache	pistachio
framboise	raspberry	poire	pear
fruit de la passion	passion fruit	pomme	apple
grenade	pomegranate	prune	plum
groseille rouge/ blanche	red/white currant	pruneau	prune
kaki	persimmon	raisin	grape
mangue	mango	reine-claude	greengage
marron	chestnut		

FRUIT DISHES AND TERMS

beignet	fritter *or* doughnut	flambé	set aflame in alcohol
compôte	stewed fruit	frappé	iced
coulis	sauce of puréed fruit	macédoine	fruit salad
crème de marrons	chestnut purée		

DESSERTS (DESSERTS OR ENTREMETS), PASTRIES (PÂTISSERIE) AND RELATED TERMS

bavarois	refers to the mould, could be a mousse or custard	glace	ice cream
		île flottante/oeufs à la neige	soft meringues floating on custard
bombe	moulded ice-cream dessert		
brioche	sweet, high-yeast breakfast roll	macaron	macaroon
		madeleine	small sponge cake
charlotte	custard and fruit in lining of almond fingers	mousse au chocolat	chocolate mousse
		omelette norvégienne	baked Alaska frozen mousse, sometimes ice cream
clafoutis	cake-like fruit tart		
coupe/boule	a serving of ice cream		
crème à l'anglaise	custard	pâte	pastry or dough
crème Chantilly	vanilla-flavoured and sweetened whipped cream	petit-suisse	a smooth mixture of cream and curds
		poires belle hélène	pears and ice cream in chocolate sauce
crème fraîche	sour cream		
crème pâtissière	thick, eggy pastry-filling	sablé	shortbread biscuit
crêpe	pancake	savarin	a filled, ring-shaped cake
crêpe suzette	thin pancake with orange juice and liqueur	tarte	tart
		tartelette	small tart
fromage blanc	cream cheese	tarte tatin	upside-down apple tart
gaufre	waffle	yaourt, yogourt	yogurt
gênoise	rich sponge cake		

WINE TERMS (VIN)

barrique	oak barrel for maturing wine	cave	wineshop/cellar
		cépage	grape variety (e.g. Merlot, Pinot noir)
blanc	white		

chais	wine cellars
corsé	full-bodied
cuvé	vat for fermenting wine
cuvée	a specially blended wine
dégustation	tasting
doux/moelleux	sweet
fin	delicate
fort	strong
léger	light
millésime	vintage
mousseux	sparkling
riche	rich
rosé	rosé
rouge	red
sec	dry
vendange	harvest
vignes	vines
vignoble	vineyard

Glossary

GENERAL VOCABULARY AND TERMS

abbaye abbey

abri prehistoric rock shelter

appellation AOP (appellation d'origine protégée) wine classification indicating that the wine meets strict requirements regarding its provenance and methods of production

auberge country inn, frequently offering accommodation

auberge de jeunesse youth hostel

autoroute motorway

bastide new town founded in the thirteenth and fourteenth centuries, built on a grid plan around an arcaded market square (see box, p.244)

boules popular French game played with steel balls (see p.34)

cabane, borie or **gariotte** dry-stone hut, probably used by shepherds

Capétien Capetian royal dynasty founded by Hugh Capet, which ruled France from 987 to 1328

causse limestone plateau extending from Dordogne *département* south through Lot and into Aveyron

chambre d'hôte bed-and-breakfast accommodation in a private house

chartreuse one-storey building typical of the Bordeaux wine region, slightly raised up and built on top of a half-buried *chai*; also a Carthusian monastery

château castle, mansion, stately home

château fort castle built for a specifically military purpose

collégiale church that shelters a community of priests

colombage traditional building style consisting of a timber frame filled with earth and straw or bricks

commune the basic administrative region, each under a mayor (very occasionally, a mayoress)

confiserie confectioner's (shop)

dégustation tasting (wine or food)

département mid-level administrative unit run by a local council – the equivalent of a county in Britain

dolmen Neolithic stone structure, generally held to be a tomb, consisting of two or more upright slabs supporting a horizontal stone

donjon castle keep

église church

falaise cliff

ferme auberge farm licensed to provide meals in which the majority of the produce must come from the farm itself

foire large market held once or twice monthly in some country towns

formule restaurant menu with two courses, usually comprising a choice of starter and main course or main and dessert

fouille archeological excavation

gabare or **gabarre** traditional wooden boat used to transport goods on the Dordogne and Lot rivers up until the late nineteenth century

gavage process of force-feeding ducks and geese to make foie gras

gisement deposit, stratified layers of an archeological excavation

gîte self-catering accommodation

gîte d'étape basic accommodation, usually restricted to walkers, pilgrims and cyclists

gouffre limestone chasm or sinkhole

grotte cave

halle(s) covered market (hall)

hôtel hotel, but also an aristocratic townhouse or mansion

lauze small limestone slabs, a traditional roof covering in the Périgord

navette shuttle-bus, for example connecting a town with its airport

Occitan language (and associated culture) formerly spoken throughout most of south and southwest France

pétanque variation of the game of boules (see p.34)

pigeonnier dovecote, often built on stilts and used to collect droppings for fertilizer

pisé traditional Périgordin floor made out of small lime-stone slabs inserted upright into a bed of clay or lime

porte gateway

retable altarpiece

seneschal chief administrator and justice in medieval times, the representative of the king

table d'hôte meals served to residents of a *chambre d'hôte*. Also, a set menu with choices, at a fixed price.

tour tower

version originale (VO) film shown in its original language and subtitled in French

ARCHITECTURAL TERMS

ambulatory passage around the outer edge of the choir of a church

apse semicircular or polygonal termination at the east end of a church

Baroque High Renaissance period of art and architecture, distinguished by extreme ornateness

chevet east end of a church

Classical architectural style incorporating Greek and Roman elements: pillars, domes, colonnades, etc, at its height in France in the seventeenth century and revived in the nineteenth century as Neoclassical

Flamboyant very ornate form of Gothic

fresco painting in watercolour on a wall or ceiling while the plaster is still wet

Gallo-Roman period and culture of Roman occupation of Gaul (1st century BC to 4th century AD)

Gothic architectural style prevalent from the twelfth to sixteenth century, characterized by pointed arches and ribbed vaulting

machicolations parapet on a castle, fortified church, gateway, etc, with openings for dropping stones and so forth on attackers

Merovingian dynasty (and art, etc) ruling France and parts of Germany from the sixth to mid-eighth century

narthex entrance hall of church

nave main body of a church

Renaissance architectural and artistic style developed in fifteenth-century Italy and imported to France in the sixteenth century by King Francis I

Romanesque early medieval architecture distinguished by squat, rounded forms and naive sculpture, called *Roman* in French (not to be confused with *Romain* – Roman)

stucco plaster used to embellish ceilings, etc

transept transverse arm of a church, at right angles to the nave

tympanum semicircular panel above the door of a Romanesque church, usually with sculpture

REGIONAL NAMES

Aquitaine Originally a Roman administrative region extending from Poitiers and Limoges south to the Pyrenees. It later became a duchy, which, at its apogee in the twelfth century, covered roughly the same area, though it fluctuated enormously. In the 1960s the name was resurrected with the creation of regional administrative units. Modern Aquitaine is based around Bordeaux and comprises the *départements* of Dordogne, Gironde and Lot-et-Garonne, among others

Gascony The region to the west and south of the River Garonne, named after a Celtic tribe (the Vascons). In the early tenth century it became an independent duchy but was soon subsumed into the duchy of Aquitaine, though still retained its own identity

Guyenne a corruption of the name "Aquitaine" originating during the period of English rule. Prior to the Revolution, the province of Guyenne extended from Gironde to Aveyron. Nowadays, it is occasionally used to refer to an area roughly encompassing Entre-Deux-Mers and St-Émilion, although there is no strict demarcation

Midi-Pyrénées the modern administrative region to the east of Aquitaine, based on Toulouse and incorporating the *départements* of Lot, Tarn-et-Garonne and Aveyron, among others

Périgord the confines of Périgord have changed little since pre-Roman times, when it was the home of the Gaulish tribe, the Petrocori. In the eighth century Périgord became a county, and then a province of France until the name was officially changed to Dordogne when *départements* were created in 1790 (each *département* was named after its principal river). However, Périgord is still used frequently, especially in tourist literature. These days it is often subdivided into Périgord Vert (Green Périgord; the *département's* northern sector); Périgord Blanc (White; the central strip along the Isle valley including Périgueux); Périgord Pourpre (Purple; the southwest corner around Bergerac); and Périgord Noir (Black; the southeast, including Sarlat and the Vézère valley)

Quercy former province roughly equivalent to the modern *départements* of the Lot and the north part of the Tarn-et-Garonne. The latter is often referred to as Bas-Quercy, while Haut-Quercy comprises the Lot's northern region. Like the Périgord, the Quercy was originally named after its Gaulish settlers, the Cadurci tribe. The name is still in regular use today and the sense of burning pride remains. A native of Cahors is still referred to as a Cadurcien

Small print and index

A ROUGH GUIDE TO ROUGH GUIDES

Published in 1982, the first Rough Guide – to Greece – was a student scheme that became a publishing phenomenon. Mark Ellingham, a recent graduate in English from Bristol University, had been travelling in Greece the previous summer and couldn't find the right guidebook. With a small group of friends he wrote his own guide, combining a highly contemporary, journalistic style with a thoroughly practical approach to travellers' needs.

The immediate success of the book spawned a series that rapidly covered dozens of destinations. And, in addition to impecunious backpackers, Rough Guides soon acquired a much broader readership that relished the guides' wit and inquisitiveness as much as their enthusiastic, critical approach and value-for-money ethos.

These days, Rough Guides include recommendations from budget to luxury and cover more than 200 destinations around the globe, as well as producing an ever-growing range of eBooks and apps.

Visit **roughguides.com** to see our latest publications.

Rough Guide credits

Editor: Lucy Kane
Layout: Jessica Subramanian
Cartography: Rajesh Mishra
Picture editor: Natascha Sturny
Proofreader: Jennifer Speake
Managing editor: Monica Woods
Assistant editor: Prema Dutta
Photographer: Jean-Christophe Godet
Production: Charlotte Cade
Cover design: Nicole Newman, Jessica Subramanian

Editorial assistant: Olivia Rawes
Senior pre-press designer: Dan May
Design director: Scott Stickland
Travel publisher: Joanna Kirby
Digital travel publisher: Peter Buckley
Operations coordinator: Helen Blount
Publishing director (Travel): Clare Currie
Commercial manager: Gino Magnotta
Managing director: John Duhigg

Publishing information

This fifth edition published May 2013 by
Rough Guides Ltd,
80 Strand, London WC2R 0RL
11, Community Centre, Panchsheel Park,
New Delhi 110017, India
Distributed by the Penguin Group
Penguin Books Ltd,
80 Strand, London WC2R 0RL
Penguin Group (USA)
345 Hudson Street, NY 10014, USA
Penguin Group (Australia)
250 Camberwell Road, Camberwell,
Victoria 3124, Australia
Penguin Group (NZ)
67 Apollo Drive, Mairangi Bay, Auckland 1310,
New Zealand
Penguin Group (South Africa)
Block D, Rosebank Office Park, 181 Jan Smuts Avenue,
Parktown North, Gauteng, South Africa 2193
Rough Guides is represented in Canada by Tourmaline
Editions Inc. 662 King Street West, Suite 304, Toronto,
Ontario M5V 1M7
Printed in Malaysia by Vivar Printing Sdn Bhd

© Jan Dodd, 2013
Maps © Rough Guides
No part of this book may be reproduced in any form
without permission from the publisher except for the
quotation of brief passages In reviews.
328pp includes index
A catalogue record for this book is available from the
British Library
ISBN: 978-1-40936-278-4
The publishers and authors have done their best to
ensure the accuracy and currency of all the information
in **The Rough Guide to the Dordogne and the Lot**,
however, they can accept no responsibility for any loss,
injury, or inconvenience sustained by any traveller as a
result of information or advice contained in the guide.
3 5 7 9 8 6 4 2

Help us update

We've gone to a lot of effort to ensure that the fifth edition
of **The Rough Guide to the Dordogne and the Lot** is
accurate and up-to-date. However, things change – places
get "discovered", opening hours are notoriously fickle,
restaurants and rooms raise prices or lower standards. If
you feel we've got it wrong or left something out, we'd like
to know, and if you can remember the address, the price,
the hours, the phone number, so much the better.

Please send your comments with the subject line
"Rough Guide the Dordogne and the Lot Update" to
✉ mail@uk.roughguides.com. We'll credit all contributions
and send a copy of the next edition (or any other Rough
Guide if you prefer) for the very best emails.

Find more travel information, connect with fellow
travellers and book your trip on ⓦ roughguides.com

ABOUT THE AUTHOR

Jan Dodd arrived in southwest France by accident in 1992 and has been there ever since, eager to ascertain whether duck fat, red wine and garlic really are the key to longevity. She has co-written several guidebooks, including *The Rough Guide to Japan* and *The Rough Guide to Vietnam*, and updated many more. These days she divides her time between travelling and writing about renewable energy.

Acknowledgements

Jan Dodd would like to thank Amanda and Norm (Darren) for their hard work helping to update this edition, and Lucy for her excellent editing.

Amanda Lawrence would like to thank Jan Dodd for initiating the adventure, Lucy Kane for patient editing, Kim Harvey for an ear for detail, Pat Lockett for creative navigation, the staff of numerous establishments for rooting out obscure information, and finally C, for just about everything else.

Darren Longley would like to thank Lucy Kane for skillfully guiding us through this new edition, not to mention her incredible patience throughout. Massive thanks to Régine Chassagne in Tulle and Micheline Morrison in Périgueux for their invaluable assistance, while thanks are also due to Clémence Djoudi and Cédric Nieuvarts in Brive, and Magali and Marie-France in Périgueux.

Readers' letters

Thanks to all the readers who have taken the time to write in with comments and suggestions (and apologies if we've inadvertently omitted or misspelt anyone's name):

Beebe Bahrami; Carolyn Haneberg; Dr P Hutchinson; and Carin and Paul Summer

Photo credits

All photos © Rough Guides except the following:
(Key: t-top; c-centre; b-bottom; l-left; r-right)

p.1 Corbis/Louis Laurent Grandadam
p.2 Alamy/Hemis
p.4 Corbis/Patrick Escudero (tr); Peet Simard (tl)
p.5 SuperStock/Photononstop
p.9 Alamy/Neiliann Tait (c); Corbis/Lionel Lourdel/
Photononstop (t); Peet Simard (b)
p.11 Alamy/Per Karlsson/BKWine.com (b); Getty Images/
Azam/AgenceImages (t); SuperStock/Photononstop (c)
p.12 Alamy/Art Kowalsky
p.13 Corbis/Jean-Pierre Lescourret (b); Julian Kumar/
Godong (c); Louis Laurent Grandadam (t)
p.14 Alamy/Les Ladbury (tr); Robert Harding Picture
Library Ltd (tl); Corbis/Patrick Escudero/Hemis (b);
Getty Images/P. Giraud (c)
p.15 Alamy/Hemis (c); Corbis/Olimpio Fantuz/SOPA (t)
p.16 Alamy/CW Images (c); Corbis/Jean-Paul Azam/
Hemis (t); SuperStock/JD Dallet (b)
p.17 Alamy/SFL Travel (bl); Corbis/Jean-Paul Azam/
Hemis (t); Sylvain Sonnet/Hemis (br)
p.18 Alamy/Hemis (tl); Jean-Daniel Sudres/Hemis (tr)
p.42 Corbis/Philippe Body

p.63 Corbis/Christophe Boisvieux (tl); Getty Images/
AFP (b)
p.103 Alamy/Andrew Duke (t); Corbis/Patrick Escudero/
Hemis (b)
p.119 Corbis/Christophe Boisvieux
p.145 Alamy/Martin Jenkinson (bl)
p.159 Corbis/Francis Cormon/Hemis
p.181 Corbis/Ellen Rooney/Robert Harding World
Imagery (t)
p.215 Corbis/Philippe Body/Hemis (t); Rene Mattes/
Hemis (b)
p.248 Corbis/Amar Grover/JAI
p.267 SuperStock/Photononstop (b)

Front cover River Dordogne © Alamy/CW Images
Back cover Domme, Dordogne Valley © Alamy/David
Norton; St Étienne cathedral © Corbis/Sylvain Sonnet;
Grapes at Château Monbazillac © Alamy/Imagebroker

Index

Maps are marked in grey

Map symbols

The symbols below are used on maps throughout the book

✈	Airport	◐	Cave	⛭	Lighthouse	⚊⚊	Tourist train
★	Bus/taxi	∴	Ruins	⊤	Gardens	⇨	Church
▮	Building	⋔	Abbey	⛰	Mountain range	▥	Building
@	Internet café/access	⚑	Windmill	≍	Bridge	☐	Park/national park
✉	Post office	♀	Fortress	•–•	Cable car	⊤	Cemetery
ⓘ	Tourist office	⛫	Château	⊠–⊠	Gate	⎯	River
✚	Hospital	♟	Tower	⎍⎍⎍	Steps	––	Ferry route
⧫	Place of interest	⚶	Viewpoint	▬	Wall		

Listings key

◼ Accommodation

● Eating and drinking

◼ Bar/Club

Published in 1982, the first Rough Guide – to Greece – was a student scheme that became a publishing phenomenon. Mark Ellingham, a recent graduate in English from Bristol University, had been travelling in Greece the previous summer and couldn't find the right guidebook. With a small group of friends he wrote his own guide, combining a highly contemporary, journalistic style with a thoroughly practical approach to travellers' needs.

The immediate success of the book spawned a series that rapidly covered dozens of destinations. And, in addition to impecunious backpackers, Rough Guides soon acquired a much broader and older readership that relished the guides' wit and inquisitiveness as much as their enthusiastic, critical approach and value-for-money ethos.

These days, Rough Guides feature recommendations from shoestring to luxury and cover more than 200 destinations around the globe. Our ever-growing team of authors and photographers is spread all over the world, particularly in Europe, the US and Australia.

Rough Guides now number around 200 titles, including Pocket city guides, inspirational coffee-table books and comprehensive country and regional titles, plus technology guides from iPods to Android. As well as print books, we publish groundbreaking apps and eBooks for every major digital device.

Visit ⓦroughguides.com to see our latest publications.

Rough Guide travel images are available for commercial licensing at ⓦroughguidespictures.com.

SO NOW WE'VE TOLD YOU
HOW TO MAKE THE MOST
OF YOUR TIME, WE WANT
YOU TO STAY SAFE AND
COVERED WITH OUR
FAVOURITE TRAVEL INSURER

WorldNomads.com
keep travelling safely

GET AN ONLINE QUOTE
roughguides.com/insurance

MAKE THE MOST OF YOUR TIME ON EARTH™

ROUGH GUIDES
A CHRONOLOGY

1982 The First *Rough Guide to Greece* – written and researched by Mark Ellingham, John Fisher and Nat Jansz – is published, shortly followed by Spain and Portugal
1983 *Amsterdam* – written by Martin Dunford – is published **1986** The first Rough Guides' offices set up in Kennington, South London **1987** Rough Guides set up as independent company **1989** BBC2 commission a Rough Guides TV series presented by Magenta Devine and Sankha Guha

1990 Rough Guides first published in the US under the name The Real Guides
1994 The first Reference titles – *World Music*, *Classical Music* and *The Internet* – are published • World Music Network starts selling Rough Guides compilation CDs
1995 roughguides.com is launched **1997** New York office set up

2001 First eBooks launched **2002** Rough Guides moves to Penguin headquarters at 80 Strand, London • Delhi office established • Rip-proof city maps series launched **2003** New colour sections added to the guides • First commissioned photographic shoots take place **2004** The *Rough Guide to a Better World* published in association with DFID **2006** First full-colour Rough Guide – *World Party* – is published • **2007** 25s series launched in honour of the 25th anniversary • *Make the Most of Your Time on Earth* becomes best-selling RG and is nominated in Richard and Judy Book Club awards **2008** A new RG TV series is broadcast on Channel 5 **2009** The first hardback picture book – *Earthbound* – featuring our commissioned photography goes on sale

2010 All guides are printed on FCO approved paper **2011** The new full-colour Pocket Guides series is launched • The first city guide iPhone/iPad apps are released **2012** Rough Guides' travel books are relaunched in time for our 30th anniversary, using full colour throughout • The first Rough Guide eBooks made specifically for the iPad go on sale **2013** roughguides.com is relaunched

ROUGH GUIDES

MAKE THE MOST OF YOUR TIME IN BRITAIN

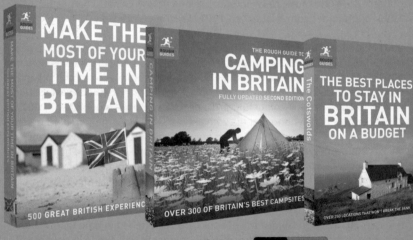

WITH OVER 700 **BOOKS, EBOOKS, MAPS** AND **APPS** YOU'RE SURE TO BE INSPIRED

Start your journey at **roughguides.com**
MAKE THE MOST OF YOUR TIME ON EARTH™